PROOF OF THE
ACCURACY OF THE BIBLE

PROOF OF THE ACCURACY OF THE BIBLE

Based on Chronological, Organizational, Prophetic and Legal Analyses

by

ELIHU A. SCHATZ

JONATHAN DAVID PUBLISHERS
Middle Village, N.Y.

PROOF OF THE
ACCURACY OF THE BIBLE
Copyright © 1973
by
ELIHU A. SCHATZ

No portion of this book may be reprinted in any form without the prior written consent of the publisher. Address all inquiries to:

JONATHAN DAVID PUBLISHERS
68-22 Eliot Avenue
Middle Village, N.Y. 11379

Library of Congress Catalogue Card No. 73-10726
ISBN 0-8246-0161-0

Printed in the United States of America

To the Jewish people, so they may learn to value their Biblical heritage.

PREFACE

Much original thinking and extensive research have gone into developing the ideas herein contained for proving the accuracy of the Bible. These ideas have evolved slowly, over a period of eighteen years, and are not the result of a sudden, concentrated effort. It was considered worthwhile, for the reader's understanding, to note in this preface some of the general thought processes that went into the writing of this book.

The present work is arranged in a straightforward logical order. First, in Part I, is presented a study of Biblical chronology, wherein are established precise dates based on both Biblical and extra-Biblical sources. Then, in Part II, a detailed analysis is given of the authorship and organization of the books of the Bible. In the analysis many of the conclusions reached in the study of the chronology are used. Part III of the book explains the Messianic passages in the Bible, and employs many facts derived from the previous two parts. Finally, in Part IV, the rationale for the Biblical laws is given in great detail. These four divisions of the book provide different approaches to prove the accuracy and correctness of the Bible.

Although this work is arranged in the above-stated logical order, the actual development by the author of the different parts was in an entirely different sequence. Initially, about 18 years ago, some success was achieved in interpreting many of the difficult numbers and dates in the Book of Daniel, using traditional chronology as a basis. Afterwards, the author became aware of the fact that for no period of Biblical chronology did the traditional dates exactly agree with those dates supplied by historical sources. This necessitated a thorough examination of the reasons for the discrepancies. Eventually the research led to the resolution of the chronological difficulties, as expounded in Part I of this book.

While doing the research on the chronology, it became apparent that Biblical higher criticism had greatly undermined the belief of the general public in the authenticity of the Bible. The author felt that the arguments of the critics were obviously fallacious, and an entirely different system of logic could be developed. The simplest and most direct method of countering the incorrect assumptions of the critics was to properly elucidate the authorship and organization of the books of the Bible. The resultant analysis of each of the Biblical works is presented in Part II of this book.

Then the author realized that to a large degree he had verified the accuracy of many aspects of the Bible. What yet needed to be explained was the rationale for the regulations found in the Pentateuch. Only if there were significant benefit in the observance of the Biblical laws, could one expect to convince the masses that it was to their own advantage to follow the commandments. As a result, Part IV was written, explaining the reasons for practically all the Biblical laws.

It was now possible to return to the Book of Daniel and complete the commentary on the prophetic portions. Clarification of the predictions of Daniel allowed the attainment of a bare outline of the events to happen in the Messianic era. What was yet needed was supplementary information on these events. Therefore, all prophecies in the Bible relative to Messianic times were interpreted. A clear picture then emerged of future events concerning the State of Israel. The resultant prophetic analysis was designated Part III of the book. In writing this section, verification was also obtained that prophecies found in the Bible were true prophecies.

These four complete parts now could be combined into one book showing conclusively that the Bible is an accurate and reliable document.

To a great extent the inspiration for this book may be attributed to the topics taught to me by my father, Rabbi Morris Schatz, z"l. His interests in the Bible, Jewish history, chronology, and traditional Judaism were the seeds that eventually flowered within me to produce the present work. I would moreover like to acknowledge the assistance of my wife, Freida, who not only typed the manuscript, but also patiently listened to many of my ideas as they were being evolved. Sincere gratitude is also given to all those who knowingly or inadvertently supplied concepts which have been used in the text.

E. S., November, 1971

CONTENTS

PREFACE — v

INTRODUCTION — xix

PART I ACCURACY OF BIBLICAL CHRONOLOGY — 1

Chapter I CREATION ERA — 3

- 1.1 Interpretation of Creation Passages in Genesis — 4
  - 1.1.1 Creation of the World — 4
  - 1.1.2 History of Man Before the Deluge — 5
  - 1.1.3 The Deluge and Subsequent Events — 8
- 1.2 Extra-Biblical Evidence Interpreted on Basis of Genesis — 10
- 1.3 Evolutionary Theory Disproved — 13
- 1.4 Fallacies in Scientific Methods for Determining Age of the World — 15
- 1.5 Chronology of Creation Era Based on the Bible — 16
- 1.6 Extra-Biblical Support for Creation History — 21
  - 1.6.1 Mythological Literature — 21
  - 1.6.2 Historical Literature — 23

Chapter II TIME OF ABRAHAM — 29

- 2.1 Abraham Identified as Hammurabi — 29
  - 2.1.1 Chronological Agreement — 29
  - 2.1.2 Other Points of Agreement — 34
  - 2.1.3 Problems in Identification — 37
- 2.2 Supplemented History of Abraham — 38
- 2.3 Biblical Chronology from Time of Abraham until Exodus from Egypt — 39
- 2.4 Significance of the Term "Generation" — 41

	2.4.1 Length of an Average Generation	42
	2.4.2 Rapid Growth of the Israelite Population	43

Chapter III HISTORY OF ISRAEL IN EGYPT 46

3.1 Comparison of the Chronologies 46
    3.1.1 Biblical Chronology 46
    3.1.2 Egyptian Chronology 47
3.2 Comparison of Biblical and Egyptian Histories 49
    3.2.1 Hyksos Period 49
    3.2.2 Eighteenth Dynasty 51
        3.2.2.1 Moses Identical to Senmut 53
        3.2.2.2 Thutmose III is the Pharaoh of the Exodus 54
    3.2.3 Amarna Age 55
3.3 Summary 57

Chapter IV PERIOD OF THE JUDGES 58

4.1 Length of Rule of Joshua 58
4.2 Periods of Subjugation 59
4.3 Length of Judgeship by Samuel 62
4.4 Age of Saul When He Became King 63
4.5 Verification of the Developed Chronology 63

Chapter V CHRONOLOGY OF THE KINGS 65

5.1 The First Day of the Year 65
    5.1.1 Nisan as the Beginning of the Year 66
    5.1.2 Nisan as the First Month 68
    5.1.3 Cheshvan as the Beginning of the Year for the Kings of Israel 69
    5.1.4 The Tenth of the Seventh Month as the Beginning of the Agricultural Year 69
5.2 Chronology of the Kings Based on the Bible 70
    5.2.1 Variant Information from Chronicles 82
    5.2.2 Times Elapsed Relevant to the Period of the Kings 84
5.3 Comparison of Biblical and Assyrian Dates 86

Chapter VI BABYLONIAN EXILE AND THE PERIOD OF THE SECOND TEMPLE 93

6.1 Reason for Disagreement of Traditional Dates from those of World History 93

6.2	Babylonian Period	95
	6.2.1 Date of the Destruction of the Temple	95
	6.2.2 Clarification of Passages Related to Babylonian Kings	97
6.3	Persian Period	98
	6.3.1 Identification of Darius the Mede with Darius I	98
	6.3.2 Identification of Ahasuerus with Hystaspes	99
	6.3.3 Identification of Mordechai with Zoroaster	102
	6.3.4 Identification of Persian Kings Mentioned in the Bible	103
6.4	Seventy Year Spans	105
6.5	Summary of Key Dates	106
6.6	High Priests During Second Temple	108

Chapter VII   SABBATICAL AND JUBILEE YEARS   111

7.1	Historical Dates for the Sabbatical and Jubilee Years	112
	7.1.1 First Entrance into the Land of Israel	112
	7.1.2 Second Entrance into the Land of Israel	114
	7.1.3 Third Entrance into the Land of Israel	115

Chapter VIII   SUMMARY OF DATES FOR MAIN EVENTS   116

PART II   AUTHORSHIP AND ORGANIZATION OF THE BOOKS OF THE BIBLE   119

Chapter IX   ASSUMPTIONS AND CONCLUSIONS   120

9.1	Authorship	120
9.2	Organization	120
9.3	Chronology	121
9.4	Textual Considerations	126
9.5	References	127

Chapter X   THE PENTATEUCH   129

10.1	Genesis	130
10.2	Exodus	136
10.3	Leviticus	142
10.4	Numbers	144
10.5	Deuteronomy	150
10.6	Early Names of the Books of the Pentateuch	152

x CONTENTS

Chapter XI EARLY PROPHETIC WORKS 165

    11.1 Joshua 165
    11.2 Judges 168
    11.3 Samuel 173
    11.4 Kings 184

Chapter XII LATER PROPHETS 193

    12.1 Isaiah 193
    12.2 Jeremiah 210
    12.3 Ezekiel 231
    12.4 The Twelve Prophets 240

Chapter XIII PSALMS, PROVERBS AND JOB 252

    13.1 Psalms 252
    13.2 Proverbs 281
    13.3 Job 300

Chapter XIV THE FIVE SCROLLS 304

    14.1 Song of Songs 304
    14.2 Ruth 306
    14.3 Lamentations 308
    14.4 Ecclesiastes 311
    14.5 Esther 321

Chapter XV DANIEL, EZRA-NEHEMIAH, AND CHRONICLES 323

    15.1 Daniel 323
    15.2 Ezra-Nehemiah 326
    15.3 Chronicles 331

PART III THE REALITY OF PROPHECY 356

Chapter XVI COMMENTARY ON PROPHETIC CHAPTERS OF THE BOOK OF DANIEL 358

    16.1 Chapter 2 of Daniel 360
    16.2 Chapter 7 of Daniel 365
    16.3 Chapter 8 of Daniel 377
    16.4 Chapter 9 of Daniel 389
    16.5 Chapter 10 of Daniel 407
    16.6 Chapter 11 of Daniel 414

16.7	Chapter 12 of Daniel	439
16.8	Modern Events Prophesied in Book of Daniel	448

Chapter XVII   COMMENTARY ON MESSIANIC CHAPTERS OF EZEKIEL   450

17.1	War-of-Gog (Chapters 38–39)	450
17.2	Development of the Land of Israel (Chapters 34–37)	452
17.3	Design of the Third Temple (Chapters 40 1–43 17; 46 19–47 12)	453
	17.3.1 Introductory and Explanatory Statements	453
	17.3.2 The Outermost Wall	453
	17.3.3 Entryways to the Outer and Inner Courts	454
	17.3.4 The Inner Court and the Temple	454
	17.3.5 The Outer Court and Its Relation to the Inner Court and the Temple	461
	17.3.6 Heights of Buildings	465
	17.3.7 The Altar	465
	17.3.8 Water Source from Jerusalem (47 1–12)	466
17.4	Supplementary Regulations	467
	17.4.1 Sacrifices (43 18–27; 45 18–46 15)	467
	17.4.2 Laws for the Leader of the Nation	469
	17.4.3 Laws for the Priests (44 6–31)	472
	17.4.4 Distribution of the Land (45 1–8; 47 13–48 35)	474
17.5	Summary of Messianic Prophecies in Book of Ezekiel	477

Chapter XVIII   COMMENTARY ON MESSIANIC PORTIONS OF THE TWELVE PROPHETS   479

18.1	Book of Joel	479
18.2	Malachi (Chapter 3)	481
18.3	Book of Obadiah	482
18.4	Micah (Chapters 4–7)	484
	18.4.1 Chapters 4–5	484
	18.4.2 Chapters 6–7	486
18.5	Amos (Chapter 9 7–15)	487
18.6	Hosea (Chapters 2 15–3 5)	488
18.7	Zephaniah (Chapter 3 8–20)	489
18.8	Zechariah (Chapters 9–14)	490
	18.8.1 Chapters 9–11	490
	18.8.2 Chapters 12–14	493
18.9	Messianic Predictions Derived from Book of Twelve Prophets	495

Chapter XIX COMMENTARY ON MESSIANIC CHAPTERS OF ISAIAH — 497

- 19.1 Chapter 2 2–4 — 497
- 19.2 Chapters 11 1–12 6 — 497
- 19.3 Chapter 19 1–25 — 499
- 19.4 Chapters 24 1–27 13 — 499
- 19.5 Chapters 32–35 — 502
- 19.6 Chapters 49–66 — 505
  - 19.6.1 Chapter 49 1–13 — 505
  - 19.6.2 Chapters 49 14–50 11 — 506
  - 19.6.3 Chapter 51 1–11 — 506
  - 19.6.4 Chapters 51 12–52 12 — 507
  - 19.6.5 Chapters 52 13–53 12 — 508
  - 19.6.6 Chapter 54 1–17 — 509
  - 19.6.7 Chapters 55 1–56 8 — 509
  - 19.6.8 Chapters 56 9–57 21 — 510
  - 19.6.9 Chapters 58 1–59 21 — 511
  - 19.6.10 Chapter 60 1–22 — 512
  - 19.6.11 Chapters 61 1–62 12 — 513
  - 19.6.12 Chapter 63 1–6 — 513
  - 19.6.13 Chapters 63 7–65 25 — 514
  - 19.6.14 Chapter 66 1–24 — 516
- 19.7 Messianic Predictions Derived from Book of Isaiah — 517

Chapter XX MESSIANIC PASSAGES IN JEREMIAH AND THE PENTATEUCH — 519

- 20.1 Commentary on Messianic Chapters of Jeremiah — 519
  - 20.1.1 Chapters 30 4–31 39 — 519
  - 20.1.2 Prophecies by Jeremiah Against the Nations — 522
    - 20.1.2.1 Prophecy to Moab — 522
    - 20.1.2.2 Prophecy to the Children of Ammon — 522
    - 20.1.2.3 Prophecy to Edom — 523
    - 20.1.2.4 Prophecy to Elam — 524
- 20.2 Messianic Passages in the Pentateuch — 524
  - 20.2.1 Leviticus 26 44–45 — 524
  - 20.2.2 Numbers 24 14–19 — 524
  - 20.2.3 Deuteronomy 4 25–31 — 525
  - 20.2.4 Deuteronomy 30 1–10 — 525
  - 20.2.5 Deuteronomy 31 29 — 525
  - 20.2.6 Deuteronomy 32 34–43 — 525

Chapter XXI DETAILED PICTURE OF THE MESSIANIC
ERA 527

21.1 Early Events Leading to Establishment
of the State of Israel 527
21.2 The Situation Prior to the War-of-Gog 529
21.3 The War-of-Gog 530
21.4 Consequences of Israel's Victory 533

PART IV RATIONALE FOR THE BIBLICAL LAWS

Chapter XXII MONOTHEISTIC PRINCIPLES 539

Chapter XXIII EDUCATIONAL PRACTICES 543

Chapter XXIV GOVERNMENTAL RESTRICTIONS 546

Chapter XXV HEALTH REGULATIONS 549

25.1 Dietary Restrictions 550
    25.1.1 Animal Foods 550
    25.1.2 Blood and Fat Avoidance 556
    25.1.3 Contaminated Meat 558
    25.1.4 Miscellaneous Cases 559
25.2 Psychological Measures 563
25.3 Sex Prohibitions 568
    25.3.1 Prevention of Disease Transmission 569
    25.3.2 Elimination of Inherited Defects 571
    25.3.3 Protection of the Society 574
25.4 Additional Regulations Concerning Disease Prevention 578
25.5 Priestly Statutes 590
    25.5.1 Responsibilities of the Priests and Levites 591
    25.5.2 Requirements for Officiating 592
    25.5.3 Special Prohibitions 594

Chapter XXVI PHYSICAL PROTECTION OF THE
POPULATION 597

26.1 Accident Prevention 597
26.2 Crime Control 599
    26.2.1 Laws to Promote Justice 600

		26.2.1.1 Regulations for Judges	600
		26.2.1.2 Laws Concerning Witnesses	602
	26.2.2	Commensurate Punishments for Criminal Actions	604
		26.2.2.1 Crimes Punishable by Death	604
		26.2.2.2 Crimes Punishable by Payments	605
		26.2.2.3 Crimes Against Parents	608
		26.2.2.4 Penalties for Bodily Damages	609
		26.2.2.5 Damages to Animals or Inaminate Objects	612
		26.2.2.6 Crimes Punishable by Lashes	615
26.3	Military Requirements		615

Chapter XXVII ECONOMIC POLICIES 624

27.1 Land Ownership 624
27.2. Taxes 628
    27.2.1 Tithes 628
    27.2.2 Priestly Portions 632
27.3 Slavery Regulations 635
27.4 Aiding One's Fellow Man 638
    27.4.1 Lending Laws 638
    27.4.2 Aid for the Poor 640
    27.4.3 Lost Objects 642
    27.4.4 Emergency Aid 643
27.5 Vow Obligations 643
27.6 Agricultural Ordinances 647

Chapter XXVIII RITUALISTIC PROCEDURES 653

28.1 Sacrifices 653
28.2 Festivals 682
28.3 Temple Design and Components 686
28.4 Priestly Garments 692

PART V CONCLUDING REMARKS 696

ABBREVIATIONS 700

REFERENCES 701

INDEX 723

LIST OF TABLES

Table		page
1.5.1	Chronology from Creation until Death of Levi	18
1.6.2.1	Antediluvian Leaders	24
1.6.2.2	Genealogical Table for the Formation of Nations after the Deluge	26
2.1.1	Revised Dating for Assyrian Kings	31
2.1.2	Time Spans Recorded by Assyrian Kings	35
3.1	Chronology of the Egyptian Period Based on the Bible	47
3.2	Chronology of the Egyptian Period Based on Extra-Biblical Sources	48
3.3	Biblical Personalities Described in Egyptian Inscriptions	56
4.1	Chronology of the Period of the Judges	60
5.2.1	Dates for the Kings of Judah and Israel	74
5.2.1.1	Ages of Kings of Judah at the Beginning of their Reigns	83
5.3.1	Correlations between Biblical and Assyrian Dates	88
5.3.2	Corrected Dates for the Assyrian Kings	91
6.1	Babylonian and Persian Chronology	94
6.5.1	Key Dates During Babylonian Exile and Second Temple	107
6.6.1	High Priests Subsequent to Destruction of the Temple	109
8.1	Summary of Main Events During Biblical Period	117
9.1	Authors of the Books of the Bible	122
9.2	Organization of the Books of the Bible	124
10.1.1	Organization of Genesis	131
10.3.1	Logical Arrangement of Topics in Leviticus Obtained by Modifying Position of **16 1–17 16**	144
10.6.1	Titles Used in the Bible for the Books of the Pentateuch	154
10.6.2	Other Titles Used for the Books of Deuteronomy and Leviticus	160
11.2.1	Arrangement of Judges **1 1–2 5** According to Similarity of Phrases between Adjacent Sentences	169

11.3.1	Early Events in David's Career Described in the Appendix to the Book of Samuel	176
11.3.2	Contents and Authorship of Book of Samuel	178
11.3.3	Organization of Appendix to Book of Samuel According to Similarity of Phrases	183
11.3.4	Events in the Reign of David	184
11.4.1	Probable Authors of the Sections of the Book of Kings	190
12.1.1	Prophecies in the Book of Isaiah for which the Dates of Revelation are Indicated	194
12.1.2	Arrangement of the Book of Isaiah	196
12.1.3	Similarity of Phrases between Adjacent Sections in the Book of Isaiah	200
12.2.1	Dated Prophecies in the Book of Jeremiah	212
12.2.2	Organization of the Book of Jeremiah	214
12.2.3	Similarity of Phrases between Adjacent Sections of the Book of Jeremiah	216
12.3.1	Dates in the Book of Ezekiel	232
12.3.2	Similarity of Phrases between Adjacent Sections in the Book of Ezekiel	234
12.4.1	Approximate Times of the Twelve Prophets	241
12.4.2	Similarity of Phrases between Sections in the Book of Hosea	244
12.4.3	Similarity of Phrases between Sections in the Book of Amos	246
12.4.4	Similarity of Phrases Between Sections in the Book of Zechariah	250
13.1.1	Dates of Events Referred to in the Book of Psalms	253
13.1.2	Arrangement of Book of Psalms by Author and Heading	257
13.1.3	Similarity of Phrases Between Adjacent Chapters in the Book of Psalms	264
13.2.1	Similarity in Sounds of the Consecutive Proverbs in the Second Section of the Book of Proverbs	283
13.2.2	Similarity in Sounds of the Consecutive Proverbs in the Third Section of the Book of Proverbs	295
14.3.1	Analogous Phrases between the Books of Lamentations and Jeremiah	309
14.3.2	Analogous Descriptions of Life of Writer of Chapter Three with Life of Jeremiah	310
14.4.1	Similarity of Words between Neighboring Sentences in the Book of Ecclesiastes	314
15.1.1	Dates of Occurrence of the Chapters in the Book of Daniel	324

15.2.1	Identification of Persian Kings mentioned in Ezra-Nehemiah	328
15.3.1	References for Additional Information on the Kings of Judah	334
15.3.2	Parallel Passages to those in Chronicles	344
15.3.3	Variant Numbers in Parallel Accounts	355
16.0.1	Words Used for Specific Time Spans	359
16.6.1	Rulers of the Houses of Seleucus and Ptolemy	415
17.4.1.1	Sacrifices Brought by the Leader	470
28.1.1	Basic Types of Burnt-and Peace-Offerings	654
28.1.2	Basic Types of Sin and Guilt Sacrifices	656
28.1.3	Meal-Offerings	658
28.1.4	Sacrifices at Set Times of the Year	660
28.1.5	Sacrifices Brought under Special Circumstances	664
28.2.1	Biblical Festivals	680
28.3.1	Components of the Tabernacle	688
28.3.2	Auxiliary Items for Use at the Tabernacle	691
28.4.1	Garments Worn by the Priests	693

ILLUSTRATIONS

		page
Figure 17.3.3.1	Dimensions of Entryway Along Outer Wall (Ez. **40** 6–16)	455
Figure 17.3.3.2	Dimensions of Entryway Along North Inner Wall (Ez. **40** 6–16, 38–43)	456
Figure 17.3.4.1	Design of the Inner Court and the Temple	457
Figure 17.3.5.1	The Temple and the Outer and Inner Courts	462
Figure 17.3.7.1	Side View of the Altar	466
Figure 17.4.4.1	Schematic Diagram of Apportionment of Land of Israel Among the Tribes	476

INTRODUCTION

One of the basic premises of the Jewish religion is that the entire Bible was developed under Divine inspiration. Although what is meant by Divine inspiration is controversial and has been variously interpreted, nevertheless, the fact that God was somehow involved in the development of the Bible surely implies that the twenty-four Biblical books must be reliable documents and their contents must be correct. Furthermore, the premise is made that the laws contained in the last four books of the Pentateuch were transmitted directly from God to Moses. Consequently, these laws, in particular, must be perfect and should be obeyed in every detail.

Now if on the contrary, it should be able to be established that the Bible has major imperfections, either historical, organizational or legal, then the very foundations of Judaism would be severely undermined. How could intelligent people believe in Divine guidance in the development of the Bible if it were possible to prove that fundamental errors existed?

In recent centuries much evidence has been uncovered and numerous works have been written which supposedly point out many examples of clearcut Biblical inconsistencies. Beginning in the middle half of the eighteenth century[1,2] there has developed the system of Biblical criticism which purportedly establishes the illogical organization and multiple authorship of even the less conplicated Biblical books. Scholarly and well-documented texts[3] attempt to show hundreds of examples of textual problems. It is claimed that many of the books of the Bible are unhistorical, and written by unknown persons, as if the authors were writing novels.

Archaeological discoveries within the past 200 years[4] have also confronted the believers in Biblical accuracy with serious difficulties. Although the archaeological finds have in general confirmed the correctness of historical information found in the Bible[5], significant disagreements have arisen in the developed datings. For not a single historical period is there exact agreement between the Biblical and extra-Biblical chronologies. For example, the traditional view, based on Dan. 9 24–27, is that the Second Temple lasted 420 years, while extra-Biblical sources[6] ascribe approximately 585 years to this era.

Even modern scientific knowledge poses questions that are difficult to answer. The evolutionary theory[7], which is well accepted in scientific literature, assumes that higher forms of animals evolved slowly from lower forms over many millions of years. Supporting this theory is the extreme age of the world of approximately five billion years, calculated by radioactive dating methods[8]. The conclusions reached by the evolutionary theory and radioactive dating obviously contradict the story of creation in Genesis (1 1–2 3), and disagree with the age of the world of about 6,000 years derived from the Biblical data.

In addition, modern scientific information seems to indicate that observance of the Biblical laws does not necessarily result in great benefits. What could possibly be the purpose of many of the laws, such as bringing of sacrifices, regulations on purity and impurity, and numerous agricultural ordinances? Even when benefits are known to result from some laws, such as prevention of trichinosis by avoidance of eating pork, still the same results could possibly be achieved by other means, such as the thorough cooking of pig's meat before eating it[9].

The evidence from numerous fields of knowledge therefore appears to point to inconsistencies, historical errors, and illogical development of the Bible. Truly, the intelligent observant Jew is faced with a serious challenge to his fundamental beliefs.

Two approaches have been commonly used to answer these problems. The ultra-orthodox Jew assumes the Bible is correct and true in spite of any criticisms. No matter how great is the evidence presented against the veracity of the Bible, still it is claimed that the Bible is absolutely correct In fact, it is considered that there is no point in even studying those fields of knowledge which result in basic questions as to the authenticity of the Bible. The second approach, by the modern orthodox Jew, is to interpret the Bible in broad general terms so that almost any contradictory information can be fitted into the Biblical text. For example, the six days of creation may really have been six eras of creation; and hence there is no contradiction between the Bible and the five billion years that the earth is purported to have existed according to the evolutionary theory and dating by radioactivity.

Neither of these approaches is completely satisfactory to the inquiring mind. The evidence from both the Biblical and extra-Biblical sources needs to be examined carefully, and a clear-cut decision made as to whether or not the entire Bible is a factual document. Questions need to be asked such as: "Is or is not the Biblical chronology correct?"; "Are the books of the Bible organized in a logical manner?"; and "Are there plausible explanations for the Biblical laws?".

It should be realized that it is only such fundamental questions as those above that result in disrespect for the Bible, when left unanswered. Occasional minor difficulties in wording of the text need not be considered as serious problems, since they can be explained as arising from uncertainty as to what the original Hebrew wording meant, or possibly from rare copyist errors occurring during the more than 2,300 years since completion of the Bible.

Examination of the criticisms levelled against the Bible reveals that the main problems posed to its truth fall into four categories. The first and most damaging involves the historical, and especially the chronological, disagreements between the Bible and other sources of ancient history. Next comes the supposed illogical organization of the individual books, and the numerous otherwise unknown authors assumed to have written the text. Thirdly, during the past 2,300 years no true prophet of God has been known, and it is therefore hard to conceive that prophecy, as described in the Bible, really can occur. Lastly, there are often no apparent rational reasons for the Biblical regulations, thus seemingly making it senseless to observe the laws.

If satisfactory answers could be supplied to the problems above, then the veracity of the Bible would be established. It was with this in mind that the four main parts of this book were written. They are entitled:

Part I   Accuracy of Biblical Chronology
Part II Authorship and Organization of the Books of the Bible
Part III Reality of Prophecy
Part IV Rationale for the Biblical Laws

Part I is concerned with establishing the accuracy of Biblical chronology by comparing dates derived from the Bible with those obtained from archaeological and other historical sources. Six periods are considered, namely: (A) Creation era; (B) Time of Abraham; (C) History of Israel in Egypt; (D) The Judges; (E) The Kings; and (F) The Babylonian Exile and the Second Temple. For each of these times, either by reinterpretation of the Biblical information or by reinterpretation of the historical sources, or both, exact agreement is obtained between Biblical and extra-Biblical chronology. The correctness of the Biblical Chronology is established to an extent not believed possible even by the most ardent traditionalists.

In Part II, each of the twenty-four books of the Bible is carefully analyzed to determine the organization and identify the authors. Such factors as logical coherence, chronological order, and similarity of phrases are used in the arrangement of the books, while the authors are frequently the key individuals described in the texts, or are mentioned in the Book of Chronicles. For each book of the Bible significant original explanations are presented which have been overlooked by others and solve numerous textual problems that have arisen.

Part III tries to establish the reality of prophecy. Many critics assume that true prophecy is non-existent, and that the recorded Biblical predictions were either written after the event or were educated guesses made shortly before the happening described. Naturally, it is impossible to go back in history to determine exactly when each prophecy was made. However, there are numerous predictions which refer to events after completion of the entire Bible. In particular such prophecies are (A) contained in the last six chapters of the Book of Daniel, or (B) found in numerous places in the prophetic books, and refer to the reestablishment of the Jewish state in Messianic times. Therefore this third part of the book contains first a detailed explanation of the last six chapters in the Book of Daniel, showing clearly how such events as the rise of Mohammad, World War I, and World War II are described. Second, all the prophecies throughout the Bible relevant to the reestablishment of the Jewish state are explained. As a result numerous predictions can be made for events in the near future, concerning the Messianic era. If these predictions turn out to be even approximately correct, they will establish the reality of Biblical prophecy, and indirectly prove that the predictions of events which happened during Biblical times also involved true prophecy.

Part IV explains all the laws in the Pentateuch on the basis of modern scientific knowledge. Since the Biblical regulations were developed by God for man's well-being, all the laws should be of a beneficial nature. The Bible itself promises that observance of the regulations will make the Jewish people greater than any nation; will eliminate sickness and crime; and will result in great economic and military benefits. Such promises are not based on miracles, but are a direct consequence of adherence to the Biblical statutes. In this fourth part are explained, within the limitations of modern knowledge, exactly how the laws are beneficial.

As a result of the careful analyses presented in the four main parts of this book, the author feels confident that the authenticity and correctness of the Bible have been proved. An observant Jew need not feel that there is any doubt as to the fundamental truth of the Bible and the principles proclaimed therein.

PROOF OF THE
ACCURACY OF THE BIBLE

PART I

ACCURACY OF BIBLICAL CHRONOLOGY

Comparison of the dates derived from Biblical information with dates derived from other historical sources reveals that there is no period for which exact agreement exists. In some cases, such as the period of the Kings, the discrepancies are only about 30 years; for other periods differences of a hundred or more years are common. These disagreements raise serious doubts as to the accuracy and reliability of the Bible. How can the Bible be so much in error? In general, historians tend to ignore the Biblical data when it disagrees with the developed chronology. In contrast, Biblical commentaries often completely ignore the extra-Biblical evidence. Neither approach is satisfactory. Both the Bible and the extra-Biblical sources, when they present the chronology for the same events, should be in exact agreement. At most, the differences should amount to a year or two, because of limited information and personal bias on the part of the recorders of the events.

Many works exist describing how the Biblical history is approximately verified by extra-Biblical sources. Correlations are made between geographical locations, similarity in stories, and other general features. Nevertheless, no attempt is made to show agreement between the chronologies. It is believed, perhaps, that such an agreement cannot be obtained. This section, entitled "Accuracy of Biblical Chronology," attempts to show that an exact agreement can be achieved, and that no fundamental differences exist in the chronologies derived from these two sources. To accomplish this task it has often been necessary to reinterpret the Biblical as well as the historical information. In some cases, such as the period of the Second Temple, complete reinterpretation of the Bible is necessary. For other cases, however, such as the time of Abraham, the historical sources need reexamination. By following these approaches, it has been possible to obtain almost perfect agreement for every historical period.

The Biblical chronology has, for convenience, been divided into six subsections. These divisions are as follows: (A) Creation Era—Creation to after the Deluge; (B) Time of Abraham; (C) History of Israel in Egypt—Joseph to after the Exodus; (D) Period of the Judges—Joshua to construction of the First Temple; (E) Chronology of the Kings of Judah and Israel; and (F) Babylonian Exile and

Period of Second Temple up to Simon, the high priest. In addition, sections are presented clarifying the Sabbatical and Jubilee Years of the Bible, and summarizing the important dates in the Biblical period. These divisions have been selected because they allow fairly sharp distinctions between one period and the next, and usually require considerably different approaches. The earlier the period considered, the less exact is the extra-Biblical information, and the more approximate the agreement that is attainable.

Emphasis has been placed mainly on questions of chronology. Agreements between historical events, geographical locations or other particulars have not been emphasized unless they present direct evidence on the chronology. Numerous tables are presented to organize the data in a relatively simple form. As is the approach throughout the book, no special attempt has been made to survey the various explanations and possibilities. Rather, the emphasis has been to find and supply the correct solutions to the chronological problems.

Chapter One

CREATION ERA

The term "Creation Era" is here used for the early period in the earth's history during which sudden and catastrophic changes occurred. Included in this era are such events as the creation of the world, the Deluge, the confusion of languages at the time of the Tower of Babel, and the separation of the single land mass into the seven continents. Covered in this chapter is a period of time of over 2,000 years.

Comparison of the Biblical data as to the time of creation with information derived by scientific methods leads to astounding discrepancies. According to calculations based on Biblical statements, the world was created at the start of 3922 B.C.E.*, which is less than 6,000 years ago. In contrast, the most modern scientific methods lead to a value of five billion years for the age of the world[1]. No reliable extra-Biblical history is available to help resolve the chronological discrepancy. Many people have tried to interpret the Bible so as to allow agreement with the high age values arrived at by scientific methods; but such interpretations do not represent the plain meaning of the Biblical text, since the word יום, meaning one day, rather than זמן, or another term meaning era, is used (Gen. 1 5,8,13,19, 23,31; 2 2,3). In the following development it will be shown how the Biblical description explains the available evidence, while the scientific method leaves many unanswered questions, and therefore the age of the world is approximately 6,000 years rather than five billion years.

When considering dates as far back as the time of creation or of the Deluge, precise extra-Biblical history is almost completely lacking. It is therefore impossible to provide exact agreement for the chronology of this era. However, as will be

---

* The date 3922 is derived by using the date 586 for the destruction of the First Temple, as a reference point. The construction of the Temple occurred 409 years earlier in 995; the Exodus from Egypt 480 years before that; and the birth of Isaac 400 years earlier in 1875. One hundred years previously, in 1975, Abraham was born, which was the 1948th year after Creation. Hence Creation occurred at the beginning of 3922. Verification and justification of these dates are presented subsequently when discussing the revelant periods (See Sections 1.5; 2.3; 4.5; and 5.2).

shown subsequently, methods are available for obtaining approximate agreement with the Deluge date calculated from the Bible.

It should be noted that it is especially in relation to the period of the Creation and Deluge that Biblical history is not believed. All too often, the narratives are treated as myths or fables. The emphasis here for the Creation Era is therefore placed not only on clarifying the chronology, but also on demonstrating the veracity of the history.

1.1 INTERPRETATION OF CREATION PASSAGES IN GENESIS

1.1.1 Creation of the World

A detailed explanation of the method of creation of the world is presented in the first chapter of Genesis. Frequently the description is dismissed by many authors as mythology, not worthy of detailed analysis. However, if the description is taken literally, as it is here, and considered as a historical record of what transpired, then upon interpreting the words from a scientific viewpoint, knowledge can be gained of the sequence and nature of events at the time of creation. The interpretation presented below follows closely the wording in Genesis 1, and supports the generally accepted scientific theory that the earth solidified from the molten state[2].

In the beginning God created space (שמים) and matter (ארץ). Now the matter, which probably was very hot, was without order or arrangement, and the only form of energy was the wind of God hovering over the melt (מים). Then God created electromagnetic energy (אור), which manifests itself visibly as light. Next, wave motion was created which allows the distinction to be made between the presence and absence of electromagnetic energy, and thus allows the existence of darkness. The concept of time was then introduced—light was called day, and darkness was called night. These creations were completed during one day, and the changes were gradual (ערב, בקר) rather than instantaneous.

Then God developed the laws governing liquids, such as surface tension and cohesive forces, which result in the formation of a membrane-like interface (רקיע) between liquids. The liquids below the interface of the earth's surface were then separated from those above the interface. The interface itself was designated as the beginning of the sky. This creation occurred gradually on the second day.

By the third day the earth had cooled sufficiently so that water was the dominant liquid. God then developed the laws of gravity and viscosity, which resulted in the waters being gathered together in one place, and the appearance of dry land (יבשה). This dry land was called the continent (ארץ), the only one at that time, and the gathered waters were called the seas. Fundamental laws of botany, including the principles of capillary rise and osmosis of liquids, were developed next, resulting in the formation of plant and tree life of all types, all able to reproduce themselves. These creations occurred gradually on the third day.

God then created light sources in the sky to distinguish between day and night, and to serve as signs and for the determination of the seasons and years. This involved the development of the laws of universal gravitation as well as the means for supplying the radiated energy from the light souces. In particular, the sun (מאור הגדול) was made to be dominant during the day, and the moon (מאור הקטן) and stars to be dominant at night. All these heavenly bodies were fixed in specific trajectories in the sky relative to the earth. These accomplishments were performed gradually on the fourth day.

God then caused the water to produce all types of fishes and water creatures, and all types of flying birds. Thus were created the large sea animals, all crawling creatures of the water, and all the birds. The necessary chemical and biological laws were developed to allow these living things to be created. God blessed the living creatures, and told them to be fruitful, and multiply, and fill the water and land. These accomplishments were performed gradually on the fifth day.

God then developed the necessary zoological laws to cause the land to produce living animals of all types, namely cattle, crawling creatures, and non-domesticated beasts. Finally man was created to rule over the air, land, and water creatures. Man was created in God's image, i.e., with intelligence—male and female. God blessed man and told him to be fruitful, multiply, fill the land and conquer it. The human being was allowed to eat from all plants and trees, and the animals could eat all green plants. No permission, however, was given to eat any type of living creature. The above creations were accomplished gradually on the sixth day.

Creation of the world was completed by the seventh day, and God rested. The seventh day was then set aside as holy because on that day God rested from all His work.

As explained in more detail in Section 10.1, the above account (Gen. 1 1–2 3) was written by God and handed to Adam. Thus it is an accurate description of the events during the six days of Creation, and offers the only reliable record of the sequence of happenings.

1.1.2 History of Man before the Deluge

The Biblical text, beginning with Gen. 2 4, presents the description written by Adam. Some of the most interesting aspects are discussed below.

When man was created he was placed in the Garden of Eden (Gen. 2 7,8). Originally man was created to live forever (Gen. 2 17), which means that no aging process existed to cause the human being to grow old and weak after he matured. That such immortality is possible is known from the fact that trees presently exist which are over 4,000 years old[3]. From Adam's point of view, the animals and birds were created for man's benefit. Also woman was created after man although still on the sixth day of Creation (Gen. 2 18–23).

Then Eve and Adam ate from the fruit of the tree of knowledge of good and evil (Gen. 3 6,7). Now before eating from the forbidden fruit, man had no shame at being naked (Gen. 2 25), and had no concept of evil. However, afterwards Adam and Eve became aware that they were naked (Gen. 3 7) and acquired the capacity for doing evil. Furthermore, they were no longer destined to live forever, but only for a maximum of about 970 years (see Gen. 5). These acquired changes, contrary to the findings of scientists concerning other traits, were inherited, as is evidenced by the fact that all subsequent generations had the choice of doing good or evil (i.e. free will), were aware of nakedness, and did not live forever. As a result of eating the forbidden fruit and disregarding God's command, woman's punishment was to suffer pain during menstruation, pregnancy, and labor; to have desire for her husband; and to be ruled by him (Gen. 3 16). These factors explain, for example, why relatively few women have become great. Thus, although many women undoubtedly have had the capability to achieve greatness, they usually, especially when married, have not had the ambition to persevere sufficiently to attain fame. Man was punished, in that the soil was made less productive. Originally the ground would produce a high yield of produce with little care or attention. Now it would become necessary to work the soil with great effort, and to eliminate thorns and weeds (Gen. 3 17–19).

The foregoing curses explain some of the major supposed imperfections of the world, namely: (A) the human being does not live forever; (B) criminal actions of man; (C) suffering of woman during the natural processes of menstruation, pregnancy, and labor; (D) low creativity of woman; and (E) low agricultural efficiency of the soil, with resultant food shortages.

The possibility still existed for man to eat from the tree of life and live forever. Adam and Eve were therefore driven out from the Garden of Eden, and prevented from returning (Gen. 3 22–24). It should be noted that this story verifies that, in theory at least, some chemical can be developed which will stop the aging process and allow the human being to live forever.

From the Biblical narrative it is obvious that man was created with the power of speech. For example, Adam named the animals and birds (Gen. 2 20), and quotations are ascribed to him (Gen. 2 23,24) and his wife (Gen. 3 2,3). Furthermore, the Biblical description, from Gen. 2 4 to 4 26 (see Section 10.1) was probably written by Adam, and therefore he was created with the knowledge of writing. Also, by implication, the original language was Hebrew, since the text and quotations are in Hebrew.

The origin of specialized skills probably arose sometime between 99 and 130 years after Creation. Thus we find (Gen. 4 20–22) that Jabal was the first cattle raiser; Jubal was the first musician—for both string and wind instruments; and Tubal-cain was the first metal worker with copper and iron. These persons were the eighth generation from creation (Gen. 4 17–22). The order was: (A) Adam; (B) Cain; (C) Enoch; (D) Irad; (E) Mehujael; (F) Methushael; (G) Lamech; (H) Jabal, Jubal, and Tubal-cain. Now Cain was the eldest son of Adam; he could have been born one year after Creation, and his future wife the next year. Allowing fourteen years as a minimum for each generation, Lamech could possibly have fathered his three sons by two wives within eighty-six years after the Creation. Thirteen years later, i.e. in year 100 A.M.,* all three sons could have matured, and it would be the earliest possible time for them to have developed their special skills. It then follows in the text (Gen. 4 25; 5 3) that Seth was born to Adam in 130 A.M. Thus, probably by that date all the sons had surely exhibited their special talents.

Archaeological evidence supports the statement that Tubal-cain originated the use of copper tools. Thus, archaeology shows that man originally used stone tools and bone tools. Then came the Bronze Age where tools of copper, and occasionally of bronze (an alloy of copper and tin) were also used. The Early Bronze Age started about 3300 B.C.E.[4] It should be realized that the archaeological date is extremely approximate, and may be in error by many hundreds of years.

The above evidence corresponds to the information that Tubal-cain was the originator of copper tools (Gen. 4 22). As previously discussed, he probably matured about 100 A.M., or 3823, and invented copper tools by about 3800. The spread of this ability, to the extent that archaeology would subsequently uncover plentiful evidence of these tools, may have taken several hundred years (ca. 3500). Thus the archaeological date of 3300 agrees, within a reasonable margin of error, with the Biblical date (ca. 3800) for the beginning of the Bronze Age.

According to Gen. 4 22, Tubal-cain also initiated the use of iron tools. However from archaeological evidence, the Iron Age began much later, about 1500. This discrepancy can be reconciled by assuming that the use of iron did not spread as rapidly as the use of copper.

It should be realized that although people then lived to over 900 years of age (Gen. 5), they matured at the same age that people do at the present time. The extra length of life was due to slower aging rather than slower maturing. Afterwards, because of man's sins, God reduced the average life expectancy to 120 years (Gen. 6 3), which would be the average life expectancy at the present time if illness, accidents, and crime were eliminated. The modification to a 120 year lifetime was gradual, however (Gen. 11 10–32), so as not to have the annoying situation of some people living to 900 years and others to 120, with none living intermediate life spans. The potential, at the present time, for an average life expectancy of 120 years is supported by two points. First, the maximum human longevity is now about 115 years, and many unauthenticated cases have been reported where people lived to over 150

---

*A.M. = Anno Mundi = years from Creation; the year of Creation is 1 A.M.

years[5]. Second, mammals usually live five or six times the period it takes for them to mature. If humans followed this ratio they would have an average life span of 100 to 125 years[6].

1.1.3 The Deluge and Subsequent Events

Because of the evil ways of man, God decided to destroy mankind, animal life, and birds (Gen. 6 5-7) by a Deluge. However Noah, his wife, his three sons, and their wives were saved (Gen. 6 18; 7 13). In addition, one pair of each impure species of animal and crawling creature, and seven pairs of each species of birds and clean animals were saved (Gen. 7 2,3). The remainder of the living animals were destroyed by the waters that rose 15 cubits above the tops of the highest mountains (Gen. 7 19-23). If we assume that Mount Everest, the highest mountain in the world (which is 29,028 feet high) was referred to, and that a cubit is about 20 inches, then the waters rose to an approximate height of 29,050 feet. The Deluge covered the entire dry land, since there was then only one continent. Furthermore, at that time man did not kill animals, except cattle for sacrifices (Gen 4 4, 8 20), and man, animals and birds only ate from plants and trees (Gen. 1 29,30). Therefore, the animals and birds were tame, did not fear man, and were easily convinced to enter the ark with him to escape the Deluge.

It should be realized that the dimensions of the ark were surely large enough to accommodate all the required animals and birds. According to Gen. 6 15,16, the ark was 300 cubits long, fifty cubits wide and thirty cubits high. Furthermore the height was divided into three stories of about ten cubits each. Thus the total interior area suitable for use by animals was $300 \times 50 \times 3 = 45,000$ square cubits. If we arbitrarily assume that on the average ten square cubits (approximately twenty-eight square feet) were necessary for each animal including its food, then a total of 4,500 animals, or about 2,200 pairs of animals, could be comfortably taken care of in the ark. This amount of room would surely be enough for the number of distinct animal species presently known[7]. Note that in considering distinct species such animals as the polar bear, grizzly bear and brown bear are all of the same species.

After the Deluge, Noah, his family, the animals and birds left the ark, and were commanded by God to be fruitful and multiply (Gen. 8 16,17; 9 1). Permission was now given for man to eat not only plant life, but all types of animals, birds and fish; and as a result these creatures would fear man (Gen. 9 2,3). Subsequently, Nimrod became the first mighty hunter, about thirty years after the Deluge (Gen. 10 6-10).

Another major modification of nature which occurred after the Deluge was the appearance of the rainbow. God promised never again to destroy all living creatures (Gen. 8 21), and He modified the world so that a Deluge could not recur. This change also resulted in the appearance of a rainbow in the sky after a rain (Gen. 9 8–17).

From a scientific viewpoint the rainbow is caused by refraction and internal reflection of the sun's rays by the raindrops. The phenomenon depends on the size of the water drops. With very small drops, whose diameter is 0.1 mm. or less, the colors become superimposed, and the rainbow becomes almost a pure white. On the other hand, if the raindrops are too large a colored rainbow also does not occur[8].

Size of the water drop is also of importance when considering rainfall. An average raindrop has a mass equivalent to several million cloud droplets. Because of their large size, raindrops have significant falling speeds and are able to survive the fall from the cloud to the ground, without completely disappearing by re-evaporation[9].

We may now postulate that the appearance of the rainbow, and the impossibility of the occurrence of another Deluge, arose from the same phenomenon, namely the change in the size of the raindrop. Perhaps some fundamental modification in such laws as that for surface tension occurred, which resulted in smaller size drops. Consequently, less complete precipitation resulted, allowing storage of much water in the sky, which otherwise could flood the land.

After the Deluge, man multiplied and spread throughout the one continent (Gen. 9 19; 10 32). The nations that were formed were named mainly after the children and grandchildren of Shem, Ham, and Japheth (Gen. 10 1–32). If we assume an average of about ten years until boys and girls were born to the sons of Noah, and an additional twenty years for each succeeding generation, then it would be expected that new nations having a reasonable population (of perhaps fifty people) would not be formed until at least fifty years after the Deluge. As will be subsequently established (Section 1.5), the Deluge occurred in 1656 A.M., equivalent to 2267 before the Common Era. Therefore the earliest date for the formation of new nations can be very approximately set as 2215.

At about 2200, the people of the world desired to build a tower to the sky rather than to spread out over the continent (Gen. 11 4). God therefore confused their speech, resulting in numerous languages and in the spread of the people throughout the land (Gen. 11 1–9). Up until that time the people spoke and wrote only Hebrew. Shortly after confusion of the languages, in 2166, i.e. 101 years* after the Deluge (Gen. 11 10–16), Peleg was born. Within thirty years after his birth (Gen. 11 18), and most probably beginning in the year of his birth (2166), the one continent began splitting to form the

---

* Two years until Arpachshad was born, thirty-five years more until Shelah was born, thirty years more until Eber was born, thirty-four years more until Peleg was born.

seven continents that are presently known; as it is stated in Gen **10** 25 that the first son of Eber was called Peleg because in his days the continent was divided (נפלגה הארץ). Nations and tribes then grew up independently on each isolated land mass. The splitting of the land into seven continents marks the approximate end of the Creation Era when unprecedented catastrophic changes, such as a Deluge and confusion of language, occurred.

1.2 EXTRA-BIBLICAL EVIDENCE INTERPRETED ON BASIS OF GENESIS

Let us now consider some of the effects and ramifications of the described history of the Creation Era.

Originally man and woman were created by God with numerous genes for each characteristic. As a minimum there were two genes carried by Adam and two genes by Eve for every human characteristic, or four possible different genes. Furthermore, many, if not most, human traits are controlled by multiples of two genes, and therefore it is possible that eight, twelve, or more different genes were originally available to control certain characteristics. For example, skin color is considered to be determined by four, five or six gene pairs[10]. Children inherit half of the genes of each parent. By the third generation— the grandchildren of Adam and Eve—it was possible for children to be born with duplicate genes for particular characteristics. Numerous large variations between individuals were therefore possible, from skull size to height to skin color. Similar considerations apply to each distinct species of animal created by God.

Because of the bad deeds of man, God decided to destroy man, animal, and bird, by means of a Deluge. Only representative living creatures of each type survived by being carried on the ark built by Noah. In particular, there were eight people (Noah, his wife, his three sons and their wives), two of each kind of impure animal, and fourteen of each type of bird and pure animal, that went aboard the ark. In the case of man, there were actually available for rebuilding mankind the genes from the equivalent of only five people, since the three sons of Noah inherited their genes from their parents. Undoubtedly, the surviving people carried many duplicate genes, and therefore numerous types of characteristics, with which Adam and Eve were created, were lost forever. The same concept applies to an even greater extent to the impure animals, for which only two of each species survived. In the case of the pure animals, such as cattle, fourteen animals survived, and therefore very few genes would be expected to have been lost. As a result of the loss of gene types, numerous variations of animals, man, and birds, that occurred before the Deluge, could no longer recur. Thus, anthropologists find human skulls that are similar to present-day types of man, yet sufficiently different to lead to numerous false concepts, such as the theory of evolution. Similarly, numerous variations in the horse and elephant have been uncovered; all these fossils in truth only verify the story of the Deluge. Furthermore, it may have happened that in a few cases the surviving pair of animals did not have any offspring, resulting in the disappearance of a complete species, some of whose skeletons are recovered by paleontologists.

Another effect of the Deluge was to kill off at one time thousands, perhaps millions, of animals and birds of various types. Since animals of one type tend to keep together, and their ability to survive the Deluge would be similar, it would be expected that layers of skeletons would be uncovered with many of the same species found in the same location. For example, some animals in trying to survive the Deluge would climb trees, others would climb mountains, others might be able to swim for hours or even days, others would fly, and so forth. To an approximate extent the more complex and bigger the animal, the longer it would survive. Therefore, the skeletons of the simpler animals would usually be found in lower levels than those of more developed animals. Now this layer arrangement may vary depending on the environment; for example the presence or absence of tall trees and mountains would affect which animals would survive the longest. When these layers of skeletons of animals are found by paleontologists, they verify the story of the Deluge, although the data are misinterpreted to indicate that the different animals developed by evolution during millions of years.

It should be realized that the Deluge did not kill off fish, vegetation, and insect life. Insects, for example, may have survived as tiny eggs. In the case of fish peculiar effects could have resulted. For example, all land areas, even those not usually covered with water, became flooded. Many fish may have swum to these areas. When the waters receded and dried up after the Deluge, many fish may have been unable to return to their original water areas, resulting in their dying in a normally land area. Discovery by paleontologists of the fossils of such fish has been used to suggest evolutionary changes of the earth's surface. More probably, these finds support the story of the Deluge.

A catastrophic event, such as the Deluge, would also be expected to cause the deposition of a thick layer of sediment in numerous locations, by transporting the soil from one area to another. The first uncovering of such a sediment was reported by the archaeologist, Sir Leonard Woolley, who found an eight foot stratum of mud between layers from different civilizations[11]. Subsequently, layers of silt were found in various other sites, such as Kish, Uruk, Lagash, and Shuruppak[12]. Such thick layers of silt clearly verify that a great flood did occur.

It is often stated that about one-fourth of the land masses of the earth were once covered with sheets of ice during the period known as the Ice Age. The evidence for the Ice Age is based on: (A) heterogeneous deposits of earth, stones and boulders spread over the earth's surface, which are characteristic of material deposited by ice sheets; and (B) bedrock which is smoothed, scratched and abraded in the manner peculiar to glaciers. Prior to the glacial hypothesis, the above evidence was attributed to the Biblical Deluge[13]. For example, the flood waters may have floated and dispersed huge blocks of ice, found in the colder regions of the earth and on tops of mountains, and subsequently deposited them in warmer land areas where they eventually melted[14]. It should be realized that at the present time, there may well be sufficient ice to cover a good portion of the land areas, just as in the past. For example, it has been calculated that if all the ice presently on earth melted it would cause a rise in sea level of 250 to 300 feet![15] Thus, the evidence for an Ice Age can just as well be attributed to the Deluge, which is an historical event recorded not only in the Bible but in many extra-Biblical sources (see Section 1.6).

The concept that the present land masses were originally one continent was initially proposed in 1912 (C.E.) by A. Wegener, a German meteorologist[16]. In recent years this concept has been revived based on the almost perfect jigsaw puzzle fit of the continental shelves of the opposing parts of South America and Africa[17]. Antartica and Australia would also fit nicely with Africa and Asia[18]. Additional support for the concept is gained from the similarity of the rock sequences of widely separated lands, and the similarities of fossil and plant life on corresponding sections of distant continents[19]. All this scientific evidence supports the historical fact stated in Gen. 10 25, that in the days of Peleg the one continent was split apart.

The splitting apart of a single continent accounts for many otherwise puzzling facts. For example, it explains how mankind arose on what are now isolated islands and land masses. Thus, subsequent to the Deluge, the surviving persons multiplied and spread over the continent. Then when the break up of the land did occur, the people were trapped on the particular areas where they settled. Civilizations thereupon arose out of necessity on all the newly formed continents and islands. The story of the Deluge was transmitted from parent to child in all the civilizations, which explains how tales of the flood arose in practically every locality of the world, including remote, isolated islands.

The picture that is obtained is that the water of the Deluge set up forces which eventually led to the breakup of the single continent. It has, for example, been stated that water can trigger volcanic eruptions, and that the water literally explodes, carrying with it lava and a variety of gases, when pressure is released[20]. The single continent split into four major land masses, namely: (A) Asia-Europe-Africa; (B) North America-South America; (C) Antartica; and (D) Australia. Numerous smaller islands were also formed. Possibly when North America-South America and Asia-Europe-Africa were drifting apart, the movement was stopped when the west coast of Alaska encountered underwater the east coast of Siberia at the Bering Strait.

If we assume that some land masses ended up below the sea after the split of the one continent, then the discovery of mammal skeletons in the ocean can be explained. Thus, the animals were drowned at the time of the Deluge, and then buried in the sea when the land separated.

Historical support for the story concerning the construction of the Tower of Babel and the subsequent confusion of languages is obtained by two different approaches. First, archaeologists have uncovered in southern Mesopotamia towers known as ziggurats. In fact, the word ziggurat[21] comes from a verb meaning "to build high." These towers were composed of immense cubes of sun-dried bricks piled up one on the other and diminishing in size up to the top. In particular, the most famous ziggurat was known as Etemenanki, meaning the House of the Foundation of Heaven and Earth, and is believed to have been the Tower of Babel[22]. This tower had a base of 298 feet square, with seven stages which reached a total height of 295 feet[23]. It should also be noted that the Egyptian pyramids, which must have originated at about the same time, have an analagous design to that of the ziggurat, and may be a distortion of the original style of the Tower of Babel.

A second support for the story of the Tower of Babel arises from the similarities between languages. For example, all of the known alphabets are considered to be derived from one original alphabet[24]. Although there are conflicting opinions as to which alphabet was the original, there are good grounds to conclude that the Hebrew alphabet is the oldest[25]. This information agrees with the contention that there was originally only one language, which was Hebrew.

Moreover, the languages of the world, of which there are approximately 3,000, can be classified in about two dozen principal language families. A few examples of families are Indo-European, Semitic, and Hamitic. Languages within any family are considered to have evolved from a single language[26]. Furthermore, common elements exist even between different language families. Thus, the languages themselves show the probability that there was originally only one language, from which the others arose, in agreement with the story of the Tower of Babel.

1.3 EVOLUTIONARY THEORY DISPROVED

The evolutionary theory has been used to explain the origin of life on this earth in a manner which conflicts with the Biblical description. The theory assumes that life started with the simplest type of microorganism, and slowly evolved to higher and higher forms, with the eventual development of man. However, many very difficult problems arise which cannot be satisfactorily explained by the evolutionary theory, although they pose no difficulty for the Biblical description. The main problems are:

(A) What initiated the beginning of life, so that it would not only arise spontaneously, but that it could also reproduce and continue developing? Even assuming that living material could develop spontaneously, which has never been scientifically found to occur in nature, the developed life would soon die out since it would not be able to reproduce.

(B) By what mechanism could one species* modify itself so as to form other species? The inheritance of acquired characteristics, as originally suggested in the eighteenth century C.E. by the naturalist Jean B. Lamarck, has been disproved genetically. The alternate explanation of botanist Hugo DeVries that rare inheritable variations called mutations begin new species is untenable since all the evidence shows that the mutations which do occur are degenerative and produce unfitness rather than improvement of the species[27]. Nevertheless, at the present time, the proponents of evolution claim that the mechanisms of evolution involve mutations and natural selection. However, according to the *Encyclopedia of X-Rays and Gamma Rays*[28], mutations which are able to surpass species limits have neither been observed in nature nor induced by any mutagens. This is because the species-specific structure of the DNA macromolecule limits mutations to only slight structural changes within species limits.

(C) The succession of fossils in the geological strata is used to imply the descent of higher species from lower organisms: however, there is a notable absence of intermediate species to bridge the gaps between fossils. Furthermore, it is not legitimate to claim that the fossil record is incomplete, since fossil representatives have been uncovered of all but a few living phyla and of most living orders and families[29]. Also, fossils are often found in different arrangements in different locations. Thus, the fossil record disproves any succession from one species to the next[30].

(D) Numerous cases of symbiotic relationships are known. These involve partnerships between dissimilar organisms, often between organisms of different evolutionary periods. In many cases the lower organism would not be able to survive without the assistance of the more developed organism. For example, a vast series of plant-animal associations occur, where insects are necessary for the fertilization of certain plants[31]. The evolutionary theory has to develop elaborate schemes to explain the survival of the lower organisms until the much later development of the higher organisms.

From a scientific viewpoint these problems present serious difficulties to the evolutionary theory, which in any other field of science would be sufficient to invalidate the theory. However, in the case of evolution it is impossible to perform experiments to verify the theory. Still, the only reason the evolutionary hypothesis does survive is because of the unawareness of a better explanation for the facts. On the previous pages we have shown how the Biblical historical presentation explains the data, and therefore a much better explanation is in actuality available. For example, the beginning of life and the existence of different species is explained as the way God created life on earth. Symbiotic relationships are feasible

---

* Two forms are here assumed to belong to the same species if they can interbreed and produce fertile offspring. Members of a species are usually separated from members of other species by differences of structure and appearance. (See John W. Klotz, *Genes, Genesis and Evolution*, Concordia Pub. House, St Louis, Missouri, 1955, Chapter 3).

since all organisms were created within four days. The fossil record arises from the death of all animals because of the Deluge. The discovery of skeletons of variant animal species arises from loss of genetic possibilities because of the Deluge, or the non-reproduction by the remaining animals of the species after the Deluge.

In general, the evolutionary theory taxes one's logical faculties by assuming that complicated living organisms could be created by pure chance, though from our own experiences we know that even such a relatively simple item as a chair does not arise spontaneously.

1.4 FALLACIES IN SCIENTIFIC METHODS FOR DETERMINING AGE OF THE WORLD

The age of the world has been variously given by scientists as millions or billions of years, where different methods produce different values. Methods that have been used in the past, but are now discounted, are based on such factors as rate of salt washed into the oceans, rate of sedimentation, time for the earth to cool from a molten mass, and rate of expansion of the universe. Involved in the calculations are so many unknowns that all these methods are now considered unreliable[32]. The only so-called reliable methods are based on radioactive dating, which result in a value of about five billion years for the age of the world. The radioactive isotopes of greatest interest are uranium-238, uranium-235, thorium-232, potassium-40, rubidium-87 and carbon-14. The ages of samples are calculated based on the ratio of the amount present of the radioactive isotope to that of its decay product. For example, one of the widely used methods involves uranium-238 and its decay product lead-206, where the assumption is made that no lead-206 was present at the time of formation of the sample. The assumption that none of the decay product was originally present is also made for all the other radioactive isotopes except for carbon-14. For the latter isotope, the method assumes that a constant level exists in the atmosphere, as well as in living things during their lifetimes. However, after death the amount of carbon-14 decreases as it forms carbon-12. The ratio of carbon-14 to carbon-12 in the sample allows the calculation of how long ago an organism died. Unlike the other methods, the carbon-14 method cannot be used to measure ages greater than about 50,000 years[33].

Some of the major problems in radioactive dating are as follows[34,35]:

(A) Except for the carbon-14 method, no knowledge is available as to how much of the end product of the radioactive series, or of intermediate products, existed at the time of creation. In the case of carbon-14 the assumption is made that the concentration of radiocarbon in the exchange reservoir is the same at present as in the past. This is because carbon-14 is continually formed in the upper atmosphere by cosmic ray bombardment of nitrogen.

(B) There is always the possibility of selective leaching or contamination of the sample. All rocks have some porosity which allows interchange by seepage of water. Also, if gases are part of the radioactive series, they may escape into the atmosphere.

(C) The assumption is made that the rate of decay of the radioisotope has always been the same as at present.

In the case of all the radioisotopes (except carbon-14) the arbitrary assumption has been made that none of the decay products were formed at the same time as the parent radioisotope. Why, for example, could there not have been initially an equal amount of decay product and radioactive isotope? This problem (A) alone, invalidates all the calculated dates for the age of the world.

In contrast, the general validity of radiocarbon dating, which often gives ages over 10,000 years, is firmly established. Corroboration of the method for samples a few thousand years old have been obtained using tree-ring counting or materials of known historical age. However, when considering samples dating from before the Deluge, then problem (B) becomes a serious difficulty. Thus, the Deluge caused water to be over all the land, and to cover the tops of all mountains, which would have resulted in pressures equivalent to approximately 850 atmospheres (about 29,000 feet of water). The resultant leaching and contamination would significantly modify the compositions of carbon-bearing specimens. Therefore, the fundamental assumption that samples dating back more than about 4,200 years (when the Deluge occurred) have not been disturbed or modified is incorrect. As a result, any date prior to the Deluge obtained by radiocarbon methods is unreliable.

Although scientists often quote ages for the earth of many billions of years, reliable evidence is lacking. The extreme age for the earth is used to support the evolutionary theory, and the evolutionary theory is used to support the extreme age for the earth. The historical evidence from the Bible, however, disproves both these theories. As mentioned previously, the earth is less than 6,000 years old, and the evolutionary concept does not explain the available facts. It is the Biblical evidence which is much stronger and more reliable than the scientific calculations and assumptions. The Biblical record is a historical account by eyewitnesses of what occurred (see Section 10.1). The scientific theories are, in contrast, guesses that cannot be tested satisfactorily, as to what may have happened.

1.5 CHRONOLOGY OF CREATION ERA BASED ON THE BIBLE

The chronology for the Creation Era is based on the ages of the fathers when their sons were born. Sufficient data are supplied in the Bible to allow a continuous succession of ages until the death of Levi in 2334 A.M. A tabulation of the available information, including the dates (A.M. and B.C.E.) and the references, is presented in Table 1.5.1. It should be noted that the year of the Deluge was the 600th of Noah, or 1656 A.M.

It has here been assumed that creation of the world began on the first day of the first month, i.e., on the first of Nisan, since this day was considered as the beginning of the year throughout almost the entire Bible (see Section 5.1). The ages for the listed persons are assumed to be based on the number of firsts-of-Nisan during which they lived*, as can be concluded from the data presented in Gen. 5. It is found there in each of the nine cases, that the sum of the father's age when his son was born, plus the years he lived afterwards, exactly equals the total years of the father's life. Thus, Adam was 130 when Seth was born, and he lived for an additional 800 years, for a total life of 930 years. Although the arithmetic seems obvious, it tells us the type of counting system used. For example, if the ages were counted from the day of birth, and were rounded off to the nearest year, then there would probably be cases of one-year discrepancies. As an illustration, assume that the stated 130 years for Adam were actually 129–5/8 years until Seth was born, and the additional 800 years were really 799–5/8, then the total number of years of Adam's life would be $929\frac{1}{4}$, or when rounded off, 929 rather than 930 years. Similarly, if an age of N years represents a number between N−1 and N, then if Adam was actually 129–3/8 when Seth was born, and he lived an additional 799–3/8 years, his total number of years would be $928\frac{3}{4}$, or rounded off to 929 years. Thus for any system that used other than a fixed day of the year for counting the ages of people, it would be expected that ages would not always be additive. That we find the years are additive in each of the given nine cases indicates that a fixed day, such as the first of Nisan, is used for counting people's ages. Hence all dates based on people's ages can be added together without introducing any error.

Many people have been tempted to explain the long life spans of over 900 years, for people during the creation era, as resulting from a much shorter year than at present. However, the Biblical statements clearly establish that the length of a year was the same then as now. Thus, the Deluge began on the seventeenth day of the second month (Gen. 7 11). One hundred and fifty days later (Gen. 7 24; 8 3), on the seventeenth day of the seventh month (Gen. 8 4), the waters subsided to the extent that the ark rested upon the mountains of Ararat. Hence, the 150 days were five months, or each month had thirty days. Furthermore, the text indicates that there were twelve months in a year at that time. Thus, on the first day of the tenth month (Gen. 8 5) the tops of mountains were seen. Subsequently there are waiting periods mentioned of forty days until the raven was sent forth (Gen. 8 6), seven days until the dove was sent out the first time (Gen. 8 8, 10), seven days until the dove was sent out the second time (Gen. 8 10), and seven more days until the dove was sent forth the third time (Gen. 8 12). These additional sixty-one days bring the time to the beginning of the twelfth month. Shortly thereafter, on the first day of the first month of the next year the waters were no longer on the land (Gen. 8 13).

We thus have shown that a year at that time consisted of about twelve months of

---

* For simplicity it is here assumed that Adam counted his first year from the sixth of Nisan, when he was created, and subsequent years from the first of Nisan.

Table 1.5.1
Chronology from Creation until Death of Levi

Person	Age When Son Born (Yrs.)	Years Lived After Son Born	Total Years	Son's Name	Reference in Genesis	Time When Lived (A.M.)*	Dates When Lived (B.C.E.)*
Adam	130	800	930	Seth	5 3–5	1–930	3922–2993
Seth	105	807	912	Enosh	5 6–8	131–1042	3792–2881
Enosh	90	815	905	Kenan	5 9–11	236–1140	3687–2783
Kenan	70	840	910	Mahalalel	5 12–14	326–1235	3597–2688
Mahalalel	65	830	895	Jared	5 15–17	396–1290	3527–2633
Jared	162	800	962	Enoch	5 18–20	461–1422	3462–2501
Enoch	65	300	365	Methuselah	5 21–23	623–987	3300–2936
Methuselah	187	782	969	Lamech	5 25–27	688–1656	3235–2267
Lamech	182	595	777	Noah	5 28–31	875–1651	3048–2272
Noah	{500 / 502	450	950	Shem, Ham, Japheth	5 32;9 29 / 11 10;7 6	1057–2006	2866–1917
Shem	100	500	600	Arpachshad	11 10–11	1559–2158	2364–1765
Arpachshad	35	403	438	Shelah	11 12–13	1659–2096	2264–1827
Shelah	30	403	433	Eber	11 14–15	1694–2126	2229–1797
Eber	34	430	464	Peleg	11 16–17	1724–2187	2199–1736
Peleg	30	209	239	Reu	11 18–19	1758–1996	2165–1927
Reu	32	207	239	Serug	11 20–21	1788–2026	2135–1897
Serug	30	200	230	Nahor	11 22–23	1820–2049	2103–1874

CREATION ERA

Nahor	29	119		Terah	11 24–25	2073–1926
Terah	70	135	205	Abram	11 26, 32	2044–1840
Abraham	100	75	175	Isaac	21 5; 25 7	1974–1800
Isaac	60	120	180	Jacob	25 26; 35 28	1874–1695
Jacob	85	62	147	Reuben	30 25; 31 41; 47 9, 28; 29 32	1814–1668
	86	61		Simeon	29 33	
	87	60		Levi	29 34	
	88	59		Judah	29 35	
	ca. 88	ca. 59		Dan	30 6	
	ca. 89	ca. 58		Naphtali	30 8	
	89	58		Gad	30 11	
	90	57		Asher	30 13	
	89	58		Issacher	30 18	
	90	57		Zebulun	30 20	
	91	56		Dinah**	30 21	
	91	56		Joseph	30 24	
	ca. 105***	ca. 42		Benjamin	35 18; 31 41	
Joseph	ca. 31	ca. 79	110	Manasseh	50 26; 41 46, 51	1723–1614
Levi	—	—	137	—	Ex. 6 16	1727–1591

* In this tabulation only the years actually counted as full years are listed. In most cases the persons were born in the middle of the year just prior to the one first listed.
** Daughter
*** See Section 10.1, Organization

thirty days, for a total of approximately 360 days. This establishes that the $29\frac{1}{2}$ day synodic revolution of the moon, and the $365\frac{1}{4}$ day revolution of the earth around the sun, were the same at the time before the Deluge as at present. Hence the long life spans which people lived during the creation era were based on years of the same duration as nowadays. Furthermore, after the Deluge God promised that while the earth exists, the seasons and day and night will not cease (Gen. 8 22). Implied in this statement is also that the seasons and the length of day were the same as at present.

It should be realized that the solar calendar at the time of Noah was not necessarily in error by $5\frac{1}{4}$ days ($365\frac{1}{4}$ minus 360). Possibly an extra month of thirty days was added about every six years to maintain the seasons in their proper positions. Alternatively, five or sometimes six days (not part of any specific month) may have been added at the end of the year, to maintain an average of $365\frac{1}{4}$ days per year.

The Greek translation of the Bible, known as the Septuagint, gives variant ages for the fathers when their sons were born. Thus instead of the Biblical numbers (Gen. 5) of 130, 105, 90, 70, 65, 162, 65, 187, and 182, we find 230, 205, 190, 170, 165, 162, 165, 187, and 188, in the Septuagint. It should be noted that an extra 100 years had been added to numbers of 130 or less. This can be explained on the basis that the writers of the translation considered the extreme ages in the Hebrew text, of up to 969 years, to be based on a year one-tenth as long as nowadays. Then the oldest person listed, namely Methuselah, would have really lived to 96.9 (or almost 97) years, in approximate agreement with the maximum lifetime at present. However, this assumption would also result in some persons becoming fathers before reaching the age of fourteen. The translators therefore modified the Hebrew numbers on the basis that 100 years had to be added to the ages when people became fathers, if they happened to be below 140. As explained previously, it is incorrect to assume that the length of the year during the Creation Era was different from the present. Therefore, the numbers found in the Septuagint are unreliable and should be ignored.

The order of birth of Shem, Ham, and Japheth, the three sons of Noah, needs to be clarified. According to Gen. 5 32, Noah was 500 years old when he became father of Shem, Ham, and Japheth, with the implication from the text that Shem was the oldest and Japheth the youngest. However, in Gen. 11 10 is stated that two years after the Deluge Shem was 100 years old; and we know from Gen. 7 11 that Noah was 600 when the Deluge occurred. These facts lead to the conclusion that Shem was not the oldest son, and perhaps was the youngest since he was born when Noah was 502.

Now, in Gen. 10 1-31 are first listed the descendants of Japheth, then those of Ham, and lastly the descendants of Shem. This arrangement supports the previous conclusion that Shem was the youngest, and also establishes that Japheth was the first-born, and Ham was the middle son. We can now infer that

Noah became father to Japheth when he was 500, to Ham when he was 501 and to Shem when he was 502.

In addition, we find in Gen 10 21 a statement that can be interpreted in two ways, either that Japheth is the oldest, or that Shem is. However, we are forced to say that it is Japheth who is the first-born, since from Gen. 11 10 we have concluded that Shem was not the oldest.

On the basis of the above deductions, we must conclude that the phrase in Gen. 9 24, "And he [Noah] knew what his youngest son had done for him," refers to Shem. What is meant is that Noah knew that Shem had covered his nakedness and not, as usually interpreted, that Noah knew of the sin of Ham.

The reason that the Biblical text always lists Shem first and Japheth last may be explained by the fact that Shem turned out to be the greatest of the three sons of Noah. However, we would then expect Ham to be placed last, rather than second, since he was the least great. An alternate explanation is that at that time children were listed in reverse chronological order—the youngest first and the oldest last. However, we find that the sons of Japheth (Gen. 10 2-4) and Ham (Gen. 10 6, 7, 13, 15) are listed in chronological order, while the sons of Shem (Gen. 10 22-24) are listed in reverse chronological order. Therefore we can not generalize and say that the usual order is reverse chronological. Upon combining both reasons, we get a satisfactory explanation for the arrangement of the listing of the three sons of Noah. Shem was the greatest and was therefore listed first. Since the usual order was now upset, the arrangement was then made according to a reverse chronological order.

The age of Jacob when each of his children was born is not given specifically, but can be deduced from the available data. According to Gen. 47 9, Jacob was 130 when he and his family descended into Egypt. At that time Joseph was thirty-nine years old, since he was thirty when made second to Pharaoh (Gen. 41 46), and he had ruled for nine years (Gen. 41 53, 54; 45 6). Thus Jacob was 91 when Joseph was born (130 minus 39). From the story presented in Gen. 29 30-30 25 it can be deduced that all the children of Jacob, except for Benjamin, were born within a seven year period. Furthermore sufficient details are given to be able, in most cases, to specify the year when each child was born. For example, Reuben was born at the end of the first of these seven years, Simeon in the second, Joseph in the seventh, and so forth. On this basis were calculated the ages for Jacob given in Table 1.5.1. The age of Jacob when Benjamin was born is arrived at according to the considerations subsequently presented in Section 10.1.

1.6 EXTRA-BIBLICAL SUPPORT FOR CREATION HISTORY

1.6.1 Mythological Literature

The mythological literature from numerous nations is one major source for verifying the Biblical history of the Creation Era. The fact that so many civilizations have legends identical in many respects to the Biblical accounts, indicates that the origin of the stories arises from actual experience. Among the legends described are found numerous narratives which have marked similarities to the Biblical descriptions of Creation, the Deluge, the Garden of Eden, the Tower of Babel and the confusion of tongues. A detailed compilation of the mythological tales is found in the book by Theodor H. Gaster[36].

It should be realized that the Biblical account was written by the persons involved, such as Adam, his descendants, and Noah and his children (see Section 10.1). In contrast, the extra-Biblical stories were usually handed down for at least several generations before they were finally recorded. Undoubtedly they arose before the separation of the one land mass into many continents, for otherwise such accounts as the Deluge stories would not be found among the inhabitants of islands and widely scattered locations. During the process of transmittal many variations in the historical facts have arisen and as a result the stories are considered mythology rather than history. Nevertheless, there are still suffcient similarities with the Biblical account to indicate a common origin.

Some examples of the extent of extra-Biblical legends about the creation of the world are as follows: The concept that water preceded all things occurs all over the world; among the Babylonians, Egyptians, and numerous American Indian and African tribes. Separation of heaven from earth is indicated in the Mesopotamian Epic of Creation, the Hittite story of Ullikummi, and Egyptian myths, as well as among the Hindus, the Maoris of New Zealand, and the Bihors of India. It is also found in parts of western Africa, in Chinese folklore, and myths in the Pacific region and Japan. The creation of man from earth or clay is a theme encountered among Mesopotamians, Babylonians, Egyptians, Greeks, natives of Australia, New Zealand, Tahiti, Melanesia, and American Indians. Similarly, there are numerous sources for legends about a garden with special foods, and four streams emanating from a central river[37].

Support for the Biblical Deluge history from mythological sources is even more striking. Deluge or great flood stories are found in almost all primitive mythologies: they are found in Babylonia, Greece, Egypt, Wales, Lithuania, Iceland, India, Tibet, China, Burma, Indochina, Malaya, the Indian archipelago, Australia, New Guinea, the islands of Melanesia, Polynesia, and Micronesia, and in South, Central and North America[38]. In fact, over forty-five pages of fine print are required to give short summaries of all the various Deluge accounts[39]. Most of these stories include: (A) a warning to the "Noah" of the coming disaster; (B) the flood; (C) "Noah" escapes with his family on a ship or by ascending a high mountain; (D) if on a ship, he sends out birds to see if the flood has subsided; and (E) no survivers other than "Noah" and his family[40].

The closest parallel to the Biblical Deluge history is found in the eleventh and the twelve tablets which make up the Epic of Gilgamesh. In the story, Utnapishtim is the Babylonian equivalent of Noah. The tale describes many factors which are identical to the Biblical account, such as the construction of a ship, bringing all types of animals aboard, the Deluge, grounding on top of a mountain, sending out birds—including a dove and a raven—to find dry land, and presenting food offerings[41].

Legends which resemble the Biblical history of the Tower of Babel occur in several parts of the world. The stories are found among the Ba-Luyi tribe of the upper Zambesi, the Bambala of the Congo, the Kulwe, a Bantu tribe near lake Rukwe in Tanganyika, the Njamwezi of Tanganyika, the Ashanti, the Anal clan of the Kuki tribe in Assam, the Lepcha of Sikkim, Hindus, Mexicans, and Hittites. Furthermore, the building of the tower to heaven is associated with subsequent confusion of tongues in much primitive folklore. A very striking example is related by the Gherko Karens who live in Burma. They claim that they were separated from the Red Karens in the 13th generation after Adam, when the people decided to build a pagoda up to heaven. The plan was, however, frustrated by God who confounded their tongues. Other mention of the confusion of tongues to explain the diversity of languages, but not associated with construction of a tower, is found in about five other examples[42].

1.6.2 Historical Literature

In addition to the mythological literature, there also exist historical records which parallel the Biblical account. The first similarity to be considered occurs with respect to the number of generations which preceded the Deluge. The Bible presents ten generations (Gen. 5), and so do two of the three available extra-Biblical antediluvian lists[43,44]. The other list has eight generations. These tabulations are: (A) the list of Chaldean kings handed down by Berossus, as preserved in the writings of Eusebius and Syncellus, who obtained their data from writings of Apollodorus, Abydenus, and Polyhistor; (B) the Sumerian king-list (Larsa List No. 1); and (C) a tablet of the Ashmolean Museum (Larsa List No. 2).

A common feature of these extra-Biblical lists is the use of time units called *sars* and *ners*. Usually a *sar* is interpreted to mean 3,600 years, and a *ner* 600 years. This, however, results in reigns for the antediluvian kings of anywhere between 10,000 and 70,000 years—highly unlikely values considering that the world is less than 6,000 years old. An alternate result can be obtained by realizing that a *sar* is only a numerical figure with a value of 3,600, and is also used as a measure of volume[45]. Now if we assume that instead of 3,600 years, a *sar* represents 3,600 days, which is equivalent to ten years (since the basic year had 360 days—see Section 1.5), we arrive at more reasonable reigns. A tabulation of the extra-Biblical kings and their reigns, based on a *sar* equivalent to ten years, is presented in Table 1.6.2.1. Also listed are the comparable Biblical personalities, and their ages when they became fathers. It should be noted that even though the lengths of the reigns are not in exact agreement, there is still

Table 1.6.2.1
Antediluvian Leaders

Biblical	Years
1. Adam	130
2. Seth	105
3. Enosh	90
4. Kenan	70
5. Mahalalel	65
6. Jared	162
7. Enoch	65
8. Methuselah	187
9. Lamech	182
10. Noah	500
Total	1556

Berossus List	sars	Years
Aloros	10	100
Alaparos	3	30
Amelon	13	130
Ammenon	12	120
Megalaros	18	180
Daonos the shepherd	10	100
Euedorakhos	18	180
Amempsinos	10	100
Ardatas	8	80
Xisouthros	18	180
Total	120	1200

Larsa List No. 1	sars	Years
A-lu-lim	8	80
A-la-gar	10	100
En-me-en-lu-an-na	12	120
En-me-en-gal-an-na	8	80
Dumuzi the shepherd	10	100
En-sib-zi-an-na	8	80
En-me-en-dur-an-na	5 (+5 ners)	58
Ubar-tu-tu	5 (+1 ner)	52
Total	67	670

Larsa List No. 2	sars	Years
A-lu-lim	18	180
A-la-gar	20	200
[. . .]-kiduum-nu-sa-kin-kin	20	200
—	6	60
Dumuzi the shepherd	8	80
En-me-en-lu-an-na	6	60
En-sib-zi-an-na	10	100
En-me-dur-an-na	20	200
Sukurlamgi	8	80
Ziud-sudra	10	100
Total	126	1260

sufficient qualitative similarity to support the Biblical data. An exact agreement should not be expected, since the extra-Biblical data do not agree among themselves.

Of particular interest is the fact that the Sumerian king-list, after presenting the data for the eight antediluvian kings, then states[46], "The flood then swept over the land. After the flood, kingship descended from heaven." This wording parallels the description given in the Bible.

Another historical means for verifying the presented Biblical chronology would be to show that the dates of formation of the different nations are subsequent to the date for the Deluge. As previously explained (Section 1.1.3), the Deluge occurred in 2267 B.C.E., and new nations would be expected to be formed by approximately 2215. The particular nations which were formed are given in Gen. **10**, and are summarized in Table 1.6.2.2. If sufficient data were available showing that the histories of the listed nations arose around 2200 or afterward, then the Biblical date for the Deluge would be established. Unfortunately, only inexact dates are usually available when going so far back in time, and the inaccuracy is admittedly several hundred years. Nevertheless, for the nations of Egypt (son of Ham), Babylon, and China (grandson of Ham), there is sufficient information available to attempt to specify the date of formation.

EGYPT

According to the chronological outline for Egyptian history developed by E. Meyer[47], the first dynasty of Egypt under the leadership of Menes began about 3400[48]. This date was fairly well accepted for a long time. However, recently an increasing amount of evidence has shown that some Egyptian kings before 2000 were contemporaneous rather than successive, resulting in a general lowering of the dates prior to the Twelfth Dynasty[49]. Furthermore, the chronology before the Eleventh Dynasty (which goes back to before 2160) is now considered to be completely uncertain[50]. Therefore, the use of the usual historical methods for determining the beginning of the Egyptian nation is not possible.

An alternate approximate method for determining the start of the Egyptian nation can be obtained from the first recorded mention of the star Sothis. As explained later in Section 3.1.2, the Egyptian calendar was based on a 365-day year, which was one-fourth of a day shorter than the actual solar year. Occasionally, sightings of the reappearance of the star Sothis (Sirius) were made, which involved a $365\frac{1}{4}$ day annual cycle. Now, according to O. Neugebauer the Egyptians were interested in knowing when to expect the annual Nile inundations[51]. Since the Nile flooding lasts for several months and does not recur at exactly the same time each year (although it is based on the solar-year cycle), it would take about two or three centuries before sufficient error would accumulate to require a criterion, other than the 365-day calendar. The new criterion that was eventually selected was the annual reappearance of the star Sothis. We know that the first record of the heliacal rising of Sothis was about 1880[52]. Three centuries before this

Table 1.6.2.2.
Genealogical Table for the Formation of Nations after the Deluge

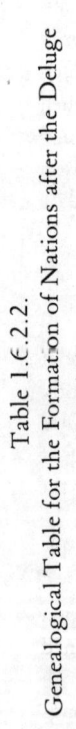

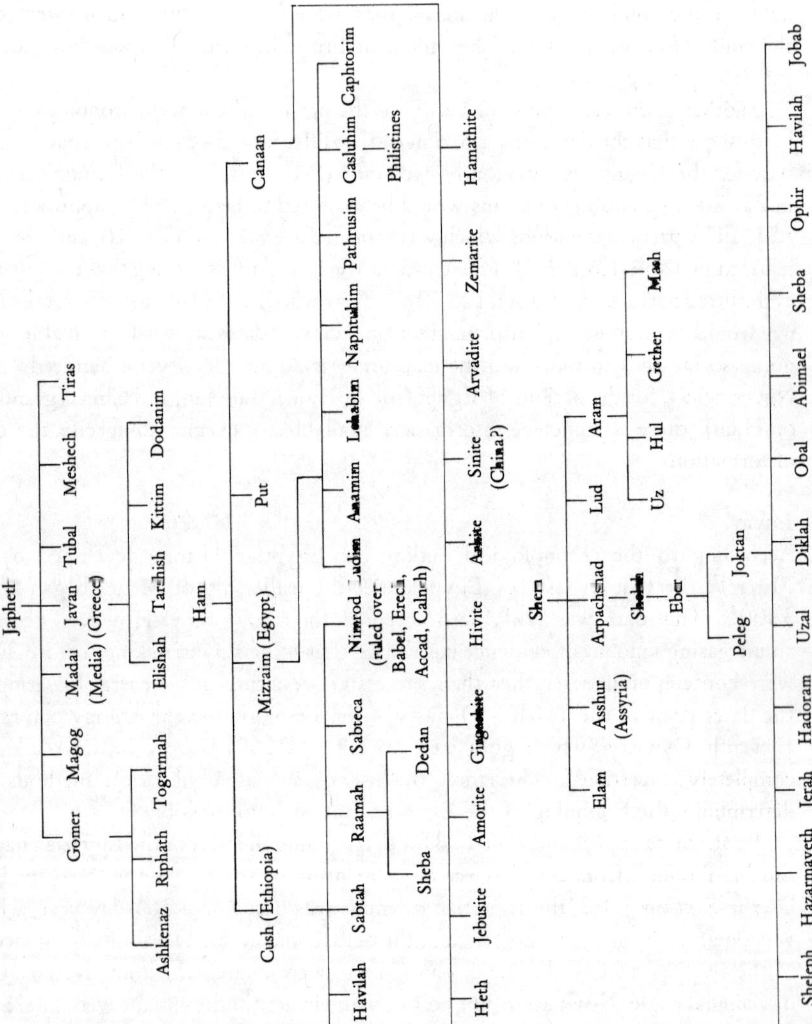

date would be roughly 2180, in agreement with the approximate date for the beginning of the nations based on the Deluge information.

Babylon and Sumerian Cities

As will be subsequently explained in great detail (Section 2.1.1), the correct dates for the First Dynasty of Babylon are 2049–1750. These dates are subsequent to 2215, and therefore are in agreement with the time for the Deluge. However, from the Sumerian king-list[53] it would appear that many of the dynasties of the other listed cities, such as Erech, Ur, Awan, Kish Hamasi, Adab, Mari, Akshak, Lagash, Agade, and Gutium would even have preceded 2267, the calculated date of the Deluge. Nevertheless, we have to keep in mind that there are serious difficulties with the king-list. Although many of the dynasties are stated to be successive, we know that in a number of cases they were contemporaneous. For example, from the king-list we learn that the first three dynasties after the flood were those of Kish, Erech, and Ur, in that order. Yet, from epic and hymnal lore it is learned that several kings of these dynasties were contemporaneous[54]. A second difficulty is that the king-list ascribes to many rulers after the flood exceedingly long reigns, up to 1,500 years, which results, for example, in the first dynasty of Kish lasting for 24,510 years! Although it may be possible that some of the kings lived for over 1,000 years (just as Noah lived to be 950), still their reigns would surely have been contemporaneous rather than successive.

The evidence thus establishes that if the Sumerian king-list is to be used for chronological purposes, care must be taken to realize that many of the listed reigns for any city, as well as dynasties of different cities, may have been contemporaneous. A similar conclusion was also reached for the early Egyptian dynasties.

It therefore seems that the formation of nations after the Deluge was a gradual process. At first, in each nation, there were only on the order of ten families because of the limitations set by the number of people born. Perhaps, each head of household was considered a king, and therefore many kings ruled simultaneously. The listed lengths of reign were in actuality the life-spans of these rulers. After another generation or two, it was necessary, for practical reasons, to select one king over the entire nation. Thereafter, the listed kings were successive. Egyptian and Sumerian historians, in reconstructing the chronology from the limited records available, have failed to recognize the early situation involved in these developing nations, and have frequently arrived at dates many hundreds of years earlier than was actually the case. It is only because of the more recent archaeological discoveries that some recognition of the historical situation has arisen.

China

The earliest historical record in China is the *Shu Ching* or the *Book of History*, which covers the 28th to the eighth centuries B.C.E. Of particular interest is the date

2205 given for the founding of the first dynasty, the Hsia, by Yü, who is said to have successfully dealt with the problem of draining away the waters of a great flood. Yü is considered to have been one of a trio of emperors, Yao, Shun, and Yü[55,56].

The above accounts show a remarkable agreement both chronologically and historically with the Biblical account. Shun, Yü, and Yao correspond to the three sons of Noah, namely Shem, Ham, and Japheth; the date 2205 for the founding of the Chinese nation is in excellent accord with the date 2215 for the approximate time of the formation of nations.

We have now established that available historical chronologies from Egyptian, Babylonian, and Chinese sources are in accord with an approximate date of 2215 for the formation of nations after the Deluge. These cases are those for which fairly reliable dates are available, that go back to before 2000. For practically all other nations, the dates around that time, when available, are dependent upon much guesswork and cannot be relied on for the required accuracy.

Chapter Two

TIME OF ABRAHAM

The time of Abraham is the next chronological period that lends itself to exact verification from extra-Biblical sources. From the Biblical evidence we determine that Abraham was born in 1975 B.C.E.*. In 1905 when seventy years old, he left Ur of the Chaldees at God's command. He lived to be 175 years old (Gen. 25 7), and died in 1800. (See Sections 2.2 and 2.3 for further elaboration.)

2.1 ABRAHAM IDENTIFIED AS HAMMURABI

In the following paragraphs will be presented strong evidence for showing that Abraham is identical with the famous Babylonian king known as Hammurabi. The identification is based on such factors as chronological agreement, similarity of names, analagous personalities, and the fact that the history of Abraham shows that he observed the laws found in the Code of Hammurabi.

2.1.1 Chronological Agreement

The dates for Abraham can be corroborated by proving that Abraham and Hammurabi are the same person. Hammurabi, the sixth king of the Amorite or West Semite dynasty of Babylonia, reigned forty-three years. If we accept the dates, based on astronomical calculations, of 2049–1750 for the first Babylonian dynasty, then Hammurabi ruled from 1947–1905. Thus, the year that Abraham left Ur of the Chaldees was the same year that Hammurabi ended his rulership there. Furthermore, since Hammurabi reigned forty-three years, it is quite reasonable to assume that he was seventy years old, the same age as Abraham, at the conclusion of the reign. Thus from a chronological viewpoint a perfect fit with the Biblical data for Abraham is possible.

It should be realized, however, that much controversy exists about the dates for Hammurabi. Astronomical calculations based on ancient tablets relating to the planet Venus, permit four main possibilities for the reign: specifically 1947–1905, 1848–1806, 1792–1750, or 1728–1686[1]. For a while, the dating by Eduard-Meyer of Hammurabi's reign to 1947–1905 was well accepted[2]. Then docu-

---

* See footnote on first page of Chapter One.

ments found in the ancient city of Mari showed that Hammurabi was a contemporary of the Assyrian King Shamshi-Adad I, and started ruling about twenty years after the beginning of Shamshi-Adad's reign. From the list of Assyrian kings found at Khorsabad, the dates of Shamshi-Adad I were calculated to be as late as 1748–1716, which resulted in the date of Hammurabi being moved forward to 1728–1676[3]. Thus the time of Hammurabi was shifted by as much as 219 years.

However, the Khorsabad List, which records the number of years ruled by the kings of Assyria from Shamshi-Adad I (No. 39 on the list), until Assur-nirari V (No. 107), has several imperfections. The lengths of reigns of kings Nos. 42 through 47, 84 and 85, are specified with the word *tuppu*, the meaning of which is unknown. Also, the length of the reigns of kings Nos. 65 and 66 have been effaced. Thus the lengths of reign of ten intermediate kings on the list are not known[4]. A. Poebel assumed that all these ten monarchs ruled for zero years, and it is on this basis that the date of Shamshi-Adad I comes out to be about 1748–1716 (actually 1739–1707).

Let us now see what would be required to make the dates of Shamshi-Adad I become 1967–1935, so that the reign of Hammurabi would be 1947–1905. The difference between 1967 and 1739 is 228 years. As will be explained in great detail in Section 5.3, twenty-eight years have to be added to the usually accepted dates of all the Assyrian kings up to Assur-nirari V, (No. 107) because the eclipse on which the absolute years are based occurred in 791, rather than 763 as generally accepted. The other 200 years needed to bring us back to 1967 would be found if we assume that the ten kings whose length of reign are unknown ruled an average of twenty years each. The value of twenty years may very well have been meant by the word *tuppu*, especially if we realize that none of the other kings included in the Khorsabad list ruled exactly 20 years, although lengths of reigns of e.g. 16, 17, 18, 19, 21, 23, 24, and 25 years do occur. Furthermore, twenty years is reasonable, since the average length of reign of the listed kings is seventeen years, with some ruling forty or more years. On the basis of the above assumptions, the dates for the Assyrian kings of interest are as presented in Table 2.1.1. Some inexactness still exists, however, since three copies of the Assyrian king-list exist, with occasional variants in the lengths of reign[5]. The varying lengths have been indicated in the Table with the word "var."

There are two ways in which the dates presented can be approximately verified. The first method is through knowledge that certain Assyrian kings were contemporaries of other monarchs whose dates are fairly well established. Thus it is known, based on the Tel-el-Amarna letters (see Section 3.4), that Assur-uballit I (No. 73) was a contemporary of one of the Egyptian Pharaohs, Amenhotep III (1412–1375) or Amenhotep IV (1375–1358). Our dates for Assur-uballit I, 1433–1398, show a partial overlapping in time with Amenhotep III. Similarly it is known that Puzur-Assur III (No. 61) was a contemporary of the Kassite King Burnaburias

TIME OF ABRAHAM 31

Table 2.1.1
Revised Dating for Assyrian Kings

No.	King	Length of Reign (yrs.)	Standard Dates (B.C.E.)	Revised Dates (B.C.E.)
32.	Ilusuma			
33.	Erisum I	40		
34.	Ikunum			
35.	Sargon I			
36.	Puzur-Assur II			
37.	Naram-Sin			
38.	Erisum II			
39.	Shamshi-Adad I	33	1739–1707	1967–1935
40.	Isme-Dagan I	40 (var. 50)	1706–1667	1934–1895
41.	Assur-dugul	6	1666–1661	1894–1889
42.	Assur-apla-idi	(20)	1661	1888–1869
43.	Nasir-Sin	(20)	1661	1868–1849
44.	Sin-namir	(20)	1661	1848–1829
45.	Ipqi-Istar	(20)	1661	1828–1809
46.	Adad-salulu	(20)	1661	1808–1789
47.	Adasi	(20)	1661	1788–1769
48.	Belu-bani	10	1660–1651	1768–1759
49.	Libaja	17	1650–1634	1758–1742
50.	Sarma-Adad I	12	1633–1622	1741–1730
51.	Iptar-Sin	12	1621–1610	1729–1718
52.	Bazaja	28	1609–1582	1717–1690
53.	Lullaja	6	1581–1576	1689–1684
54.	Kidin-Ninua	14	1575–1562	1683–1670
55.	Sarma-Adad II	3	1561–1559	1669–1667
56.	Erisum III	13	1558–1546	1666–1654
57.	Shamshi-Adad II	6	1545–1540	1653–1648
58.	Isme-Dagan II	16	1539–1524	1647–1632
59.	Shamshi-Adad III	16 (var. 15)	1523–1508	1631–1616
60.	Asur-nirari I	26	1507–1482	1615–1590
61.	Puzur-Assur III	24 (var. 14)	1481–1458	1589–1566
62.	Enlil-nasir	13	1457–1445	1565–1553
63.	Nur-ili	12	1444–1433	1552–1541
64.	Assur-saduni	1 mo.	1433	1541

Table 2.1.1 (continued)

No.	King	Length of Reign (yrs.)	Standard Dates (B.C.E.)	Revised Dates (B.C.E.)
65.	Assur-rabi I	(20)	1433	1540–1521
66.	Assur-nadin-ahhe I	(20)	1433	1520–1501
67.	Enlil-nasir II	6	1432–1427	1500–1495
68.	Assur-nirari II	7	1426–1420	1494–1488
69.	Assur-bel-nisesu	9	1419–1411	1487–1479
70.	Assur-rim-nisesu	8	1410–1403	1478–1471
71.	Assur-nadin-ahhe II	10	1402–1393	1470–1461
72.	Eriba-Adad I	27	1392–1366	1460–1434
73.	Assur-uballit I	36	1365–1330	1433–1398
74.	Enlil-nirari	10	1329–1320	1397–1388
75.	Arik-den-ili	12	1319–1308	1387–1376
76.	Adad-nirari I	33 (var. 32)	1307–1275	1375–1343
77.	Shalmaneser I	30	1274–1245	1342–1313
78.	Tukulti-Ninurta I	37	1244–1208	1312–1276
79.	Assur-nadin-apli	4 (var. 3)	1207–1204	1275–1272
80.	Assur-nirari III	6	1203–1198	1271–1266
81.	Enlil-kudurri-usur	5	1197–1193	1265–1261
82.	Ninurta-apil-Ekur	13 (var. 3)	1192–1180	1260–1248
83.	Assur-dan I	46 (var 36)	1179–1134	1247–1202
84.	Ninurta-tukulti-Assur	(20)	1134	1201–1182
85.	Mutakkil-Nusku	(20)	1134	1181–1162
86.	Assur-res-isi I	18	1133–1116	1161–1144
87.	Tiglath-Pileser I	39	1115–1077	1143–1105
88.	Asarid-apil-Ekur	2	1076–1075	1104–1103
89.	Assur-bel-kala	18	1074–1057	1102–1085
90.	Eriba-Adad II	2	1056–1055	1084–1083
91.	Shamshi-Adad IV	4	1054–1051	1082–1079
92.	Assurnasirpal I	19	1050–1032	1078–1060
93.	Shalmaneser II	12	1031–1020	1059–1048
94.	Assur-nirari IV	6	1019–1014	1047–1042
95.	Assur-rabi II	41	1013–973	1041–1001
96.	Assur-res-isi II	5	972–968	1000–996
97.	Tiglath-Pileser II	33 (var. 32)	967–935	995–963
98.	Assur-dan II	23	934–912	962–940

Table 2.1.1 (continued)

No.	King	Length of Reign (yrs.)	Standard Dates (B.C.E.)	Revised Dates (B.C.E.)
99.	Adad-nirari II	21	911–891	939–919
100.	Tukulti-Ninurta II	7	890–884	918–912
101.	Assurnasirpal II	25	883–859	911–887
102.	Shalmaneser III	35	858–824	886–852
103.	Shamshi-Adad V	13	823–811	851–839
104.	Adad-nirari III	28	810–783	838–811
105.	Shalmaneser IV	10	782–773	810–801
106.	Assur-dan III	18	772–755	800–783
107.	Assur-nirari V	10	754–745	782–773

I[6]. However, the time for Burnaburias I can only be given very approximately as ca. 1550, which is in reasonable agreement with our dates for Puzur-Assur III of 1589–1566. It should be noted that the dates of the Kassite kings are partially determined by correspondence with Assyrian rulers. By our modification of the Assyrian dates, a corresponding modification is necessary in the dates of the Kassite monarchs.

The second method for corroborating the dates is through time-spans mentioned in Assyrian inscriptions. However, these time-spans are considered as highly unreliable since there are numerous contradictory lengths of duration. For example, Esarhaddon reckons 434 years from reconstruction of a temple by Shamshi-Adad I (No. 39) until a later reconstruction by Shalmaneser I (No. 77); but Shalmaneser I ascribes 580 years to the same period[7]. The known time-spans are summarized in Table 2.1.2. Because of the contradictions among the time-spans, it is impossible to propose any scheme which would agree with all the given statements. Below are explained only those time-spans which are in reasonable accord with the listed dates.

(A) Tiglath-Pileser I (No. 87) states that sixty years passed from Assur-dan I (No. 83) to the beginning of his own reign[8]. According to our dating, Assur-dan I ended his reign in 1202, and Tiglath-Pileser I began ruling in 1143, which is a difference of sixty years, if the years 1202 and 1143 are both included.

(B) Sennacherib (704–681) refers to finding, after conquest of Babylon, a 600 year old seal of Tukulti-Ninurta I (No. 78)[9]. Since we do not know the exact years in the reigns of Sennacherib and Tukulti-Ninurta I which are referred to, the 600 years could have begun anytime between 1304 and 1281. This is in accord with our dates of 1312–1276 for the reign of Tukulti-Ninurta I.

(C) Sennacherib states that after his eighth campaign he brought back to Assyria what had been taken from Tiglath-Pileser I (No. 87) by Marduk-nadin-ahe, king of Babylon, 418 years previously[10]. Now, the eighth campaign occurred in Sennacherib's fourteenth year (691) or possibly in his nineteenth year (686); since both years are dated by the same *limmu**, namely Bel-emurani[11]. If we arbitrarily assume that 686 is the year in question, then the 418 years are from 1105, the last year of Tiglath-Pileser I, until 686.

(D) As mentioned previously, Shalmaneser I ascribes 580 years to the interval from Shamshi-Adad I (No. 39) until Shalmaneser I (No. 77). Now, 580 years prior to 1342, the beginning of Shalmaneser's reign, is 1922. However, according to our listing, Shamshi-Adad I ruled from 1967 to 1935. The thirteen year discrepancy can be considered small, especially in comparison to discrepancies as great as 100 years occurring in other specified time-spans. In particular, the thirteen year disagreement can be attributed to variant records of the lengths of reign of the Assyrian kings which were available to Shalmaneser I.

2.1.2 Other Points of Agreement

In addition to the possible perfect chronological agreement between the dates of Hammurabi and Abraham, there are numerous other factors which are strong evidence for establishing that these two great persons are one and the same.

Both Abraham and Hammurabi originated in Babylonia. Abraham came from the city of Ur of the Chaldees (Gen. 11 28, 31); Hammurabi, king of Babylon, unified the separate cities of the region into one Babylonian realm, and obviously came from one of these cities.

Especially interesting are the similarities between the names "Abraham" and "Hammurabi," which are extremely alike in sound and construction. The meanings of the names are analagous. "Hammurabi" can be interpreted as meaning "the family is great,"[12] which is in approximate agreement with the meaning of the name "Abram"—"a great father"—or "Abraham"—"a father of many nations" (Gen. 17 5). Furthermore, the name Hammurabi is found with and without the beginning "H," which parallels the fact that the names Abraham and Abram differ by an "H" sound (Gen. 17 5)[13].

Another king with the name Ammurabi or Hammurapih is found in the Canaanitish kingdom of Hana, whose capital Tirga is the modern Asharah on the middle Euphrates, near the mouth of the Habur. The Hana kingdom is contemporary with the Kassite dynasty of Babylon[14]. The usual dates for the Kassite dynasty are approximately 1748–1172. Because of the modifications in the Assyrian dates presented in Section 2.1.1, the period of the Kassite dynasty is more probably aound 1790 to 1214. Therefore, the Hana kingdom may have been flourishing as early as 1850. Now, Abraham died in 1800 at the age of 175.

---

* See section 5.3 for explanation of the *limmu* lists as used in Assyrian chronology.

Table 2.1.2
Time Spans Recorded by Assyrian Kings

Statement by King	Span	Years	Reference
Shalmaneser I (77)	From Erisum I (33) until Shamshi-Adad I (39)	159	ARAB I p. 41
	From Shamshi-Adad I (39) until beginning of reign of Shalmaneser I (77)	580	ARAB I p. 41
Tukulti-Ninurta I (78)	From Ilusuma (32) until beginning of reign of Tukulti-Ninurta I (78)	780	ARAB I p. 62, 63
Tiglath-Pileser I (87)	From Shamshi-Adad III (59) until Assur-dan I (83)	641	ARAB I p.88
	From Assur-dan I (83) until beginning of reign of Tiglath-Pileser I (87)	60	ARAB I p.88
Sennacherib (dates: 704–681)	From Tiglath-Pileser I (87) until after 8th campaign of Sennacherib	418	ARAB II p. 152
	From Tukulti-Ninurta I (78) until Sennacherib	600	ARAB II p. 158–9
Esarhaddon (dates: 680–669)	From Erisum I (33) until Shamshi-Adad I (39)	126	ARAB II p. 272–3
	From Shamshi-Adad I (39) until Shalmaneser I (77)	434	ARAB II p. 272–3
	From Shalmaneser I (77) until Esarhaddon	580 (or 586)	ARAB II p. 271–3

Also, we know that God promised Abraham that his children would inherit the land from the river of Egypt to the Euphrates (Gen. 15 18). The coincidences of the time, the location, and the name, indicate that the Hammurapih of Hana was also the same person as Abraham, and that Abraham became king there toward the end of his life.

The attitudes and actions of Hammurabi, King of Babylon, are analagous to those of Abraham in many respects. Firstly, Hammurabi insisted on justice for the people. His second year is called the year he established justice in the country, and is probably when he initially promulgated the famous laws known as the Code of Hammurabi[15]. This Code follows a more ordered arrangement than other ancient codes of law, and in many cases is extremely similar to the Biblical laws[16]. We find that a statue of Hammurabi was called "King of Justice."[17] Also, Hammurabi investigated trivial complaints and disputes among the humbler classes, and rigidly enforced his legal code. The provisions of the laws reflect the king's support of the humble and oppressed[18].

Similarly, we find that Abraham was a champion of justice. He separated from his nephew Lot so as to avoid disputes (Gen. 13 8), and refused to take booty for himself after the battle in which Lot was rescued (Gen. 14 23). It is specifically mentioned that God knows that Abraham "will command his children and his household ... to do righteousness and justice" (Gen. 18 19). Of particular interest is the conversation between Abraham and God, where Abraham states it is unbelievable God would not do justice with respect to any people of Sodom who are righteous (Gen. 18 25). Furthermore, Abraham insisted on paying the full price for the field of Ephron, rather than obtain it free (Gen. 23 16).

Secondly, we find that Hammurabi was a great administrator. He unified the separate cities, dug canals vital to the Babylonian irrigation system, built temples, made an end of war, and governed in peace[19,20]. Similarly, we observe Abraham's great administrative ability in settling the dispute between his shepherds and Lot's (Gen. 13 5–12), in leading an attack to save Lot (Gen. 14 14–16), in circumcizing himself as well as all the men in the household (Gen. 17 24–27), in making arrangements for feeding unexpected guests (Gen. 18 2–8), in arranging for the burial of Sarah (Gen. 23 3–20), in commanding his servant to find a suitable wife for Isaac (Gen. 24 2–9), and in distributing the main part of his possessions to Isaac (Gen. 25 5, 6).

Thirdly, Hammurabi was a great military leader. In his sixth and seventh years he conquered the cities of Isin, Uruk, and Iamutbal. Subsequently, around his thirtieth year, he conquered Larsa, and became master of all Babylonia. Within a few more years he defeated Mari and other Assyrian allies[21]. Similarly, we find that Abraham was very capable militarily. When his nephew Lot was captured by the combined army of four kings, Abraham with only 318 men defeated the army and rescued Lot (Gen. 14 1–16).

Of extreme importance to the identification of Abraham with Hammurabi is the fact that several occurrences during Abraham's life show his observance of the Code of Hammurabi[22]. According to Articles 144–147 of the Code, a barren wife may offer one of her maidservants to her husband as a concubine. If the servant bore children, boasted of them, and thus became a rival of the wife, then the wife could reduce the concubine back to the position of servant. Now when Sarah did not bear any children, she offered her Egyptian handmaid, Hagar, to Abraham as a wife. Hagar, upon becoming pregnant, despised Sarah. Abraham then gave Sarah permission to reduce Hagar back to the position of handmaid (Gen. 16 1–6).

Article 146 states that if the wife is displeased with the concubine, she cannot sell the concubine for money, but can reduce her to servitude. When Sarah became once again displeased with Hagar, she wanted to expel Hagar from the household, which would be a legal loophole from the law. Abraham disliked this idea, but acquiesced after being told to do so by God (Gen. 21 10–14).

Article 165 allows the father to give a special gift to his preferred son, which is above the equal shares that all the sons receive upon the father's death. Article 171, however, permits the father not to recognize as his own the children of a servant-girl. In such a case the children of the servant-girl do not inherit from the father. Before Abraham died he made Isaac his full heir, and gave gifts to the sons from his other wives (Gen. 25 5–6), whom he did not recognize as his true sons; a clever way of meeting the requirements of the Code of Hammurabi.

2.1.3. Problems in Identification

Up until now, only arguments showing strong reasons for identifying Hammurabi as Abraham have been presented. However, there are a few items in the life of Hammurabi which might at first make one believe that the identification is incorrect. Below are given means for resolving such difficulties.

(A) Hammurabi is known to have been an idol-worshipper. For example, at the beginning of the inscription of the "Code of Hammurabi" he is shown receiving the commission to write the lawbook from the sun god, Shamash[23]. Yet we know that Abraham was a strict monotheist. In actuality, the paradox is readily resolved, for in Josh. 24 2, 3 is stated that Abraham worshipped other gods before being taken out of Ur of the Chaldees by God.

(B) Hammurabi was succeeded as ruler of Babylonia by his son Samsu-iluna, yet Abraham did not father any children before he reached the age of eighty-six (Gen. 11 29, 30; 16 16).

Tablets found at Nuzi in northern Mesopotamia, dating to the first half of the second millenium, reveal that adoption was frequent, even when the original parents were still alive. In particular, childless couples often adopted a son who would be heir to their estate, and in return would care for them when they were old. It was specified, however, that if after the adoption they had a son of their own, the adopted son would have to give way to the real son as the chief heir[24].

Also, laws with respect to adoption of sons are given in Articles 185–191 of the Code of Hammurabi. There, also, it is implied that the adopted son would care for the foster parents and in return be heir to the estate[25].

If, therefore, we assume that Samsu-iluna was Hammurabi's adopted son, then the problem is solved. Support for this contention is found in Gen. 15 2, 3, where Abraham states that he has no children, and that Damesek-Eliezer, the son of the administrator of his house, is his heir. Samsu-iluna can now be identified with Damesek-Eliezer, and this identification gains additional support from the moderate similarity of the names.

(C) Hammurabi's father and predecessor was Sin-muballit, yet Abraham's father is known as Terah (Gen. 11 26). Possibly Terah is identical with Sin-muballit although the names seem entirely different. Alternatively, Hammurabi may have been an adopted son of Sin-muballit.

(D) What evidence is there that Hammurabi was still alive when his son Samsu-iluna became king? A badly damaged letter proves that Hammurabi was alive when Samsu-iluna became king. In the letter Samsu-iluna writes "The king, my father is s[ick] and I sat myself on the throne in order to . . . the country."[26]

2.2 SUPPLEMENTED HISTORY OF ABRAHAM

Upon combining the known histories of Abraham and Hammurabi we obtain the following picture for the selection of Abraham by God. Abraham was a capable administrator and honest ruler of Babylonia who tried his utmost to maintain and enforce justice. In his second year he developed a legal system known as the Code of Hammurabi, which was the most advanced legal system up to that time, and which was amazingly similar to the Biblical laws given subsequently by God. All this time Abraham was an idol-worshipper who believed in many gods. When Abraham was seventy years old, after 43 years of rulership over Babylonia, God revealed himself and commanded Abraham to leave the country over which he ruled and where he was born, and to go to a new land (Gen. 12 1, 2). As a reward, Abraham would become the father of a great nation. He listened to God, and left Babylonia with his father Terah and his nephew Lot (Gen. 11 31). Five years later Abraham left his father in Haran (Gen. 12 4), and proceeded to the land of Canaan.

On several occasions Abraham was promised that his descendants would inherit the land (Gen. 12 7; 13 15; 15 4). This raised the problem that he had no children, and that his adopted son Samsu-iluna (Gen. 15 2) inherited his rulership in Babylonia. God answered that Abraham would have children, and it would take 400 years before they would become a nation (Gen. 15 13). Abraham withstood many trials and difficulties, as detailed in the Bible, and proved himself to be a staunch believer in God. As a result, Abraham was promised that his descendants would be too numerous to be counted (Gen. 22 17, 18).

Eventually Isaac was born, and married a suitable wife, Rebekah (Gen. 24 67).

Abraham's task with respect to becoming the father of a great nation, was now completed. He remarried (Gen. 25 1), and established himself as King of Hana. Abraham lived to be 175 years old, and was buried in the Cave of Machpelah (Gen. 25 7–9).

2.3 BIBLICAL CHRONOLOGY FROM TIME OF ABRAHAM UNTIL EXODUS FROM EGYPT

The chronology of the Creation Era was based upon the ages of the fathers at the time of birth of the children. Sufficient data were supplied to allow such calculations from Creation through the birth of the twelve sons of Jacob. Then a break in the system of dating arises. No longer is it known how old the father is when the child is born. Instead, the dating continues by giving the lengths of time from one event to another.

The first such interval occurs at the time of Abraham, and spans the period until the Exodus from Egypt. Thus, Abraham was told by God, "Know that your descendants will be aliens in a land that is not theirs, and they will be enslaved and afflicted, for 400 years" (Gen. 15 13). Also, at the time of the Exodus of the Israelites from Egypt it is stated (Ex. 12 40), "The settlement of the Israelites, those who dwelt in Egypt, lasted 430 years." Although it is not perfectly obvious where the 400 and 430 years begin, it is clear that they end at the time of the Exodus.

Some insight as to when these periods begin can be obtained from the information supplied about Levi and his descendants (Ex. 6 16–20). Levi lived to be 137 years old, and was father of Gershon, Kohath, and Merari. Kohath lived to be 133 years old, and was father of Amram, Izhar, Hebron, and Uzziel. Amram lived to be 137 years old, and was father of Miriam, Aaron, and Moses. Also, from Ex. 7 7 and Deut. 1 3; 34 7, we know Moses was eighty, and Aaron eighty-three at the time of the Exodus.

The maximum number of years that the Israelites resided in Egypt can be calculated as follows, assuming it is possible (although extremely unlikely) for each father to have a child born in the last year of his life. When Levi and the other brothers arrived in Egypt, Kohath was already born (Gen. 46 11). Since he had a younger brother Merari, Kohath was then at least one year old. Also Amram had three younger brothers, and therefore must have been at least three years old at the time of the death of his father Kohath. Then, based on the meager available data, the maximum total number of years is 346 (132 for Kohath, 134 for Amram, 80 for Moses), which is fifty-four years less than 400.

We thus learn that the 400 years specified in Gen. 15 13 refers not to the period of the sojourn in Egypt, but to the length of time *that the descendants of Abraham would be aliens in a land not their own.* Abraham was told by God that the Land of Canaan would be given to his children (Gen. 12 7; 13 15). God modified the statement (Gen. 15 13), however, by letting Abraham know that the children will not inherit the land until after 400 years. The beginning of the 400 years must then be from the birth of Isaac, the child through whom came the descendants of Abraham (Gen. 17 19).

The period of 430 years must begin thirty years before the birth of Isaac. We know that Abraham entered the land of Canaan at the age of seventy-five (Gen. 12 4–5), which was twenty-five years before Isaac was born (Gen. 21 5). The event of importance thirty years before the birth of Isaac must then be the departure of Abraham from Ur of the Chaldees (Gen. 11 31; 21 1), at the calculated age of seventy. Leaving Ur of the Chaldees was momentous, since it marked the beginning of the Israelite people. Reference to this event is found, for example, in Gen. 15 7 and Neh. 9 7. Thus the phrase "settlement of the Israelites" (Ex. 12 40) refers to the departure of Abraham from Ur 430 years before the Exodus.

Support for the above conclusions can be obtained by calculating the maximum and minimum probable lengths for the stay of the Israelites in Egypt. The maximum can be calculated on the assumption that the oldest average age for people living at that period to become fathers was ninety years. Thus Jacob was ninety-one when Joseph, his next to youngest child, was born (see Table 1.1); Abraham considered 100 years unusually old to beget a child (Gen. 17 17), but saw nothing unusual about his becoming a father at eighty-six (Gen. 16 16). Following this line of reasoning, the maximum probable length of the stay in Egypt is 256 years (89 for Kohath, 87 for Amram, and 80 for Moses).

The minimum probable length can be calculated as follows. According to Ex. 1 6, 8 a new king arose over Egypt who enslaved the Israelites after the death of all the twelve sons of Jacob as well as their entire generation. It was during the period of enslavement that Moses was born (Ex. 2). Now, Levi died at the age of 137 (Ex. 6 16), and was 43 years old when the family of Jacob arrived to settle in Egypt (Jacob was 130 at that time, and was 87 when Levi was born). Thus Levi lived 94 years in Egypt. Furthermore, Moses lived 80 years in Egypt before the Exodus (Ex. 7 7). With fair certainty we may also assume that not only Moses but also his older sister Miriam were born after the death of the generation of the sons of Jacob. At the time Moses was born, his sister is called a young lady (עלמה) (Ex. 2 8) implying that she was at least twelve. The total minimum stay in Egypt then becomes 186 years (94 for Levi, 80 for Moses, 12 for Miriam before the birth of Moses).

We have now established that in all probability the Israelites resided in Egypt, not more than 256 years nor less than 186 years. According to our explanation for the sentence specifying 400 years, the actual stay in Egypt was 210 years (400 years, minus 60 years until Isaac fathered Jacob [Gen. 25 26], minus 130 years until Jacob settled in Egypt [Gen. 47 9]). Thus the available chronological data are in accord with the interpretation presented.

2.4 SIGNIFICANCE OF THE TERM "GENERATION"

In addition to being told that his descendants would be aliens for 400 years (Gen. 15 13), Abraham was also informed that the fourth generation would return to the promised land (Gen. 15 16). The problem arises as to what is meant by the term "generation," and when the counting of the four generations begins.

The term "generation" usually signifies the time for a father to be succeeded by his child, and the term will be used in that sense in the following discussion. According to this definition it is impossible to assume that the four generations begin with the birth of Isaac. We know that Isaac was succeeded by Jacob, the twelve brothers, and their children—and the latter three generations descended to Egypt (Gen. 46 8–27). The Israelites resided in Egypt for 210 years; this requires that at least one generation was born in Egypt, since the maximum lifetime at that historical period was approximately 137 years (Ex. 6 16,18,20). Thus there were a minimum of five generations before the Exodus. Furthermore, a sixth generation must be counted, because the entire generation who were over the age of twenty at the time of the Exodus died in the desert (Num. 14 29; 26 64).

We have now proved that the four generations do not begin with the birth of Isaac. Probably what was meant by the text was that some of the fourth generation of those who descended to Egypt would return to the promised land. The following three definite examples of the return of the fourth generation can be obtained from the Biblical data:

(A) Eleazar, son of Aaron, son of Amram, son of Kohath (see Ex. 6 18, 20, 23; Num. 26 57–60; I Chr. 5 27–29): Kohath was among those who descended to Egypt (Gen. 46 11), while Eleazar was buried in the land of Israel (Josh. 24 33).

Alternatively, Eleazar can be considered as the son of Aaron, son of Jochebed (wife of Amram), daughter of Levi (see Ex. 6 20; Num. 26 59). Here Eleazar must be considered as the fourth generation from Levi, who descended to Egypt (Gen. 46 11), since Jochebed was born in Egypt (Num. 26 59).

(B) Achan (or Achar), son of Carmi, son of Zabdi (or Zimri), son of Zerah (see Josh. 7 1; I Chr. 2 6, 7): Zerah was among those who descended to Egypt (Gen. 46 12), while Achan was among those who returned to the land of Israel since he was a mature individual, the father of sons and daughters (Josh. 7 24), shortly after the entrance into the land.

(C) Sons of Korah, son of Izhar (or Amminadab), son of Kohath (see Ex. 6 18, 21, 24; Num. 16 1; I Chr. 6 7): Kohath was among those who descended to Egypt (Gen. 46 11), while the sons of Korah returned to the land of Israel. Evidence that the sons of Korah actually entered the land is found in Ps. 85 2, where a Psalm written by the original sons of Korah mentions the reestablishment in the land of the settlement of Jacob (see Section 13.1, Authorship).

It should be realized that although some of the fourth generation returned to the promised land, the majority of the Israelites at that time were descended from more intervening generations. For example, Joshua was of the tenth generation from Ephraim (I Chr. 7 23, 25-27). The genealogy for Joshua is as follows: Joshua, son of Nun, son of Elishama, son of Ammihud, son of Ladan, son of Tahan, son of Telah, son of Rephah, son of Beriah, son of Ephraim.

2.4.1 Length of an Average Generation

Although Abraham did not become a father until the age of eighty-six (Gen. 16 16), Isaac until the age of sixty (Gen. 25 26), and Jacob until the age of eighty-five (see Table 1.1), yet most of the sons of Jacob became fathers when they were in their teens. Let us now consider the available evidence for the ages when the twelve brothers and their descendants became parents.

When Judah descended to Egypt he was forty-two years old (three years older than Joseph, who was then thirty-nine [Gen. 41 46, 48; 45 6]). During these forty-two years, he married, had three children (Gen. 38 2-5), the youngest already matured (Gen. 38 14). In addition, Judah fathered twins named Perez and Zerah (Gen. 38 29, 30), and Perez had two children (Gen. 46 12). We can conclude that the age of maturity of the males was twelve years, for otherwise it would be difficult to explain the data. Assume that Judah married at twelve, had three children by the time he was fifteen, and the youngest son matured when Judah was twenty-seven. The next year Perez and Zerah were born, and fourteen years later Perez had his second child when Judah was forty-two. Thus, in three instances the age of maturity was twelve, and the length of a generation was thirteen years.

When Benjamin descended to Egypt he was the father of ten children (Gen. 46 21). At that time he was about twenty-five years old, since he was approximately fourteen years younger than Joseph (see Section 10.1, Organization). Assuming that Benjamin had all ten children from one wife, and allowing one year for the birth of each child, we must conclude that he was married by the age of fifteen, and the oldest son was born when Benjamin was no older than sixteen.

For the descendants of Ephraim, the son of Joseph, we find a generation to be a maximum of nineteen years. Thus, Ephraim was born when Joseph was thirty-two, or at the most, thirty-seven (Gen. 41 45, 46, 50-52). Joseph lived to be 110 (Gen. 50 22). During the period of seventy-eight years (110 minus 32) Ephraim had fourth generation descendants (Gen. 50 23). Hence four generations occurred within seventy-eight years, or nineteen years per generation.

The above three cases indicate that, except in unusual circumstances such as occurred with Joseph, the sons of Jacob and their descendants married young, and became parents before the age of twenty. This information is useful in comprehending the rapid growth of the Israelite people from the seventy persons who descended to Egypt into a population containing over 600,000 males.

2.4.2 Rapid Growth of the Israelite Population

When Jacob and his descendants settled in Egypt, there were sixty-eight males and two females among the seventy persons listed in Gen. **46** 8–27. In the second year after the Exodus, which was 212 years later, the number of males over twenty years of age was 603,550 (Num. **1** 46); in 192 years (212 minus 20) the number of males increased by a factor of 8,876 (603,550 divided by 68). Following the line of reasoning in Section 2.4.1, let us assume that on the average the total number of children per family per generation were born within twenty-five years. Then if x represents the number of male children per family per generation, which is also equal to the factor by which the population increases in twenty-five years, we obtain the equation $x^{192/25} = 8,876$. Upon solving this equation, we find $x = 3.3$. Since the average family had an equal number of boys and girls, then approximately seven children must have been born per family for the population to increase to 603,550. People married young, and it therefore is quite feasible that the average family had seven children within a generation of twenty-five years.

It should be realized that the above numbers are very approximate, and are presented to show that the Israelite population could easily grow by the large factor of 8,876 within 192 years. Implicit in the calculations is that none of the parents—those of the previous generation—are surviving among the 603,550 males. In actuality many did survive, some even lived to be over 120 years old. Therefore, the calculated number of children per family is the maximum necessary to explain the large growth rate, unless there was a large fatality rate among the children born. C. Tietze in "Population Studies" concludes that in a society not using contraceptive methods, with allowance made for still births, infertility, and delayed marriages, women would have an average of 7.2 live births[27]. This rate is said to correspond roughly to the present situation in certain parts of Africa and Asia. Furthermore, according to D. M. Kiefer a married couple in the United States around 1800 had between eight and ten children on the average during their lifetime.[28]. It is thus seen that the described increase in the Israelite population is not unusual.

Approximately two years before the birth of Moses, the King of Egypt told the two Hebrew midwives to kill all male Hebrew babies (Ex. **1** 15, 16). We can conclude from this that only two midwives were then necessary for the entire Israelite population. At that time it was 128 years (210 minus 82) after the sixty-eight males in the family of Jacob settled in Egypt. Using the values of 3.3 boys, 25 years per generation, and a time span of 128 years, we can calculate that the population increased by a factor of 452 ($=3.3^{128/25}$) over the original sixty-eight males. Hence the population was approximately 68 × 452 × 2 = 61,472. According to C. Tietze, for a population where women have an average of 7.2 live births, the annual birth rate is 50.7 per 1,000 of population.[29]

Using this value, we calculate that in a population of 61,472 there would be approximately 3,117 births per year, or an average of one birth every 2.8 hours. Two midwives could handle this rate, assuming they worked long hours. Also, at that time the Hebrew women were very healthy and gave birth rapidly (Ex. 1 19), thereby not requiring much assistance during labor. Shortly thereafter, with the increase of the Hebrew population, houses or hospital facilities were built for the midwives (Ex. 1 21) to enable them to care for the increasing number of births.

Just as the average number of children per family was calculated for the entire Israelite population, so the average number per family for each tribe can be determined. In Gen. **46** 8–27 the number of males per tribe is given at the time of settling in Egypt, and in Num. 1 an exact counting of the number of males over the age of twenty is given for each tribe during the second year in the desert. Let us consider the two extreme cases. For the tribe of Benjamin there is the smallest increase. Benjamin had ten sons, giving a total of eleven males when the family descended to Egypt. In the year after the Exodus, the tribe of Benjamin had 35,400 males over the age of twenty, or a growth by a factor of 3,218. As figured previously, $x^{192/25} = 3,218$, or $x = 2.9$. Thus the average family in the tribe of Benjamin had six children. At the other extreme is the tribe of Dan, for which there is the greatest increase. Dan had only one son, giving a total of two males when the Israelites went to Egypt. In the year after the Exodus there were 62,700 males over the age of 20 in the tribe of Dan, a growth by a factor of 31,350. Then $x^{192/25} = 31,350$, or $x = 3.9$. Thus the average family of the tribe of Dan had eight children.

The average number of three to four male children per family is in approximate agreement with the average number of the male children listed. For example, the average number of male children is $4\frac{1}{4}$ for the twelve sons of Jacob (see Gen. **46** 8–27), and $2\frac{2}{3}$ for members of the tribe of Levi (Ex. **6** 17–25).

A problem arises from the number of first-born male children listed in Num. 3 43. The number of first-born males over one month of age is given as 22,273. At this time there were 603,550 males over the age of twenty and additional males below that age who were not counted. This leads to an average of one first-born son for more than thirty men; if we consider the people under the age of twenty, the number of first-born males is closer to one for sixty men in the population. Furthermore, in Num. 3, where the Levites were substituted for the first-born, the actual total of the Levites is 22,300 (Num. 3 22, 28, 34), although the text gives the sum as 22,000 (Num. 3 39). The logical explanation for the discrepancy is that the 300 Levites not included were first-born. Hence there would be 300 first-born males out of 22,000, or one first-born per seventy-three men. However, according to our previous conclusion that there were about four male children per family (and realizing that half the time the eldest child is a girl) we would expect about one eldest male per eight men.

In trying to resolve this problem, it is very difficult to assume that the eldest children were so much more subject to death that their ratio was decreased from one out of eight to approximatly one out of seventy. Rather, the first-born males referred to in the text must have been a select group of the first-born who had special responsibilities. This elite group of first-born must have consisted of about one out of eight of the actual first-born males.

Chapter Three

HISTORY OF ISRAEL IN EGYPT

3.1 COMPARISON OF THE CHRONOLOGIES

Various dates, differing by as much as 250 years, have been proposed by historians for the period of Egyptian history when the Israelites dwelt in Egypt. None of these dates, however, correspond exactly to the traditional interpretation of the Biblical passages. Below will be described a means for making the Biblical and Egyptian chronologies coincide, which in addition allows the identification in Egyptian history of such personalities as Jacob, Moses, Aaron, the Pharaoh who enslaved the Israelites, and the Pharaoh of the Exodus. The chronologies will be presented first, followed by comparison based on other historical data.

3.1.1 Biblical Chronology

The chronological outline of the time from Joseph until after the Exodus can be established using the date of the destruction of the First Temple as a starting point. On the basis of Babylonian history, the destruction of the Temple occurred in 586 B.C.E. The foundations of the Temple were laid 409 years previously (see Section 5.2, Conclusion) which was 480 years after the Exodus (I Kings 6 1). This sets the date of the Exodus as 1475 (586 + 409 + 480), or more exactly, the beginning of 1474. The Israelites were in Egypt for 210 years (see Section 2.3), making 1685 the year when Jacob and his family settled in Egypt. Joseph was acting as second to Pharaoh for nine years prior to the arrival of the rest of his family (Gen. 41 53,54; 45 6), from 1694. In addition, we can establish (A) that the Israelites were enslaved after the death of Levi and before the birth of Miriam, Moses' sister, sometime between 1591 and 1567 (see Section 2.3); (B) that Moses was born in 1555, eighty years before the Exodus (Ex. 7 7); and (C) that the entrance into the land of Canaan occurred at the beginning of 1434, after a forty-year journey through the desert (Deut. 1 3; 34 7). Subsequently, in Section 4.1, we will establish that Joshua ruled for fifty-two years, and therefore the conquest of the land of Canaan continued under his leadership until 1383. A summary of these dates is presented in Table 3.1.

Table 3.1
Chronology of the Egyptian Period Based on the Bible

Year (B.C.E.)	
1694	Joseph becomes ruler of Egypt, second to Pharaoh
1685	Arrival of Jacob and family in Egypt
Between 1591 and 1567	Enslavement of the Israelites
1555	Birth of Moses
Beginning of 1474	Exodus from Egypt
Beginning of 1434	Entrance into land of Canaan
1434–1383	Conquest of land of Canaan under Joshua

3.1.2 Egyptian Chronology

The Biblical chronology was based on an historical written record. Such is not the case for Egyptian chronology. No reliable account of Egyptian history, written by ancient historians, has survived. The Egyptian history written by Manetho, a priest who flourished under Ptolemy I (305–285), is quoted by Africanus, Eusebius, and Josephus. However, the original work written in Greek has perished. Manetho's division of the reigns of the Pharaohs into thirty dynasties is still used because of the convenience of the classification. Nevertheless, the chronology and much of the history described by Manetho is inexact and often completely wrong, as attested by inscriptions of contemporary monuments[1] and the criticism of Josephus[2].

Present knowledge of Egyptian history is mainly reconstructed from inscriptions, and the results of much of the findings are described in the works of J. H. Breasted[3,4]. For the period concerned (the Eighteenth Dynasty), the chronology is fairly exact in many instances because of recorded cases of correspondence of the annual cycle of the heliacal rising at sunrise of the star Sothis (a $365\frac{1}{4}$ day cycle) with the Egyptian calendar (a 365-day cycle). In the Egyptian calendar the months gradually lost all relation to the seasons because an extra day was not intercalated every four years. Instead the seasons were determined by the Sothic cycle, which closely corresponds to the solar year. In general 1,461 calendar years equals 1,460 Sothic years, and it is possible to figure out the actual year to within four years at most. Modern historians give these astronomical data interpretations that vary by as much as thirteen years from the dates used by Breasted. Furthermore, since the time of Breasted, there has been additional clarification of events in the Eighteenth Dynasty. For our purposes, the key dates of the Eighteenth Dynasty will be based on those of Breasted, but slight modifications will be made in other dates according to more recent discoveries. A summary of the Egyptian chronology relevant to the Israelite period is presented in Table 3.2. The dates of

1580 for the start of the Eighteenth Dynasty, and 1479 for the beginning of Thutmose III's sole reign, are the key dates in the present discussion. Explanation of some of the data listed in the Table are presented below with respect to the beginning of the Hyksos period, and the co-regnancies during the Eighteenth Dynasty.

In general, the start of the Hyksos period is usually given as circa 1700. However, more exact dates can be specified. According to the Turin Papyrus, the Hyksos kings reigned for 108 years; while Eusebius and the Scholia of Plato allow 103 years for the Hyksos[5]. We know that the Hyksos' reign ended around the third year of Ahmose I, the first ruler of the Eighteenth Dynasty, when he captured the city of Avaris[6] Therefore, the beginning of Hyksos rule is 1685 or 1680, i.e. circa 1685. In addition, an inscription erected by Ramses II (1292–1225) commemorates 400 years of worship of the Hyksos god Seth near the end of the reign of Seti I (1313–1292)[7,8]. If we assume that the 400th year was 1294, two years before the end of Seti's reign, then the introduction of worship of Seth by the Hyksos was in 1694.

Table 3.2
Chronology of the Egyptian Period
Based on Extra-Biblical Sources

	Dates (B.C.E.)
Hyksos Period	
Beginning of worship of Seth	ca. 1694
Reign of Hyksos kings	ca. 1685–1580
Eighteenth Dynasty	
Ahmose I	1580–1557
Amenhotep I	ca. 1557–1540
Thutmose I and Princess Ahmose	ca. 1540–1511
Thutmose II and Hatshepsut	ca. 1511–1501
Thutmose III and Hatshepsut	1501–1479
Thutmose III	1479–1447
Amenhotep II	1448–1420
Thutmose IV	1420–1412
Amarna Age	
Amenhotep III	1412–1375
Amenhotep IV (Ikhnaton)	1375–1358

The co-regnancies listed for the Eighteenth Dynasty are based on the following information[9]. Originally it was not permitted for a woman to be the main ruler of Egypt. When Amenhotep I died without any children, the right to the crown fell to Amenhotep's sister, the Princess Ahmose, who was married to Thutmose I. Since she could not be the Pharaoh, her husband became the ruler, while she was called the "Great Royal Wife," a title reserved for the official queen. It was also required, according to Egyptian tradition, that only the children of Thutmose I by the Princess Ahmose, had a legitimate right to the throne. From their marriage, only Princess Hatshepsut survived as lawful heir. However, from a second marriage of Thutmose I with a Princess Mutnofret, a son named Thutmose (II) was born. To allow this son to rule, he was married to his half-sister Hatshepsut. After the death of Thutmose I, Thutmose II began to rule, but he was dominated by the Queen-Mother Ahmose and his wife Hatshepsut. Then a similar situation occurred again: Thutmose II only had daughters by his wife Hatshepsut, although by another wife he had a son, the future Thutmose III. Thutmose III was appointed co-regent with Thutmose II, and was married to his half-sister Merytre, who was Thutmose II's daughter by Hatshepsut. When Thutmose II died, Thutmose III became ruler, with his mother-in-law Hatshepsut as the official "king." Subsequently, she became the dominant ruler of Egypt until her death.

Comparison of the dates presented in Table 3.1 based on the Bible, with the dates presented in Table 3.2 based on Egyptian inscriptions, indicates the following: (A) the Hyksos rulers were none other than Joseph, his father's family, and their successors; (B) the Israelites were enslaved at the time of Ahmose I; (C) the Exodus from Egypt occurred in the fourth year of the reign of Thutmose III; and (D) the conquest of the land of Canaan by Joshua occurred prior to and during the Amarna Period of the Eighteenth Dynasty. These conclusions are based solely on the comparative chronologies. However, strong corroboration of these inferences can be gained from a detailed study of the corresponding historical data. In the next section, such a comparison will be made.

3.2 COMPARISON OF BIBLICAL AND EGYPTIAN HISTORIES

3.2.1 Hyksos Period

Based on the Biblical data the following historical description can be given concerning the Hyksos period. In 1694 B.C.E. Joseph, who had for eight years (see end of section 10.1) been in prison, correctly interpreted the dream of Pharaoh, King of Egypt (Gen. 41 1–32). Joseph ascribed his ability to interpret dreams to God (Gen. 41 16,25), and as a consequence Pharaoh recognized the God of Joseph (Gen. 41 38,39). Joseph was rewarded by becoming the second most important leader of Egypt. In actuality, Joseph was made "King" of Egypt while Pharaoh retained the title of "Pharaoh" for himself (Gen. 41 40–46; 42 6; 44 18; 45 8,9). In 1685 Jacob and his descendants (seventy persons in addition to wives—Gen. **46** 26,27) settled in Egypt. Because the brothers of Joseph were shepherds, the Israelites settled in the land of Goshen (Gen. **45** 10; **47** 6), which was also called the land of Rameses (Gen. **47** 11). Some of the brothers were placed in high positions, as is evidenced by their becoming officers in charge of the cattle of Pharaoh (Gen. **46** 6). At about this time, Joseph brought almost all of Egypt into servitude and tribute in return for food during the years of famine (Gen. **47** 20–26). The rulership of the Israelites continued until at least 1591, the year that Levi, the brother of Joseph, died. The family of Jacob and his descendants were acting in the capacity of king of Egypt all that time. This is implied from Ex. **1** 6 where it is stated that Joseph, his brothers, and that entire generation died; and then in Ex. **1** 8 is told that a new king of Egypt arose who did not know Joseph, and enslaved the Israelites. The new king of Egypt formed a new dynasty since he replaced the Israelite leadership.

Based on Egyptian history, the following parallel description of the Hyksos period is obtained. Around 1694, the worship of the Hyksos God Seth (or Sutekh) began. About nine years later, in 1685 the reigns of the Hyksos kings started. The name Hyksos is explained by Manetho as meaning "shepherd kings,"[10] although it is now believed to have meant "rulers of foreign countries."[11] The Hyksos ruled from the city of Avaris (or Tanis), which is considered to be in the land of Goshen[12]. These rulers were Semites who became rulers of Egypt without a fight. They placed all Egypt under tribute. Simultaneously with the Hyksos period, the Egyptian Pharaohs ruled from Thebes. Around 1580, Kamose, the last Pharaoh of the Seventeenth Dynasty, and then Ahmose I, the first Pharaoh of the Eighteenth Dynasty, besieged, attacked, and eventually conquered and enslaved the Hyksos people[13].

In addition to the chronological and general historical agreement between the Israelite rulership in Egypt and the Hyksos kings, there are the following additional points which help establish the identity of the two groups.

(A) Josephus identifies the Hyksos kings with Joseph and his brothers[14].

(B) Scarabs (beetle-shaped amulets) of the Hyksos have been found on which are inscribed such Semitic names as Jacob-el and Hur[15]. These Hyksos rulers would correspond to Jacob, father of Joseph; and perhaps to Hur (Ex. **17** 10; **24** 14), the leader of the Israelites after the Exodus, who may have been a long-lived Hyksos ruler. Furthermore, Thutmose III enumerates in an inscription the localities conquered by him in Palestine. Among the places listed are found the names Joseph-el and Jacob-el[16]. This strongly indicates the greatness of Joseph and Jacob, as well as the fact that they preceded the time of Thutmose III.

(C) There is strong evidence that the Hyksos were monotheists. According to the Papyrus Sallier, the Hyksos ruler Apophis "made Sutekh his Lord, serving no other God."[17] Furthermore, Manetho states that the Hyksos demolished the temples of the gods[18]; and Queen Hatshepsut writes in an inscription that the Hyksos ruled without the Egyptian god, Re[19]. It is possible that the Hyksos God

Sutekh is identical with the Biblical name Shaddai for the Israelite God (Ex. 6 3). (D) At the beginning of the Eighteenth Dynasty, the land system attributed in the Bible (Gen. 47 20–22) to Joseph's administration was the prevailing one. The Pharaoh was the owner of all land in the kingdom with the exception of the temple properties[20].

(E) The first reference in an Egyptian text to the horse is found at the end of the Hyksos period[21]. In particular, the war chariot with horse was first encountered during the wars against the Hyksos[22]. Similarly, the first Biblical mention of horses occurs when Joseph gave food to the Egyptian people in exchange for animals including horses (Gen. 47 17). Subsequently, mention of horse and chariot is found at the time of the Exodus (Ex. 14 9).

3.2.2 Eighteenth Dynasty

From the Biblical description of the period during which the Israelites were enslaved in Egypt, the following outline of events during the Eighteenth Dynasty can be derived. Sometime between 1591 and 1567, a new Egyptian dynasty arose. The new King of Egypt conquered and enslaved the Israelites, and used them for building the cities of Pithom and Raamses (Ex. 1 11). Afraid of the rapid natural increase of the Israelite population, the succeeding Pharaoh decreed that all new-born males should be thrown into the Nile River (Ex. 1 22). During the short time that the decree was in effect Moses was born from the tribe of Levi, hidden in a small ark on the edge of the river, and found and adopted by the daughter of Pharaoh (Ex. 2 3–10). The birth of Moses occurred in 1555, eighty years before the Exodus. His older brother Aaron was born three years previously (1558) (Ex. 7 7), when the decree to drown the new-born males was not yet in effect. Although Moses was adopted by the daughter of Pharaoh, he still was cognizant of his Israelite origin, since he was nursed and raised for a number of years by his own mother (Ex. 2 7–10).

Because of his adoption by the daughter of Pharaoh, Moses was appointed, when he grew up, as an officer over his people (Ex. 2 14). In this capacity he killed an Egyptian, and had to flee to Midian in fear for his life, since the latest Pharaoh wanted to kill him (Ex. 2 15). Moses remained in Midian for many years, until at least one Pharaoh and one King of Egypt died (Ex. 2 23; 4 19). God reveals himself to Moses and tells him to return to Egypt and speak to Pharaoh to free the Israelites (Ex. 3 10). At that time the offices of Pharaoh and King of Egypt were held by two different persons, as can be concluded from Ex. 5 4–5, where one sentence is stated by Pharaoh, and the next by the King of Egypt. When the request to free the Israelites is made, Pharaoh does not heed the request but instead increases the burden on the Israelite slaves (Ex. 5 6–9). Subsequently, after the death of the King of Egypt, Moses is commanded by God to speak to Pharaoh, King of Egypt (Ex. 6 11); Pharaoh has now assumed the additional office of King of Egypt.

By the beginning of 1474, the year of the Exodus (Ex. 7 7), Moses had become a very important personality in Egypt. He was considered as a god to Pharaoh (Ex. 7 1), and was great in the eyes of the servants of Pharaoh and in the eyes of the Egyptians (Ex. 11 3). The ten plagues were inflicted on Pharaoh and the Egyptians, until finally the Israelites were released to go for three days into the desert to worship God (Ex. 7 19–12 36). When it was evident that the Israelites were not going to return (Ex. 14 5), Pharaoh pursued them with horses, riders, and his entire chariot force (Ex. 14 7). The sea split to allow the Israelites to pass, but then returned to its usual position and drowned the entire army and chariots that chased after the Israelites (Ex. 14 21–28). Nevertheless, Pharaoh was not drowned, since otherwise this fact would have been specifically mentioned (see e.g., Ex. 15 4,19,21). The Israelites then spent forty years in the desert under the leadership of Moses and the protection of God, and entered the land of Canaan at the start of 1434.

Numerous supplementary facts from Egyptian history can be added to the above Biblical description of events during the Eighteenth Dynasty. These data are based on the list of Egyptian rulers presented in Table 3.2, as well as relevant inscriptions. We will here specifically try to identify the particular Pharaohs and Kings of Egypt referred to in the Biblical description.

Ahmose I (1580–1557) is clearly the Pharaoh who enslaved the Israelites. From inscriptions we learn that Kamose, the last Pharaoh of the Seventeenth Dynasty, initiated attacks on the Hyksos. He captured an enemy stronghold at Neferusy, as well as a fleet of Hyksos ships[23]. The taking of Avaris was not, however, accomplished by Kamose, but by his younger brother and successor Ahmose I, founder of the Eighteenth Dynasty. Ahmose I besieged the city of Avaris and eventually conquered it. Many of the Hyksos then retreated to the city of Sharuhen in southern Palestine, where they were eventually conquered. Records indicate that the Hyksos were taken as slaves[24]. It is also recorded that in the twenty-second year of Ahmose I new workings in the quarries of Ayan were started in order to secure stone for building purposes[25]. This additional stone was needed for construction performed by the slaves.

The Pharaoh who decreed that new-born Israelite male children should be thrown into the Nile is undoubtedly Amenhotep I (1557–1540). Aaron was born in 1558 prior to the edict, while Moses who was born in 1555 had to be hidden so as not to be drowned. The daughter of Pharaoh, who discovered Moses when he was placed in an ark on the edge of the Nile, is probably the Princess Ahmose, daughter of the preceding Pharaoh, Ahmose I. The "daughter of Pharaoh" could not be a daughter of Amenhotep I, since he died without any children[26]. Subsequently, after the death of Amenhotep I, Princess Ahmose and her husband Thutmose I became the King and Pharaoh of Egypt, respectively. It was during their reign that Moses killed an Egyptian and ran away to Midian, and therefore Thutmose I was the Pharaoh who wanted to kill Moses. Not until the death of

Thutmose II did Moses return to Egypt. This latter point will be deduced from knowledge of the life of Senmut (or Sennemut), who will now be shown to be identical with Moses.

3.2.2.1 Moses Identical to Senmut

Senmut was a famous person in Egypt at the time of Hatshepsut, after the death of Thutmose II[27]. The family of Senmut is essentially identical to that of Moses. Thus, Senmut's ancestors were not found in writing, i.e., his parentage was not distinguished[28]. Four members of his family are recorded, his father Ramose, his mother Hatnufer, his brother Senmen, and his sister A'h-hotpe. His father and mother are buried in tomb No. 71, which Senmut prepared for himself on the hill Sheikh Abd el Kurneh; but neither he nor his brother or sister are buried in the locations set aside for them[29]. Similarly, we know that Moses' ancestors were not of the royal line of the Eighteenth Dynasty, and that his father was Amram, his mother Jochebed, his brother Aaron, and his sister Miriam (Ex. 6 20; 15 20). Undoubtedly, Moses' parents died and were buried in Egypt; but Moses, his brother and sister left Egypt and died forty years later (Num. 20 1, 28; Deut. 34 5).

During the reign of Hatshepsut, Senmut was the most powerful official. He is called "The greatest of the great in the entire land." He was the chief royal architect, and was in charge of all building construction. His titles include "Overseer of the two granaries," "Controller of works," "Overseer of the fields," and "Steward of Hatshepsut." Senmut was on the most intimate terms with Egypt's ruling family, and conducted himself as if he were a member of the family. He had tutored Thutmose III as a child, and taught Hatshepsut's daughter Nefrure. Also, Senmut's brother, Senmen, was an important official[30,31].

The parallel account of Moses' life in the Bible indicates that Moses and Senmut were the same person. Moses, as stated previously, was the adopted son of the Princess Ahmose. As wife of Thutmose I, Ahmose gave birth to Hatshepsut. Thus, Moses was the foster-brother of Hatshepsut, and they were both reared by the same mother. When Moses returned to Egypt, after the death of Thutmose II, Hatshepsut made him an important official. Because of Moses' great capability, he became one of the greatest persons in the land, and by the time of the Exodus Moses was "very great in the eyes of the servants of Pharaoh and in the eyes of the Egyptians" (Ex. 11 3). As foster-brother of Hatshepsut, Moses had easy access to the royal family, and was therefore able to come and go at will, as indicated by the ease with which Moses announced to Pharaoh of oncoming plagues. Aaron (Senmen), Moses' brother, was also of importance because of the high position occupied by Moses.

A final point that proves the identity of Senmut and Moses, is the fact that Thutmose III, after the death of Hatshepsut, had the names of Hatshepsut, Senmut, and Senmen chiselled away or otherwise erased from all their monuments and inscriptions[32]. Such an act of hatred by Thutmose III indicates that he suffered a severe setback because of these persons, such as at the time of the Exodus when his entire chariot force was destroyed. The names of Senmut and Senmen were erased because they were none other than Moses and Aaron; while the name of Hatshepsut was destroyed because of her ardent support for these officials.

3.2.2.2 Thutmose III is the Pharaoh of the Exodus

Now to continue with the supplementary information to the Biblical account obtained from Egyptian history. After the death of Thutmose II, Moses returned to Egypt and spoke to Thutmose III, the Pharaoh, and to Hatshepsut, the King of Egypt, to allow the Israelites to travel three days in the desert to offer sacrifices to God. However, Thutmose III did not heed Moses' request but instead increased the work load of the slaves (Ex. 5 1–9). Many years later, after the death of Hatshepsut in 1479, Thutmose III assumed the titles of both Pharaoh and King of Egypt. Then almost every year, for twenty years, he embarked on a major campaign[33]. However, no record is found of his fourth campaign, which would have occurred in late 1475, or early 1474, in the year of the Exodus. Several factors support the contention that Thutmose III suffered a major defeat that year. Firstly, Thutmose III protests more than once his deep respect for the truth. He states, "I have not uttered exaggeration in order to boast of something I have not done."[34] The absence of the records of his fourth campaign, therefore, indicates that an unsuccessful campaign occurred. Secondly, there is a three-year gap between the calculated time of the fourth campaign in Thutmose III's twenty-sixth year, and the time of the fifth campaign in his twenty-ninth year. This gap is the longest between any of the successive campaigns and indicates that it took several years to recover from the defeat. Thirdly, the fifth campaign began a new period of wars. Previously the fighting was in the south. Now in the fifth campaign begin wars in the north[35]. Furthermore, beginning with the fifth campaign, and continuing for many years thereafter, the army was transported by ship, and no mention is made of the Egyptians using horses. In contrast, the use of horses is described in the account of the first campaign[36]. This information fits in with the fact that all the chariots and horses of Egypt were destroyed at the time of the Exodus (Ex. 14 28; 15 4).

There are a number of additional points which support the contention that Thutmose III was the Pharaoh at the time of the Exodus. Thutmose III is known to have been one of the greater Egyptian builders. He employed captives on his construction projects and had untiring energy. Secondly, in the later campaigns of Thutmose III we find an influx of slaves[37], probably to replace the Israelites who were released at the time of the Exodus. Thirdly, we know from the Biblical account that Pharaoh was not drowned in the Red Sea. Similarly, we know that Thutmose III survived the time of the Exodus. Fourthly, the oldest son of Pharaoh, who was to succeed him on the throne, was killed in the plague of the first-born

(Ex. 11 5; 12 29). Now the successor of Thutmose III was Amenhotep II, who ascended the throne at the age of eighteen[38]. Thutmose III ruled for twenty-eight years after the Exodus, and therefore Amenhotep II was born subsequent to that event, in agreement with the Biblical information.

3.2.3 Amarna Age

The Israelites entered the land of Canaan in the beginning of 1434 and began the conquest of the country under the leadership of Joshua. As will be established in Section 4.1, Joshua ruled fifty-two years, from 1434 to 1383. After the first seven years (Josh. 14 10), i.e. by 1428, the cities of Jericho, Ai, Lachish, Hebron, and others were destroyed. However, such cities as Jerusalem, Gezer, Beth-Shean, Ibleam, Dor, En-dor, Taanach, Megiddo, Zidon, and Acco remained to be conquered (Josh. 15 63; 16 10; 17 11,12; Jud. 1 27–36). Even Othniel the son of Kenaz (1383–1344), the ruler who succeeded Joshua, encountered much territory yet to be acquired (Jud. 3 1–11).

Corresponding to the time of conquest of the land of Canaan are the tablets found at Tel El-Amarna, in Egypt. There are 378 tablets, of which 356 consist of letters from the archives of Amenhotep III (1412–1375) and Amenhotep IV (1375–1358). These letters include correspondence between city-states in Syria, Phoenicia, and Palestine, and the Egyptian leaders, although the specific Egyptian king is not mentioned by name[39]. Six letters were sent by Abdi-hiba, ruler of Jerusalem, who mentions the threat of the Habiru. He writes to the King of Egypt such statements as, "The Habiru plunder all the countries of the king . . . the countries of the king will be lost," and "The country of the king is fallen away to the Habiru"[40]. In general, Abdi-hiba requested assistance from Egyptian troops lest the entire country be conquered by the Habiru. These letters from Abdi-hiba are the only Amarna texts to make explicit mention of the Habiru. However, from other letters it can be deduced that the Habiru are the same as the SA-GAZ. According to Rib-adda, the ruler of Byblos (Gebal) in Phoenicia, from whom we have fifty-three letters, the SA-GAZ had been encroaching on the Egyptian empire since the closing years of Thutmose IV (1420–1412)[41].

We thus see that the threat of the Habiru against the Egyptian empire in the region of the land of Canaan occurred approximately between the years 1415 and 1358. These times correspond fairly well to the dates 1428 to 1343, when the danger from the Israelites, under the leadership of Joshua and Othniel, was felt by the neighboring cities in Canaan. Thus, the Habiru can be identified with the Israelites. Furthermore, the word Habiru is considered phonetically identical to the word Hebrew (עברי). Many historians have at least partially accepted this identification, although others have encountered chronological difficulties with such an interpretation because of their erroneous dating of the period of the Exodus.

In addition to the above points, it should be noted that numerous cities are mentioned in the Amarna letters. Among those mentioned are the Biblical cities of Acco, Ashkelon, Arvad, Aroer, Ashtaroth, Beth-shean, Gebal, Gezer, Gath, Gaza, Jerusalem, Joppa, Keilah, Lachish, Megiddo, Sharon, Shechem, Tyre, Taanach, Zidon, and Zorah. Reference is also made to the city of Beth-Ninurta, which is considered in all probability to be the same as Bethshemesh[42]. In most cases, just the cities mentioned in the books of Joshua and Judges as remaining to be conquered, are the ones so mentioned in the Amarna letters. The Biblical cities in this category are Acco (Jud. 1 31), Ashkelon (Josh. 13 3), Beth-shean (Josh. 17 11), Gebal (Josh. 13 5), Gezer (Josh. 16 10), Gath (Josh. 13 3), Gaza (Josh. 13 3), Jerusalem (Josh. 15 63), Joppa (Josh. 19 46), Megiddo (Josh. 17 11), Taanach (Josh. 17 11), Zidon (Jud. 1 31), and Bethshemesh (Jud. 1 33). However, the cities of Lachish and Shechem are mentioned in the letters by Abdi-hiba as belonging to the Habiru; and these same cities are described in the book of Joshua as having been conquered by the Israelites (**10 32; 24 1**).

Table 3.3
Biblical Personalities Described in Egyptian Inscriptions

Biblical Characterization	Egyptian Equivalent
Joseph and family	Hyksos kings
King who enslaved the Israelites	Ahmose I
Pharaoh who decreed that all newborn Israelite boys should be thrown into the Nile	Amenhotep I
Daughter of Pharaoh who found Moses	Princess Ahmose, daughter of Ahmose I.
Pharaoh who wanted to kill Moses	Thutmose I
Moses	Senmut
Aaron	Senmen
Amram, father of Moses	Ramose
Jochebed, mother of Moses	Hatnufer
Pharaoh and King of Egypt who Moses originally approached to release the Israelites	Thutmose III and Hatshepsut
Pharaoh, King of Egypt, at time of Exodus	Thutmose III
Egyptian rulers at time of conquest of land of Canaan	Thutmose IV, Amenhotep III and Amenhotep IV
Israelites (Hebrews) who conquered the land of Canaan	Habiru

Similarly, King Abi-milki of Tyre states that the King of Hazor has espoused the cause of the Habiru, in agreement with the conquest of Hazor by Joshua (Josh. 11 10,11)[43].

We have now established that the name Habiru, as used in the Amarna letters, is equivalent to the name Hebrew, and refers to the Israelites who conquered the land of Canaan around the time of Joshua. However, the name Habiru, and its variants Apiru or Aperu, have been found in documents from many periods, such as in the first dynasty of Babylon, at the time of Hammurabi, in the Amarna letters, and at the times of Thutmose III and later Egyptian rulers such as Ramses II, III, and IV [44]. Thus the name Habiru has been found in documents dating from about 2000 to 1150.

In the Bible we find the name Hebrew (עברי) first used concerning Abram (Gen. 14 13), and afterwards to refer to Joseph (Gen. 39 14) and to the Israelites in Egypt (Ex. 1 15-19; 2 11). The name probably indicates a descendant of Eber (עבר) (Gen. 10 21,24,25; 11 16,17). Eber was born sixty-seven years after the Deluge (2200) and lived for 464 years until 1736. Originally the name Hebrew (Habiru) applied to any descendant of Eber, but subsequently became more specific and referred only to the Israelites. The Biblical information as to the origin of the name Habiru explains the occurrence of the name as early as the first Babylonian dynasty (ca. 2000), and the continuance of its use for centuries thereafter.

3.3 SUMMARY

We have now proved numerous identifications between persons described in the Bible and those mentioned in Egyptian inscriptions. These identifications have been arrived at on the basis of chronological and historical evidence. For convenience, the identifications are summarized in Table 3.3.

Chapter Four

PERIOD OF THE JUDGES

The "period of the judges" strictly refers to the time from the beginning of the rule of Othniel, the successor to Joshua, until the start of the monarchy under Saul. However, from a chronological viewpoint it is desirable to include in our discussion the rule of Joshua, as well as the reigns of Saul, David, and Solomon. In this way the period under discussion covers the era from the death of Moses until the division of the monarchy into the Kingdoms of Judah and Israel.

No exact extra-Biblical dates are available with which to compare the period of the judges. At best a rough comparison can be made between the time of Joshua and the Amarna Age, as has already been done in Section 3.2.3. Otherwise, there is insufficient comparable historical evidence; therefore no disagreement for the period of the judges exists between the Biblical chronology and world history.

The main problem of this period is to present a straight-forward explanation of the Biblical data so as to obtain a system which is consistent with all the facts. In particular, the following points are the main ones which have caused difficulty in obtaining an accurate interpretation of the Biblical record:

(A) The length of the rule of Joshua is not specified.
(B) In the Book of Judges numerous periods of subjugation are stated. However, it is not clear from the text whether or not the periods of subjugation occurred simultaneously with the years of rulership by the judges.
(C) The length of rule by the Prophet Samuel is not specified.
(D) The length of the reign of King Saul, although specified in I Sam. **13** 1, is considered very unreliable since in the same sentence it is stated that Saul was only one year old when he became king.

Below are presented solutions to these four problems, which allow a consistent chronology to be developed. The resultant chronology is summarized in Table 4.1.

4.1 LENGTH OF RULE OF JOSHUA

Although the length of rule of Joshua is not specified in the Bible, nevertheless the number of years can be calculated based on Joshua's age. As will presently be proved, he started ruling when he was 59; he continued ruling until his death at the age of 110 (Josh. **24** 29,31). Thus, he ruled for 52 years.

His age when he started ruling can be derived from his age in the second year in the desert. At that time (Num. 10 11), Joshua, Caleb, and other tribal leaders were sent as spies to investigate the nature of the land of Canaan and to determine the fortifications therein (Num. 13 1–20). When the spies returned, the majority reported that the Israelites would not be able to overcome the occupants of the land (Num. 13 31). Only Joshua and Caleb considered it possible to conquer the land (Num. 14 6–8). As a result, the Israelites were disheartened and rebelled (Num. 14 9–11). As punishment for their lack of faith, God decreed that all people who were mature (i. e., twenty years or older*) at the time of the Exodus, as well as younger persons who had despised God, would not live to see the land of Canaan (Num. 14 22–23). The people, however, continued to murmur against God (Num. 14 27), and were consequently punished even more severely. Now, even those who reached twenty years of age in the second year of the desert when the census was taken, would not enter the land of Canaan (Num. 14 29,30; 1 1–3). Interestingly enough, only Caleb was excluded from punishment among those who were twenty at the time of the Exodus (Num. 14 22,24; Deut. 1 35,36), while both Caleb and Joshua were excluded from punishment among those who were twenty in the second year of the desert (Num. 14 29,30; 32 11,12). This establishes that Joshua was nineteen years old at the time of the Exodus, and twenty years old in the second year of the desert, when he was sent out as a spy. Support for this relatively young age for Joshua is obtained from Ex. 33 11 where he is called a young man (נער). Since Joshua was nineteen at the time of the Exodus, he obviously was fifty-nine when he began to rule forty years later.

4.2 PERIODS OF SUBJUGATION

Although the text in the Book of Judges is unclear whether the periods of subjugation occur simultaneously with, or subsequent to, the rulership of the judges, it is logical to assume that there were no extended gaps of more than a few months during which the country was without a leader. The chronology presented in Table 4.1 bears out that this assumption is not only logical but also results in self-consistent dates. Otherwise, the period of the judges would have to be increased by 111 years (8 + 18 + 20 + 7 + 18 + 40), i.e., by the sum of the years given for the six mentioned subjugations, resulting in numerous inconsistencies.

The term "the land was quiet" (ותשקט הארץ) used in connection with the judgeships of Othniel, Ehud, Deborah, and Gideon (Jud. 3 11,30; 5 31; 8 28), is often explained to refer to peace from foreign domination and war. This explanation would, however, imply that the periods of subjugation did not occur during the rule of the judges. It is therefore better to explain the term "the land was quiet" as referring to quiet from internal disputes concerning who should be the leader of the country.

---

*The word "men (אנשים) refers to people 20 years of age or older, as indicated in Num. 32 11.

Table 4.1
Chronology of the Period of the Judges

Ruler (or Event)	Dates (B.C.E.)	Duration (Yrs.)	Reference	Concurrent Subjugation by	Subjugation (No. of Yrs.)	Reference
Desert Stay	1474–1435	40	Num. 14 34			
Joshua	1434–1383	52	See Discussion			
Othniel son of Kenaz	1382–1343	40	Jud. 3 11	Cushan-rishathaim, King of Aram	8	Jud. 3 8
Ehud son of Gera	1342–1263	80	Jud. 3 30	Eglon, King of Moab	18	Jud. 3 14
Shamgar son of Anath	1263	0	Jud. 3 31			
Deborah	1262–1223	40	Jud. 5 31	Jabin, King of Canaan	20	Jud. 4 3
Gideon (Jerubbaal)	1222–1183	40	Jud. 8 28	Midian	7	Jud. 6 1
Abimelech son of Gideon	1182–1180	3	Jud. 9 22			
Tola son of Puah	1179–1157	23	Jud. 10 2			
Jair, the Gileadite	1156–1135	22	Jud. 10 3	Philistines and Children of Ammon	18	Jud. 10 7, 8
Total No. of Years Beginning with Joshua		300	Jud. 11 26			

PERIOD OF THE JUDGES

Jephthah, the Gileadite	1134–1129	6	Jud. 12 7	
Ibzan of Bethlehem	1128–1122	7	Jud. 12 9	
Elon, the Zebulunite	1121–1112	10	Jud. 12 11	
Abdon son of Hillel	1111–1104	8	Jud. 12 14	
Samson son of Manoah	1103–1084	20	Jud. 15 20; 16 31 } Philistines 40	Jud. 13 1
Eli	1083–1044	40	I Sam. 4 18	
Samuel	1043–1041	3	See Discussion	
Saul	1040–1039	2	I Sam. 13 1	
David	1038–999	40	II Sam. 5 4	
Solomon (until Temple begun)	998–995	4	I Kings 6 1	
Total No. of Years from Exodus } 480			I Kings 6 1	
Solomon (entire reign)	998–959	40	I Kings 11 42	

4.3 LENGTH OF JUDGESHIP OF SAMUEL

The number of years that Samuel ruled independently is not specified. The reason for this is probably that a large portion of his career was during the judgeship of Eli. We can nevertheless show from the text that Samuel ruled independently a minimum of two years and a maximum of eleven years. Subsequently, from the available chronological data it will be proved that he ruled exactly three years.

The minimum number of years of rule by Samuel is obtained from the events specified to have occurred after the death of Eli. Thus, the Ark of the Lord remained with the Philistines for seven months (I Sam. 6 1), and was returned in the season of the wheat harvest (I Sam. 6 13). When Saul became king, succeeding Samuel, it was also the time of the wheat harvest (I Sam 12 17). We know from Ex. 34 22 that the time of the wheat harvest is around the time of the Feast of Weeks, about the third month, Sivan. Hence, the specified one year and seven months must have included two firsts-of Nisan, and therefore would be counted as two years of rule (see Section 5.1.1).

The calculation of the maximum number of years of independent rule by Samuel is based on the statement that the Ark of the Lord remained at Kiriath-Jearim for twenty years (I Sam. 7 2) after the death of Eli. The next transfer of the ark (II Sam. 6 3; I Chr. 13 5) occurred during King David's reign, after the judgeship of Samuel, the two year rule by Saul (I Sam. 13 1), the seven year reign of David in Hebron (II Sam. 5 4,5) and after an unspecified number of years of reign by David in Jerusalem. The maximum length of rule for Samuel is then eleven years (i.e. $20-2-7=11$), if it is assumed that the transfer of the Ark occurred shortly after David began ruling from Jerusalem.

That Samuel ruled independently for exactly three years is calculated from I Kings 6 1 where it is stated that construction of the Temple was begun 480 years after the Exodus. A three-year judgeship for Samuel (see Table 4.1) allows perfect agreement with this time span.

At first thought, a three-year rule for Samuel seems to be inconsistent with the description presented in I Sam. 7 15–8 3. However, not all the events and descriptions mentioned happened after the death of Eli. Samuel began serving in the capacity of prophet during the judgeship of Eli (I Sam. 3 20), and perhaps even appointed his sons as local rulers (I Sam. 8 1–5) during Eli's lifetime. The text of I Sam. 7 15–8 3, therefore summarizes events in the life of Samuel, whether or not the events occurred during Samuel's independent rule.

Let us now clarify the history of Samuel. It is probable that he was conceived while Eli acted as priest, but before Eli became the judge (I Sam. 1). At that time Eli was a minimum of thirty-five years old, since he had to be at least fifteen when his second son was born, and the sons would not be expected to serve as priests before the age of twenty (I Chr. 23 24,27; Num. 4 23; 8 24). A year later, when Eli was a minimum of thirty-six, Samuel was born (I Sam.

1 20). Now, Eli died at ninety-eight (I Sam. 4 15,18). Therefore Samuel could possibly have been sixty-two when Eli died. Samuel ruled for three years until he was sixty-five; and he lived for another year (I Sam. 25 1; 27 7; 13 1) until the age of sixty-six. This analysis of the maximum age for Samuel, explains the use of the words "old" and "white-haired" (I Sam. 8 1,5; 12 2) in describing him.

4.4 AGE OF SAUL WHEN HE BECAME KING

It is stated in I Sam. 13 1 that Saul was one year old when he became king, and he ruled two years over Israel. Biblical critics have assumed that the sentence is imperfect; just as it is obvious that Saul was more than one year old when he became king, so also Saul ruled longer than two years. Support for a long rule by Saul is supposedly gained from the extensive description of his reign, occupying nineteen chapters (I Sam. 13–31). However, the lengthy description only indicates that the reign of Saul was well documented because he was the first king. All the specified events could easily have transpired within two years.

The term "one year" used in the sentence to specify Saul's age, really means fifty-two years, corresponding to the fifty-two weeks in one solar year. The word "year" (שנה), when used in a context where it could not possibly mean one year, had the meaning of fifty-two years. A similar usage for the word "years" (שנים) is found in Dan. 11 6,8,13, as explained in Section 16.5.

That Saul was fifty-two when he became king can be calculated as follows. In II Sam. 2 10 it is stated that Ish-bosheth, the son of Saul, was forty years old when he became king. This occurred immediately after the death of Saul (II Sam. 1 1), who had reigned two years. If we assume that Saul was fourteen years old when Ish-bosheth was born, then Saul was fifty-two when he became king. This is quite probable if Ish-bosheth was the oldest, or next to the oldest child (see Section 2.4.1). However, from I Chr. 8 33; 9 39 and I Sam. 14 49 we learn that Jonathan was the eldest son of Saul. Furthermore, in I Chr. 8 33; 9 39, Ish-baal (or Ish-bosheth) is listed last of the four sons. Nevertheless, it is still reasonable to assume that Ish-bosheth was next to the oldest child. Thus, in I Sam. 14 49 Ishvi (which is probably another name for Ish-bosheth) is presented as the second son. The reason he is listed last in Chronicles may be his lesser greatness; for example, he did not fight in the battle against the Philistines in which his father and three brothers were killed (I Sam. 31 2; I Chr. 10 2). Based on the above arguments we can now conclude that Jonathan, the oldest son, was born when Saul was thirteen, and Ish-bosheth, the next oldest, was born a year later when Saul was fourteen.

4.5 VERIFICATION OF THE DEVELOPED CHRONOLOGY

There are two time-spans that allow a check of the years of rule of the individual leaders. The first was stated at the beginning of Jephthah's reign (Jud. 11 8,11).

At that time Jephthah claims that 300 years have passed since the Israelites conquered Sihon, King of the Amorites (Jud. 11 26). Now, from Num. 21 23, 24, we determine that the conquest of Sihon occurred after the death of Aaron (Num. 20 28); and from Num. 33 38 we know that Aaron died in the fifth month of the fortieth year after the Exodus. Thus, there are 300 years from the beginning of Joshua's rule until the start of the judgeship of Jephthah. Corroboration of this number is given in Table 4.1.

The second time-span is found in I Kings 6 1, where it is stated that construction of the Temple was begun in the second month of the fourth year of Solomon, which was 480 years after the Exodus. Although this number is corroborated in Table 4.1, we should keep in mind that the exact number of years of Samuel's rule was based on it. Otherwise, there was a leeway of anywhere between two and eleven years for Samuel's judgeship (see Section 4.3). Nevertheless, the 480 year time-span confirms within ten years the developed chronology for the period of the judges, and shows the reasonableness of the assumptions involved.

Chapter Five

CHRONOLOGY OF THE KINGS

The period of the kings during the time of the First Temple requires detailed analysis. To obtain satisfactory agreement between the Biblical data and Assyrian history it is necessary to reinterpret the Bible as well as the extra-Biblical information. Both sources have not been properly explained, leading to the discrepancies which have arisen. Before proceeding with these interpretations, it is desirable to establish the time for the beginning of the year as used throughout the entire Bible. This is an important point for understanding the chronology, especially of the kings, and has often been stated incorrectly.

5.1 THE FIRST DAY OF THE YEAR

Numerous opinions have been expressed as to the dating systems used in the Bible. Some people are of the opinion that Nisan begins the year; others believe that Tishri begins the year. The idea has also been proposed that the time of the beginning of the year was changed during the Biblical period. These opinions are only partially correct, as will be explained.

Careful examination of the available information leads to the following conclusions:

(A) Dates throughout the Bible are, in general, based upon the first of Nisan as the beginning of the year.

(B) However, after the split of the monarchy, the kings of Israel counted their regnal years from the first of Cheshvan, the eighth month; the kings of Judah still counted their regnal years from the first of Nisan.

(C) The agricultural year officially began on the tenth of Tishri, the seventh month.

(D) Throughout the Bible, the numbering of the months is based on Nisan as the first month.

The evidence and reasoning supporting these conclusions are presented in the ensuing paragraphs.

5.1.1 Nisan as the Beginning of the Year

In nearly all cases throughout the Bible, the years begin on the first of Nisan, i.e. the first day of the first month. Ages of people, intervals elapsed, and lengths of rule, are calculated from this starting point. The evidence supporting this conclusion is summarized below.

(A) In the genealogies in Gen. 5, the total number of years for the lifetime of each person is exactly equal to the sum of the person's age when his son was born, plus the number of years he lived after the son's birth. As explained in greater detail in Section 1.5, this establishes that ages are determined from a definite time, such as the first day of the year, rather than from the day of birth.

(B) The implication from Gen. 7-8 is that the year at the time of Noah began on the first day of the first month. Thus, in Gen. 7 11 is given the date for the start of the Deluge as the seventeenth day of the second month in the 600th year of Noah. Subsequently, are mentioned the seventh month (Gen. 8 4), the tenth month (Gen. 8 5), and sixty-one days afterwards (40 + 14 + 7—Gen. 8 6,10,12)—i.e., the beginning of the twelfth month. In all these cases it is implied that the year is still the 600th in the life of Noah. Then, in Gen. 8 13 the date is given as the first day of the first month of the 601st year, strongly indicating that the new year began on the first day of the first month.

(C) At the time of Moses there are several relevant passages. It is explicitly stated in Ex. 12 2 that the first month is the beginning of the year. Also in Ex. 40 17 the date is given as the first day of the first month of the second year (in the desert), indicating that the first day of the first month started the new year.*

Furthermore, in Num. 33 38 it is stated that Aaron died on the first day of the fifth month of the fortieth year, and in Deut. 1 3 is stated that Moses spoke on the first day of the eleventh month of the fortieth year. Thus, no change in the year occurred between the fifth and eleventh months. Similarly, it can be concluded from Ex. 16 1 and Ex. 19 1 that no change in the year occurred between the first and third months. Hence, the only possible months for the beginning of the year are the first, fourth, fifth and twelfth, which strongly supports the above-mentioned evidence that the new year started on the first day of the first month.

(D) In I Kings 6 1 it is stated that construction of the Temple was begun in the fourth year, in the *second month of Solomon's reign*. However in II Chr. 3 2 the same event is dated in the *second month (of the year)*, in the fourth year of Solomon's reign. Therefore the second month of Solomon's reign is the second month of the year, establishing that the first month is the beginning of the regnal year.

---

* Although the Exodus from Egypt occurred on the fifteenth of the first month, the counting of the years in the desert began on the first day of the first month, when the statement in Ex. 12 2 was made.

In addition, we find described in II Kings 22 3–23 23 and II Chr. 34 8–35 19 events which occurred in the eighteenth year of King Josiah. The King ordered that the Temple be repaired, and as a result a Book of the Law was found. The contents of the book caused the King to order the purification of the land from all types of idolatry. Subsequently, on the fourteenth day of the first month (II Chr. 35 1) the Passover sacrifice was brought. The argument has been put forward that if the year began in the first month, there was insufficient time to perform all the described tasks, and therefore the year began in some other month. However, in actuality the tasks described are of such a nature that they could easily have been performed within two weeks, as would be expected because of the urgency given the matter by the king. Thus we may assume that on the first day of the first month of the eighteenth year King Josiah initiated the series of events which was culminated on the fourteenth of the first month with the observance of the Passover sacrifice.

(E) In Jer. 1 3 it is stated, "until the end of the eleventh year of Zedekiah ... until the exile of Jerusalem in the fifth month." The phrasing thus indicates that the year began before the fifth month.

Furthermore in Jer. 28 1 the date is given as the fourth year of Zedekiah, in the fifth month. Then in Jer. 28 17 it is stated that the false prophet Hananiah died in the same year in the seventh month. Thus, no change in the year occurred between the fifth and seventh months; or the new year did not begin in the sixth or seventh months.

(F) In Hag. 1 1,15 the date is given as the sixth month of the second year of Darius. Later (Hag. 2 10) the date is given as the ninth month of the second year of Darius. Thus no change in the year in Darius' reign occurred between the sixth and ninth months.

Similarly, in Zech. 1 1 the date is specified as the eighth month of the second year of Darius, and in Zech. 1 7 as the eleventh month of the second year of Darius. Thus there is no change in the year between the eighth and eleventh months during the reign of Darius.

(G) It is stated in Est. 3 7 that a lot was cast on the first month of the twelfth year of Ahasuerus, which fell on the twelfth month. Subsequent dates, such as the twenty-third of the third month (Est. 8 9), and the thirteenth of the twelfth month (Est. 8 12), do not mention the year, indicating that it is the same as previously mentioned, i.e. the twelfth of Ahasuerus. Thus, there is no change in the year between the first and twelfth months.

(H) In Ezr. 3 1 it is stated that the people were already settled in the cities when the seventh month arrived; and in Ezr. 3 6 the people began on the first day of the seventh month to bring sacrifices. Then in Ezr. 3 8 the date is given as the second month of the second year of their coming to Jerusalem, indicating that the second year began not on the first day of the seventh month, but some time later before the subsequent second month.

There is one case where it is clear that the year did not begin on the first of Nisan. In Neh. 1 1 the date is given as the month of Kislev of the twentieth year (of Artaxerxes II). Then in Neh. 2 1 the date is given as the month of Nisan of the twentieth year of Artaxerxes. The events of the second chapter followed those of the first, and therefore, the indication is that Nisan was not the first month of the year at the time of Artaxerxes II.

Evidence from Persian history allows an explanation for this exception. Originally the Persians, just like the Babylonians, made the first of Nisan the beginning of the year. Subsequently, a new calendar system, known as the Zoroastrian or Young Avesta calendar, was adopted. The exact date for the change is not known, but is believed to be about 441 B.C.E. At about that time the beginning of the year became the first of Farvadin, which did not coincide exactly with the first of Nisan[1]. It should here be noted that the time of Artaxerxes II (404–359), who is referred to in the Book of Nehemiah, was subsequent to the time the calendar system was changed.

5.1.2 Nisan as the First Month

In all the above cases it has been implicitly assumed that throughout the Bible the first month of the year is the spring month Nisan, rather than Tishri for example. Sufficient evidence is available to establish that this is indeed true.

Firstly, in Ex. 12 2–20 it is stated that the month of the Exodus from Egypt is the first month of the year, and the event is to be commemorated by the Passover sacrifice and the Feast of Unleavened Bread. Also, in Deut. 16 1–8 it is stated that this holiday should be observed in the spring. Thus we know that the first month occurs in the spring, and therefore the first month is the spring month, Nisan. The months in which the other festivals occur, such as Tabernacles, are specified in Lev. 23 4–44 and Num. 28 16–29 39; the numbers of the months are based on the occurrence of the Passover sacrifice and the Feast of Unleavened Bread in the first month.

One way, then, to establish that the counting of the months used throughout the Bible is based on Nisan as the first month is simply to show that the festivals noted in the Bible occur in the same numbered months as specified in Leviticus and Deuteronomy. Such is the case for the observance of the Passover sacrifice (Josh. 4 19, 5 10; Ez. 45 21; Ezra 6 19; II Chr. 30 2; 35 1), the Feast of Tabernacles (I Kings 8 2,65; Ezra 3 1,4; Neh. 8 14; II Chr. 5 3, 7 8–10) and the Day of Blowing of the Shofar (Neh. 8 2,9,10).

Another means for establishing that the numbers of the months are based on Nisan as the first month, is by the correspondence of the numbered months with the names of the months. Thus, based on Nisan as the first month we know for example that Sivan is the third month, Kislev the ninth month, etc. Such correspondences are found for many of the months in the books of Zechariah and Esther. Thus, Nisan is called the first month in Est. 3 7; Sivan is called the third month in Est. **8** 9; Kislev is called the ninth month in Zech. **7** 1; Tebet is called the tenth month in Est. **2** 16; Shevat is called the eleventh month in Zech. **1** 7; and Adar is called the twelfth month in Est. **3** 7,13; **8** 12; **9** 1.

A final indication that the first month was Nisan rather than for example Tishri, is obtained from Jer. **36** 22. There it is stated that the king was sitting in the winter-house in the ninth month. Now the ninth month would be in the winter if the first month were Nisan, but not if the first month were Tishri.

The above evidence establishes that the counting of the months is based on Nisan as the first month at the times of Moses, Joshua, the kings, the Babylonian Exile, and the time of Ezra and Nehemiah. Thus throughout the Biblical period the numbering of the months is based on Nisan as the first month.

5.1.3   Cheshvan as the Beginning of the Year for the Kings of Israel

Despite the overwhelming evidence showing that the first day of the first month was the beginning of the year, there are two categories where such was not the case. The first category involves the regnal years of the kings of Israel at the time when the monarchy was divided into two kingdoms. As will be explained in greater detail in Section 5.2, the kings of Israel counted their regnal years from Cheshvan, the eighth month. This assertion is supported by the numerical evidence based on the synchronistic dating, as well as the statement in I Kings **12** 32,33 that Jeroboam established a new holiday in the eighth month, a month which he had devised from his own heart.

5.1.4   The Tenth of the Seventh Month as the Beginning
of the Agricultural Year

The second category where Nisan is not the beginning of the year refers to the start of the agricultural year. The Biblical evidence supports the contention that the agricultural new year began on the tenth of the seventh month. Thus, in Lev. **25** 9,10 it is stated that the jubilee year should be announced on the tenth of the seventh month, on the Day of Atonement. The implication there is that the jubilee year begins on the day when the announcement is made. Furthermore in Ex. **23** 16 it is stated that the Feast of Ingathering is when the year starts (צאת השנה). Also, in Ex. **34** 22 the Feast of Ingathering is called the time of recycling of the year (תקופת השנה). Now the Feast of Ingathering commences on the fifteenth day of the seventh month (Lev. **23** 39), which is in essential agreement with the concept that the year begins on the tenth of the seventh month. The statement in Ez. **40** 1 which sets the beginning of the year (ראש השנה) on the tenth of the month supports the tenth day of the seventh month (rather than the fifteenth day) as the beginning of the agricultural year.

Frequently the term "return of the year" (תשובת השנה) is found in the Bible (II Sam. **11** 1; I Kings **20** 22,26; I Chr. **20** 1; II Chr. **36** 10). By "return of the year" is meant half the cycle of the agricultural year, that is, in the spring, around

Nisan. In particular, in II Sam. 11 1; I Chr. 20 1 the term is clarified with the phrase "when the kings go out [to battle]," which is usually in the spring when the weather becomes suitable for long trips. On the other hand, the term "recycling of the year" used in II Chr. 24 23, refers to the time of the seventh month, as explained above.

Archaeological evidence also supports Tishri as the beginning of the agricultural year. A tablet known as the Gezer calendar, written in Hebrew, in approximately the tenth century, relates the months of the year to the agricultural events. The Gezer calendar begins with the two months of ingathering (around Tishri) and ends with the month of summer fruit (around Elul), essentially the same as explained above[2].

5.2 CHRONOLOGY OF THE KINGS BASED ON THE BIBLE

The chronology of the kings during the period of the First Temple is the most complicated of any of the periods of Biblical chronology. Two kingdoms flourished simultaneously, the Kingdom of Israel and the Kingdom of Judah. In the Book of Kings are given not only the number of years that each king reigned, but also the year in the reign of the contemporary king in which the first king began to rule. The complicating feature is that there are numerous cases in which there are seemingly discrepancies of one or more years. Many interpretations have been proposed to explain the numbers, but none, not even by traditional commentaries, can satisfactorily explain all the data involved. Below is presented a systematic method of explaining the numbers and dates in the Book of Kings, and elsewhere in the Bible, relevant to the period of the kings. The specified assumptions are based on the data and have been arrived at on the basis of the history presented in the text and in extra-Biblical sources. These assumptions have been made as simple as possible to explain all the facts. Numerous other possible explanations have been tried but have not made possible as perfect an explanation as presented below.

BASIC ASSUMPTIONS AND THEIR EXPLANATIONS

(A) In the Books of Kings and Chronicles there is mention of three books supplying supplementary information. These books are:

    i. Book of the Kings of Judah and Israel;
    ii. Book of the Chronicles of the Kings of Judah;
    iii. Book of the Chronicles of the Kings of Israel.

The internal evidence supports the contention that our present Book of Kings is the Book of the Kings of Judah and Israel, that our present Book of Chronicles is the Book of the Chronicles of the Kings of Judah, and that the Book of the Chronicles of the Kings of Israel is unfortunately lost. Firstly, the Book of Kings deals with both the kings of Israel and Judah while the Book of Chronicles deals only with the kings of Judah. Even the genealogies at the beginning of the Book of Chronicles emphasize the tribe of Judah. Secondly, in the Book of Kings we find no reference to the Book of the Kings of Judah and Israel, but only to the Book of the Chronicles of the Kings of Judah, and the Book of the Chronicles of the Kings of Israel. Similarly, the Book of Chronicles contains references to the Book of the Kings of Judah and Israel, and the Book of the Kings of Israel, and no reference to the Book of the Chronicles of the Kings of Judah. Thirdly, every time the Book of Kings mentions that supplementary information is found in the Book of the Chronicles of the Kings of Judah, then supplementary information is found in Chronicles; and similarly when the Book of Chronicles mentions that supplementary information is found in the Book of the Kings of Judah and Israel, then supplementary information is found in the Book of Kings. In addition, when reference is made to the Book of the Chronicles of the Kings of Israel, no information of that nature is found elsewhere in the Bible, indicating that the Book of the Kings of Israel is lost. (See Section 15.3 for additional details.)

One result is that a more detailed knowledge of the kings of Judah is available than of the kings of Israel.

(B) Two slightly different counting schemes exist for the kings of Judah and for the kings of Israel. The kings of Judah count the beginning of their reigns from the first month, the month of Nisan, while the kings of Israel count their years of rule from the eighth month, the month of Cheshvan. Thus, if it is stated that a particular king of Judah ruled for N years, this means that he was king on N consecutive firsts-of-Nisan. Actually, the data only require that the month of the beginning of the year of the king of Judah should be a few months apart from that for the king of Israel irrespective of which particular months are involved. However, Biblical evidence (Ex. 12 2) supports the idea that Nisan is the beginning of the year for all except agricultural purposes, while the tenth of Tishri is the agricultural New Year (Lev. 25 9) (see Section 5.1). Now, when Jeroboam I became king of Israel he wanted to be independent of the Kingdom of Judah, and therefore established the month of Cheshvan as the beginning of his regnal year. This month is only a few weeks after the agricultural New Year, and therefore was readily accepted by the people. Evidence for the change is found in I Kings 12 32,33 where mention is made of the establishment by Jeroboam of a new holiday which occurred in the eighth month of the year, a month which he had devised from his own heart. It is interesting to note that the Babylonians at this time considered Nisan as being the first month of the year and the beginning of the regnal year[3].

Two pieces of evidence support the contention that the counting system used is one where the number of years listed is the number of consecutive times that the king has ruled at the beginning of the year.

David is stated, in II Sam. 5 5 and I Chr. 3 4, to have ruled seven and one-half years in Hebron, while in I Kings 2 11 and I Chr. 29 27 it is stated that he ruled seven years in Hebron. Thus seven years and seven and one-half years are equivalent in the counting system.

In I Kings 6 1,37 and II Chr. 3 2 it is stated that the building of the Temple was begun in the fourth year and second month of the reign of Solomon, and in I Kings 6 38 that it was completed after seven years, in the eleventh year and eighth month of Solomon. The actual time of building is seven and one-half years, and yet is considered to be seven years, again indicating that the system of counting is only accurate to one year and is counted from the first month of the year.

(C) A slight modification in the counting scheme for the kings of Israel occurs around the time of Jehoram, King of Israel. Prior to Jehoram, the kings of Israel, whose regnal year began from the month of Cheshvan, counted the months between the date of accession and the month of Cheshvan as their first year. The first of Cheshvan began their second year of rulership. This explains, for example, the fact that Nadab, who began ruling in the second year of Asa of Judah, and ruled for two years, completed his reign not in the fourth year of Asa but in the third year. Thus, the kings are credited with ruling one more year than actually occurred. After Jehoram of Israel, no longer did the kings of Israel count the years between the date of accession and the first of Cheshvan as a full year. Evidence of the transition occurs during the reign of Jehoram. King Ahaziah of Judah originally is stated to have begun ruling in the twelfth year of Jehoram (II Kings 8 25); and subsequently (II Kings 9 29) to have begun ruling in the eleventh year of Jehoram. Thus the change occurred during the reign of Jehoram of Israel, probably at the time of Ahaziah of Judah, and the time from the accession of Jehoram until the beginning of Cheshvan is from then on not counted as a year of rulership. The result is that the twelfth year of Jehoram became the eleventh year. Among the Assyrians and Babylonians a similar situation occurred. The general practice was to count the regnal years from the next New Year's day after accession, and to call the period between the accession day and the first New Year's day "the beginning of the reign," while the New Year's day began the "first year." Nevertheless, for several Assyrian and Babylonian rulers there are cases where the year of accession is considered as the first year, thus giving two reckonings for their reigns[4].

For the kings of Judah no such problem exists. In all cases the first year begins from the month of Nisan after the king's accession.

(D) The years given for any king refer to the actual number of years ruled according to the counting scheme. This refers not only to the length of rule given for each king but also to the synchronistic years; i.e. the year in the contemporary reign of the king of the parallel kingdom.

(E) Even upon following the basic assumptions listed above there will occur many discrepancies. These discrepancies can all be explained on the basis of co-regnancy of the son with his father, hinted at in the text, or on the basis of unusual circumstances described in the text. For the kings of Judah a more complete description of events is available since the texts of Kings and Chronicles supplement each other on this topic; but for the kings of Israel only the Book of Kings supplies information. It is therefore reasonable to assume that the occurrence of a co-regnancy or some unusual event in the reign of a king of Judah will be known to us, but not necessarily for the kings of Israel, and a hint of the text may be the only record available other than the chronological difficulty.

(F) In Table 5.2.1 is presented the proposed explanation for the reigns of the kings of Israel and Judah. The explanation of unusual situations is given subsequently for each case. The notation 9:959 and 2:939 mean, respectively, the ninth month of the year 959 and the second month of the year 939. However, the actual dates often cannot be determined more precisely than the nearest half-year. What is meant by the second month is sometime between the beginning of counting of an additional year for the king of Judah (after the first of Nisan, the first month) and prior to counting of an additional year for the king of Israel (before the first of Cheshvan, the eighth month). Similarly, the ninth month signifies sometime after the counting of an additional year for the king of Israel but before the counting of an additional year for the king of Judah. In actuality, in nearly all cases any time between the second day of Nisan and the eighth month such as the second, third, fourth, fifth, sixth or seventh month is equivalent to that of the first month for the purpose of the calculations; and similarly the ninth, tenth, eleventh and twelfth months would be the same as the eighth. The use of the second and ninth months, in nearly all cases, is a matter of convenience and is not meant to exclude the possibility of the event occurring on a different month that would be equivalent chronologically. It should be noted that the dates presented in the Table are based on the year beginning in Nisan (March or April), as was the case in ancient times.

(G) It is further assumed that in cases where co-regnancy occurs, that the number of ruling years for the co-regent begins from the time of the beginning of the co-regnancy, rather than, e.g., after the death of the older king. Thus Jehoshaphat, who ruled two years during the reign of his father Asa, begins counting the twenty-five years of his reign from the beginning of his co-regnancy, rather than from after the death of Asa. Only in cases where a discontinuous reign occurs is this procedure not followed. The dates of such events are placed in parenthesis to indicate lack of continuity. Such is the case for Jehoram of Judah and Jeroboam II of Israel. In all other cases the listed years of reign begin from the year of co-regnancy. An unusual situation occurs in the case of Hoshea of Israel who ruled in two stages, and the years listed in his case begin from the second stage when he began ruling from Samaria.

Notes on Table 5.2.1

Below are explained the reasons for the datings given for particular kings in Table 5.2.1. The letters identifying the paragraphs correspond to the notes

Table 5.2.1
Dates for the Kings of Judah and Israel

King		Reign (Yrs.)		Accession Yr. in Reign of-		Other Data (Notes)	Biblical References		Dates (B.C.E.)
Judah	Israel	Judah	Israel	Judah	Israel		Kings	Chronicles	
Rehoboam		17				(A)	I 14 21	II 12 13	9:959–9:942
	Jeroboam		22				I 14 20		9:959–2:937
Abijam (Abijah)		3			18	(B)	I 15 1, 2	II 13 1, 2	9:942–2:939
Asa		41			20	(D)	I 15 9, 10	II 16 13	2:939–2:898
	Nadab		2	2			I 15 25		2:937–2:936
	Baasa		24	3			I 15 28, 33		2:936–2:913
	Elah		2	26			I 16 8		2:913–2:912
	Zimri		(7 days)	27			I 16 10, 15		2:912
	Omri		12	31		(C) 6 yrs. in Tirzah	I 16 23		2:912–9:908 −2:901
	Ahab		22	38			I 16 29		2:901–9:881
Jehosha-phat		25			4	(D)	I 22 41, 42	II 20 31	9:900–2:898 −9:875
	Ahaziah		2	17		(E)	I 22 52		9:881–9:880
	Jehoram (Joram)		12	18		2nd of Jehoram	II 1 17; 3 1		9:880–9:868
Jehoram (Joram)		8			5	(F)	II 8 16, 17	II 21 5, 20	(9:882) 9:876 −2:868

CHRONOLOGY OF THE KINGS

Ahaziah	1	12	(G) 11th of Jehoram	II 8 25, 26; 9 29	II 22 2	9:869–2:868 –9:868
Athaliah	6		(H)	II 11 3, 4	II 22 12; 23 1	9:868–12:862
Jehu	28			II 10 36		9:868–2:839
Jehoash (Joash)	40	7	(H)	II 12 2	II 24 1	1:861–2:822
Jehoahaz	17	23		II 13 1		2:839–2:822
Jehoash (Joash)	16	37	(I)	II 13 10		9:825–2:822 –2:808
Amaziah	29	2	(J) Lived 15 yrs. after death of Jehoash of Israel	II 14 1, 2 17	II 25 1, 25	8:823–2:822 –9:794
Jeroboam II	41	15	(K, L)	II 14 23		(9:821) 2:811 –2:808–12:771
Azariah (Uzziah)	52	27	(L)	II 15 1, 2	II 26 3	2:809–9:794 –9:757
Zechariah	6 mos.	38	(M)	II 15 8		12:771–6:770
Shallum	1 mo.	39		II 15 13		6:770–7:770
Menahem	10	39	(M)	II 15 17		8:770–2:759
Pekahiah	2	50		II 15 23		2:759–2:757

Table 5.2.1 (continued)

King Judah	King Israel	Reign (Yrs.) Judah	Reign (Yrs.) Israel	Accession Yr. in Reign of: Judah	Accession Yr. in Reign of: Israel	Other Data (Notes)	Biblical References Kings	Biblical References Chronicles	Dates (B.C.E.)
	Pekah		20				II 15 27		2:757–2:737
Jotham		16		52	2	(N)	II 15 5, 32, 33	II 26 21; 27 1, 8 1 5 17	9:757–9:756 –9:741
	Hoshea		9		17		II 16 1, 2 II 15 30; 17 1; 18 10	II 28 1	9:741–2:725 2:737–9:729 –2:719
Ahaz		16		12		(O) 20th of Jotham			
Hezekiah		29			3		II 18 1, 2, 9, 10	II 29 1	2:725–2:696
Manasseh		55					II 21 1	II 33 1	2:696–2:641
Amon		2					II 21 19	II 33 21	2:641–2:639
Josiah		31				(P)	II 22 1	II 34 1 Jer. 25 3	2:639–2:608
Jehoahaz		3 mos.					II 23 31	II 36 2	2:608–5:608
Jehoiakim		11				(Q)	II 23 36	II 36 5	5:608–9:597
Jehoiachin (Jeconiah)		3 mos.				(R)	II 24 8	II 36 9, 10	9:597–12:597
Zedekiah		11					II 24 18	II 36 11 Jer. 52 1	12:597–5:586

indicated in the Table. Specific emphasis is here given to exceptional cases, such as when a co-regnancy occurs.

(A) Rehoboam and Jeroboam began ruling at the same time, immediately after the death of Solomon. Rehoboam reigned seventeen years, and Jeroboam twenty-two years. The problem then arises why Abijam, son of Rehoboam, began ruling in the eighteenth year immediately after the death of his father. On the assumption that the kings of Israel counted the months between the time of accession and the month of Cheshvan as a full year, the explanation becomes simple. What is the seventeenth year of Rehoboam is the eighteenth year of Jeroboam.

(B) Abijam, King of Judah, began ruling in the eighteenth year of Jeroboam and reigned for three years. Yet his son Asa began ruling in the twentieth year of Jeroboam. This is explained as follows: Abijam began ruling in the ninth month of the year, or later, and reigned until e.g. the second month of the year. The actual time of rule is about two and one-half years. According to the counting system of the kings of Judah this is three years, but according to the counting system of the kings of Israel this is only two years. (Numerous similar cases exist and will not further be explained individually.)

(C) Omri, King of Israel, began ruling immediately after the death of Zimri and ruled twelve years. Zimri ruled seven days and began ruling in the twenty-seventh year of Asa. Yet it is stated that Omri began ruling in the thirty-first year of Asa and ruled for six years from Tirzah, until he moved the capital to Samaria.

The situation is explained as follows: The six years that Omri ruled in Tirzah are from the twenty-seventh year of Asa until the thirty-first year of Asa. In actuality, the duration was only four and one-half years, but because of the counting system it is called six years. One extra year because of the months between the date of accession and the month of Cheshvan, and a second extra year if the rule of Omri is assumed to begin in the second month, and the six years to end in the ninth month.

(D) The reign of Jehoshaphat is the first where a co-regnancy is necessary to explain the chronology. Jehoshaphat must have ruled two years during the reign of his father Asa, at the later stages of Asa's painful affliction in his feet (II Chr. 16 12; I Kings 15 23).

Care must be taken not to assume that Asa became afflicted in his feet in the 39th year of his *reign*. In II Chr. 16 12 it is stated that Asa became afflicted in his feet in the thirty-ninth year of his *kingdom*. Other dates of Asa are also given in terms of his *kingdom*; thus in II Chr. 15 10 is mentioned the fifteenth year, in II Chr. 15 19 the thirty-fifth year, and in II Chr. 16 1 the thirty-sixth year; all dated with respect to the "kingdom" of Asa. In no other cases are dates given with respect to the *kingdom* of a king, but rather with respect to the reign. The dating with respect to the kingdom is obviously different from that with respect to the reign, since II Chr. 16 1 states that Baasa, King of Israel, attacked Asa in the thirty-sixth year of the kingdom of Asa. However, according to Kings (I Kings 16

6,8) Baasa died in the twenty-sixth year of the reign of Asa. Hence the dating of the kingdom of Asa obviously precedes that of the reign of Asa by a minimum of ten years. The dating of the kingdom of Asa cannot, however, precede that of the reign of Asa by more than fifteen years, since Asa was ruling in the fifteenth year of his kingdom (II Chr. 15 10). The problem then arises as to what likely event begins the dating of the kingdom of Asa. Preceding the rule of Asa was Abijam who reigned three years, and he was preceded by Rehoboam who reigned seventeen years. Sometime between the fifth and tenth year of Rehoboam must be the date for the beginning of the kingdom of Asa. From I Kings 14 25 and II Chr. 12 2 we know that in the fifth year of Rehoboam, Shishak king of Egypt attacked Judah and removed the treasures of the kingdom. No other intermediate date is given during the reign of Rehoboam. A logical assumption then can be made that the kingdom of Asa begins from the fifth year of Rehoboam. This information leads to the conclusion that the fifteenth year of the kingdom of Asa is the first year of the reign of Asa, and that the thirty-ninth year of the kingdom of Asa is the twenty-fifth year of the reign of Asa, and is the year that the affliction in his feet began. Fourteen years later, two years before his death, Asa made his son Jehoshaphat co-regent with him because of excessive trouble with his feet.

(E) In II Kings 1 17 it is stated that Jehoram, son of Ahab, of Israel began ruling in the second year of Jehoram, son of Jehoshaphat, of Judah, while II Kings 3 1 states that Jehoram son of Ahab began ruling in the eighteenth year of Jehoshaphat. This indicates that Jehoshaphat and his son Jehoram ruled simultaneously. The dates can be explained as follows: when Jehoshaphat went to visit Ahab in Samaria (I Kings 22 2 and II Chr. 18 2) he set up his son Jehoram as king. This was in the middle of the sixteenth year of Jehoshaphat. After the death of Ahab, Jehoshaphat returned to Judah and resumed sole rulership.

(F) In II Kings 8 16 it is stated that Jehoram son of Jehoshaphat of Judah began ruling in the fifth year of Jehoram son of Ahab of Israel and also when Jehoshaphat was king of Judah. This information, combined with the numerical data, is equivalent to the statement that Jehoram son of Jehoshaphat began ruling as king of Judah one year before the death of Jehoshaphat. Support for this conclusion is gained from II Chr. 21 3 where is stated that Jehoshaphat gave the kingdom to Jehoram because he was the first-born; thus indicating that Jehoram was made king before Jehoshaphat died.

(G) Ahaziah son of Jehoram of Judah is stated to have begun ruling in the twelfth year of Jehoram of Israel (II Kings 8 25) and in the eleventh year of Jehoram (II Kings 9 29). This seeming contradiction is explained by the assumption that during the reign of Jehoram of Israel there was a modification in the counting system. Prior to Jehoram the months between accession and the month of Cheshvan are counted as a full year. Afterwards they are not counted as a year. The change from the twelfth to the eleventh year of the reign of Jehoram is to inform us that the change had been made during the time that Ahaziah of Judah ruled.

The above explanation coupled with the numerical information makes it necessary that Ahaziah, son of Jehoram, began ruling over Judah during the reign of his father. This agrees with the fact that Jehoram of Judah suffered extreme intestinal sickness at the end of his reign (II Chr. 21 19). Therefore Ahaziah ruled during the last few months of the life of Jehoram as a co-regent.

(H) It is stated that Athaliah ruled over Judah for six years (II Kings 11 3, II Chr. 22 12). However, it is also stated that Jehoash the son of Ahaziah revolted in the seventh year (of Athaliah). The text implies that it was at the very beginning of the seventh year, i.e. on the first of Nisan, that the revolt took place. This first day of Nisan is therefore counted for the reign of Jehoash rather than for the reign of Athaliah.

(I) Jehoash, King of Israel, is said to have begun to rule in the thirty-seventh year of Jehoash, King of Judah. This requires that Jehoash reigned two years during the reign of his father Jehoahaz of Israel. The only hint of a co-regnancy during the rulership of Jehoahaz is deduced from II Kings 13 5 where it is stated that God sent Israel a deliverer; and from II Kings 13 25 where it is implied that the deliverer was Jehoash. It should be remembered that no information supplementary to that in the Book of Kings exists for the kings of Israel. Therefore the lack of a clear hint of co-regnancy in the text, other than the numerical data, does not exclude the possibility that a co-regnancy did occur.

(J) The numerical data require that Amaziah reigned a short while during the reign of his father Jehoash of Judah. This is supported by the statement in II Chr. 24 25 that Jehoash was left with many diseases by the army of Aram, and was subsequently assassinated by his servants. During the time that Jehoash suffered from his diseases, Amaziah must have reigned jointly with Jehoash. Since it is stated in II Chr. 24 23 that the attack by Aram occurred at the time of "recycling of the year," i.e., around the middle of the seventh month (see Section 5.1.4), we here assume that Amaziah began his co-regnancy in the eighth month.

(K) The reign of Jeroboam II, son of Jehoash of Israel, involves several phases as indicated by the numerical information. The first phase involves the co-regnancy of Jeroboam with his father, beginning with the second year of his father's sole reign. At that time Jeroboam was of secondary importance and therefore his length of rule is not counted from then. Three years prior to the death of Jehoash, Jeroboam became a dominant factor and therefore the years of rule of Jeroboam begin from that time. The third phase begins at the time of the death of his father when Jeroboam became sole ruler.

Evidence for the co-regnancy, other than from numerical data, is given in II Kings 13 13 where it is stated that Jeroboam sat on the throne, implying prior to his father's death. This is in contrast to the phraseology used in II Kings 14 16 where it is stated that Jeroboam ruled after the death of his father.

(L) A complicating factor in the calculation of the years of rule of Azariah of Judah and of Jeroboam II of Israel is that they both ruled many years as co-regents with their fathers. In other cases of co-regnancy only one of the kings ruled jointly with his father at a time, except in cases of co-regnancies of less than one year.

The texts of II Kings **14** 22 and II Chr. **26** 2 state that Azariah built Elath after the death of his father Amaziah. This clearly implies that Azariah ruled Judah during the lifetime of his father. Secondly, it is implied that Amaziah was not the dominant ruler during the last fifteen years of his life (II Kings **14** 17; II Chr. **25** 25) since the term "lived" rather than "ruled" is used. The numerical data require a minimum of twelve years of co-regnancy for Azariah, and upon allowing three years co-regnancy of Jeroboam II of Israel during the reign of Jehoash, a co-regnancy of fifteen years for Azariah is obtained in agreement with the hint from the text. It is necessary to assume that Azariah, when he began ruling fifteen years prior to the death of Amaziah, was sixteen years old, (II Kings **14** 21; II Chr. **26** 1) rather than after the death of Amaziah; for otherwise Azariah would have been one year old when he was co-regent with his father.

(M) Menahem of Israel began ruling in the thirty-ninth year of Azariah and ruled for ten years. However, his son Pekahiah began ruling in the fiftieth year of Azariah. To explain this, one might at first assume that Menahem actually ruled ten and one-half years; and though he ruled on ten consecutive months of Cheshvan, he also ruled on eleven consecutive months of Nisan.

There is, however, a difficulty involved in the above explanation. In particular, Shallum who preceded Menahem reigned one month, and Zechariah who preceded Shallum reigned six months. This situation makes it impossible to arrange the reign of Menahem according to the above-described system.

Another possible explanation is that Shallum, who reigned one month, reigned from the middle of the seventh month to the middle of the eighth month (Cheshvan). Then, in actuality, Shallum would have reigned a full year according to the counting system of the kings of Israel, which is not in agreement with the statement that he ruled only one month.

The preferable explanation, which is here used, is that about a month passed between the death of Shallum and the official beginning of the reign of Menahem. Thus in II Kings **15** 16 it is stated that Menahem had to conquer the city of Tiphsah because it did not open to him. During this interim time occurred the eighth month, adding another year.

(N) Jotham, King of Judah, began ruling in the second year of Pekah, King of Israel. However Azariah, who preceded Jotham, reigned fifty-two years, and Pekah began ruling in the fifty-second year of Azariah. This would, at the latest, make Jotham begin ruling in the first year of Pekah, since Pekah revolted against Pekahiah and could not have begun ruling prior to the death of Pekahiah. A simple explanation is that in actuality Azariah lived a year after his fifty-two years of reign were concluded. As stated in II Kings **15** 5 and II Chr. **26** 21, Azariah was afflicted with leprosy, resided in a separate place, and his son Jotham presided over the people. Also, Isa. **6** 1 dates a prophecy as "the year of the death of

Azariah," rather than the last year of the reign of Azariah. Thus Jotham began ruling while Azariah was alive. The assumption here made is that the fifty-two years of the reign of Azariah do not include the time when Azariah was a leper. The statement that Jotham began ruling in the second year of Pekah refers to the time when Azariah died and Jotham became absolute ruler.

(O) Hoshea, King of Israel is said to have begun ruling in the twentieth year of Jotham, King of Judah (II Kings 15 30), and also in the twelfth year of Ahaz, King of Judah (II Kings 17 1). These dates make the entire reign of Hoshea eighteen years, rather than the nine years stated in II Kings 17 1. It is therefore necessary to explain that there were two stages in the reign of Hoshea. In the twentieth year of Jotham, Pekah was killed and Hoshea began ruling, but not from the capital city of Samaria. Probably the rule by Hoshea was not accepted by all the people since he had rebelled against Pekah. Nine years later, in the twelfth year of Ahaz, Hoshea began ruling from Samaria as specifically stated in II Kings 17 1; and the years of his reign are dated from this latter event. The reason the date of the twentieth year of Jotham is used, even though Jotham reigned only sixteen years, is not to confuse the reader with two different dates based on the reign of Ahaz.

The statement in I Chr. 5 17 that the genealogies presented were reckoned in the days of Jotham, King of Judah, and in the days of Jeroboam, King of Israel, does not necessarily mean that Jotham and Jerobaom II ruled at the same time. The dates from the Book of Kings establish that they did not rule at the same time. The statement merely relates that the genealogy of the tribes residing in Israel were reckoned during the reign of Jeroboam II, and those of the tribes in Judah were reckoned during the reign of Jotham. Supporting this explanation is the possible indication from I Chr. 4 41 that genealogies were also taken during the reign of Hezekiah, King of Judah.

(P) A check on the reigns of the last kings of Judah is obtained from the statement in Jer. 25 3 that the length of time from the thirteenth year of Josiah, King of Judah, through the fourth year of Jehoiakim is twenty-three years. Josiah reigned thirty-one years, followed by Jehoahaz who reigned three months, followed by Jehoiakim who reigned eleven years. If both the thirteenth year of Josiah and the fourth year of Jehoiakim are included, exactly twenty-three years are obtained. This confirms that no co-regnancies occurred between Josiah and Jehoahaz, or between Jehoahaz and Jehoiakim.

(Q) A second check on the reigns of the last kings of Judah is obtained from the correspondence to the reign of Nebuchadnezzar. The fourth year of Jehoiakim, King of Judah, is the first year of King Nebuchadnezzar (Jer. 25 1). The three months in which Jehoiachin ruled occurred in the eighth year of King Nebuchadnezzar (II Kings 24 12). The eleventh year of Zedekiah is the nineteenth of King Nebuchadnezzar (II Kings 25 8; Jer. 52 12) (see explanation at end of Section 12.2). Therefore, between the fourth year of Jehoiakim and the eleventh year of Zedekiah is eighteen years. This agrees with the lengths of rule given in Kings and

Chronicles; Jehoiakim reigned eleven years, followed by Jehoiachin who reigned three months, followed by Zedekiah who reigned eleven years. It can therefore be concluded that the listed years of reign for Jehoiakim, Jehoiachin, and Zedekiah refer to the years of sole rulership.

(R) In II Chr. 36 10 it is stated that Jehoiachin was captured by Nebuchadnezzar at the time of the "return of the year." As explained in Section 5.1.4 this phrase refers to the springtime, or approximately the first month. However, if Jehoiachin was captured in the first month, then he would have ruled a full year. Therefore, it is necessary to assume that Jehoiachin was actually made captive sometime in the twelfth month. This conclusion is supported by the Babylonian Chronicle, where it is stated that the conquest was accomplished on the second of Adar, i.e., in the twelfth month[5].

CONCLUSION

The scheme presented above can be fitted to the 410 years claimed by Jewish tradition (Babylonian Talmud, Tractate *Yoma* 9a) for the time the First Temple existed. Thus in I Kings 6 1 and II Chr. 3 2 it is stated that the building of the Temple began in the second month of the fourth year of Solomon. Solomon ruled forty years. Hence the building of the Temple began thirty-six years before the end of the rule of Solomon (or thirty-six years before the beginning of the reigns of Rehoboam and Jeroboam). According to the chronological scheme presented, Rehoboam began ruling in 8:959. Thirty-six years earlier is 995. From 995 through 586 is only 409 years; the year 995 is not included, since construction of the Temple was begun in the second month. However, the specified 410 years for the duration of the Temple may be calculated on a slightly different basis, i.e. by counting part of a year as a full year. From the second month of 995 until the fifth month of 586 is 409 years three months, which would then be equivalent to 410 years.

Also, upon comparing the years of rule presented here to those obtained by A. Akabya based on the interpretations of Rashi and Elijah of Wilna, one finds a disagreement in the years of reign of the kings of no more than two or three years[6]. This indicates that the chronological scheme here presented agrees fairly well with the traditional interpretations, since both schemes are based on a literal explanation of the Biblical statements.

5.2.1 Variant Information from Chronicles

The lengths of reign and the ages of the kings of Judah, as specified in the Book of Chronicles, agree exactly with the values given in the Book of Kings, with but two exceptions. These exceptions are for the ages of Kings Ahaziah and Jehoiachin at the time they began to rule. According to Kings, Ahaziah and Jehoiachin were twenty-two and eighteen years old respectively, while according to Chronicles they were forty-two and eight years old respectively. The ages of the

Table 5.2.1.1
Ages of Kings of Judah at the Beginning of their Reigns

King	Age	References Kings	II Chronicles
Rehoboam	41	I 14 21	12 13
Jehoshaphat	35	I 22 42	20 31
Jehoram (Joram)	32	II 8 17	21 5, 20
Ahaziah	22 (42 according to Chronicles)	II 8 26	22 2
Jehoash (Joash)	7	II 12 1	24 1
Amaziah	25	II 14 2	25 1
Azariah (Uzziah)	16	II 15 2	26 1, 3
Jotham	25	II 15 33	27 1, 8
Ahaz	20	II 16 2	28 1
Hezekiah	25	II 18 2	29 1
Manasseh	12	II 21 1	33 1
Amon	22	II 21 19	33 21
Josiah	8	II 22 1	34 1
Jehoahaz	23	II 23 31	36 2
Jehoiakim	25	II 23 36	36 5
Jehoiachin	18 (8 according to Chronicles)	II 24 8	36 9
Zedekiah	21	II 24 18	36 11

kings of Judah at their accession are tabulated in Table 5.2.1.1, where the instances of discrepancies are specified.

The discrepancy in the case of Jehoiachin can be simply explained by assuming that he was co-regent with his father Jehoiakim for ten years. The age of eighteen given in Kings refers to the time when Jehoiachin became sole ruler, while the age of eight mentioned in Chronicles refers to the time when he became co-regent. Probably the dangers from Pharaoh Necho, who had previously killed Josiah (II Kings 23 29; II Chr. 35 20–24) and captured Jehoahaz (II Kings 23 33, 34; II Chr. 36 4), prompted Jehoiakim in the second year of his reign to make his eight-year-old son Jehoiachin co-regent.

The discrepancy in the case of Ahaziah is not easily explained. Jehoram, Ahaziah's father, was thirty-two years when he became king and he ruled for eight years; thus Jehoram was forty when he died. The age of twenty-two for

Ahaziah given in II Kings 8 26 is reasonable, even when considering that he had older brothers (II Chr. 21 17), since he would be eighteen years younger than his father. However, the age of forty-two specified in II Chr. 22 2 is impossible since it would make Ahaziah older than his father. No simple solution seems possible for the age of forty-two, and probably the text should read twenty-two in agreement with the Book of Kings.

One other case needs comment. Hezekiah was twenty-five years old when he became king, which was only eleven years younger than his father Ahaz (twenty plus sixteen equals thirty-six). This small difference in age does not pose a serious difficulty, since it is very possible for Ahaz to have matured early at the age of ten. Furthermore, if Ahaz were born shortly after Nisan, and Hezekiah shortly before Nisan, there would actually be almost a full twelve years difference in age between father and son, making the data even more plausible.

In addition to the ages for the kings of Judah which are listed in Table 5.2.1.1 the ages of Kings Saul, David, and Solomon who ruled over the united monarchy can be ascertained. Saul was fifty-two years old when he became king as explained in great detail in Section 4.4; David was thirty, as specifically stated in II Sam. 5 4; and Solomon was fifteen, as approximated very closely in the discussion at the end of Section 11.3.

5.2.2 Times Elapsed Relevant to the Period of the Kings

Two passages, which present times elapsed during the period of the kings, need to be interpreted. The first passage occurs in Ez. 4, where it is described how Ezekiel is to lie on his left side for 390 days to represent the 390 years of iniquity of the "House of Israel," and then to lie on his right side for forty days to symbolize the forty years of the iniquity of the "House of Judah."

These numbers of 390 and 40 have offered great difficulty to commentators. To explain the numbers it is necessary to realize that the terms "House of Israel" and "House of Judah" do not necessarily correspond to the divided kingdoms of Israel and Judah. Thus, in the fifth year of the exile of Jehoiachin (Ez. 1 2), Ezekiel is told to speak to the "House of Israel" (Ez. 3 4). Obviously the "House of Israel" does not correspond to the Kingdom of Israel, since this occurred long after the exile of the northern tribes. The group referred to can be understood on the basis of other sections in the Bible. In general the term "Children of Israel" is used to include the entire Israelite population, while the term "House of Israel" refers only to the heads of the households. For example, the "House of Israel" named the food found in the desert manna (Ex. 16 31), although all the "Children of Israel" ate the manna (Ex. 16 35). It is also clear that "House" refers only to males, since in I Kings 12 21, Rehoboam gathered the "House of Judah" to fight with the "House of Israel." In this case "House of Judah" refers to the heads of the households of the tribe of Judah, and "House of Israel" refers to the heads of the housholds of the other tribes.

The Biblical text indicates that the end of the 390 and 40 year periods occurs in 586 at the time of the destruction of the Temple, since the symbolism used refers to the siege and attack on Jerusalem (Ez. 4 1–3). Three hundred and ninety years before 586 is 975, the year when King Solomon completed construction of the palace and the Temple. Thus, Solomon (999–959) began building the Temple in his fourth year (I Kings 6 1) and completed the palace and the Temple twenty years later (I Kings 9 10) in 975. Similarly, forty years before the destruction of the Temple is 626, which corresponds to the thirteenth year of King Josiah when Jeremiah began to prophesy (Jer. 1 2).

There is a common element in the times beginning 390 and 40 years before the destruction of the Temple. At the time of the former date, when the Temple and the king's palace were completed, God appeared to Solomon (I Kings 9 1–9) telling him that if he observed the laws his kingdom would last forever, but if he turned from the correct path then the Temple would be destroyed. We know from the Bible that Solomon and his descendants did not truly follow the correct path, and therefore the iniquity of 390 years marks the period from this revelation until the destruction of the Temple. Similarly, the latter date (626) marks the beginning of the prophecies of Jeremiah to the people of Judah. He states (Jer. 4 1–9) that the people should repent, lest Jerusalem and Judah be destroyed. This prophecy is in contrast to the revelation to Solomon. During the last forty years, the people of Judah were sinning and needed to repent lest they be destroyed, while at the time of Solomon the people were acting correctly and needed to continue to do so for fear that the Temple be destroyed.

The second passage requiring interpretation occurs in Isa. 7 8, where is stated that in another sixty-five years the people of Ephraim (i.e. the people of the Kingdom of Israel) will be destroyed. The prophecy was stated during the reigns of Ahaz, king of Judah, and Pekah, king of Israel (Isa. 7 1), which limits the time to the years between 741 and 737. The date when the prophecy was revealed can be further delimited since it is also stated (Isa. 7 14–16) that the young woman will become pregnant, give birth to a son, and before the child will know how to differentiate between right and wrong the two kings, namely Pekah of Israel and Rezin of Aram, will be removed. Now the approximate time specified is one year for pregnancy and two years until the son matures sufficiently to know right from wrong, or a total of three years. Therefore the prophecy must have been received approximately in 740, three years before the death of Pekah.

Sixty-five years after 740 is 675; but no obvious event is known for that year. However, Manasseh (696–641) king of Judah, was then reigning. In II Chr. 33 11–13 it is mentioned that Manasseh was captured by Assyrian officers, led to Babylonia, and subsequently returned to Jerusalem. It is further stated (II Chr. 33 18) that additional information about Manasseh is written in the Book of the Kings of Israel. This establishes that some portions of the Kingdom of Israel still remained at the time of Manasseh. From Assyrian history (see Table 5.3.1) we can estimate the time of Manasseh's capture as 676 or shortly thereafter. If we assume that it was about this time (675) that the Kingdom of Israel and its people were completely destroyed, to an even greater extent than at the end of Hoshea's reign, then the sixty-five years becomes meaningful.

An indirect conclusion from the above discussion is that the Book of the Chronicles of the Kings of Israel (which as we have stated in Section 5.2 is lost to us) was not completed in its entirety until after 675.

5.3 COMPARISON OF BIBLICAL AND ASSYRIAN DATES

Upon comparing the presented chronology of the kings, based on the Biblical sources, with corresponding events dated from Assyrian history, significant discrepancies are noted. The main cases where such comparisons can be made are specified in Table 5.3.1. Where the sources do not allow the giving of an exact date, the period of time in which the event must have occurred based on the reigns of the monarchs is then given. Let us examine the basis for the Assyrian chronology to determine where modifications can be made so as to allow exact agreement between the Biblical and Assyrian dates.

Assyrian chronology is based on "eponym" or *limmu* lists, whereby each year is assigned to an important person known as an eponym. A continuous list covering a period of over 250 years, until 659 B.C.E., can be established based on several somewhat damaged inscriptions[8]. The absolute dates of the years are set on the basis of the statement opposite the eponym Pur-Sagale that in Sivan there was an eclipse of the sun. Limitations based on geographical location, the month of Sivan, and data from other inscriptions leave only a few possible dates for the eclipse. It is usually identified with the eclipse of June 15, 763, although two other possibilities exist. According to the calculations of Theodore Von Oppolzer solar eclipses seen over Assyria also occurred in the month of June in the years 791 and 809[9]. By assuming that the eclipse for the eponym Pur-Sagale really occurred in June 24, 791, agreement with the Biblical dates is obtained for the events ascribed to the reign of Shalmaneser III. The resulting one year discrepancy (see Table 5.3.1) for the time when tribute was sent by Jehu (869 rather than 868) can be explained by assuming that the tribute was actually sent in Shalmaneser's nineteenth year, since the campaign which was begun in Shalmaneser's eighteenth year probably extended into the next year of his reign.

It should be further noted that the extra twenty-eight years gained by selection of the eclipse of 791, allows agreement for the first two correlations ascribed to Tiglath-Pileser III, but not to the last two. To explain this discrepancy it is necessary to realize the existence of another problem in Assyrian chronology. According to the Bible, there existed an Assyrian king named Pul who ruled immediately before Tiglath-Pileser III. This is indicated by (A) the mention in I Chr. 5 26 that Pul, king of Assyria and Tiglath-Pileser, king of Assyria exiled the tribes of Reuben, Gad, and half of Manasseh; and by (B) the mention that

Menahem gave tribute to Pul (II Kings 15 19), and that Pekah, who was king of Israel shortly after Menahem, ruled at the same time as Tiglath-Pileser III (II Kings 15 29). However, no mention of a king named Pul is found either in the eponym list or in Assyrian inscriptions. Historians, for lack of a better assumption, identify Tiglath-Pileser III with Pul, based on the use in Babylonia by Tiglath-Pileser III of the name Pulu. This is concluded from the Babylonian Chronicle which states that Tiglath-Pileser seated himself on the throne of Babylon and ruled for two years, and from the Babylonian king list A which specifies for those same two years that Pulu reigned[10]. Although Tiglath-Pileser may have used the name Pulu in Babylonia, it is definitely incorrect to identify Tiglath-Pileser with the Biblical Pul, since these two kings are mentioned together in the same Biblical sentence (I Chr. 5 26). George Smith states, "the inability to identify the king called Pul in the Bible is a grave difficulty and lends support that he was a monarch whose name is not in the eponym list."[11]

An additional difficulty is the imperfection of the inscriptions of Tiglath-Pileser III. According to Daniel D. Luckenbill: "The annals of Tiglath-Pileser were engraved upon the slabs of the rebuilt central palace at Caleh. These slabs were later removed by Esarhaddon to be used in his southwest palace of the same city. As a result of the removal and retrimming of the stone, the annals have come down to us in a fragmentary state. Without the aid of the eponym-list it would have been impossible to arrange the fragments in their chronological order, and even so, future discoveries are likely to show that the arrangement now generally accepted is wrong."[12] It should also be pointed out that the beginnings and ends of the royal annals, the sections which identify the king and the year, especially had been chiselled off[13].

A reasonable conclusion to be drawn is that the annals of Pul have been confused with those of Tiglath-Pileser III. It may very well have been that Tiglath-Pileser, upon becoming king, removed all of the records relating to Pul from the eponym-list, as well as the name Pul from all the inscriptions. As subsequently shown (Section 12.4), the Assyrian king who repented at the time of the prophet Jonah, was probably Pul. This break by Pul with Assyrian tradition may very well have been the reason for the obliteration of all mention of Pul's name in the inscriptions. Modern historians, in reconstructing the annals, have mixed up some of the inscriptions of Pul with those of Tiglath-Pileser III. The result is that Menahem's and Azariah's contacts with Tiglath-Pileser, based on Assyrian inscriptions, should really be between them and Pul. This is corroborated by the statement in II Kings 15 19 that Menahem paid tribute to Pul. However, the Assyrian records which mention contacts of Pekah and Ahaz with Tiglath-Pileser, are corroborated by II Kings 15 29 and 16 7.

The evidence shows that an Assyrian king named Pul, whose records have been either damaged or destroyed, preceded Tiglath-Pileser III. The length of Pul's reign is probably twenty-eight years, which exactly fills in the time-gap that would

Table 5.3.1
Correlations between Biblical and Assyrian Dates

Assyrian King	Yr. of Reign	Event	Standard Date (B.C.E.)	Historical Refs.	Date From Bible (B.C.E.)	Biblical Refs.	Difference (Yrs.) Min.	Max.
Shalmaneser III	6	Contact with Ahab	853	ARAB I p. 222–3	Bet. 901 and 881	—	28	48
Shalmaneser III	18	Tribute from Jehu	841	ARAB I p. 243	Bet. 868 and 839	—	−2	27
Tiglath-Pileser III	3	Tributes from Azariah and Menahem	742	ARAB I p. 272–6	Bet. 770 and 759	—	17	28
Tiglath-Pileser III	8	Tribute from Menahem	737	TP p. 5ff	Bet. 765 and 759	—	22	28
Pul	—	Tribute from Menahem	—	—	Bet. 770 and 759	II Ki. 15 19	—	—
Tiglath-Pileser III	—	Pekah killed; Hoshea made king	Bet. 744 and 727	ARAB I p. 293	737	II Ki. 15 29–30	—	—

CHRONOLOGY OF THE KINGS

		Event	Date	Reference	Date	Bible ref	
Tiglath-Pileser III	—	Tribute from Ahaz	Bet. 744 and 727	ARAB I p. 287	Bet. 741 and 737	II Ki. 16 7; II Chr. 28 16-21	—
Sargon II	1	Samaria conquered	721	ARAB II p. 2	719	II Ki. 17 3-6; 18 10	-2
Sennacherib	4	War with Hezekiah	701	ARAB II p. 142-3	711	II Ki. 18 13-19 36	10
Esarhaddon		Contact with Manasseh	ca. 676	ARAB II p. 265-7; DOTT p. 73	Bet. 696 and 641	II Chr. 33 11-13	—
Assurbanipal	1	Tribute from Manasseh	668	ARAB II p. 340	Bet. 696 and 641	—	—
Babylonian King							
Merodach-baladan		Contact with Hezekiah	Bet. 721 and 710; 703	—	711	II Ki. 20 5, 6, 12	—

have otherwise been left by placing the eclipse of the eponym year Pur-Sagale twenty-eight years prior to the usually accepted time. The corrected dates for the Assyrian monarchs, based on the foregoing discussion, are tabulated in Table 5.3.2.

Reexamination of Table 5.3.1 reveals that most of the discrepancies listed in the Table have now been resolved. Thus, the contact of Ahab with Shalmaneser III occurred in 881; the tributes from Azariah and Menahem were to Pul, rather than to Tiglath-Pileser III, and were presented in 770, and subsequently another tribute was presented by Menahem in 765. However, two discrepancies still need to be reconciled: namely the date when Samaria was conquered, and the date when Sennacherib threatened the kingdom of Judah during the reign of Hezekiah.

According to Table 5.2.1, based on II Kings **17** 6, Samaria was conquered in the ninth year of Hoshea, in 719. The conquest occurred after three years of siege by the Assyrians, which was initiated by King Shalmaneser V in 722 (II Kings **17** 3–5). However, according to the usual interpretation of the Assyrian inscriptions, the three-year siege was begun in 724 by Shalmaneser V, and completed in 721 by Sargon II.

In actuality, the discrepancy may only be a matter of interpretation of the Assyrian inscriptions. No data are available stating that Shalmaneser V besieged Samaria for three years. The eponym list which shows that Shalmaneser went on campaigns during his last three years, is sufficiently damaged so that the places which he attacked are not recognizable. The insertion of "Samaria" as the name of the place attacked[14] is conjectural, based on the three-year siege mentioned in II Kings **17** 3–5, and the fact that Sargon II, in a damaged inscription, seems to claim that he conquered Samaria in his first year of reign[15]. Nevertheless, in the second year of Sargon's reign[16] there was still some fighting in Samaria, indicating that the campaign against Samaria had not been completed[17].

We can, therefore, assume that the siege of Samaria was begun by Shalmaneser V in his last year in 722. The siege was continued by Sargon II until the beginning of 719, when Samaria was captured, and the Israelite people carried away.

The last discrepancy that needs to be reconciled is that concerned with the attack by Sennacherib against Hezekiah, King of Judah. According to the annals, Sennacherib captured forty-six of the walled cities of Judah from King Hezekiah in the year 701[18]. In contrast, the Biblical account states that the capture of the cities occurred in the fourteenth year of Hezekiah, i.e. in 711 (II Kings **18** 13). The problem is even stronger since the Bible states that Shalmaneser was king of Assyria in the fourth year of Hezekiah, and Sennacherib was king of Assyria in the fourteenth year of Hezekiah (II Kings **18** 9,13). This allows a maximum of only ten years for the rule of Sargon II, who we know from well substantiated Assyrian records reigned for seventeen years.

A solution to these questions can be formulated by reexamination of the state-

Table 5.3.2
Corrected Dates for the Assyrian Kings

Assyrian King	Standard Dates (B.C.E.)	Corrected Dates (B.C.E.)
Shalmaneser III	858–824	886–852
Shamshi-Adad V	823–811	851–839
Adad-nirari III	810–783	838–811
Shalmaneser IV	782–773	810–801
Assur-dan III	772–755	800–783
Assur-nirari V	754–745	782–773
Pul	–	772–745
Tiglath-Pileser III	744–727	744–727
Shalmaneser V	726–722	726–722
Sargon II	721–705	721–705
Sennacherib	704–681	704–681
Esarhaddon	680–669	680–669
Assurbanipal	668–627	668–627

ments in Kings in the light of the Assyrian records. In the fourteenth year of Hezekiah, 711, Sennacherib invaded and captured forty-six of the fortified cities of Judah (II Kings 18 13). At that time Sennacherib was probably a regent for his father Sargon II. We know, for example, that Sennacherib was regent in Kalhu while his father Sargon was annexing Babylonia[19]. Sennacherib was willing to stop the attack if given 300 talents of silver and thirty talents of gold (II Kings 18 14). Hezekiah, in his eagerness to rid himself of the Assyrian army, sent Sennacherib the required gold and all available silver (II Kings 18 15), which amounted to 800 talents[20]. Sennacherib did not record the event since he was only the regent. Neither did Sargon record the victory since he was only interested in describing his own achievements.

For ten years, the Assyrian army stayed away from Jerusalem. Meanwhile, in 704 Sennacherib became king upon the death of Sargon II. Then in 701 Sennacherib launched an attack against Jerusalem, which is described in detail in II Kings 18 17–19 36, Isa. 36 2–37 37, and II Chr. 32 9–21. The texts in Kings and Isaiah do not make the distinction in time between the first and second attacks on Judah. However, in Chronicles, the second episode is introduced with the phrase "after this" (אחר זה), which as explained in Sections 9.3 and 11.3 usually indicates a time gap of at least three years. In the attack Sennacherib was unsuccessful, and his army was miraculously destroyed. He returned to Assyria terribly shamed, and in order to save face, he wrote in his account of the campaign the victory against Judah ten years previously, when he was only a regent, rather than the present defeat. Twenty years later, in 681, Sennacherib was assassinated by two of his sons[21,22]. The Biblical description of Sennacherib's death again does not mention that a time-gap existed (II Kings 19 37, Isa. 37 38, II Chr. 32 21), but rather describes the event as if it happened almost immediately.

In summary, the Biblical narrative of the attacks against Hezekiah by Sennacherib, and Sennacherib's subsequent assassination, are correctly described in the Bible. However, insufficient care was taken to let the reader know that the events did not all happen in one year. Similarly, with respect to the conquest of Samaria initiated by Shalmaneser V and completed by Sargon II, the Bible describes the events correctly, but makes no effort to tell the reader that the conquest was completed by Sargon. The Bible's lack of clarity on these points is probably due to the author's feelings that such points were not of great importance in understanding the history of the Kingdoms of Judah and Israel. However, because of the inexactness of the Biblical description, coupled with insufficient historical data from the Assyrian sources, the chronology of the events has been imperfectly interpreted, resulting in the apparent discrepancies according to the usual dating. The above revised interpretations allow the Biblical and Assyrian records to supplement each other, and also to agree chronologically.

Emphasis has here been given to correlations between Biblical and Assyrian chronology, since the Assyrian chronology is sufficiently exact, and has been developed independently, so as to make a comparison meaningful. Exact comparison with other histories, such as the Egyptian, is not warranted at present. For example, we learn from the Bible that Sheshonk I began ruling by at least the last year of Solomon (I Kings 11 40), and reigned for a minimum of five more years (I Kings 14 25; II Chr. 12 2). According to Table 5.2.1, this means that Sheshonk I was king of Egypt in the years between 959 and 954. Yet, Sir Flinders Petrie gives 952 as the earliest possible date for Sheshonk I[23]; and J. H. Breasted assumes that Sheshonk I reigned from 945 to 924[24]. It should, however, be realized that the dates of the Egyptian monarchs at this period are not necessarily more accurate than within fifteen years, and therefore no effort is needed to reconcile the apparent discrepancies.

Chapter Six

BABYLONIAN EXILE AND THE PERIOD OF THE SECOND TEMPLE

In this section will be considered mainly the period of the Babylonian and Persian dominations of Judea, from 586 to 331 B.C.E. Examination of the Jewish traditional interpretation of this period reveals sharp disagreements with extra-Biblical history. According to tradition, the Second Temple existed for 420 years (Babylonian Talmud, Tractate Yoma 9a), and the Persian domination lasted fifty-two years[1,2]. Yet according to well documented extra-Biblical history the Persian period lasted 208 years (539 to 331) and the Second Temple existed for 585 years (from 516 B.C.E. to 70 C.E.). Thus the traditional dating is shorter by about 165 years than that obtained from extra-Biblical evidence. Furthermore, according to tradition a Darius the Mede ruled for about one year before Cyrus[3], although such a Darius is unknown in Persian history. In addition, King Ahasuerus, who ruled over the Persian empire from India to Ethiopia (Est. 1 1), is unknown in Persian history.

The above problems have created much disrespect for Biblical accuracy, and have suggested that the Biblical authors were ignorant of world history. In actuality, however, the Biblical data are correct. It will presently be shown that by simple reinterpretation of the texts it is possible to obtain exact agreement with world history.

The relevant dates from Babylonian and Persian history[4,5] are presented for reference in Table 6.1. These dates are considered highly reliable; at most there are uncertainties of two years. The two main sources for the chronology of the New Babylonian and Persian empires are: (A) the canon of the Greek historian Ptolemy; and (B) the reckoning on tablets[6]. In general, the reckoning of Babylonian and Persian regnal years was from the first of Nisan after a king's accession. Months or days prior to the first Nisan of his reign were reckoned "beginning of kingship." Note that the reigns listed in Table 6.1 do not include the year of accession, except where the reign was less than a year.

6.1 REASON FOR DISAGREEMENT OF TRADITIONAL DATES FROM THOSE OF WORLD HISTORY

The traditional dating which ascribes 420 years for the Second Temple is probably based on the passage in Dan. 9 24–27 concerning "seventy *shavuim*" (שבעים). A

Table 6.1
Babylonian and Persian Chronology

	Years (B.C.E.)
New Babylonian Empire	
Nabopolassar	625–605
Nebuchadnezzar II	604–562
Evil-Merodach	561–560
Neriglissar	559–556
Labashi-Marduk	556
Nabonidus	555–539
Belshazzar	552–539
Persian Empire	
Cyrus II	559–530
Cyrus II (from beginning of empire)	538–530
Cambyses II	529–522
Pseudo-Smerdis (or Bardiya)	522
Darius I	521–486
Xerxes I	485–465
Artaxerxes I	464–424
Darius II	423–405
Artaxerxes II Memnon	404–359
Artaxerxes III Ochus	358–338
Arses	337–336
Darius III	335–331
Events Relevant to Jewish History	
Exile of Jehoiachin	597
Destruction of Temple	586
Cyrus captures Babylon	539

common interpretation is that the period referred to is seventy weeks of years, i.e. 70 × 7 = 490 years. Seventy of the years are assumed to refer to the Babylonian exile, leaving 420 years for the duration of the Second Temple. However, this interpretation is incorrect since it cannot accurately explain many of the specified subdivisions, such as seven and sixty-two *shavuim*. As shown in Section 16.4, the word *shavuim* really means a forty-nine-year span, and the seventy *shavuim* has no direct connection with the period of the Second Temple. Hence there is no Biblical evidence for the duration of the Second Temple.

Inaccurate knowledge by the Jews of the history of the Persians helped to support the 420-year period, which is 165 years shorter than the actual duration of about 585 years for the Second Temple. By coincidence this figure of 165 years is close to the time-span between Darius I and Darius III, who both had the same name and were both defeated twice by the Greeks. The rule of Darius I ended in 486, and that of Darius III in 331, an interval of 155 years. By simply shortening the period of Persian domination by this amount it was possible to obtain a chronology for the Second Temple that was fairly correct in most other details. Thus, *Seder Olam Zuta* (Chapter 7) states that the Greeks started ruling in the fifty-second year of Persia. From 538, when Cyrus began his first year of rule over Judea, until 486, when the reign of Darius I ended, is fifty-two years. Since Darius I and Darius III were mistakenly assumed to be the same person, this brings the chronology to the Greek period.

The above discussion shows that the traditional chronology is incorrect, and is based on erroneous interpretation. In the ensuing paragraphs a modified interpretation of the Biblical information will be presented, which will agree with historical sources in all details. It will thus be shown that the Biblical chronology is correct, although the usual interpretations of it have been wrong.

Before proceeding with analysis of the Persian period, wherein the major chronological discrepancies exist, we will first consider the Babylonian period in which a number of relatively minor problems occur, usually involving one-year discrepancies.

6.2 BABYLONIAN PERIOD

6.2.1 Date of the Destruction of the Temple

Fundamental to the development of much of the chronology of this book is the assumption that the destruction of the First Temple occurred in 586 B.C.E. There are those historians, however, who maintain that this event occurred one year earlier in 587. Let us examine the evidence for these dates, and show that the preponderance of the data favors 586.

Fairly reliable data[7] establish that the reign of Nebuchadnezzar lasted from 604 to 562, and his accession year was 605. Then, based on the statement (II Kings **25** 8,9; Jer. **52** 12,13) that the destruction of the Temple occurred in the nineteenth year of King Nebuchadnezzar, we obtain the date 586. Furthermore, there are several correlations of dates between Nebuchadnezzar's reign and those of the kings of Judah, which support the nineteenth as the correct year. Thus, the first year of Nebuchadnezzar is the fourth of Jehoiakim (Jer. **25** 1); the eighth year of Nebuchadnezzar is the year in which Jehoiachin reigned for three months (II Kings **24** 12): the eighteenth year is the tenth of Zedekiah (Jer. **32** 1); and the nineteenth year is the eleventh and last year of Zedekiah (II Kings **25** 2,8; Jer. **52** 5,12). These correlations are all consistent with the reigns of the kings of Judah, as explained in Section 5.2, Note Q.

However, in Jer. **52** 28 the event previously ascribed to the eighth year of

King Nebuchadnezzar, is dated as the seventh of Nebuchadnezzar; and in Jer. 52 29 the event previously ascribed to the nineteenth year of *King* Nebuchadnezzar is dated in the eighteenth of Nebuchadnezzar. The one-year discrepancies can be resolved by assuming that dates based on the reign of *King* Nebuchadnezzar refer to 604 as his first year, while years dated with respect to Nebuchadnezzar consider 603 as his first year (see discussion near end of Section 12.2). Now the year 604 as the first year of reign is the correct year, and needs no further explanation. The year 603 as the first year may be based on the conquest of Jehoiakim by Nebuchadnezzar in the middle of the previous year, as can be surmised from the Babylonian Chronicle[8], in combination with the statement that Jehoiakim was subservient to Nebuchadnezzar (II Kings 24 1).

The situation is further complicated by the fact that the Babylonian Chronicle attributes the exile of Jehoiachin to the seventh year of Nebuchadnezzar[9], in agreement with Jer. 52 28, but not with II Kings 24 12. At first we might assume that the date in the Babylonian Chronicle is based on 603, rather than 604, as the first year of Nebuchadnezzar. However, this is impossible since the same Babylonian Chronicle places the first year of Nebuchadnezzar immediately after his accession year, i.e. in 604[10]. Several different methods have been suggested to reconcile the difficulty, such as assuming that (A) the Babylonian year and the Jewish year started in different months; or that (B) the three-month reign of Jehoiachin should be considered as a full year, and that Nebuchadnezzar's first year was the fifth, rather than the fourth year of Jehoiakim. These assumptions are, however, not acceptable according to our present chronological development. Instead we have to assume that the campaign described in the Babylonian Chronicle lasted for over a full year. Thus, in his seventh year, Nebuchadnezzar mustered his troops in the month of Kislev, and besieged Jerusalem for about a year before capturing the city in Adar, which was then the eighth year of Nebuchadnezzar (597).

Another problem arises concerning the date of the Battle of Carchemish, fought between the Egyptian and Babylonian armies. According to the Babylonian Chronicle the battle occurred in the accession year of Nebuchadnezzar (605) before he became king[11]. However, according to Jer. 46 2 the battle occurred in the fourth year of Jehoiakim, which we know from Jer. 25 1 to have been the first year of Nebuchadnezzar (604). The one-year discrepancy can be reconciled by reinterpreting the passage of Jer. 46 1,2. Instead of assuming that the text states that the Battle of Carchemish occurred in the fourth year of Jehoiakim, we may assume that it says that the prophecy concerning the Egyptians was received by Jeremiah in the fourth year of Jehoiakim. Then, the mention of the Battle of Carchemish is to let us know that the prophecy refers to the Egyptian army which fought in the battle during the previous year (605).

The same Babylonian Chronicle continues with the statement that Nebuchadnezzar, after becoming king, returned in his accession year (605) to the Hattiland (the land west of the Euphrates including Syria and Palestine), marched victoriously through it, and took heavy tribute back to Babylon[12]. This description is in agreement with that found in Dan. 1 1,2, where it is described how King Nebuchadnezzar in the third year of Jehoiakim (605) besieged and conquered Jerusalem, and took back to the land of Shinar (Babylonia) many of the vessels of the Temple.

6.2.2 Clarification of Passages Related to Babylonian Kings

Additional passages involving Babylonian kings which need explanation are clarified below.

In Dan. 2 1 the date is given as the second year of the "kingdom of Nebuchadnezzar." By this expression is meant 603, the second year of the reign of Nebuchadnezzar. This date is the third year after Daniel was brought to Babylonia in 605, and corresponds to the three years of growth mentioned in Dan. 1 5. The term "kingdom of Nebuchadnezzar" must refer to 605, the accession year of Nebuchadnezzar, rather than 586 when the Temple was destroyed, as many commentaries assume, because of the statements in Ez. 14 14, 20. There, Ezekiel in 591 (see Ez. 8 1 for date) considers Daniel as a pious man. Now, Daniel became renowned only after the events described in Dan. 2; and therefore these events must have occurred prior to 591. A similar argument can be made based on Ez. 28 3, where Daniel is considered a great man, and the statement was made in 586 before the destruction of the Temple (Ez. 26 1).

No mention is found in Babylonian records of the seven years, described in Dan. 4, during which Nebuchadnezzar behaved as an animal. Nonetheless, it is possible to specify the exact seven years of Nebuchadnezzar's forty-three-year reign when this occurred. In general, historical records describing events during Nebuchadnezzar's rule occur for the years from 605 until 573. No historical records exist from 573 onward, except for a fragmentary text that tells of an encounter in 568 between Nebuchadnezzar and Pharaoh Amasis of Egypt[13]. Hence, the only seven consecutive years during which nothing is known about Nebuchadnezzar's reign are from 568 through 562; and therefore these years must have been the time when he acted like an animal. Actually, from the Biblical text, it appears that it was not a full seven years that Nebuchadnezzar behaved irrationally, but only slightly longer than six years* (Dan. 4 26,31). Then, we may conclude that from 568 through the beginning of 562 he behaved as an animal. He then recovered and wrote the contents of Dan. 4. Shortly thereafter he died and was succeeded by Evil-Merodach.

According to Babylonian history, Evil-Merodach reigned from 562, his accession year, through about the eighth month of 560 (Table 6.1). Yet, based on the usual interpretations of II Kings 25 27 and Jer. 52 31, we would expect that

---

* The word יומיא (days) in Dan. 4 31 has the meaning of six years. See Section 16.5.

his first year of reign would be 560. Thus, it is stated in the Biblical passage that the twelfth month of the thirty-seventh year from the exile of Jehoiachin corresponds to the (first) year of Evil-Merodach's reign; and we know from our previous discussion that the exile of Jehoiachin occurred in 597. A possible way to reconcile the one-year discrepancy is to assume that the year 597 is included in the counting, and the thirty-seventh year therefore refers to 561. This solution is not entirely satisfactory, since from a comparison of Ez. 1 2; 24 1,2 with II Kings 25 1 we learn that dates based on the exile of Jehoiachin do not include the year 597. An alternate solution might be that Evil-Merodach's first year is actually 560, but this solution is also difficult to justify. Further research is necessary to reconcile the one-year discrepancy satisfactorily.

The name of Nabonidus is not mentioned in the Book of Daniel, although the name of Belshazzar, who ruled jointly with him, is mentioned (Dan. 5 ;7 1; 8 1). The reason is that Belshazzar was the acting king in Babylonia, while his father Nabonidus resided in western Arabia[14]. Verification that the author of the Book of Daniel did realize that Belshazzar was a co-regent comes from Dan. 5 29. There, on the day of Belshazzar's death, Daniel was made to rule as one of three in the kingdom, implying that Daniel would have power equal to that held by Belshazzar and Nabonidus.

One might at first conclude from Dan. 5 2,11,13,18,22 that Belshazzar was the son of Nebuchadnezzar. However, Babylonian inscriptions clearly establish that Belshazzar was the oldest son of Nabonidus[15]. Furthermore, Nabonidus was known not to be a descendant of Nebuchadnezzar[16]. The most reasonable solution to the problem, which has been suggested by many, is to assume that Nabonidus was married to a daughter of Nebuchadnezzar, and therefore Belshazzar was a grandson of Nebuchadnezzar. The Hebrew expression for "son" or "father" is often used in the Bible to denote a "grandson" or "grandfather," which fits in with this explanation. Support for this solution is gained from Jer. 27 6,7. It is there prophesied that the nations will serve Nebuchadnezzar, his son, and his grandson (literally his son's son), until the end of the Babylonian kingdom. This is what happened: Evil-Merodach was the son, and Belshazzar the grandson of Nebuchadnezzar, and during Belshazzar's reign the kingdom of Babylonia was conquered by the Persians.

6.3 PERSIAN PERIOD

6.3.1 Identification of Darius the Mede with Darius I

Let us first establish that Darius the Mede, mentioned in Dan. 6 1; 9 1; 11 1, is the same ruler as Darius I, rather than a king unknown to Persian history. The main problem with this identification is that in Dan. 6 1 is stated:

ודריוש מדאה קבל מלכותא כבר שנין שתין ותרתין.

The word "כבר" is usually interpreted to mean "of the age." Then the sentence is translated "Darius the Mede received the kingdom when sixty-two years of age." From the history by Herodotus (I, 209) we know that Darius I was about twenty at the time of the death of Cyrus, and therefore about twenty-eight when he began to rule. Based on the interpretation of the word "כבר" as "of the age" it is obvious that Darius the Mede is not Darius I. However, if we interpret the word "כבר" to mean "already," then the sentence can be translated "Darius the Mede received the kingdom, when it was already the sixty-second year (from the destruction of the Temple)." This indicates that Darius the Mede became king in 524 B.C.E. (586−62 = 524), which is in good agreement with the commonly accepted date of 522 for the accession year of Darius I. Thus, by interpreting the word "כבר" as "already" it becomes apparent that Darius the Mede is the same person as Darius I.

The two-year discrepancy between the Biblical date of 524 and the historical date of 522 can be reconciled as follows. The statement in Dan. 6 1 does not actually say that Darius the Mede became king, but only that he received the kingdom, i.e. he was designated to be the prospective king. We know that in 525 Cambyses went on an expedition to conquer Egypt[17]. At about that time Cambyses had his younger brother and heir Bardiya, killed[18]. Therefore it was necessary for Cambyses to designate a successor in case of his death. According to Persian law a monarch had to appoint a successor before he dared to risk his life in a foreign war[19]. Based on Dan. 6 1, we can state that Darius the Mede was the one designated in 524 to succeed Cambyses. We similarly know that Cyrus appointed Cambyses as his successor before starting on the dangerous campaign of conquest towards Central Asia[20], and that Nabonidus appointed Belshazzar as co-regent before going on a campaign against Harran[21]. It was, however, not until 522 that Darius fought and achieved the kingship.

6.3.2 Identification of Ahasuerus with Hystaspes

According to Dan. 9 1, Darius the Mede was the son of Ahasuerus. Similarly it is known from the Behistun inscription and Herodotus (III,70) that Darius I was the son of Hystaspes[22]. Since we have shown that Darius the Mede is none other than Darius I, we must also conclude that Ahasuerus is none other than Hystaspes.

This identification is supported by our knowledge about these two persons. Ahasuerus was a ruler of Persia (Est. 1 1), was a contemporary of Mordechai who was exiled from Judea in 597 (Est. 2 5,6), and ruled sometime after Cyrus and before Darius I (Ezra 4 5,6). Analagously, Hystaspes ruled the provinces of Bactria and Hyrcania under Cyrus, and as shown in the Behistun inscription, he ruled over Parthia and Hyrcania under Darius I[23].

Certain similarities between the reigns of Ahasuerus and Darius are to be noted. Ahasuerus ruled from India to Kush (Est. 1 1; 8 9), and Darius ruled from Scythia to Kush and from India to Sardis[24]. Also, we find in Dan. 6 2 that

Darius appointed 120 satraps to rule his kingdom. This number is almost identical to the 127 districts over which Ahasuerus ruled (Est. 1 1). Although Herodotus (III, 90–95) divides the Persian empire into only twenty provinces, he then enumerates about seventy subdivisions that paid taxes, and implies that other subdivisions exist. Thus the number given by Herodotus does not contradict the Biblical number of 120.

According to the Behistun inscription there was a double line of kings which sprang from Teispes, king of Anshan. The lines of descent are as follows[25]:

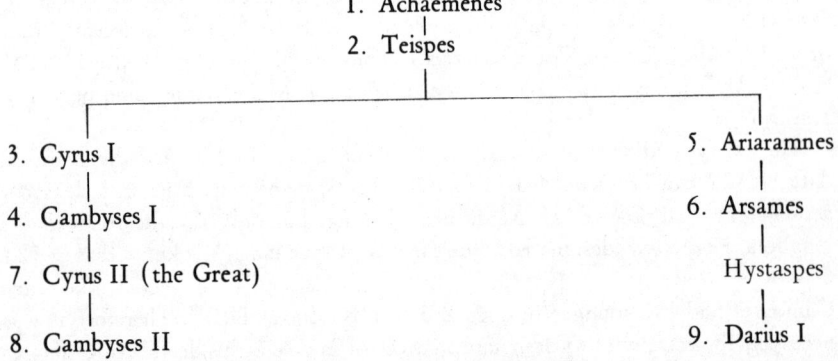

Both Cyrus II and Hystaspes were great-grandchildren of Teispes and were of the royal line. Cyrus was originally known as King of Anshan, but after his conquests of 546 he was referred to as King of Persia[26]. In contrast, Hystaspes was never the sole ruler of Persia, although as a satrap he may on occasion have been designated as king. At the end of the reign of Cambyses II, son of Cyrus, there arose a pretender to the throne, Pseudo-Smerdis. Hystaspes recognized that it was time for him to assert his claim to the throne. However, Hystaspes was too old to fight for the crown, and therefore he had his son Darius I fight and gain the rulership. It was after the death of Cambyses that Darius I, who had been spear-bearer to Cambyses in Egypt, hastened to Media to press his claim to the throne[27]. Probably Darius I was also known as Darius the Mede because his original start as ruler was in Media. Once Darius I became king, his father Hystaspes (Ahasuerus) gained an almost equivalent position, as attested to by Est. 1 1; 8 9. Support for the contention that Ahasuerus was never the main king is given in Ezra 4 5–7. There, Cyrus, Darius, and Artachshast are all separately denoted as kings of Persia, while Ahasuerus is not mentioned with this title. Also the fact that Ahasuerus, in the beginning of his reign, did not respond to the written accusations against the Jews, possibly indicates that at that time he had little power to act on this matter. However, after Darius became king, Ahasuerus was a co-regent, as attested by Est. 5 3; 7 2 where Ahasuerus promised up to half the kingdom, the limit of his power, to Esther.

Based on the above identification of Ahasuerus with Hystaspes, it is possible to specify the approximate years of his reign as 531-518, and his accession year as 532. Orignally, in 532, Hystaspes became a satrap under Cyrus. In 530 (or 529) Cyrus died, and Hystaspes gained in power under the rulership of Cambyses. Therefore in 529 Hystaspes held a grand party to celebrate the third year of rule (Est. 1 3). Later, some time after the seventh year of reign (Est. 2 16), possibly in the tenth year, i.e. 522, there was a plot against the life of Ahasuerus (Est. 2 21). At this time Cambyses was in Egypt, and Pseudo-Smerdis, a pretender to the throne, arose and claimed to be the rightful king, son of Cyrus. Filled with apprehension lest his true identity be revealed, Pseudo-Smerdis slew many who had known the true Smerdis[28]. Now, Hystaspes, as adviser to Cyrus, must have known the true Smerdis, and it is therefore possible that this was the reason for the attempt on the life of Hystaspes.

In 521, the eleventh year of Hystaspes, Darius was considered King of Persia, and therefore his father Hystaspes, who was satrap over Shushan, also acquired equivalent power (Est. 5 3). Then in 520, at the beginning of the twelfth year of Hystaspes (Est. 3 7), it was possible for Haman, the Agagite, with the consent of Hystaspes, to try to destroy the Jews in the entire Persian empire (Est. 3 6-15). Because of Esther's intervention, it turned out instead that Haman was hanged (Est. 7 10), and the Jews were given permission to fight for their lives (Est. 8 11). On the thirteenth and fourteenth of the twelfth month the Jews succeeded in defeating their enemies (Est. 9 1-18).

The actual event of Purim is similarly described on the Behistun inscription. It is there written how, in one of the first years of Darius I (ca. 520), a man named Martius, from the Persian city Cyganaca, arose in the state of Susiana. He said "I am Imanes King of Susiana." Then the people of Susiana, fearing Darius, seized Martius and slew him. Subsequently, a revolt in Parthia and Hyrcania, was suppressed by Hystaspes on the twenty-second day of Viyakhana (the 12th month)[29].

The above description corresponds to the events described in the Book of Esther. Thus, Shushan is either Susiana or Susa, Haman is Imanes,* and Agag is Cyganaca. The hanging of Haman corresponds to the slaying of Imanes by the people. The later revolt against Hystaspes involved the battle by the Jews in defending their lives. The discrepancy between the fourteenth day and the twenty-second day of the twelfth month may possibly be accounted for by slight differences between the Jewish and Persian calendars.

It should be noted that the date of the Imanes uprising is considered to be 520 —according to the opinion that all events in the first four columns of the Behistun inscription occurred in the same year—or at most seventeen months after Darius' accession to kingship[30].

---

* The name Imanes is written by some authors as Ummanish or Umman.

6.3.3 Identification of Mordechai with Zoroaster

We have established that Ahasuerus is none other than Hystaspes. As a consequence, we can also conclude that Mordechai, the second to King Ahasuerus (Est. 10 3) is identical with Zoroaster, the advisor to King Hystaspes (Vishtaspa).

Although there is some question as to whether the Hystaspes who was patron of Zoroaster is the same as the father of Darius I, several points establish the identity. Firstly, no earlier Hystaspes is known in Persian history. Secondly, the writer Ammianus Marcellinus of Antioch (Amm. xxiii 6,32) quite clearly makes this identification[31]. Thirdly, Darius I, son of Hystaspes, was the first main king to worship Ahura Mazda, the god of whom Zoroaster preached. Other worshippers were his immediate successors, Xerxes I and Artaxerxes I [32].

Zoroaster was the founder of the religion known as Zoroastrianism. Although his teachings developed into a dualistic religion, Zoroaster originally taught the belief in one god named Ahura Mazda[33]. The name Zoroaster is the corrupt Greek form of the Iranian Zarathustra, and of the new Persian Zardushi[34]. Note the similarity of the name Zardushi with the Hebrew name Mordechai. Furthermore, we know that Zoroaster was not a native of Persia, for he complained that he was persecuted in his homeland and had to flee[35]. Similarly, Mordechai was exiled from Jerusalem at the time of the exile of Jeconiah (Jehoiachin) (Est. 2 5,6).

The traditional date assigned to Zoroaster is 258 years before Alexander the Great (336–323). In addition, Zoroaster is said to have lived seventy-seven years[36]. This information makes the dates for Zoroaster from 594 to 518. From the Book of Esther, and the previous discussion concerning Hystaspes, we can set the dates for Mordechai from 597 when exiled from Judea (Est. 2 10), and perhaps a few years later when he arrived in Persia, until 518, the approximate end of the reign of Hystaspes. Thus, within the accuracy of the available data, the dates for Mordechai and Zoroaster are identical.

Furthermore, according to the Avesta, the bible of Zoroastrianism, Zoroaster found a woman who accepted him and believed in his mission. She was Hutaosa, consort of Vishtaspa, and was the intermediary in winning over the king[37]. This description corresponds exactly to that of Queen Esther (Est. 2 5–20; 8 1,2). Her other name Hadassah (Est. 2 7) is almost a perfect transliteration of Hutaosa.

There are numerous similarities between Judaism and Zoroastrianism. Zoroaster taught that there was only one god, Ahura Mazda, who created heaven, earth, and mankind. (The name Ahura Mazda may possibly be a transliteration of the Hebrew term *Makom-Aher* (מקום אחר), meaning "another place," used by Mordechai to refer to God (Est. 4 14)). Opposing Ahura Mazda was an antagonist who may be compared to the Satan of Judaism. Worship of images was forbidden by both Judaism and Zoroastrianism. A tendency towards the formation of an organized angelic hierarchy, and reward and punishment after death, are common to both religions. However, years after the death of Zoroaster, the religion developed into a dualistic belief and involved many deities, so that the original purity of the teachings of Zoroaster were completely corrupted[38,39].

We find in Est. **8** 17 the statement that many of the Persian leaders converted to Judaism at the time of Mordechai because the fear of the Jews fell on them. Thus, we may assume that Zoroastrianism originally arose as a form of Judaism, and only later did the religion become corrupted by the Persians. In this regard, it should be noted that Darius I promulgated a law that everyone in his kingdom should worship the God of Daniel (Dan. **6** 27,28), because He is everlasting, delivers and saves people, and performs wonders in the heaven and on earth. We also know from Persian history that Darius I was an adherent of Zoroastrianism. Hence, this information supports the contention that Zoroastrianism was originally a form of Judaism.

6.3.4 Identification of Persian Kings Mentioned in the Bible

In addition to Cyrus, Darius the Mede, and Ahasuerus, there are several other Persian kings mentioned in the Bible. These kings are Artachshast (ארתחששתא) (Ezra **4** 7; **6** 14); Artachshaste* (ארתחשסתא) (Ezra **7** 1, 11; **8** 1; Neh. **2** 1; **5** 14; **13** 6); and Darius the Persian (Neh. **12** 22).

From Ezra **4** 5–7,23,24 it is obvious that Artachshast was a king of Persia who ruled after Cyrus (538–530) and before Darius I (521–486). The only rulers who fit these limitations are Cambyses (529–522) and Pseudo-Smerdis (522). Most probably Artachshast is Cambyses, since the term "in the days of" (Ezra **4** 7) is used, implying that Artachshast ruled more than one year. Furthermore, if the name Artachshast represented Pseudo-Smerdis, there would be a gap of eight years during the reign of Cambyses which would not be accounted for. In contrast, Pseudo-Smerdis ruled less than one year, and the omission of his name would not be unexpected.

In Ezra **6** 14 is stated that Artachshast supported the building of the Second Temple, which seems to contradict Ezra **4**. However, in Ezra **4**, Artachshast only stopped the building of the city of Jerusalem (Ezra **4** 21). Based on the king's edict, the enemies of the Jews then forcefully stopped the Temple construction. Alternatively, the support for the Temple construction stated in Ezra **6**, refers to the early part of Artachshast's reign, before he suspended the building effort.

Mention of Darius the Persian occurs in Neh. **12** 22. This Darius is obviously not Darius I, since we have previously established that the king called Darius the Mede is Darius I. Nor can he be Darius III (335–331), since Darius III was

---

* The two different kings, Artachshast and Artachshaste, are here spelled slightly differently to correspond to the slightly different Hebrew spellings. Usually both Hebrew names are translated as Artaxerxes, but this is not entirely correct, as is here clarified.

after Artaxerxes II; and we will presently show that Artaxerxes II was the king at the time of Ezra and Nehemiah when the Book of Ezra-Nehemiah was completed. Furthermore, if Darius the Persian were Darius III then we would also expect mention of Alexander the Great, a more renowned contemporary. Since there were only three Persian kings named Darius, we must conclude that Darius the Persian must be Darius II (423–405).

It should also be noted that in Neh. **12** 22, where Darius the Persian is mentioned, it is also stated that Johanan was one of the high priests. Thus, the sentence there states, according to a possible translation from the Hebrew, "The Levites in the days of Eliashib, were Joiada, Johanan and Jaddua, who were recorded as heads of fathers' houses; and these priests were at the time of the reign of Darius the Persian." Now, from a papyrus from Elephantine, we learn that the high priest Johanan was at the time of Darius II[40]. Hence, Darius the Persian must be identical to Darius II. (Also see Section 6.6.)

The Artachshaste mentioned in the Book of Ezra-Nehemiah (Ezra **7**,8; Neh. **2** 1; **5** 14; **13** 6) must correspond to King Artaxerxes II (404–358). From Neh. **13** 6 we learn that Artachshaste ruled for more than thirty-two years. This fact alone limits the identification to the only two Persian kings after Darius I who had such a long reign, namely Artaxerxes I (465–424) and Artaxerxes II (404–358). Artaxerxes I, is however eliminated since we find mention of Darius the Persian (i.e. Darius II) in the Book of Nehemiah (**12** 22). Now Darius II (423–405) was after Artaxerxes I, and Artachshaste was still ruler when the Book of Nehemiah was completed. Hence Artachshaste cannot be Artaxerxes I, but must be Artaxerxes II.

Support for the identification of Artachshaste with Artaxerxes II comes from comparison of the available information about these rulers. Artachshaste was sympathetic to Ezra, and supplied him with a letter of rescript and all his requests (Ezra **7** 6,11–26); and was sympathetic to Nehemiah, and supplied him with official letters and armed soldiers (Neh. **2** 9). Similarly, Artaxerxes II was known to be mild in temperament, good natured, affectionate and well meaning. Incapable of resisting entreaty, he granted gifts which he should have refused and condoned offenses which it would have been proper to punish[41].

In the twentieth year of Artachshaste (385), Nehemiah hears that Jerusalem was invaded, Jews captured, the walls of Jerusalem broken, and the gates set afire (Neh. **1** 1–3). Similarly, between 391 and 379 disaffection and revolt were exhibited by Cyprus, Phoenicians, Cilicians, Carians, and the Idumaean Arabs[42].

During the thirty-second year of Artachshaste (373), Nehemiah returned to Persia from Judea (Neh. **13** 6). At about that time, in 372, it was necessary for Artaxerxes II to prepare an imperial rescript prescribing the terms on which the existing hostilities among the Greeks should cease[43]. Some factor connected with this event could possibly have been the reason for the return of Nehemiah to Persia.

From Neh. 2 2 we see that Artachshaste was afraid of treachery in his court. We also know that the court of Artaxerxes II was a scene of horrors and atrocities. Parysatis, the queen-mother, was its presiding spirit; and the long catalogue of her cruel and bloody deeds is almost without a parallel. The members of the royal household became the special objects of jealousy to one another; family affection had disappeared; and executions, assassinations, and suicides decimated the royal stock[44].

There is the unusual statement in Neh. 2 6 that the "queen" (שגל) was sitting near the king. The statement becomes significant if we assume that the queen-mother, rather than the queen, is meant. Now Parysatis, the queen-mother, had poisoned Statira, the original queen, in 400, because of jealousy of Statira's influence over the king. Artaxerxes II was horrified and banished Parysatis, but soon she was back at the court[45]. The mention in the text of the presence of the queen-mother in the court implies that she was an extra obstacle for Nehemiah to overcome in order to obtain the king's approval.

A few additional passages related to Persian kings, found in the Book of Daniel, have often been misinterpreted and need to be explained. In Dan. 11 2 it is stated that there will be three additional Persian kings, and then the fourth king will be much richer. The three kings are to be counted from after Cyrus (Dan. 10 1), and are Cambyses, Pseudo-Smerdis and Darius I. The fourth king is Xerxes, who is known to have amassed much wealth. (See Section 16.5 for further details.)

The phrase in Dan. 1 21 that "Daniel was until the first year of King Cyrus" informs us that Daniel was of importance under Babylonian rule from the time of King Nebuchadnezzar until the conquest of Babylonia by Cyrus in 539. The phrase was not meant to say anything concerning how long Daniel lived, since we know he lived much longer, till at least 517 (Dan. 9 1). The similar expression in Dan. 6 29, stating that Daniel was successful during the reign of Darius and in the reign of Cyrus the Persian, means that Daniel was successful not only during Darius' reign, but also previously during the reign of Cyrus. There was no intention in the text to indicate that Darius preceded Cyrus, contrary to the actual history.

6.4 SEVENTY YEAR SPANS

In many places of the Bible, time-spans of seventy years are specified for events during the period of the Babylonian exile. Explanations of the stated time-spans are presented below.

In Jer. 25 11,12 it is stated that the nations will be subservient to Babylonia for seventy years until Babylonia will be destroyed. Similarly, in Jer. 29 10 it is stated that upon completion of seventy years for Babylonia, God will remember the Jewish people to return them to the land of Israel. The period referred to is from 609 when Nabopolasser, king of Babylonia, entrusted the command of the army to his son Nebuchadnezzar[46], and which marks the beginning of the Babylonian conquests, until 539 when Cyrus, king of Persia, conquered the Babylonian empire. In 538, when the seventy years had passed, Cyrus allowed the Jews to return to their land (II Chr. 36 22,23).

In II Chr. 36 21,22 is stated that the land laid desolate and rested for seventy years to fulfill the word of God that the land will desire her Sabbaths. Also stated is that the seventy years were completed in the first year of Cyrus. Here, in addition to the previously explained sentences in the Book of Jeremiah, the passage in Jer. 17 27 is referred to, where it is stated that if the Jews do not observe the Sabbath then Jerusalem will be destroyed. The seventy years are again from 609 to 539.

From Zech. 1 7,12 we learn that the second year of Darius I corresponds to seventy years after the destruction of the Temple in 586. This correlation is equivalent to stating that the first year of Darius' reign is 517. However, from historical records we know that the first year of Darius is 521. We must therefore say that the Bible considers the years of Darius to begin with 517, because it is the first year of the sole rule of Darius after the death of his father Hystaspes in 518 (see Section 6.3.2). On this basis the date for erection of the foundations of the Second Temple is 516 (Hag. 2 10,18), marking the end of the seventy years of the Temple's destruction. Completion of construction of the Temple occurred four years later in the sixth year of Darius (Ezr. 6 15), i.e. in 512.

We also learn from the Book of Zechariah (Zech. 7 1,5) that seventy years of fasting in the fifth and seventh months had occurred by the ninth month of the fourth year of Darius, i.e. by the end of 514. Thus, official fasting for events relevant to the destruction of the Temple and exile from the land did not start until 583, three years after 586.

Daniel states in Dan. 9 2 "I examined the scriptures; 'the number of years that the word of the Lord was told to Jeremiah the prophet' was to complete for the desolations of Jerusalem 70 years." Here Daniel refers to the duration mentioned in Jer. 25 3 where is stated "it is twenty-three years that the word of the Lord was told to me [Jeremiah]." Thus, Daniel states he calculated that the twenty-three years mentioned by Jeremiah will complete seventy years for the destruction of the Temple. From 538 when Cyrus permitted the Jews to return until 516 when the foundations of the Second Temple were laid is twenty-three years. Thus the seventy years of the desolation of Jerusalem are from 586 to 516. This calculation by Daniel was performed in the first year of Darius (517), one year before the calculated time. Daniel saw no signs of the end of the desolation, and therefore prayed for the forgiveness of the sins of the Jews.

6.5 SUMMARY OF KEY DATES

In Table 6.5.1 are summarized the dates for the key events relevant to the period of the Babylonian exile and the Second Temple. These dates are mainly concerned with events referred to in the Bible, and which have previously been explained.

Table 6.5.1
Key Dates During Babylonian Exile and Second Temple

Date (B.C.E.)	Event
609	Nebuchadnezzar general for his father, King Nabopolasser; Beginning of Babylonian expansionist policy
609–539	Seventy years of Babylonian empire
604–562	Reign of Nebuchadnezzar
597	Exile of Jehoiachin
594–518	Mordechai (Zoroaster) in Persia
586	Destruction of First Temple
586–516	Seventy years during which Temple lay in ruins
561–560	Reign of Evil-Merodach
559–530	Reign of Cyrus
539	Cyrus conquered Babylon
538	Cyrus edict permitting return to Judea
538–511	Zerubbabel governor of Judea
531–518	Reign of Ahasuerus (Hystaspes)
521–486	Reign of Darius I (Darius the Mede)
520	Year of Purim event; Haman (Imanes) killed
517	First year of Darius I according to Biblical dating
516	Start of construction of Second Temple; Prophecies by Haggai and Zechariah
516 B.C.E.–70 C.E.	585 year duration of the Second Temple
512	Second Temple completed
423–405	Reign of Darius II (Darius the Persian)
404–359	Reign of Artaxerxes II
398	Ezra comes to Judea from Babylon
398–385	Ezra acts as leader
385	Nehemiah comes to Judea from Shushan; the Great Assembly
385–ca. 370	Nehemiah serves as governor of Judea

It should be noted that the time of the Great Assembly, when Ezra and Nehemiah led a religious reawakening (Neh. 8–10), is here put at 385, about 60 years later than the usually accepted date. Furthermore, the time gap from the approximate end of the governorship by Zerubbabel (511), until the beginning of the leadership by Ezra (398), is 113 years; and they are definitely not contemporary as often assumed according to Jewish traditional interpretation. We thus notice that the Bible supplies practically no details as to what happened and who were the leaders during the first hundred years after construction of the Second Temple.

6.6 HIGH PRIESTS DURING SECOND TEMPLE

One test of the chronology described for the period of the Babylonian exile and the Second Temple is to show the feasibility of working out a satisfactory chronology for the high priests up to and including Simon the Just. In general, there is very meager evidence as to how long and exactly when they served. The main sources of information are: (A) Neh. 12 10,11 which presents the genealogies; (B) Occasional statements in the biblical books of Nehemiah, Ezra, Chronicles, Zechariah and Haggai concerning individual high priests; (C) Incidental remarks by Josephus in Antiquities xi and xii; (D) A few facts mentioned in the Talmud; and (E) A papyrus from Elephantine of the time of Darius II. Based on the foregoing references we have developed the very approximate dates for the high priests which are presented in Table 6.6.1. Although many of these dates may be off from the true situation, perhaps by as much as twenty years, still they show that our prescribing the times of Ezra and Nehemiah during the reign of Artaxerxes II, rather than at the time of Artaxerxes I, does not prevent the attainment of a satisfactory chronology for the priests.

In particular, it should be noted that according to Neh. 12 22, the High Priests Eliashib, Joiada, Johanan, and Jaddua served contemporaneously as early as the time of Darius II. This is reasonable, although they represented four successive generations, since people married young, and could have been fathers by the age of fourteen. Thus Eliashib may possibly have been only forty-two years older than his great-grandson Jaddua. Then if Eliashib began serving as high priest when about sixty years old, it would be feasible for all of the four generations, including Jaddua, to be sufficiently old, about thirty years, to act as high priests during the latter part of the reign of Darius II. That Johanan acted as high priest at the time of Darius II is supported by the papyrus from Elephantine, written during the reign of Darius II, which mentions the high priest Johanan. Further support is gained from the Talmud which ascribes an eighty-year term to Johanan, allowing the possibility that he officiated when still young while his father or grandfather was the main high priest.

In the same Elephantine papyrus, dated to 407, mention is made of Sanballat, the governor of Samaria[48]. Now Sanballat is also mentioned in the Book of Nehemiah as a leader of Samaria around the twentieth year of Artaxerxes II (385) (Neh. 2 10; 3 33,34). We thus learn that Sanballat ruled Samaria for at least twenty-two years, from 407 to 385.

The dates for Simon the Just are based on the Talmud, supplemented with information supplied by Josephus. In *Yoma* 69a, the story is told how Alexander the Great (332) bowed down to Simon the Just. Now, in *Ant.* xi,8 the same story is related, except that Jaddua is the high priest to whom Alexander bowed. If we assume, in order to reconcile the contradiction, that both high priests were involved, then both were occupying this position in 332. We furthermore know from Ant.

Table 6.6.1
High Priests Subsequent to Destruction of the Temple

High Priest	Very Appr. Dates (B.C.E.)	References	Corresponding Times
Jehozadak	590–540	I Chr. 5 41	Destruction of Temple (586)
Jeshua	540–480	Ezr. 1 1; 2 1,2 Hag. 1 1; Zech. 1 7; 3 1	First year of Cyrus (538) Second year of Darius (516)
Joiakim	480–430	*Ant.* xi, 5, par. 1* Neh. 12 10, 26	Reign of Xerxes I (485–465) Prior to Ezra (before 398)
Eliashib	430–370	Neh. 12 22 Neh. 2 1; 3 1 Neh. 13 4, 6	Reign of Darius II (423–405) Twentieth year of Artaxerxes II (385) 33rd year of Artaxerxes II (372)
Joiada	430–370	Neh. 12 22 Neh. 13 28	Reign of Darius II (423–405) After 33rd year of Artaxerxes II (ca. 370)
Johanan	430–350	Neh. 12 22 Elephantine Papyrus[47] *Yoma* 9a Ezr. 10 6; 7 7	Reign of Darius II (423–405) 14th and 17th years of Darius II (410, 407) High priest for 80 years Seventh year of Artaxerxes II (398)
Jaddua	410–325	Neh. 12 22 *Ant.* xi, 8, par. 5 *Ant.* xi, 8, par. 7	Reign of Darius II (423–405) Reign of Alexander the Great (332) Died at about same time as Alexander (323)
Onias I	ca. 345–315	*Ant.* xii, 2, par. 5 *Ant.* xi, 8, par. 7	Preceded Simon the Just Succeeded Jaddua
Simon the Just	332–292	*Yoma* 69a *Yoma* 9a *Ant.* xii, 2, par. 5	Reign of Alexander the Great (332) High Priest for 40 years Reign of Ptolemy I (305–285)

* Josephus, *Antiquities of the Jews*

xii 2 that Simon the Just died during the reign of Ptolemy I (305–285), and from *Yoma* 9a that Simon officiated for forty years. The dates of Simon the Just may then be approximately specified as 332 to 292.

Another point of information is the statement in Mishnah *Aboth* 1,2 that Simon the Just was one of the last survivors of the Great Assembly (כנסת הגדולה)*. The Great Assembly probably refers to the large gathering of the Jewish people in the twentieth year of Artaxerxes II (385) as described in Neh. **8–10**. Now, we have previously shown that Simon the Just lived till about 292. Therefore, the statement that he "was one of the last survivors of the Great Assembly" indicates that he lived ninety-three years after the time of the Great Assembly, to an age of about 110 years. It should be noted that the preceding interpretation of the meaning of the Great Assembly would not be possible, because of chronological difficulties, if the Persian king in the Book of Nehemiah had been assumed to be Artaxerxes I, as many historians claim.

Examination of the number of years the high priests officiated, as presented in Table 6.6.1, indicates that many of them lived long lives, perhaps even as old as 110 years. Thus, for example, if Johanan began serving when 30 years old, and he served for eighty years, then he would have lived to be 110. Such long lifetimes for the high priests are not completely unexpected. Because of their high office the high priests were required to maintain extreme degrees of purity which, as explained in Part IV, would minimize their exposure to disease-causing microorganisms, and result in long life expectancies. In particular, we know that the High Priest Eli lived to be ninety-eight (I Sam. **4** 15,18), and the High Priest Jehoiada (II Chr. **24** 15) lived to be 130.

---

* In other places in the Talmud the term "people of the Great Assembly" (אנשי כנסת הגדולה) is often used. In those cases, the people who attended the large gathering are being referred to.

Chapter Seven

SABBATICAL AND JUBILEE YEARS

A useful check on the dating that has been developed can be obtained by consideration of the Sabbatical and Jubilee years. The laws pertaining to these events are presented in Lev. 25 2–12. In each seventh or Sabbatical year the land is to lie fallow, and agricultural tasks are not to be performed. The cycle continues for seven periods of seven years, for a total of forty-nine years. Then comes the fiftieth or Jubilee year, when again agricultural pursuits are not permitted. Thus, for two consecutive years, the forty-ninth and fiftieth, the land lies fallow.

As explained in Section 5.1.4 the agricultural years begin with the tenth day of the seventh month (Tishri). In particular it is stated in Lev. 25 10 that the Jubilee year should be announced on that day. On the other hand, the regnal years and most other historical dates are based on the year beginning with the first day of the first month (Nisan). This difference in the starting time between the agricultural and regnal years should be kept in mind when corresponding the Sabbatical or Jubilee years with historical dates.

The usually accepted opinion is that during the First Temple period the Sabbatical-Jubilee cycle lasted fifty years, and the Jubilee year followed the seventh Sabbatical year; but during the time of the Second Temple the cycle lasted only forty-nine years, and the Jubilee year coincided with the seventh Sabbatical year[1]. Nevertheless, such an interpretation does not correspond with the Biblical text, and is also not self-consistent. Instead we will here show that a perfectly acceptable system for the periods of the First and Second Temples can be obtained by assuming that for both periods the Jubilee year followed the seventh Sabbatical year, and therefore the cycle was fifty years long. It should be noted that the traditional authority Rabbenu Tam (*Tosafot*, Tractate *Gitin* 36a) claims that the Jubilee year was observed also during the Second Temple, in agreement with our present assumption.

7.1 HISTORICAL DATES FOR THE SABBATICAL AND JUBILEE YEARS

7.1.1 First Entrance into the Land of Israel

According to Lev. 25 2-12, the laws of the Sabbatical and Jubilee years are to be observed from the time the people of Israel enter into the land of Israel. The first occasion, when the people as a group entered the land, was in Nisan 1434 B.C.E., after forty years in the desert; and they remained until the destruction of the Temple in Ab 586. Now the agricultural years begin from Tishri. The question therefore arises as to whether the six months from Nisan 1434 to Tishri 1434 should or should not be counted as a year. We will here assume that the six months are considered as a full year in order to obtain a better fit with the available data. Then the Jubilee years, which recur every fiftieth year, begin with Tishri of: 1386, 1336, 1286, 1236, 1186, 1136, 1086, 1036, 986, 936, 886, 836, 786, 736, 686, 636, (586). Similarly, the Sabbatical years, which occur seven times within each Jubilee period, at seven-year intervals, begin with Tishri of:

1429, 1422, 1415, 1408, 1401, 1394, 1387
1379, 1372, 1365, 1358, 1351, 1344, 1337
1329, 1322, 1315, 1308, 1301, 1294, 1287
1279, 1272, 1265, 1258, 1251, 1244, 1237
1229, 1222, 1215, 1208, 1201, 1194, 1187
1179, 1172, 1165, 1158, 1151, 1144, 1137
1129, 1122, 1115, 1108, 1101, 1094, 1087
1079, 1072, 1065, 1058, 1051, 1044, 1037
1029, 1022, 1015, 1008, 1001, 994, 987
979, 972, 965, 958, 951, 944, 937
929, 922, 915, 908, 901, 894, 887
879, 872, 865, 858, 851, 844, 837
829, 822, 815, 808, 801, 794, 787
779, 772, 765, 758, 751, 744, 737
729, 722, 715, 708, 701, 694, 687
679, 672, 665, 658, 651, 644, 637
629, 622, 615, 608, 601, 594, 587

There are four cases in the Bible where the calculated date for the historical happening is one of the above-listed Sabbatical or Jubilee years, and the events described involve famines or other situations which would be expected to occur, at least occasionally, in a year when the soil was not worked.

The first case involves the distribution of the land of Israel among the people at the time of Joshua. We know that the year was the seventh of Joshua (1428) from the statement by Caleb (Josh. **14** 10) that it was forty-five years from the time he was sent by Moses as a spy. Now the spies were sent during the second year in the desert (Num. **10** 11; **13** 2), and an additional thirty-eight years passed (Num. **14** 33) before the people entered the land of Israel under the leadership of Joshua. Hence the year was the seventh of Joshua (45−38 = 7). According to our calculations, the first half of 1428 corresponds to the last half of the Sabbatical year beginning in Tishri 1429. It is only logical to assume that the land distribution would occur in a Sabbatical year, so that no one could complain that he tilled the soil, and the produce went to the new owner.

The second case occurs at the time of King David. According to a subsequent analysis (see Section 11.3) the three years of famine mentioned in II Sam. **21** 1 happened during the first few years of David's rule. If we take into consideration that a Sabbatical and a Jubilee year occurred at that time, the probable date for the three-year famine is from 1037 to 1035, from the second to fourth years of David's reign. Thus 1037 was a Sabbatical year, and 1036 was a Jubilee year, when agricultural crops were not raised, and a food shortage would not be too unexpected. However, when hunger continued in the next year, 1035, David sought divine help, as described in II Sam. **21** 1.

The third case arises when the army of Sennacherib, king of Assyria threatened the city of Jerusalem ruled by King Hezekiah. According to our discussion in Section 5.3, the event occurred in 701, which we now know was also a Sabbatical year. Furthermore, by comparison of the wording in the Book of Kings with that in Leviticus, we learn that it definitely was a Sabbatical year.* Thus, the prophet Isaiah states (II Kings **19** 29), "Eat this year *that which grows by itself,* and in the second year that which is self-sown, and in *the third year sow* and reap, plant vineyards and eat their fruit." This phraseology is extremely similar to that used in Leviticus to describe the situation in a Sabbatical year. Thus in Lev. **25** 5 is stated *"That which grows by itself* you shall not reap"; and in Lev. **25** 21,22 is stated, "And it shall bring forth produce for *the three years*; and you shall *sow* in the eighth year . . . ." This example is the only clear allusion in the Bible to an historical event occurring in a Sabbatical year.

The final case supporting our dating for the Sabbatical and Jubilee years arises at the time of the destruction of the Temple. At that time, during the siege of Jerusalem, it is stated in II Kings **25** 3 that the famine was severe in the city. Now we know that the fifth month of 586 (II Kings **25** 8), the month of the destruction of the Temple, was near the end of the Sabbatical year starting in Tishri 587. Hence, the combined effect of the siege of Jerusalem and the observance of the Sabbatical year resulted in the severe famine.

---

* In both places, the rare word ספיח, which means "that which grows by itself," is used.

7.1.12 Second Entrance into the Land of Israel

The second occasion when the people entered into the land of Israel occurred in early 538, after the decree of Cyrus permitting the return of the exiles (Ezra 1 1-2 2). If we assume, as at the first entrance into the land, that the half year from the beginning of 538 until Tishri 538 is counted as a full year, and we remember that there is no year zero in the counting system, then the Jubilee years during the Second Temple begin with Tishri of: 490, 440, 390, 340, 290, 240, 190, 140, 90, and 40 B.C.E.; 11 and 61 C.E.

Similarly, the Sabbatical years begin with Tishri of:

(B.C.E.)

533, 526, 519, 512, 505, 498, 491
483, 476, 469, 462, 455, 448, 441
433, 426, 419, 412, 405, 398, 391
383, 376, 369, 362, 355, 348, 341
333, 326, 319, 312, 305, 298, 291
283, 276, 269, 262, 255, 248, 241
233, 226, 219, 212, 205, 198, 191
183, 176, 169, 162, 155, 148, 141
133, 126, 119, 112, 105, 98, 91
 83, 76, 69, 62, 55, 48, 41
 33, 26, 19, 12,   5

(C.E.)

3, 10, 18, 25, 32, 39, 46, 53, 60, 68

There are a number of cases—based on information from the Bible, the Book of the Maccabees, the writings of Josephus, and the Talmud—which lend support to the above dates for the Sabbatical and Jubilee years during the Second Temple.

According to Ezra 6 15 the Second Temple was completed in the twelfth month of the sixth year of Darius I. As explained in Section 6.4, the reign of Darius is counted from 517 and therefore the Temple was completed near the end of 512. Now our calculations showed that this time was a Sabbatical year which began in Tishri 512. The coincidence that the Temple was completed in a Sabbatical year is not altogether unexpected. More manpower was then available from the persons freed from agricultural pursuits, which allowed the construction to proceed more rapidly.

From Ezra 7 1,8; 10 9 we learn that all the men of Judah and Benjamin gathered in Jerusalem for three days during the ninth month of 398. Such a meeting was possible because it was a Sabbatical year, and the men were therefore released from many agricultural tasks.

Based on *Ant.* xi, 8, par. 5, combined with information from Greek history, it is learned that in 332 Alexander the Great excused Judea from payment of tribute in Sabbatical years in accordance with the request of the high priest. It can be deduced from this that 332 was the end of a Sabbatical year, in agreement with our presented calculation which shows a Sabbatical year beginning in Tishri 333.

The First Book of Maccabees supplies the strongest support for the prescribed Sabbatical years. In I Mac. 6 20,49,53 it is explicitly stated that the year 150 of the Seleucid era (i.e. 162 B.C.E.) was a Sabbatical year. This date is in exact agreement with the calculated Sabbatical year beginning in Tishri 162.

According to Josephus (*Ant.* xiii, 8, par. 1) a Sabbatical year occurred some time after John Hyrcanus assumed the position of high priest. From I Mac. 16 14 we learn that John Hyrcanus accepted the high priesthood at the end of 135 (the eleventh month of the 177th year of the Seleucid era). Therefore the Sabbatical year should have begun in Tishri 134 or at the latest Tishri 133. Our calculated dates agree with the assumption that the specified Sabbatical year began in Tishri 133.

Josephus also implies (*Ant.* xiv, 16, par. 2) that approximately the third year of Herod (i.e. 37) was a Sabbatical year. This dating is, however, inconsistent with our calculations. The reliability of the statement by Josephus that the year was a Sabbatical year is therefore suspect.

Lastly, in Tractates *Taanith* 29a and *Erechin* 11b is stated that the years when the First and Second Temples were destroyed were post-Sabbatical years. We have ignored the information concerning the First Temple because it was based on a different calculation from ours, and was definitely not based on eyewitness accounts. However, the information for the Second Temple may very well have been handed down, and not have been based solely on calculation. Now the Second Temple was destroyed in the fifth month of 70 C.E. which according to our calculations is the year after the Sabbatical year of Tishri 68 to Tishri 69 C.E., in agreement with the Talmudic statement.

7.1.3   Third Entrance into the Land of Israel

By analogy with the preceding discussion the counting of the Sabbatical and Jubilee years for the period ushering in the construction of the Third Temple, will commence with the mass return of the Jewish people from exile; and the first half-year between Nisan and Tishri will be counted as a full year.

Chapter Eight

SUMMARY OF DATES FOR MAIN EVENTS

Dates for the events which occurred during the different Biblical periods, arrived at on the basis of historical and logical considerations, have been presented in Chapters One through Seven. Additional dates are also occasionally given in Chapters Ten through Fifteen, where the authorship and organization of the books of the Bible are discussed. For convenience, as well as for clarity, the dates for the main events during the Biblical period are summarized in Table 8.1. These dates serve as a framework to which others can be added if so desired. In particular, if additional information is needed, use should be made of Table 1.5.1 for the creation era; Table 4.1 for the period of the judges; Table 5.2.1 for the time of the kings; Table 10.3.4 for events during King David's reign; Table 6.5.1 for the history of the Second Temple; and Section 7.1 for the dates of the Sabbatical and Jubilee years. To have included the information from these and other sources in Table 8.1 would have made it too long and cumbersome for practical purposes.

It should be pointed out that the traditional Jewish dates, based on the time of the creation of the world, are too low by 162 years when used for post-Biblical events. For example, the year 1972 C.E. could also be called 5732 A.M., based on the interpretation of the author of the book *Seder Olam*. However, based on the chronology developed within this book the year 1972 C.E. is in actuality 5894 A.M. (since 1 A.M. = 3922 B.C.E.; or 1 C.E. = 3923 A.M.). Thus the world has actually existed for 162 years longer than would be indicated from the traditional dates.

Table 8.1
Summary of Main Events During Biblical Period

	Date (B.C.E.)
Creation of the world	Nisan, 3922
Life of Adam	3922–2993
Development of special skills—cattle-raising, music, metal-working	ca. 3800
Life of Noah	2866–1917
Life of Shem	2364–1765
The Deluge	2267
Formation of the nations after the Deluge	ca. 2215
Tower of Babel—confusion of languages	ca. 2200
Life of Eber	2199–1736
Break-up of the single continent (birth of Peleg)	2166
Life of Terah	2044–1840
Life of Abraham (Hammurabi)	1974–1800
Reign of Hammurabi over Babylonia	1947–1905
Abraham leaves Ur of the Chaldees	1905
Arrival of Abraham in land of Canaan	1900
Life of Isaac	1874–1695
Life of Jacob	1814–1668
Life of Levi	1727–1591
Life of Joseph	1723–1614
Joseph becomes second to Pharaoh	1694
Descent of Jacob and his family to Egypt—known as Hyksos rulers	1685
Enslavement of the Israelites by the Egyptians	ca. 1580
Pharaoh who enslaved the Israelites—Ahmose I	1580–1557
Life of Aaron (Senmen)	1557–1475
Life of Moses (Senmut)	1554–1475
Pharaoh at time of Exodus—Thutmose III	1501–1447
Exodus from Egypt	Nisan, 1474
Forty years in the desert	1474–1435
Entrance into land of Canaan	Nisan, 1434
Rule of Joshua	1434–1383
Period of the Judges (from Othniel until Saul)	1382–1041
Samuel, judgeship of	1043–1041
Reign of Saul, the first king	1040–1039
Reign of David	1038–999

Table 8.1 (continued)

	Date (B.C.E.)
Birth of Solomon	1014
Reign of Solomon	998–959
First Temple, construction begun	995
First Temple, construction completed	988
Division of the monarchy into two kingdoms	959
Duration of Kingdom of Israel	959–719
Exile of ten tribes	719
Duration of Kingdom of Judah	959–586
Seventy years of Babylonian Empire	609–539
Exile of Jehoiachin	597
Babylonian exile	586
Seventy years during which Temple lay in ruins	586–516
Cyrus conquered Babylon	539
Cyrus edict permitting return to Judea	538
Zerubbabel governor of Judea	538–511
Reign of Ahasuerus (Hystaspes)	531–518
Reign of Darius I (Darius the Mede)	521–486
Year of Purim event—Haman killed	520
First year of Darius I according to Bible	517
Beginning of construction of Second Temple— prophecies by Haggai and Zechariah	516
Second Temple completed	512
Reign of Artaxerxes II	404–359
Ezra comes to Judea from Babylon	398
Ezra acts as leader	398–385
Nehemiah comes to Judea from Shushan	385
The Great Assembly	385
Nehemiah serves as governor of Judea	385–ca. 370

PART II
AUTHORSHIP AND ORGANIZATION OF THE BOOKS OF THE BIBLE

Each book of the Bible will here be discussed to try to ascertain who the probable authors were, and the basis for the textual arrangement. All too often Biblical critics have selected as authors unknown persons living hundreds of years after the time indicated from the Biblical work, and have also assumed that many of the books are arranged in a nonsystematic, illogical manner. In contrast, the Jewish traditional commentaries de-emphasize the topics of authorship and organization and are mainly concerned with the meaning of the text. When the authorship is discussed in traditional sources, as for example in Babylonian Talmud, Tractate *Baba Bathra* 14b, the basis for numerous conclusions are not presented, and an over-simplified picture is given. Here will be presented for each book of the Bible, logical, well documented reasons for the conclusions as to author and arrangement; reasons which are acceptable from a traditional viewpoint, and yet answer the questions raised by the Biblical critics. However, no specific effort has been given to stating clearly the arguments of the critics, for otherwise it would have been necessary to write several times as much, and the result would be a work that emphasizes the critics' viewpoints. Instead, the emphasis has been on writing a logical, self-consistent presentation which solves fundamental questions that have undermined the beliefs of many in the veracity of the Bible.

In the discussion of each book, the headings "authorship" and "organization" are used. Sometimes the heading "authorship" is given first, and in other cases the heading "organization" is first, depending on the logical requirements for properly interpreting the particular book. Numerous tables are also presented for clarification.

Chapter Nine

ASSUMPTIONS AND CONCLUSIONS

9.1 AUTHORSHIP

In arriving at the author of a particular Biblical book numerous suppositions have been made. Firstly, it is assumed that the author has only in rare instances remained completely anonymous. Usually he is a key person named in the text, or is specified in the Book of Chronicles. Some indications from the text itself are as follows:

(A) A person who was familiar with most of the details described because he was intimately involved in the happenings, is likely to have been the author. In particular, a statement that the events described were told to some key person often establishes that the one to whom the description was given is the author.

(B) If a section is written in the first person, then the speaker is clearly the author, although someone else may have subsequently edited the text. However, a section written in the third person does not indicate anything for or against authorship, since this is the most common style of Biblical writing.

(C) The events described in a historical book, covering a period of time much longer than the lifetime of any of the mentioned persons, such as several hundred years, must obviously have been written by many individuals, where each individual recorded the events in which he was involved.

A summary of the conclusions reached as to the authors of each of the books of the Bible is presented in Table 9.1. Many of the historical works, such as Genesis, Judges, Samuel, Kings, and Chronicles, were each composed by numerous authors. In contrast, the prophetic writings were usually written by the prophets themselves; for example, the Book of Ezekiel was authored by Ezekiel. Also to be noticed are the number of books in which Moses, Joshua, Samuel, and Solomon were significantly involved.

9.2 ORGANIZATION

When discussing the organization of the Bible, the implicit assumption is made that each book was arranged in a sensible manner. Some typical factors for a meaningful order are chronology, similarity of topics, logical considerations, and similarity of phrases in adjacent passages. A chronological arrangement can be either approximate or exact. When the arrangement is approximately chronological, then some exceptions to an exact chronological order are to be found. If, however, an exact chronological order is followed then no events are placed out of chronological order.

Similarity of topics is one example of a logical arrangement. A logical arrangement implies that the book is arranged according to a prominent feature or other characteristic, such as is the case in the debates in the Book of Job.

Similarity of phrases is a very important factor in the arrangement of numerous of the Biblical books and has been overlooked by most commentators. Even when not overlooked, the importance of this factor is not realized. Many of the prophetic works are arranged, at least partly, on this basis. However, it is often difficult to know where one prophecy ends and the next one begins. This problem frequently arises, for example, in the Book of Isaiah. What may seem to be one prophecy may actually be two, and vice versa. Often separate prophecies similar in context or wording may be placed next to each other without any introductory separating heading. Sometimes in the tables showing the similarity of phrases, arbitrary separations into prophecies have been used based on a reasonable understanding of the text. These arbitrary separations have been used to establish that the book is partly organized by similarity in phrases, rather than to show where separate prophecies begin or end. Frequently the tables showing similarity of phrases are presented in the original Hebrew, because not always are the same Hebrew roots, when conjugated differently, translated by the same English terms. Preferably all these tables should be in Hebrew. However, in a number of instances the phrases have been translated into English for the benefit of those not familiar with Hebrew.

A summary of the arrangements used in the books of the Bible is presented in Table 9.2. It should be noted that the historical books are usually organized according to chronological considerations, modified by logical requirements. In contrast, the prophetic works are often organized by similarity of topics as modified by similarity of phrases. Also of interest is the fact that for some books, different parts are arranged according to varying criteria.

9.3 CHRONOLOGY

Frequently, chronological information in addition to that presented in Part I aids in selecting the author or in clarifying the organization. Some assumptions used, besides cases where actual dates are given, are as follows:

(A) People are assumed to have married upon becoming physically mature, unless contrary information is available. In the average case, the male matures at thirteen, and the female at twelve years of age.

(B) The phrases "and it later came to pass" (ויהי אחרי כן) or "after these things" (אחרי הדברים האלה), where the word "after" (אחרי) is used, often indicate a time span of three years. These phrases could, however, also refer to other much longer durations, depending upon the context.

Table 9.1
Authors of the Books of the Bible

Book	Final Editor	Authors of Sections	Main Author
Genesis	Judah or Moses	God, Adam, Cain, Adam's descendants, Noah, Noah's sons, Shem, Shem's descendants, Terah, Abraham, Lot, Isaac, Ishmael and his sons, Rebekah, Jacob, Esau, Descendants of Esau, Joseph, Judah	
Exodus	Joshua	Moses, Joshua	Moses
Leviticus	Joshua or Moses	Moses	Moses
Numbers	Joshua	Moses, Balaam, Joshua	Moses
Deuteronomy	Joshua	Moses, Joshua	Moses
Joshua	Samuel	Joshua	Joshua
Judges	Samuel	Samuel, Ehud, Deborah, Gideon, Jotham, Jephthah, Samson's mother, Micah, The Levite	
Samuel	Nathan	Samuel, Gad, Nathan	
Kings	Baruch	Nathan, Ahijah, Iddo, Shemaiah, Hanani, Jehu, Elijah, Micaiah, Elisha, Jonah, Isaiah, Hozai, Huldah, Jeremiah, Baruch	
Isaiah	Isaiah	Isaiah	Isaiah
Jeremiah	Baruch	Jeremiah, Baruch	Jeremiah
Ezekiel	Ezekiel	Ezekiel	Ezekiel
The Twelve Prophets			
Hosea	Hosea	Hosea	Hosea
Joel	Joel	Joel	Joel
Amos	Amos	Amos	Amos
Obadiah	Obadiah	Obadiah	Obadiah
Jonah	Jonah	Jonah	Jonah

ASSUMPTIONS AND CONCLUSIONS   123

Micah	Micah	Micah	Micah	Micah	Micah
Nahum	Nahum	Nahum	Nahum	Nahum	Nahum
Habakkuk	Habakkuk	Habakkuk	Habakkuk	Habakkuk	Habakkuk
Zephaniah	Zephaniah	Zephaniah	Zephaniah	Zephaniah	Zephaniah
Haggai	Haggai	Haggai	Haggai	Haggai	Haggai
Zechariah	Zechariah	Zechariah	Zechariah	Zechariah	Zechariah
Malachi	Malachi	Malachi	Malachi	Malachi	Malachi
Psalms	David	David	David, Moses, Sons of Korah, Heman, Asaph, Ethan, Jeduthun, Solomon		David
Proverbs	Solomon and Men of Hezekiah	Solomon, Agur, Lemuel			Solomon
Job	Elihu	Elihu; and possibly Eliphaz, Bildad, Zophar, Job			Elihu
Song of Songs	Solomon	Solomon			Solomon
Ruth	Boaz	Boaz			Boaz
Lamentations	Jeremiah	Jeremiah			Jeremiah
Ecclesiastes	Solomon	Solomon			Solomon
Esther	Mordechai	Mordechai			Mordechai
Daniel	Daniel	Daniel, Nebuchadnezzar, one of the three companions of Daniel			Daniel
Ezra-Nehemiah	Nehemiah	Zerubbabel, Ezra, Nehemiah			
Chronicles	Zerubbabel, Nehemiah	Adam, Adam's descendants, Noah, Noah's sons, Shem, Shem's descendants, Abraham, Ishmael, Ishmael's sons, Isaac, Jacob, Esau, Esau's descendants, Judah, Moses, Joshua, Boaz, Samuel, Nathan, Hur, Nehemiah, Gad, The Levites, Asaph, Ahijah, Iddo, Shemaiah, Hanani, Azariah son of Oded, Micaiah, Jehu, Jahaziel, Elijah, Eliezer son of Dodavahu, Elisha, Jonah, Isaiah, Zechariah the visionary, Azariah the priest, Oded the prophet, Hozai, Huldah, Jeremiah, Baruch, Zerubbabel			Iddo and others

Table 9.2
Organization of the Books of the Bible

Book	Section	Main Arrangement Principle	Secondary Factor
Genesis		Essentially chronological	
Exodus		Essentially chronological	
Leviticus		Essentially chronological	
Numbers		Essentially chronological	
Deuteronomy		Essentially chronological	
Joshua		Essentially chronological	
Judges	1 1–2 5	Similarity of phrases	
	2 6–16 31	Essentially chronological	
	17 1–21 25	Similarity of phrases	
Samuel	I Sam. 1 1–II Sam. 20 26	Essentially chronological	
	II Sam. 21 1–24 25	Similarity of phrases	
Kings		Essentially chronological	
Isaiah		Topical	Similarity of phrases
Jeremiah		Topical	Similarity of phrases
Ezekiel		Topical	Similarity of phrases
Twelve Prophets			
Hosea		Topical	Similarity of phrases
Joel		One prophecy	
Amos		First words of prophecies	Similarity of phrases
Obadiah		One prophecy	
Jonah		Chronological	
Micah		Logical	

ASSUMPTIONS AND CONCLUSIONS   125

Nahum		One prophecy
Habakkuk		Logical
Zephaniah		One prophecy
Haggai		Chronological
Zechariah		Topical
Malachi		One prophecy
Psalms		Authors and headings of poems
Proverbs	1 1–9 18	Topical
	10 1–29 27	Similarity of words, sounds or sentence construction
	30 1–31 31	Proverbs by authors other than Solomon
Job		Logical
Song of Songs		Logical
Ruth		Chronological
Lamentations		Logical
Ecclesiastes		Mainly logical
Esther		Chronological
Daniel		Logical
Ezra-Nehemiah	Ezra 1 1–6 22	Chronological
	Ezra 7 1–10 44	Chronological
	Neh. 1 1–13 31	Logical
Chronicles	I Chr. 1 1–9 44	Logical
	I Chr. 10 1–II Chr. 9 31	Essentially chronological
	II Chr. 10 1–36 23	Essentially chronological

Similarity of phrases (Nahum)
Similarity of phrases (Zechariah)

Alphabetical order
Similarity of words and phrases

(C) In calculating exact dates of the Hebrew months, it is assumed that the length of the months are the same as at the present time. Thus the first, third, fifth, seventh, and eleventh months have thirty days, and the second, fourth, sixth, tenth, and twelfth months have twenty-nine days. Furthermore the eighth and ninth months may have either twenty-nine or thirty days; and in leap years the twelfth month has thirty days, and the thirteenth month twenty-nine days. Naturally, in Biblical times, these month lengths were not as yet established, but the above arrangement is as good an assumption as any when other data are lacking, and at most introduces an error of only a few days.

Evidence as to the date of completion of a book is based on the following assumptions:

(A) The time of completion of a book is shortly after the latest event mentioned in the text, unless other evidence indicates otherwise.

(B) Evidence based on linguistics is highly conjectural. Our knowledge of early and late Hebrew arises from the Biblical books, and therefore it is usually impossible to say what are actually early or late Hebrew words. Occasionally, foreign words, such as Persian, indicate a very approximate time, but even then such evidence should only be used to verify conclusions reached by other means, and should never be used to contradict clearly stated times.

(C) The present order of the Biblical books relative to each other does not give definitive information as to the time of completion, since the arrangement is arbitrary in many instances, and varies in different compilations. However, the relative positions of books within a book, such as within the Twelve Prophets, or within Ezra-Nehemiah, does offer significant information.

(D) Specific dates within the text are mainly presented to clarify events described. However, when prophecies about the Messianic Era are presented, or events of a non-historical type are related, then frequently no dates are given.

9.4 TEXTUAL CONSIDERATIONS

In interpreting the text numerous basic assumptions about the books have been made. These are:

(A) The present Masoretic Hebrew text is as close to the original text as we can attain at the present time. Not only are the wordings to be considered the same as in the original, but also the arrangement within each book. To a very great extent the accuracy of the Hebrew text has been verified by the Dead Sea Scrolls. The Septuagint and Vulgate translations, for example, are to be considered as translations, where significant textual alterations were permitted to explain difficulties in the Hebrew original. Needless to say, the explanations implied in the translations are not necessarily correct.

(B) The Books of Samuel, Kings, Chronicles, and Ezra-Nehemiah, which are now each divided into two parts, were each originally one book. This is attested to by early Hebrew manuscripts, as well as in the Talmudic discussion of authorship (*Baba Bathra* 14b). The division of these four works into two parts each goes back to the first printed Hebrew bible in 1518 C.E., where the divisions in the Septuagint were followed. When considering authorship and organization of these books, they must be treated as originally written and not as presently divided. Similarly, the chapter divisions are of late origin, and do not necessarily indicate correct separations of ideas.

(C) In interpreting the text, it is assumed that the simple meaning is to be taken in all cases. Complex twisting of wording, and brilliant Midrashic interpretations, although of great homiletic value, are not to be used in reaching conclusions. Furthermore, statements of the text, including dates, should be taken literally, unless other considerations establish that a less literal explanation is warranted.

(D) Since this commentary is mainly written in English, it has often been necessary, in order to elucidate a point, to modify existing English translations slightly to give a more literal rendering of the Hebrew.

(E) In considering prophetic works, it should be assumed that all the Divine revelations received by a prophet have survived, and they contain all the messages from God of historical importance received by the prophet. Many prophets, such as those in the Book of the Twelve Prophets, received only one revelation. It is not a reasonable question to ask why the prophet did not discuss other topics of importance to his generation. Such a question implies that the revelations were not from God, but were educated guesses. We should realize that the topics in the prophecies are limited to those messages received from God.

9.5 REFERENCES

In developing the ideas and concepts presented in this Part II, use has been made of numerous commentaries and discussions in addition to the Biblical text. Traditional as well as critical references have been frequently consulted for information and ideas. However, the resultant discussions and conclusions have been developed according to the premises just summarized, rather than on the basis of the conclusions in the references. In fact, sharp variations in approach and conclusions occur for all books of the Bible between the explanations presented here and those in the references. The main works consulted are listed below, although on occasion other discussions on the Biblical books have also been examined.

1. *Soncino Books of the Bible*, edited by A. Cohen.
2. א.ש. הרטום, מ.ד. קאסוטו "תורה נביאים כתובים" הוצאת יבנה, תל-אביב, 1961–1963.
3. S. R. Driver, *Introduction to the Literature of the Old Testament*.
4. Articles on the Biblical books, in *The Jewish Encyclopedia*.
5. W. O. E. Oesterley and T. H. Robinson, *Introduction to the Books of the Old Testament*.

6. Articles on the Biblical books in *Encyclopaedia Britannica*.
7. Articles on the Biblical books in *Harper's Bible Dictionary*, edited by M. S. Miller and J. L. Miller.
8. י. אמוראי, ז. בהרב, א.א. עקביא "תנ"ך מקרא מפרש" הוצאת שלמה שרברק, תל-אביב.
9. מ.צ. סגל "תורה נביאים כתובים" הוצאת דביר, תל-אביב

Chapter Ten

THE PENTATEUCH

In considering the authorship and organization of the five books of the Pentateuch, it is convenient to consider the Book of Genesis separately. As will presently be clarified, Genesis is a work presenting the history for a period of 2,309 years, which contains the writings of such people as Adam, Noah, Abraham, Isaac, Jacob, Joseph, and Judah. The final editing of Genesis could have been accomplished either by Judah or Moses. In contrast, the next four books, namely Exodus, Leviticus, Numbers, and Deuteronomy, were written by Moses and edited by Joshua. The authorship by Moses is clear since he is the main person described in the four books, and often would be the only one aware of many of the mentioned incidents and revelations. Furthermore, in numerous places (Ex. **17** 14; **24** 4; **34** 27; Num. **33** 2; Deut. **31** 9,22,24; Josh. **8** 32) it is specifically mentioned that Moses wrote down certain sections. Several factors, however, also point to the editorship of Joshua. In Ex. **16** 35 it is stated that the manna was eaten for forty years until the people came unto the borders of the land of Canaan; and from Josh. **5** 12 we know that the manna stopped after the death of Moses. Secondly, in Numbers **12** 3 it is stated that Moses was the most modest man on the earth. No person could honestly write such a statement about himself, and therefore someone other than Moses must have written the sentence. Finally, in Deut. **34** 8,9 are described events after the death of Moses. We thus find that in the Books of Exodus, Numbers, and Deuteronomy there are sentences clearly written by someone other than Moses, namely Joshua. It is only logical to draw the conclusion that Joshua edited not only these three books, but all four of the last books of the Pentateuch. Furthermore, we find explicitly stated in Josh. **24** 26 that Joshua wrote in the Book of the Law of Elokim. As will be subsequently proved, this latter book is the same as Genesis, and shows that Joshua had the right to add comments to the entire Pentateuch. This generalized understanding of the authorship of the Pentateuch will be of value when discussing the authorship of the five individual books.

    The Pentateuch is clearly organized according to a chronological sequence. The Book of Genesis begins at the time of creation and slowly leads up to the time immediately preceding the entry of the Israelites into the Land of Israel after the death of Moses, which is detailed at the end of Deuteronomy. In general, each described event occurs later in time than that described immediately prior to it. However, in a number of cases, incidents are placed slightly out of chronological order to maintain a logical coherence. It should be noted that the exceptions to a strict chronological order in Genesis are mainly with respect to the statements about the deaths of individuals. In the other four books, items placed not in strict chronological order are concerned mainly with retaining topical unity. Cases where the chronological order is not maintained are explained when discussing the arrangement of each of the five books.

10.1 GENESIS

Authorship

The Book of Genesis, the historical accuracy of which has been verified in Part I, covers the period of time from creation to the death of Joseph, which is a period of 2,309 years. This period is much too long to have been covered by one individual, since even Methusaleh, who lived longer than any other recorded person, only lived 969 years (Gen. 5 27). The conclusion therefore arises that the text of Genesis was written by many people, each one recording the events in which he was involved. Otherwise, how could such an accurate historical document have been prepared? Surely people who lived thousands of years after the events could not have written the book from their imagination or based on distorted verbal accounts transmitted orally for numerous generations.

Genesis is divided into twelve sections, the last eleven of which begin in the first or second sentence with the words "these are the histories" (אלה תולדות), or with a very similar phrase. The arrangement is presented in Table 10.1.1. It should be noted that the phrase "these are the histories" is found elsewhere in the Bible only in Num. 3 1, concerning the histories of Aaron and Moses, and in Ruth 4 18, concerning the descendants of Perez. Hence the frequent use of this phrase is a characteristic feature of this book.

The first section of the book (Gen. 1 1–2 3) describes the creation of the world in seven days, and must have been composed by God since no one else was present; at least until the sixth day, when man was created. God uses only the word "Elokim" to describe Himself. God passed the information to Adam either verbally or more probably in writing.

The second section (Gen. 2 4–4 26) relates the history of Adam and his sons Cain and Seth and the descendants of Cain. The author of Gen. 2 4–3 24 is clearly Adam, since until children were born only he and Eve were around to record the events. The history of Cain and his descendants (Gen. 4 1–24) probably was recorded by Cain and edited and completed by Adam. Adam lived 930 years (Gen. 5 5) and surely lived long enough to edit the recorded events of the lives of his grandchildren. Adam calls God "YHWH Elokim" showing the eternal qualities of God in comparison to the transient nature of man. The use of the

Table 10.1.1
Organization of Genesis

No.	Section	Key Opening Phrase	Events Described	Probable Author(s)
1.	1 1–2 3	In the beginning	Creation of the world by God	God
2.	2 4–4 26	These are the histories of the heaven and the earth	History of Adam, and his sons Cain and Seth, and the descendants of Cain	Adam and Cain
3.	5 1–6 8	This is the book of the history of Adam	Genealogy of Adam until Noah	Adam, his descendants, and completed by Noah
4.	6 9–9 29	These are the histories of Noah	Life of Noah, the Deluge, until death of Noah	Noah, and completed by his sons
5.	10 1–11 9	These are the histories of the sons of Noah.	Genealogies of the sons of Noah, and story of Tower of Babel	Sons of Noah
6.	11 10–11 25	These are the histories of Shem	Genealogy of Shem until birth of Abraham	Shem and his descendants, completed by Jacob
7.	11 26–25 11	These are the histories of Terah	History of Abraham, Lot, and Isaac	Initially by Terah, remainder mainly by Abraham; Chap. 19 by Lot; completed by Isaac
8.	25 12–25 18	These are the histories of Ishmael	History of Ishmael and his sons	Ishmael and his sons
9.	25 19–35 29	These are the histories of Isaac	History of Isaac and Jacob	Isaac, Rebekah, and Jacob
10.	36 1–36 8	These are the histories of Esau who is Edom	History of Esau	Esau
11.	36 9–36 43	These are the histories of Esau founder of Edom	History of descendants of Esau	Descendants of Esau
12.	37 1–50 26	These are the histories of Jacob	History of children of Jacob	Jacob and his children; main authors Joseph and Judah

names Cush and Ashur (Gen. 2 13,14) indicates the early origin of these names, even prior to the birth of individuals with the identical names (Gen. 10 6,11), and does not indicate later editorship. Obviously since Adam wrote this second part of the book, he was created not only with the ability to speak but also to write.

The third section (Gen. 5 1–6 8) presents the genealogy of Adam's descendants until Noah. This is clearly a composite work initiated by Adam, with subsequent information as to the length of the lives of the persons added by Adam's descendants. Adam lived only till the fifty-sixth year of Lamech, while the descendants listed all lived to later times. Thus Adam could not have recorded the duration of his own life and the lives of his descendants. Furthermore, it is obvious that Noah completed the listing, since Methuselah died in the year of the Deluge when only Noah, of those listed, remained alive.

The next section (Gen. 6 9–9 29), beginning with the phrase "these are the histories of Noah," deals with the events in the life of Noah until his death, including the detailed description of the Deluge. All the described events were probably written down by Noah. Only the last two sentences of the section, detailing the length of Noah's life, need to be ascribed to one of his sons; even these two sentences could possibly have been written by Noah, when he realized that his death was imminent.

The fifth section (Gen. 10 1–11 9) is introduced with the phrase "these are the histories of the sons of Noah" and relates the genealogies of the three sons: Shem, Ham, and Japheth as well as the story of the Tower of Babel. Since these three lived long lives, Shem for example lived 502 years after the Deluge (Gen. 11 10,11), it is quite probable that this section was written only by the sons of Noah. Up to the event of the Tower of Babel everybody spoke Hebrew. This is obvious since the Creation chapters are written in this language. After the confounding of the languages, Shem and his descendants still spoke Hebrew since the subsequent section, which is written by them, is also in this language. According to this reasoning, we may conclude that the story of the Tower of Babel was written by Shem, since it is written in Hebrew.

The sixth section (Gen. 11 10–25), beginning with the phrase "these are the histories of Shem," presents the genealogy of Shem until the birth of Abram. Now, Shem and Eber lived till the fiftieth and seventy-ninth years of Jacob, respectively. This was a later time than for any of the other persons listed. It is therefore possible that Shem recorded all the lifetimes listed, except those for himself and Eber. The latter information probably was supplied by Jacob.

The following section (Gen. 11 26–25 11) begins with the phrase "these are the histories of Terah." The first few sentences (Gen. 11 26–31), dealing with the life of Terah, were probably written by Terah. The remainder of the section presents the history of Abraham, Lot, and Isaac. The majority of the contents were written by Abraham. However, Chapter 19, which describes details concerning the escape of Lot from destruction in Sodom, was written by Lot, with additional comments (Gen. **19** 27–29) added later by Abraham. Chapter 24, which describes how the servant of Abraham found a wife for Isaac, was written by Isaac. This is implied by the statement (Gen. **24** 66) that the servant told Isaac all that the servant accomplished. It is reasonable to assume that Isaac concluded this section by writing Gen. **25** 1–11, although the first several sentences of Chapter 25 could also have been written by Abraham, since they describe the children of Abraham born to his wife Keturah.

The eighth section (Gen. **25** 12–18) presents the history of Ishmael and his sons, and begins with the phrase "these are the histories of Ishmael." Probably Ishmael wrote this section, and it was completed by one of his sons or perhaps by Isaac. It is unlikely that Ishmael finished the section, since Ishmael's age at the time of death is given.

The ninth section (Gen. **25** 19–**35** 29) begins with the phrase "these are the histories of Isaac," and presents the history of Isaac and Jacob. It is not clear whether the beginning part (Gen. **25** 19–34) was written by Isaac. Possibly it was written by Rebekah, the wife of Isaac, since she is described as seeking information concerning her pregnancy and also probably was aware of the details of the sale of the birthright by Esau to Jacob. Chapter 26, describing the stay of Isaac and Rebekah in Gerar, seems to have been written by Isaac. Afterwards, Isaac's vision became so poor he could not tell Jacob from Esau (Chapter 27). Naturally he could also not see well enough to write. Therefore Gen. **27** 1–**28** 9 is here attributed to Rebekah. It is specifically mentioned that she overheard Isaac talking to Esau (Gen. **27** 5), and was told of Esau's plan to kill Jacob (Gen. **27** 42). Also, she was responsible for Jacob instead of Esau receiving the blessings from Isaac. The subsequent events (Gen. **28** 10–**35** 29) describe the history of Jacob's trip to the house of Laban until Jacob's return to his father's house. These events were obviously written by Jacob, the only person familiar with all the details.

The tenth section (Gen. **36** 1–8) beginning with the phrase "these are the histories of Esau, who is Edom" describes the children of Esau born in the land of Canaan. The details were probably written by Esau. The next section (Gen. **36** 9–43) begins with the phrase "these are the histories of Esau the founder of Edom in the mountain-land of Seir," and describes the histories of the descendants of Esau, and of the inhabitants of Seir. This section was probably written by one of the descendants of Esau. A copy of both these sections about Esau could subsequently have been obtained by the family of Jacob.

The last section of the book (Gen. **37** 1–**50** 26) starts the second sentence with the phrase "these are the histories of Jacob," and describes the history of the children of Jacob. The main personalities of the story are Jacob, Joseph, and Judah, and this section is the combined work of all three. Joseph undoubtedly wrote the parts where he was the main personality, including the description of his stay in Egypt. Accounts attributable to Joseph are: Gen. **37** 1–17,36; **38** 18–35; **39** 1–**41** 57; **42** 6–26; **43** 16–**44** 6; **45** 1–24; **46** 28–**50** 22. Judah probably wrote the parts describing the actions of the brothers and himself; Gen. 37 18-35; 38 1-30; 42 1-5; 42 27-43 15; 44 7-34; 45 25-28; 50 23-26. It has been assumed that Judah outlived Joseph, and, therefore, could describe the death of Joseph. Jacob wrote the description of God's message to him and the list of the seventy members of his family who went to Egypt; i.e. he wrote 46 1-27. The result of the combined efforts of Jacob, Joseph, and Judah is a masterful, interesting history of the children of Jacob.

The development of the Book of Genesis can now be clarified. The described history was written by the key personalities in the text; in many cases they were the only ones familiar with all the details. Main authors of different sections include God, Adam, Cain, Noah, Shem, Terah, Abraham, Lot, Isaac, Ishmael, Rebekah, Jacob, Esau, Joseph, and Judah. These sections were transmitted in writing and brought to Egypt and completed there by the family of Jacob. Upon leaving Egypt, Moses carried the material, and possibly edited the information into the form we now have it, if it had not previously been completed by Judah. Indication of the common authorship of Genesis, and the remaining books of the Pentateuch written mainly by Moses, is indicated by the use of the phrase "these are the histories of Aaron and Moses" in the Book of Numbers (Num. 3 1). It is here suggested that the phrase "these are the histories" may have been used by Moses in the Book of Genesis to indicate the beginning of new documents or scrolls.

The possibility that the Book of Genesis was supplied in its entirety by God to Moses on Mount Sinai, or subsequently, is untenable. First, there is no indication in the Bible that such was the case. Secondly, part if not all of the text of Genesis was available before Moses received the Ten Commandments. This is indicated by the exact quotation at the time of the Exodus from Egypt (Ex. 13 19) of the words of Joseph (Gen. 50 25) "God will surely remember you, and you shall bring my bones from here." These words could have been quoted 139 years after the death of Joseph only if a written record existed, namely the Book of Genesis.

The fact that different sections of the Book of Genesis were written by different authors explains numerous variations in style within the book. For example, the genealogy of Adam and his descendants (Gen. 5) lists the ages of the fathers when the children were born, the number of years lived by the fathers after the birth of the children, and the total number of years lived. In contrast, the genealogy of Shem and his descendants (Gen. 11 10-25) lists the same information but omits the total number of years lived. Another example is the differences in the name of God used in Gen. 1 1-2 3 and in Gen. 2 4-3 24. In the former case the name used is *Elokim*, and in the latter *YHWH Elokim*. Numerous other examples of variations in style can be attributed to the different authors.

ORGANIZATION

The Book of Genesis is not arranged in a strict chronological order of events, but rather in the chronological order of the key personalities described. A rigid chronological arrangement would require the interruption of narratives to mention the deaths of important persons previously mentioned. However, the age of death is often given immediately after conclusion of the description of the history of the person concerned, even though his death may have occurred many years later. Numerous examples of this occur. For example, Adam died at the age of 930 (Gen. 5 5) in the fifty-sixth year of Lamech. However, the event of Adam's death is mentioned immediately after the birth of Adam's son Seth, rather than when discussing the life of Lamech. Similar considerations apply to the statements of the deaths of the descendants of Adam (Gen. 5 6–31), the death of Noah (Gen. 9 29), the deaths of Shem and his descendants (Gen. 11 11–25), and the death of Terah (Gen. 11 32), Abraham (Gen. 25 7–10), Ishmael (Gen. 25 17), and Isaac (Gen. 35 28,29). It should be realized that this type of exception to a strict chronological arrangement was made so as to present a more orderly description of events, without having to interrupt the narratives subsequently. Similarly, we find the description of Judah's marriage and his relations with Tamar (Gen. 38 1–30) placed separately from the description of Joseph's experiences in Egypt, although the events were contemporaneous, and overlapped timewise in numerous instances. The same is true for the history of Esau and his descendants (Gen. 36 1–30), which overlapped the history of Jacob.

Details of the dates and chronology in Genesis with respect to the Creation and Deluge eras have been previously discussed in sections 1.1 and 1.5. Information in Genesis concerning the time of Abraham and subsequent dated events is presented below.

Abraham was seventy years old when he left Ur-Casdim and seventy-five years old when he left Haran to go to the land of Canaan (Gen. 11 31; 12 1–5; see also section 2.2). Ten years later he married Hagar (Gen. 16 3). Ishmael was born when Abraham was eighty-six (Gen. 16 16). When Abraham was ninety-nine (Gen. 17 1,24) he was told that Isaac would be born, and to circumcize himself and the males in his family. The next year, when Abraham was 100 and his wife Sarah ninety, Isaac was born (Gen. 17 17, 21 5). Thirty-seven years later, Sarah died at the age of 127 (Gen. 23 1). Three years later, when Isaac was forty, he married Rebekah (Gen. 25 20), and when he was sixty, Esau and Jacob were born (Gen. 25 26). Abraham died fifteen years later at the age of 175 (Gen. 25 7). This statement was placed slightly out of place so as not to interrupt the narrative of the history of Jacob. Esau married when he was forty (Gen. 26 34); i.e. when Isaac was 100. At the age of 137, Isaac blessed Jacob and sent him to the house of Laban (Gen. 37,38 5). The age of Jacob was then seventy-seven, based on the statement that Jacob was 130 when Joseph was thirty-nine (Gen. 47 9; 45 6; 41 46), and that Joseph was born fourteen years after arrival of Jacob at house of Laban (Gen. 30 25; 31 41). After twenty years (Gen. 31 41), when he was ninety-seven years old, Jacob took his family and left Laban. At that time, Dinah was six years old. Jacob stayed in Shalem, the city of Shechem (Gen. 33 18) for about six years, until Dinah was about twelve and went out to see the land (Gen. 34 1). At that time Simeon was seventeen and Levi sixteen, and they killed the inhabitants of Shechem (Gen. 34 25). Jacob was then 103 and Isaac 163. About two years later when Jacob was 105, Benjamin was born (Gen. 35 16–18). When Jacob was 108, Joseph who was seventeen was sold into slavery in Egypt (Gen. 37 1,28). Twelve years later when Jacob was 120 and Joseph twenty-nine, Isaac died at the age of 180 (Gen. 35 28). The death of Isaac is placed slightly out of place so as not to interrupt the history of Joseph. The next year, when Joseph was thirty he became renowned in Egypt (Gen. 41 46). Nine years later (Gen. 45 6), when Jacob was 130 (Gen. 47 9), he and his family settled in Egypt. After seventeen years in Egypt, Jacob died at the age of 147 (Gen. 47 28). At that time Joseph was fifty-six. Joseph lived for another fifty-four years until the age of 110 (Gen. 50 26).

In addition to the above chronological analysis of the Book of Genesis, it is possible to pinpoint events in the lives of Joseph and Judah more exactly. Joseph was seventeen years old when sold into slavery (Gen. 37 2). About two years later Joseph was appointed as head of the household of Potiphar (Gen. 39 1–6). Three years later (based on the phrase "after these things" [Gen. 39 7]) when Joseph was twenty-two, he was imprisoned because of the false accusations by Potiphar's wife (Gen. 39 14–20). In about two years, Joseph was made responsible for all the prisoners (Gen. 39 21–23). Three years later (Gen. 40 1) when Joseph was twenty-seven, the royal baker and butler were put in prison for one year. At the age of twenty-eight Joseph correctly interpreted the dreams of these officers. Two years later (Gen. 41 1) when Joseph was thirty (Gen. 41 46), he correctly explained Pharaoh's dream, and was appointed ruler over all Egypt (Gen. 41 41).

In the case of Judah, the events described in Gen. 38 force the following chronology. When Judah was twelve he married the daughter of Shua (Gen. 38 2). The sons Er, Onan, and Shelah were born when Judah was thirteen, fourteen, and fifteen years old, respectively (Gen. 38 3–5). When Er was twelve and Judah twenty-five, Er married Tamar (Gen. 38 6). Shortly thereafter, Er and Onan died (Gen. 38 7,10). When Shelah was twelve years old and Judah twenty-seven (Gen. 38 11,14) Judah had relations with Tamar. The next year, Perez and Zerah were born (Gen. 38 27–30). Perez married when he was twelve and Judah forty. Within two years, Perez fathered Hezron and Hamul (Gen. 46 12). At that time Judah was forty-two, three years older than Joseph who was thirty-nine. This was the year when Jacob and all the family went to live in Egypt.

The preceding detailed analysis of the dates for events described in Genesis is presented to support the general chronological arrangement of the book, and to point out people's ages at the time when key events occurred.

10.2 EXODUS

The Book of Exodus follows that of Genesis, yet there is a time gap of thirty-four years between the death of Joseph (Gen. 50 26) and the beginning of the new

Egyptian dynasty (Ex. 1 8) which enslaved the Israelite people. This time gap between the books probably arose because of the absence of an author to accurately record the events during the interval. Moses, who subsequently was the recorder of the historical events, was not born until fifty-nine years after the death of Joseph. Nevertheless, a few historical details were preserved during the time gap. For example, the length of the life of Levi is given (Ex. 6 16), even though his death occurred after that of Joseph and prior to the birth of Moses. (See section 3.1 for discussion of the chronology.) It is very probable that Moses, after he had matured, acquired the information from personal acquaintances familiar with the details.

The Book of Exodus describes the enslavement of the Israelites by a new Egyptian king; the birth and growth of Moses; how Moses was selected by God as leader of his people; the events leading to the Exodus from Egypt; the receiving of the Ten Commandments at Mount Sinai; and the setting up of the Tabernacle in the desert. From the time of enslavement of the Israelites (1580 B.C.E.) until the completion of the Tabernacle (1473) is a period of 107 years, which would seem to be too long a time to have been described by one person. However, if we take into consideration the fact that the events described prior to the manhood of Moses could have been told him by his parents and sister, then the book could have been written by Moses. In this respect, it should be noted that Moses lived to be 120 years old, and was eighty years at the time of the Exodus (Ex. 7 7).

Authorship

The contents of the Book of Exodus devolve around the life of Moses. Details are given about the birth of Moses, his early manhood, and the revelations from God that he received. Many of these details could have been known only to Moses. Other facts, such as the description of his birth, could have easily been acquired from his immediate family. Therefore, based on content alone, it is clear that Moses was the main author. In addition, several statements specifically mention the writing down by Moses of the details of particular events. Thus Moses is told by God to write down that God will erase the remembrance of Amalek (Ex. 17 14), and to write the words of the covenant (Ex. 34 27). Furthermore, it is stated (Ex. 24 4) that Moses wrote all the words of the Lord.

In addition to the above facts, there is also strong evidence that Joshua was the one who edited the Book of Exodus. The statement (Ex. 16 35) that the manna was eaten for forty years until the people came to the borders of the land of Canaan, could not have been written by Moses, since the manna stopped after his death (Josh. 5 12). The most probable person to have written the sentence therefore is Joshua. Furthermore, the statement in 11 3 that Moses was very great in the eyes of the servants of Pharoah and in the eyes of the people, is unlikely to have been written by Moses since he was a very modest man (Num. 12 3). Probably, this sentence was also written by Joshua.

In addition, the passage of Ex. 33 7–11 may have been added by Joshua. The passage describes how Moses would receive revelations from God at the Tent of Meeting. However, this section is presented before the Tabernacle was built. Furthermore, mention is made of Joshua who ministered to Moses. These points indicate the possibility that this passage is also a later addition by Joshua. It should be noted that here in Ex. 33 7 as well as in Num. 11 24–30 we find that the Tent of Meeting was outside the camp. However in Num. 2 17 it is stated that the Tent of Meeting was in the midst of the camps. Nevertheless, no contradiction exists. "Outside the camp" meant away from where the people lived; "in the midst of the camps" meant that the Tent of Meeting was surrounded by people on all sides, but they were so far away that they were considered as being in another camp.

Naturally, numerous other phrases, words, and sections may have been added or modified by Joshua. One likely possibility is Ex. 34 29–35 which describes how the face of Moses became roughened (קרן) and he therefore had to wear a veil. This passage somewhat interrupts the narrative, and appears to be a later addition. In particular it is mentioned (Ex. 34 29) that Moses did not know that his face was roughened, which would indicate that someone other than Moses wrote the sentence. It should be pointed out however that we could also claim that Moses wrote the sentence later, after realizing what happened. In general it is not now possible to specify all the places in the Book of Exodus where Joshua might have added a section or modified the wording.

ORGANIZATION

The general chronological order of the book, from the enslavement of the Israelites till completion of the Tabernacle, has been indicated in the previous discussions. In a number of cases, however, exact dates are available to show the chronological arrangement in more detail. These cases are as follows.

On the first day of the first month (12 2) God commanded Moses to tell the Israelites to select sheep on the tenth day of the month (12 3), and to keep the animals until the fourteenth day (12 6). The sheep were to be slaughtered that evening (12 9) at the beginning of the fifteenth day. The same night (12 29) the Egyptian first-born died, and Pharaoh allowed the Israelites to leave Egypt in accordance with Moses' previous request (12 31); i.e. to travel three days in the desert to bring sacrifices to God (8 23). On the nineteenth day (allowing three days plus one day of travel) a messenger informed Pharaoh that the Israelites had run away (14 5). The Egyptian army ran after the Israelites and overtook them (14 9), probably at the end of the twentieth day. That night (14 21), the twenty-first day of the month, the Israelites walked over the dried land of the sea. The army of Egypt, which followed in the early morning (14 24), was drowned by the returning waters. The events from the fifteenth day when the Israelites left Egypt until the twenty-first day when the Egyptian army was drowned correspond to the days of the Festival of Matzos (12 18).

After three days of travel in the desert (15 22) the people came to Marah, and afterwards arrived at Elim (15 27). On the fifteenth day of the second month they reached the Desert of Sin (16 1). There they stayed for about a week or more, and the supply of manna began (16 26). The Israelites then travelled to Rephidim (17 1). They finally reached the Desert of Sinai on the first day of the third month (19 1,2).

That very day Moses alternately spoke to God and to the Israelites, and Moses told the people to prepare for the third day (19 15). On the third day of the third month (19 16) God spoke the Ten Commandments. The next day (24 4,12) Moses went near the mountain and stayed there for six complete days (24 16). On the tenth day of the month Moses went up the mountain, and was on the mountain for forty days (24 18), until the twentieth day of the fourth month. When he came down he discovered that the people had made a golden calf. The next day (32 30) Moses told the people they had sinned greatly. The following day (34 2,4) on the twenty-second day of the fourth month, Moses again went up the mountain. There he stayed for forty days (34 28), until the third day of the sixth month. Then Moses commanded the people to begin construction of the Tabernacle (35 4–20). Slightly less than six months later, on the first day of the first month of the second year in the desert (40 1,17), the Tabernacle was completed.

Although the Book of Exodus in general is arranged according to chronological order, there are many sections which are not placed in their correct chronological position because of logical considerations. The first such case is the listing of genealogies relevant to Moses and Aaron (Ex. 6 14–28). This listing is there presented so as to not interrupt the ensuing narrative concerning the ten plagues and also to precede the mention of the ages of Moses and Aaron (7 7). Since this genealogical section interrupts the narrative, a concise summary of 6 2,10–12 is presented in 6 29,30 so as to bring the reader back to the main topic.

A second case occurs in Chapter 11. In the middle of a conversation between Moses and Pharaoh (10 24–11 9) there is inserted a message from God to Moses (11 1–3). Undoubtedly this message was received by Moses prior to his meeting with Pharaoh, but was inserted in the middle of the conversation because of the relevance of the topic to the next statement by Moses (11 4–9) concerning the plague of the first-born.

Another exception to chronological order is found in 16 32–34 where mention is made that a jar full of manna was placed before the Testimony (the Tablets on which were written the Ten Commandments). Now the Tablets of the Testimony were not obtained until afterwards (32 15; 34 29). Furthermore, in 16 35 it is stated that the manna was eaten for forty years. These statements at the end of Chapter 16 were undoubtedly written afterwards, but were placed here for continuity of the story about the manna.

The most significant deviation from chronological order occurs in 18 1–27 where the visit of Jethro, the brother-in-law* of Moses, is described. This visit occurred when the Israelites were in the desert near the mount of God (**18** 5). However, they did not reach the desert of Sinai where the mount of God was located until later. Thus in **17** 8 the Amalekites fought the Israelites in Rephidim, and in **19** 1,2 it is stated that the Israelites left Rephidim and arrived in the desert of Sinai. Furthermore, shortly after Jethro arrived, Moses was informing the people of the laws of God (**18** 16). This probably refers to the laws received on the mount of God, which are described later (**20** 1–14; **21** 1–**23** 33). In addition, Jethro brought sacrifices (**18** 12) without mention of building an altar, indicating that the event was after the altar of the people (Lev. **9** 1–24) was built and used (i.e. after the eighth day of the first month of the second year). The actual date for the visit of Jethro can be delimited even further. In Deut. **1** 6–9 it is stated that the appointment of judges, as suggested by Jethro in Ex. **18** 14, occurred shortly before leaving Horeb (i.e. the desert of Sinai). Now, the Israelites left the desert of Sinai on the twentieth of the second month of the second year (Num. **10** 11,12). Hence we can conclude that Jethro's visit occurred sometime between the eighth day of the first month and the twentieth day of the second month of the second year in the desert. The reason the section concerning Jethro's visit is placed out of chronological order is the emphasis during his visit on the miracles performed by God against the Egyptians (**18** 1,8–11), which were described in detail in the Book of Exodus. However, the correct place chronologically for describing the visit of Jethro would probably be somewhere in the middle of the Book of Leviticus, or near the beginning of the Book of Numbers.

A minor case where chronological order is not perfectly followed occurs in **32** 1–6, where it is described how the people and Aaron formed a golden calf while Moses was on the mount of God. In actuality, the preparations for worshipping the golden calf took at least two days (**32** 5,6), and therefore overlapped some of the laws told by God to Moses. However, for simplicity of presentation the events concerning the construction of the golden calf are not intermingled with the laws presented to Moses.

A sixth case where chronological order is not followed occurs in **33** 7–11, where it is described how Moses set the Tent of Meeting outside the camp. Now the Tent of Meeting was not completed until over a half-year later (Chapter 40). The section about the Tent of Meeting is placed here because of its relevance to the statement in **33** 5 that if God goes in the midst of the people, He will destroy them. As a result, although it occurred over a half-year later, Moses set the Tent of Meeting outside the camp so that the people would not be destroyed. Because of the connection of this act of Moses (**33** 7) with God's statement (**33** 5), the section concerning the Tent of Meeting is not in chronological order.

---

* The Hebrew word חתן, usually translated "father-in-law" actually means a "male related by marriage." Jethro was the brother-in-law and Reul the father-in-law of Moses (see **2** 18; **3** 1).

Laws Given on the Mountain of Sinai
The information contained in the Book of Exodus allows the specification of which laws were received on Mount Sinai. Initially God spoke the Ten Commandments from Mount Sinai to the people of Israel (20 1-14). Then Moses approached the darkness of the mountain (20 18), and was told the laws contained in 20 19-23 33, which are mainly concerned with regulations between man and man (משפטים). These regulations were written down by Moses (24 4) and were called the Book of the Covenant (24 7).

Moses then went up Mount Sinai (24 12) for forty days to receive the stone tablets, the laws (תורה), and the commandments (מצוה) which God wrote. It is explicitly stated in numerous other places that God wrote the words found on the tablets (31 18; 32 15,16; 34 1,28). Furthermore, it is indicated that the laws (תורה), and the commandments (מצוה) were written by God (24 12; 32 32, 33). The term "book" is used in 32 32,33 and refers to the sections Ex. 25 1-31 17 concerning the building of the Tabernacle, and Lev. 6 1-7 38 concerning the sacrificial rules. The former is called the "commandments" as indicated by use of the term "command" (תצוה) (Ex. 27 20); and the latter is called the law (תורה) as stated in Lev. 7 37,38. When Moses descended from the mountain after his first forty-day stay there, he brought down not only the tablets on which were written the Ten Commandments, but also a written record of Ex. 25 1-31 17 and Lev. 6 1-7 38.

A day later Moses went near the mountain to request atonement from God for the people's sins (32 30,31); and the next day Moses went up the mountain for a second stay of forty days (34 28). During this second stay Moses received a duplicate copy of the Ten Commandments, as well as a written copy of Ex. 34 5-26; Lev. 25 1-26 46; and Lev. 27 1-34. The section Ex. 34 5-26 is concerned with miscellaneous laws dealing with conquest of the land of Israel, monotheism, and the festivals, and was written down by Moses (34 27). The other two sections were not included in the Book of Exodus because their contents were not relevant to the construction of the Tabernacle. Thus Lev. 25 1-26 46 deals with the laws of the Sabbatical and Jubilee years, and the dire punishment awaiting the people if they do not observe the laws. The other section in Leviticus (27 1-34), deals with vows and gifts to the sanctuary. These sections were added as an appendix to the Book of Leviticus, since they are mainly concerned with laws which apply in the Land of Israel. It is not specified whether these sections in Leviticus were initially written by God, or told orally to Moses and then written down by Moses.

When Moses came down after his second stay on Mount Sinai, he carried out the commandments concerning the construction of the Tabernacle (Ex. 35 1-39 43). The Book of Exodus ends with the completion of the Tabernacle.

FULFILLMENT BY GOD OF HIS PROMISE TO ABRAHAM, ISAAC, AND, JACOB

Incorrect conclusions have been drawn by Biblical critics concerning God's names from the passage Ex. 6 2-8, where God states to Moses "I am YHWH; and I appeared to Abraham, Isaac and Jacob as God Almighty, but by My name YHWH I made Me not known to them...." In actuality what the passage states is as follows: Although when I appeared to Abraham, Isaac, and Jacob using the name God Almighty I did not use the name YHWH; still I, who am called YHWH, will carry out that covenant to provide them with the Land of Canaan.

Support for this interpretation is gained from Gen. **17** 1, **28** 3, **35** 11 and **48** 3 where God appears to Abraham, Isaac, and Jacob using the name God Almighty (and not the name YHWH) to tell them that they would inherit the land of Canaan. It is clearly not the intention of the text to imply that the name YHWH was completely unknown to Abraham, Isaac, and Jacob, since, for example, Abraham calls the mountain of Moriah "YHWH will see " (Gen. **22** 14), and in Gen. **15** 7, God states to Abraham "I am YHWH who has taken you out from Ur of the Chaldees."

10.3 LEVITICUS

The Book of Leviticus relates laws mainly concerned with the bringing of sacrifices, sanctification of the priests, and requirements for purity. These laws were, in general, told to Moses shortly after erection of the Tabernacle, since they were necessary for the proper performance of the sacrificial procedures. A few historical events are also described, such as the initiation of Aaron and his sons as priests (**8** 1-**9** 24), the deaths of Nadab and Abihu (**10** 1-20), and the punishment of the blasphemer of God (**24** 10-23).

ORGANIZATION

Most of the events described in the Book of Leviticus occurred within one month's time, and are arranged in chronological order. The book begins immediately after the completion of the Tabernacle on the first day of the first month of the second year (Ex. **40** 2, 17); describes the initiation procedure for the priests on the eighth day of the month (Lev. **9** 1); and ends before the first day of the second month of the second year, the time at which the Book of Numbers begins (Num. **1** 1). Only a few accounts in Leviticus, such as the laws written in Lev. **6** 1-**7** 38; **25** 1-**26** 46; and **27** 1-34, were presented previously to Moses. The regulations in Lev. **6** 1-**7** 38 give the details for bringing the different sacrifices, and were told to Moses on his first forty-day stay on Mount Sinai. However, as stated in Lev. **7** 38, these regulations were told by Moses to the Israelites after the completion of the Tabernacle. The contents of the passage were placed immediately after Lev. **1** 1-**5** 26 because both sections are concerned with the laws for the different sacrifices.

The regulations in Lev. 25 1–26 46, concerning the Sabbatical and Jubilee years, as well as the rewards for observance, and the punishments for non-observance of the laws, were most probably told Moses on his second forty-day stay on Mount Sinai (26 46). Also the regulations in Lev. 27 1–34, concerning vows to the sanctuary, were received by Moses at the same time (27 34). These regulations mainly apply only in the Land of Israel, and were stated with the implication that although the Israelites had sinned by worshipping a golden calf still they would arrive safely and settle in the land. However, if they then sinned they would be severely punished and even exiled. Since these regulations were not particularly relevant to the immediate problems in the desert they were placed not in chronological order in the Book of Exodus but as an appendix to the Book of Leviticus. Then follows the Book of Numbers which describes the events leading to the settlement in the land of Israel.

The section 16 1–17 6 was also not placed in chronological order. As stated in 16 1, the subsequent laws were told to Moses by God after the death of Nadab and Abihu, the two sons of Aaron. Most probably, the laws that are placed out of order are 16 1–17 16, which contain phrases such as "he (the high priest) shall atone for himself and his household" (16 6), and "Speak to Aaron and his sons" (17 2). For Moses to relate such statements immediately after the deaths of two of Aaron's sons would be a cruel act. Instead, Moses delayed in telling these laws until later when some of the agony of the deaths would have abated. These laws were then placed according to the date when Moses related the laws rather than on the date when the laws were told to Moses. It should be noted that if the section 16 1–17 16 was in its proper place, there would be a significant improvement in the logical arrangement of the laws. The order of the text would then be 10 1–20; 16 1–34; 17 1–16; 11 1–47; 12 1–15 33; 18 1–30. The logical connection between these passages is shown in Table 10.3.1.

In addition to the previously mentioned cases, it is also possible that the section (24 10–23) about the blasphemer of God is not in chronological order. The section may be considered as an appendix to the Book of Leviticus, placed prior to the other appendices received by Moses on Mount Sinai (25 1–27 34). Alternatively, the story of the blasphemer of God may have occurred shortly before the first day of the second month of the second year (Num. 1 1), and therefore may be in its correct chronological place.

AUTHORSHIP

No explicit mention is made as to who wrote down any of the sections in the Book of Leviticus. However, since all the laws in the book were told to Moses by God, and since Moses was involved in all the described events, it is obvious that Moses was the author. Furthermore there are no passages or sentences in the book that need be ascribed to someone other than Moses, and it is therefore possible that Moses was the final editor. Nevertheless, since we have established that Joshua

Table 10.3.1
Logical Arrangement of Topics in Leviticus
Obtained by Modifying Position of 16 1–17 16.

Passage	Contents
10 1–20	Deaths of Nadab and Abihu for bringing an unprescribed sacrifice
16 1–34	The high priest should come into the Holy of Holies only once a year, and should bring prescribed sacrifices
17 1–16	All sacrifices should only be brought in front of the Tabernacle; also, do not eat blood, nor animals which die by themselves, or that are torn by beasts
11 1–47	Laws as to which animals, fish, fowl, and insects may be eaten, and related purity laws
12 1–15 33	Impurity laws concerning a woman after childbirth, a leper and leprous objects; also impurity laws if a man has an issue from his flesh, or a flow of semen, or a woman has an issue of blood
18 1–30	Restrictions on sexual intimacies, such as between certain relatives, and certain types of sexual perversions

edited the Books of Exodus, Numbers, and Deuteronomy, it is possible that Joshua also edited the Book of Leviticus.

10.4 NUMBERS

The Book of Numbers contains historical details concerning the travels and tribulations of the Israelites in the desert after the setting up of the Tabernacle. Information is contained about such events as the first (1 1–4 49) and second (26 1–51) census of the people; the sending of spies to investigate the land of Canaan (13 1–14 45); the rebellion of Korah (16 1–17 15); the deaths of Miriam (20 1) and Aaron (20 22–29); the conquests by Israel of the Canaanites (21 1–3), Amorites (21 21–32), people of Bashan (21 33–35), and Midianites (31 1–54); the blessings by Balaam (22 2–24 25); the appointment of Joshua as successor to Moses (27 15–23); and the itinerary of the travels in the desert (33 1–49).

In addition the book contains laws dealing with many subjects, such as numerous cases where special sacrifices are involved (5 11–31; 6 1–21; 7 1–89; 8 5–22; 9 9–14; 15 1–16; 15 22–31; 19 1–22; 28 1–30 1); the phrases to be used by priests in blessing the people (6 22–27); the procedure for lighting the lamps (8 1–4); the uses of the two silver trumpets (10 1–10); setting of fringes in the corners of garments (15 37–41); portions allotted for the priests and levites (18 8–32); method of division of the land (26 52–56); inheritance laws for daughters (27 1–11; 36 1–13); regulations concerning vows (30 2–17); boundaries of the land of Israel (34 1–15); and refuge cities for those who kill by accident (35 9–34).

As indicated by the above brief summary, there is a great diversity of material within the text, much greater than in the Book of Leviticus. This greater diversity corresponds to the longer historical period covered by the Book of Numbers.

ORGANIZATION

The Book of Numbers begins with the first day of the second month of the second year after the Exodus (Num. 1 1), and covers the period until the first day of the eleventh month of the fortieth year (Deut. 1 3). No details are given of events from the third to the end of the thirty-ninth year, except for such facts as the places in the desert where the Israelites camped (Num. 33).

The book is arranged in chronological order. However numerous exceptions occur to maintain a logical narrative. These exceptions mainly involve the presentation of background information to the topics under consideration. Thus, the genealogy of the priests is given in 3 1 as of the time when Moses was on Mount Sinai, i.e. in the third month of the first year. Then is mentioned (3 4) the death of two of the sons of Aaron, which we know from Lev. 9 1–10 7 occurred on the eighth day of the first month of the second year. Hence the genealogies presented refer to events prior to the beginning of the Book of Numbers (1 1), i.e. prior to the first day of the second month of the second year. However, the genealogies of the priests are presented as background information to the initiation of the Levites, where the priests Aaron and his sons are mentioned (3 9,10).

A second case occurs in 7 1, where the date of the setting-up of the Tabernacle is given. From Ex. 40 17 this event is known to have occurred on the first day of the first month of the second year, which is one month prior to the date given in the beginning of the book (1 1). However, this early date is supplied as background to the offerings by the princes of the tribes (7 12–89). These offerings were brought beginning with the first day of the second month and completed on the twelfth day, which is subsequent to the book's beginning. It should be noted that the offerings of the princes could not have been brought until after the inauguration of the priests on the eighth day of the first month. Since the offerings were brought from the first to the twelfth days, it is implied that the offerings were begun on the first day of the second month and completed on the twelfth day.

A third example where events are not in perfect chronological order occurs in

9 1–8. Moses is told the laws of Passover on the first day of the first month of the second year (**9 1**), so that the Passover sacrifice would be brought on the fourteenth day of the first month (**9 3,5**). These dates are prior to the beginning of the book. The laws, however, are given as background for observance, by persons who were impure, of the Passover sacrifice on the fourteenth of the second month (**9 9–14**), which is thirteen days after the time at the beginning of the book.

Still another case occurs in **9 15**, where the event of setting-up the Tabernacle is mentioned, which we know from Ex. **40 17** to have occurred on the first day of the first month of the second year, one month prior to the time at the beginning of the book. The passage (**9 15–23**), however, describes the cloud over the Tabernacle, and is background information (along with **10 1–10**) for **10 11**, where it is mentioned that the cloud moved from the Tabernacle on the twentieth day of the second month, nineteen days after the time at the beginning of the book.

Thus we find that the key dates mentioned at the beginning of Numbers are as follows:

| | | Date from Exodus | |
Reference	Day	Month	Year
1 1	1	2	2
7 12–89	1–12	2	2
9 9–14	14	2	2
10 11	20	2	2

These dates are obviously in chronological order. As previously explained, the other dates which refer to earlier events are supplied as background material, and are only mentioned incidentally.

The Book of Numbers then proceeds in clear chronological order. The Israelites travelled from the desert of Sinai on the twentieth of the second month of the second year (**10 11**). They travelled for three days (**10 33**), and then ate meat for thirty days (**11 20**). Afterwards they journeyed to Hazeroth (**11 35**) where the people waited for seven days until Miriam recovered from leprousy (**12 15**). Then the people journeyed to the desert of Paran (**12 16**). Based on the previously presented information, the Israelites would have reached Paran on the first day of the fourth month at the earliest. Shortly thereafter, spies were sent out to investigate the land of Canaan. It was then the time of the beginning of the ripening of grapes (**13 20**), which dates the events within about two weeks before or after the beginning of the fifth month. Forty days later (**13 25**) the spies returned. Afterwards are described the unsuccessful fight against Amalek (14 45); the death of the man who gathered wood on the Sabbath (15 32-36); and the rebellion by Korah, Dathan, and Abiram (16 1-17 5). The rebellion by Korah was sometime shortly after the event of the spies, since mention is made that the people will die in the desert and not arrive in the land of Canaan (16 13,14). This sorrowful information was first stated after the expedition of the spies (14 29). Events occurring in the second year of the desert are completed with God telling Moses and Aaron the laws concerning purification with the ashes from the red heifer (19 1-22).

It should be noted that the regulations about the ashes of the red heifer are not out of place chronologically. These laws were first told to Moses sometime near the end of the second year. The prior use of the term "water of purification" (מי חטאת) (8 7) in connection with purification of the Levites refers to sprinkling of ordinary water on the Levites, and not to the use of "water of sprinkling" (מי נדה) (19 9,13,20,21) as in the case of the red heifer. This distinction is clear not only because of the use of different terms, but also because the "water of sprinkling" requires seven days for completion (19 12), which was not the case when the Levites were purified (8 5-22). In contrast, when the people and booty were purified after the conquest of Midian, the term "water of sprinkling" was used (מי נדה) (31 23), and mention is also made that it takes seven days for purification (31 19,24). Prior to the giving of the regulations concerning the ashes of the red heifer, a person who touched a dead body was considered impure (Lev. 22 4-7; Num. 5 2; 6 9; 9 6), but no purification procedure was specified.

Between the end of Chapter 19 and the beginning of Chapter 20 there is a skip of thirty-seven years to the first month of the fortieth year (20 1). This thirty-seven-year gap arises because few, if any, laws were given then; and few historical events of significance occurred then. Originally God intended that the Israelites be in the desert for only about two years. However, because of the sin of the spies, the people were required to stay forty years in the desert (14 33). Nevertheless, there was no corresponding increase in the number of laws received by Moses from God, and hence a resultant time-gap in the text of thirty-seven years.

Passages subsequent to 20 1 appear to be in perfect chronological order. Thus the deaths of Miriam and Aaron, the conquest of countries in Transjordan, the blessings by Balaam, the second census of the people, the writing by Moses of the itinerary of the journeys, as well as other specified events and laws all occurred in the fortieth year in the desert. The death of Aaron (20 28) is one event which can be precisely dated, as occurring on the first day of the fifth month of the fortieth year, as stated indirectly in 33 38. In this connection it should be noted that several past events, such as the escape of the Israelites from Egypt (33 3,4), the death of Aaron (33 38), and the encounter with the King of Arad (33 40), are mentioned indirectly when listing the places of travel of the Israelites (33 1–49). Similarly, several past events such as the rebellion by Korah, Dathan, and Abiram (26 9–11), and the death of Nadab and Abihu, the sons of Aaron (26 61), are mentioned indirectly when tabulating the results of the census (26 1–65).

AUTHORSHIP

Nearly the entire Book of Numbers describes episodes in which Moses was involved, or relates laws told to Moses by God. In many of these cases Moses was the only one who would have known the information, and it is therefore obvious that Moses was the main author of the Book of Numbers. Furthermore, it is explicitly stated (33 2) that Moses wrote the places of travel of the Israelites (33 1–49) by the commandment of God. There are, however, two cases in which Moses was not directly involved. Firstly, the laws concerning the priests and Levites, presented in 18 1–24, are stated to have been told by God only to Aaron, and not to Moses. It is very probable, however, that Aaron subsequently told these laws to Moses, and then Moses incorporated these laws in the Book of Numbers. Secondly, the problem arises as to who wrote down the section concerning the blessings by Balaam (22 2–24 25). The events described were completely independent of the Israelites. The probable answer is that Balaam wrote an account of the events, which was subsequently discovered by the Israelites in their successful attack on Midian (31 1–12). It is specifically mentioned (31 8) that Balaam was killed at that time. Moses subsequently edited the writings of Balaam, and placed them in their proper chronological position. In particular, Moses connected the plague of Peor with the incident of Balaam (31 16), and therefore placed the story of Balaam just prior to the description of the plague of Peor (25 1–9).

There are, however, many sentences in the Book of Numbers which imply that someone other than Moses, such as Joshua, was the final editor of the book. The statement (12 3) that Moses was the most modest man on earth is a paradox if Moses wrote it. How could a truly modest man write how modest he is? It must, therefore, be assumed that Joshua subsequently added the sentence for clarification. Another example is the passage (10 35,36) stating the phrase used by Moses when the Ark was carried and when it was set down. The passage, which appears to have been added as an afterthought, is enclosed between two inverted Hebrew letters *nun*. Now Joshua's father's name was Nun, and very probably the inverted letters are to let us know that the sentences were written by Joshua.

A third section possibly written by Joshua is 9 15–23, which explains how the position of the cloud over the Tabernacle was the signal for travelling or camping. As explained previously, this section is not in chronological order. Furthermore, this section is a later addition since it mentions cases when the cloud was over the Tabernacle for a year or more (9 22). Yet in a following passage (10

11) the date is given as the twentieth day of the second month of the second year, which is less than two months after the construction of the Tabernacle. It should be noted that this passage has similarities to the passage Ex. 33 7–11 which also mentions the cloud over the Tabernacle, and which we have considered as probably written by Joshua. The sum total of these factors provides a strong possibility that 9 15–23 was authored by Joshua.

Other probable additions by Joshua are 32 34–42 and 36 10–12. In 32 34–42 are mentioned the cities built by the tribes of Gad, Reuben, and Manasseh. Now, they received the land in the last half-year of the life of Moses, and it is improbable that all the cities named were built before Moses died. Similarly, in 36 10–12 it is mentioned that the five daughters of Zelophehad married within the tribe of Manasseh, as Moses commanded. Now, there probably was at least a four-year difference in age between the youngest and oldest daughters; and probably the youngest daughter had not yet matured. Hence the youngest girl would not have married until several years after the death of Moses. Thus both of these passages contain information which occurred after Moses' death, and therefore the passages were probably added by Joshua.

MALE POPULATION OF THE ISRAELITES IN THE DESERT
The number of the males over twenty years old was found to be 603,550 during the second half of the first year in the desert (Ex. 38 26; 40 2). The exact same number 603,550, was obtained from a census conducted on the first day of the second month of the second year (Num. 1 1,45,46). At first it seems surprising that the numbers were identical even though obtained in different years. In between the two counts occurred the first day of the first month when all people became one year older (see Section 1.5). Thus the number of male deaths between the times of the counts must have been just compensated by the number of males reaching twenty years of age.

In actuality, however, the fact that the numbers are identical is not surprising. Firstly, the initial count is based on the collection of half-shekels (Ex. 30 11–16; 38 26), which probably occurred shortly after Moses came down from Mount Sinai for the second time; i.e. in the beginning of the sixth month of the first year (see Exodus, Organization, Section 10.2). The second count occurred in the second month of the second year, or about eight months later. Secondly, about thirty-eight and one-half years later, in the fortieth year in the desert, the census of the male population over twenty years was 601,730 (Num. 26 2,51). Thus there was a change of only 1,820 (603,550–601,730) in the count in thirty-eight and one-half years, or on the average a decrease of only forty-seven people per year. Thirdly the number 603,550 is rounded off to the nearest fifty (or even to the nearest 100), as is evident from the fact that none of the numbers for the individual tribes (Num. 1) is more exact than to the nearest fifty; and in only one case is it more exact than to the nearest 100 (Num. 1 25). It can thus be seen that it is quite likely that in an eight-month period, the number of males over twenty years of age might not change by a sufficiently large number to change the rounded-off number of 603,550.

In this connection it should be noted that the census in the second month of the second year did not include the Levites (1 49), and it therefore must be assumed that the number 603,550 obtained in the count of the first year also did not include the Levites.

10.5 DEUTERONOMY

The Book of Deuteronomy mainly describes the occurrences during the last thirty-six days of the life of Moses. During that time Moses presented to the Israelites a code of law (5 2–28 69) which supplemented the laws previously given in the desert. Prior to presenting the code, Moses recounted the historical background for the code (1 6–4 40). We also find that Moses taught a historical song (32 1–43) to the people; and shortly before his death, he blessed the tribes (33 1–29). In addition to these messages by Moses, the Book of Deuteronomy relates such events as the setting aside of cities of refuge (4 41–43), the appointment of Joshua as the future leader (31 7,8,14,23), and the death of Moses (34 1–12).

The period of time covered by the Book of Deuteronomy can be calculated from the dates of the first and last mentioned events of the book. The last mentioned event of the book can be dated from the statement in Josh. 4 19 that the Israelites crossed the Jordan on the tenth day of the first month. The crossing occurred three days after Joshua received the command from God (Josh. 1 2,11; 3 2). Based on Deut. 34 8 we know that this command was received a minimum of thirty days after the death of Moses. Hence, the latest possible date for Moses' death is the sixth day of the twelfth month of the fortieth year in the desert (assuming a twenty-nine day month); and the contents of Deuteronomy describe events that occurred through the seventh day of the first month of the forty-first year. The date of the first mentioned event of the Book of Deuteronomy, i.e. the time of the first discourse by Moses, is specifically given as the first day of the eleventh month of the fortieth year (1 3). Thus the entire book covers a period of at most two months and six days; and if the last five sentences of Deuteronomy are excluded, the book covers a time span of only thirty-six days.

Organization

The available evidence indicates that the Book of Deuteronomy is arranged in chronological order. As explained previously, the book begins with the first discourse of Moses on the first day of the eleventh month of the fortieth year; continues until the death of Moses on the sixth day of the twelfth month; and is completed with the end of the thirty-day mourning period. Even though no other specific dates can be derived, still the text shows a general chronological arrangement. Initially, in the first discourse (1 6–4 40), Moses presented a historical background to the code of law. In particular, it is stated that Moses first clarified the law-code (באר את התורה הזאת) (1 5). Afterwards, in the second discourse he related the laws in the code (וזאת התורה אשר שם משה) (4 44). The code is presented in section 4 44 to 28 69. A covenant was then made between God and Israel based on the law-code (29 1–30 20). Subsequently, Moses wrote down the law-code (31 19,22), and spoke the words of the song to the people (31 30–32 45). God then commanded Moses to go up Mount Nebo where he would die (32 48–52). Before obeying God's command, Moses blessed the Israelites (33 1–29). Then he went up the mountain and died (34 1–8). The book ends with Joshua assuming leadership over the people (34 9–12).

Only the section 31 24–29 is slightly out of place chronologically. The section states that after Moses wrote down the law-code he commanded the Levites to place the written law-code next to the Ark. This section should be placed after 31 13, before the introduction to the historical song (31 14–23). However, we find in this misplaced section the phrase "and call heaven and earth to witness" (31 28). This phrase is similar to that found at the beginning of the song, "Give ear you heavens, . . . and let the earth hear." Because of the similarity, the section 31 24–29 was placed immediately preceding the song (32 1–43).

It should be noted that the term "this law (התורה הזאת) which occurs numerous times in Deuteronomy (1 5; 4 8,44; 17 18,19; 27 3,8,26; 28 58,61; 29 20,28; 30 10; 31 9,11,12,24,26; 32 46), refers to the second discourse (4 44–28 69), and includes the blessings and curses specified in 27 11–28 68. The command by Moses to the people (27 1–8) to write the law-code on big rocks; the orders by Moses and the priests to obey the laws (27 9,10); and the command by Moses to the people to stand on the mountains of Gerizim and Ebal (27 11–13), should not be construed as indicating the end of the second discourse, but as minor pauses necessary to properly convey certain laws.

AUTHORSHIP
In numerous instances the authorship of particular sections is attributed to Moses. The first discourse (1 6–4 40) is clearly stated to have been spoken by Moses (1 5). The second discourse (5 1–28 68) is also presented as a speech by Moses (5 1). Furthermore it is specifically mentioned (31 9,24) that he wrote down the law-code, i.e. the contents of the second discourse. The third discourse (29 1–30 20), where the covenant between God and Israel is described, is stated to have been spoken by Moses (29 1); as well as other specific commands, such as 31 1–6; 31 7–8; 31 10–13; 31 23; and 31 26–29. Next we find that the historical song (32 1–43) was spoken by Moses (31 30; 32 44,45), and also written down by him (31 22). Finally, the blessing of the people of Israel (33 2–29) is stated to have been spoken by Moses. Thus nearly the entire Book of Deuteronomy was the composition of Moses.

Nevertheless, the last eight sentences of Deuteronomy could not have been written by Moses, since they describe events after his death. We must therefore say that Joshua completed the Book of Deuteronomy. Furthermore, it is quite probable that much of the introductory material and explanatory sentences were written by Joshua, especially when we consider that much of the book describes events which happened only a few days before Moses died. It thus seems logical to assume that Joshua compiled the book into its present form, even though the main contents were stated, and often written down, by Moses. Some sections probably added by Joshua are: the introduction to the first discourse (1 1-5); the introduction to the second discourse (4 41-49); and the concluding chapter describing the death of Moses (34 1-12). It should be pointed out that at the end of the book Joshua probably went up Mount Nebo with Moses, for otherwise how would it be known what parts of the land of Canaan were shown to Moses, what was said to him before his death, and the approximate place where he was buried (see 34 1-6)? It should also be realized that numerous explanatory phrases, such as **27** 1,9,11; **29** 1; **31** 1,7,9,22,24,25,30; **32** 44,45; **33** 1, may have been added by Joshua also.

10.6 EARLY NAMES OF THE BOOKS OF THE PENTATEUCH

In numerous places in the Bible reference is made to particular books of the Pentateuch. Genesis is called "The [Book of the] Law of God"; Exodus is called "The [Book of the] Law of the Lord"; Leviticus is called "The Law of Moses, the Man of God"; Numbers is called "The Law of Moses, the Servant of God"; and Deuteronomy is called "The [Book of the] Law of Moses." Because of the similarity of the names used to specify the different books, these identifications have been completely overlooked by all commentaries. In Table 10.6.1 are presented the cases in the Bible where these names are used, and the cited phrases from the Pentateuch when quotations are given. In general, the persons who quoted from the Pentateuch did not strive for exactness, and therefore slight variations in wording occur between the original and the quoted text. This in no way detracts from the fact that statements in the Pentateuch are being cited.

The selection of the particular names for the different books can be explained as follows: Genesis is called "The Book of the Law of *God*" because of the emphasis on the name God (*Elokim*) in the text. Thus, in the description of the creation of the world (Gen. 1 1-2 3) only the name *Elokim* is used. Furthermore, throughout the book the name *Elokim* is mentioned about 170 times, and the book concludes with a reference to *Elokim* (50 25).

Exodus is similarly called "The Book of the Law of the *Lord*" because of the emphasis on the name Lord (YHWH) throughout the book. Thus, in Ex. **6** 2 God tells Moses "I am the Lord," and in Ex. **20** 2, the Ten Commandments begin with the phrase "I am the Lord thy God." In addition the name Lord is used in the book about 350 times; and most statements from God to Moses begin in the book with a phrase such as "and the Lord spoke to Moses." It should be noted, for comparison, that the name *Elokim* is used only about sixty times in Exodus, while the name Lord is used about 150 times in Genesis.

In Leviticus we find the interesting fact that throughout the book Moses is told (about twenty-five times) numerous messages by God to relate to either the Israelites or the priests. For example, in Lev. 1 1,2 God tells Moses to speak to the Israelites. We thus find that Moses is the intermediary between God and the people, and can therefore be considered "the Man of God." A suitable title for Leviticus is then "The Law of Moses, the Man of God."

On the other hand, in Numbers we find that most of the messages from God to Moses involve actions to be performed. For example in Num. 1 1,2, Moses is told to count the population. Thus we find Moses acting as the servant of God, in following God's instructions. A suitable title for Numbers is therefore "the Law of Moses, the Servant of God."

The style of Deuteronomy is somewhat different from that of the previous books. We do not find it stated that God spoke to Moses. Rather, Moses speaks to the people seemingly on his own initiative; although naturally the laws were communicated to him by God. The book consists dominantly of speeches by Moses to the Israelites. A suitable title for Deuteronomy is therefore "the Book of the Law of Moses."

According to the above explanations, the early names for the books of the Pentateuch were based on prominent characteristics, rather than on the author. Nevertheless, the presence of the name Moses in three of the titles, surely does not contradict our conclusion that Moses was the main author of Exodus, Leviticus, Numbers, and Deuternomy.

In addition to the above-listed names, reference is made to Deuteronomy or parts thereof, by such titles as "Copy of the Law of Moses" (משנה תורת משה), "the Book of the Covenant," "Book of the Law of the Lord given by Moses," and "This Book of the Law." Furthermore, the Book of Leviticus is once referred to by the phrase "The Law that the Lord had Commanded by Moses." A summary of these and similar cases are presented in Table 10.6.2.

Awareness of the names used in the Bible to refer to the different books of the Pentateuch helps explain several otherwise difficult passages.

Joshua is stated to have written down the covenant of the people to worship God, in the "Book of the law of God" (Josh. 24 26), i.e. in Genesis. Joshua recorded the event in this book, because of the emphasis in the passage on historical events mentioned in the Book of Genesis (Josh. 24 2-4,14,15), such as reference to Abraham, Isaac, and Jacob.

The book of the law found at the time of King Josiah (II Kings 22 8-23 24; II Chr. 34 14-33) is described by various names such as "the Book of the Covenant," "Copy of the Law of Moses," "Book of the Law of the Lord given by Moses," and "This book of the Law." As substantiated in Table 10.6.2, these

Table 10.6.1
Titles Used in the Bible for the Books of the Pentateuch

Title Used	Reference	Phrase Used	Reference Quoted	Phrase Quoted
For Genesis:				
In the book of the Law of God	Josh. 24 26			
In the book, in the Law of God	Neh. 8 8			
In the book of the Law of God	Neh. 8 18			
The Law of God	Neh. 10 29			
For Exodus:				
In the Law of the Lord, the God of Israel.	II Kings 10 31	The sins of Jeroboam, wherewith he made Israel to sin	Ex. 32 31	This people have sinned a great sin, and have made them a god of gold
The Law of the Lord	Ezra 7 10	To teach in Israel statutes and ordinances	Ex. 15 25	He made for them a statute and an ordinance
In the book of the Law of the Lord their God	Neh. 9 3			
In the Law of the Lord	I Chr. 16 40	To offer burnt-offerings unto the Lord upon the	Ex. 29 38, 39, 42	Upon the altar . . . continually . . . the one

		altar of burnt-offering continually morning and evening		lamb you shall offer in the morning, and the other lamb you shall offer in the evening... a continual burnt-offering
The Law of the Lord thy God	I Chr. 22 12, 13	Observe to do the statutes and the ordinances	Ex. 15 25	He made for them a statute and an ordinance
The Law of the Lord	II Chr. 12 1 (I Kings 14 23)	(They also built them high places and pillars, and Asherim)	Ex. 34 13	You shall break down their altars, and dash in pieces their pillars, and you shall cut down their Asherim
The book of the Law of the Lord	II Chr. 17 9			
Written in the Law of the Lord	II Chr. 31 3, 4	The king's portion of his substance for the burnt-offerings	Ex. 10 25	You (Pharaoh) must also give into our hand sacrifices and burnt-offerings, that we may sacrifice unto the Lord our God
Written in the Law of the Lord	II Chr. 35 26			
For Leviticus: As it is written in the Law of Moses the man of God	Ezra 3 2, 4	To offer burnt-offerings thereon... They kept the feast of Tabernacles	Lev. 1 3–13; 6 1–6 Lev. 23 33–44	This is the law of the burnt-offering.... The feast of Tabernacles....

Table 10.6.1 (continued)

Title Used	Reference	Phrase Used	Reference Quoted	Phrase Quoted
The Law of Moses the man of God	II Chr. 30 16, 17	The priests dashed the blood, which they received of the hand of the Levites. Killing the Passover lambs....	Lev. 1 3–17 Lev. 23 5–8	The priests shall dash its blood.... Passover....
For Numbers: Written in the Law of Moses the servant of God	Dan. 9 11	Been poured out upon us the curse and the oath	Num. 5 21	Make thee a curse and an oath
Law of God, which was given by Moses the servant of God	Neh. 10 30	And entered into a curse and an oath	Num. 5 21	Make thee a curse and an oath
For Deuteronomy: Written in the book of the Law of Moses	Josh. 8 31	An altar of unhewn stones, upon which no man had lifted any iron;	Deut. 27 5,6	An altar of stones; you shall lift up no iron tool upon them. Unhewn stones
Written in the book of the Law of Moses	Josh. 23 6	That you turn not aside therefrom to the right or to the left	Deut. 17 20	That he turn not aside from the commandment to the right or to the left

THE PENTATEUCH 157

Written in the law of Moses	I Kings 2 3	(a) To walk in His ways, to keep His statutes and His commandments and His ordinances and His testimonies (b) That you may prosper in all that you do, and wherever you turn yourself	Deut. 26 17	(a) To walk in His ways and to keep His statutes and His commandments and His ordinances and hearken to His voice (b) That you may prosper in all that you do									Deut. 29 8
Written in the book of the Law of Moses	II Kings 14 6	The fathers shall not be put to death for the children, nor the children be put to death for the fathers, but every man shall be put to death for his own sin	Deut. 24 16	The fathers shall not be put to death for the children. nor the children be put to death for the fathers, every man shall be put to death for his own sin
The entire Law of Moses	II Kings 23 25	With all his heart and with all his soul and with all his might	Deut. 6 5	With all your heart and with all your soul and with all your might
Remember the Law of Moses, My servant	Mal. 3 22	Which I commanded unto him in Horeb for all Israel, even statutes and ordinances	Deut. 4 8–10	Statutes and ordinances . . . take heed . . . lest thou forget . . . the day that thou stood before the Lord thy God in Horeb

Table 10.6.1 (continued)

Title Used	Reference	Phrase Used	Reference Quoted	Phrase Quoted
Written in the Law of Moses	Dan. 9 13	All this evil is come upon	(Deut. 28 15 –29 68) Deut. 29 26	To bring upon it all the curse
Written in the book of Moses	Ezra 6 18	And they set the priests in their divisions and the Levites in their courses, for the service of God, which is at Jerusalem	Deut. 18 1–8	Has chosen him (the priest) . . . to minister in the name of the Lord . . . The Levites who stand there before the Lord
Skilled scribe in the Law of Moses	Ezra 7 6			
Book of the Law of Moses	Neh. 8 1			
The book of Moses	Neh. 13 1, 2	An Ammonite and a Moabite should not enter into the assembly of God forever because they met not the children of Israel with bread and with water, but hired Balaam	Deut. 23 4–7	An Ammonite and a Moabite should not enter into the assembly of the Lord . . . forever, because they met you not with bread and with water . . . and because they hired against thee

	against them to curse them, but our God turned the curse into a blessing		Balaam ... to curse thee ... but the Lord thy God turned the curse into a blessing
II Chr. 23 18 Written in the Law of Moses	To offer the burnt-offerings of the Lord ... with rejoicing	Deut. 12 11–14	Thither shall you bring ... your burnt-offerings ... and you shall rejoice
II Chr. 25 4 Written in the Law in the book of Moses	The fathers shall not die for the children neither shall the children die for the fathers; but every man shall die for his own sin	Deut. 24 16	The fathers shall not be put to death for the children, neither shall the children be put to death for the fathers; every man shall be put to death for his own sin
II Chr. 35 11, 12, 16 Written in the book of Moses	To keep the Passover-sacrifice, and to offer burnt-offerings upon the altar of the Lord For the children of the people to present unto the Lord	Deut. 12 11	(a) The place which the Lord your God shall choose to cause his name to dwell there, thither shall you bring ... your burnt-offerings, and your sacrifices
		Deut. 16 2	(b) You shall sacrifice the Passover-offering unto the Lord thy God of the flock and the herd, in the place which the Lord shall choose to cause his name to dwell there

Table 10.6.2
Other Titles Used for the Books of Deuteronomy and Leviticus

Title Used	Reference	Phrase Used	Reference Quoted	Phrase Quoted
For Deuteronomy				
This book of the Law	Josh. 1 8		Deut. 31 26	Take this book of the Law
Copy of the Law of Moses	Josh. 8 32	Which he wrote before the children of Israel	Deut. 17 18 Deut. 31 24	Copy of this law in a book When Moses completed writing the words of this law in a book
Written in the book of the Law	Josh. 8 34	All the words of the Law, the blessing and the curse	Deut. 11 26	I set before you this day a blessing and a curse
The words of the book of the Covenant which was found in the house of the Lord	II Kings 23 2, 3	To walk after the Lord, and to keep His commandments, and His testimonies and His statutes, with all the heart and all the soul	Deut. 28 69 Deut. 31 26 Deut. 10 12, 13	These are the words of the covenant Take this book of the Law, and put it by the side of the Ark of the covenant of the Lord To walk in all His ways . . . with all thy heart and with all thy soul, to keep the commandments of the Lord and His statutes

THE PENTATEUCH

II Kings 23 21	Written in the book of the Covenant	Perform the passover-sacrifice unto the Lord your God	Deut. 16 1	Perform the Passover-sacrifice unto the Lord your God
II Kings 23 24	Words of the law which were written in the book.... found in the house of the Lord	They that divine by a ghost or a familiar spirit ... all the detestable things	Deut. 18 9–12	You shall not learn to do the abominations ... and one that consults a ghost or a familiar spirit or necromancer ... these abominations
II Chr. 34 14	Book of the law of the Lord given by Moses			
II Chr. 34 21	Concerning the words of the book that is found	Because our fathers have not observed the word of the Lord to do	Deut. 5 29	You shall observe to do as the Lord your God has commanded you
II Chr. 34 24	Written in the book which they have read before the King of Judah	I will bring evil upon this place ... all the curses that are written	Deut. 27 15–16	Cursed be the man ....
			Deut. 28 15–68	All these curses shall come upon thee, and overtake thee

Table 10.6.2 (continued)

Title Used	Reference	Phrase Used	Reference Quoted	Phrase Quoted
The words of the book of the Covenant that was found in the house of the Lord	II Chr. 34 30, 31	To walk after the Lord and to keep His commandments, and His testimonies, and His statutes with all his heart, and with all his soul	Deut. 28 69 Deut. 10 12, 13	These are the words of the covenant To walk in all His ways ... with all thy heart and with all thy soul, to keep the commandments of the Lord and His statutes
For Leviticus Written in the Law, that the Lord had commanded by Moses	Neh. 8 14, 15	The children of Israel should dwell in booths in the feast of the seventh month ... and fetch olive branches, and branches of wild olive, and myrtle branches, and palm branches, and branches of thick trees	Lev. 23 40–42	You shall take ... the fruit of goodly trees, branches of palm-trees, and boughs of thick trees, and willows of the brook ... a feast ... in the seventh month ... You shall dwell in booths

names refer to passages in Deuteronomy. The question arises, however, why was not the usual title for Deuteronomy, namely "the Book of the Law of Moses," used to describe the book found in the Temple? The answer is that the discovered text was not the entire Book of Deuteronomy, but only a part thereof. Thus we find (as explained in Section 10.5) that Moses wrote down (Deut. 31 24) the text of his second discourse (Deut. 5 1–28 68), and commanded that this written law-code be placed beside the Ark of the Tabernacle. It is natural to assume that this book written by Moses was later transferred to the Temple. Hence the book found at the time of King Josiah was the copy of the second discourse in Deuteronomy written by Moses himself, and was not the entire book of Deuteronomy. The discovery of the original text, written in Moses' own handwriting, made a deep impression on King Josiah in that it verified the historical correctness of the Book of Deuteronomy. However, the Book of Deuteronomy had not been lost, as has often been assumed by many expositors of the Bible, as is evident from the reference to the "Law of Moses" (i.e. Deuteronomy) by the prophet who recorded the historical events (II Kings 23 25).

In the Book of Daniel we find a quotation stated to have been written in the "Law of Moses the Servant of God" (9 11); and two sentences later we find another quotation, but this time stated to have been written in the "Law of Moses" (9 13). Only if these two titles refer to different books of the Pentateuch, specifically Numbers and Deuteronomy, can we understand the variations in language. (Also see commentary on these sentences in Section 16.4.)

Similarly, we find that Ezra was an expert scribe of the "Law of Moses" (7 6), i.e. the Book of Deuteronomy. Then, Ezra set himself the task of studying the "Law of the Lord" (7 10), i.e. the Book of Exodus. Without the knowledge that two different books of the Pentateuch are being mentioned, it would have been unclear as to what the text really meant.

A final and very important case where the knowledge of the different names of the Pentateuch elucidates the text occurs in the Book of Nehemiah. First we find mention of a public reading by Ezra, on the first day of the seventh month, of the "Book of the Law of Moses" (8 1,3), i.e. Deuteronomy. Next, the leaders read "in the book, in the Law of God" (8 8), i.e. in Genesis. The following day the text of "the Law that the Lord has commanded by Moses" (8 14), i.e. Leviticus, was read. Subsequently, we find the statement that the "Book of the Law of God," i.e. Genesis, was read for the seven days of the Festival of Tabernacles. At another gathering a few days later, on the twenty-fourth of the seventh month, the "Book of the Law of the Lord their God" (9 3), i.e. Exodus, was read, followed by a prayer by the Levites which mentions historical events described in the Books of Genesis, Exodus, and Deuteronomy, as well as in Judges, Kings, and possibly other books of the Bible. Afterwards, the books of the "Law of God" (10 29) and the "Law of God which was given by Moses the Servant of God" (10 30), i.e. Genesis and Numbers, are specified. Still on the same day, the twenty-fourth of the seventh month, the "Book of Moses" was read (13 1). We thus find that between the first and twenty-fourth days of the seventh month, public readings were held of all five books of the Pentateuch, some books more than once. Without knowledge of the different names of the Pentateuch, it would be extremely unclear as to the purpose of all the public readings.

The realization that the books of the Pentateuch are frequently referred to throughout the Bible, is strong verification of the early completion of the Pentateuch. The Book of Joshua clearly mentions Genesis and Deuteronomy; Kings cites Exodus and Deuteronomy; Daniel quotes Numbers and Deuteronomy; Ezra-Nehemiah refers to all five books; and Chronicles mentions Exodus, Leviticus, and Deuteronomy. Furthermore, there are numerous cases where statements in the Pentateuch are quoted, without mention of the specific book (see e.g. Josh. 1 13–15; 14 2; 21 2,8; 22 5; I Kings 8 53,56). We thus see that the books of the Pentateuch were in existence at the time of Joshua, and were still written on separate scrolls as late as the time of Ezra-Nehemiah. Those Biblical critics who try to postpone the date of completion of the books of the Pentateuch to the period of the kings, such as the time of King Josiah, obviously are presenting an untenable assumption.

Chapter Eleven

EARLY PROPHETIC WORKS

11.1 JOSHUA

The Book of Joshua describes the conquest and distribution of the land of Canaan under the leadership of Joshua, the successor of Moses. After approximately seven years of conquest, the acquired land was distributed by lot to the tribes of Israel.

As explained in the chronological section (Section 4.0), Joshua was twenty years old when sent as a spy in the second year of the stay in the desert. Thirty-nine years later, when his first year of rule began, he was fifty-nine years old. Since he lived until the age of 110 (Josh. **24** 29), his length of rule is fifty-two years. Thus the Book of Joshua, which relates the main events during the rule of Joshua, covers a period of fifty-two years.

ORGANIZATION

The book is arranged in chronological order, although a few minor exceptions occur to maintain logical coherence. The chronological arrangement is shown as follows: for three days (**1** 11; **3** 2) the Israelites prepared for the crossing of the Jordan River, which occurred on the tenth day of the first month of the first year of the rule of Joshua (**4** 19). During these three days, the two men who had previously been sent to spy on the city of Jericho, returned (**2** 1–24). The male population was then circumcized (**5** 2–9) in preparation for observance of the Passover sacrifice on the fourteenth of the first month (**5** 10). Subsequently the cities of Jericho (**6** 1–27) and Ai (**7** 1–**8** 29) were conquered; and the Biblical blessings and curses were read in the vicinity of Mounts Gerizim and Ebal (**8** 30–35). A peace agreement was then made with the city of Gibeon (**9** 1–27). Afterwards, numerous kings were conquered (**10** 1–**11** 23), and a summary is given of all the territory and kings conquered by Israel (**12** 1–24).

This first section of the book (Chapters **1–12**), which describes the conquests of the land, contains a few cases which are not in exact chronological order. From **2** 22 we learn that the spies were away from the Israelite camp for more than three days, which means that the spies were sent by Joshua prior to the beginning of the book. However, they probably returned after the beginning of the three-day preparation for crossing the Jordan (**1** 11). The entire story of the two spies is combined for the sake of clarity, and is inserted prior to the crossing of the Jordan, based on the time when the spies returned. A second case which is not in its proper chronological position is the appearance of the war-angel of God to Joshua (**5** 13–15). This event occurred when Joshua was in Jericho (**5** 13), although the passage is placed before Jericho was conquered. The story of the angel was placed just before the conquest of Jericho (**6** 1–27) so as not to interrupt the narrative of the conquest. A third case is the sentence **10** 15 (repeated in **10** 43) which states that Joshua and all Israel returned to Gilgal. Afterwards (**10** 16–42) is recounted what happened before the return to Gilgal. A simple explanation is that the return to Gilgal is mentioned in **10** 15 to indicate that the return occurred after the sun finally set one day later than usual (**10** 13). Then in **10** 16–42 are described the events which occurred during the extra day's fighting that occurred because the sun did not set on time. A last example of a section not in exact chronological order occurs in **12** 1–24. In this chapter are summarized all the kings conquered by the Israelites. In the summary are included the kings conquered by Moses (**12** 1–6)—events which occurred before the beginning of the book. It is, however, obvious that the summary should mention the kings that Moses conquered so as to include all the territory occupied by the Israelites.

After the previously described conquests, Joshua had aged sufficiently so that he no longer could lead the people out to battle (**13** 1). God then told Joshua to distribute the land among the tribes (**13** 1–7). Caleb, the son of Jephunneh, then approached Joshua with the request that Hebron be given him as an inheritance (**14** 6–15). Caleb remarks that it is now forty-five years since Moses sent the twelve spies (**14** 10), which is equivalent to it being the seventh year of Joshua's rule. We thus learn that the main conquest of the land of Canaan occurred within seven years; and that Joshua at the age of sixty-five (20 + 45) was too old to lead the people in battle.

The division of the land of Canaan, which probably was completed within about a year, is described in the second section of the book, Chapters 13 to 22. The listings of the territories of the tribes is arranged according to the order in which the tribes received their portions. The tribes of Reuben, Gad, and half of Manasseh, (**13** 8–33) are listed first because they received their allotments first, at the time of Moses. Next are listed the tribes of Judah, Ephraim, and the second-half of Manasseh (**14** 1–**17** 18), who received their portions at Gilgal (**14** 6). The remaining seven tribes received their portions at Shiloh (**18** 1–10), and are listed last (**18** 11–**19** 51). Miscellaneous details concerning the division of the land are then presented. These details concern the assignment of cities of refuge (**20** 1–9); the providing of cities for the Levites and priests (**21** 1–43); and the return of the soldiers of Reuben, Gad, and half of Manasseh to their allotted land, with the subsequent building of an altar as a memorial (**22** 1–34). Although the land division is presented in chronological order, still numerous details which may have occurred at other times are included for completeness. For example, the conquests of Caleb and Othniel (15 13-19), and the inability to conquer the Jebusites (15 63) and the Canaanites (16 10; 17 12,13), may very well have been events which occurred some years after the initial division of the land. In contrast, the tribes of Reuben, Gad, and half of Manasseh received their territory about seven years previously, but the details are presented in 13 8-33 for completeness.

The last division of the book, Chapters 23-24, describes two gatherings of the people with the purpose of reinforcing their belief in God, and their observance of the Biblical commandments. The dates for these gatherings are not given, although they probably occurred sometime between the twelfth and forty-ninth years of Joshua, based on the indefinite durations given in 23 1 and 24 29. The first gathering (23 1-16) mainly emphasizes observance of the Biblical laws, while the second gathering emphasizes belief in God. Joshua considered the covenant made in the second gathering as so important that he added the description of the event to the Book of Genesis (Book of the Law of God)(24 26). Subsequently (24 29-33) are mentioned the death of Joshua, and miscellaneous details such as the place where Joseph's bones were buried, and the place where Eleazer, the priest, was buried. The burials of Joseph's bones and of Eleazer the priest did not necessarily occur after Joshua's death.

Authorship

The obvious author for the Book of Joshua is Joshua himself. Many passages where God speaks directly to Joshua, such as (1 1-9; 3 7-8; 4 15,16; 5 2,9; 6 2-5; 7 10-15; 8 1-2,18; 10 8; 11 6; 13 1-7; 20 1-6) could only have been known by Joshua. Also, as leader of the people, he would undoubtedly be familiar with all the places and events mentioned in the book. In fact he was personally involved in most of the happenings described. It is specifically mentioned that the spies related to Joshua all that transpired (2 23). Evidence of the writing ability of Joshua is given in 24 26 where it is stated that the events described were written by him in the Book of Genesis (Book of the Law of God).

In numerous places in the book, such as (4 9; 5 9; 6 25; 7 26; 8 28,29; 9 27; 10 27; 13 13; 14 14; 16 10; 22 3,17; 23 8,9) the phrase "unto this day" is used. This phrase often implies that an addition to the text was made many years afterwards, and the one who made the addition testifies that the item being discussed exists until his time. Not necessarily, however, does the presence of this phrase imply a later editor than Joshua. It should be remembered that Joshua ruled for fifty-two years, while the majority of the events of the book occurred within eight years (seven years of conquest, and one year of distribution of the land). Thus the comment "unto this day" could have been added by Joshua himself forty or more years after the events.

It should be noted that the phrases used in the Book of Joshua are frequently very similar to those used in Deuteronomy. The similar phrases may be attributed to familiarity by Joshua with the Book of Deuteronomy. In addition we have ascribed the final editing of the Pentateuch to Joshua, and therefore it is not unexpected that he would often use phrases in the Book of Joshua similar to those used in Deuteronomy.

The problem arises as to who wrote the last section of the book (24 29–33), which mentions the death and burial of Joshua. Now it should be noticed that in Judg. 2 6–9 we find a passage essentially identical with 24 28–31, which indicates a common author for the two books. When discussing the Book of Judges, we show that the editor is probably the prophet Samuel. Similarly, we can conclude that the passage mentioning the death of Joshua was added later by Samuel based on historical records. It should also be noted that 24 1–28, about the covenant of the people with God, is stated to have been written by Joshua, not in the Book of Joshua but in the Book of Genesis (24 26); yet we find the passage in the Book of Joshua. It is therefore possible that Samuel removed this passage from Genesis and placed it in the Book of Joshua where it is much more appropriate.

11.2 JUDGES

The Book of Judges covers the historical period from the death of Joshua to the death of Samson, which is a duration of 299 years (see Section 4.0). During this time-span twelve different judges ruled the people of Israel. Particularly detailed accounts are presented concerning the judgeships of Ehud, Deborah, Gideon, Abimelech, Jephthah, and Samson; while very short descriptions are given about the judgeships of Othniel, Tola, Jair, Ibzan, Elon, and Abdon. Although the emphasis of the book is on events which occurred during this period of 299 years, nevertheless some events going back to the time of Joshua, and other events as late as the time of Eli, or even afterwards, are mentioned, as will be discussed later.

The chronology presented in the Book of Judges has been considered very inadequate by historians and critics. However, a simple explanation of the chronology has been given in Section 4.0. There it is shown that there were no time gaps between judges; the judges succeeded each other within a short time. The periods of subjugation to other nations, which are specified frequently in the book, all occurred concurrently with a judge's rule, and should not be added to the total number of years of the period.

There are two characteristics which differentiate the type of rule of the judges from that of the later kings. First, the rule of the judges was not hereditary; rather, the most capable person available was selected as judge. Secondly, the judges did not govern from one central location, but each judge ruled from his local area. Thus Deborah ruled from the hill-country of Ephraim (4 5), Gideon ruled from Ophrah (6 11; 8 27), Abimelech from Shechem (9 1,6), Tola from Shamir (10 1,2), Jephthah from Mizpah (11 34), Ibzan from Bethlehem (12 8,10),

Table 11.2.1
Arrangement of Judges 1 1–2 5,
According to Similarity of Phrases between Adjacent Sentences

Section	Sentence	Phrase	Section	Sentence	Corresponding Phrase
1 1–7	1 7	ויהודה 1 4; ירושלם	1 8–9	1 8	ויהודה; בירושלם
1 8–9	1 9	ויהודה; ההרה	1 10–15	1 10	ויהודה; חברון
1 10–15	1 15	הנב	1 16	1 16	הנגב
1 16	1 16	לך ואבי	1 17–19	1 17	וילך אתו
1 17–19	1 19	אתם	1 20	1 20	וילא
1 19	1 19	יושב העמק	1 21	1 21	היבוסי ישב
1 21	1 21	לא הורישו	1 22–26	1 26	לא הוריש
1 21	1 21	וישבו היבוסי	1 27–28	1 27	לא הוריש
1 27–28	1 28	ולמיתר והעלהו	1 29–33	1 29	וישב הכנעני
1 29–33	1 33	מם לבס	1 34–36	1 35	ותכבד יד
1 34–36	1 36	הגבול	2 1–5	2 1	ויעל מלאך

Elon from Zebulun (**12** 11,12), Abdon from Pirathon (**12** 13,15), and Samson from between Zorah and Eshtaol (**13** 25; **16** 31). It may also be surmised from the general descriptions that the judges had less power than the kings, and therefore each local area usually made its own decisions concerning national problems.

ORGANIZATION

The Book of Judges consists of three separate parts. The first part (**1** 1–**2** 5) presents background information to the book. In it are described the places of the country still unconquered, as well as information relevant to later statements in the book. Thus the victory of Othniel (**1** 13) foreshadows his becoming leader of the people (**3** 9–11); and mention of the children of the Kenite (**1** 16) is relevant to their later importance in connection with the defeat of Sisera, the military leader of Hazor (**4** 11,17). This first part of the book is arranged according to the similarity of phrases between adjacent sentences, or groups of sentences on the same topic, as established in Table 11.2.1, and is clearly not arranged in chronological order. That the first part of the book is not in chronological order can be seen as follows: the campaigns by the tribes of Judah and Simeon against Bezek and Zephath (**1** 1–7,17) are specifically stated to have occurred after the death of Joshua (**1** 1). In contrast, numerous sentences of this first part of the book are nearly identical to those in the Book of Joshua, and hence describe events which occurred during the lifetime of Joshua. For example, compare **1** 10–15 with Josh. **15** 13–19; **1** 20 with Josh. **14** 13; **1** 21 with Josh. **15** 63, **18** 28; **1** 27,28 with Josh. **17** 11–13; and **1** 29 with Josh. **16** 10. Therefore, numerous sentences are not in correct chronological order.

The events in the Book of Joshua which are repeated in the Book of Judges must have occurred at the time of Joshua, and not at the time of the judges, based on the following reasoning. Caleb was eighty-five years old in the seventh year of Joshua's reign (Josh. **14** 10). Joshua died forty-five years later (since he ruled fifty-two years); at that time Caleb, if still alive, would have been 130 years. At such an advanced age Caleb could not possibly have fought in battle. Thus the described battle (Judg. **1** 10; Josh. **15** 13,14) must have occurred before the death of Joshua. We may therefore also assume that the events in the other passages found in both of the Books of Joshua and Judges also occurred during Joshua's lifetime.

The second part of the book (**2** 6–**16** 31) contains the historical description of the main events which occurred during the period of the judges. The narrative begins (**2** 6–9) with a repetition of the end of the Book of Joshua (Josh. **24** 28–31) to let us know that the historical theme has begun. Then the narrative continues with a summary of the degenerate spiritual condition of the people and their consequent punishment by God during the entire period of the judges (**2** 10–**3** 6). This summary is written from the point of view of a historian looking at the period in retrospect. Then the history continues with detailed historical information concerning the judges, and the most notable events during their reigns (**3** 7–**16** 31), and is essentially arranged in chronological order. Thus the judgeships of Othniel, Ehud, Deborah, Gideon, Abimelech, Tola, Jair, Jephthah, Ibzan, Elon, Abdon, and Samson are described successively, in the order in which they ruled. Nevertheless, the periods of subjugation are not necessarily placed in strict chronological arrangement. For example, the Israelites were subjugated by the Philistines for forty years (**13** 1), at about the time of Samson. However, Samson ruled only twenty years (**15** 20; **16** 31), and he did not succeed in completely removing the Philistine subjugation. Therefore, some of the forty years must have been after the death of Samson during the judgeship of Eli, although the text does not supply sufficient information to enable specifying the number of years of subjugation by the Philistines before and after Samson. Similar inexactness occurs in many cases for the other periods of subjugation mentioned in the book. Furthermore, the birth of Samson (**13** 1–25) must have preceded the eight-year rule of Abdon (**12** 14) and part of the ten-year rule of Elon (**12** 11), since Samson who succeeded them could not have become the judge before his maturity at thirteen years of age. Similarly, the expulsion of Jephthah by his brethren (**11** 1–3) preceded his becoming judge, and therefore is not in strict chronological order. Based on the above discussion it is reasonable to conclude that this second part of the book is arranged in strict chronological order except for such items as the beginning summary (**2** 10–**3** 6), the durations of the periods of subjugation (**3** 8; **3** 14; **4** 7; **6** 1; **10** 7,8; and **13** 1), the story of the birth of Samson (**13** 1–25), and the expulsion of Jephthah (**11** 1–3).

The third part of the Book of Judges (**17** 1–**21** 25) relates two stories which are placed as appendices. The first story (**17** 1–**18** 31) describes how the idol of Micah was placed in the city of Dan, and remained there until the time of the ruin of Shiloh. The second story (**19** 1–**21** 25) describes how the death of a concubine at Gibeah almost resulted in the complete extinction of the tribe of Benjamin. These stories were preserved because of the information they provide as to the chaotic situation existing at the time of the judges. The events described are not dated, and therefore the exact time when they occurred can not be ascertained. However, the events are probably not in chronological order, and probably did not occur after Samson's death (**16** 30,31). Rather the arrangement is by similarity of phrases, just as for the first part of the book. Thus in **16** 31 it is mentioned that Samson was buried between Zorah and Eshtaol. These same place names are mentioned in the first story concerning the idol of Micah (**18** 2). Similarly, both of the appendices refer to a "Levi" and to the "hill-country of Ephraim" (**17** 7,8 and **19** 1).

AUTHORSHIP

Since the Book of Judges covers a period of over 299 years, the historical events described could not have been recorded by one person. Rather, the individual sections must have been recorded by persons living at the respective times, and the book was subsequently organized and edited into its present form.

There is strong evidence that the prophet Samuel was the one who compiled the book. Firstly, we find that Samuel was familiar with the history of the judges since he mentions several of the events and leaders during the period (I Sam. **12** 9–11). Secondly, at the time of King David, Joab is acquainted with the story, which occurred 164 years previously, concerning Abimelech (II Sam. **11** 21), which indicates that the Book of Judges was surely completed by about the twenty-third year of David's reign (see Table 11.3.4). Thirdly, the book must have been completed not earlier than the beginning of King Saul's reign. This is indicated by such statements as "In those days there was no king in Israel" (**17** 6; **18** 1; **19** 1; **21** 25); "until the day of the exile of the land . . . all the time that the house of God was in Shiloh" (**18** 30,31). These statements establish that the book was completed after Shiloh was destroyed, and after Saul was anointed as the first king. Furthermore, in **2** 11–23 a general summary is given of the situation during the time of the judges, which indicates that the summary was written after the period of the judges. In addition, the forty years of subjugation of the Israelites by the Philistines (**13** 1), as explained previously, possibly requires that the sentence was written as much as twenty years after the beginning of Eli's rule. All these factors point to Samuel as the most likely person to have been the compiler; which agrees with the traditional view (*Baba Bathra* 14b). Since Samuel died in the first year of Saul's reign (I Sam. **25** 1; **27** 7; **13** 1), we must conclude that the Book of Judges was completed in the year of Samuel's death.

Although Samuel was the editor of the Book of Judges, still the history of the individual sections was recorded shortly after the events, and manuscripts were maintained. It is reasonable to assume that in many cases where detailed accounts are found, such as for Ehud (**3** 12–30), Deborah (**4** 1–**5** 31), Gideon (**6** 1–**8** 28), and Jephthah (**10** 6–**12** 7), the history was written by the judges themselves. In particular, the Song of Deborah is attributed to Deborah (**5** 1), and is written in the first person as if by her (**5** 7,12). The history of Abimelech (**8** 29–**9** 57), however, was more likely to have been written by Jotham than by Abimelech; especially since Abimelech died in his last battle (**9** 54) and could not have recorded the last happenings. Similarly, the history of Samson (**13** 1–**16** 31) was probably not recorded by Samson, since he was blinded (**16** 21) and eventually died (**16** 30), and therefore could not have written the section **16** 4–31. Also, Manoah, Samson's father, was dead at that time (**16** 31) and therefore could not have been the author of the final section on Samson. A very likely possibility is Samson's mother, who plays a very important role in the beginning (**13** 2–**14** 20), and would naturally have been curious to find out the background details of her son's death.

The histories of the other judges, namely Othniel (**3** 7–11), Tola (**10** 1,2), Jair (**10** 3–5), Ibzan (**12** 8–10), Elon (**12** 11,12), and Abdon (**12** 13–15), are extremely concise. The main details presented are the name of the judge and the number of years of rule. It is probable that an official record was kept of the years that each judge ruled, and this document served as the main basis for the history of these rulers. This official record probably was also used by Samuel to supplement the history of the other better-described judges, for otherwise the problem arises as to who recorded the number of years each judge ruled; surely not the judges themselves after they died.

The story of the idol of Micah (17 1–18 31) was possibly recorded by Micah; and the story of the concubine at Gibeah (19 1–21 25) possibly by the Levite. Other manuscripts which may have existed could be descriptions of 1 1–9,16–19, 22–26,30–36; 2 1–5, i.e. those early sections not borrowed from the Book of Joshua. One passage clearly written by Samuel without the aid of previous manuscripts is 2 11–3 6 which summarizes the history of the entire period of the judges.

Considering the varied sources available, and the different styles of writing used in the manuscripts, we must give Samuel great credit for compiling an excellent, well-organized book.

11.3 SAMUEL

The two Books of Samuel, which were originally one work, cover the period from the time of the birth of Samuel to the last year of the kingship of David. Included in this period are the forty years of the judgeship of Eli, the three years of Samuel's rule, the two years of Saul's reign, and the forty years of David's reign, for a total of eighty-five years. As explained in section 4.3, Samuel was probably born about twenty years before Eli became judge. Therefore, the Book of Samuel covers about 105 years, and really starts at the time of the beginning of Samson's judgeship.

Authorship

Clarification of the authorship of the Book of Samuel is obtained from I Chr. 29 29,30 where it is stated that the complete history of David is written in the "records of the prophets Samuel, Nathan and Gad." As will be presently shown, it is reasonable to assume that this title was the original name for the Book of Samuel; and we thus have a clear statement that Samuel, Nathan, and Gad were the authors. The names of these three prophets are found numerous times in the Book of Samuel. For example, in the first nineteen chapters of I Sam., Samuel is mentioned over 100 times as an active participant in the events described. Similarly, the name Gad is found in I Sam. 22 5, and II Sam. 24 11,13,14,18,19; and Nathan is mentioned in II Sam. 7 2–4,17; and 12 1,5,7,13,15,25.

From the Bible it is evident that Nathan was later than Gad. Mention of Gad is only found relevant to the early years of David, such as when David was running from Saul (I Sam. 22 5). Mention of Nathan is, however, found in the later years of David; such as when David wanted to build the Temple (II Sam. 7; I Chr. 17), which occurred after David was a firm ruler over all Israel; after the sin of

David with Bathsheba (II Sam. 12; Psalms 51 2); and during the last year of David's reign (I Kings 1). Also, Nathan is listed among the chroniclers of Solomon's reign (II Chr. 9 29). Furthermore, in II Chr. 29 25, Gad is mentioned before Nathan, supporting the conclusion that Nathan was later than Gad.

The problem then arises why in I Chr. 29 29 Nathan is listed before Gad as a recorder of the history of David. A probable explanation is that many of the sections written by Gad are placed at the end of the Book of Samuel; i.e. the order of the authors given in I Chr. 29 29 is according to the order of the sections written by these authors. To verify this explanation it is necessary to establish which sections of the Book of Samuel were written by Samuel, which by Nathan, and which by Gad.

The beginning of the Book of Samuel, from I Sam. 1 to 19, was probably written by Samuel. The background of Samuel's birth (1 1–2 12) was told to him by his mother, Hannah. (The use of the terms "king" and "anointed" [2 10] possibly refers to Eli, the anointed priest and leader.) The descriptions of Eli and Samuel involve events that Samuel himself witnessed (2 13–3 21). The details of the battle with the Philistines and the capture of the Ark (4 1–7 1) could have been obtained from eyewitnesses. However, the sentence stating that the Ark remained in Kiriath-jearim for twenty years (7 2) could not have been written by Samuel, since he died before the twenty years were completed. This sentence was most probably added later by the prophet Nathan. Subsequent passages (7 3–19 24) describe events in which Samuel was directly involved; or stories told him by Saul and David; or information readily available to the population. It is specifically mentioned (19 18) that David told Samuel all that Saul had done to David. Also it is specifically mentioned (10 25) that Samuel wrote down the regulations of the monarchy. Therefore, it is quite reasonable to ascribe these first nineteen chapters to Samuel. One additional exception should, however, be noted. The sentence which states that Saul ruled two years (13 1) must have been added later by Gad (or Nathan), since Samuel died before Saul.

The last contact of David with Samuel, before Samuel's death (25 1), is described in Chapter 19. It is therefore reasonable to assume that the succeeding passages beginning with I Sam. 20 1 were written by Gad, the prophet who followed Samuel. In 22 5 we find Gad specifically mentioned, when he told David to leave the stronghold. Later, it is stated in 27 6 that "the city Ziklag belonged to the kings of Judah until this day." What is meant is that the city of Ziklag remained under David's control during his seven-year rule over Judah. It is implied that the author of the sentence, namely Gad, died before the end of David's seven-year rule over Judah. If that were the case, we must attribute II Sam. 2 to Nathan rather than Gad, since in 2 11 it is mentioned that David ruled over Judah for seven years. Hence the chapters from I Sam. 20 through II Sam. 1 are reasonably ascribed to Gad.

The text from II Sam. 2 through 20 was probably written by the prophet

EARLY PROPHETIC WORKS   175

Nathan. Described in these passages are events from the beginning of David's reign to his fortieth year. Points which indicate that even the chapters describing the first seven years of David's reign (II Sam. 2 1–5 3), when Gad was possibly still alive, were written by Nathan rather than by Gad, are as follows: first, in 2 11 it is mentioned that David ruled over Judah for seven and one-half years, which as explained previously could not have been written by Gad. Secondly, in 2 12-32 is described the event when Asahel was killed by Abner; and in 3 6–39 the subsequent death of Abner. As will be presently shown, based on II Sam. 23 24, Gad only described events prior to Asahel's death. Thirdly, in 3 2–5 are listed all the children born to David in Hebron. This list must have been completed after the seven-year stay of David in Hebron, and therefore could not have been written by Gad. In addition, the history in 4 1–5 3 is subsequent to 3 6–39, and hence must have been written by Nathan. It has now been shown that the text after 2 11 was written by Nathan and not by Gad. Only the text from 2 1 to 2 10 may have been written by Gad, but for simplicity is here attributed to Nathan. After the chapters describing the initial years of David's reign, we find Nathan mentioned in II Sam. 7 and 12, supporting his authorship. Furthermore the statement in 5 4 that David ruled for forty years indicates that it must have been written by Nathan, who we know from I Kings 1 and II Chr. 9 29 to have been active at the end of David's rule.

The chapters from II Sam. 21 through 24 are placed as an appendix to the Book of Samuel. These chapters do not affect the main historical narrative and are not clearly dated. Sufficient information is supplied, however, to show that these passages refer to events not later than about the fifth year of David's reign, and were probably written by Gad. Thus the appeasement of the Gibeonites by David (21 1–14) possibly occurred in the fifth year of David's reign (21 1) (see Section 7.1.1). The battles with the Philistines described in II Sam. 21 15–22 should be compared with those described in I Sam. 18 26–30; 19 8; and 23 1–5, and would date these events as the first year of Saul's reign. The words of the song spoken by David upon being saved from Saul (II Sam. 22 1–51) would appropriately have been written in the second year of Saul's reign, after Saul's death. "The last words of David" (23 1–7) probably means the last poetry composed by David as a private individual before officially becoming King of Judah, and would therefore also have been composed in the second year of Saul, after Saul's death. The list of David's military heroes (23 8–39) refers to events and persons at about the first year of Saul's reign. In particular, the cave of Adullam and the stronghold are mentioned (II Sam. 23 13,14) which should be compared to I Sam. 22 1–5. Also, Asahel is listed as one of the heroes (II Sam. 23 24), which dates the text as prior to the death of Asahel (II Sam. 2 23). Finally, the census of Israel and Judah ordered by David (24 1–25) may have occurred after the two-year rule of Ish-bosheth over Israel (II Sam. 2 10), i.e. in the third year of David's reign. The census surely occurred before the conquest of the Jebusites by David

(5 6–10), since David, to stop a plague, purchased the threshing-floor of Araunah, the Jebusite (**24** 24). A summary of the dates of the events described in the appendix is presented in Table 11.3.1.

The authorship of the appendix by Gad can be deduced by the following reasoning. First, the described events are those during the early years of David's career, when Gad was the dominant prophet. Secondly, Gad is specifically mentioned as being involved in the events described in II Sam. 24. Thirdly, Gad was present when David was in the stronghold (I Sam. **22** 5), and this event is referred to in II Sam. **23** 13,14.

We have now shown that the order of authorship for the Book of Samuel is

Table 11.3.1
Early Events in David's Career Described in the Appendix to
the Book of Samuel
(II Sam. **21** 1–**24** 25)

Reference	Event	Approximate Date
II Sam. **21** 1–14	Three years of famine because Saul killed many Gibeonites	Second to fourth years of David's reign
II Sam. **21** 15–22	Battles with the Philistines (Compare with I Sam. **18** 26–30; **19** 8; **23** 1–5)	First year of Saul's reign
II Sam. **22** 1–51	Song by David upon being saved from Saul	Second year of Saul's reign
II Sam. **23** 1–7	Last words of David, before officially becoming king	Second year of Saul's reign
II Sam. **23** 8–39	List of David's military heroes (compare II Sam. **23** 13, 14 with I Sam. **22** 1–5; II Sam. **23** 18 with I Sam. **26** 6; II Sam. **23** 24 with II Sam. **2** 23)	First year of Saul's reign
II Sam. **24** 1–25	Census of Israel and Judah ordered by King David (occurred before conquest of the Jebusites (**24** 18); probably after the two years of rule of Ish-bosheth over Israel)	Third year of David's reign

Samuel (I Sam. 1–19), Gad (I Sam. 20–II Sam. 1), Nathan (II Sam. 2–20), and again Gad (II Sam. 21–24). A summary of the contents and authors of the book are presented in Table 11.3.2 for clarity. The order of authorship thus corresponds to that given in I Chr. 29 29, i.e. Samuel, Nathan and Gad; even though Gad was a younger contemporary of Nathan. Nevertheless, since Nathan was the last of the three prophets, he undoubtedly was the final editor and compiler of the book.

ORGANIZATION

The Book of Samuel consists of two parts. The first part (I Sam. 1 –II Sam. 20 26) contains the main historical narrative, and describes the histories of Eli, Samuel, Saul, and David. In this section the stories are presented in chronological order, although occasional minor exceptions occur. For example, in II Sam. 3 2–5 are listed all the sons born to David in Hebron. If a strict chronological order were maintained, it would have been necessary to intersperse the births of the sons with the events during the seven years at Hebron. Similar comments can be made concerning the list of sons born to David in Jerusalem (II Sam. 5 14–15). Furthermore, Solomon is mentioned among those born in Jerusalem, although his actual birth is described subsequently (II Sam. 12 24) in its correct sequence.

It should be noted that in the Book of Samuel the years of rule of the leaders are usually given at the beginning of the historical events, and therefore not in strict chronological order. Thus the lifetime-judgeship of Samuel (I Sam. 7 15), the two-year rule by Saul (I Sam. 13 1), the two-year rule by Ish-bosheth (II Sam. 2 10), the seven-year rule of David from Hebron (II Sam. 2 11) and the thirty-three-year rule by David from Jerusalem (II Sam. 5 5) are all stated before the descriptions of the events for the specified periods. The only exception is the forty-year judgeship of Eli (I Sam. 4 18) which is stated after Eli's death. Even the sixteen-month stay of David in the Philistine camp (I Sam. 27 7) is mentioned before the actual events are described.

Another example where the presentation is not in strict chronological order is the description of the consultation by Saul at En-dor with the spirit of Samuel (I Sam. 28 3–25). Now this occurred after the Israelite army camped at Gilboa (I Sam. 28 4), where the actual battle with the Philistines occurred (31 1,8). Yet in the next chapter (29 1–11) we find the Israelites camped at Jezreel. Hence the events described in Chapter 28 occurred after those described in Chapter 29. The reason the story of Saul's consultation with Samuel's spirit is placed slightly out of chronological order, is so as not to interrupt later the story of David's conquest of the Amalekites and retrieval of the captured possessions (30 1–31).

The realization that the text is not in strict chronological order allows an easy explanation for the apparent contradiction between I Sam. 16 14–23 which states that David played the harp to remove the evil spirit from Saul, and the later description (I Sam. 17 55–58) where Saul asks who David is at the time of the battle with Goliath. How could Saul not know who David was if David played the

Table 11.3.2
Contents and Authorship of Book of Samuel

Chapter (I Sam.)	Contents	Author	Supplier of Additional Details to Author
1 1–2 11	Background of birth of Samuel; blessing of Hannah by Eli; song of thanks by Hannah	Samuel	Hannah, mother of Samuel
2 12–3 18	Sins of sons of Eli; service of Samuel under Eli; prophecies of punishment to family of Eli	Samuel	Eli, and personal experiences of Samuel
3 19–4 22	Samuel prophet of God; war against Philistines; capture of Ark of God; Death of Eli and his sons	Samuel	Eye-witnesses
5 1–7 1	Stay of Ark of God in land of Philistines; return of Ark	Samuel	Philistines, and Eyewitnesses
7 2	Twenty-year stay of Ark at Kiriath-jearim	Nathan	
7 3–17	Success against Philistines; judgeship of Samuel	Samuel	
8 1–22	Request by the people to Samuel for establishment of a monarchy	Samuel	
9 1–10 16	Private anointment of Saul by Samuel	Samuel	Some information supplied by Saul
10 17–27	First public announcement of Saul as king	Samuel	
11 1–12 25	Saul leads people in victory against Ammon; confirmation of Saul as king by Samuel and people	Samuel	Eye-witnesses
13 1	Length of Saul's reign	Gad	
13 2–14 46	Sin of Saul at Gilgal; victory	Samuel	Saul, and

Table 11.3.2 (continued)

Chapter (I Sam.)	Contents	Author	Supplier of Additional Details to Author
	over Philistines led by Jonathan and Saul		Jonathan
14 47–52	General description of Saul's reign	Samuel	
15 1–35	Battle against Amalek; sin of Saul	Samuel	
16 1–23	Private anointment of David by Samuel; spirit of God leaves Saul and alights on David	Samuel	David
17 1–58	David kills Goliath; victory over Philistines	Samuel	David
18 1–19 24	Service of David under Saul; Saul's jealousy of David; plan by Saul to kill David; escape of David to Ramah to Samuel	Samuel	David
20 1–42	Jonathan finds out that his father, Saul, definitely wants to kill David	Gad	Jonathan or David
21 1–22 5	David goes to Nob, the city of the priests; from there he flees to Gath, and feigns madness to prevent being killed; then he runs to the cave of Adullam; then to Mizpeh of Moab, where Gad warned David to run away	Gad	David
22 6–23	Saul has the priests and inhabitants of Nob killed because they helped David	Gad	Abiathar or David

Table 11.3.2 (continued)

Chapter (I Sam.)	Contents	Author	Supplier of Additional Details to Author
23 1–24 23	David defeats the Philistines who were fighting against Keilah; David travels from Keilah; then from the woods in the wilderness of Ziph; then from the wilderness of Maon; then from the strongholds of En-Gedi to escape from Saul	Gad	David
25 1–44	Samuel dies; story of David versus Nabal; David marries Abigail, widow of Nabal	Gad	David
26 1–25	David spares Saul's life at Hachilah	Gad	David
27 1–28 2	David settles for 16 months in Ziklag, city of Achish, King of Gath	Gad	David
28 3–25	Saul inquires of a fortune-teller about outcome of battle with Philistines	Gad	Eyewitness
29 1–11	The Philistines refuse to allow David to accompany them to battle	Gad	David
30 1–31	David saves the captives and booty from the Amalekites	Gad	David
(II Sam.)			
31 1–1 27	Saul and Jonathan killed in battle with the Philistines	Gad	David
2 1–4 12	David anointed in Hebron as king over Judah; conflict between House of David	Nathan	Eyewitnesses

Table 11.3.2 (continued)

Chapter (I Sam.)	Contents	Author	Supplier of Additional Details to Author
	and House of Saul; David's rule from Hebron		
5 1-10 19	Events from eighth to twenty-second years of David's reign	Nathan	David and Eye-witnesses
11 1-20 26	Sin of David with Bathsheba, and consequent punishment of David, including Absalom's revolt	Nathan	David and Eye-witnesses
21 1-14	Apeasement of Gibeonites by death of seven of Saul's descendants	Gad	David
21 15-22	Early battles with the Philistines	Gad	David
22 1-51	Song by David when saved from the hand of his enemies	Gad	David
23 1-7	Song by David upon becoming King of Judah	Gad	David
23 8-39	Early military heroes of David	Gad	David
24 1-25	Census of people ordered by David, and consequent plague	Gad	David

harp for him? In actuality David did not play the harp for Saul until after the battle with Goliath the Philistine. Thus in connection with removal of the evil spirit (I Sam. 16 18) it is stated that David was a man of valor and a man of war, which would only be true after the battle with Goliath. Also in I Sam. 18 2, after the death of Goliath it is stated that Saul took David, and did not let him return to his father's house. This corresponds to the time when Saul took David to play the harp to remove the evil spirit. The reason that the taking of David by Saul to play the harp is mentioned before the battle with Goliath is to maintain the logical coherence of the stories. Thus David played the harp after the battle with Goliath to calm the evil spirit that had often visited Saul even before the battle with Goliath.

However, the evil spirit of Saul was connected with the anointing of David and the Godly-spirit of David (I Sam. 16 13), and therefore the topic was placed separately for clarity.

The second part of the Book of Samuel is the appendix written by Gad (II Sam. 21 1-24 25). This section is not arranged chronologically (see Table 11.3.1), but rather by similarity of phrases, as shown in Table 11.3.3. The appendix describes events during the early career of David which if placed in their proper place in the first part of the book would have interrupted the flow of the narrative.

The dates of the historical events described during David's reign are not usually given. However a close approximation can be obtained based on the statement in I Kings 14 21 that Rehoboam was forty-one years old when he became king. Now his father Solomon ruled forty years (I Kings 12 44), which means that Rehoboam was born one year before Solomon became king. Thus, Solomon was at least fifteen years old when he began to rule, assuming that he did not marry before the age of thirteen. The first relationship between David and Bathsheba (II Sam. 11) occurred about two years before Solomon's birth (II Sam. 12 24), since Solomon was the second son of Bathsheba (II Sam. 11 27). Hence the initial relationship of David with Bathsheba occurred seventeen years before David's death, or in the twenty-third year of David's reign. Subsequent events can now be easily dated, assuming that the term "and it later came to pass" (ויהי אחרי כן), refers to a period of about three years. Based on the above discussion, the birth of Solomon occurred in David's twenty-fifth year (II Sam. 12 24). The story of Amnon and Tamar happened about three years later (II Sam. 13 1) in David's twenty-eighth year; two years later Absalom had Amnon killed (13 23), in David's thirtieth year; Absalom resided in Geshur (13 38) for three years until the thirty-third year of David, and two years in Jerusalem (14 28) until the thirty-fifth year of David. About three years later (15 1) Absalom found favor in the people's eyes, i.e. in the thirty-eighth year of David; and Absalom rebelled in David's fortieth year of rule (15 7). The rebellion and related events are described from 15 7 to 20 26.

Another point from which events during David's reign can be dated is the bringing of the Ark from the house of Abinadab (II Sam. 6 3). This event occurred twenty years (I Sam. 7 2) and seven months (I Sam. 6 1) after the death of Eli; which includes three years for Samuel, two years for Saul (I Sam. 13 1), and fifteen years for David. Then the next event, in II Sam. 7 1, when David wanted to build the Temple, occurred in about the sixteenth year of David. About three years later (II Sam. 8 1) in the nineteenth year of David, numerous battles transpired. At about the same time (II Sam. 9) David showed kindness to Mephibosheth, the son of Jonathan. About three years later (II Sam. 10 1) in the twenty-second year of David, a war with the Children of Ammon occurred; and the next year (II Sam. 11 1) in the twenty-third of David, the initial relationship

EARLY PROPHETIC WORKS 183

Table 11.3.3
Organization of Appendix to Book of Samuel, According to Similarity of Phrases

(II Sam.) Section	Sentence	Phrase	(II Sam.) Section	Sentence	Phrase
20 1–26	20 19	לאמה... בישראל	21 1–14	21 4	לי... בישראל
	20 21	דוד... איש		21 6	אתן... יהוה
21 1–14	21 12	דוד... בנו		21 15	דוד ובעבדים
21 15–17	21 15	ויהי עוד מלחמה...		21 18	ויהי אחרי כן מלחמה...
		פלשתים			פלשתים
21 15–22	21 16	אמר להכות את דוד	22 1–51	22 1	דוד... שירה... את
22 1–51	22 1	דוד דבר... דברי			כל איבו
23 1–7	23 7	ישבו	23 1–7	23 1	ויקם... ונעים
	23 1	ואלה... דוד		23 8	שמות
23 8–39	23 18	שלשה 19 ;23 ואהי		23 8	אל ישראל
	23 8	שמות הגברים	24 1–25	24 2	דן... באר
				24 9	שמות הגברים

between David and Bathsheba took place. Thus, using the age of Rehoboam as a starting point, or using the length of stay of the Ark at the house of Abinadab as a basis, results in the same date for the meeting of David and Bathsheba.

The events in the early years of David are not specified as clearly as for the later years. However, it is fairly obvious that the text in II Sam. 2 1 to 5 3 describes the first seven and one-half years of David's reign when he ruled from Hebron; and 5 6–12,17–25 describes events between the eighth and fourteenth years of David. A summary of the dates of the events in David's reign is presented in Table 11.3.4.

11.4 KINGS

The two Books of Kings, which were originally one work, describe the history of the period from the end of the fortieth year of David's reign to the thirty-seventh year of the captivity of Jehoiachin; which is from 999 to 560 B.C.E. or 440 years.

Table 11.3.4
Events in the Reign of David

Year of David's Reign	Event	Reference (II Sam.)
0 to 7	Rule of David from Hebron	2 1–4 12
8 to 14	Reign of David over all Israel; conquest of Jerusalem; battles with the Philistines	5 1–25
15	Ark of God brought to Jerusalem	6 1–22
16	Desire to build the Temple by David	7 1–17
19	Battles against Philistines, Moab, Zobah, and Aram	8 1–6
22	War against Ammon	10 1–14
23	Marriage of David to Bathsheba	11 1–27
24	Death of child of Bathsheba	12 15–18
25	Birth of Solomon	12 24
28	Desire of Amnon for Tamar	13 1–14
30	Absalom has Amnon killed	13 23–33
31–33	Absalom stays three years in Geshur	13 38
34–35	Absalom remains two years in Jerusalem	14 28
38	Absalom popular among the people	15 1–6
40	Rebellion by Absalom against David	15 7– 19 11

Described in the book are the reigns of King Solomon, and of the subsequent kings of Judah and Israel after the split of the monarchy.

The chronology of the period of the kings has already been clarified in Section 5.2. As explained there, and also subsequently in Section 15.3, the "Book of the Kings of Judah and Israel," as mentioned in Chronicles, refers to our present Book of Kings. The "Book of the Chronicles of the Kings of Judah," as mentioned in Kings, refers to our present book of Chronicles. The "Book of [the Chronicles of] the Kings of Israel" as mentioned in both Kings and Chronicles, refers to a book that has been lost. These identifications show that there is cross-referencing between the Book of Kings and the Book of Chronicles, which often supplies the needed information to identify the authors of particular sections in the Book of Kings.

AUTHORSHIP

The period of 440 years covered by the Book of Kings is much too long to have been described by only one person, and must have been recorded by numerous people. Let us examine the book and determine, according to the available information, who was the likely author of each section.

Information as to the authors of the history of King Solomon (I Kings 1–11) is gained from the Book of Chronicles. From II Chr. 9 29 we learn that the events of Solomon's reign were "written in the words of Nathan the prophet; and in the prophecy of Ahijah the Shilonite; and in the visions of Iddo (or Jedo) the seer concerning Jeroboam the son of Nebat." Nathan the prophet is mentioned numerous times in I Kings 1, and he undoubtedly wrote that chapter. Similarly, Ahijah the Shilonite is mentioned in I Kings 11 29, and therefore this chapter, the last one dominantly concerned with Solomon, was written by Ahijah. The intermediate chapters, 2 through 10, which mainly cover the first twenty years of Solomon's reign (I Kings 9 10), were probably also written by Nathan who prophesied during the early years of Solomon's reign. This conclusion is supported by the wording in II Chr. 9 29 which indicates that Nathan wrote a large portion of Solomon's history, while Ahijah only wrote one prophecy.

The part written by Iddo the seer, as stated in II Chr. 9 29, is concerned with Jeroboam the son of Nebat, which corresponds to I Kings 12 1–20; 12 25–14 20. Only incidental mention is made in these chapters about Solomon; for example in I Kings 12 4,10,11,14 reference is made to the high taxes that Solomon imposed upon the people. It should be noted that although Iddo wrote the history of Jeroboam, the King of Israel, there are included in the text also the story involving the elderly prophet (13 1–32), and the prediction by Ahijah the Shilonite concerning the son of Jeroboam (14 1–16). Probably, Iddo recorded these stories based on oral statements from the individuals involved. Certainly Ahijah could not have written down the events concerning the death of Jeroboam's son since Ahijah could not see at that time (14 4).

The authors of the history of Rehoboam, King of Judah (I Kings 12 21–24;

14 21–31) are given in II Chr. 12 15, where it is stated that the history of Rehoboam is written in the words of Shemaiah the prophet and of Iddo the seer after the manner of genealogies. The part written by Shemaiah is clearly I Kings 12 21–24 which describes a short prophecy by him. The section written by Iddo must then be 14 21–31. No genealogies are, however, given. Probably the genealogies were included in I Chronicles 1–9.

The next section (I Kings 15 1–8), concerning the reign of Abijam, King of Judah, was written also by Iddo. Thus in II Chr. 13 22 it is stated, "And the rest of the history of Abijah, and his ways and his history, are written in the commentary [*midrash*] of the prophet Iddo." The word *midrash* is used to refer to the comment in I Kings 15 3–5 about the comparison of the bad qualities of Abijam with the good qualities of David. Thus, the prophet Iddo was the main historian describing the events from the time of Jeroboam to the end of the reigns of Abijam and Jeroboam, or a total of about twenty-one years.

The writer of the history of Asa, King of Judah, (I Kings 15 9–24) is not indicated in the Book of Kings. Also, the author is not specified in the Book of Chronicles; although in II Chr. 16 11, it is stated that the history of Asa is "written in the Book of the Kings of Judah and Israel," which as previously explained corresponds to our present Book of Kings. This "Book of the Kings of Judah and Israel" is now mentioned in Chronicles for the first time, indicating that the author of the history of Asa expanded on the previous writings of Iddo and others, to lay the foundation for our present book of Kings. The probable author of the history of Asa can, nevertheless, be selected based on information from Chronicles. In II Chr. 16 1–6, the passage in I Kings (15 17–22) describing the war with Baasa is repeated with only minor variations. Then this passage is followed in Chronicles with a prophecy by Hanani the seer (II Chr. 16 7), indicating that the latter was the author not only of the passage in Chronicles in which his name occurs, but also of the entire historical description of Asa's reign.

Meager information as to authorship also exists for the reigns of Nadab (I Kings 15 25–32), Baasa (15 33–16 7), Elah (16 8–14), Zimri (16 15–20), and Omri (16 21–28), the kings of Israel contemporary to Asa. Based on the facts that (A) Jehu the son of Hanani received a prophecy concerning Baasa (16 1,7), (B) the writings of Jehu were included in the lost book of the Kings of Israel (II Chr. 20 34), and (C) that Jehu lived until after the death of Jehoshaphat the son of Asa (II Chr. 19 2; 20 34), we may conclude that Jehu was the recorder of the histories of these kings of Israel. Thus the amazing situation arises that Jehu recorded the history of the kings of Israel at the same time that his father Hanani recorded the history of Asa, King of Judah.

Beginning with the reign of Ahab, King of Israel, and including the reigns of Jehoshaphat, King of Judah, and Ahaziah, King of Israel, the text of Kings offers clear evidence from its content that the history was recorded mainly by Elijah the Tishbite. This period of about twenty-six years is covered in I Kings 16 29–

II Kings 1 18. However, the events described in I Kings 20 1–43 were probably written by the anonymous prophet mentioned in that chapter. Similarly, the description of the death of Ahab, I Kings 22 1–38, was probably written by the prophet Micaiah the son of Imlah, who was a participant in some of the happenings. These narratives were inserted in their proper chronological position within the parts written by Elijah. The statement in II Chr. 20 34 that the history of Jehoshaphat was written by Jehu the son of Hanani, refers only to the description in the book of the Kings of Israel, the records of which are lost, and does not refer to the present Book of Kings.

The following sections (II Kings 2 1–13 19), which describe the histories of Jehoram, Jehu, Jehoahaz, and Jehoash, of Israel, and Jehoram, Ahaziah, Athaliah, and Jehoash, of Judah —a period of about sixty years— were recorded by the prophet Elisha. This is evident from the context, where miracles and prophecies of Elisha predominate. It should be noted that the reference given in II Chr. 24 27 concerning the reign of Jehoash, King of Judah, does not refer to the present Book of Kings. It is there stated "Now concerning his sons, and the multitude of the burdens [taxes] from him, and the foundation of the house of God, they are written in the Midrash (commentary) of the Book of Kings." The meaning is that additional information to that given in II Chr. 24 3 about the number of the children of Jehoash, and to that found in II Chr. 24 6,11 relative to the tax on the people, and to that presented in II Chr. 24 13,14 about the money used for strengthening the foundation of the Temple, are found in the Midrash on the Book of Kings. Records of these items are not found in the present Book of Kings, and therefore the reference is to some unknown work.

It is unclear from the text who recorded the end of the reign of King Jehoash of Israel, and the history of King Amaziah of Judah and King Jeroboam of Israel (II Kings 13 20–14 29)—a period of about fifty years. Based on the mention of the Prophet Jonah (II Kings 14 25), the history of these kings is attributed to him, although other prophets not mentioned by name could also have recorded the described events.

The next section (II Kings 15 1–20 21) concerning Azariah, Jotham, Ahaz, and Hezekiah, kings of Judah, and Zechariah, Shallum, Menahem, Pekahiah, Pekah, and Hoshea, kings of Israel, was very probably written by Isaiah. Thus, in II Chr. 26 22 it is stated that Isaiah recorded the history of King Uzziah (Azariah) of Judah. Similarly in II Chr. 32 32 it is stated that the history of King Hezekiah of Judah was written by Isaiah in the Book of the Kings of Judah and Israel (our present Book of Kings). Furthermore, the superscription of the Book of Isaiah (Isa. 1 1) states that Isaiah prophesied during the reigns of Uzziah (Azariah), Jotham, Ahaz, and Hezekiah, Kings of Judah. We may therefore conclude that Isaiah recorded the histories not only of Azariah and Hezekiah, but also of the intermediate kings of Judah, Jotham and Ahaz. Additional support for this conclusion is gained from the involvement of Isaiah in the story of Hezekiah, as recorded both in the Book of Kings (II Kings **18** 17–20 19) and the Book of Isaiah (**36** 1–39 8). Since no evidence is available concerning the author of the history of the contemporary kings of Israel, namely Zechariah, Shallum, Menahem, Pekahiah, and Hoshea, their events are also considered to have been recorded by Isaiah.

No evidence is available in the Book of Kings concerning the author of the history of Manassah, King of Judah (II Kings **21** 1–18). However in II Chr. **33** 18,19 it is stated that further information about Manasseh's reign is given in two places: (A) the history of the Kings of Israel, and (B) the history by the prophet Hozai. The former work as explained previously, is lost. It remains to be clarified if the latter work is in existence. In particular we find stated concerning Manasseh, (II Chr. **33** 19), "His prayer, and how God was entreated of him, and all his sin and his transgression, and the places wherein he built high places and set up the Asherim and the graven images before he humbled himself; behold, they are written in the history by Hozai." Now, in II Kings **21** 1–18 we do not find mention of "his prayer, and how God was entreated of him"; however, we do find descriptions which could very well correspond to "all his sin and his transgression, and the places wherein he built high places and set up the Asherim and the graven images." It is therefore a reasonable assumption that the description in II Kings concerning Manasseh's fifty-five-year reign was partially, but not completely, taken from the writings of Hozai. Possibly the description of "his prayer" was omitted in Kings, to prevent duplication of the description of "his prayer" contained in the Book of the Kings of Israel (see II Chr. **33** 18). We will also here assume, for lack of other evidence, that the two-year rule of Manasseh's son, King Amon (II Kings **21** 19–26) was recorded by the prophet Hozai.

The history of the reign of King Josiah (II Kings **22** 1–23 30) was probably recorded by Huldah the prophetess. She is mentioned in II Kings **22** 14; and it is clear from her prophecy that she was aware of all the details described in Chapter 22. Undoubtedly, she was also aware of the details presented in Chapter 23 concerning King Josiah, since the events described mainly occurred within a two-week period, i.e. from the first of Nisan (II Kings **22** 3) to the fourteenth of Nisan (II Kings **23** 21).

The remainder of the Book of Kings (II Kings **23** 31–25 30) which describes the reigns of Jehoahaz, Jehoiakim, Jehoiachin, and Zedekiah, Kings of Judah, and covers a period of twenty-two years, does not offer any clear evidence as to authorship. The most notable clue as to the author is the essential identity of much of the description with that written in the Book of Jeremiah. For example, compare II Kings **24** 18–25 21 with Jer. **52** 1–27; II Kings **25** 22–26 with Jer. **40** 6–9; **41** 1–3; **41** 17–42 1; **43** 5–7; and II Kings **25** 27–30 with Jer. **52** 31–34. Also, note the slight similarity between II Kings **24** 12–16 and Jer. **52** 28. Thus it is very probable that the author of the descriptions in the Book of Jeremiah is the one who wrote the corresponding descriptions in Kings. Any variations in information may possibly be attributed to the writing of the material in a form most appropriate for each book. According to this approach, the author of the histories of Jehoahaz through Zedekiah would be Baruch, the son of Neriah, who based much of his writing on that of Jeremiah (see Section 12.2). This identification also makes Baruch the final redactor of the Book of Kings.

The previously presented opinions as to the authors of the different sections of the Book of Kings are summarized in Table 11.4.1. It should be realized that the above assumptions are logical conjectures, based on the limited evidence available. Only when the authors of the sections, such as for the reigns of Solomon, Jeroboam, Abijam, Azariah, and Hezekiah, are specifically stated in Chronicles; or where the authors, such as Elijah, Elisha, and Huldah, are involved in the transpired events, is there any certainty as to the given authors. Furthermore, we have frequently assumed that the entire history of a king was recorded by one person. It may have often happened, however, that the concluding description of a king's reign was added by someone else after the main author's death, especially for kings who reigned long periods. Despite the above shortcomings, we have here clarified the authorship of the individual sections of the Book of Kings, and the probable person who was the final redactor of the text.

ORGANIZATION

The main purpose of the Book of Kings is to present the histories of the kingdoms of Judah and Israel. To achieve this goal it would be very difficult to present the events in strict chronological order, since the two kingdoms flourished simultaneously. Instead, the approach taken is to give the story of one king from accession to death, and then all the kings of the other kingdom who came to the throne during his reign. Occasionally this results in a king of the other kingdom being mentioned before his accession has been recorded. Thus King Jehoshaphat of Judah is mentioned when describing the reign of King Ahab of Israel (I Kings 22 1–38), even though the accession of King Jehoshaphat is not related until I Kings 22 41–51. A similar case occurs for King Ahaziah of Israel (I Kings 22 50; 22 52). Also, we find that the history of King Jehoram of Israel (II Kings 3 1–8 15; 9 14–26) is interrupted at II Kings 8 16 to give an account of the reigns of Kings Jehoram and Ahaziah of Judah, so as to be able later to describe how Jehu slew King Jehoram of Israel and King Ahaziah of Judah in one day (II Kings 9 21–29). We thus see that the arrangement of the kings of either kingdom is in chronological order. However, the places where the history of one kingdom is interrupted by that of the other kingdom is dependent on logical considerations.

One noteworthy feature of the book is the synchronistic data giving the year in the reign of the corresponding king when the king of the other kingdom began to rule. An elaborate explanation of the dates, and the solution to the apparent difficulties has already been presented (Section 5.2).

The cross-referencing between the Book of Kings (Book of the Kings of Judah

Table 11.4.1

Probable Authors of the Sections of the Book of Kings

Section	Probable Author	Described Reigns		Approximate Time-Span (years)
			Israel	
I Kings 1–10	Nathan the prophet	David and Solomon		20
I Kings 11 1–43	Ahijah the Shilonite	Solomon		20
I Kings 12 1–20;		Judah		
12 25–14 20			Jeroboam	
I Kings 12 21–24	Iddo the seer	Rehoboam		⎫
I Kings 14 21–31	Shemaiah the prophet	Rehoboam		⎬ 21
I Kings 15 1–8	Iddo the seer	Abijam		⎭
I Kings 15 9–24	Iddo the seer	Asa		41
I Kings 15 25–16 28	Hanani the seer		Nadab, Baasa,	36
	Jehu son of Hanani		Elah, Zimri,	
			Omri	
I Kings 16 29–	Elijah the Tishbite	Jehoshaphat	Ahab	⎫
II Kings 1 18			Ahaziah	⎬ 26
I Kings 20 1–43	Anonymous prophet		Ahab	⎭
I Kings 22 1–38	Micaiah son of Imlah		Ahab	
II Kings 2 1–13 19	Elisha the prophet	Jehoram	Jehoram	60
		Ahaziah	Jehu	
		Athaliah	Jehoahaz	
		Jehoash	Jehoash	

Table 11.4.1 (continued)

Section	Probable Author	Described Reigns		Approximate Time-Span (years)
II Kings 13 20–14 29	Jonah son of Amittai	Amaziah	Jehoash Jeroboam	50
II Kings 15 1–20 21	Isaiah son of Amoz	Azariah Jotham Ahaz Hezekiah	Zechariah Shallum Menahem Pekahiah Pekah Hoshea	75
II Kings 21 1–26	The prophet Hozai	Manasseh Amon		57
II Kings 22 1–23 30	Huldah, the prophetess	Josiah		31
II Kings 23 31–25 30	Jeremiah the prophet and Baruch son of Neriah	Jehoahaz Jehoiakim Jehoiachin Zedekiah		22

and Israel), and the Book of Chronicles (Book of the Chronicles of the Kings of Judah) poses a difficult problem as to how it was achieved. Two explanations seem probable. Either the corresponding sections were written contemporaneously, or the cross-references were added after the completion of both books. The latter possibility is excluded because in several cases very specific titles are used to refer to the Book of Kings. These titles are (A) the histories of Shemaiah the prophet and Iddo the seer (II Chr.]12 15); (B) the commentary of the prophet Iddo (II Chr. 13 22); and (C) the vision of Isaiah the prophet the son of Amoz upon the Book of the Kings of Judah and Israel (II Chr. 32 32). These variant names for the different sections of the Book of Kings would not have been known to anyone except a contemporary of the original writer. The conclusion therefore arises that the cross-referenced parts of Chronicles and Kings were written contemporaneously, though by different authors. See Section 15.3 for a more detailed discussion.

Chapter Twelve

LATER PROPHETS

12.1 ISAIAH

The Book of Isaiah presents prophecies and historical details concerning more periods of history than any of the other prophetic books. Details are presented concerning the times of the attack on Judah by Aram and Israel (740 B.C.E.), the Assyrian invasion of the Kingdom of Israel (719), the unsuccessful Assyrian invasion of Judah (701), the Babylonian conquest of Judah (586), the resettlement of the land at the time of Cyrus (538), and the Messianic era (after 1948 C.E.). The general theme of the book is that the Kingdom of Israel will be destroyed by Assyria (719), but the Kingdom of Judah will survive the subsequent attack (701). However, the sins of Judah will increase until the nation will be conquered by the Babylonians (586). Then in 539-8 Cyrus, the King of Persia, will conquer Babylonia and allow the reestablishment of the Jewish nation. In much later times (1948 C.E.) the State of Israel will be established to last forever.

Because of the varied periods prophesied in the book, and because of a disbelief in the existence of true prophecy, many critics have assumed that the book was written by at least two authors who lived over 100 years apart. In particular, Chapters 40-66 which are concerned with the reestablishment of the Jewish state after the Babylonian Exile and with the situation during Messianic times, are ascribed to a later author than Isaiah. However, it will here be shown that the book is organized in a logical manner, indicating that the book was written by only one author, namely Isaiah.

ORGANIZATION

The organization of the Book of Isaiah is not easily discernible. The book is definitely not arranged on a chronological basis, as is evident from the information listed in Table 12.1.1. In the Table, there are presented eight cases where the dates when the prophecies were received are able to be derived from the text. Obviously they are not arranged in any time sequence. It should also be noted that the majority of the prophecies of the book are not dated. Dates are given only when the information is useful in understanding the prophecies. For example, in 6 1 the

Table 12.1.1
Prophecies in the Book of Isaiah for which the Dates of Revelation are Indicated

Sentence	Passage	Date (B.C.E.)
1 1	In the days of Uzziah, Jotham, Ahaz, and Hezekiah, kings of Judah	appr. 757–709
1 7	Your country is desolate, your cities are burned with fire, strangers devour your land (compare II Kings 18 13)	711
6 1	In the year that King Uzziah died	756
7 1,14–16	Rezin, king of Aram, and Pekah, king of Israel went up to Jerusalem to war against it (compare II Kings 6 5)	740
8 4	Before the child shall have knowledge to cry father and mother, the riches of Damascus and the spoil of Samaria shall be carried away before the King of Assyria	721
14 28	In the year that King Ahaz died	725
20 1	In the year that Tartan came to Ashdod, when Sargon, King of Assyria sent him	711
36 1	In the fourteenth year of King Hezekiah, Sennacherib, King of Assyria came against all the fortified cities of Judah, and took them	711

year of the death of King Uzziah is specified, to inform us that it is the first prophecy received by Isaiah. Similarly, the dates given in 7 1 concerning the attack on Judah by Aram and Israel, and in 20 1 concerning the capture of Ashdod by Assyria are presented to make possible the calculation of the specified elapsed times (sixty-five years in 7 8; two years in 7 16; and three years in 20 3). In other cases such as 1 7, 14 28, and 36 1 the dates supplied are given to enable proper understanding of the historical events described. In contrast, prophecies concerning such events as the Messianic Era or the Babylonian Exile are undated because the dates when the prophecies were received are completely irrelevant to understanding of the prophecies.

The Book of Isaiah is also not arranged according to the time when the prophesied events would occur. Thus prophecies concerning the Messianic era, and the conquest of Judah by the Babylonians are distributed within the book. Clarification of these points will be presented in subsequent paragraphs.

Rather, the book is arranged according to the nature of the prophecies; and six separate groupings are discernible (see Table 12.1.2). The first group, Chapters 1-12, presents prophecies to the Jewish people where detailed historical information is included, such as the date, or the political and moral situation at the time. The second group, Chapters 13-27, presents prophecies to the different nations, such as Babylonia, Assyria, Philistia, Moab, Damascus, Cush, Egypt, Desert of the Sea, Dumah, Arabia, Kedar, Jerusalem, and Tyre. The Third group, Chapters 28-35, again provides prophecies about the Jewish people, but the prophecies contain meager historical background. In this group the prophecies usually begin with the word "Woe" (הוי). In these three groupings, we find that first are presented prophecies referring to the Babylonian period (ca. 586), followed by events concerning the attacks and conquests of Assyria (ca. 719), and concluded by prophecies concerning the Messianic era (after 1948 C.E.). Only minor exceptions to this generalization occur. Following the first three groups, comes the fourth division, Chapters 36-39, which presents an historical account of the events in the lifetimes of Isaiah and King Hezekiah. This account supplies information for understanding the historical situation during the Assyrian and Babylonian periods described in the previous sections. Thus, the attacks by Assyria against Judah (36 1) and Israel (36 19), and the future conquest by Babylonia (39 6), are mentioned. Furthermore, the fourth section serves as an approximate dividing line between prophecies referring to events up to the destruction of Judah by Babylonia, and the reestablishment of the Jewish people after the destruction. The fifth section, Chapters 40-48, describes the prophecies of events after the Babylonian Exile, when Persia will conquer Babylonia (538), and the Jews will be reestablished in Israel. The sixth and concluding group, Chapters 49-66, then presents the description of the Messianic era, when complete and permanent restoration of the land of Israel will occur (see Chapter Eighteen for interpretation and clarification of the Messianic prophecies).

In addition to the above criteria for the organization of the Book of Isaiah, the prophecies are also arranged according to similarity in phrases. Within each grouping, and from grouping to grouping, there is found that adjacent prophecies contain numerous similar words and phrases, as presented in Table 12.1.3. It should be pointed out, however, that it is not always entirely clear from the text where one theme or prophecy ends and another begins. The divisions into chapters, which are of relatively late origin, are quite often misleading. The separations indicated in Table 12.1.3 are not necessarily the actual division of the book into separate revelations, although considerable care has been used to approach this goal as closely as possible.

The above description shows that the book was organized according to a logical plan, and therefore one, and only one person, was responsible for the arrangement of the book.

Table 12.1.2
Arrangement of the Book of Isaiah

Section	Main Historical Topic of Prophecy	Appr. Date of Prophesied Event*
Group I—Prophecies Containing Detailed Historical Information		
1 1–31	Destruction of Judah and Jerusalem because of their sins, and reestablishment after Babylonian Exile.	586
2 1–4 6	In the Messianic times Jerusalem will be looked up to by all the nations. Now, however, the people have sinned, and therefore Judah and Jerusalem will be destroyed.	1973 C.E. 586
5 1–30	The people of Judah and Jerusalem will be exiled because of their sins by the Babylonians.	586
6 1–13	The Kingdom of Israel will be destroyed because of its sins. Afterwards the Kingdom of Judah will also be destroyed.	719 586
7 1–25	In 740 Israel and Aram attacked Judah. Isaiah prophesied that in sixty-five years (675) Israel will be bereft of her people; and within three years (737) the two rulers Rezin of Aram and Pekah of Israel will no longer exist. Furthermore, Assyria will attack and partially conquer Judah (711).	675 737 711
8 1–23	Within about three years Damascus and Samaria will be conquered by Assyria. Furthermore, Assyria will attack and partially conquer the Kingdom of Judah.	737 711
9 1–6	The people of Judah saw the light of salvation from the Assyrian oppression. Hezekiah, the future king, has been born (750), under whom the salvation shall occur.	701
9 7–10 4	The Kingdom of Israel continues to sin despite the punishments that it receives. Therefore Israel will be destroyed.	719
10 5–34	Assyria will attempt to conquer Judah as it has previously conquered other countries. However, the Assyrian army will be destroyed.	701

* All dates are B.C.E. except when indicated otherwise.

Table 12.1.2 (continued)

Section	Main Historical Topic of Prophecy	Appr. Date of Prophesied Event*
11 1–12 6	In the Messianic times, David will rule justly and the enemy will be destroyed. The Jews will praise God.	1973 C.E.
	Group II—Prophecies to the Nations	
13 1–14 23	Babylonia will be destroyed by the Persians, and the Jews will be reestablished on their land.	539
14 24–27	Assyria will be destroyed on Judean territory.	701
14 28–32	The land of Philistia, which suffers under the hand of the Judean kings, will be destroyed by Assyria.	711
15 1–16 14	Moab will be destroyed by Assyria. Moab will request help from Judah, but Judah will refuse. The second part of the prophecy (**16 14**) was received three years before the destruction.	ca. 719
17 1–11	Damascus will be destroyed by Assyria. Also, Ephraim will be destroyed by Assyria.	737 / 719
17 12–18 7	The Assyrian army attacking Judah will be suddenly destroyed. The Ethiopians will recognize the miracle of God, and will bring gifts.	701
19 1–25	In the Messianic times Egypt will be severely punished, and will eventually serve God in cooperation with Assyria and Israel.	1973 C.E.
20 1–6	In 711, after Ashdod was captured by Assyria, Isaiah went naked as a sign that Egypt and Ethiopia would be conquered by Assyria.	670
21 1–10	Babylon will be conquered by Persia.	539
21 11–12	Prophecy on Dumah (uncertain as to meaning).	
21 13–17	Kedar and Arabia will be conquered within a year.	ca. 719
22 1–14	The Assyrian army will attack Jerusalem, but the Jewish people will be merry.	701
22 15–25	Shebna, who is over the house, will be replaced by Eliakim the son of Hilkiah.	ca. 715
23 1–18	Tyre and Zidon will be conquered by Assyria. After seventy years Tyre will be reestablished.	ca. 719 / ca. 649

Table 12.1.2 (continued)

Section	Main Historical Topic of Prophecy	Appr. Date of Prophesied Event*
24 1–27 13	Describes the Messianic times when all the enemy nations will be destroyed and Israel will become great (see detailed explanation in Chapter Eighteen).	1973 C.E.
Group III—Prophecies with a Minimum of Historical Detail		
28 1–29	The Kingdom of Israel will be destroyed because of her sins. So also the Kingdom of Judah. However, God will not permanently destroy the Jewish people, just as a farmer does not continuously plow or thresh his field.	719 586
29 1–24	The Assyrian army will attack Jerusalem, because of the sins of the people. However, the attacking army will disappear, and Judah will be saved.	701
30 1–31 9	The Jewish people foolishly turn to Egypt for help against Assyria. It will however be God who will quietly and miraculously save Jerusalem from Assyria.	701
32 1–35 10	Shortly after the Messianic king begins to rule, the army of Gog will prepare to attack Israel. As a result the crops in Israel will not be tended and the cities will be deserted. Then God will destroy the attacking nations. In particular, the territory of Edom (Jordan) will be destroyed. Then the land of Israel will flourish, and the Jewish exiles will return to the land of Israel (see Chapter Eighteen for more details).	1973 C.E.
Group IV—Historical Events in the Lives of Isaiah and Hezekiah		
36 1–37 38	Historical account of how Sennacherib, King of Assyria, threatened to destroy Jerusalem. Hezekiah prayed to God. Then Isaiah prophesied that Sennacherib would not succeed.	

Table 12.1.2 (continued)

Section	Main Historical Topic of Prophecy	Appr. Date of Prophesied Event*
	And so it happened, that overnight 185,000 Assyrian soldiers died, and the Assyrians returned to Assyria.	701
38 1–22	Hezekiah became sick and prayed to God for help. Isaiah prophesied that Hezekiah would recover, and would live for fifteen more years (until 696).	711 696
39 1–8	Isaiah prophesied to Hezekiah that the Babylonians would conquer Judah, and bring the Judean captives to Babylonia.	586
Group V—Prophecies Concerning Return After Babylonian Exile		
40 1–48 22	After the set time for the Babylonian Exile, Babylonia will be conquered by Cyrus, king of Persia, and the Jewish state will be reestablished.	539–8
Group VI—Prophecies Concerning the Messianic Era		
49 1–66 24	In the Messianic times, Israel will win in the war against Gog. The country will prosper once again, and the exiled Jews will return to the land of Israel (see Chapter Eighteen for detailed explanation).	1973 C.E.

AUTHORSHIP

The heading of the book (1 1) ·clearly implies that Isaiah was the author. It should be noted that the heading has two parts. The first part "the vision of Isaiah the son of Amoz which he saw concerning Judah and Jerusalem" refers only to the contents of Chapter 1. However the second part, "in the days of Uzziah, Jotham, Ahaz, and Hezekiah, Kings of Judah," refers to the time when Isaiah prophesied, and is a superscription for the entire book.

In addition to the book's heading, Isaiah is specifically mentioned in 2 1; 7 3; 13 1; 20 2,3; 37 2,5,6,21; 38 1,4,21; and 39 3,5,8. Also the writing of Chapters 6, 8, and 21 in the first person establishes authorship by Isaiah. Although

Table 12.1.3
Similarity of Phrases between Adjacent Sections in the Book of Isaiah

Section	Sentence	Phrase	Section	Sentence	Phrase
1 1–31	1 27	ציון במשפט	2 1–4 6	2 3,4	למשפט ושפט
2 1–4 6	3 14	במשפט; ובזקני	5 1	5 1	כרמי
	4 4	במשפט		5 16	במשפט
5 1–30	5 16	ישפט		5 3	כרם
	5 10	וזרע ל׳ אבנים	6 1–13	6 3	מלוא ה׳ כבודו
6 1–13	6 4	מלא		6 13	זרע
	6 9	ואמרת		7 2	וינע
7 1–25	7 16	ובטרם ידע	7 13	ואמר ביתו
	7 14	בן…ובקראת		8 4	בטרם ידע
	7 17	מלך אשור		8 3	בן…ובקרא את
	7 4	וישעון		8 4	מלך אשור
8 1–23	8 6	מימי		8 6	וישעון
	8 3	ובאכלתו אם		9 1	ענף
9 1–6	9 4	כל סאון		9 5	שם
	9 6	שם		9 18	ובאכלתו ה׳ צבאות
9 7–10 4	9 18	ובאכלתו ה׳ צבאות		9 18	כל סאון
	9 8	ואמרו		10 6	ומ
9 17	מלך …אשור אשכב	10 12	וחשב
	9 12	וחרב	10 17	ובער…חרב הושב אשור
	10 4	וה	10 24	במפה
				10 21	בצדק

LATER PROPHETS

		נחמתי		
		נראו		
		ניבו		
		יקר		
		במרה צעיר		
		רעב		
	11 16	לבארותיה		
	11 15	אבחר		
	11 11	ניבו		
11 1-12 6	13 2	עשו: ד' צבאות		
	13 20	ירפט ד'		
13 1-14 23	14 24	כל גאות: כן יהיה	10 24	וידבר
14 24-27	14 25	ורגלי	10 27	תאמרו: כברו מאמרם
	14 26			
14 28-32	14 29	ראש	11 15	
15 1-16 14	15 1	משאדן	11 7	
	15 3	רבה	14 23	
	15 5	לפליטה	14 21	
	15 9	עמש	14 19	
17 1-11	17 1	לעטרת	14 7	
	17 5	כל יכול	14 18	
		בארות	14 25	
17 12-18 7	18 5	וסגם	14 28	
	18 6	טעם	14 31	
	18 7	ויראעית: ירקני	14 31	
	18 3	יד קודש	14 29	
19 1-25	19 6		14 30	
		על פני מים: הרעים	15 1	
			16 9	
			16 10	
			17 5,11	
			17 9	
			17 7	
			18 2	ויהי בהם וחתת: בבךר מאמרם
			17 12-18 7	

Table 12.1.3 (continued)
Similarity of Phrases between Adjacent Sections in the Book of Isaiah

Section	Sentence	Phrase	Section	Sentence	Phrase
19 1–25	19 25	ברוך	20 1–6	19 8	נכרתו
	19 24	מצרים; אשור		20 4	ארץ
	19 20	בתוך מצרים		20 6	מצרים; אשור
20 1–6	20 2	לך		20 3	אות
21 1–10	21 1	ממדבר בא	21 1–10	21 3	מדבר 216
21 11–12	21 8	אמר	21 11–12	21 11	אתא
21 11–12	21 11	נאמן; משמרתי; ונצפיה		21 11	אלי; אמר; משא
21 13–17	21 12	אמר		21 13	חדר
	21 11	אתא		21 14	חבקה
21 13–17	21 13	משא	22 1–14	21 16	כי
	21 17	נעז		22 1	משא
	21 15	מפלטי		22 3	מקשת
	21 14	מים	22 15–25	22 2	עלזה
22 1–14	22 1	לך		22 9	בית
	22 12	אז	22 15–25	22 16	לך אבנה; בית וחדר
22 15–25	22 25	ביום ההוא נאם		22 25	כי
	22 15	לך	23 1–18	23 1	נכרי
	22 20	מעבדי; בית וחדר		23 15	ביום ההוא
	22 18	כי	23 9	אלף
	22 23	נאמן	23 8	נכרי

23 1–18	23 1		24 1–27 13	24 10	כל אמור
	23 18	גלות		24 5	טורה
	23 17	המלכות ואנשיה		24 21	הצבו

24 1–27 13	27 6	ארץ	28 1–29	28 1	יקרת
	24 9			28 1	שמעו
	25 6	שמרים		28 17	וככריו ואמתו
	25 4	אשתמו			
28 1–29	28 1	כפר	29 1–24	29 9	אפוא
	28 10	אכניהו		29 17	האם חלכה
	28 4	יבל		29 10	וחשבו ועלי על פיהם
	28 7				
29 1–24	29 10	עיף	30 1–31 9	30 1	עגל
	29 21	הואסם אלהי		30 5	בלבבי
	29 22	ישע		30 8	מחטיה ואמתו
	29 12	קם			
30 1–31 9	30 15	לקחו	32 1–35 10	32 17	אלם
	30 30	מסח		33 11	חצבי
	30 8	משכיו		33 10	עכבים
	31 2				
32 1–35 10	35 7	ענאי	36 1–37 38	36 6	חוחים
	35 8	שליע		36 2	אנחה
	35 9	נתב		36 1	חשבו
	35 5			36 11	חרשים
36 1–37 38	37 37	משמה	38 1–22	38 6	ברך הבכוו

Table 12.1.3 (continued)
Similarity of Phrases between Adjacent Sections in the Book of Isaiah

Section	Sentence	Phrase	Section	Sentence	Phrase
	37 30	הזה לך האות		38 7	הזה לך האות
	37 21	ישעיהו; ויאמר		38 4	ישעיהו
				38 5	ויאמר
38 1–22	38 1	חזקיהו; חלה	39 1–8	39 1	חזקיהו; חלה
	38 2	חזק		39 2	חזק
	38 1	לאמר; ישעיהו		39 3	ישעיהו; לאמר
39 1–8	39 8	אמר		40 1	יאמר
	39 5	ישראל		40 4	אמר
	39 8	יהי		40 5	יקרא
	39 7	ילקחו		40 2	לקחה
40 1–31	40 31	יגעו; ייעפו	41 1–42 4	41 1	אי'ם; לאמים; יעפו
	40 27	משפטי		41 2	ארץ
	41 15	תדוש; אתה			
41 1–42 4	42 4	משפט	42 5–43 13	42 5	ארץ
	41 1	אי'ם		42 10	אי'ם
	41 4	אני יי		43 3	אני יי
42 5–43 13	43 1	יעקב; ישראל; ויאמר	43 14–44 5	43 14	יעקב; ישראל; אמר יי
				43 15	ישראל
				43 16	אמר
43 14–44 5	43 2		44 6–23	44 6	יעקב; ישראל; אמר יי
	43 14	קדוש; משכם; ישראל			

LATER PROPHETS   205

44 6–23	43 16		ותאבל
	44 6		אומללה
	44 7		המון
	44 25		קדרי
44 24–28	44 28	44 24–28	ועד
	44 26	44 12	אכלה
	44 24	44 24	ויקדיש
45 1–13	45 5	44 25	ובבל; בבלים
	45 6	44 22	
	45 7	45 1	בני יהודה; בני עילם
45 14–25	45 21	45 4	עילם
	45 19	45 7	
	45 21	45 21	דמשק
46 1–47	47 8	45 22	כי ארבע, קל ואדר א'
	46 10	45 18	לקדר
48 1–16	48 14	46 9	וגוי חצור
	48 1	46 11	עמוני ועדני
48 17–22	48 20	46 7	ולאדום; אדומים
	48 17	48 1	לאמון: אמונה
		48 12	עמון
49 1–13	49 1	48 20	עמי
	49 6	48 18	כי אצר ד' אתכן
	49 7	49 3	גלעד
		49 6	מואב
		49 7	חי אנכי ד' ואני כל
		49 14–50 3	סוף
		49 15	
		49 25	
		49 26	

Table 12.1.3 (continued)
Similarity of Phrases between Adjacent Sections in the Book of Isaiah

Section	Sentence	Phrase	Section	Sentence	Phrase
49 14–50 3	49 8	שמועה		49 19	ולקולה אשלך
	50 3	אשר	50 4–11	50 7	ידעי
	49 26	וכאסיס		50 9	כאסם
	50 2	הן		50 9	הן
50 4–11	50 9	לבשו; בגדי עש	51 1–11	51 6	בגדי עיני לבלבש עם
51 1–11	51 9	עורי עורי לבשי עז	51 12–52 12	52 1	עורי עורי לבשי עז
	51 11	ציון		51 16	ציון
	51 3	שמח		51 23	שמח
	51 3	מים		51 12	מכם
51 12–52 12	51 12	מנחם מנחם; ארם	52 13–53 12	52 14	מעני
	51 14	למחת		52 15	עלי
	52 7	מלך			
52 13–53 12	53 10	יגל	54 1–17	54 3	ירשי
	53 6	נברל		54 8	נברל
	53 11	אלה		54 17	אלה
	(52 9)	יצחו יחדיו		(54 1	יצחו יחדיו)
54 1–17	54 1	אלהי ישראל	55 1–13	55 12	אלהי ישראל
	54 3	וזרע		55 10	ולזרע
	54 5	יקרא		55 5	יקרא
	54 8	מים		55 3	מכם

LATER PROPHETS   207

55 1-13	55 12	עץ	
	55 3	ואכלותו פוה רוד לדוד	
	55 13	פלח	
56 1-8	56 3	עץ	56 3 עץ
	56 4	כדי	56 4
	56 5	אוכם	56 5
	56 7	ובבתי	
56 9-57 21	57 11	ותחומים: ור קדמי	56 9-57 21
	57 21	קמסלי	57 5
	57 17	ואת	57 8
	57 4	דם	57 11
	56 12	ומסתי קמסי	57 13
58 1-14	58 8	חטלומר	57 7
	58 4	קלי	58 2
	58 1	כבוד	58 4
	58 2	קדר	58 6
	58 8	חמר	58 5
	58 14	ככוה	
59 1-21	59 9	האני: דוסכו	59 1
	59 1	אוכם	59 12
	59 9	עדיר	59 4
	59 20	חמר	59 9
	59 21	קלי	59 20
	59 20	כככי	60 1
			60 2
			60 14
			60 15
			60 16
			60 17

Table 12.1.3 (continued)
Similarity of Phrases between Adjacent Sections in the Book of Isaiah

Section	Sentence	Phrase	Section	Sentence	Phrase
60 1–22	59 9				
	59 8	צדקה			יקוה מש
	60 21	לעולם; צדיקם כלם	61 1–11	61 3	ונקרא...נטע יהוה להתפאר
	60 11	כל גוי		61 6	אל יהוה
	60 16	חות		61 7	עולם תהיה
	60 19	עולם			
61 1–11	61 10	אנ...שוש	62 1–12	62 5	ישיש...א'
	61 2	יום		62 6	יום
	61 3	לעולם כלם		62 2	לכל גוים
	61 4	מחרבות		62 4	מחרבת
	61 10	כחתן וככלה		62 5	כי כבחור
62 1–12	62 12	גאולי	63 1–6	63 4	גאולי
	62 11	ישועה		63 1	ישועה
	62 6	יום		63 4	יום
	62 10	עמים		63 6	עמים
63 1–6	63 1	ישועה	63 7–65 7	63 8	ישועה
	63 4	כל		63 9	כל
	63 1	רב		63 7	רב
63 7–65 7	64 3	עין לא ראתה; יעשה	65 8–25	65 8	טוב
	63 19			65 12	ורע בעיני יהוה
	65 2			65 15	אשר

65 14	ונאמר לא ונצרך ההרר
66 20	לא מעמי ונקטו וילך וצרוי
66 4	מי פראי ואן אבחי ובחרתי
	מחרב
66 1-24	
65 25	הפצרי ההרחם
65 12	ויל בארי ונאמר לא
	בחרתי לא מעמתי וניצאו
	מי פראי לא אבחי
	הי קשוי
65 8-25	

Isaiah's name is not mentioned in Chapters 40–48 which describe the reestablishment of the Jewish state after the Babylonian Exile, his name is mentioned (13 1) as author of a prophecy about the doom of Babylon, and revival of the Jewish nation. Thus the evidence is clear that he foretold events not only with respect to the Assyrian empire but also concerning the Babylonian empire.

The question arises, however, if Isaiah is the author of the book, why are the historical descriptions in Chapters 36–39 presented only about the life of King Hezekiah and not about the other kings of Judah who reigned during the time that Isaiah prophesied? It is clearly stated in Chronicles that Isaiah wrote the history of King Uzziah (II Chr. 26 22) as well as the history of King Hezekiah (II Chr. 32 32); and it is only logical to assume that Isaiah also authored the history of the intermediate kings, Jotham and Ahaz, as well as the contemporary kings of Israel (see Section 11.4). Secondly, why are Chapters 36–39 almost, but not entirely, identical to the description in Kings (II Kings 18 13–20 19)? The major difference between the accounts is that the song of Hezekiah (Isa. 38 9–20) is not found in Kings. The answers to these questions are fairly simple. Isaiah in writing his book of prophecies also included the historical account of the reign of Hezekiah because several of Isaiah's prophecies are included in the narrative, and the history is relevant to understanding many of the other prophecies by Isaiah concerning the attacks by Assyria and Babylonia. The extra section containing Hezekiah's song is presented only in the Book of Isaiah because of the more poetic nature of the book, as well as the lack of additional historical information in the song. The slight variations in wording between the descriptions in the Books of Isaiah and Kings are because the emphasis in Kings is on historical detail. The accounts of the histories of Uzziah, Jotham, and Ahaz found in Kings (II Kings 15 1–17 41), and here attributed to Isaiah, are not included in the Book of Isaiah because the accounts do not contain any of Isaiah's prophecies.

From the headings of Chapter 6, "the year of the death of Uzziah" (756), and Chapter 20, "the year that Tartan came to Ashdod" (711), we can conclude that Isaiah prophesied for a period of at least forty-five years.

12.2 JEREMIAH

The prophecies in the Book of Jeremiah were delivered during a period of forty years, from the thirteenth year of Josiah (626 B.C.E.) to after the destruction of the Temple (586) (Jer. 1 1–3; 41 1). During that time the prophecies of Jeremiah describe events concerning the capture of Jerusalem, the exile of the Jews by Nebuchadrezzar, king of Babylon, and the conquest of other nations by Nebuchadrezzar. In addition, prophecies are also given concerning the conquest of Babylonia by the Medes, the reestablishment of the Jewish settlement (after seventy years of Babylonian conquest), and the eventual permanent redemption of the Jewish people.

Organization

The Book of Jeremiah is clearly not arranged in chronological order, as can be determined from the data presented in Table 12.2.1. For example, Chapter 24 is dated at the time of the exile of Jeconiah (597), while the following chapter, Chapter 25, is dated the fourth year of Jehoiakim (604), i.e. seven years earlier. Numerous similar examples are readily apparent. Rather, the book is arranged in a logical order according to the subject matter of the prophecies (Table 12.2.2). Four major groupings are apparent.

Group I (Chapters 1–36)

The first major grouping involves prophecies about the future destruction of Judah and Jerusalem, and is further subdivided into six categories. Chapter 1 contains introductory prophecies, detailing the initiating visions to Jeremiah, where he is promised that God will be with him to save him from all enemies. Chapters 2 through 12 contain prophecies about the destruction of Judah and Jerusalem, presented in general terms with a minimum amount of historical and symbolic details.

The third subgrouping, Chapters 13 through 19, contains prophecies where symbolic examples are significant parts of the prophecies. Some of the more obvious key symbolisms are: a linen girdle (13 1); a bottle filled with wine (13 12); droughts (14 1); intercession of Moses and Samuel (15 1); not to marry (16 1); not to carry on the Sabbath (17 21); clay vessel in the hand of the potter (18 4); potter's earthen bottle (19 1).

The fourth subgrouping, Chapters 20 through 22, continues with prophecies about the destruction of Jerusalem, and makes specific mention of prominent individuals. The names presented are: Pashhur the son of Immer (20 1); King Zedekiah, Pashhur the son of Malchiah, and Zephaniah the son of Maaseiah (21 1); King of Judah (22 1); King Shallum (22 11); King Jehoiakim (22 18); and King Coniah (22 24).

The next subgrouping, Chapters 23 through 33, contains prophecies of consolation and future redemption in addition to prophecies on the destruction of Judah. The concept of redemption is found, for example, in Jer. 23 3–8, 19–20; 24 5–7; 25 12–15; 26 3,13; 27 22; 28 6; 29 10–14,32; 30 3,8–25; 31 3–39; 32 15,37–44; and 33 6–26.

The sixth and final subgrouping of Group I, Chapters 34 through 36, contains additional prophecies about the destruction of Judah and Jerusalem, in relation to miscellaneous topics. For example, Chapter 34 discusses freeing of slaves, Chapter 35 refers to the righteousness of the house of Rechabites, and Chapter 36 presents details concerning the writing of certain sections of the Book of Jeremiah. A common feature of this subgrouping is that in each case the manner of death of certain individuals is prophesied. Thus, King Zedekiah will not die by

Table 12.2.1
Dated Prophecies in the Book of Jeremiah

Chapter	Stated Time	Date (B.C.E.)
1 2	Thirteenth year in the reign of Josiah	626 to
1 3	Until exile of Jerusalem in the fifth month	586
3 6	In the days of King Josiah	626 to 608
21 1,2	Nebuchadrezzar warred against Zedekiah	588
22 11	Shallum (i.e. Jehoahaz) son of Josiah	608
22 18	Jehoiakim, King of Judah	608 to 597
22 24	Coniah (i.e. Jehoiachin), King of Judah	597
24 1	After exile of Jeconiah by Nebuchadrezzar	597
25 1	The fourth year of Jehoiakim which was the first year of Nebuchadrezzar	604
26 1	Beginning of the reign of Jehoiakim	about 608
27 1	Beginning of the reign of Jehoiakim	about 608
27 12	I spoke to Zedekiah, King of Judah	593
28 1	Fourth year, fifth month of the reign of Zedekiah	593
28 17	Fourth year, seventh month of Zedekiah	593
29 1,2	After exile of Jeconiah by Nebuchadnezzar	597
32 1	The tenth year of Zedekiah which is the eighteenth year of Nebuchadrezzar	587
33 1(32 2)	Jeremiah still captive in the court of the guard	587
34 1	The army of Nebuchadrezzar fighting against Jerusalem	587
35 1,11	In the days of Jehoiakim, King of Judah; When Nebuchadrezzar came against the land.	probably about 597
36 1	Fourth year of Jehoiakim, King of Judah	604
36 9	Fifth year, ninth month of Jehoiakim	603
37 1	During the reign of Zedekiah	597 to 586
38 28	Jeremiah remained in the court of the guard until the capture of Jerusalem	586
39 1	Ninth year, tenth month of Zedekiah	588
39 2	Eleventh year, fourth month, ninth day of Zedekiah	586
40 1	Captives of Jerusalem and Judah being exiled to Babylon	586
41 1	Seventh month (of eleventh year of Zedekiah)	586
44 1	To the Jews who dwell in Egypt	586
45 1	Fourth year of Jehoiakim, King of Judah	604

Table 12.2.1 (continued)

Chapter	Stated Time	Date (B.C.E.)
46 2	Defeat of Pharaoh Necho of Egypt by Nebuchadrezzar in the fourth year of Jehoiakim	604
47 1	Before Pharaoh smote Gaza	Exact date not known
49 34	Beginning of the reign of Zedekiah, King of Judah	about 597
51 59	Fourth year of Zedekiah	593

the sword (34 4,5); the leaders and people, who forced back into slavery their freed slaves, will be killed, and the dead bodies will be food for the birds and the beasts (34 20); no descendant of Jonadab the son of Rechab will die a premature death (35 19); and the dead body of King Jehoiakim will be cast out in the day to the heat and in the night to the frost (36 30).

Group II (Chapters 37–45)

The second major grouping of the Book of Jeremiah, with the exception of Chapter 45, is arranged in approximate chronological order, and describes the prophecies of Jeremiah at the time preceding the destruction of Jerusalem and shortly thereafter. These chapters present an excellent description of the historical situation of this period, and give a clear picture of the trials that Jeremiah underwent. At the end of this grouping we find the prophecy to Baruch the son of Neriah telling him that his life would be spared (Chapter 45). Logically it would seem that this chapter would have been more appropriately placed at the end of Chapter 36, where Baruch is described as writing down Jeremiah's prophecies. However, Chapter 45 serves the purpose of bringing the story back to the time of the fourth year of Jehoiakim, the same time as the prophecy of Chapter 46, implying that Chapter 46 was included among the prophecies initially dictated to Baruch by Jeremiah in the fourth year of Jehoiakim.

Group III (Chapters 46–51)

The third major grouping contains prophecies by Jeremiah to other nations than Judah, namely Egypt, Philistia, Moab, Children of Ammon, Edom, Damascus, Kedar, Hazor, Elam, and Babylon. Details are given concerning the impending

Table 12.2.2
Organization of the Book of Jeremiah

Group I—Prophecies on the destruction of Judah and Jerusalem—
(Chapters 1-36)
Chapter 1 —Introductory Prophecies
Chapter 2-12—Prophecies with minimal historical details and symbolism
Chapter 13-19—Prophecies with symbolic examples
Chapter 20-22—Mention of individuals
Chapter 23-33—Prophecies containing consolation and mention of future redemption
Chapter 34-36—Miscellaneous topics—prophecies about deaths of individuals

Group II—Prophetic chapters presenting the history and trials of Jeremiah—
(Chapters 37-45)
Chapter 37-44—Arranged in approximate chronological order
Chapter 45-Appendix—about Baruch the son of Neriah

Group III—Prophecies on the Nations—(Chapters 46-51)
Chapter 46-49—The nations of Egypt, Philistia, Moab, Ammon, Edom, Damascus, Kedar, Hazor will be conquered by Babylonia
Chapter 50-51—Babylonia will be conquered by Media

Group IV—History of period from Zedekiah to release of Jehoiachin by Evil-Merodach—(Chapter 52)
Chapter 52—History of period, without any prophecies

---

destruction of these countries. All these nations will be destroyed by Babylon. Babylon, however, will be conquered by Media.

It should be noted that each of the three major groupings ends with a section concerning a son of Neriah. The first grouping ends with an account relating how Baruch the son of Neriah wrote down the prophecies for Jeremiah (36 32); the second grouping ends with a prophecy to Baruch the son of Neriah telling him that his life would be spared (45); and the third grouping ends with the command by Jeremiah to Seraiah the son of Neriah to bring the prophecies concerning Babylon to Babylon (51 59-64). It is probable that Chapter 45 was placed somewhat out of logical sequence to enable each major grouping to end with mention of a son of Neriah, because of the indebtedness felt by Jeremiah to these brothers.

Group IV (Chapter 52)

The final major grouping contains a historical account of the reign of Zedekiah (597-586) until the release of Jehoiachin by Evil-Merodach (560). Described in detail are the events concerning the destruction of Jerusalem, which was emphasized throughout the book in the prophecies of Jeremiah. The history is presented here (similarly to the historical account in the Book of Isaiah [Isa. 36-39]) to clarify the historical events relative to the presented prophecies.

It should be pointed out that in addition to the general outline presented, there are many fine points for the organization within the groupings and subgroupings. Similarity of episodes, as well as similarity of phrases between adjacent sections, have been used as the basis for much of the book's arrangement. In Table 12.2.3 many of the similarities of phrases between adjacent sections are tabulated. Note that numerous remarkably similar phrases occur in adjacent sections. Naturally these similarities in phrases have been of secondary importance in the book's organization, relative to the systematic arrangement of the book described above.

The present organization of the Book of Jeremiah is not necessarily the same as that used by Jeremiah when he dictated prophecies to Baruch the son of Neriah in the fourth and fifth years of Jehoiakim (36 1,2,9,27,28,32). At that time the resultant book could not possibly have included any of the prophecies received subsequently. Based on the datings of the chapters listed in Table 12.2.1 it is obvious that sections 1 3; 21 1-14; 22 20-30; 24 1-10; 27 12-29 32; 32 1-35 19; 37 1-44 30; 49 34-39; 51 59-64; and 52 1-34 were not included. On the other hand, the sections 1 1,2; 1 4-20 18; 22 1-19; 23 1-40; 25 1-27 11; 30 1-31 39; 36 1-32; 45 1-49 33; and 50 1-51 58 or parts thereof, may have been included, since the contents could have been in existence by the fifth year of Jehoiakim. It would, however, be reasonable to assume that the order of these earlier prophecies was the same as the present arrangement, and that the later prophecies were inserted in appropriate places according to the scheme previously outlined. Hence, for example, Chapter 45, which was a prophecy to Baruch when he transcribed the dictation of Jeremiah (45 1), would have directly followed the description of the events concerning the transcribing of the words of Jeremiah (36 1-32). Subsequently Chapters 37-44 were inserted immediately after Chapter 36 to indicate that just as the Book of Jeremiah was burned (36 23), so the city of Jerusalem would be burned (37 10).

In Jer. 25 13 it is stated that God will bring destruction to the land "as it is written in this book which Jeremiah prophesied against all the nations." Usually the above phrase is interpreted as referring to the prophecies of Jeremiah against the different nations as presented in Jer. 46-51. This interpretation would pose problems as to the logical organization of the book, since then Chapter 25 should immediately precede Chapter 46. However, such an interpretation of Jer. 25 13

Table 12.2.3
Similarity of Phrases between Adjacent Sections of the Book of Jeremiah

Section	Sentence	Phrase	Section	Sentence	Comparable Phrase
1 1–10	1 7	Whatsoever I command you, you will speak	1 11–19	1 17	And you shall speak to them, all that I command you
	1 8	For I am with you to save you		1 19	For I am with you, says God, to save you
1 11–19	1 15	All the families of the kingdoms of the north	2 1–3 5	2 4	All the families of the house of Israel
	1 18	Against the kings of Judah, the princes, the priests		2 26	Their kings, their princes, and their priests
2 1–3 5	3 2	And you have polluted the land with your harlotries	3 6–4 4	3 9	Because of the sound of her harlotry, the land was polluted
3 6–4 4	3 18	And they will come from the land of the north	4 5–6 30	6 22	A people comes from the land of the north
4 5–6 30	6 12–15	And their houses will be turned to others, fields and wives together . . . Because from the smallest unto the greatest, everyone is greedy for gain, and from prophet unto priest everyone deals falsely. And they have healed the hurt of my people lightly, saying	7 1–9 25	8 10–12	Therefore I will give their wives to others, their fields to those who will possess them, because from the small unto the great everyone is greedy for gain, from prophet unto priest everyone deals falsely. And they have healed the hurt of the daughter of my

7 1–9 25			"Peace, Peace" but there is no peace. Are they ashamed because they have committed abominations? They are not at all ashamed, neither know they how to blush. Therefore they shall fall among those who fall; at the time that I punish them they shall stumble, said God.
	9 23		
	8 19	For I am the Lord	
		With their idols, with strange vanities	
10 1–25	10 1	Hear the word which the Lord spoke to you	
	10 3	For a tree from the forest	
11 1–12 13	12 7	I have cast off My heritage	
11 1–12 13	11 4	And you shall be unto Me a people	
13 1–27	13 10	This bad people	
	13 17	And my eye will run down with tears	

			people lightly, saying "Peace, peace", but there is no peace. Are they ashamed because they have committed an abomination? They are not at all ashamed, neither know they how to blush. Therefore they shall fall among those who fall; at the time of their punishment they shall stumble, said God.
10 1–25	10 10	For the Lord is the true God	
	10 15	They (the idols) are vanity	
11 1–12 13	11 1,2	The word that came to Jeremiah from the Lord saying "Hear . . ."	
	12 8	As a lion in the forest	
12 14–17	12 15	I will bring them back every man to his heritage	
13 1–27	13 11	To be unto Me a people	
14 1–22	14 11	For this people for good	
	14 17	Let my eyes run down with tears	

Table 12.2.3 (continued)
Similarity of Phrases Between Adjacent Sections of the Book of Jeremiah

Section	Sentence	Phrase	Section	Sentence	Comparable Phrase
14 1–22	14 12	Because I will consume them by the sword and by the famine	15 1–21	15 2	And such as are for the sword, to the sword; and such as are for the famine, to the famine
15 1–21	15 3	The sword to slay ... and the fowl of the heaven and the beasts of the earth to eat and to destroy	16 1–17 4	16 4	And they shall be consumed by the sword and by the famine; and their carcasses shall be for eating by the fowl of the heaven and the beasts of the earth
16 1–17 4	16 2	You should not have sons and daughters	17 5–18	17 11	Broods (over eggs) which she has not brought forth
	16 11	And they have forsaken Me		17 13	All those who forsake You
	16 11	And you should say to them		17 20	And you should say to them
17 5–14	17 9	It is woeful; who can know it?		17 16	A woeful day; You did know it
17 5–18	17 5	Cursed is the man that trusts in man	17 19–27	17 24	If you diligently listen to Me
	17 7	Blessed is the man that trusts in the Lord		17 27	But if you do not listen to Me
17 19–27	17 19	Go and stand in the gate	18 1–23	18 2	Arise and go down to the potter's house

LATER PROPHETS 219

	17 27	But if you do not listen to Me	18 10	So as not to listen to My voice
18 1–23	18 16	To make their land an astonishment and a perpetual hissing; everyone who passes it by will be astonished and shake his head	19 1–20 18 19 8	And I will make this city an astonishment and a hissing; everyone who passes it by will be astonished and hiss
	18 4	And the vessel that he makes of clay was ruined in the hand of the potter	19 11	As one breaks a potter's vessel
19 1–20 18	20 1	Pashhur the son of Immer	21 1	Pashhur the son of Malchiah
	20 4	I will give all Judah into the hand of the king of Babylon	21 10	It shall be given into the hand of the King of Babylon
21 1–14	21 12	Thus said God: Execute justice in the morning and deliver the stolen item out of the hand of the oppressor	22 3	Thus said God: Do justice and righteousness, and deliver the stolen item out of the hand of the oppressor
22 1–12	22 3	Do justice and righteousness	22 15	And he did justice and righteousness
	22 11	Thus said God to Shallum the son of Josiah King of Judah	22 18	Thus said God to Jehoiakim the son of Josiah, King of Judah
22 13–19	22 18	Jehoiakim the son of Josiah, King of Judah	22 24	Coniah the son of Jehoiakim King of Judah
22 20–30	22 15	Your father	22 26	You and your mother

Table 12.2.3 (continued)
Similarity of Phrases Between Adjacent Sections of the Book of Jeremiah

Section	Sentence	Phrase	Section	Sentence	Comparable Phrase
22 20–30	22 30	No child of the king will succeed to the throne of David, and rule over Judah	23 1–8	23 5,6	God will raise unto David a righteous shoot who will reign as king . . . and Judah will be saved
23 1–8	23 1	Woe unto the shepherds who mislead the sheep	23 9–40	23 9,13	The prophets . . . have misled the people of Israel
23 9–40	23 39,40	I will forsake them and the city that I gave unto you and your ancestors . . . and I will bring an everlasting reproach	24 1–10	24 9,10	I will make them . . . as a reproach . . . until they be consumed from off the land that I gave to them and their ancestors
24 1–10	24 10	Until they be consumed from off the land that I gave to them and their ancestors	25 1–38	25 5	Dwell in the land that God has given to you and your ancestors
25 1–38	25 4	And God has sent to you all His servants the prophets, early and often, but you have not listened	26 1–24	26 5	To listen to the words of My servants the prophets, whom I send to you, even early and often, but you have not listened
26 1–24	26 15	Because in truth God has sent me to you (to prophesy)	27 1–22	27 15	Because I have not sent them says God, and they prophesy falsely in My name

LATER PROPHETS 221

27 1–22			
	27 21,22	Concerning the vessels that remain in the House of God ... shall be carried to Babylon	28 3	All the vessels of the House of God ... and they were carried to Babylon
	27 2	Make bands and bars, and place them on your neck		
28 1–17			28 1–17	
	28 15	God has not sent you, and you have made the people trust in falsehood	28 10	He took ... the bar from off the neck of the prophet Jeremiah
	28 4	I will bring them and all the exiles of Judah back to this place says God	29 9	Because they prophesy falsely to you in My name; I have not sent them, says God
29 1–32			29 14	And I will bring you back to the place from which I have exiled you
	29 14	I will reestablish your settlements ... and I will bring you back to the place from which I have exiled you		
30 1–3			30 3	I will reestablish the settlement of My people Israel and Judah ... and I will bring them back to the land that I gave to their ancestors
	30 3	And I will reestablish the settlement of my people Israel and Judah, said God		
30 4–25			30 4	That God said to Israel and Judah
	30 10	Because I will save you from afar	31 2	From afar God appeared to me
31 1–13				
	30 17	She is Zion, no one seeks her	31 5	Arise and we will go to Zion
31 14–39	31 12	Then shall the virgin rejoice in the dance	31 20	Return virgin of Israel

Table 12.2.3 (continued)
Similarity of Phrases Between Adjacent Sections of the Book of Jeremiah

Section	Sentence	Phrase	Section	Sentence	Comparable Phrase
31 14–39	31 8	And Ephraim is my firstborn		31 19	Ephraim is a darling son to Me
	31 22	When I reestablish their settlements	32 1–44	32 44	Because I will reestablish their settlements
	31 30	And I will make a new covenant		32 40	And I will make an everlasting covenant
	31 31	To bring them out of the land of Egypt		32 21	And You did bring Your people Israel out of the land of Egypt
	31 37	Hananel		32 7	Hananel
32 1–44	32 2	And Jeremiah was imprisoned in the court of the guard	33 1–26	33 1	And he was still imprisoned in the court of the guard
	32 42	I will bring upon them all the good that I speak for them		33 9	That will hear all the good that I do to them
	32 40	I will make with them an everlasting covenant		33 20,21	If you can break My covenant with the day . . . then also My covenant with David can be broken
33 1–26	33 5	They come to fight with the Chaldeans . . . from this city	34 1–7	34 1	Nebuchadrezzar King of Babylon . . . are fighting against Jerusalem

				LATER PROPHETS
33 14–34 7				
	33 20	If you break My covenant with the day	34 2	This city
			34 18	Who have transgressed My covenant
	34 4	Zedekiah, King of Judah.... You will not die by the sword	34 21	Zedekiah, King of Judah,.... I will give (them) into the hands of their enemies
34 8–22	34 8–22			
	34 14,15	But your ancestors did not listen to Me, nor did they incline their ears. And you returned this day and have done that which is right	35 15	Return now every man from his evil way... But you have not inclined your ears, nor listened to Me
35 1–19	35 14	Until this day	36 2	And until this day
	35 17	All the evil that I have spoken unto them	36 3	All the evil that I think to do unto them
	35 15	Return now every man from his evil way	36 7	And everyone will return from his evil way
36 1–32	36 4	Baruch wrote from the mouth of Jeremiah all the words of the Lord, which He had spoken unto him	37 2	The words of the Lord, which He spoke by the prophet Jeremiah
	36 14	The son of Shelemiah	37 3	The son of Shelemiah
	36 32	Had burned in the fire	37 8	And burn it with fire
37 1–21	37 3	Jehucal the son of Shelemiah	38 1	Jucal the son of Shelemiah

Table 12.2.3 (continued)
Similarity of Phrases Between Adjacent Sections of the Book of Jeremiah

Section	Sentence	Phrase	Section	Sentence	Comparable Phrase
	37 8	And the Chaldeans shall return, and fight against this city . . . and burn it with fire		38 18	This city shall be given into the hand of the Chaldeans, and they shall burn it with fire
	37 17	Then Zedekiah the King sent and took him . . . and he said . . . You shall be delivered into the hand of the King of Babylon		38 14	Then Zedekiah the King sent and took Jerusalem . . . and he said
	37 21	And Jeremiah abode in the court of the guard		38 23	But shall be taken by the hand of the King of Babylon
				38 28	And Jeremiah abode in the court of the guard
38 1–28	38 18	The hand of the Chaldeans, and they shall burn it with fire	39 1–14	39 8	The Chaldeans burned . . . with fire
	38 19	That are fallen away to the Chaldeans		39 9	That fell away to him
	38 28	And Jeremiah dwelt in the court of the guard		39 14	And they took Jeremiah out of the court of the guard
38 1–28	38 12	And Ebed-melech the Ethiopian said	39 15–18	39 16	And speak to Ebed-melech the Ethiopian
	38 19	Lest they deliver me into their hand		39 17	And you shall not be delivered into the hand of the men

LATER PROPHETS 225

39 1–18	39 13	Nebuzaradan the captain of the guard sent	40 1–43 7	40 1	After Nebuzaradan the captain of the guard had sent him away
	39 14	Gedaliah the son of Ahikam, the son of Shaphan		40 5	Gedaliah the son of Ahikam, the son of Shaphan
	39 14	And he dwelt among the people		40 6	And dwelt with him among the people
40 1–43 7	43 7	Tahpanhes	43 8–13	43 8	Tahpanhes
	42 17	To go to Egypt to sojourn there, they shall die by the sword, by the famine, and by the pestilence		43 11	And shall smite the land of Egypt; such as are for death to death, . . . and such as are for the sword to the sword
42 7–43 13	43 8	Tahpanhes	44 1–30	44 1	Tahpanhes
	42 17	That set their faces to go to Egypt to sojourn there they shall die by the sword, by the famine, and by the pestilence; and none of them shall remain or escape		44 12	That set their faces to go to . the land of Egypt to sojourn there . . . they shall die by the sword and by the famine
				44 14	And none shall escape or remain
	42 18	And you shall be an execration, and an astonishment and a curse and a reproach		44 12	And they shall be an execration, and an astonishment and a curse and a reproach

Table 12.2.3 (continued)

Similarity of Phrases Between Adjacent Sections of the Book of Jeremiah

Section	Sentence	Phrase	Section	Sentence	Comparable Phrase
44 1–30	44 14	And none shall escape or remain . . . for they will not return except for the few who escape	45 1–5	45 5	And I will give you your life as a prey in all the places where you go
44 1–45 5	44 30	Pharaoh Hophra, King of Egypt	46 1–12	46 2	Pharaoh Necho King of Egypt
	45 1	In the fourth year of Jehoiakim the son of Josiah, King of Judah		46 1	In the fourth year of Jehoiakim the son of Josiah King of Judah
44 1–45 5	44 1	In the land of Egypt, who dwell in Migdol and in Tahpanhes, and in Noph	46 13–28	46 14	Declare in Egypt and announce in Migdol, and announce in Noph and Tahpanhes
46 1–28	46 25	Pharaoh	47 1–7	47 1	Pharaoh
	46 8	A city and its inhabitants		47 2	A city and its inhabitants
47 1–7	47 5	Baldness is come . . . How long will you cut yourself?	48 1–47	48 37	Because every head is bald . . . upon all hands are cuttings
48 1–47	48 2	Heshbon	49 1–6	49 3	Heshbon
	48 47	And I will reestablish the settlement of Moab . . . says God		49 6	I will reestablish the settlement of the children of Ammon says God
48 1–49 6	49 1	Thus said God, Does Israel have no sons?	49 7–22	49 7	So said God . . . Has counsel perished from the sons?

48 24	Bozrah	49 13	Bozrah
48 40, 41	Behold, he shall swoop down as a vulture, and spread his wings... And the heart of the mighty men of Moab at that day will be as the heart of a woman in her pangs	49 22	Behold, he shall come up and swoop down as the vulture and spread his wings. And the heart of the mighty men of Edom, at that day will be as the heart of a woman in her pangs
49 7–22	As the heart of a woman in her pangs	49 24	Anguish and pangs have taken hold of her, as a woman in travail
49 7–27	Flee, turn back, dwell deep you inhabitants of Dedan	49 8	Flee, wander exceedingly, dwell deep, you inhabitants of Hazor
	No man shall abide there, neither shall any son of man dwell therein	49 33	No man shall abide there, neither shall any son of man dwell therein
48 1–49 33, 48 47	And I will reestablish the settlement of Moab in the aftermath of the six-year era, says God	49 39	And it will be in the aftermath of the six-year era that I will reestablish the settlement of Elam, says God
49 1–39	Behold he will arise as a lion from the thickets of the Jordan to the strong habitation. For I will suddenly make him run away from it, etc.	50 1–51 64, 50 44–45	Behold he will arise as a lion from the thickets of the Jordan to the strong habitation. For I will suddenly make them run away from it, etc.

Table 12.2.3 (continued)
Similarity of Phrases Between Adjacent Sections of the Book of Jeremiah

Section	Sentence	Phrase	Section	Sentence	Comparable Phrase
	49 26	Therefore her young men shall fall in her broad places, and all the men of war shall be brought to silence in that day, says the Lord of hosts		50 30	Therefore her young men shall fall in her broad places, and all her men of war shall be brought to silence in that day says the Lord
	49 18	As in the overthrow of Sodom and the neighbor cities thereof, says the Lord; No man shall abide there, neither shall any son of man dwell therein		50 40	As when God overthrew Sodom and Gomorrah and the neighbor cities thereof, says the Lord; so shall no man abide there, neither shall any son of man dwell therein
50 1–51 64	51 59	Zedekiah the King of Judah to Babylon	52 1–34	52 3	Zedekiah rebelled against the King of Babylon

is incorrect since Chapter 25, which includes mention of Elam (25 25), was stated in the fourth year of Jehoiakim (604), while the date given for the prophecy against Elam (49 34) is the beginning of the reign of Zedekiah (597). Instead, the phrase "the book which Jeremiah prophesied against all the nations" actually refers to Jer. 25 15–38, which is stated (25 15) to be a prophecy against all the nations. No difficulty therefore arises as to the placement of Chapter 25.

Authorship

Numerous factors establish that the author of the Book of Jeremiah is Jeremiah himself. In the first place, the heading of the book (1 1) states "the words of Jeremiah"; and at the end of the next to the last chapter (51 64) it is stated "until here are the words of Jeremiah." Thus the contents of Chapters 1 through 51 are explicitly stated to be authored by Jeremiah.

Secondly, we find that numerous sections were dictated or written by Jeremiah. From Chapter 36 and 45 1, it may be deduced that all prophecies predating the fourth or fifth year of Jehoiakim were originally dictated by Jeremiah and written down by Baruch the son of Neriah. In addition, Chapters 50 1–51 58, which are prophecies against Babylon, were personally written down by Jeremiah as stated in 51 60. Also we find Jeremiah capable of writing a deed of land purchase (32 10). This information indicates that the prophecies received up to the ninth month of the fifth year of Jehoiakim (36 9) were originally written down by Baruch, but subsequent prophecies were written down by Jeremiah himself. Only because Jeremiah was imprisoned (36 5) was it necessary for the earlier prophecies to be transcribed by Baruch. Support for this supposition is gained from Jer. 30 2; 36 2,28; where Jeremiah is commanded to write down the prophecies, and no mention is made of dictating them to Baruch.

Two other points verify the authorship by Jeremiah. First, the name Jeremiah is used as the central personality over 100 times throughout the book. Secondly, many sections and sentences are written in the first person, with the speaker clearly indicated as Jeremiah. Typical cases occur in Jer. 1 4–6 30; 11 6–13 27; 14 11–17 27; 18 3–23; 20 7–18; 24 1–10; 28 1; and 35 3–11.

Although the Book of Jeremiah was written by Jeremiah it is clear, based on the phrase at the end of Chapter 51 "until here are the words of Jeremiah," that the last chapter, Chapter 52, was written by someone other than Jeremiah. The most probable person to have written this chapter is Baruch the son of Neriah who accompanied Jeremiah and the remnant of Judah to Egypt after the exile (43 6). Not only was Baruch present at the appropriate time and place, but he also had the capability (36 4), and was a disciple of Jeremiah (43 3). Chapter 52 describes events until the thirty-seventh year of the exile of Jehoiachin (560), which indicates that Baruch lived till after this date, in accordance with the prophecy of Jeremiah (45 5) that Baruch would survive the calamities of all the places where he goes. It should be noted that Baruch used in the writing of Chapter 52 many of the phrases written by Jeremiah. Thus, Jer. 52 4–16 is almost identical with Jer. 39 1–10.

Chapter 52 is identical in most respects with II Kings 24 18–25 30, establishing that Baruch also completed the Book of Kings. The slight variations in the accounts arise from his writing in a form most appropriate for consistency with each book. The major differences between the accounts in Kings and Jeremiah are with respect to the dates in Nebuchadrezzar's reign. In Jer. 52 28,29 the successful conquests by Nebuchadrezzar are attributed to the seventh and eighteenth years of Nebuchadrezzar, while in II Kings 24 12; 25 8, the same events are attributed to the eighth and nineteenth years of *King* Nebuchadnezzar.* A distinction must therefore be made between years dated with respect to Nebuchadrezzar and those with respect to *King* Nebuchadrezzar. The seventh and eighteenth years of Nebuchadrezzar are respectively the eighth and nineteenth years of *King* Nebuchadrezzar. Probably the dates based on the years of *King* Nebuchadrezzar are counted as usual, while the years based on Nebuchadrezzar start the counting system one year later (see Section 6.2).

It should be pointed out that in the seventh year of Nebuchadrezzar (i.e. the eighth of *King* Nebuchadrezzar) it is stated in Jer. 52 28 that 3,023 people were exiled; while in II Kings 24 12–16 is stated that 7,000 soldiers, and a total of 10,000 people (including soldiers) were exiled. Thus the 3,023 people mentioned in Jeremiah omits the 7,000 soldiers also exiled at the same time. The total of 10,000 given in II Kings is a rounded number, accurate to the nearest 100.

Sufficient information is available to estimate how long Jeremiah lived. His first prophecy was in the thirteenth year of Josiah (626) (1 2). At that time he was a young man (נער)** (1 6), or very roughly twenty-one plus or minus seven years old. His last mentioned dated event was in the seventh month of 586 (44 1). Hence Jeremiah lived from about 647 to about 580, or approximately

---

* Nebuchadnezzar is a variant form of the name Nebuchadrezzar.
** The term נער when referring to a mature person indicates a young man. In general the term is usually used for men between the ages of fourteen and twenty-eight, or roughly twenty-one plus or minus seven. Examples of the use of this word in the Bible, where the ages of the individuals referred to are known at least approximately are as follows:

Gen. 21 12—Ishmael—about seventeen years
Gen. 37 2—Joseph—seventeen years
Gen. 41 12—Joseph—twenty-eight years
Gen. 44 22—Benjamin—twenty-five years
Gen. 48 16—Ephraim and Manasseh—about twenty-two years
Ex. 33 11—Joshua—twenty years
I Sam. 17 33—David—twenty-eight years
II Sam. 18 12—Absalom—about thirty-seven (used affectionately by his father David)
I Kings 3 7—Solomon—fifteen years
I Chr. 22 5—Solomon—fourteen years
II Chr. 34 3—Josiah—sixteen years

sixty-seven years. Undoubtedly Jeremiah did not live until the thirty-seventh year of the exile of Jehoiachin (560) (52 31), or otherwise he would have written the contents of Chapter 52 himself.

It is clear from the previous discussion that Baruch the son of Neriah lived until at least 560, and must have been a younger contemporary of Jeremiah. Probably the Book of Jeremiah was completed by him around 560. References to the Book of Jeremiah, indicating that the book was completed, are found in Dan. 9 1,2 in the first year of Darius (517) and in II Chr. 36 21,22 and Ezra 1 1 in the first year of Cyrus (538).

12.3 EZEKIEL

The Book of Ezekiel relates the prophecies experienced by Ezekiel in the land of Babylon. His prophecies concern the impending destruction of Jerusalem and Judah by Nebuchadnezzar, the destruction of other countries by Nebuchadnezzar, and the detailed situation to occur at the time of the Messianic era. The prophecies were received over a period of twenty-two years, i.e. from the fifth year of the exile of Jehoiachin (1 2) to the twenty-seventh year (29 17) (592 to 570 B.C.E.). Probably the book was completed shortly after 570.

AUTHORSHIP

The author of the book is specified as Ezekiel, the son of Buzi (1 3), and he is again mentioned in 24 24. There are no problems to accepting Ezekiel as the author, since the entire book, with the exception of one sentence (1 3), is written in the first person. Furthermore typical phrases, such as "son of man" and "the word of the Lord came to me" are used throughout, and show a common style and single authorship.

ORGANIZATION

The book can be subdivided into three main sections. The first division, Chapters 1–24, describes the sins and consequent punishment of the people of Judah. Jerusalem will be destroyed, and the people exiled. The second section contains prophecies concerning the destruction in the near future of the nations of Ammon, Moab, Edom, Philistia, Tyre, Zidon, and Egypt (Chapters 25–32). The last division contains prophecies relevant to the distant future and the restoration of the Jewish state in Messianic times (Chapters 33–48).

A superficial examination of the book might make one believe that an approximate chronological order has been followed. With only three exceptions the order of the prophecies seem to be based on the dates when they were received by Ezekiel. In Table 12.3.1 these dates are listed. Note that only the dates mentioned in 26 1, 29 17, and 33 21 are not in chronological order. However, more careful consideration reveals that a logical rather than a chronological arrangement has been used, and each subdivision has been arranged on a somewhat different logical basis.

Table 12.3.1
Dates in the Book of Ezekiel

Reference	Date (B.C.E.)	Years from Exile of Jehoiachin			Probable Month if not Specified	Notes
		Year	Month	Day		
1 1,2	592	5	4	5		Equivalent to thirtieth year, fourth month, fifth day
8 1	591	6	6	5		
20 1	590	7	5	10		
24 1	588	9	10	10		Compare to II Kings 25 1 Jer. 52 4
26 1	586	11	—	1	6	Year called עשתי עשרה
29 1	587	10	10	12		
29 17	570	27	1	1		
30 20	586	11	1	7		Year called אחת עשרה
31 1	586	11	3	1		Year called אחת עשרה
32 1	585	12	12	1		
32 17	585	12	—	15	12	
33 21	585	12	10	5		
40 1	572	25	Beginning of the year	10	7	Fourteenth year after the city was smitten

Before describing the arrangements in the different sections, it should be noted that the entire book has as one basis for its order the similarity in phrases between adjacent prophecies. In Table 12.3.2 some of the main similar wordings between adjacent prophecies are tabulated. The prophecies have been separated based on the criteria that they are separate revelations and are not direct continuations of previous topics. The similarities of phrases were used for some of the fine arrangements within the three divisions.

The first section (1–24) contains prophecies concerning the impending punishment of Judah, and is arranged in approximate chronological sequence. Specifically, all the dated prophecies are in order. However, the intermediate undated prophecies, are not necessarily in exact chronological arrangement, but may have been arranged by similarity of phrases. It should still be noted that since these twenty-four chapters cover numerous variations of the same theme, it was difficult to use a topical sequence, and instead a chronological arrangement was used.

The second section, concerning the impending punishment of other nations by the Babylonians (25–32), is arranged by geographical location of the nations. An approximately clockwise sequence is followed. Ammon, which is east of Israel, is mentioned first (25 1–7), followed by Moab (25 8–11) which is south of Ammon. Then comes Edom (25 12–14) which is even further south. Next is Philistia (25 15–17) which is to the southwest of Israel, followed by Tyre (26 1–28 19) to the north, and Zidon (28 20–24) which is further north. A brief mention is then made of Israel (28 25–26) which is located in the center of the previously mentioned countries. Then are presented prophecies against Egypt (29 1–32 32), which is south of Israel.

By following the above arrangement, the author succeeded in arranging the prophecies against the nations not only by geographical location, but also in approximate chronological order. Thus only two of the seven dates given in this section are out of place (see Table 12.3.1). Furthermore this arrangement allowed the maintaining of the similarity of phrases between adjacent prophecies.

The third subdivision (33–48) contains descriptions of the Messianic era. These Messianic prophecies are the most detailed and clearly explained of all the Messianic prophecies throughout the Bible. A thorough explanation of their meaning is presented in Chapter Seventeen of this book. It should be noted that although this subdivision begins with Chapter 33, it is only with Chapter 34 that the Messianic prophecies begin. In fact, the statement in 33 21,22 that the fugitive from Jerusalem had come to Ezekiel, would form an excellent continuation of 24 27 where Ezekiel is told by God that the fugitive would eventually come. The problem therefore arises, why was Chapter 33 concerning the destruction of Jerusalem not placed after Chapter 24? The answer is two-fold. First, Chapter 33 (33 21) is dated in the twelfth year, and fits in chronologically much better after the prophecies against the nations. Secondly, the present placement of Chapter 33 allows an excellent arrangement based on the similarity of phrases (see Table 12.3.2). In general, the prophecies within this last subdivision are arranged mainly by similarity of phrases, and they do not accurately reflect the sequence in which the events will occur (see Chapter Seventeen). Additionally, the third subdivision may be considered as separated into two parts. The first part (Chapters 33–39) concerns itself with the historical events during the Messianic Era. The second part (Chapters 40–48) which is one long prophecy, mainly concerns itself with

Table 12.3.2
Similarity of Phrases between Adjacent Sections in the Book of Ezekiel

Passage	Sentence	Phrase	Passage	Sentence	Phrase
1 1–5 17	5 7	הנה רוח סערה באה מן	6 1–10	6 3	הנה אני מביא עליכם חרב
6 1–10	6 9	הנזונים אשר נשבו שם בכל	6 11–14	6 11	בכל תועבות רעות בית
	6 6	במושבותיכם; הערים			
6 11–14	6 11	תחרבנה	7 1–4	6 13	בתוככם; הריגליכם
	6 14	ביד כל עובר			
7 1–4	7 2	על ארבע כנפות	7 5–27	7 3	ועל אחד
7 5–27	7 8	וחרבנתיך	8 1–11 25	7 4	ועליך
				7 6	קץ בא, בא הקץ
8 1–11 25	11 25	התועבות	12 1–16	8 6,13,15	תועבות גדולות
12 1–16	12 16	וחרב ברעב ובדבר	12 17–20	12 3	גולה
12 17–20	12 19	את אדמתה מלאה	12 21–25	12 20	ישראל
12 21–25	12 24	כל חזון שוא ומקסם חלק	12 26–28	12 22	אמר אלי; חזון ומקסם
12 26–28	12 27	בתוך בית ישראל	13 1–23	12 27	בית ישראל
				13 2	ונבאו
				13 6	וקסמו
13 1–23	13 2	אל נביאי ישראל הנבאים מלבם	14 1–11	14 9	יבאו
14 1–11	14 9	חטאתם אש עוון דרש	14 12–23	14 13	ועוונם; ידי עליו
14 12–23	14 13	בהם רעב	15 1–8	15 8	ונתתי את הארץ שממה
	14 16	ונתנו הארץ שממה			
15 1–8	15 6	נתתיו לאכל	16 1–63	16 2	דמים
16 1–63	16 44	כמה כתה	17 1–24	17 2	מות נפשות
17 1–24	17 2	חוד חידה ומשל משל	18 1–19 14	18 2	מה לכם אתם משלים

LATER PROPHETS

18 1–19 14	18 5	ויהי דבר ה׳		20 7	ויהי דבר ה׳ אלי
	19 8	אלי לאמר: בן־אדם		20 23	גם־אני: כל־בשר ידעו
20 1–44	20 31	על שמי	20 1–44	21 3	אמר
	20 32	אמר	21 1–5	21 7	ונתתי
21 1–5	21 2	ונתתי	21 6–12	21 14	ונאם
21 6–12	21 7	נאם	21 13–22	21 14,16,17	מאחז; ואנה אנא; מחזיק
21 13–22	21 8,9,10	נבואה; אל קטון גדול	21 23–37	21 25	רבה
21 23–37	21 14,16,17		22 1–16	22 4	דמים
	21 36	ועצמי; יהיו חדים		22 5	רבת
	21 25	רבה	22 17–22	22 22	אתא ברורה
22 1–16	22 16	ונחלת בי; אני ה׳	22 23–31	22 31	נתתי
	22 4			23 38	עמו
22 17–22	22 21	וכנסתי אתכם; ונפחתי		24 2	כתוב לך
22 23–31	22 22	בהתך	24 1–14	24 13	בחנתך; ויהנו
	22 26	מפרשת; ואצל	24 15–27	24 24	ויבא
23 1–49	23 15	בכן		24 26	יבא
	23 48	ונוסדו	25 1–7	25 3	אמא
24 1–14	24 14	יבא	25 8–11	25 8	בית
	24 2	כתב		25 10	ונתתיה
24 15–27	24 21	אשר; ובנתיכם	25 12–14	25 12	אשם; על ישי
25 1–7	25 3	אמא		25 14	אשם
	25 4	בני־קדם			
25 8–11	25 8	כבית יהודה			
	25 11	עשה			

Table 12.3.2 (continued)

Passage	Sentence	Phrase	Passage	Sentence	Phrase
25 12–14	25 12	יען עשותו בקם דמי	25 15–17	25 15	כים וגוי
	25 14	את נקמתי		25 17	אנה
25 15–17	25 16	לכל בקר לא היה וגוי	26 1–14	26 3	וגוי
26 1–14	26 3	כלה יענני; וגון כי אני ה׳	26 15–21	26 19	בלכתי
	26 5			26 17	בלכל
26 15–21	26 17	וידעו כני אני ה׳	27 1–36	27 3	היי׳
	26 18			27 3	אני
	26 21	פלכל עת תואלת לה		27 36	וכלו עליך מלכים
27 1–36	27 25,26,27	לבם ברעש	28 1–10	28 2,8	לכל עם פלי
28 1–10	28 4	החכמה		28 12	וכלכוך
	28 4	וחב		28 13	וכלי
	28 5	ברכלך		28 16	ברעל
28 11–19	28 16	וגואתי; ממם		28 23	בהעותי ואמחת׳ וכלו כי
	28 18	ובלמעי		28 22	נכבדתי
	28 22	בלגבן ברי אני ה׳		28 26	עלי לי
28 25–26	28 25	ברכל אמ ברת ישראל; ונכלל	29 1–16	29 5	כים וגוי
29 1–16	29 16,13	כלה יענני; וגון כי אני ה׳		29 6	אני
29 17–21	29 13	משם	29 17–21	29 21	
	29 21	מוצא הברים		29 17	
			30 1–9	30 9	

LATER PROPHETS 237

30 1-9		30 10-12	ראשי פרקים והבטחות
30 10-12	30 7	30 13-19	התוכחות והבטחות
	30 10		נחמה
30 13-19	30 12	30 20-26	מאמר
30 20-26	30 18	31 1-18	מאמרי; אלמנה
31 1-18	30 22	32 1-16	גלות
32 1-16	31 6 הימים באים ועבדו את ה'	32 17-32	מאמר; איני
	32 16		נחמה
	32 12		ציון
	31 18 ידעתי אבי כנגד אהבת עולם	33 1-20	נחמה
32 17-32	32 20-32	33 21-33	נחמה ואת עבדי דוד]...]
33 1-20	33 7		מי
	33 7	34 1-31	דור אל דור
33 21-33	33 32		מאמר
	33 28		הלוי
34 1-31	34 2		מאמרי; אכל
	34 10		דוד
	34 17		משה
	34 6	36 16-38	מאמרי; מאמרי
35 1-36 15	36 6		מאמרי; אלמנה
	36 6		נבואה
	36 6		משנה בנין
	36 4		עבודה; מאמר
36 16-38	36 17	37 1-14	מאמרי; אלמנה

30 10-12	30 12
30 13-19	30 13
	30 14
30 20-26	30 21
31 1-18	31 18
32 1-16	32 4
32 17-32	32 20
	32 20,21
	32 32
33 1-20	33 2,3,4,6
33 21-33	33 22
	33 32
34 1-31	34 7
	34 6
35 1-36 15	35 2
	35 3
	35 11
	36 4
36 16-38	36 17
	36 18
	36 22,32
	36 35
37 1-14	37 12

Table 12.3.2 (continued)

Passage	Sentence	Phrase	Passage	Sentence	Phrase
	36 24	ויוצא אתכם מאברתם		37 12	ויוצא אתכם מאדמה
37 1–14	37 7	והקרבו		37 17	וקרב
	37 12	מקברותיכם את עמי והעליתי אתכם	37 15–28	37 21	ויבאתי אתם אל
		אדמה			אדמתם
37 15–28	37 21	וקבצתי	38 1–39 29	38 8	תקבץ
	37 25	לעולם		38 8	לה; אל
	37 22,23	גוי אחד		39 28,29	גוי
38 1–39 29	38 21	לגלגלתם	40 1–48 35	40 2	בראש ההר
	39 29			40 4	הנה הנה
	38 11	מאת הנחה		40 5	הנה הנה

procedural details such as the design of the Temple, special sacrifices to be brought, and special laws to be followed.

COMMENTS ON THE DATED PROPHECIES

Clarification needs to be given for the dates presented in the book of Ezekiel (Table 12.3.1). In general, events are dated from the exile of Jehoiachin (597) as stated in 1 2. The only exception is the date of the thirtieth year presented in 1 1, which refers back to the eighteenth year of Josiah (621) when a book of the Torah was found and reforms were instituted (II Kings 22, 23). The year 621 is considered as the first year of this counting system, and therefore the thirtieth year is 592.

A comparison of Ez. 24 1 with II Kings 25 1 and Jer. 52 4, shows that the event of the siege of Jerusalem by Nebuchadnezzar is dated as the ninth year of the exile of Jehoiachin, as well as the ninth year of Zedekiah. This offers no difficulty since the exile of Jehoiachin and the beginning of the reign of Zedekiah occurred in the same year.

It is readily observed that only those prophecies of special historical importance, or needing the specific year of occurrence for clarification, were dated. The date of the first chapter (1 1,2) was given so as to provide the year when the first revelation was received by Ezekiel. Chapter 8 was dated to establish that abominations were occurring at the Temple shortly before its destruction. Chapters 20 and 24 are dated, because special note was made in each of the prophecies, of the day the events occurred (20 31; 24 2). The prophecies against the nations (Chapters 25-32) are dated in numerous cases because specific historical events are being described. Finally, the date of the vision of Chapters 40-48 is specified so as to point out that it was the Day of Atonement (see below), on which day the high priest is able to enter the holy of holies. Therefore, it was permissible for Ezekiel to obtain the dimensions of the holy of holies (41 4) in the vision.

In two cases (26 1 and 32 17) the year and day are given but not the month. This is because the month can be understood from the context. In 26 2,4 it is implied that Jerusalem was already destroyed, which occurred in the fifth month (II Kings 25 8-10). Therefore the prophecy was probably received in the sixth month. In the case of 32 17, the date probably followed that given in 32 1, of the twelfth month, first day. Hence the twelfth month, fifteenth day is being referred to. It should also be noted that the term "beginning of the year" (40 1) denotes the beginning of the agricultural year, and therefore the seventh month is being indicated (see Section 5.1.1).

In 26 1 the eleventh year is called "עשתי עשרה" while in 30 20, and 31 1 the eleventh year is called "אחת עשרה". This difference in wording may simply be to denote that the event in Chapter 26 is not in chronological order, while the events in Chapters 30 and 31 are in chronological order.

12.4 THE TWELVE PROPHETS

The book of the Twelve Prophets contains the prophetic works of twelve different individuals who prophesied between about 790 and 490 B.C.E. The twelve separate prophetic works were compiled into one book, so as to include the writings of those prophets whose compositions were too short to form a book of their own (in contrast to the case for Isaiah, Jeremiah, and Ezekiel), and whose contents were not suitable for inclusion in the historical books of Kings and Chronicles.

The arrangement of the twelve works within the book of the Twelve Prophets is based on the dates of the first revelations received by the prophets. Thus, the first prophecy of Haggai (Hag. 1 1) was received in the sixth month of the second year of Darius, two months prior to the first prophecy of Zechariah (Zech. 1 1). Accordingly the Book of Haggai precedes that of Zechariah. It should be noted that the arrangement is not based on the last revelations received, since we find that the Book of Amos is placed later than the Book of Hosea, even though the later prophecies of Hosea were received after those of Amos (compare Hos. 1 1 with Am. 1 1).

The dates when the prophecies were received are presented in the headings of the Books of Hosea, Amos, Micah, Zephaniah, Haggai, and Zechariah. In contrast, the Books of Joel, Obadiah, Jonah, Nahum, Habakkuk, and Malachi are undated. However, Jonah can be dated on the basis of the statement in II Kings 14 25 that he was at the time of Jeroboam the son of Joash, King of Israel. Also Nahum can be dated, since he mentions the destruction of No-Amon (661) as a past event (Nah. 3 8), and he describes the destruction of Nineveh* (612) as a future event (Nah. 3 7). The times for the other undated books can be approximated from their relative positions in the book of the Twelve Prophets. For example, Joel must have begun prophesying after Hosea and before Amos. In Table 12.4.1 the approximate dates are presented for the books based on the above reasoning.

The fact that the dates of six of the twelve books are not specified is not an oversight by the authors, but rather to let us know that the dates are irrelevant to understanding the prophecies. In contrast, six of the books are dated, and they thereby let us know that at least one prophecy within the book concerning the Jewish people is better understood because of the date.

The Books of Hosea, Amos, Micah, Zephaniah, Haggai, and Zechariah are dated. In each of these cases there is reference in the text to an approaching historical event concerning the Jewish people. Hosea predicts the destruction of the kingdom of Israel (Hos. 1 4); Amos predicts the exile of the Kingdom of Israel, and the violent death of Jeroboam (Am. 7 11); Micah foresaw the destruction of Samaria (Mic 1 6), Jerusalem, and the Temple (Mic. 3 12); Zephaniah

---

* The date of the destruction of Nineveh as 612 is based on the Babylonian Chronicle where it is stated that Nineveh was conquered in the fourteenth year of Nabopolassar, king of Babylonia[1].

Table 12.4.1 Approximate Times of the Twelve Prophets

Prophet	Specified Time	Reference	Approx. Period of Prophesying (B.C.E.)	Date of First Prophecy (B.C.E.)
Hosea	Uzziah (794–757) Jotham (757–741) Ahaz (741–725) Hezekiah (725–696) Jeroboam (808–771)	Hos. 1 1	790–720	ca. 790
Joel	—	—		
Amos	Uzziah (794–757) Jeroboam (808–771) 2 years before the earthquake	Amos 1 1 (Zech. 14 5)	786 782	ca. 786 ca. 782
Obadiah	—	—		
Jonah	Jeroboam (808–771)	II Kings 14 25	778	ca. 778
Micah	Jotham (757–741) Ahaz (741–725) Hezekiah (725–696)	Mic. 1 1 Jer. 26 18	774 750–710	ca. 774 ca. 750
Nahum	After the destruction of No-Amon (661) and before the destruction of Nineveh (612)	Nah. 3 7,8	650	ca. 650
Habakkuk	Mention of the Chaldeans indicates a date after 625, when Nabopolassar founded the Chaldean dynasty	Hab. 1 6	625	ca. 625
Zephaniah	Josiah (639–608) Probably prior to 621 before religious reforms were instituted	Zeph. 1 1 (II Kings 22 3–23 30)	621	ca. 621
Haggai	Second year of Darius	Hag. 1 1,15; 2 1,10,18,20	516	516
Zechariah	Second and fourth years of Darius	Zech. 1 1,7; 7 1	516–514	516
Malachi	—	—	490	ca. 490

foretold the destruction of the Kingdom of Judah (Zeph. 1 4); Haggai is concerned with construction of the Second Temple (Hag. 1 1–2 20); and Zechariah needs the dates to clarify the seventy-year durations which he mentions twice (Zech. 1 12, 7 8). Additional historical events may be found in several cases, which also would warrant the specification of dates.

In contrast, the Books of Joel, Obadiah, Jonah, Nahum, Habakkuk, and Malachi are undated. No major historical event occurring to the Jews in the immediate future is mentioned in any of these cases. Joel and Obadiah prophesy concerning the Messianic era—events in the far-distant future. Jonah warns of the destruction of Nineveh. However the people repent, the city is saved, and no major historical event occurs. Nahum predicts the destruction of Nineveh, and the prophecy is fulfilled within fifty years. However, no prophecy concerning the Jewish people is given. Habakkuk presents the philosophical problem, "Why does wickedness prosper?" The mention of the Chaldeans as destroyers of nations (Hab. 1 6), is only incidental to the philosophical discussion. Malachi rebukes the priests without mention of any historical events, and then later speaks concerning the Messianic era. In none of these cases would the prophecies be any clearer if the dates of the books were given.

Authorship

The only persons sufficiently familiar with the contents of the prophecies are the individual prophets, and therefore it is only logical to assume that each of the twelve books was authored by the prophet named. Furthermore, in each case, the heading indicates that the prophet was the author of his book. The fact that the introductory headings are written in the third person does not imply editorship by some unknown person. It is characteristic of the prophetic literary style to write in an impersonal manner. Nevertheless, in a few cases, some of the prophecies are written in the first person, as is the case for Hos. 3, Amos 7–9, and Zech. 1–6, further substantiating that the prophets were the authors.

In certain cases the names of the prophets are mentioned not only in the headings, but also in the book itself. This is clearly the case in the Books of Jonah and Haggai, where the prophets' names are mentioned frequently throughout. Also in the Books of Amos (Am. 7 8,10,11,12,14; 8 2), Zechariah (Zech. 1 7, 7 1,8), and Habakkuk (Hab. 3 1), mention of the prophets is found in the text. This is further evidence that these prophets are the only ones sufficiently knowledgeable of the events mentioned to have authored the books.

Organization

In presenting the organization of the twelve books, it is best to discuss each book separately. Two books are arranged in chronological order; five are arranged in a logical order; and five contain only one prophecy, and no explanation of the arrangement is necessary. While discussing each of the books, clarification will be made of numerous relevant factors.

Hosea

The dominant theme of the Book of Hosea is that the Kingdom of Israel will be destroyed because of the people's sins. In addition the Kingdom of Judah will also be punished (see e.g. 5 5, 12–15). Incidental mention is also made of the situation to occur in the Messianic times (2 16–25; 3 5).

The book is arranged in a logical manner, and the sequence of the different prophecies is partly based on the similarity of phrases, as presented in Table 12.4.2. In most prophetic books the Messianic passages are placed at the end. Here, however, the Messianic prophecies are intertwined with the prophecies of condemnation and punishment, and fit in more logically within the text. A detailed explanation of the Messianic passages is given in Chapter Eighteen.

The heading of the book (1 1) states that Hosea prophesied during the reigns of Uzziah, Jotham, Ahaz, and Hezekiah, Kings of Judah, and in the days of Jeroboam the son of Joash, King of Israel. The question arises why are the kings of Judah emphasized? Hosea prophesied mainly to the Kingdom of Israel, and to a much lesser extent to the Kingdom of Judah. Should not the kings of Israel, namely Zechariah, Shallum, Menahem, Pekahiah, Pekah and Hoshea, who reigned after Jeroboam II and who were contemporaries of the listed kings of Judah, also be mentioned? A probable explanation involves the fact that many of these kings of Israel ruled for very short times. Thus Shallum ruled one month, Zechariah six months, and Pekahiah two years. Very probably Hosea might not have received any revelations from God during these short reigns. As a result their names would be omitted, causing a non-continuous listing of the kings of Israel. Instead, the names of the kings of Judah, all of whom ruled at least sixteen years, were given so as to allow a continuous listing of monarchs to be presented.

Hosea may have been as young as thirteen years old when he received his first prophecy (1 2), since he was commanded to marry a woman of harlotry, and later (3 1) told to marry another wife. It is thus implied that he was not married, and yet was of marriageable age, which would be the case at the age of thirteen. Support for this contention is gained from the fact that he prophesied for a period of about seventy years (see Table 12.4.1), which would only be possible if he were extremely young at the time of the first prophecy.

It should also be noted that the events described in the first chapter must have taken at least five years. During this time three children were conceived and born; and furthermore the third child was not conceived until after the second child was weaned (1 8). Usually a child was nursed for at least two years.

Joel

The entire Book of Joel is one prophecy describing the War of Gog. The enemy attacking Israel is compared to a plague of locusts. A detailed explanation of the book is given in Chapter Eighteen. The book contains only one prophecy, and therefore no explanation of the book's arrangement is necessary.

Table 12.4.2
Similarity of Phrases between Sections in the Book of Hosea

Section	Sent.	Phrase	Section	Sent.	Phrase
1 1–9	1 9	לא עמי	2 1–25	2 1	לא עמי
	1 4	יזרעאל		2 2	יזרעאל
	1 6	רחמה		2 3	רחמה
2 1–25	2 4	אשתי; ינאפופיה	3 1–5	3 1	אהב אשה; ומנאפת
	2 7	מאהבי			
3 1–5	3 1	ומנאפת	4 1–19	4 2	ונאף
				4 13	תנאפנה
	3 3	תזני		4 10	הזנו
4 1–19	4 10	הזנו	5 1–7	5 3	הזנית
	4 11	זנונים		5 4	זנונים
	4 1	שמעו; הכהנים		5 1	שמעו 9; ככהן
5 1–7	5 1	המשפט	5 8–15	5 11	משפט
	5 5	יהודה; ישראל ואפרים		5 9	אפרים; ישראל
				5 10	יהודה
5 8–15	5 15	אשובה; ישחרנני	6 1–7 7	6 1	ונשובה; טרף
	5 14	אטרף		6 3	כשחר
6 1–7 7	7 2		7 8–16	7 10	שבו; בפניו
	7 7	ואכלו		7 9	אכלו
	7 3	ברעתם		7 15	רע
7 8–16	7 14	זעקו אלי	8 1–14	8 2	לי יזעקו
	7 13	פשעו		8 1	פשעו
	7 9	אכלו זרים		8 7	זרים
				8 13	ויאכלו
8 1–14	8 13	מצרים ישובו; ויאכלו; זבחי	9 1–9	9 4	זבחיהם
				9 3	ושב; מצרים; יאכלו
9 1–9	9 1	ישראל; אהבת	9 10–17	9 10	ישראל; כאהבם
	9 3	אפרים		9 11	אפרים
9 10–17	9 16	פרי	10 1–8	10 1	פרי
10 1–8	10 8	חטאת ישראל		10 9	חטאת ישראל
	10 3	והמלך	10 9–15	10 15	מלך

Table 12.4.2 (continued)

Section	Sent.	Phrase	Section	Sent.	Phrase
	10 1	פרי		10 13	פרי
10 9-15	10 14	בנים	11 1-7	11 1	לבני
11 1-7	11 5	לא ישוב; ואשור	11 8-11	11 9	לא אשוב
	11 7	למושבתי		11 11	אשור
	11 2	הלכו		11 10	ילכו
11 8-11	11 11	ממצרים; אשור	12 1-14	10 12 2	אשור; למצרים
	11 8	אפרים; ישראל		12 1	אפרים; ישראל

Amos

The Book of Amos contains prophecies describing the impending destruction of the Kingdom of Israel. The book is arranged in a logical order based mainly on the first words of the prophecies, and the similarity in ideas and words between adjacent sections. The first prophecy (1 2-2 16) repeatedly uses the words "Thus says the Lord." Next come three prophecies (3 1-15; 4 1-13; and 5 1-17) all beginning with the phrase "Hear this word"; two prophecies (5 18-27; and 6 1-14) beginning with the exclamation "Woe"; and four prophecies (7 1-3; 7 4-6; 7 7-9; and 8 1-14) beginning with the statement "Thus the Lord God showed me." A separate section (7 10-17) is inserted after the prophecy given in 7 7-9, because the added section describes (7 11,12) how Amos was threatened by Amaziah for stating (in 7 9) that the house of Jeroboam would be destroyed by the sword. The prophecies against the people of Israel are completed with a revelation beginning with the words "I saw" (9 1-6). The book is then ended with a message of hope (9 7-15) wherein are described the permanent resettlement of the people in Messianic times. In addition to the arrangement based on the first words of the prophecies, the book is also arranged by the similarity in phrases between adjacent sections, as presented in Table 12.4.3.

Obadiah

The entire Book of Obadiah, consisting of just one chapter, describes the treacherous role and consequent destruction of Edom at the time of the War of Gog. A detailed explanation of the book is given in Chapter Eighteen. The book contains only one prophecy, and therefore no explanation of the book's organization needs to be given.

Jonah

Jonah is commanded by God to tell the city of Nineveh that it would be destroyed. Jonah, however, tries to avoid carrying out this task, and travels by ship to a

Table 12.4.3
Similarity of Phrases between Sections in the Book of Amos

Section	Sent.	Phrase	Section	Sent.	Phrase
1 1–2 16	1 2	יהי קולו; ישאג	3 1–15	3 4	ישאג... קולו
3 1–15	3 9	השמעו; 3 14 ופקדי	4 1–13	4 1	עשק; דל 4 4 ופשעו
4 1–13	4 4	מזבח; אל הבקר	5 1–17	5 5	מזבח; הגלגל
5 1–17	5 16	ונהי; 5 7 צדקה	5 18–27	5 18	יום; יהוה
	5 8	יום; ישועה		5 24	צדקה
5 18–27	5 18	יום; 5 19 יהוה	6 1–14	6 1	ונהי
	5 27	והגלתי		6 7	יגל
6 1–14	6 14	כי הנה אקים עלי	7 1–3	7 1	קום; הנה
7 1–3	7 2	סלח נא; מי יקום	7 4–6	7 5	סלח נא; מי יקום
7 4–6	7 3	נחם יי על; לא תהיה		7 6	נחם יי על
	7 5	סלח נא; מי יקום	7 7–9	7 9	אקום בחרב
	7 4	באש; ואכלה		7 7	הנה; נצב
7 7–9	7 9	אקום בחרב	7 10–17	7 10	אמציה... ישראל
	7 8	הנני; משליך... בקרב		7 10	בקרב
7 10–17	7 17	בקרב; ישראל	8 1–14	8 2	אמציה
	7 10	ארץ ישראל		8 11	הנני
	7 12	אמצי; יהודה		8 8	ארץ
8 1–14	8 12	מים עד ים	9 1–6	9 3	הים
	8 8	הארץ		9 6	הארץ
9 1–6	9 5	והגל	9 7–15	9 13	והגלתי
	9 1	מזבח		9 10	מזבח

distant land (1 3). A storm arises (1 4), Jonah is thrown into the waters (1 15), and swallowed alive by a huge fish (2 1). After three days the fish vomits Jonah safely onto shore (2 11). Once again Jonah is commanded to proclaim God's message to Nineveh (3 2). This time Jonah carries out his mission and states that Nineveh will be destroyed in forty days (3 4). However, the residents of the city repent (3 8), and God does not destroy the city (3 10).

The book clearly describes an historical event, and is presented in chronological order. Although the survival of Jonah within a big fish for three days is hard to believe, it should be realized that numerous cases, not necessarily well substantiated, have been reported of people surviving being swallowed by a whale*. The story in the book is therefore not impossible.

Based on the chronology of the Assyrian kings presented in Section 5.3, and the approximate date for Jonah of 774 given in Table 12.4.1, the Assyrian ruler who commanded the people of Nineveh to repent (3 6-9) would be either Assurnirari V (782-773) near the end of his reign, or Pul (772-745) at the beginning of his rule. Probably it is Pul, since his name was subsequently not placed on the eponym list, and his inscriptions were destroyed (see Section 5.3), indicating that subsequent monarchs were resentful of Pul's leadership.

MICAH

The Book of Micah may be considered to contain four prophecies (1 1-16; 2 1-3 12; 4 1-5 14; 6 1-7 20). The first two are prophecies rebuking the people of Israel and Judah for their sins, while the last two are Messianic prophecies. The book is arranged in a logical order according to the following plan. The first prophecy (1 1-16) states that Samaria will be destroyed (1 6) and Jerusalem will be threatened severely (1 9) because of their sins. The second prophecy (2 1-3 12) provides detailed descriptions of the people's sins, and mentions that Zion, Jerusalem, and the Mountain of the Temple will be destroyed (3 12). The third prophecy begins the descriptions of the Messianic era. In contrast to the previous revelation, it is stated (4 1,2) that the Mountain of the Temple will be firmly established, and instruction will come forth from Zion and Jerusalem. The fourth and concluding prophecy (6 1-7 20) describes the sins and subsequent repentance of the people, and states that a day will come (7 11-17) when the enemies of Israel will be destroyed in the Messianic era. It should be noted that in the second revelation (2 1-3 12), the sentences (2 12-13) are not a prophecy of redemption by Micah, but rather a quotation of what the false prophets say. Micah then denounces the false prophets (3 5-8). Chapter Three then is a logical continuation of Chapter Two.

---

* Though strictly speaking a whale is a mammal and not a fish, still the term "big fish" as used in the Book of Jonah would include a whale.

The book is arranged on the following basic assumptions:

(A) The two prophecies of rebuke should be placed first, and the two Messianic prophecies should be placed last.

(B) The two prophecies of rebuke should be placed next to each other.

(C) The two Messianic prophecies should be placed next to each other.

(D) The third prophecy should be placed next to the second prophecy because they both refer to the Mountain of the Temple, Zion and Jerusalem.

These four points result in the present arrangement of the four prophecies of the Book of Micah, as the only possible arrangement.

Nahum

The Book of Nahum consists of one prophecy predicting the fall of Nineveh. The book begins with a narration of God's power and vengeance (1 1–14) and then continues with a description of the destruction of Nineveh (2 1–3 19). The first chapter is arranged in an imperfect but discernible alphabetic arrangement. From 1 3 through 1 13 each half-sentence begins with a succeeding letter of the Hebrew alphabet, as is plain for the letters ג, ה, ו, ח, ט and מ. In some cases the second or third word of the half-sentence begins with the desired alphabetical letter, as occurs for א, ב, ז, כ and ס. In other cases the alphabetical letter is contained within a word, as for י, צ, ש and ת; and possibly for ל, נ and ר. A few letters, such as ד, ע, פ and ק are omitted. An imperfect alphabetical arrangement has also been used in Psalms 9–10. Such imperfections only indicate that the authors did not limit themselves to the alphabetical constraint if it prevented proper expression of the ideas.

No explanation of the book's arrangement need be given since it contains only one prophecy.

Habakkuk

The Book of Habakkuk is arranged in a logical order. The book can be considered as a discourse between Habakkuk and God. Habakkuk asks (1 2–4) "Why does wickedness prosper?" God states (1 5–11) that the Chaldeans will destroy the wicked nations, but then the Chaldeans will be guilty and will themselves be destroyed. Habakkuk then asks (1 12–2 1) "How could the wicked Chaldean nation be allowed to destroy other nations which are more righteous?" God answers (2 2–20) that the wicked will be punished, the righteous will survive, the Chaldeans will be destroyed—and God will reside in the Temple. Habakkuk then praises God (3 1–19) for saving His nation, even when other nations are to be destroyed. This chapter of praise is written in a form typical of many of the Psalms.

Zephaniah

The Book of Zephaniah contains one prophecy consisting of two parts. The first part (1 1–3 7) describes the impending destruction by the Babylonians of the

Kingdom of Judah, as well as of the surrounding and neighboring countries of Philistia, Moab, Children of Ammon, Cushim, and Assyria. The specified countries are approximately the same as those specified in Jer. **46–49** to be destroyed by Babylonia, namely Egypt, Philistia, Moab, Ammon, Edom, Damascus, Kedar, and Hazor; and those specified in Ez. **25–32**, namely Ammon, Moab, Edom, Philistia, Tyre, Zidon, and Egypt.

Incidental mention is made that the Jewish remnant will inherit the nations of Philistia (2 7), Moab, and Children of Ammon (2 9). This may refer to the conquests of these territories during the Second Temple, for example by the Hasmonaiim; or to the conquest of these territories at the time of the Messianic era.

The second part of the prophecy (3 8–20) describes the Messianic era. The contents of the passage are explained in detail in Chapter Eighteen.

No explanation of the arrangement of the book need be given, since the book contains only one prophecy.

The approximate maximum age of Zephaniah when he received his prophecy can be calculated as follows. Zephaniah is stated to have been the fourth generation to Hezekiah, since he was the son of Cushi, the son of Gedaliah, the son of Amariah, the son of Hezekiah. Undoubtedly King Hezekiah was meant, otherwise the lineage of Zephaniah would not have been traced back so far. Now when Hezekiah died in 696 he was succeeded by his son Manasseh (probably his eldest son) who was twelve years old (II Kings 21 1, II Chr. 33 1). Hence, the Amariah son of Hezekiah, mentioned here, was not older than eleven years in 696. In 693, when Amariah was fourteen, he could possibly have fathered Gedaliah. In turn, Cushi could have been born in 679, and Zephaniah in 665. As presented in Table 12.4.1, the prophecy of Zephaniah was received about 621, which would make Zephaniah a maximum of forty-four years old at that time. It would be more logical to assume, however, that Zephaniah was thirty plus or minus ten years when he received the revelation.

Haggai

The Book of Haggai is arranged in chronological order. Each prophecy and its related descriptions is dated, and all the specified dates are during the second year of Darius (516). They are the first day of the sixth month (1 1); twenty-fourth day of the sixth month (1 15); twenty-first day of the seventh month (2 1); and twenty-fourth day of the ninth month (2 10,18,20). The book covers a period of only three months and twenty-three days, and recounts prophecies and events relative to the building of the Second Temple, and concerning Zerubbabel, the governor of Judea.

Zechariah

The Book of Zechariah is arranged according to a logical order. The book may be divided into two parts. The first part (1 1–8 23) concerns itself with prophecies

250 PROOF OF THE ACCURACY OF THE BIBLE

Table 12.4.4
Similarity of Phrases between Sections in the Book of Zechariah

Section	Sentence	Phrase	Section	Sentence	Phrase
1 1-6	1 2	קצף ;קצף	1 7-6 8	1 15	קצף ;קצף
	1 3	שובו		1 16	שובו
1 7-6 8	1 16	ובנתה בה לבנות י'	6 9-15	6 15	ובנה את היכל י'
6 9-15	6 15	לשכן		7 3	הבכה
	6 11	הבכה			
7 1-7	7 7	הדברים האראשונים	7 8-14	7 12	הדברים האראשונים
7 8-14	7 10	ואיש את רעת אחיו	8 1-17	8 17	ואיש את רעת רעהו
		אל תחשבו בלבבכם			מחשבות רעהו
8 1-17	8 10	שלום ;8 16 שלום... אמת	8 18-23	8 19	האמת והשלום
	8 8	לעמי		8 22	לבקש
	8 13	והוששתם		8 23	לכת
8 18-23	8 19	שמים ;8 22 שמים	9 1-11 17	9 10	עמים ;גוים
9 1-11 17	11 14	ישראל ;יהודה	12 1-14 21	12 5	יהודה ;ישראל
	11 10	עמים כל	12 2	מנערת	

relevant to the rebuilding of the Temple and revival of the Jewish nation. This first part is mainly arranged in chronological order. The chronological arrangement is evidenced by the specified dates. Thus we have the dates, eighth month of second year of Darius (1 1); twenty-fourth day of the eleventh month of second year of Darius (1 7); and fourth day of the ninth month of fourth year of Darius (7 1). The dates were presented for the cases where they would clarify the described historical events.

The second part of the book (9 1–14 21) concerns the Messianic era. A detailed explanation of these chapters is found in Chapter Eighteen.

In addition to the arrangement described above, the entire book is also arranged by similarity of phrases between adjacent sections, as presented in Table 12.4.4. It is possible that a few of the short prophecies in the first part of the book, are not arranged according to a chronological arrangement in order to maintain the similarity in phrases.

Malachi

The Book of Malachi contains only one prophecy, in which are described the sins of the priests (1 6–2 17), and the Messianic time when Eliyah (Elijah) will reestablish the priesthood and purify the priests so sacrifices can be reinstituted (3 1–24). In describing the sins of the priests, the covenant between God and the Jewish people is compared to the youthful marriage of the people against which they have rebelled (2 10–16). A detailed explanation of the Messianic section (3 1–24) is presented in Chapter Eighteen. In the book written by Malachi (1 1) we also find the word "Malachi" (3 1) used to mean messenger, and to refer to Eliyah the prophet.

Chapter Thirteen

PSALMS, PROVERBS, AND JOB

13.1 PSALMS

The Book of Psalms is a collection of 150 poems which recognize the influence of God in the success of the individual and the nation. Many of the poems have headings which state the author, the historical event, the musical accompaniment or the type of song.

In the headings for Chapters 7 and 18 (see also II Sam. 22) it is clearly stated, using the preposition "ל" preceding the name, that David authored the poems of these chapters under particular historical circumstances. Therefore, in general, the preposition "ל" in a heading before a name, as is used throughout the book, specifies the author of the poem, rather than for example the person about whom or for whom the poem was written. This conclusion is further substantiated by the statement at the end of Chapter 72 "the prayers by David, son of Jesse, are completed," implying that David was the author of numerous poems. In the headings of the book, seventy-three poems are ascribed to David, twelve to Asaph, eleven to the sons of Korah, two to Solomon, and one poem each to Heman the Ezrahite, Ethan the Ezrahite, and Moses. Also Jeduthun is mentioned three times, and this name probably refers to the chief musician.

Numerous terms are used in the headings to designate the type of musical accompaniment and which musical instrument should be used. The type of music is described by such terms as *mizmor, shiggaion, michtam, tefillah, shir, maschil, lehazkir,* and *shir hamaaloth.* Musical instruments which are mentioned are *neginoth, nehiloth, sheminith, gittith, muth-labben, aijeleth-hashahar, shoshannim, alamoth, mahalath, mahalath-leannoth, jonath elem rehokim, al tashheth,* and *shushan-eduth.* The exact meaning of all these terms is not clear. Attempts to use any of these descriptive terms for clarification of the purpose of the poem, such as is often done with the words *shir hamaaloth,* will lead to erroneous conclusions, until further general clarification of the expressions is accomplished.

ORGANIZATION

The over-all organization of the Book of Psalms is not immediately apparent. The book is not arranged according to chronology, topic, length of poem, or grouping together of those chapters following an alphabetical order. That the book is not arranged chronologically is obvious from Table 13.1.1 where the historical dates for the chapters (based on the analysis of the Book of Samuel) are assigned when possible. For example Chapter 51 was written in the twenty-third year of David's reign, Chapters 52, 53, 54, 56, 57, 59 in the first year of Saul's reign, and Chapter 60 in the nineteenth year of David's reign. A topical arrangement is not used as can be discerned from Chapters 136–139. Chapter 136 is a hymn of praise based on past historical events; Chapter 137 is a plea by Jewish captives for revenge against the enemy; Chapter 138 is a praise of God by David for personal help; and Chapter 139 is a description of the omniscient powers of God. In general, there is no topical connection from one chapter to the next. Furthermore it would be extremely difficult to arrange the poems by subject matter since many of the poems can be categorized in several ways. That the length of poem is not used as a basis of arrangement is obvious from Chapters 118–120. Chapter 118

Table 13.1.1
Dates of Events Referred to in the Book of Psalms

Chapter	Quotation	Reference	Date
3 1	When David fled from his son Absalom	II Sam. 15 14	40th yr. of David
*7 1	Concerning the words of Cush, a Benjamite	II Sam. 18 31	40th yr. of David
*9 1	Concerning death to the son	II Sam. 12 14	24th yr. of David
*14 1	Nabal said in his heart	I Sam. 25 37	1st yr. of Saul
14 7	From out of Zion	II Sam. 5 7	8th yr. of David
18 1	On the day that the Lord saved David from all his enemies and from Saul	II Sam. 1 4	2nd yr. of Saul
27 10	My father and mother have left me	I Sam. 22 3	1st yr. of Saul
30 1	Dedication of the house of David	II Sam. 5 11	ca. 10th yr. of David
34 1	When David changed his demeanor before Abimelech who drove him away, and he departed	I Sam. 21 14– 22 1	1st yr. of Saul
42 1,7	Sons of Korah; From the land of Jordan; and the Hermons, from the hill Mizar	Deut. 3 8	1435 B.C.E.

* The date given is based upon one possible interpretation of the text.

Table 13.1.1 (continued)

Chapter	Quotation	Reference	Date
47 1,5	Sons of Korah; God chooses our inheritance	See e.g. Deut. 26 1	ca. 1435 B.C.E.
51 2	When the prophet Nathan came to David after he had gone in to Bathsheba	II Sam. 12 1	23rd yr. of David
52 2	When Doeg the Edomite came and told Saul that David came to the house of Ahimelech	I Sam. 22 9	1st yr. of Saul
*53 2	Nabal said in his heart	I Sam. 25 37	1st yr. of Saul
53 7	From out of Zion	II Sam. 5 7	8th yr. of David
54 2	When the Ziphites came and said to Saul "Does not David hide himself with us?"	I Sam. 23 19	1st yr. of Saul
55 14,25	You are a man of my equal, my leader and my familiar friend.	II Sam. 3 27–30,39	ca. 6th yr. of David
	Men of blood and deceit	I Kings 2 5	
56 1	When the Philistines caught David in Gath	I Sam. 21 11	1st yr. of Saul
57 1	When David fled from Saul in the cave	I Sam. 24 9	1st yr. of Saul
59 1	When Saul sent, and they watched the house to kill David	I Sam. 19 11	1st yr. of Saul
60 2	When David strove with Aram-Naharaim and with Aram-Zobah; and Joab returned and smote Edom in the Valley of Salt	II Sam. 8 5,13,14	19th yr. of David
61 7,8	May the King sit forever before God	II Sam. 7 16	16th yr. of David
63 1	When David was in the wilderness of Judah	II Sam. 15 23,28	40th yr. of David
72 1	By Solomon: God give your judgments to the King and your righteousness to the King's son	I Kings 1 33–37,48	40th yr. of David

Table 13.1.1 (continued)

Chapter	Quotation	Reference	Date
85 1,2	Sons of Korah: Lord you have desired your land, you have reestablished the settlement of Jacob	See e.g. Deut. 28 11,12	ca. 1434 B.C.E.
89 39, 45	You have been angry with David your anointed; You have cast his throne to the ground	II Sam. 15 -17	40th yr. of David
90 1	Prayer of Moses the man of God	Deut. 33 1	
96 1-13	(Essentially identical to passage in Chronicles)	I Chr. 16 23-33	15th yr. of David
105 1-15	(Essentially identical to passage in Chronicles)	I Chr. 16 8-22	15th yr. of David
106 1, 47,48	(Essentially identical to passage in Chronicles)	I Chr. 16 34-36	15th yr. of David
110 6	He crushes a head on the land of Rabbah	II Sam. 12 26-31	25th yr. of David
126 1	When the Lord re-established the settlement of Zion	II Sam. 5 7 I Chr. 11 5	8th yr. of David
127 1,3	Solomon; If the Lord does not build a house; children are a heritage of the Lord	I Chr. 28 5,6,10	40th yr. of David
132 11	The Lord swore unto David, of the fruit of your body will I set upon the throne	II Sam. 7 12,16	16th yr. of David
137 1,7	By the rivers of Babylon; Remember Lord concerning the children of Edom	II Sam. 8 3,14	19th yr. of David
142 1	When David was in the cave	I Sam. 24 4	1st yr. of Saul

In addition, the use of the word Zion in Chapters 2, 20, 48, 50, 65, 69, 74, 76, 78, 84, 87, 97, 99, 102, 125, 128, 129, 133, 134, 135, 146, 147, and 149 establishes that these chapters were written sometime between the eighth and fortieth years of David.

has twenty-nine sentences, Chapter 119 has 176 sentences, and Chapter 120 only seven sentences. Common features, such as alphabetical arrangements, are also no criterion since only Chapters 9, 10, 25, 34, 37, 111, 112, 119 and 145 are arranged alphabetically.

One obvious division of the book is into five separate sections which begin from Chapters 1, 42, 73, 90, and 107. The last four sections are indicated by phrases that include such words as "blessed be the Lord," "for everlasting" and "amen and amen," which are placed at the end of the preceding chapters. A typical closing sentence is Psalm **89** 53 "Blessed be the Lord for evermore, amen and amen."

A second factor of importance in the book's arrangement is the author of the individual poem, or a common term in the heading, such as *shir hamaaloth* or *hallelujah*. The authors and headings of the chapters are tabulated in Table 13.1.2. It should be noted however that there are numerous exceptions to a systematic order based on author or heading. For example the poems by Asaph are Chapters 73–83; yet a poem by Asaph is also found in Chapter 50. Furthermore, at the end of Chapter 72 it is stated "the prayers by David, son of Jesse, are completed," although numerous poems by David occur in later chapters.

A third key factor in the arrangement of the book is gained by observation that similar phrases are used in consecutive chapters. A listing of the similar expressions is presented in Table 13.1.3. Some very striking examples are Chapters 103 and 104 both containing "Let my soul bless the Lord"; 106 and 107 containing "Give thanks unto the Lord for He is good, for His mercy is forever"; and 130 and 131 containing "Israel have hope in the Lord." In other cases the same phrases are used in different grammatical constructions, while at worst the same unusual word is found in two consecutive chapters. Naturally, occasional poor fits will result when arranging 150 chapters in this manner, and sometimes better similarity of phrases occurs between chapters which are two apart.

The following method for arrangement of the book can now be given. Originally the poems were collected and grouped according to author and heading. Then the poems were rearranged with a minimum number of relocations according to the similarity of phrases between chapters. Subsequently the book was divided into five sections so that the poems by a particular author, with only minor exceptions, were together within each section. The division into sections also allowed each section to begin with a different author of importance. Thus, Section I is authored by David; Section II begins with the sons of Korah; Section III begins with Asaph; Section IV begins with Moses; and Section V mainly contains anonymous poems. The phrase at the end of Chapter 72 "the prayers by David, son of Jesse, are completed" signifies that this chapter ends the groupings based on the authorship by David. Subsequent poems by David are out of place to maintain the similarity in phraseology.

Table 13.1.2
Arrangement of Book of Psalms by Author and Heading

Chap.	Author	Type Song	Musical Accompaniment or Historical Event
		Section I—Chapters 1–41	
Introductory Chapters			
1			
2			
Chapters authored by David			
3	David	Mizmor	When he fled from his son Absalom
4	David	Mizmor	To the music leader, with *neginoth*
5	David	Mizmor	To the music leader, with *nehiloth*
6	David	Mizmor	To the music leader, with *neginoth* on the *sheminith*
7	David	Shiggaion	Concerning Cush, a Benjamite
8	David	Mizmor	To the music leader, upon the *gittith*
9	David	Mizmor	To the music leader, upon *muth-labben*
10			
11	David		To the music leader.
12	David	Mizmor	To the music leader, on the *sheminith*
13	David	Mizmor	To the music leader
14	David		To the music leader
15	David	Mizmor	
16	David	Michtam	
17	David	Tefillah	
18	David		To the music leader; when he was delivered from his enemies, and from Saul
19	David	Mizmor	To the music leader
20	David	Mizmor	To the music leader
21	David	Mizmor	To the music leader
22	David	Mizmor	To the music leader, upon *aijeleth-hashahar*
23	David	Mizmor	
24	David	Mizmor	
25	David		
26	David		
27	David		

Table 13.1.2 (continued)

Chap.	Author	Type Song	Musical Accompaniment or Historical Event
28	David		
29	David	*Mizmor*	
30	David	*Mizmor Shir*	Dedication of the house of David
31	David	*Mizmor*	To the music leader
32	David	*Maschil*	
33			
34	David		When David changed his demeanor before Abimelech
35	David		
36	David		To the music leader
37	David		
38	David	*Mizmor Lehazkir*	
39	David	*Mizmor*	To the music leader, for Jeduthun
40	David	*Mizmor*	To the music leader
41	David	*Mizmor*	To the music leader

Section II—Chapters 42–72

Chapters authored by Sons of Korah

42	Sons of Korah	*Maschil*	To the music leader
43			
44	Sons of Korah	*Maschil*	To the music leader
45	Sons of Korah	*Maschil Shir Yedidut*	To the music leader, upon *shoshannim*
46	Sons of Korah	*Shir*	To the music leader, upon *alamoth*
47	Sons of Korah	*Mizmor*	To the music leader
48	Sons of Korah	*Shir Mizmor*	

PSALMS, PROVERBS, AND JOB 259

Table 13.1.2 (continued)

Chap.	Author	Type Song	Musical Accompaniment	Historical Event
49	Sons of Korah	*Mizmor*	To the music leader	
50	Asaph	*Mizmor*		

Historical chapters authored by David

Chap.	Author	Type Song	Musical Accompaniment	Historical Event
51	David	*Mizmor*	To the music leader	When Nathan the prophet came to David
52	David	*Maschil*	To the music leader	When Doeg the Edomite told Saul
53	David	*Maschil*	To the music leader upon *mahalath*	Nabal said in his heart
54	David	*Maschil*	To the music leader with *neginoth*	When the Ziphites said to Saul
55	David	*Maschil*	To the music leader with *neginoth*	(You are a man of my equal)
56	David	*Michtam*	To the music leader upon *jonath elem rehokim*	When the Philistines took David in Gath
57	David	*Michtam*	To the music leader *al-tash-heth*	When David fled from Saul in the cave
58	David	*Michtam*	To the music leader *al-tash-heth*	
59	David	*Michtam*	To the music leader *al-tash-heth*	When Saul sent, and they watched the house
60	David	*Michtam*– to teach	To the music leader upon *shushan-eduth*	When David strove with Aram-Naharaim and Aram-Zobah

Table 13.1.2 (continued)

Chap.	Author	Type Song	Musical Accompaniment	Historical Event
61	David		To the music leader upon *neginoth*	(May the king sit forever before God)
62	David	*Mizmor*	To the music leader for jeduthun	
63	*David*	*Mizmor*		When David was in the wilderness of Judah

Concluding chapters authored by David

Chap.	Author	Type Song	Musical Accompaniment	Historical Event
64	David	*Mizmor*	To the music leader	
65	David	*Mizmor, Shir*	To the music leader	
66		*Shir, Mizmor*	To the music leader	
67		*Mizmor Shir*	To the music leader	
68	David	*Mizmor Shir*	To the music leader upon *neginoth*	
69	David		To the music leader upon *shoshannim*	
70	David	*Lehazkir*	To the music leader	
71				
72	Solomon			(The prayers of David the son of Jesse are ended)

Section III—Chapters 73–89

Chapters authored by Asaph

Chap.	Author	Type Song	Musical Accompaniment
73	Asaph	*Mizmor*	
74	Asaph	*Maschil*	
75	Asaph	*Mizmor, Shir*	To the music leader, *al-tashheth*
76	Asaph	*Mizmor, Shir*	To the music leader on *neginoth*
77	Asaph	*Mizmor*	To the music leader for jeduthun
78	Asaph	*Maschil*	
79	Asaph	*Mizmor*	
80	Asaph	*Mizmor*	To the music leader upon *shoshannim*, a testimony
81	Asaph		To the music leader upon the *gittith*
82	Asaph	*Mizmor*	
83	Asaph	*Shir Mizmor*	

PSALMS, PROVERBS, AND JOB

Table 13.1.2 (continued)

Chap.	Author	Type Song	Musical Accompaniment
Chapters authored by Sons-of-Korah			
84	Sons of Korah	Mizmor	To the music leader upon the *gittith*
85	Sons of Korah	Mizmor	To the music leader
86	David	Tefillah	
87	Sons of Korah	Mizmor Shir	
88	Sons of Korah Heman the Ezrahite	Shir Mizmor, Maschil	To the music leader upon *mahalath-leannoth*
89	Ethan the Ezrahite	Maschil	
Section IV—Chapters 90–106			
Chapter authored by Moses			
90	Moses	Tefillah	
Anonymous Chapters with few details in the Headings			
91			
92		Mizmor Shir for the Sabbath day	
93			
94			
95			
96			
97			
98		Mizmor	
99			
100		Mizmor of thanksgiving	
101	David	Mizmor	
102		Tefillah of the afflicted	

Table 13.1.2 (continued)

Chap.	Author	Type Song	Musical Accompaniment or Historical Event
103	David		
104			
105			Hallelujah (at the end)
106		Hallelujah	Hallelujah (at the end)

Section V—Chapters 107–150

Connecting chapters authored by David

107			
108	David	Shir Mizmor	
109	David	Mizmor	To the music leader
110	David	Mizmor	

Hallelujah chapters

111		Hallelujah	
112		Hallelujah	
113		Hallelujah	Hallelujah (at end)
114			
115			Hallelujah (at end)
116			Hallelujah (at end)
117		Hallelu	Hallelujah (at end)
118			
119			

Shir Hamaaloth chapters

120		Shir Ha-maaloth	
121		Shir La-maaloth	
122	David	Shir Ha-maaloth	
123		Shir Ha-maaloth	
124	David	Shir Ha-maaloth	
125		Shir Ha-maaloth	
126		Shir Ha-maaloth	When the Lord re-established the settlement of Zion

Table 13.1.2 (continued)

Chap.	Author	Type Song	Musical Accompaniment or Historical Event
127	Solomon	*Shir Ha-maaloth*	
128		*Shir Ha-maaloth*	
129		*Shir Ha-maaloth*	
130		*Shir Ha-maaloth*	
131	David	*Shir Ha-maaloth*	
132	David	*Shir Ha-maaloth*	
133	David	*Shir Ha-maaloth*	
134		*Shir Ha-maaloth*	

Connecting chapters authored by David

135		*Hallelujah*	*Hallelujah* (at end)
136			
137			By the rivers of Babylon
138	David		
139	David	*Mizmor*	To the music leader
140	David	*Mizmor*	To the music leader
141	David	*Mizmor*	
142	David	*Maschil, Tefillah*	When David was in the cave
143	David	*Mizmor*	
144	David		
145	David	*Tehillah*	

Chapters with Hallelujah at beginning and end

146		*Hallelujah*	*Hallelujah* (at end)
147		*Hallelujah*	*Hallelujah* (at end)
148		*Hallelujah*	*Hallelujah* (at end)
149		*Hallelujah*	*Hallelujah* (at end)
150		*Hallelujah*	*Hallelujah* (at end)

Table 13.1.3
Similarity of Phrases between Adjacent Chapters in the Book of Psalms

Chapter	Phrase	Chapter	Similar Phrase
1 1	Happy is the man	2 12	Happy are all they,
1 6	The way of the wicked shall perish		And you perish in the way
2 6	Upon Zion My holy mountain	3 5	His holy mountain
3 3	There are many that say	4 7	There are many that say
4 4	The Lord will hear	5 4	The Lord in the morning You shall hear
5 4	The Lord in the morning You shall hear my voice	6 9	The Lord has heard the voice
6 5	Return Lord, deliver my soul,	7 2,5	Save me; I have delivered
6 8,11	Save me My adversaries; My enemies	7 6,8	My adversary; the enemy pursue my soul; return
7 5,6	My adversary; the enemy pursue	8 3	Your adversaries, to still the enemy
8 2	How glorious is Your name	9 3	I will sing praise to Your name
8 3	To still the enemy	9 7	The enemy, they are ended
9 20	Arise O Lord	10 12	Arise O Lord
10 3	For the wicked boasts of his soul's desire	11 5	The wicked and he that loves violence, His soul hates
11 2	The wicked; the upright in heart	12 3	With a heart and a heart
11 4	The children of men	12 9	the wicked; to the children of men
12 6	I will set (אשית)	13 3	Will I set (אשית)
12 6	Now I will arise says the Lord	13 2	For how long Lord will you forget me
13 6	My heart shall rejoice in Your salvation	14 7	The salvation of Israel; Let Jacob rejoice
14 1,3	There is none that does good	15 3	He did not do evil to his fellow
15 3	He did not take	16 4	And I will not take
15 5	He did not give; He will never be moved	16 8,10	I shall not be moved; He will not give

Table 13.1.3 (continued)

Chapter	Phrase	Chapter	Similar Phrase
16 11	Satisfaction of joy in Your face	17 15	I will behold Your face, I shall be satisfied
17 6	I called You; Incline Your ear to me, hear my speech	18 7	I will call upon the Lord; He will hear; into His ears
18 3,14	My God is my Rock; in the heavens	19 15,2	The Lord is my Rock; the heavens
18 16	The world (תבל)	19 5	The world (תבל)
18 42	They cried but there was none to save, unto the Lord but He did not answer them	20 10	Save, Lord, the King will answer us on the day that we call
18 51	Salvation to His being; mercy to his anointed	20 7	The Lord has saved his anointed
20 6	We will shout for joy in Your salvation	21 6	His glory is great through Your salvation
20 7	With mighty acts	21 14	We will praise Your might
21 8	For the king trusts in the Lord	22 29	For the kingdom is the Lord's
21 5	Length of days	23 6	For length of days
22 11	You are my God	23 4	For You are with me
23 3	He restores my soul	24 4	Not taken My soul in vain
24 4	Not taken My soul in vain	25 1	I take my soul
25 2	My God, in You I have trusted	26 1	And I have trusted in the Lord
25 7,16	As Your mercy; be gracious to me	26 3,11	For Your mercy; Be gracious to me
26 1,5	And I have trusted in the Lord; evil-doers	27 3,2	In this I trust; evil-doers
26 11	And be gracious to me	27 7	And be gracious to me
27 1	The Lord is my light and salvation; The Lord is the stronghold of my life	28 8	The Lord is a strength to them, and a stronghold of salvation
27 7	Hear O Lord when my voice calls	28 2	Hear the voice of my supplication

Table 13.1.3 (continued)

Chapter	Phrase	Chapter	Similar Phrase
28 8	The Lord is a strength to them	29 11	The Lord will give strength to His people
29 10	The Lord sat as a king forever	30 13	The Lord is my God, I will give thanks to you forever
29 11	The Lord will give strength	30 8	The Lord has established strength for my mountain
30 3	I cried to You	31 23	When I cried to You
30 7	As for me I said	31 23	As for me I said
30 8	You did hide Your face	31 21	You will hide them in the covert of Your face
31 7	And I trusted in the Lord	32 10	And he that trusts in the Lord
32 11	And rejoice you righteous, and shout for joy	33 1	Shout for joy you righteous
33 8	Let all the earth fear the Lord	34 10	Fear the Lord you his holy ones
33 16	A mighty man is not delivered by great strength	34 20	But the Lord delivers him out of them all
34 3	My soul shall glory in the Lord	35 9	And my soul shall be joyful in the Lord
34 8,11	The angel of the Lord; Young lions	35 5,17	And the angel of the Lord; From the young lions
34 21	All his bones	35 10	All my bones
35 19	They that hate me; wink with the eye;	36 3	In his eyes; to be hated
35 24	Judge me Lord my God according to your righteousness	36 7	Your righteousness is like the mountains of God, your judgments
36 7	Your righteousness; Your judgments	37 6	Your righteousness; and Your judgments
37 7	And hope in Him	38 16	For in You O Lord have I hoped
37 39,40	And the salvation of the righteous is of the Lord; and the Lord helped them	38 23	Make haste to help me, the Lord is my salvation

Table 13.1.3 (continued)

Chapter	Phrase	Chapter	Similar Phrase
38 16	For in You O Lord do I hope	39 8	O Lord, My hope, it is in You
39 8	Lord, what have I waited for?	40 2	I waited patiently for the Lord; and He heard my cry
39 13	Hear my prayer; give ear to my cry		
40 5, 8, 12	Happy; then I said; You O Lord	41 2, 5, 11	Happy; As for me I said; and You O Lord
41 2, 5, 6	In the day; my soul; when	42 4, 2, 3	All the day; my soul; when
42 10	Why have you forgotten me, why go I mourning under the oppression of the enemy?	43 2	Why have you rejected me, why go I mourning under the oppression of the enemy?
42 12	Why is my soul bowed down, and why do you moan within me? Hope in God, for I shall yet thank him, the salvation of my face and my God	43 5	Why is my soul bowed down, and why do you moan within me? Hope in God, for I shall yet thank him, the salvation of my face and my God
43 2	Why have you rejected me; the oppression; For you are the God of my strength	44 24, 25	Why, Don't reject forever; and our oppression
		44 5	You are my king, O God
44 2	We have heard with our ears	45 11	Hear; incline your ear
44 9	And we will give thanks to your name forever	45 18	Your name; nations will give thanks to you forever
45 3, 8, 18	Therefore (על כן)	46 3	Therefore (על כן)
45 17	You shall make them princes in all the land	46 9	Who has made desolations in the land
46 8, 12	The God of Jacob, Selah	47 5	Jacob whom He loves, Selah

Table 13.1.3 (continued)

Chapter	Phrase	Chapter	Similar Phrase
46 7, 10	With His voice; the land	47 6, 3	With the voice; the land
47 9	God sat on His holy throne	48 2	In the city of our God, His holy mountain
47 3, 8	All the land; For God is the King	48 3, 15	All the land; For such is God
48 9	We have heard; We have seen	49 2, 10	Hear; He won't see.
48 14, 15	Set (שיתו); death	49 15	Have set (שתו); death
49 2, 13	Hear this all you peoples; like cattle	50 7, 10	Hear, my people; cattle
50 8	Not because of your sacrifices; and your burnt-offerings	51 18	You do not want sacrifice; burnt-offering
50 23	I will show him the salvation of God	51 16	God of my salvation
51 3	God according to Your mercy	52 10	In the mercy of God
51 6	Be righteous in your speech	52 5	Than speaking righteousness
52 11	You have done, and I hope for Your name for it is good	53 2, 4	There is none that does good
53 2, 4	There is none that does good	54 8	For it is good
53 5	They did not call upon God	54 5	They have not set God before them
54 3	God save me with Your name	55 17	I will call upon God, and the Lord will save me
54 4	God hear my prayer, give ear	55 2	Give ear God to my prayer
55 20	And they feared not God	56 5	In God I trusted, I will not be afraid
55 24	As for me, I will trust in You.	56 4	I will put my trust in You
55 24	As for me, I will trust in You.	56 5	In God I trusted, I will not be afraid
56 2	Be gracious to me God	57 2	Be gracious to me God

Table 13.1.3 (continued)

Chapter	Phrase	Chapter	Similar Phrase
56 3	They trample (שאפו)	57 4	He that would trample me (שאפי)
57 5	Their teeth are spears and arrows	58 7,8	Their teeth; his arrows
58 6,7,11	Will not hear; in their mouth; in the blood	59 8,13,3	Who hears; their mouth; blood
59 3,7	Save me; they return; and go around the city	60 7,2,11	Save; and he returned; fortified city
60 6,12	Selah; You God	61 5,6	Selah; You God
61 3,4,9	In a rock; a refuge; so I may pay	62 8	The rock of my strength and my refuge
		62 13	Will pay
62 2,6	My soul	63 2,9,10	My soul
62 8	And my glory, the rock of my strength	63 3	Your strength and Your glory
63 12	Will rejoice in God, All who swear by him shall glory	64 11	The righteous shall rejoice in the Lord; and all the upright in heart shall glory
64 2,10	Hear; and all men feared	65 3,9	You that hears; and they feared
65 2	And to You is fulfilled the vow	66 13	I will fulfill to you my vows
65 3	The one who hears prayer	66 19	Heard; my prayer
66 8	Bless our God, peoples	67 4	Let the peoples give thanks to God
66 20	Blessed be God	67 7,8	May God bless us
67 2	God will be gracious to us and bless us	68 20	Blessed be the Lord; the God who is our salvation, Selah
67 3	Selah; Your salvation		
67 7,8	May God bless us	68 27,36	Blessed be God
68 2	His enemies; They that hate Him	69 5	They that hate me; my enemies.
68 4	And the righteous will be glad	69 29,33	Righteous; will be glad

Table 13.1.3 (continued)

Chapter	Phrase	Chapter	Similar Phrase
68 20	The God who is our salvation	69 30	Your salvation, God
68 23	I will bring back	69 5	I will bring back
69 7	Let those who seek You not be ashamed	70 3	Those who seek my soul; and be ashamed
69 20	My reproach and my shame	70 3	They will be ashamed and reproached
69 30	Your salvation, God	70 5	God; they that love Your salvation
70 2	Lord make haste to help me	71 12	God make haste to help me
70 3	They will be ashamed and reproached those who seek my soul, they will be turned back and abashed those who delight in my hurt	71 13	They will be ashamed and consume those who are adversaries to my soul, they will be covered with reproach and abashment those who seek my hurt
71 19	And Your righteousness God	72 1	God; and Your righteousness
72 3,4,5	Peace; oppressor; all generations	73 3,8,15	Peace; oppression; generation
72 16	In the land	73 9	In the land
73 9,14	In the land; all the day	74 12,22	The land; all the day
73 17,18	The sanctuaries; to utter ruin	74 7,3	Your sanctuary; to utter ruin
74 17,21	All the borders of the land; Your name	75 9,2	All the wicked of the land; Your name
75 2,3	We gave thanks; I will judge	76 11,10	Will give thanks to you; to judgment;
75 10	To the God of Jacob	76 7	God of Jacob
76 5,7	Enlightened; Jacob	77 19,16	Lighted; Jacob
76 9	The land feared and was still	77 19	The land trembled and shook
77 6,15	The days of old; does wonders	78 2,12	From times of old; did wonders
77 16	The sons of Jacob and Joseph	78 5,67	In Jacob; Joseph

Table 13.1.3 (continued)

Chapter	Phrase	Chapter	Similar Phrase
78 4	To the last generation they tell the praises of the Lord	79 13	We will tell of Your praise to all generations
79 6	To the nations; that did not call upon Your name;	80 9,19	Nations; and we will call upon Your name.
79 9	God of our salvation	80 4	God; and we will be saved
80 2,19	Joseph; and we will call upon Your name	81 6,8	Joseph; You did call in trouble
81 5	A judgment of the God of Jacob	82 1	In the midst of God (angels) He judges
82 6	And all of you are sons of the Most High	83 19	The Most High over all the land;
82 8	For You (כי אתה)		That You (כי אתה)
83 5,6,12	Ever (עוד); heart; make their	84 5,3,7	Ever (עוד); my heart; they will make it
83 8	They that dwell	84 5	They that dwell
84 12	The Lord will give, no good thing will he withhold	85 13	The Lord will give the good thing
85 11	Mercy and truth	86 15	Mercy and truth
86 12	And I will glorify Your name forever	87 3	Glorious things are spoken of You
87 3,6;4	Selah; I will remember	88 11,6	Selah; remember them
88 2	God of my salvation	89 27	My God, and the rock of my salvation
88 15,13	Why do you cast off; Your wonders	89 39,6	You have cast off; Your wonders
88 12	Your mercy; Your faithfulness	89 2	The mercies of; Your faithfulness
89 2,12	To all generations; the earth, the world	90 1,2	In all generations; the earth and the world
90 4,10	A thousand; the days of our years	91 7,16	A thousand; length of days
91 1,9	The Most High; for You Lord	92 2,9	Most High; And You; Lord
92 9	And You Lord are on high forever	93 4,2	The Lord on high is mighty; You are forever

Table 13.1.3 (continued)

Chapter	Phrase	Chapter	Similar Phrase
92 14	In the house	93 5	To Your house
93 1,5	Majesty (גאות); Lord for evermore	94 2,3	Proud (גאים); Lord how long
92 8	All the workers of iniquity	94 4	All the workers of iniquity
92 12	The evil-doers that rise up against me	94 16	Who will rise up for me against the evil-doers?
94 9	Will he not hear? if	95 7	If you would hearken to His voice
94 2, 20,22	The land; create; to a rock	95 4,5,1	Land; created; to a rock
95 3	For the Lord is a great God, and a great King above all gods	96 4	For great is the Lord; He is to be feared above all gods
96 10,11	The Lord reigns; and the land will rejoice	97 1	The Lord reigns, the land will rejoice
97 5,6	From before the Lord; and all the peoples have seen	98 9,3	Before the Lord; All the ends of the earth have seen
97 9	All the land	98 4	All the land
96 1	Sing unto the Lord a new song	98 1	Sing unto the Lord a new song
96 13	Before the Lord, for He has come, For He has come to judge the land, He will judge the world with righteousness, and the peoples with his faithfulness	98 9	Before the Lord, for He has come to judge the land, He will judge the world with righteousness and the peoples with equity
98 9	He will judge the world with righteousness; equity	99 4	Equity; justice and righteousness
99 9	For the Lord our God is holy	100 3	That the Lord He is God
100 1	Shout unto the Lord	101 1	Unto the Lord will I sing
100 2	Come before His presence with singing	101 2	When will You come to me?
100 3	Know that	101 4	I will not know

Table 13.1.3 (continued)

Chapter	Phrase	Chapter	Similar Phrase
101 2,7	You will come to me; He will not sit	102 2,13	Will come to You; Will sit forever
102 5,13	For I forgot; forever; and Your remembrance	103 2,9,14	And don't forget; forever; It is remembered
102 14,15	Will have compassion; her dust	103 2,9,14	As a father has compassion; dust
102 16,20	Will fear the name of the Lord; His holy place	103 13,1	The Lord, on those that fear Him; His holy name
103 1,2,22	Let my soul bless the Lord	104 1,35	Let my soul bless the Lord
104 31	The Lord will rejoice in his works	105 3	The heart of those who seek the Lord will rejoice
104 33	I will sing to the Lord	105 2	Sing to Him
105 2,3,23	His wonders; Glory; Egypt, the land of Ham	106 7, 5,21,22	Your wonders; To glory; in Egypt; in the land of Ham
105 26, 29,32	Moses, Aaron; to blood; fire	106 16, 38,18	Of Moses, of Aaron; blood; fire
106 1	Give thanks to the Lord for He is good, For His mercy is forever	107 1	Give thanks to the Lord for He is good, For His mercy is forever
107 1,2	Give thanks to the Lord; redeemed them from the hand of the adversary	108 4,13	I will give thanks to You Lord; help against the adversary
108 4	I will give thanks to you Lord	109 30	I will give great thanks to the Lord
108 5,7	Your mercy; Save with Your right hand	109 21,31	Your mercy; to the right hand; to save
109 6,31	Stand at his right hand	110 1,5	Sit at My right hand; at your right hand
110 4,6,7	Forever; among the nations	111 5,6	Forever; of the nations
109 30	I will give great thanks to the Lord with my mouth	111 1	I will give thanks to the Lord with all my heart
111 4	Gracious and compassionate	112 4	Gracious and compassionate

Table 13.1.3 (continued)

Chapter	Phrase	Chapter	Similar Phrase
111 10	Fear of the Lord;	112 1	Who fears the Lord
112 2	Shall be blessed; in the land	113 2,6	Be blessed; and in the land
112 6,10	forever; shall see	113 2,6	Forever; to see
113 6	To see; and in the land	114 3,7	Saw; land
114 1,2,7	Israel; land	115 9,15	Israel; and land
113 2	From now and until forever	115 18	From now and until forever
115 5	But they do not speak; eyes	116 10,8	When I speak; my eye
115 7	Their feet, but they walk not	116 8,9	My foot; I shall walk
115 2,1	The nations; Your mercy, Your truth	117 1,2	All nations; His mercy, and the truth
117 2	For His mercy is great toward us, and the truth of the Lord is forever	118 1,29	Give thanks to the Lord for He is good, for His mercy is forever
118 1,29	For His mercy is forever	119 98	For it is with me forever
118 10	In the name of the Lord	119 55	Your name, Lord
118 21	And You were a salvation to me.	119 94	I am Yours, save me
118 26	Blessed be he that comes in the name of the Lord	119 12	Blessed are You, Lord
119 145	I have called with my whole heart, answer me Lord	120 1	In my distress I called to the Lord, and He answered me
120 2	Lord deliver my soul from lying lips	121 7	The Lord will watch you from all evil; He will watch your soul
120 7	I am peace, and when I speak	122 8	I will now speak peace
122 5	Sat	123 1	Sit
121 1	I will lift my eyes to the mountains	123 1	To You I lifted up my eyes
123 4	Our soul	124 4,5,7	Our soul

Table 13.1.3 (continued)

Chapter	Phrase	Chapter	Similar Phrase
121 2	My help comes from the Lord, who makes the heaven and earth	124 8	Our help is in the name of the Lord, who makes the heaven and earth
124 1	Israel	125 5	Israel
122 2,3,8	Jerusalem; peace	125 2,5	Jerusalem; peace
125 1	Zion	126 1	Zion
124 3,4,5	Then	126 2	Then
126 1,4	Settlement (שיבת)	127 2	Sit (שבת)
126 1	As dreamers	127 2	Sleep
127 3,5	Children; happy is the man	128 6,4	Children; will the man be blessed
128 5	The Lord will bless you from Zion	129 8,5	The blessing of the Lord; Zion
128 6	Israel	129 1	Israel
129 1	Israel	130 7	Israel
128 1	Happy are all who fear the Lord	130 4	That you may be feared
130 7	Israel have hope in the Lord	131 3	Israel have hope in the Lord
131 1,2	My eyes; If	132 4,3	To my eyes; If
131 3	Forever	132 12	For ever
132 13,17	For the Lord chose Zion; there	133 3	Zion, for there the Lord commanded
133 1,3	Behold; the Lord commanded the blessing	134 1	Behold, bless the Lord
134 1,2	Bless the Lord	135 19,20	Bless the Lord
134 3	The Lord will bless you from Zion, He who makes the heaven and earth	135 21	The Lord is blessed from Zion
		135 6	Made, in heaven and in earth
135 10	And slew mighty kings	136 18	And He slew mighty kings
135 11	Sihon king of the Amorites, and Og King of the Bashan	136 19 136 20	Sihon king of the Amorites; And Og King of the Bashan
135 12	And gave their land for a heritage, A heritage to Israel his people	136 21 136 22	And gave their land for a heritage A heritage to Israel his servant

Table 13.1.3 (continued)

Chapter	Phrase	Chapter	Similar Phrase
135 21	Blessed be the Lord from Zion	137 1	When we remembered Zion
	Who dwells at Jerusalem	137 5	If I forget you Jerusalem
137 4	How shall we sing the Lord's song	138 5	They shall sing in the ways of the Lord
138 7	You will stretch forth Your hand, and Your right hand will save me	139 10	Your hand will lead me, and Your right hand will hold me
139 7, 14,19	From Your presence; knows; the wicked	140 14, 13,5	In Your presence; I knew; the wicked
140 5	Keep me Lord from the hands of the wicked	141 9	Keep me from the hands of the snare
140 6	A snare for me; they have set traps for me	141 9,3	And the traps; set
140 7	Give ear, Lord, to the voice	141 1	Give ear to my voice
141 1	My voice when I call to You;	142 2	My voice will cry to the Lord;
141 8	For my eyes are to You, God the Lord, in You I have taken refuge, pour not out my soul	142 6	I cried to You Lord, I said You are my refuge
		142 5	No one cares for my soul
141 9	Snare	142 4	Snare
142 7	Deliver me from my persecutors	143 9	Deliver me from my enemies
142 8	My soul	143 3,6	My soul
143 5,6	Your hands; My hands	144 7,1	Your hands; My hands
143 9	Deliver me	144 11	And deliver me
144 1	Blessed be the Lord	145 1	And I will bless Your name
144 3,7	Son of man; Your hands	145 12,16	To the sons of man; Your hand
145 14	And raises up all who are bowed down	146 8	The Lord raises up those who are bowed down

Table 13.1.3 (continued)

Chapter	Phrase	Chapter	Similar Phrase
145 20	The Lord preserves all who love Him	146 8	The Lord loves the righteous
146 7	Gives bread to the hungry	147 9	Gives to the cattle their bread
146 10	Your God, Zion; praise God	147 12	Praise Your God, Zion
147 4,8,9	Of the stars; mountains; to the cattle	148 3, 9,10	All the stars; the mountains; and all cattle
147 16	Snow	148 8	Snow
148 5,13	They will praise the name of the Lord	149 3	They will praise His name
148 11	Kings of the earth and all peoples	149 8,7	Their kings; upon the peoples
148 14	For his people; a praise for all His saints	149 4,9	In His people; for all His saints, praise
149 3	They will praise His name in the dance, they will sing to Him with the timbrel and harp	150 3	Praise Him with the psaltery and harp
		150 4	Praise Him with the timbrel and dance

One further point that needs clarification is the almost exact duplication of chapters or parts of chapters in different places of the book. Thus, Chapters 14 and 53, **40** 14–18 and Chapter 70, as well as **57** 8–12 and **60** 7–14 with Chapter 108, are essentially identical. A simple explanation is that the duplicate sections were set to different music. In all these cases of duplication the musical headings are different. The slight variations in wording between the otherwise identical sections were probably to obtain a better fit to the music.

AUTHORSHIP

The fact that a simple explanation to the organization of the Book of Psalms can be given, establishes that all the poems were arranged at one time by one editor. There are two ways to establish the time of the editor. First, he must have been a contemporary, or lived shortly after the time of the latest of the listed authors. Secondly, the editor must have compiled the book after the time of the last historical event described in the poems. We shall presently show that the editor was King David, and he completed the book during his fortieth and last year as king.

The earliest author listed is Moses (Psalms **90** 1), and he probably was the originator of the psalm-style of poetry. Only once is he specified as an author. Another early author is the "sons of Korah" (Chapters 42, 44–49, 84, 85, 87, and 88) who were contemporaneous with Moses. It is specifically mentioned in Num. **26** 10,11 that the sons of Korah did not die at the time that their father was swallowed up by the earth, thus indicating their great righteousness. However it should be noted that there are two groups of people going under the title of sons of Korah. The first group are the actual sons of Korah who lived at the time of the stay of the Israelites in the desert. Chapters 42, 47, and 85 clearly were written by these original sons of Korah. Thus in **42** 7 is mentioned "from the land of Jordan, and the Hermons," which is reminiscent of Deut. **3** 8 "beyond the Jordan, from the valley of Arnon to Mount Hermon." The phrase in **47** 5 "He chooses our inheritance" corresponds to the time before entering the land of Canaan under the leadership of Joshua. Similarly the phrases in **85** 2,3 "Lord, You have desired Your land, You have reestablished the settlement of Jacob; You have forgiven the iniquity of Your people" refers to the time shortly after entering the land of Canaan under Joshua. Chapters 44 and 49 may also have been written by the original sons of Korah, although the chapters could have been written much later too.

The second group using the title "sons of Korah" were contemporaneous with David, and were descendants of Korah. In particular, Heman who authored Chapter 88, was a descendant of Korah (I Chr. **6** 16–23). The other chapters ascribed to the sons of Korah, namely Chapters 45, 46, 48, 84, and 87 were written by a contemporary of David, such as Heman, because of the use of words not known at the time of the original sons of Korah. Thus, the word Zion which was first used in the time of David (II Sam. **5** 7) is mentioned in **48** 3, 12, 13; **84** 8; and **87** 2,5, in addition to other terms in these chapters indicating their composition at the time of David. Similarly, the terms "king" and "Tyre" used in **45** 12,13; and the term "city of God" used in **46** 5, indicate that Chapters 45 and 46 were written by a contemporary of David.

Other authors than Heman who are mentioned in the book of Chronicles as musicians are Asaph, Ethan, and Jeduthun. From I Chr. **6** 16–33; **15** 16–19 we learn that the chief musicians for David were Heman descendant of Kohath, Asaph descendant of Gershom, and Ethan descendant of Merari. These three authors represented the three divisions within the tribe of Levi (Num. **3** 17). We subsequently find (I Chr. **16** 37–42; **25** 1–7) that Jeduthun replaced Ethan as one of the chief musicians. Furthermore, we find that Ethan the Ezrahite and Heman were famous for their wisdom, and preceded the time of King Solomon (I Kings **5** 11). Thus, in addition to Heman and the later sons of Korah, the authors Asaph (**50**, **73**–**83**), Ethan (**89**), and Jeduthun (mentioned in **39**, **62**, and **77**) are contemporaneous with King David.

Let us not overlook David himself, King of Israel, who was the author of seventy-three poems. He was a gifted musician (I Sam. **16** 16–23) who played the harp; and a capable poet as indicated from the poems in II Sam. (**1** 17–27; **3** 33, 34; **22** 1–51; **23** 1–7).

The latest author mentioned is Solomon, son of David. If we assume that the two chapters ascribed to Solomon (**72** and **127**) were written after he had recently been appointed king, while his father was still alive (I Chr. **28–29**; I Kings **1** 29–**2** 10) (see Table 13.1.1 on Chapters 72 and 127), then we see that based on the names of the given authors there is no reason to doubt the assumption that David completed the Book of Psalms in his last year as king.

It should be noted that no author is specified for forty-nine of the chapters (see Table 13.1.2). In a few cases the authors may be surmised from parallel sections in other books of the Bible. For example, Psalms **96** 1–13; **105** 1–15; **106** 1,47,48 may be assumed to have been authored by Asaph and his brethren because of the essential identity of these passages with that in I Chr. **16** 7–36 attributed to Asaph and his brethren. However, in most other cases we have no information as to the authors. Some possible reasons for the anonymity of these poems are (A) that the authors were not known by David; (B) that the poems were a joint composition of numerous individuals; or (C) that the authors' names were immaterial to understanding of the poems' contents.

In order to defend the conclusion that the Book of Psalms was completed by David in the last year, we must be able to show that no event is referred to which corresponds to a time later than the reign of David. This is clearly true of those events where the historical incidents are specified in the headings (see Table 13.1.1). However, numerous phrases seem at first to refer to much later events, and have been so interpreted by all commentaries. In order to show that this is not the case we must first explain certain words and phrases used repeatedly in the book.

The term Messiah (משיח) (**2** 2; **18** 51; **20** 7; **28** 8; **84** 10; **89** 39,52; **105** 15; **132** 10,17) has often been misinterpreted, and simply refers to the anointed king. In particular, we find in **18** 51 that Messiah refers to David. Furthermore we know that David was anointed as stated in I Sam. **16** 13 and II Sam. **5** 3.

The phrase "when the Lord reestablished the settlement of Zion" ("בשוב ד' את שיבת ציון") used in **126** 1, refers to the capture of Zion, i.e. Jerusalem, by David (II Sam. **5** 7; I Chr. **11** 5). The word "re-established" implies that Zion previously belonged to the Israelites, which was the case at the time of Abraham* (Gen. **22** 2; II Chr. **3** 1) and the time of Jacob (Gen. **33** 18)**; even though not captured at the time of Joshua (Josh. **15** 63). The similar phrase "Lord return our captured" ("שובה ד' את שביתנו") used

---

* Note that God promised Abraham that all the land which he could see and upon which he would walk would be given to him and his descendants (Gen. **13** 15–17).
** It is here assumed that the Hebrew *Salem* was an early name for the city of Jerusalem.

in **126** 4 means return those who are in captivity, for example those captured by the enemy during the battles fought by David.

The word Zion, used in numerous cases throughout the book (**2** 6; **9** 12, 15; **14** 7; **20** 3; **48** 3,12,13; **50** 2; **51** 20; **53** 7; **65** 2; **69** 36; **74** 2; **76** 3; **78** 68; **84** 8; **87** 2,5; **97** 8; **99** 2; **102** 14,17,22; **125** 1; **126** 1; **128** 5; **129** 5; **132** 13; **133** 3; **134** 3; **135** 21; **137** 1,3; **146** 10; **147** 12; **149** 2) refers to the place in Jerusalem captured by David from the Jebusites. Often in the book, requests are made from God for the development of Zion. In general, the use of this word in a psalm indicates the poem was written sometime between the eighth and fortieth year of David's reign, and not at a much later historical period (such as after the destruction of the Temple in 586).

The phrases "house of the Lord" (**23** 6; **27** 4; **92** 14; **116** 1,9; **118** 26; **122** 1,9; **134** 1; **135** 2) and "house of God" (**42** 5; **52** 10; **55** 15; **84** 11; **135** 2) are often interpreted to refer to the Temple built by Solomon, and therefore would indicate that the chapters containing these phrases were written after the death of David. However, these terms are also used by David to refer to the site in Jerusalem where the temple was to be built. Thus, in I Chr. **22** 1 David says of the threshing-floor of Ornan "this is the house of the Lord God." Also in II Sam. **12** 20, the tent which housed the Ark was called "the house of the Lord." Furthermore, in Ezra **2** 68, **3** 8 the terms "house of the Lord" and "house of God" are used to refer to the site of the Temple. Hence these phrases as used in the Book of Psalms do not indicate that the Temple was constructed.

The word "מקדש" (**68** 36; **73** 17; **74** 7; **78** 69; **96** 6) usually translated as "sanctuary" really is used in the sense of "holy place." The term "holy place" could signify Mount Zion (see Ps. **78** 68,69), as well as the Tabernacle, or tent in which the Ark was kept, and the use of the word does not necessarily indicate a time after the reign of David.

In Chapters 74 and 79, both authored by Asaph, we find expressions which most commentaries explain as referring to the destruction of the Temple in 586. However this is impossible, since Asaph was a contemporary of David, and it is specifically stated in I Chr. **16** 7,37 that Asaph was appointed by David to minister before the Ark in Jerusalem. Hence the phrase in Ps. **74** 7 "they have set your holy place on fire, they have profaned to the ground the dwelling place of Your name" ("שלחו באש מקדשך לארץ חללו משכן שמך"), refers to some incident during the reign of David. Probably what is referred to are the attacks of the Philistines against David in the Jerusalem area, specifically around the Valley of Rephaim (II Sam. **5** 17–25; I Chr. **14** 8–17). It is specifically mentioned that the Philistines left behind their idols, and they were burned at the command of David. The idols were what profaned the holy places, and were the indirect cause of a fire being set to destroy the abominations. The terms "your holy place" ("מקדשך") and "dwelling place" ("משכן") do not refer to the sanctuary, but to the Jerusalem area which was considered holy. Similarly the statement in Psalms **79** 1,2, "the heathens have come into Your territory, defiled the holy places, made Jerusalem into heaps, and have given the dead bodies of Your servants as food for the birds of the heaven" (באו גוים" בנחלתך, טמאו את היכל קדשך שמו את ירושלים לעיים; נתנו את נבלת עבדיך מאכל לעוף השמים") refers to the Philistine invasion into the Jerusalem area. Obviously some Israelites were killed and their bodies were eaten by the birds, even though eventually the Philistines were beaten. The phrase "Your holy Temple" ("היכל קדשך") refers to the holiness of Jerusalem, and not to the Temple as with similar expressions which were previously explained.

One other chapter needs clarification. In **137** 1,3 it is stated, "By the rivers of Babylon ... we wept when we remembered Zion .... For there our captors asked of us words of song ..." All commentaries incorrectly assume that this poem refers to the Babylonian Exile. However, it actually refers to the incidents described in II Sam. **8** 3–14, where David conquered Hadadezer at the Euphrates river (one of the rivers of Babylon). Undoubtedly during the battles some Israelites were taken captive, even though David was victorious. These captives, who were later saved, wrote Ps. **137**. The phrase (**137** 6) "If I do not raise up Jerusalem above my highest joy" clearly indicates that Jerusalem was a flourishing city, and excludes the possibility that the event described is after the destruction of Jerusalem in 586. Also the mention of sons of Edom (**137** 7) corresponds to the mention of Edom in II Sam. **8** 14; and as clarified in I Kings **11** 15–16, Joab, the chief general of David, stayed in Edom for six months. Furthermore, the expression* (**137** 8) "the plundered daughter of Babylon" indicates that it was the enemy around Babylon who was conquered, rather than the Israelites in Jerusalem. Support for this interpretation of the chapter is gained from **87** 4, where Babylon is mentioned in a poem authored by the sons of Korah, who were contemporaries of David.

We have now shown that no authors or events later than the fortieth year of David's reign are mentioned in the book of Psalms. This information, coupled with the fact that seventy-three chapters were authored by David, offer strong evidence that the Book of Psalms was completed and edited by David himself.

13.2 PROVERBS

The Book of Proverbs contains sayings about numerous diverse topics. However, the emphasis is on such topics as wisdom, foolishness, righteousness, wickedness, wealth, poverty, happiness, sadness, kings, servants, women, and God's power. The proverbs are of two types: (A) numerous sentences involving one theme; and (B) short sentences, each presenting a different idea.

---

* The usual translation "daughter of Babylon, that art to be destroyed" is incorrect, since the Hebrew uses the present rather than the future tense.

Organization

The Book of Proverbs can be divided into five main sections. The first section (1 1–9 18), commences with the heading "The proverbs of Solomon, the son of David, King of Israel," and consists of proverbs organized according to topic. Typical themes are: a warning against crimes of violence (1 10–19); danger of immorality (5 1–23; 6 20–7 27); and benefits of wisdom and good deeds (1 20–4 27; 8 1–9 18).

The second section (10 1–24 34) has the heading "The proverbs of Solomon," and consists of individual proverbs connected not by topic but by similarities of words, sounds, or sentence construction. Sometimes the same words are repeated, as "צדיק ... תהפכות" (10 31,32). In other cases the similarity in sounds of certain words are used to connect adjacent sentences. Similarities of sound include כ and ח, ס, שׁ and ת, ב and ו, ת and ט, א and ע, כ and ק; and even less perfect matches such as פ and ב, and ז and ס. Usually there are two or more words that have similar sounds between consecutive proverbs. As an example, "עצל לא יחרש" (20 4) sounds somewhat similar to "עצה בלב איש" (20 5). In addition there are cases of rhyme between words: for example (18 21,22) "מות ... לשון" rhymes with "מצא ... רצון." Furthermore, similarities in sentence construction between proverbs occur, such as "כ ... כ ... כן ... לא" (26 1,2). In Table 13.2.1 the similarities between adjacent proverbs for this second section are presented. The Table is presented in Hebrew because it is impossible to translate the similarities in sound. Occasionally adjacent proverbs are concerned with the same topic, but these cases have not been pointed out.

At the end of the section (22 17–24 34) is found a concluding part which breaks the monotony of the unrelated proverbs. This concluding part contains numerous cases where adjacent sentences refer to the same topic.

The third section (25 1–29 27) begins with the heading "These also are the proverbs of Solomon, which the men of Hezekiah, King of Judah copied." Just as in the previous section, the proverbs are not arranged by topic but by similarities of words, sounds and sentence construction. These similarities are listed in Table 13.2.2. Nevertheless, occasional topical arrangement occurs, as for example 25 2–7 concerning kings; 26 1–12 concerning fools, and 26 13–16 concerning sluggards.

The fourth section (30 1–33) begins with the heading "The words of Agur the son of Jakeh," and presents proverbs written by Agur. Similarly, the fifth section (31 1–31) begins with the heading "The words of Lemuel Melech" and contains the proverbs written by Lemuel. Included in this last section is the famous alphabetically arranged song about the woman of valor (31 10–31).

Authorship

Based on the headings of the first three sections it is clear that Solomon was the main author of the Book of Proverbs. In all three cases the headings include the

Table 13.2.1
Similarity in Sounds of the Consecutive Proverbs
in the Second Section of the Book of Proverbs

Sentence	Phrase	Sentence	Phrase
10:1	תוגת אמו	10:2	תציל ממות
10:2	לא . . . רשע וצדקה ממות	10:3	לא . . . צדיק והות רשעים
10:3	והות רשעים יהדף	10:4	כף רמיה ויד
10:4	חרוצים תעשיר	10:5	נרדם בקציר
10:5	משכיל	10:6	חמס
10:6	צדיק . . . רשעים	10:7	צדיק . . . רשעים
10:7	צדיק לברכה	10:8	מצות ואויל
10:8	ואויל שפתים ילבט	10:9	הולך בתם ילך בטח
10:9	הולך בתם ילך בטח	10:10	ואויל שפתים ילבט
10:10	קרץ עין	10:11	מקור חיים
10:11	רשעים יכסה	10:12	פשעים תכסה
10:12	תכסה אהבה	10:13	תמצא חכמה
10:13	ושבט לגו חסר לב	10:14	ופי אויל מחתה קרבה
10:14	מחתה	10:15	מחתת
10:15	מחתת . . . ריש	10:16	רשע לחטאת
10:16	לחיים תבואת . . . לחטאת	10:17	לחיים . . . תוכחת מתעה
10:17	תוכחת מתעה	10:18	ומוצא . . . כסיל
10:18	מכסה . . . שפתי . . . כסיל	10:19	וחושך שפתיו משכיל
10:19	וחושך שפתיו	10:20	כסף נבחר
10:20	כסף נבחר לשון צדיק, לב	10:21	שפתי צדיק . . . ואוילים בחסר לב
10:21	ואוילים בחסר לב ימותו	10:22	ולא יוסף עצב עמה
10:22	ולא יוסף עצב עמה	10:23	לכסיל עשות זמה
10:23	תבונה	10:24	תבואנו
10:24	רשע . . . ותאות צדיקים יתן	10:25	סופה ואין רשע וצדיק
10:25	כ . . . ואין . . . עולם	10:26	כ . . . לעינים, כן
10:26	וכעשן לעינים	10:27	ימים ושנות
10:27	ושנות רשעים	10:28	ותקות רשעים
10:28	שמחה	10:29	ומחתה
10:29	לתם	10:30	בל ימוט
10:30	צדיק . . . ארץ	10:31	צדיק . . . תכרת
10:31	פי צדיק . . . ולשון תהפכות	10:32	שפתי צדיק . . . רשעים תהפכות

Table 13.2.1 (continued)

Sentence	Phrase	Sentence	Phrase
10:32	רצון . . . תהפכות	11:1	תועבת . . . רצונו
11:1	מאזני . . . ואבן . . . רצונו	11:2	זדון . . . ואת צנועים
11:2	ואת צנועים חכמה	11:3	תמת ישרים תנחם
11:3	תמת	11:4	ממות
11:4	וצדקה תציל	11:5	צדקת תמים
11:5	צדקת תמים תישר	11:6	צדקת ישרים תצלם
11:6	ובהות בגדים ילכדו	11:7	ותוחלת אונים אבדה
11:7	רשע תאבד	11:8	רשע תחתיו
11:8	צדיק . . . נחלץ	11:9	צדיקים יחלצו
11:9	ובדעת צדיקים יחלצו	11:10	בטוב צדיקים תעלץ
11:10	קריה, ובאבד רשעים	11:11	קרת, ובפי רשעים
11:11	ובפי רשעים תהרס	11:12	בז לרעהו חסר לב
11:12	לרעהו חסר לב	11:13	רוח מכסה דבר
11:13	ונאמן רוח מכסה	11:14	באין תחבלות
11:14	ותשועה ברב	11:15	ירוע כי ערב
11:15	תוקעים בוטח	11:16	תתמך כבוד
11:16	יתמכו עשר	11:17	ועכר שארו
11:17	ועכר שארו אכזרי	11:18	רשע עשה . . . שכר
11:18	רשע . . . צדקה . . . אמת	11:19	צדקה . . . רעה למותו
11:19	ומרדף רעה למותו	11:20	ורצונו תמימי דרך
11:20	עקשי לב	11:21	לא ינקה
11:21	וזרע . . . נמלט	11:22	וסרת טעם
11:22	יפה וסרת טעם	11:23	תקות רשעים עברה
11:23	אך . . . רשעים	11:24	מישר אך
11:24	וחשך מישר	11:25	נפש ברכה
11:25	ברכה . . . ומרוה	11:26	וברכה . . . משביר
11:26	וברכה לראש	11:27	ודרש רעה
11:27	טוב יבקש	11:28	בוטח בעשרו
11:28	בוטח בעשרו	11:29	עכר ביתו
11:29	לחכם לב	11:30	ולקח . . . חכם
11:30	צדיק עץ	11:31	צדיק בארץ
11:31	אף כי רשע וחוטא	12:1	אהב מוסר . . . ושונא
12:1	אהב מוסר	12:2	ואיש מזמות
12:2	מזמות ירשיע	12:3	אדם ברשע
12:3	בל ימוט	12:4	עטרת בעלה
12:4	בעצמותיו מבישה	12:5	תחבלות . . . מרמה
12:5	רשעים מרמה	12:6	רשעים ארב דם
12:6	רשעים ארב דם	12:7	רשעים ואינם

Table 13.2.1 (continued)

Sentence	Phrase	Sentence	Phrase
12:7	רשעים ואינם	12:8	איש ונעוה
12:8	ונעוה לב	12:9	ועבד לו
12:9	ועבד לו . . . וחסר	12:10	בהמתו . . . אכזרי
12:10	ורחמי רשעים אכזרי	12:11	ומרדף ריקים חסר לב
12:11	ומרדף ריקים	12:12	מצוד רעים
12:12	מצוד רעים . . . צדיקים	12:13	מוקש רע . . . צדיק
12:13	בפשע שפתים	12:14	פי איש ישבע
12:14	ידי אדם ישוב	12:15	ישר . . . לעצה חכם
12:15	אויל . . . בעיניו	12:16	אויל . . . יודע
12:16	יודע . . . קלון ערום	12:17	ועד שקרים מרמה
12:17	שקרים מרמה	12:18	חכמים מרפא
12:18	כמדקרות . . . ולשון	12:19	ועד ארגיעה לשון
12:19	ארגיעה לשון	12:20	חרשי רע . . . שלום
12:20	מרמה . . . רע	12:21	מלאו רע
12:21	יאנה לצדיק	12:22	אמונה רצונו
12:22	תועבת	12:23	דעת
12:23	ערום כסה דעת	12:24	ורמיה תהיה למס
12:24	תהיה למס	12:25	טוב ישמחנה
12:25	ודבר . . . ישמחנה	12:26	ודרך . . . תתעם
12:26	יתר מרעהו צדיק	12:27	יחרך רמיה צידו
12:27	יחרך . . . צידו	12:28	בארח צדקה
12:28	אל מות	13:1	מוסר אב
13:1	בן חכם מוסר	13:2	בגדים חמס
13:2	פי איש . . . ונפש	13:3	פיו שמר נפשו
13:3	נפשו . . . מחתה	13:4	מתאוה . . . נפשו
13:4	מתאוה . . . עצל ונפש	13:5	ישנא צדיק . . . יבאיש
13:5	צדיק, ורשע	13:6	צדקה . . . ורשעה
13:6	ורשעה תסלף	13:7	מתרושש
13:7	יש מתעשר	13:8	איש עשרו
13:8	עשרו ורש	13:9	ונר רשעים
13:9	צדיקים ישמח	13:10	נועצים חכמה
13:10	בזדון יתן מצה	13:11	הון . . . ימעט
13:11	מהבל ימעט וקבץ	13:12	תוחלת ממשכה . . . ועץ
13:12	ממשכה מחלה לב	13:13	יחבל לו . . . ישלם
13:13	וירא מצוה	13:14	תורת . . . מות
13:14	תורת . . . חיים לסור	13:15	שכל טוב . . . חן
13:15	שכל טוב	13:16	בדעת, וכסיל
13:16	כל ערום . . . וכסיל יפרש	13:17	מלאך . . . יפל . . . וציר

Table 13.2.1 (continued)

Sentence	Phrase	Sentence	Phrase
13:17	רשע . . . ברע	13:18	ריש . . . פורע
13:18	מוסר . . . תוכחת	13:19	ותועבת . . . סור מרע
13:19	כסילים סור מרע	13:20	ורעה כסילים ירוע
13:20	חכמים . . . ירוע	13:21	חטאים . . . רעה
13:21	ואת צדיקים . . . טוב	13:22	וצפון לצדיק . . . חוטא
13:22	טוב ינחיל בני בנים	13:23	רב אכל ניר ראשים
13:23	ויש נספה בלא	13:24	חושך . . . שונא בנו
13:24	שונא בנו . . . מוסר	13:25	לשבע נפשו . . . תחסר
13:25	רשעים תחסר	14:1	נשים בנתה
14:1	ואולת בידיה	14:2	ונלוז דרכיו בוזהו
14:2	ירא יקוה	14:3	חטר גאוה
14:3	בפי אויל חטר גאוה	14:4	באין אלפים אבוס בר
14:4	באין אלפים אבוס	14:5	עד אמונים . . . יכזב
14:5	כזבים עד שקר	14:6	בקש לץ חכמה
14:6	לץ . . . ודעת	14:7	לך . . . דעת
14:7	לאיש כסיל	14:8	ואולת כסילים
14:8	ערום הבין . . . ואולת	14:9	אולים . . . ובין ישרים
14:9	אולים יליץ אשם	14:10	לב יודע מרת
14:10	לא יתערב	14:11	ואהל ישרים
14:11	רשעים ישמד	14:12	יש דרך ישר
14:12	ואחריתה	14:13	ואחריתה
14:13	יכאב לב . . . שמחה תוגה	14:14	מדרכיו ישבע סוג לב
14:14	ומעליו איש טוב	14:15	יבין לאשרו
14:15	יבין לאשרו	14:16	ירא וסר מרע
14:16	וכסיל מתעבר	14:17	יעשה אולת
14:17	יעשה אולת	14:18	פתאים אולת
14:18	נחלו פתאים	14:19	שחו רעים
14:19	שחו רעים	14:20	עשיר רבים
14:20	לרעהו . . . ואהבי עשיר	14:21	לרעהו . . . אשריו
14:21	לרעהו חוטא	14:22	יתעו חרשי
14:22	חרשי רע . . . חרשי טוב	14:23	יהיה מותר . . . אך למחסור
14:23	בכל עצב	14:24	כסילים אולת
14:24	אולת כסילים	14:25	עד אמת . . . כזבים
14:25	כזבים מרמה	14:26	מבטח עז
14:26	ביראת ד'	14:27	יראת ד'
14:27	חיים לסור	14:28	לאם מחתת
14:28	הדרת מלך	14:29	מרים אולת
14:29	ארך אפים רב	14:30	חיי בשרים לב

Table 13.2.1 (continued)

Sentence	Phrase	Sentence	Phrase
14:30	לב מרפא	14:31	דל חרף
14:31	עשק דל חרף עשהו	14:32	ברעתו ידחה רשע
14:32	ידחה רשע	14:33	תנוח חכמה
14:33	ובקרב כסילים	14:34	וחסד לאמים
14:34	וחסד לאמים	14:35	לעבד משכיל
14:35	ועברתו תהיה	15:1	עצב יעלה
15:1	ודבר עצב	15:2	יביע אולת
15:2	חכמים תיטיב	15:3	בכל מקום . . . וטובים
15:3	מקום עיני	15:4	לשון עץ
15:4	לשון עץ	15:5	אויל ינאץ
15:5	ינאץ מוסר אביו	15:6	צדיק חסן רב
15:6	ובתבואת רשע נעכרת	15:7	שפתי . . . יזרו דעת
15:7	שפתי חכמים יזרו דעת	15:8	זבח רשעים תועבת
15:8	זבח רשעים תועבת ד'	15:9	תועבת ד' דרך רשע
15:9	תועבת . . . רשע	15:10	רע . . . תוכחת
15:10	לעזב ארח	15:11	לבות . . . אדם
15:11	אף כי לבות	15:12	יאהב . . . הוכח לו
15:12	יאהב לץ הוכח	15:13	ובעצבת לב רוח
15:13	ובעצבת לב	15:14	לב . . . אולת
15:14	לב נבון יבקש דעת	15:15	וטוב לב משתה תמיד
15:15	וטוב . . . משתה	15:16	טוב מעט
15:16	טוב . . . ביראת	15:17	טוב ארחת
15:17	ארחת . . . ואהבה שם	15:18	איש חמה . . . וארך
15:18	וארך אפים	15:19	וארח ישרים
15:19	כמשכת חדק	15:20	חכם ישמח אב
15:20	חכם ישמח אב	15:21	שמחה לחסר לב
15:21	שמחה לחסר	15:22	הפר מחשבות
15:22	הפר מחשבות	15:23	שמחה . . . פיו
15:23	שמחה . . . במענה . . . מה טוב	15:24	למשכיל למען . . . מטה
15:24	משאול מטה	15:25	גבול אלמנה
15:25	יסח ד' . . . אלמנה	15:26	תועבת ד' . . . אמרי נעם
15:26	מחשבות רע	15:27	עכר ביתו
15:27	מתנת יחיה	15:28	יהגה לענות
15:28	צדיק . . . ופי רשעים	15:29	מרשעים, ותפלת צדיקים
15:29	צדיקים ישמע	15:30	שמועה . . . עצם
15:30	שמועה טובה	15:31	שמעת תוכחת
15:31	שמעת תוכחת	15:32	ושומע תוכחת
15:32	פורע מוסר	15:33	יראת . . . מוסר

Table 13.2.1 (continued)

Sentence	Phrase	Sentence	Phrase
15:33	חכמה . . . ענוה	16:1	מערכי . . . מענה
16:1	מערכי . . . מענה	16:2	דרכי . . . בעיניו
16:2	ותכן רוחות	16:3	ויכנו מחשבתיך
16:3	גל אל ד׳ מעשיך	16:4	כל פעל ד׳ למענהו
16:4	כל . . . ליום	16:5	כל . . . ליד
16:5	תועבת ד׳	16:6	וביראת ד׳
16:6	וביראת ד׳	16:7	ברצות ד׳
16:7	ישלם אתו	16:8	בלא משפט
16:8	טוב מעט בצדקה	16:9	לב אדם . . . צעדו
16:9	לב אדם יחשב	16:10	לא ימעל פיו
16:10	מלך במשפט	16:11	ומאזני משפט
16:11	מעשהו כל אבני כיס	16:12	כי בצדקה יכון כסא
16:12	מלכים עשות	16:13	מלכים שפתי
16:13	מלכים שפתי	16:14	מלאכי מות
16:14	מלך מלאכי	16:15	מלך חיים
16:15	ורצונו כעב מלקוש	16:16	וקנות . . . נבחר מכסף
16:16	בינה נבחר	16:17	נפשו נצר
16:17	שמר נפשו . . . דרכו	16:18	לפני שבר . . . רוח
16:18	גבה רוח	16:19	שפל רוח
16:19	טוב . . . מחלק	16:20	משכיל . . . טוב
16:20	משכיל על	16:21	לב . . . ומתק
16:21	ומתק שפתים	16:22	מקור חיים שכל
16:22	חיים שכל	16:23	חכם ישכיל
16:23	ישכיל פיהו	16:24	מתוק לנפש
16:24	מתוק לנפש	16:25	לפני איש . . . מות
16:25	לפני איש	16:26	נפש עמל
16:26	עליו פיהו	16:27	ועל שפתיו
16:27	שפתיו כאש	16:28	איש תהפכות
16:28	איש תהפכות	16:29	איש חמס יפתה
16:29	חמס יפתה	16:30	לחשב תהפכות
16:30	עצה . . . תהפכות	16:31	עטרת תפארת
16:31	עטרת תפארת	16:32	טוב ארך אפים
16:32	טוב . . . מגבור	16:33	יוטל . . . הגורל
16:33	בחיק יוטל את	17:1	טוב פת חרבה
17:1	ושלוה בה, מבית	17:2	ימשל בבן מביש
17:2	בבן מביש	17:3	ובחן לבות
17:3	ובחן לבות	17:4	לשון הות
17:4	מרע מקשיב על שפת	17:5	לרש חרף עשהו

Table 13.2.1 (continued)

Sentence	Phrase	Sentence	Phrase
17:5	חרף עשהו	17:6	ותפארת
17:6	בנים, ותפארת	17:7	לנבל שפת יתר
17:7	נאוה לנבל	17:8	בעיני בעליו
17:8	השחד בעיני	17:9	ושנה בדבר
17:9	מכסה... אהבה	17:10	מהכות... מאה
17:10	מהכות כסיל	17:11	ומלאך אכזרי
17:11	ומלאך אכזרי ישלח בו	17:12	ואל כסיל באולתו
17:12	כסיל באולתו	17:13	תחת טובה, לא
17:13	משיב רעה	17:14	מים ראשית
17:14	מים ראשית	17:15	מצדיק רשע
17:15	ומרשיע צדיק	17:16	מחיר ביד כסיל
17:16	לקנות חכמה ולב	17:17	ואח לצרה יולד
17:17	עת אהב הרע, ואח	17:18	חסר לב תקע כף
17:18	לב... ערב	17:19	אהב... אהב
17:19	פשע אהב מצה	17:20	עקש לב לא ימצא
17:20	לב לא ימצא	17:21	לו ולא ישמח
17:21	ולא ישמח אבי	17:22	לב שמח ייטיב
17:22	נכאה תיבש	17:23	ארחות משפט
17:23	להטות ארחות	17:24	כסיל... ארץ
17:24	ועיני כסיל	17:25	בן כסיל
17:25	כעס לאביו	17:26	להכות נדיבים
17:26	ענוש... טוב	17:27	איש תבונה
17:27	חושך אמריו... תבונה	17:28	אטם שפתיו נבון
17:28	אויל מחריש	18:1	לתאוה יבקש
18:1	בכל... יתגלע	18:2	בהתגלות לבו
18:2	אם בהתגלות	18:3	בא גם בוז, ועם
18:3	ועם קלון חרפה	18:4	נבע מקור חכמה
18:4	פי איש	18:5	פני רשע
18:5	שאת פני... לא טוב להטות	18:6	שפתי... למהלמות
18:6	שפתי כסיל... ופיו	18:7	פי כסיל... ושפתיו
18:7	כסיל מחתה	18:8	כמתלהמים
18:8	נרגן כמתלהמים	18:9	גם מתרפה במלאכתו
18:9	במלאכתו	18:10	מגדל עז
18:10	עז... ונשגב	18:11	עזו... נשגבה
18:11	עשיר... נשגבה	18:12	שבר יגבה
18:12	שבר יגבה	18:13	משיב דבר
18:13	וכלמה	18:14	מחלהו
18:14	נכאה מי ישאנה	18:15	ואזן חכמים

Table 13.2.1 (continued)

Sentence	Phrase	Sentence	Phrase
18:15	לב . . . יקנה דעת	18:16	מתן אדם . . . לו
18:16	ירחיב לו	18:17	וחקרו
18:17	ובא . . . וחקרו	18:18	ובין . . . יפריד
18:18	מדינים ישבית . . . יפריד	18:19	נפשע . . . ומדונים כבריח
18:19	נפשע מקרית	18:20	תשבע . . . תבואת
18:20	מפרי . . . תבואת	18:21	ואהביה . . . פריה
18:21	מות . . . לשון	18:22	מצא . . . רצון
18:22	אשה . . . רצון	18:23	ועשיר יענה
18:23	ידבר רש	18:24	איש . . . דבק
18:24	ויש אהב	19:1	רש הולך
19:1	טוב רש הולך	19:2	נפש לא טוב
19:2	גם בלא דעת	19:3	אולת אדם
19:3	אולת אדם	19:4	ודל מרעהו
19:4	רעים . . . ודל . . . יפרד	19:5	שקרים . . . לא ימלט
19:5	לא ימלט	19:6	לאיש מתן
19:6	וכל הרע	19:7	כי מרעהו
19:7	אף כי מרעהו	19:8	קנה לב אהב
19:8	קנה לב אהב	19:9	כזבים יאבד
19:9	ויפיח כזבים יאבד	19:10	אף כי לעבד
19:10	אף כי לעבד	19:11	האריך אפו
19:11	שכל אדם האריך אפו	19:12	נהם ככפיר זעף מלך
19:12	וכטל על עשב	19:13	לאביו . . . כסיל
19:13	הות לאביו . . . כסיל אשה	19:14	והון . . . אבות . . . אשה משכלת
19:14	נחלת אבות	19:15	עצלה . . . תרעב
19:15	עצלה . . . ונפש . . . תרעב	19:16	מצוה . . . נפשו . . . דרכיו
19:16	מצוה שמר נפשו	19:17	מלוה . . . ישלם לו
19:17	ישלם לו	19:18	ואל המיתו
19:18	ואל המיתו . . . תשא נפשך	19:19	גרל חמה נשא ענש
19:19	כי אם תציל	19:20	שמע עצה וקבל
19:20	עצה . . . תחכם	19:21	ועצת . . . תקום
19:21	מחשבות בלב איש	19:22	וטוב רש מאיש כזב
19:22	תאות . . . חסדו . . . רש	19:23	יראת . . . לחיים . . . רע
19:23	ושבע ילין בל יפקד	19:24	אל פיהו לא ישיבנה
19:24	בצלחת . . . פיהו לא ישיבנה	19:25	לץ תכה ופתי . . . לנבון
19:25	והוכיח . . . יבין	19:26	יבריח . . . בן
19:26	בן מביש ומחפיר	19:27	בני לשמע מוסר

Table 13.2.1 (continued)

Sentence	Phrase	Sentence	Phrase
19:27	חדל בני לשמע	19:28	רשעים יבלע און
19:28	יליץ משפט	19:29	ללצים שפטים
19:29	נכונו ללצים . . . כסילים	20:1	לץ היין . . . לא יחכם
20:1	המה שכר	20:2	נהם ככפיר
20:2	מתעברו	20:3	שבת מריב
20:3	וכל אויל	20:4	מחרף עצל
20:4	עצל לא יחרש	20:5	עצה בלב איש
20:5	מים עמקים עצה . . . איש, ואיש	20:6	איש . . . ואיש אמונים מי ימצא
20:6	ואיש . . . מי ימצא	20:7	בתמו צדיק, אשרי
20:7	בניו אחריו	20:8	בעיניו כל רע
20:8	על כסא	20:9	זכיתי לבי
20:9	זכיתי לבי טהרתי מחטאתי	20:10	אבן ואבן איפה ואיפה
20:10	אבן ואבן . . . גם	20:11	גם . . . אם . . . ואם
20:11	גם . . . אם זך ואם ישר	20:12	אזן שמעת ועין . . . גם
20:12	ועין . . . שניהם	20:13	שנה . . . עיניך
20:13	אל תאהב	20:14	יתהלל
20:14	רע . . . אז	20:15	זהב ורב
20:15	זהב ורב	20:16	ערב זר
20:16	לקח . . . ערב	20:17	ערב . . . לחם
20:17	לאיש לחם	20:18	עשה מלחמה
20:18	ובתחבלות	20:19	ולפתה שפתיו
20:19	הולך רכיל	20:20	מקלל . . . ידעך
20:20	נרו באישון	20:21	בראשונה
20:21	לא תברך	20:22	וישע לך
20:22	אל תאמר . . . קוה לד'	20:23	תועבת ד' . . . מרמה לא
20:23	ד' . . . ומאזני	20:24	מד' מצעדי
20:24	ואדם מה יבין דרכו	20:25	אדם . . . נדרים לבקר
20:25	מוקש אדם	20:26	מלך חכם
20:26	מלך חכם	20:27	נשמת אדם
20:27	חפש כל	20:28	בחסד כסאו
20:28	בחסד כסאו	20:29	בחורים כחם
20:29	תפארת בחורים	20:30	חברות פצע
20:30	חברות פצע	21:1	אשר יחפץ
21:1	לב . . . כל אשר	21:2	כל . . . ישר . . . לבות
21:2	ותכן . . . ד'	21:3	נבחר לד'
21:3	נבחר לד'	21:4	ורחב לב
21:4	ורחב לב	21:5	אך למותר

Table 13.2.1 (continued)

Sentence	Phrase	Sentence	Phrase
21:5	מחשבות . . . למותר	21:6	מבקשי מות
21:6	בלשון שקר	21:7	שד רשעים
21:7	שד רשעים	21:8	דרך איש
21:8	הפכפך . . . וזר	21:9	על פנת גג . . . חבר
21:9	ובית חבר	21:10	אותה רע
21:10	לא יחן	21:11	לחכם
21:11	ובהשכיל	21:12	משכיל
21:12	משכיל	21:13	מזעקת דל
21:13	אטם אזנו	21:14	מתן . . . עזה
21:14	חמה עזה	21:15	עשות . . . ומחתה
21:15	שמחה לצדיק	21:16	מדרך השכל
21:16	מדרך השכל	21:17	מחסור אהב
21:17	איש מחסור	21:18	ותחת ישרים
21:18	לצדיק רשע, ותחת	21:19	שבת בארץ מדבר
21:19	שבת בארץ מדבר	21:20	אוצר נחמד ושמן
21:20	אוצר נחמד	21:21	רדף צדקה
21:21	רדף צדקה	21:22	וירד . . . מבטחה
21:22	עיר . . . עלה . . . מבטחה	21:23	שמר . . . ולשונו . . . מצרות
21:23	מצרות נפשו	21:24	לץ שמו
21:24	לץ . . . עושה בעברת	21:25	תאות עצל . . . לעשות
21:25	תאות . . . לעשות	21:26	תאוה . . . ולא יחשך
21:26	התאוה תאוה	21:27	תועבה . . . יביאנו
21:27	כי בזמה יביאנו	21:28	כזבים יאבד
21:28	עד . . . ואיש שומע	21:29	העז איש רשע
21:29	העז . . . הוא יכין	21:30	אין חכמה . . . עצה
21:30	חכמה . . . תבונה . . . ד'	21:31	מוכן . . . ולד' התשועה
21:31	סוס מוכן	22:1	מכסף . . . חן
22:1	מעשר רב	22:2	עשיר ורש
22:2	ורש נפגשו	22:3	עברו ונענשו
22:3	ראה . . . עברו ונענשו	22:4	עקב ענוה יראת
22:4	עקב ענוה יראת	22:5	עקש . . . נפשו ירחק
22:5	פחים בדרך	22:6	על פי דרכו
22:6	לנער . . . לא	22:7	עשיר . . . לוה
22:7	ועבד לוה . . . מלוה	22:8	עולה . . . עברתו יכלה
22:8	און, ושבט	22:9	טוב עין
22:9	כי נתן מלחמו	22:10	דין וקלון
22:10	וישבת דין	22:11	חן שפתיו
22:11	שפתיו רעהו	22:12	ויסלף דברי

Table 13.2.1 (continued)

Sentence	Phrase	Sentence	Phrase
22:12	נצרו דעת	22:13	רחבות ארצח
22:13	בתוך רחבות	22:14	שוחה...זרות
22:14	שוחה...זרות	22:15	קשורה...מוסר
22:15	אולת קשורה...מוסר	22:16	עשק דל...למחסור
22:16	דל להרבות לו	22:17	ולבך תשית לדעתי
22:17	הט אזנך ושמע	22:18	תשמרם בבטנך
22:18	בבטנך...יחדו	22:19	מבטחך, הודעתיך
22:19	להיות...הודעתיך	22:20	הלא...ודעת
22:20	הלא כתבתי לך	22:21	להודיעך קשט
22:21	להודיעך	22:22	כי דל הוא
22:22	כי...הוא ואל תדכא	22:23	כי...קבעיהם
22:23	וקבע את	22:24	תתרע את
22:24	בעל אף...חמות לא	22:25	תאלף ארחתו
22:25	תאלף...מוקש	22:26	אל תהי...משאות
22:26	בתקעי כף	22:27	משכבך
22:27	לשלם...מתחתיך	22:28	עולם...אבותיך
22:28	אל תסג	22:29	בל יתיצב
22:29	איש...לפני	23:1	אשר לפניך
23:1	תבין...לפניך	23:2	שכין בלעך
23:2	ושמת...בעל	23:3	אל תתאו
23:3	אל תתאו	23:4	אל תיגע
23:4	להעשיר, מבינתך	23:5	עיניך בו...השמים
23:5	עיניך...יעשה לו	23:6	עין, ואל תתאו
23:6	אל תלחם	23:7	בל עמך
23:7	אכול ושתה	23:8	אכלת...ושחת
23:8	אכלת...דבריך	23:9	כסיל...תדבר
23:9	באזני...אל תדבר	23:10	ובשדי...אל תבא
23:10	גבול עולם	23:11	גאלם
23:11	הוא יריב את ריבם אתך	23:12	הביאה למוסר לבך
23:12	למוסר...לאמרי	23:13	אל תמנע...מוסר
23:13	תכנו בשבט	23:14	בשבט תכנו
23:14	תכנו	23:15	גם אני
23:15	לבך...ישמח לבי	23:16	כליותי...שפתיך
23:16	ותעלזנה כליותי	23:17	ביראת...כל היום
23:17	כי אם ביראת	23:18	כי אם יש אחרית
23:18	אם יש אחרית	23:19	שמע אתה
23:19	אתה בני	23:20	אל תהי
23:20	בסבאי...בזללי	23:21	סבא וזולל

Table 13.2.1 (continued)

Sentence	Phrase	Sentence	Phrase
23:21	וזולל . . . תלביש	23:22	זה ילדך, ואל תבוז
23:22	זקנה אמך	23:23	אמת קנה
23:23	חכמה ומוסר ובינה	23:24	חכם וישמח בו
23:24	יגול אבי . . . יולד . . . וישמח	23:25	ישמח אביך . . . ותגל יולדתך
23:25	ואמך . . . יולדתך	23:26	לבך . . . ועיניך
23:26	דרכי תרצנה	23:27	צרה נכריה
23:27	כי שוחה . . . ובאר	23:28	כחתף תארב
23:28	ובוגדים באדם	23:29	אבוי . . . מדונים . . . חנם
23:29	למי חכלילות עינים	23:30	למאחרים על היין
23:30	על היין	23:31	אל . . . יין
23:31	בכיס עינו	23:32	וכצפעני
23:32	אחריתו כנחש	23:33	עיניך . . . תהפכות
23:33	ולבך . . . תהפכות	23:34	והיית . . . בלב
23:34	בלב ים . . . חבל	23:35	בל חליתי, הלמוני בל
23:35	הכוני בל	24:1	אל תקנא
24:1	ואל . . . אתם	24:2	לבם . . . ועמל
24:2	יהגה . . . תדברנה	24:3	יבנה . . . ובתבונה
24:3	ובתבונה יתכונן	24:4	ובדעת . . . כל הון
24:4	ובדעת חדרים	24:5	חכם . . . ואיש דעת
24:5	חכם . . . ואיש . . . מאמץ	24:6	מלחמה, ותשועה . . . יועץ
24:6	לך מלחמה	24:7	לאויל חכמות
24:7	לאויל חכמות	24:8	לו בעל מזמות
24:8	בעל מזמות	24:9	זמת אולת
24:9	ותועבת לאדם	24:10	התרפית ביום
24:10	צר כחכה	24:11	הצל . . . תחשוך
24:11	הצל . . . למות	24:12	הלא . . . לבות
24:12	כי תאמר	24:13	כי טוב
24:13	מתוק על חכך	24:14	חכמה לנפשך
24:14	לנפשך . . . לא תכרת	24:15	אל תארב . . . לנוה
24:15	רשע . . . צדיק	24:16	צדיק . . . ורשעים
24:16	יפול . . . יכשלו	24:17	בנפל . . . ובכשלו
24:17	בנפל אויביך	24:18	פן . . . בעיניו
24:17	אל תשמח	24:19	אל תתחר
24:19	תקנא ברשעים	24:20	נר רשעים
24:20	אחרית לרע	24:21	אל תתערב
24:21	עם שונים	24:22	שניהם מי
24:22	כי פתאם	24:23	הכר פנים

Table 13.2.1 (continued)

Sentence	Phrase	Sentence	Phrase
24:23	הכר פנים . . . לחכמים	24:24	יקבהו עמים . . . לאמים
24:24	עמים . . . לאמים	24:25	ולמוכיחים ינעם
24:25	ולמוכיחים	24:26	נכחים
24:26	שפתים . . . נכחים	24:27	הכן . . . ביתך
24:27	ועתדה . . . ובנית ביתך	24:28	והפתית בשפתיך
24:28	אל תהי	24:29	אל תאמר
24:29	אעשה לו	24:30	על שדה
24:30	כרם . . . חסר לב	24:31	כסו . . . חרלים
24:31	חרלים . . . נהרסה	24:32	לקחתי מוסר
24:32	אשית . . . לקחתי	24:33	שנות . . . חבק
24:33	מעט חבק	24:34	ומחסריך

Table 13.2.2
Similarity in Sounds of the Consecutive Proverbs
in the Third Section of the Book of Proverbs

Sentence	Phrase	Sentence	Phrase
25:2	מלכים חקר	25:3	מלכים אין חקר
25:3	וארץ לעמק	25:4	ויצא לצרף
25:4	הגו . . . לצרף כלי	25:5	הגו . . . בצדק כסאו
25:5	לפני מלך	25:6	לפני מלך
25:6	לפני מלך	25:7	לפני נדיב
25:7	לפני נדיב . . . ראו עיניך	25:8	לרב . . . רעך
25:8	אתך רעך	25:9	את רעך
25:9	וסוד אחר	25:10	יחסדך
25:10	ודבתך לא	25:11	דבר על
25:11	זהב . . . כסף	25:12	זהב . . . כתם
25:12	על אזן שמעת	25:13	נאמן לשלחיו
25:13	שלג ביום	25:14	וגשם אין
25:14	ורוח וגשם	25:15	רכה . . . גרם
25:15	בארך אפים	25:16	אכל . . . פן
25:16	פן תשבענו	25:17	פן ישבעך
25:17	מבית רעך	25:18	ברעהו
25:18	שנון . . . ברעהו	25:19	שן רעה
25:19	בוגד ביום צרה	25:20	בגד ביום קרה
25:20	לב רע . . . חמץ	25:21	רעב . . . לחם
25:21	האכילהו לחם	25:22	כי גחלים
25:22	גחלים	25:23	תחולל גשם

Table 13.2.2 (continued)

Sentence	Phrase	Sentence	Phrase
25:23	גשם, ופנים	25:24	פנת גג
25:24	על פנת; מאשת מדינים	25:25	על נפש; מארץ מרחק
25:25	מים . . . נפש; מארץ מרחק	25:26	מעין נרפש; ומקור משחת
25:26	ומקור משחת	25:27	כבדם כבוד
25:27	כבדם כבוד	25:28	איש אשר
25:28	אין . . . אין	26:1	כ . . . וכ
26:1	כ . . . וכ . . . כן לא	26:2	כ . . . כ . . . כן . . . לא
26:2	ל . . . ל	26:3	ל . . . ל
26:3	לגו כסילים	26:4	כסיל כאולתו
26:4	כסיל כאולתו	26:5	כסיל כאולתו
26:5	כסיל . . . חכם	26:6	חמס . . . כסיל
26:6	ביד כסיל	26:7	בפי כסילים
26:7	בפי כסילים	26:8	נותן לכסיל
26:8	נותן לכסיל	26:9	בפי כסילים
26:9	שכור . . . כסילים	26:10	ושכר כסיל
26:10	כל . . . כסיל	26:11	ככלב . . . כסיל
26:11	על קאו, כסיל	26:12	תקוה לכסיל
26:12	לכסיל . . . בעיניו	26:13	עצל . . . בין
26:13	עצל . . . בדרך	26:14	הדלת . . . ועצל
26:14	ועצל . . . מטתו	26:15	טמן עצל
26:15	עצל . . . להשיבה	26:16	עצל . . . משבעה
26:16	משבעה משיבי	26:17	עבר מתעבר
26:17	מתעבר . . . לא לו	26:18	כמתלהלה
26:18	כמתלהלה	26:19	הלא משחק
26:19	כן איש	26:20	תכבה אש
26:20	עצים . . . אש	26:21	ועצים לאש
26:21	לגחלים . . . לחרחר	26:22	כמתלהמים . . . חדרי
26:22	כמתלהמים	26:23	כסף סיגים
26:23	שפתים . . . ולב רע	26:24	בשפתו . . . ובקרבו
26:24	ינכר . . . ובקרבו	26:25	יחנן קולו
26:25	כי . . . כי . . . קולו	26:26	תכסה . . . תגלה . . . בקהל
26:26	תכסה . . . תגלה	26:27	כרה . . . וגלל
26:27	כרה שחת	26:28	לשון שקר
26:28	חלק יעשה מדחה	27:1	אל תתהלל . . . מחר
27:1	תתהלל; אל . . . לא	27:2	יהללך; ולא . . . ואל
27:2	ולא . . . ואל	27:3	אבן . . . אויל
27:3	וכעס אויל	27:4	אכזריות . . . אף
27:4	אכזריות חמה	27:5	תוכחת מגלה

Table 13.2.2 (continued)

Sentence	Phrase	Sentence	Phrase
27:5	מאהבה מסתרת	27:6	אוהב, ונעתרות
27:6	נאמנים . . . ונעתרות	27:7	נפש . . . ונפש
27:7	נפש . . . ונפש	27:8	נודדת . . . נודד
27:8	נודדת מן קנה	27:9	וקטרת . . . ומתק
27:9	שמן וקטרת ישמח	27:10	שכן קרוב מאח
27:10	אחיך . . . מאח	27:11	חכם . . . ושמח
27:11	ואשיבה חרפי דבר	27:12	ראה רעה נסתר
27:12	ראה . . . עברו	27:13	ערב . . . נכריה
27:13	כי ערב . . . חבלהו	27:14	מברך . . . תחשב לו
27:14	תחשב	27:15	ואשת
27:15	ביום סגריר	27:16	ימינו יקרא
27:16	צפן רוח	27:17	פני רעהו
27:17	יחד פני רעהו	27:18	פריה . . . יכבד
27:18	יאכל . . . אדניו	27:19	בן לב האדם
27:19	הפנים לפנים . . . האדם לאדם	27:20	לא תשבענה
27:20	שאול ואבדון לא	27:21	ואיש לפי מהללו
27:21	לפי מהללו	27:22	מעליו אולתו
27:22	מעליו אולתו	27:23	לבך לעדרים
27:23	ידע תדע	27:24	לדור דור
27:24	כי לא . . . חסן ואם נזר	27:25	גלה חציר ונראה
27:25	עשבות הרים	27:26	שדה עתודים
27:26	כבשים ללבושך	27:27	עזים ללחמך
27:27	ודי חלב	28:1	ואין רדף
28:1	ואין רדף	28:2	מבין ידע
28:2	רבים . . . מבין	28:3	דלים . . . ואין
28:3	רש ועשק	28:4	רשע, ושמרי
28:4	עזבי תורה . . . ושמרי תורה	28:5	לא יבינו . . . יבינו כל
28:5	רע . . . ומבקשי	28:6	רש . . . מעקש
28:6	טוב רש . . . דרכים	28:7	תורה . . . יכלים
28:7	בן מבין . . . יכלים	28:8	מרבה הונו . . . דלים
28:8	מרבה הונו בנשך ובתרבית	28:9	מסיר אזנו משמע תורה
28:9	משמע תורה	28:10	משגה . . . רע
28:10	ישרים . . . ינחלו	28:11	עשיר . . . יחקרנו
28:11	חכם . . . עשיר	28:12	ובקום רשעים
28:12	בעלץ צדיקים . . . יחפש	28:13	לא יצליח . . . ירחם
28:13	מכסה . . . לא	28:14	ומקשה לבו

Table 13.2.2 (continued)

Sentence	Phrase	Sentence	Phrase
28:14	ומקשה . . . ברעה	28:15	מושל רשע
28:15	ודב שוקק	28:16	ורב מעשקות
28:16	מעשקות	28:17	אדם עשק
28:17	עשק בדם	28:18	ונעקש דרכים
28:18	תמים יושע . . . דרכים	28:19	אדמתו ישבע . . . ריקים
28:19	עבד אדמתו	28:20	איש אמונות
28:20	להעשיר לא	28:21	הכר . . . לא
28:21	הכר פנים לא	28:22	רע עין, ולא
28:22	להון איש רע עין	28:23	לשון . . . אחרי חן
28:23	אחרי חן	28:24	ואמר אין
28:24	חבר . . . לאיש	28:25	רחב נפש
28:25	ובטח על	28:26	בוטח בלבו
28:26	בחכמה . . . ימלט	28:27	מחסור, ומעלים
28:27	לרש אין מחסור . . . רב	28:28	רשעים יסתר . . . ירבו
28:28	בקום רשעים	29:1	מקשה ערף
29:1	מקשה ערף	29:2	ובמשל רשע
29:2	ישמח העם	29:3	ישמח . . . הון
29:3	איש . . . זונות	29:4	ואיש תרומות
29:4	מלך במשפט	29:5	מחליק . . . פעמיו
29:5	מחליק . . . רעהו	29:6	רע מוקש
29:6	וצדיק ירון	29:7	צדיק . . . יבין
29:7	לא יבין	29:8	לצון . . . ישיבו
29:8	אנשי . . . וחכמים	29:9	איש חכם
29:9	איש . . . נשפט	29:10	אנשי . . . נפשו
29:10	וישרים . . . נפשו	29:11	באחור ישבחנה
29:11	כל רוחו	29:12	כל משרתיו
29:12	כל משרתיו רשעים	29:13	רש ואיש תככים
29:13	תככים נפגשו	29:14	מלך שופט
29:14	שופט באמת	29:15	שבט ותוכחת
29:15	ותוכחת . . . ונער	29:16	ברבות רשעים
29:16	ירבה פשע	29:17	יסר . . . לנפשך
29:17	בנך ויניחך	29:18	באין חזון
29:18	באין חזון	29:19	יבין ואין
29:19	בדברים . . . מענה	29:20	בדבריו . . . ממנו
29:20	בדבריו . . . ממנו	29:21	עבדו . . . מנון
29:21	יהיה מנון	29:22	יגרה מדון
29:22	ובעל חמה	29:23	ושפל רוח
29:23	גאות אדם	29:24	עם גנב

Table 13.2.2 (continued)

Sentence	Phrase	Sentence	Phrase
29:24	גנב שונא	29:25	ישגב
29:25	מוקש ... בד׳	29:26	מושל, ומד׳
29:26	איש ... מושל	29:27	איש עול
29:27	איש עול	30:1	לאיתיאל

words "The proverbs of Solomon." The question however arises as to the meaning of the words "which the men of Hezekiah, King of Judah copied," used in the heading of the third section. Clarification can be gained from I Kings 5 12,13, where it is stated that Solomon spoke 3,000 proverbs, and that he spoke of trees, animals, fowl, creeping things, and fish. Now the Book of Proverbs only contains 915 sentences, and obviously does not contain 3,000 proverbs. Furthermore, little is said in the book about trees and living creatures. The main emphasis of the book is on the actions and feelings of man. Thus most of the proverbs by Solomon are lost. The implication is that, just as with the songs of Solomon (see Section 14.1), only the most important were considered by Solomon worthy of preservation for posterity. Most probably Solomon selected the proverbs presented in sections one and two, in addition to those of Agur and Lemuel, as worthy of collating into one book. Subsequently at the time of Hezekiah (see II Chr. 31 21), examination of the original books of proverbs written by Solomon revealed another collection worthy of being preserved. This added section was inserted by the men of Hezekiah after the first two sections and before that written by Agur. Since the second and third sections of proverbs are both organized according to similarities of words, sounds, and sentence construction of consecutive proverbs, it is clear that the third section was also written in its present form by Solomon. All that the men of Hezekiah did was insert the third section in the Book of Proverbs to be preserved for posterity.

Nothing is known about Agur or Lemuel other than what is stated in the Book of Proverbs. It is however probable that they both lived at the time of Solomon, and were noted for their proverbs.

Duplication of Proverbs

In a number of cases there is almost exact duplication of particular proverbs. For example, **14** 12 = **16** 25; **21** 9 = **25** 24; **18** 8 = **26** 22; **22** 3 = **27** 12; and **20** 16 = **27** 13. Numerous other cases occur of great similarity of proverbs. For example, **10** 1 and **15** 20; **10** 2 and **11** 4; **16** 2 and **21** 2; **19** 5 and **19** 9; **19** 24 and **26** 15; and **12** 11 and **28** 19. These duplications can be explained as follows. First, duplications of proverbs between different sections, such as between section 2 (Chaps. **10–24**) and section 3 (Chaps. **25–29**), offer no difficulty since they were originally written by Solomon as completely separate collections; and section 3 was not intended by Solomon for preservation for posterity. Secondly, the duplications that occur within a section, were probably necessary for organizational purposes, so as to maintain the similarities between adjacent proverbs.

13.3 JOB

The Book of Job is a poetical discussion of the philosophical question "Why are the righteous often punished, and why do the wicked often prosper?" The book is based on an event in the life of the righteous Job, when within a short time his ten children were killed, he lost his wealth, and became afflicted with a serious skin disease.

Historical Background

Biblical critics frequently question whether the book is based on an historical event. However, the evidence is clear that Job was a real person, and the described events actually occurred. First, in Ezekiel 14 14,20, Job is mentioned as a righteous man, whose life would be saved if a major calamity occurred. This clearly indicates that Job was a famous righteous person who had actually survived a serious catastrophe. Secondly, numerous names of actual countries and individuals are mentioned in the Book of Job. These names attest to the fact that a real event is being described. In particular the lineage of Elihu is given, tracing his ancestry to the family of Ram (32 2). If a fictional story were described, there would be no need for presenting the lineage of Elihu.

The time when Job recovered from his afflictions can be ascertained from the statement in Ezekiel 14 14,20 that in a sinful country Noah, Daniel, and Job would save only themselves, and not even their children. It should be noticed that Job is listed after Daniel, indicating that the fame of Daniel preceded that of Job. The statement in Ezekiel was made in the sixth year of the exile of Jehoiachin (Ez. 8 1, 1 2), i.e. in 591 B.C.E. Now Daniel was brought to Babylon in 605 (Dan. 1 1), and became a leader there, and thereby famous, in 602 (Dan. 2 1,48). Hence, Job must have become renowned between 602 and 591, i.e. shortly before the destruction of the First Temple.

Support for placing Job at this time is gained from historical references in the Book of Job. In particular, we find mention of the land of Uz (1 1), Children of the East (1 3), Sheba (1 15), Chaldeans (1 17), Teman, Shuah, and Naamah (2 11), Tema (6 19), Ethiopia (28 19), and Buz (32 2). References to most of these places and countries are found in the Book of Jeremiah, and other Biblical works such as Lamentations and Ezekiel, written shortly after the destruction of the Temple. Some typical references for these places are: land of Uz (Jer. 25 20; Lam. 4 21), Children of the East (Jer. 49 28; Ez. 25 4), Sheba (Jer. 6 20; Ez. 27 22), Chaldeans (Jer. 52 14; Ez. 1 3), Teman (Jer. 49 7,20; Ez. 25 13),

Tema (Jer. 25 23), Ethiopia (Jer. 46 9; Ez. 30 5; Esth. 1 1), and Buz (Jer. 25 23). Only Shuah and Naamah are not mentioned elsewhere at this period of time.

A question arises since we learn from Jer. 25 20 and Lam. 4 21 that the land of Uz was conquered shortly after 586. How could Job have regained his wealth at such a time? However, it is not necessary to assume that the regained wealth was acquired immediately after his affliction. Instead, it is implied (Job. 42 12) that Job acquired great riches by the time of his death, which was possibly over 100 years later as explained in the next paragraph. By that time, the entire political situation was completely different.

The age given for Job at the time of his death, namely 140 years (Job 42 16) is not so extremely exceptional so as not to be believed. For example Jehoiada, the priest, at the time of Joash, King of Judah (about 825) lived to be 130 years (II Chr. 24 15). Now when the disasters occurred to Job, he must have been at least thirty-five years old. Thus, assume he was fourteen when his first child was born, and twenty-three when his tenth child was born. Furthermore, the description in 1 4 implies that his children were mature, i.e. at least twelve years old, making Job at least thirty-five. In addition, his wife most probably was not much over thirty-five, since subsequent to Job's recovery, she had ten more children (42 13). The child-bearing age of a woman usually is completed by about fifty years, and hence her maximum age was about forty. It is therefore reasonable to assume that Job was about forty when afflicted, and he lived for an additional 100 years. Furthermore, the statement (42 16) that Job saw four generations of children, implies that he lived for at least forty-three more years. Thus it would take a minimum of one year for the first child, fifteen years for the second generation, and forty-three years for the fourth generation. Naturally, it probably took somewhat longer till the fourth generation.

On the basis that the affliction occurred to Job some time between 602 and 591, and that he lived for an additional 100 years, the approximate date for completion of the book would be 500. This is obviously only a rough approximation to the actual date because of the numerous assumptions involved.

It can be concluded from the text that Job and his three friends, Eliphaz the Temanite, Bildad the Shuhite, and Zophar the Naamathite, were not Jewish. Thus, it is stated (1 5) that Job regularly brought sacrifices in the morning, and that God commanded the three friends (42 8) to bring sacrifices near where Job was. Now Job lived in the land of Uz (1 1), at the time when the Temple in Jerusalem was in existence (as explained previously). According to Deut. 12 13,14 sacrifices by Jews had to be brought only in Jerusalem, i.e. only in the place designated by God. Since we find in the Book of Job that God specifically commanded the bringing of sacrifices outside of Jerusalem, it is obvious that Job and his three friends were not Jewish. In contrast, Elihu was clearly Jewish since he was the descendant of Ram (32 2), who in turn was a descendant of Judah (I Chr. 2 9,25). Additional support for these conclusions are the facts that Elihu was not described as bringing sacrifices, and that no specifically Jewish laws are found in the Book of Job.

Authorship

Several factors make Elihu the most probable author of the Book of Job. Firstly, the book is written in Hebrew, and Elihu was the only Jew present during the discussions. Secondly, he was the youngest of those participating in the discussions (32 4,6,7) and therefore could have lived to write about the death of Job about 100 years later. Thirdly, no mention of Elihu occurs at the beginning of the book. This would be a likely occurrence if Elihu were the author.

The formulation of the book may be explained as follows. During the discussion Job specified his desire that the words expressed be written down (19 23,24). Perhaps some notes were taken, or otherwise the participants had excellent memories. At the end, when God spoke to the three friends, He most probably also explained the true reason for Job's suffering, as described in 1 6-12, 2 1-7. Upon Job's recovery, the three friends, and Elihu and Job, possibly got together and wrote down the ideas expressed during Job's illness. Alternatively, Elihu wrote the book himself entirely from memory. It is possible that originally much of the discussions were in prose, and only afterwards were the ideas expressed in poetic form. In any case, the book is clearly a literary description of an actual historical event.

Organization

The Book of Job is arranged in a logical manner. In the first two chapters (1-2) are presented the details of Job's righteousness and prosperity, and how he went from riches to poverty and from health to illness within a short time. The misfortunes that befell Job were to test the extent of his belief and trust in God (1 11; 2 5). Job's three friends, Eliphaz the Temanite, Bildad the Shuhite, and Zophar the Naamathite, came to offer comfort (2 11). They did not know the reason for Job's misfortunes, and an extended discussion of this problem occurred. The discussion took place in three conversational cycles. The first two cycles (3 1-14 22; and 15 1-24 34) presented statements by Job, answered alternately by Eliphaz, Bildad, and Zophar. In the third cycle (22 1-31 40), the same sequence of speeches occurred, except that there was no response by Zophar. During these discussions the three friends speak on the assumption that the calamities which occurred to Job were for serious sins he committed. With each succeeding cycle the accusations against Job increase. By the third cycle, e.g., Eliphaz accuses Job of great wickedness and of sins without end (22 5). In the last cycle the other friends, Bildad and Zophar concur with these accusations, in that Bildad makes a statement of only five sentences (25 2-6) and Zophar says nothing since he has nothing to add. During all this time Job insists that he has been righteous and that God has punished him unjustly. Then Elihu speaks up

(32 1–37 24), and is angry with Job for his protestations of righteousness before God, and is angry with the three friends for condemning Job as a wicked person (32 2,3). Elihu states that God is not unjust, and He rewards or punishes people according to their deeds (34 10,11). However, it is beyond man's ability to understand the ways of God (36 26; 37 14–16). Then God answers Job, and supports the ideas expressed by Elihu (38 1–40 2). God asks Job if he understands all the wondrous things in the world, implying that Job should not accuse God of being unjust since he does not know God's ways. Job then states that he is overwhelmed by the majesty of God and the greatness of His accomplishments (40 3–5). God again speaks (40 6–41 26), followed by an admission by Job that he spoke incorrectly concerning injustice by God (42 1–6). God then tells the three friends that they have not spoken correctly, in that they have accused Job of wickedness, and they should bring sacrifices to atone for their sins (42 7–8). Afterwards Job recovered from his illness and was rewarded for his righteousness (42 9–17).

Chapter Fourteen

THE FIVE SCROLLS

14.1 SONG OF SONGS

The Song of Songs, as interpreted below, is a drama depicting the love of a maiden for King Solomon. They eventually marry and have two children, a boy and a girl. The boy matures and falls in love, reminding the mother of her early romance. The book has usually been interpreted allegorically to justify its retention in the Bible. However, the probable reasons for its inclusion are the beauty of expression, the morals of the story, emphasizing the virtues of chastity before marriage and faithfulness after marriage, and, most important, the fact that the book is the best of the songs written by Solomon (Song 1 1).

Authorship

The author of Song of Songs is clearly Solomon, as explicitly stated in Song 1 1. He is an active participant in the story and is mentioned in Song 1 5; 3 7,9,11; 8 11,12. In addition, an analogy is made to the tower of David (4 4), which indicates that the tower was in existence, and this would have been the case during Solomon's reign. Also, mention is made of the beautiful cities of Tirzah and Jerusalem (6 4). Jerusalem became prominent after its capture by David, and was David's capital city (II Sam. 5 5–8); while Tirzah probably was prominent during the time of Solomon, and became the capital city of the ten tribes after the split of the monarchy (I Kings 14 17; 15 33), shortly after the death of Solomon. It should also be noted that the woman of the story is called Shulamit (שולמית) (7 1) with the meaning "belonging to Solomon" (שלמה).

Further support for Solomon as the author is obtained from I Kings 5 12 where it is stated that Solomon wrote 1,005 songs. Unfortunately only the Song of Songs has survived. The title of the book "Song of Songs" (1 1) indicates that it was the best of Solomon's songs, and explains why it alone was preserved.

Organization

The contents of the book have been interpreted in various ways, all of which have serious difficulties. The most straight-forward explanation, which is here clarified in detail, is that the book describes the love between King Solomon and a beautiful girl. Solomon is often called lover (דוד), while the girl is called beloved (רעיתי), bride (כלה), and Shulamit (שולמית) by Solomon, and also called fairest among the women (היפה בנשים) by the daughters of Jerusalem. The daughters of Jerusalem are the other wives of Solomon, as indicated from Song 3 10. The only speakers in the drama are Solomon, the beautiful girl, and the daughters of Jerusalem.

The girl has been brought by Solomon to the quarters of the daughters of Jerusalem. She is uncertain as to what to expect. The book opens with the Shulamit introducing herself to the daughters of Jerusalem (1 2-7) expressing her love for Solomon, the reason for her dark complexion, and her desire to see Solomon once again. The daughters of Jerusalem reply (1 8) that if you, who are so beautiful, do not know about the intentions of Solomon, then go out and seek a lover from among the shepherds. In the next scene (1 9-2 3) Solomon is conversing with the girl, and they praise each other's beauty. Subsequently (2 4-7) she tells the daughters of Jerusalem that she is love-sick for Solomon to such an extent that they should not stir up her love until the proper time.

We then find (2 8-17) Solomon again speaking to the beautiful girl. He comes with great enthusiasm and asks to marry her. She accepts the proposal, and the wedding date is set. In the next scene (3 1-5) the girl speaks to the daughters of Jerusalem, and tells them that her love for Solomon is so great that it does not let her sleep. She yearns for him and wants to bring him into her mother's chamber. Again she cautions the daughters of Jerusalem not to over-excite her love.

The appointed time for the marriage arrives (3 6-11), and the wedding ceremony takes place. In 4 1-5 1 the bridal night is described. At first the girl, who is now called the bride, is unresponsive (4 12), but then she opens up to him. The term "garden" is used to describe the bride. Her description of the bridal night, as she later relates it to the daughters of Jerusalem, is described in 5 2-8. She states that she was at first hesitant (5 3), but then opened up to her husband. The pain of loss of her virginity was as if she were beaten by the watchmen (5 7). Now she tells the daughters of Jerusalem (5 8) that the time of love has arrived, and that they should tell Solomon that she is love-sick. The conversation of the bride with the daughters of Jerusalem continues (5 9-6 3), and she describes for them the wonderful qualities of her husband. The daughters of Jerusalem ask her where he is, and she answers that he went to his other gardens, i.e. to his other wives, but she still loves him (6 1-3).

In the next scene (6 4-7 14) Solomon returns to the bride and praises her beauty. He states that he has many queens and other wives but she is the most beautiful (6 8,9). He had gone to see his other wives (6 11), but now he wants the Shulamit to return to him (7 1). She replies (7 11-14) that her desire is still for him, and her love awaits him. Then the Shulamit speaks to the daughters of

Jerusalem (8 1-4) and states that she would want to associate more closely with Solomon. She concludes (8 4) by saying that she had told them that there was no purpose in arousing her love until the right time, with the implication that the right time had come.

The scene now changes, and it is over fourteen years later. The Shulamit has a mature son and a young daughter. She sees her son walking with his sweetheart (8 5). It reminds her of the time when she gave birth to him under the apple-tree. The Shulamit speaks to her son and tells him (8 6,7) to continue to remember his mother even after he gets married. Love is very strong and it cannot be washed away by floods. The Shulamit then continues talking to her son (8 8-10), and speaks about her daughter (who is her son's sister). The daughter is not yet physically mature, but when she becomes ready for marriage we have to consider her chastity.

As for me, the Shulamit states (8 10), I was chaste when I married, and I therefore found favor with Solomon. This reminds her of the past, and she says (8 11-12) that Solomon had a thousand wives (see I Kings 11 3) as his vineyard, with many guards. She, however, is satisfied with her small vineyard, i.e. her family, and does not mind that Solomon has so many other wives.

The book concludes (8 13-14) with Solomon asking the Shulamit to speak to him. She replies "run at your own pleasure as a deer or a young hart and feel free to go on your mountains of spices" (i.e. to go to your other wives).

14.2 RUTH

This historical book tells the story of how Ruth, the widowed daughter-in-law of Naomi, came to the land of Judah and married Boaz. A son named Obed was born who was the grandfather of David, King of Israel. The book covers a period of 100 or more years, as shown by the following analysis using the age of Naomi as a reference. Assume Naomi was twelve years old when she married Elimelech, and fourteen when her second son was born (1 1). Thirteen years later when Naomi was twenty-seven, both her sons had married. For ten years the family resided in Moab (1 4). Naomi would then have been a minimum of thirty-seven, but was probably at least forty since she was past the child-bearing age (1 11,12). About a year later Ruth married Boaz. Obed was born the following year when Naomi was forty-two. Fourteen years later, when Naomi was fifty-six, Jesse was born. From I Sam. 17 12 and I Chr. 2 13-16 we learn that Jesse had ten children, eight boys and two girls, all born to one wife (see I Sam. 22 3). Now David was probably the youngest of the children (I Sam. 17 14). This would make Jesse a minimum of twenty-three when David was born, and more probably about twenty-six. David was completely unknown until he was twenty-eight and slew Goliath; and became truly famous at thirty years of age when he became king (II Sam. 5 4). It is therefore likely that the Book of Ruth was completed (Ruth 4 17-22) when David was thirty and had just become king. If

Naomi were still living she would have then been 112 years (56 + 26 + 30), exactly 100 years from the time she married at the age of twelve.

Based on the above analysis, the approximate period of the judges (1 1) when Naomi and her family lived in Moab can be determined. At that time Naomi had two mature sons and was about thirty years old, which would be eighty-two years before David became king. Based on the data presented in the chronological section (Section 4.0) this would have been during the first year of the ten-year rule of Elon the Zebulunite (Jud. 12 11), who succeeded Ibzan of Bethlehem. Ten years later, during the first year of Abdon, the son of Hillel the Pirathonite (Jud. 12 13), Naomi returned to Judah with Ruth.

Care must be taken not to draw any chronological conclusions from the genealogies of those preceding Boaz presented at the end of the book (Ruth 4 18–22). The same genealogies are presented in I Chr. 2 5–15, where is added that Nahshon the son of Amminadab was the prince of the children of Judah, i.e. the leader of the tribe of Judah at the second year in the desert (Num. 1 7). Accordingly, there are only four ancestors of David from the entrance into Israel after the desert, until the birth of David, which is a period of 366 years. This would require that each parent became a father at an average age of about ninety-one, which is extremely unlikely. It is therefore necessary to assume that many additional generations occurred between Nahshon and Boaz which are not mentioned in the texts.

Organization
The Book of Ruth is a historical account of the events leading to the marriage of Ruth and Boaz, the great-grandparents of David, and is obviously written in chronological order. None of the events of the book are out of place chronologically.

Authorship
The three main personalities of the book are Naomi, Ruth, and Boaz, and most probably one of these three is the author. Naomi can be eliminated from consideration since she would have had to be a minimum of 112 years, a very unlikely age, to complete the last sentence about David. Ruth is also unlikely because she would have had to be ninety-four years old. Thus, assume she was twelve when she married Mahlon, then she would have been twenty-three when she married Boaz. According to the previously presented calculations for Naomi, another seventy-one years need to be added before David became king, giving a total of ninety-four years.

The most likely person to have written the book is therefore Boaz, who could have been eighty-four when David became king if we assume Boaz was thirteen when he married Ruth. The fact that Boaz is described as a man (איש) (2 1) does not exclude the possibility that he was as young as thirteen, since the term man is used to contrast him with his servants who are called youths (נערים) (3 20,21). If, however, we take the description of the maturity of Boaz literally, he still could have been as young as twenty when he married Ruth, which would make him only ninety-one when David became king. The details of the events were readily available to Boaz, being the husband of Ruth and relative of the family of Naomi. It is specifically mentioned in Ruth 2 11 that Boaz was informed of the events which occurred to Naomi and Ruth, i.e. the contents of Ruth 1.

It is of course possible that Naomi, Ruth, or Boaz wrote the main part of the book, while the genealogies relating to David (Ruth 4 17-22) were added later by, for example, the prophet Samuel. However, this is unlikely, since the main purpose of the book is to give the ancestry of David.

14.3 LAMENTATIONS

There is no specific statement in the Book of Lamentations as to the historical event being described. However, the similarities between the descriptions in the Book of Lamentations with those given in the Books of Kings, Jeremiah, and Chronicles, concerning the destruction of the Temple and the exile of Judah, clearly indicate that the Book of Lamentations describes the Babylonian conquest of Judah. Thus, from II Kings 25; II Chr. 36 17-21; and Jer. 52 we learn that at the time of the Babylonian conquest there was severe famine; the Temple as well as all the houses in Jerusalem were burned; the people were exiled or killed; the treasures of the Temple and of the officials were taken as booty; and the walls of Jerusalem were broken down. Similarly, the Book of Lamentations describes in vivid detail the severity of the famine (1 11,19, 2 19; 4 5; 5 9,10); the burning of the Temple and Jerusalem (1 10; 2 3,4,7; 4 11); the exile and killing of the people (1 3,5,18-20; 2 21); the removal of the country's treasures (1 6,7,10); and the destruction of the walls of Jerusalem (1 4; 2 8,9). Thus, it is clear that the Book of Lamentations is a poetical description of the pathetic situation at the time of the destruction of the First Temple in 586 B.C.E.

Authorship

Although the Book of Lamentations is written anonymously, the evidence strongly indicates that the author was Jeremiah. The book describes the destruction of Jerusalem from similar perspectives and using similar phrases to those found in the Book of Jeremiah. Some particularly striking analogous phrases are presented in Table 14.3.1. In addition, at the time of the destruction of the Temple Jeremiah was the main, and perhaps the only, true prophet in Judah, and therefore would logically be the one to have written the Book of Lamentations. Support for this contention is obtained from II Chr. 35 25 where it is stated that Jeremiah lamented for Josiah. We thus know that Jeremiah, in addition to writing in ordinary prose as in his own book, also wrote in a style similar to that found in the Book of Lamentations. Furthermore, the third chapter of the book is a detailed description of the tribulations of the author; and the description fits the known

Table 14.3.1
Analogous Phrases between the Books of Lamentations and Jeremiah

Lamenta-tions	Phrase	Jeremiah	Phrase
1 2	Among all her lovers	30 14	All your lovers
1 8	Saw her nakedness	13 26	And her shame will be seen
1 9	In her skirts	13 26	Your skirts
2 11	Hurt of the daughter of my people	8 11	Hurt of the daughter of my people
2 18	Let tears run down like a river, day and night; let not the apple of your eye cease	14 17	Let my eyes run down with tears night and day, and let them not cease
2 22	My terrors on every side	6 25; 20 10	Terror on every side
3 14	I was a laughing-stock; all the day	20 7	I was a laughing-stock all the day
3 19	Wormwood and gall	9 14	Wormwood; water of gall
3 47	Terror and the pit	48 43	Terror and the pit
5 16	The crown of our heads has fallen	13 18	Your headtires have come down, the crown of your beauty

history of Jeremiah quite uniquely. Examples of analogous descriptions are presented in Table 14.3.2. All the foregoing reasons clearly point to the authorship of Lamentations by Jeremiah.

ORGANIZATION

The structural organization of the Book of Lamentations is readily apparent. Chapters 1, 2, and 4 each have twenty-two verses and follow a Hebrew alphabetic arrangement. Chapter 3 has sixty-six verses and follows a triple alphabet. The last chapter, Chapter 5, although not alphabetical, also has twenty-two verses. One problem to be noted is that Chapter 1 follows the common alphabetical order, but Chapters 2, 3, and 4 place the פ before the ע. This exception can simply be explained as necessary to allow better expression of the author's ideas. Biblical words beginning with פ and ע are somewhat limited. A better continuity of thought could be obtained by reversing the order. Also, in the Book of Psalms there are found numerous cases of imperfect alphabetical arrangement for the same reason. Thus Ps. 145 omits the נ; Ps. 34 omits the ו; Ps. 25 omits the ב and ו, and replaces the ק with a ר; and Ps. 9, 10, 37 have

Table 14.3.2
Analogous Descriptions of Life of Writer of
Chapter Three with Life of Jeremiah

Lamentations	Phrase	Jeremiah	Phrase
3 8	He shuts out my prayer	7 16	Pray not for this people
3 14	I was a laughing-stock to all my people	20 7	I was a laughing-stock all the day.
3 27	It is good for a man that he bear a yoke in his youth	1 7	Don't say, I am a youth
3 30	He will give his cheek to him that smites him	20 2	And Pashhur smote Jeremiah
3 48	My eye runs down with rivers of water for the hurt of the daughter of my people	14 17	My eyes will run down with tears; for the virgin daughter of my people is broken with a great hurt
3 53	They have cut off my life in the pit	38 9	They have thrown (Jeremiah) into the pit, and he is dying
3 58	You have redeemed my life	1 19	For I am with you, says the Lord, to save you
3 62	The lips of those that rise up against me and their mutterings, are against me all the day	26 11	And the priests and the prophets said; judgment of death to this man

an imperfect alphabetical arrangement. Only Ps. 111, 112, and 119 are in perfect alphabetical order. Rather than emphasizing the imperfection in the Book of Lamentations of the order of the פ and ע, credit should be given to the author for being able to fit his ideas into alphabetical arrangements, with the only required exception being the reversal of the order of the פ and ע in the second, third, and fourth chapters.

Note should be made of the extent of assonance present in Chapters 1, 2, and 4. A common feature of the sentences is that emphasis in sound is given to the key alphabetical letters of the preceding and following verses, as well as of the sentence itself. For example, Lam. 2 13 begins with a מ and emphasizes words containing the letters נ, מ, ל. This characteristic shows the greatness of the poetical effort of the book.

The individual sentences of the Book of Lamentations are not disconnected ideas, but present a logical development which concludes with the idea of repentance and prayer to God. Initially Jeremiah asks, how could it have happened that the great city of Jerusalem has been destroyed, that Judah has been exiled? It could only be because of the sins of the people (1 1–11). The city of Jerusalem answers that God in his anger has caused the desolation and destruction (1 12–16). Jeremiah agrees that God was the cause of the destruction by the enemy (1 17). The city of Jerusalem responds that nevertheless God has acted righteously because the city had rebelled against God (1 18–20); and furthermore God should punish those enemies that have rejoiced at the fate of the city (1 21–22). Jeremiah continues and asks, how could God have brought about the destruction without showing mercy? (2 1–9); the condition of the city and the survivors is pathetic (2 10–17); cry out to God wall of the city about the hungry children within (2 18,19). Jerusalem then cries out "see God what You have done on the day of Your anger, how You have unmercifully killed the city residents" (2 20–22).

Jeremiah then describes his personal experiences. He saw the anger of God, and underwent such suffering that he almost lost hope for God's help (3 1–18); but then he regained faith in God and felt the need for repentance. He realized that his suffering was a result of the people's sins (3 19–54). Jeremiah called to God for help and was answered (3 55–66).

Then Jeremiah continues "How is it that the precious children of Zion have been so degraded, that such a sharp contrast has occurred?" (4 1–10). It is a result of the sins of the leaders that the people have been punished so terribly (4 11–20). However the end of the punishment has come, God will not continue the exile of Zion, but in contrast the enemies such as Edom will be punished (4 21,22). Jeremiah continues with a prayer, saying that we and our ancestors have sinned, and God should be aware of the terrible misfortune which has befallen us (5 1–18). God should accept our repentance, and return the situation to that which existed before the calamity (5 19–22). Implied in the final plea is that just as Jeremiah was answered by God and saved from his suffering (Chapter 3), so will the people be redeemed upon praying for redemption.

14.4 ECCLESIASTES

The Book of Ecclesiastes discusses the philosophical question, "What is the purpose of man's effort and toil?" No matter what man does, still the world goes on in the same way. During the discussion in the book, particular consideration is given to the merits of wisdom, work, enjoyment and following of God's laws. The book ends with the conclusion that man should fear God and observe the commandments, because this is the purpose of man's existence.

Authorship
At the beginning of the book (Eccl. 1 1) it is stated that the author is Koheleth, the son of David, King in Jerusalem. No king, however, is known having the name

Koheleth. The possibility arises that "son of David" may also mean a descendant of David, and therefore Koheleth may have been any one of the kings residing in Jerusalem. However, the description of Koheleth given in the book is identical to that of King Solomon, son of David. Thus, Koheleth was a king in Jerusalem (1 12), was a very wise man (1 16; 12 9), and wrote many proverbs (12 9). In addition he amassed silver and gold (2 8), servants (2 7), and other material possessions (2 4–9). Similarly we find that King Solomon ruled from Jerusalem (I Kings 2 11,12), was wiser and richer than all other kings (I Kings 5 10, 10 23), spoke 3,000 proverbs (I Kings 5 12), and amassed silver and gold (I Kings 10 14–22), servants (I Kings 10 5), and other items (I Kings 10 25–11 3). Thus the description of Koheleth matches Solomon identically. Furthermore, many sayings of the book are similar in structure to those in the Book of Proverbs written by Solomon.

The problem then arises, why was the name Koheleth used rather than Solomon? A hint to the answer is obtained from II Sam. 12 25 where it is stated that Nathan the prophet called Solomon "Jedidiah." This establishes that Solomon was identified by other names. Here the name Koheleth is used as a pen-name, and possibly was a common alias for Solomon. In this particular case, the name Koheleth was selected because of its similarity in sound to such words as הבל (vanity) and הכל (everything), thereby increasing the poetic beauty of the sentence 1 2 (also see 12 8)

"הבל הבלים אמר קהלת הרל הרלים הכל הבל."

It is clear from the text that the entire book was written by Koheleth. Thus, the name Koheleth is found at the beginning (1 1,2,12), the middle (7 27), and the end (12 8,9,10) of the book. Furthermore the entire book, with the exception of the heading (1 1,2) and ending (12 8–11), is written in the first person. These points are in addition to that already mentioned, namely, that it is specifically stated that Koheleth was the author (1 1).

ORGANIZATION

The organization of the book of Ecclesiastes is not completely self-evident, and it has eluded most commentaries. Initially, Koheleth poses the problem, "What does man gain by all his toil?" The world continues in the same cyclic pattern independent of man's accomplishments (1 1–12). Then, Koheleth gives the reasons for his proficiency in this problem. As king, he actually tested and tried different means for understanding the purpose of man. In particular, he examined the merits of wisdom, pleasure, creative work, and wealth (1 13–2 26). The numerous conclusions which were reached are presented in 3 1–12 8. Some of the main topics are:

3 1–15   Everything has its appropriate time. The appropriate time for man is during his lifetime, when he should be happy and do good.

	In contrast the accomplishments of God last forever.
3 16–17	There is a limited time for the success of the wicked since God will judge the people according to their ways.
3 18–22	The fate of man is the same as the fate of the animal; both return to the dust. The best thing for man is to be happy while he lives.
4 1–12	There are several types of imperfections in the world. These are oppression, jealousy, idleness, and aloneness.
4 13–16	The reign of a king does not last forever. Eventually the king is replaced by a younger person.
4 17–11 8	Numerous one-sentence or several-sentence proverbs are presented concerning such topics as: caution in what one says, oppression, wealth, labor, wisdom, righteousness, fear of God, enjoyment, and miscellaneous ideas.
11 9–12 8	This section is a concluding summary of the main points of the book. Be happy when young and follow the ways of God. Eventually you will grow old and become physically weak. Finally you will die and return to the soil. Everything will then be vanity.
12 9–14	The final conclusion by Koheleth is that man should fear God and observe His commandments, for God judges people according to their deeds.

One of the main problems in understanding the book is the frequent lack of logical continuation of the presented proverbs. Not all the sayings on wisdom are grouped together; nor are proverbs on other topics, such as wealth, enjoyment and fear of God, always grouped together. The reason for this situation is that the book is not only arranged according to a logical order, but also according to similarity in words and phrase structure from one sentence to those immediately following. This type of association for the entire book is presented in Table 14.4.1. Thus, many of the proverbs are not entirely in a logical sequence in order to maintain the similarity in words between neighboring sentences. (For comparison see Section 13.2).

Apparent Internal Contradictions

It should be pointed out that there are no real contradictions in philosophy within the book. The concept that everything is vanity (1 2) does not contradict the idea that one should observe the commandments of God (12 13). What is implied is that despite the fact that everything is vanity, still the best course of action is to follow God's laws. Similarly there is no real contradiction between such statements as "Anger is better than laughter" (7 3); and "Remove anger from your heart" (11 10). The former phrase is used in the sense that anger or seriousness may improve a person's disposition, and does not advocate anger as a good course of

Table 14.4.1
Similarity of Words between Neighboring Sentences in the
Book of Ecclesiastes

1 1	קהלת	1 2	קהלת
1 2	הכל	1 3	בכל
	—	1 4	
1 3	בא 1 4; השמש	1 5	השמש ; ובא
1 4	ואל 1 5; הלך	1 6	הולך; אל
1 6	שב 1 6; ואל מקומו 1 5; הולך	1 7	הלכים; אל מקום; שבים
1 7	כל	1 8	כל
1 8	לא ,לא 1 8; איננו 1 7; כל	1 9	ואין כל; מה; מה; הוא; הוא
1 9	הוא 1 9; הדברים 1 8	1 10	היה; דבר; הוא
1 10	שהיה; שיהיה 1 9; היה; היה	1 11	שיהיו; יהיה; שיהיו
1 11	שיהיו	1 12	הייתי
1 12	שנעשה; תחת 1 9; על	1 13	על; נעשה תחת
1 13	נעשה תחת	1 14	שנעשו תחת
1 8	לא יוכל	1 15	לא יוכל
1 12	על כל אשר; לבי 1 13; אני ראיתי 1 14	1 16	אני; לבי; על כל אשר; ראה
1 16	ודעת 1 16; רוח 1 14; לבי; חכמה	1 17	לבי; חכמה; רוח; ודעת
1 17	הרבה 1 16; חכמה ודעת	1 18	ברב חכמה; דעת
1 16	הבל 1 14; ראה; לאמר אני לבי 1 17	2 1	אמרתי אני בלבי; וראה; הבל
2 1	הללות; זה 1 17; אמרתי; בשמחה	2 2	אמרתי מהולל ולשמחה; זה
2 2	בלבי; וראה בטוב 2 1; זה עשה ושכלות 1 17; חכמה 1 18	2 3	בלבי; בחכמה; בסכלות; אראה; זה טוב; יעשו
2 3	הגדלתי 1 16; יעשו	2 4	מעשי; הגדלתי
2 4	מעשי; נטעתי לי	2 5	עשיתי לי; ונטעתי
2 5	עשיתי לי; עץ	2 6	עשיתי לי; עצים
2 6	היה לפני; ירושלים 1 16; לי בתים 2 4; כל 2 5	2 7	לי; בית; מכל שהיו לפני בירושלם
2 7	לבני האדם 2 3; עשיתי 2 6; וגם	2 8	עשיתי לי; גם; בני האדם
2 8	מכל שהיו לפני בירושלם 2 7; לי בחכמה 2 3; הגדלתי 2 4	2 9	וגדלתי; מכל שהיה לפני בירושלם; חכמתי; לי
2 9	ולשמחה 2 2; בלבי 2 3; מכל	2 10	לבי מכל שמחה
2 10	עשיתי 2 8; מכל עמלי	2 11	בכל מעשי; ובעמל
2 11	חכמתי 2 9; ופניתי אני; שעשו	2 12	ופניתי אני; חכמה; עשוהו
2 12	אני לראות חכמה; וסכלות יתרון 2 11	2 13	וראיתי אני; יתרון לחכמה הסכלות
2 13	עיני 2 10; אני; לחכמה; החשך	2 14	החכם עיניו; בחשך; אני

Table 14.4.1 (continued)

2 15	גם אני; בלבי כמקרה הכסיל; חכמתי; יתר; הבל	2 14	החכם; והכסיל; גם אני שמקרה לבי 10 2; הבל 11 2; יתרון 13 2
2 16	לחכם; הכסיל; בשכבר; הכל	2 15	כבר 12 2; הכסיל; חכמתי 2 כלם 14 2
2 17	המעשה שנעשה; כי הכל הבל; ורעות רוח	2 11	מעשי שעשו; ורעות רוח הבל 15 2; כי; הכל 16 2
2 18	ושנאתי אני; כל עמלי; תחת השמש	2 17	ובעמל 11 2; תחת השמש; אני 15 2; ושנאתי; הכל 17 2
2 19	יודע החכם יהיה; בכל עמלי תחת השמש; הבל	2 14	הבל 15 2; לחכם 16 2; וידעתי כל עמלי; תחת השמש; שיהיה 18 2
2 20	אני; כל העמל שעמלתי תחת השמש	2 19	בכל עמלי שעמלתי;תחת השמש אני 18 2
2 21	אדם שעמלו בחכמה; גם זה הבל	2 19	לאדם 18 2; החכם; גם זה הבל העמל 20 2
2 22	כי; לאדם בכל עמלו; לבו; תחת השמש	2 20	לבי; כל; תחת השמש כי; אדם; עמל 21 2
2 23	כי כל; לא; לבו; גם זה הבל	2 21	שלא; גם זה הבל בכל; כי; לבו 22 2
2 24	באדם; בעמלו; גם זה; אני כי	2 22	אני 20 2; לאדם; עמלו כי; גם זה 23 2
2 25	כי; יאכל	2 24	שיאכל; כי
2 26	כי לאדם שטוב; הא'; גם זה הבל	2 25	גם זה הבל 23 2; כי טוב באדם; הא' 24 2
3 1	לכל; תחת	2 23	תחת 22 2; כל
3 2	ועת	3 1	ועת
3 3	עת; ועת; עת; ועת	3 2	עת; ועת; עת; ועת
3 4	עת; ועת; עת; ועת	3 3	עת; ועת; עת; ועת
3 5	עת; ועת; עת; ועת	3 4	עת; ועת; עת; ועת
3 6	עת; ועת; עת; ועת	3 5	עת; ועת; עת; ועת
3 7	עת; ועת; עת; ועת	3 6	עת; ועת; עת; ועת
3 8	עת; ועת; עת; ועת	3 7	עת; ועת; עת; ועת
3 9	עמל; הוא	2 24	היא; בעמלו
3 10	הענין; נתן הא'	2 26	נתן ענין; הא'
3 11	עשה; בעתו; אשר; הא'	3 10	עת 8 3; העושה 9 3; א'; אשר
3 12	ולעשות	3 11	עשה
3 13	וגם כל האדם; טוב; עמלו; מתת א'	3 11	הכל; נתן; הא'; האדם; גם עמל 9 3; טוב 12 3

Table 14.4.1 (continued)

3 12	העלם אשר 11 3; ידעתיכי; ולעשות בכל; הא' היא 13 3	3 14	ידעתי כי כל אשר יעשה הא' הוא; לעולם
3 14	אשר הא' הוא יהיה	3 15	שהיה; הוא ואשר; והא'
3 13	וראה	3 16	ראיתי
3 16	המשפט; הרשע; הצדק שמה והא' 15 3	3 17	הצדיק; הרשע; ישפט הא'; שם
3 17	אמרתי אני בלבי; הא' ראיתי 16 3	3 18	אמרתי אני בלבי; הא'; ולראות
3 18	בני האדם; בהמה	3 19	בני האדם; הבהמה
3 19	מקום 16 3; אחד; הכל	3 20	הכל; אחד; מקום
3 19	בני האדם; הבהמה	3 21	בני האדם; הבהמה
3 21	אין כי 19 3; האדם; היא	3 22	כי אין; האדם; הוא
3 22	אין; מאשר; וראיתי	4 1	וראה; ואין; אשר
4 1	כמות 19 3; אני; להם	4 2	אני; המתים; המה
4 1	אשר נעשים תחת השמש שיהיה; טוב 22 3	4 3	וטוב; היה; אשר נעשה תחת השמש
4 3	וראה 1 4; אני 2 4; המעשה	4 4	וראיתי אני; המעשה
4 4	את; ואת	4 5	את; את
4 5	וטוב 3 4; ורעות רוח 4 4; ידיו	4 6	טוב; ורעות רוח; כף
4 4	תחת השמש 3 4; וראיתי; הבל	4 7	ואראה הבל תחת השמש
4 7	טוב; ו1 עוד 6 4; אני; הבל	4 8	אני; עמלו; הבל; מטובה; רע
4 8	אחד; שני; עמלו; מטובה	4 9	טובים השנים; האחד; בעמלם
4 9	ואין 8 4; האחד; השנים	4 10	האחד; ואין שני
4 10	להם 9 4; אם; האחד; שני	4 11	שנים; ולאחד; אם; להם
4 11	אם; שנים; ולאחד	4 12	ואם; האחד השנים
4 12	טובים; אשר 9 4; לא	4 13	טוב; לא; אשר
4 13	כי 10 4; גם 11 4; ממלך; ילד	4 14	למלך; כי גם; נולד
4 13	השנים יעמדו 12 4; ילד; אשר	4 15	הילד השני אשר יעמד
4 14	הבל 8 4; לא 13 4; כי גם כל; אשר 15 4	4 16	לכל; אשר; גם; לא; כי; הבל
4 15	ידע 13 4; המהלכים כי; אין; אשר 16 4	4 17	כאשר תלך; כי אינם יודעים הא'; כי
4 17	הא'; כי	5 1	
4 17	דבריך מעטים; כי 1 5; הכסילים	5 2	כי; ברב דברים; כסיל
5 2	כאשר 17 4; הא' 1 5; כסיל	5 3	בכסילים; לא; כאשר
5 3	תדר שלם	5 4	תדר; תשלם
5 1	אל; לא' 3 5; פיך	5 5	ואל; הא'; פיך
5 2	הא' 5 5; כי; ברב דברים	5 6	הא'; כי ברב; ודברים

Table 14.4.1 (continued)

5 5	אל; על; כי	5 7	אל; על; כי
5 7	במדינה	5 8	ארץ
5 8	לשדה	5 9	תבואה
5 9	תבואה	5 10	אוכליה
5 10	נעבד 8 5; ישבע 9 5; אוכליה	5 11	יאכל; שבע; העבד
5 11	לעשיר	5 12	עשר
5 12	רעה; עשר	5 13	העשר; רע
5 13	מאומה; בידו	5 14	בידו; ומאומה
5 12	כשבא; ללכת 14 5; רעה חולה	5 15	רעה חולה; שבא; ילך
5 11	חולה 15 5; יאבל	5 16	יאכל; חליו
5 14	שיעמל 15 5; בעמלו כל ימיו 16 5	5 17	ימי חיו; בכל עמלו שיעמל
5 16	הא'; עמלו 17 5; גם כל	5 18	גם כל; בעמלו; א'
5 18	ימי חיו 17 5; ולשמח; הא'	5 19	הא'; בשמחת; ימי חייו
5 17	האדם; תחת השמש	6 1	תחת השמש; האדם
5 18	לאכל ממנו; הא' עשר ונכסים	6 2	הא' עשר ונכסים; לאכל ממנו
6 2	לו; איש; ממנו; לנפשו	6 3	ונפשו; ממנו; איש; לו
6 2	כי; הבל	6 4	בהבל; כי
6 1	לא 3 6; זה 2 6; השמש	6 5	שמש; לזה מזה; לא
6 5	ילך 4 6; הטובה 3 6; לא ראה	6 6	וטובה לא ראה; הולך
6 3	הכל; לא 6 6; ונפשו	6 7	הנפש; לא; כל
6 6	הולך	6 8	להלך
6 8	וגם הנפש 7 6; להלך	6 9	מהלך נפש גם
6 8	שמו 4 6; האדם 7 6; מה	6 10	מה; אדם; שמו
6 10	כי מה יותר 8 6; מה; אדם הבל 9 6	6 11	הבל; מה; לאדם; כי; מה יותר
6 11	מה שהיה 10 6; כי; מה; לאדם	6 12	מה; לאדם; כי; מה יהיה
6 12	שמו 10 6; טוב; ימי	7 1	טוב שם; ויום
7 1	ויום המות 1 7; חיי 12 6; טוב	7 2	טוב; והחי; סוף כל האדם
7 2	טוב; לבו	7 3	טוב; לב
7 3	בית אבל 2 7; לב	7 4	לב; בבית אבל
7 4	טוב 3 7; חכמים; כסילים	7 5	טוב; חכם; כסילים
7 5	משחוק 3 7; כסילים	7 6	שחק הכסיל
7 6	לב 4 7; חכם 5 7; כי	7 7	כי; חכם; לב
7 5	טוב	7 8	טוב
7 8	כעס 3 7; כסילים 5 7; רוח	7 9	ברוחך; כעס; כסילים
7 9	טוב; מראשיתו 8 7; אל; כי	7 10	אל; כי; הראשונים; טובים
7 10	טובים; מחכמה	7 11	טובה חכמה
7 11	חכמה; ויתר	7 12	החכמה; ויתרון

Table 14.4.1 (continued)

7 12	כי	7 13	כי
7 13	טובה 11 7; ראה; הא׳	7 14	ראה; הא׳; טובה
7 14	ראה	7 15	ראיתי
7 15	ויתרון 12 7; צדיק	7 16	צדיק; יותר
7 16	אל; הרבה; למה	7 17	אל; הרבה; למה
7 14	זה; זה 14 7; הכל 15 7; בטוב	7 18	טוב; כלם; בזה; מזה
7 12	החכמה	7 19	החכמה
7 18	טוב אשר	7 20	אשר; טוב
7 18	אשר; ולא 20 7; וגם	7 21	גם; אשר לא
7 21	גם לבך אשר; מקללך	7 22	גם; לבך, אשר; קללת
7 21	מזה 18 7; החכמה 19 7; לכל	7 23	כל זה; בחכמה
7 23	רחוקה	7 24	רחוק
7 22	תרשע; סכל 17 7; לבך בחכמה 23 7	7 25	חכמה; לבי; רשע כסל
7 24	טוב; יחטא 20 7; ימצאנו ממני 23 7; אני ולבי 25 7	7 26	אני; לבה; ממנה טוב; וחוטא; ומוצא
7 26	וחשבון 25 7; ומוצא	7 27	מצאתי; חשבון
7 27	ובקש 25 7; האשה 26 7; מצאתי	7 28	בקשה; מצאתי; ואשה
7 28	הא׳ 26 7; מצאתי; אדם; בקשה חשבון; ראה זה 27 7	7 29	ראה זה מצאתי; הא׳ האדם; בקשו חשבנות
7 29	האדם	8 1	אדם
7 26	הא׳ 29 7; דבר 1 8; אני	8 2	אני; דברת; א׳
8 1	עשה 29 7; דבר; פניו	8 3	מפניו; בדבר; יעשה
8 3	מלך 2 8; בדבר; אשר; יעשה	8 4	באשר דבר מלך; תעשה
8 3	יודע 1 8; בדבר רע	8 5	ידע דבר רע
8 5	רע; ועת ומשפט	8 6	עת ומשפט; רעת
8 6	באשר; ומי; לו; מה 4 8; ידע 5 8 כי	8 7	כי; ידע מה; כאשר; מי; לא
8 6	איננו 7 8; שלטון 4 8; האדם	8 8	אדם; שלטון; ואין
8 8	רעת 6 8; לו 7 8; אדם שליט עת 6 8; תעשה 4 8	8 9	מעשה; עת; שלט האדם; לרע לו
8 9	רשע 8 8; מעשה אשר; זה ראיתי	8 10	ראיתי רשעים; אשר; עשו; זה
8 9	לרע; האדם; לבי ובכן; אשר; עשו 10 8	8 11	אשר נעשה; הרעה; על כן; לב; האדם
8 11	אשר; לעשות רע	8 12	אשר; עשה רע
8 12	יהיה טוב ליראי הא׳ אשר מלפניו; ומאריך	8 13	וטוב; יהיה; יאריך; אשר; ירא מלפני א׳
8 11	נעשה; מעשה רשעים; גם זה הבל 10 8	8 14	רשעים; שגם זה הבל; נעשה; כמעשה
8 13	האדם 11 8; טוב; ימים; א׳	8 15	טוב לאדם; הא׳; ימי

Table 14.4.1 (continued)

8 14	שגם; אשר נעשה על הארץ	8 16	גם; אשר נעשה על הארץ
8 15	כמעשה 14 8; הא׳;תחת השמש; ולראות; אשר נעשה 16 8	8 17	וראיתי; מעשה הא׳; אשר נעשה; תחת השמש
8 17	החכם; הא׳; האדם; לדעת נתתי את לבי 16 8	9 1	נתתי את לבי; והחכמים; הא׳; יודע האדם
9 1	כאשר 16 8; הצדיקים;הכל טוב 15 8	9 2	הכל; לצדיק; כאשר; כטוב
9 1	אשר נעשה תחת השמש 17 8; זה הכל; לכל 2 9	9 3	זה; בכל אשר נעשה תחת השמש; לכל
9 3	כטוב 2 9; לכל; בחייהם; המתים	9 4	כל החיים; טוב; מת
9 4	איננו 2 9; כי; החיים; המת יודע 1 9	9 5	כי החיים יודעים שימתו והמתים אינם
9 1	גם אהבה גם שנאה בכל אשר נעשה תחת השמש 3 9	9 6	גם אהבתם גם שנאתם; בכל אשר נעשה תחת השמש
9 6	כבר; נעשה	9 7	כבר; מעשיך
9 6	בכל	9 8	בכל
9 6	אשר; תחת השמש; אהבתם בכל 8 9; החיים 5 9	9 9	חיים; אשר; תחת השמש; כל; אהבת
9 7	כל; אשר; אתה 9 9; מעשיך; לך	9 10	כל אשר; מעשה; אתה; הלך
9 9	עת 8 9; תחת השמש; ראה וחכמה; כי 10 9	9 11	וראה תחת השמש כי; לחכמים; עת
9 11	כי; וגם לא; לידעים; עת	9 12	כי גם לא ידע; לעת
9 11	וראה תחת שמש; לחכמים גם 12 9	9 13	גם; ראיתי חכמה תחת השמש
9 12	וגדולה 13 9; במצודה	9 14	מצודים גדולים
9 14	חכמה 13 9; עיר; ואנשים האדם 12 9	9 15	איש; חכם; העיר; ואדם
9 15	חכם; המסכן	9 16	חכמה; המסכן
9 16	וחכמת; ודבריו; נשמעים	9 17	דברי חכמים; נשמעים
9 16	טובה חכמה	9 18	טובה חכמה
9 18	מעט 14 9; חכמה	10 1	מחכמה; מעט
10 1	מחכמה; סכלות	10 2	חכם; כסיל
10 2	סכלות 1 10; לב	10 3	לבו; סכל
9 18	גדולים 14 9; מושל 17 9; וחוטא	10 4	המושל; חטאים גדולים
9 13	ראיתי; תחת השמש	10 5	ראיתי תחת השמש
10 3	הרבה 18 9; סכל	10 6	הסכל; רבים
10 3	ועשירים בשפל ישבו 6 10; הלך ראיתי 5 10	10 7	ראיתי; הלכים; ושרים הלכים כעבדים

Table 14.4.1 (continued)

9 12	כשתפול	10 8	יפול
10 8	חפר גומץ; ופרץ גדר; בו	10 9	בם; מסיע אבנים; בוקע עצים
10 9	בוקע עצים	10 10	הברזל
10 10	ישכנו נחש 10 8; ויתרון	10 11	ישך הנחש; יתרון
10 11	לחש; לבעל הלשון	10 12	דברי פי; ושפתות
10 12	דברי פי	10 13	דברי פיהו
10 13	דברי; סכלות; ואחרית	10 14	והסכל; דברים; מאחריו
10 14	כסיל 10 12; ואשר; לא ידע	10 15	הכסילים; אשר לא ידע
10 7	הארץ; ושרים	10 16	ארץ; ושריך
10 16	ארץ שמלכך; ושריך; יאכלו	10 17	ארץ שמלכך; ושריך; יאכלו
10 17	בן חורים; בגבורה	10 18	בעצלתים; ובשפלות
10 17	בעצלתים 10 18; יאכלו	10 19	לחם ויין; לשחוק
10 17	והכסף 10 19; שמלכך	10 20	מלך; עשיר
10 19	לחם	11 1	לחמך
11 1	במדער 10 20; על; כי	11 2	כי; על; תדע
11 2	על הארץ	11 3	על הארץ
11 3	העבים	11 4	בעבים
11 4	לא תדע 11 2; רוח	11 5	הרוח; לא תדע
11 4	תדע 11 5; יזרע	11 6	זרע; יודע
11 6	וראה 11 4; טובים	11 7	וטוב; לראות
11 6	הכל 11 5; כי; ואם	11 8	כי אם; כל
11 8	הא׳ 11 5; שבא; ימי	11 9	בימי; יביאך; הא׳
11 9	הבל 11 8; בילדותך; לבך; כי	11 10	מלבך; כי הילדות; הבל
11 9	רעה 11 10; בימי בחורותיך	12 1	בימי בחורתיך; הרעה
12 1	החשך 11 8; עד אשר לא האור 11 7	12 2	עד אשר לא; תחשך; והאור
12 2	בימי 12 1; תחשך	12 3	וחשכו; ביום
12 3	הטחנות	12 4	הטחנה
12 4	בשוק	12 5	בשוק
12 1	אל 12 5; עד אשר לא	12 6	עד אשר לא; אל
12 2	על; אל 12 6; ושבו	12 7	וישב; על; אל
12 4	כל	12 8	הכל
12 8	הקוהלת	12 9	קהלת
12 9	קהלת	12 10	קהלת
12 10	דברי	12 11	דברי
12 9	הרבה	12 12	הרבה
12 11	הכל 12 8; דברי	12 13	דבר הכל
12 13	הא׳; כי; כל	12 14	כי; הא׳; כל

action. Again, the phrase "There is nothing better for a man than that he should eat and drink and make his soul enjoy pleasure for his labor" (2 24), and the phrase "It is better to go to the house of mourning than to go to the house of feasting" (7 2) are not contradictory. In the former case it is meant that man should enjoy the results of his work and labor, and not that he should prefer feasting to other activities.

In general, many examples of internal contradictions within the book have been given by the critics. However, careful analysis of the statements, and not quoting out of context, reveal that the supposedly contradictory phrases are actually in agreement. (Compare, for example 9 2 with 8 12,13; 4 2 with 9 4; and 1 13 with 2 13.)

14.5 ESTHER

The Book of Esther describes the events during the reign of the Persian King Ahasuerus which resulted in the Jewish people being saved from extermination throughout the Persian empire. The major problem with the book has been the identification of King Ahasuerus and the time when he ruled. As established in the chronological section (Sections 6.2.1 and 6.2.2) Ahasuerus was the father of Darius I (521–486 B.C.E.), and was known as Hystaspes. In actuality Hystaspes was never the principal ruler of Persia, and his name is therefore not listed among the Persian kings. However, he was of the royal line, and was considered as joint ruler when his son Darius became king. The approximate dates for the reign of Hystaspes (Ahasuerus) are 532 to 518. These dates include the time when Hystaspes was not king, but only adviser to Cyrus and governor of the district of Susiana.

Authorship

It is evident from the text that the author of the Book of Esther is Mordechai. Being the cousin and foster-father of Queen Esther (2 7), second to King Ahasuerus (10 3), and a leader of the Jews (10 3), he had access to all the information reported in the book. It is twice specifically stated that Mordechai knew what transpired (2 22, 4 1). Furthermore, he was a major participant in many events, such as reporting of a plot on the King's life (2 21–23), being honored by Haman at the King's command (6 10,11), and directing the royal counter-command allowing the Jews to fight for their lives (8 8–13). In addition, the writing of several sections of the book is clearly attributed to Mordechai (8 9; 9 20,29,30).

The Book of Esther was completed in about the year 518. Thus, the book covers events till at least 519, the fourteenth year of Ahasuerus (3 7; 9 1,18,19), and must therefore have been written after this date. Also, the book was written during the reign of Ahasuerus, as indicated from the use of the word המלך (who rules) in the present tense (1 1). These points limit the date of the book's composition to within a few years after 519.

The age of Mordechai when he wrote the Book of Esther can be approximated as follows. Assume that in 597 when he was exiled from Jerusalem (2 5,6) he was between one and thirteen years, or seven (plus or minus six) years old. Seventy-nine years later in 518, when Mordechai wrote the Book of Esther, he would then be eighty-six (plus or minus six) years.

ORGANIZATION

The Book of Esther is written according to a well organized, chronological arrangement. The book starts in the third year of Ahasuerus (1 3) and tells about the feasts lasting for over half a year (1 4,5), at the conclusion of which Vashti is deposed from being queen (1 10–21). Three years later* (2 1), Esther was taken to the king's house (2 8), where she remained for twelve months (2 12), until appointed queen in the tenth month of the seventh year of Ahasuerus (2 16, 17). Three years later* (3 1), in the eleventh year of Ahasuerus, Haman was appointed second to the king and became enraged at Mordechai, the Jew (3 5). In the first month of the twelfth year (3 7,12,13) it was arranged by Haman that the Jews were to be killed on the thirteenth day of the twelfth month of that year. Subsequently Haman was hanged (7 10), and Mordechai issued a counter-command on the twenty-third day of the third month (Est. 8 9). Then on the thirteenth day of the twelfth month (9 1) and on the fourteenth day (9 15), the Jews fought for their lives and conquered their enemies. Shortly thereafter, the holiday of Purim was established as an annual commemoration of the historical events (9 26–28).

It should be noted that the second half of the first sentence of the book (1 1) is not in strict chronological order. In the sentence, Ahasuerus is described as the king who rules from India to Ethiopia. In actuality, he did not rule over this large a territory until after his son Darius became king, i.e. after 521. Ahasuerus is called king in the early parts of the book, even though he was only a satrap, because he later became co-ruler with his son Darius I.

---

* The term "After these things" denotes a time-span of at least three years.

Chapter Fifteen

DANIEL, EZRA-NEHEMIAH AND CHRONICLES

15.1 DANIEL

The Book of Daniel has been subjected to much criticism because of inaccurate interpretation of its historical information and because of inability to understand the prophecies contained therein. In actuality, however, the historical information presented is highly accurate, as explained in detail in Chapter Seven. It is there shown that the information in the Book of Daniel agrees well with the history derived from extra-Biblical sources, and no major disagreements exist. Furthermore, in Chapter Sixteen a detailed commentary on the prophetic chapters of the book of Daniel is presented which clarifies in a straight-forward manner the passages which have heretofore been imperfectly explained. It is there shown that the histories concerning the Ptolemaic and Seleucid empires, Mohammad, World War I, and World War II, as well as the United Nations, establishment of the State of Israel, and numerous other periods, are presented clearly and concisely.

Many Biblical critics postpone the date of writing of the Book of Daniel to about 165 B.C.E. because of the accurate descriptions presented of the Ptolemaic and Seleucid empires, and because of disbelief in true prophecy. In doing so, they disregard the statement by Josephus (*Ant.* xi 8, par. 5) that Alexander the Great (332) was shown the Book of Daniel. In accord with such reasoning, these same critics would have to postpone the writing of the book to modern times since accurate descriptions of events of the twentieth century are also contained in the book. It is needless to say that the arguments of these critics are faulty. It is much more logical to accept the statement of the book that Daniel lived at the time of the Babylonian Exile, and to realize that some of the most remarkable prophecies of the future were received and recorded by Daniel. The fact that Daniel is mentioned by his contemporary Ezekiel (Ez. 14 14,20; 28 3) verifies that Daniel lived during the stated time.

The Book of Daniel covers the period from the third year of the reign of Jehoiakim (605) (Dan. 1 1) to the first year of Darius (517) (Dan. 9 1), which is a period of eighty-eight years. This time-span corresponds to the active period in the life of Daniel. If he were ten years old when brought to Babylon, as indicated from Dan. 1 4,5, then he lived to be at least ninety-eight. The book describes the life of Daniel; some incidents in the life of his three companions Hananiah, Mishael, and Azariah; and numerous dreams and revelations received by Daniel concerning the distant future.

ORGANIZATION

The Book of Daniel is organized according to a logical arrangement. The first division of the book, Chapters 1–6, records the historical events of importance to Daniel and his three companions; while the second half, Chapters 7–12, relates the dreams or visions which Daniel experienced. On first examination it might be thought that within each of the two divisions the chapters are arranged chronologically. However, Chapter 9, which occurred in the first year of Darius (517), precedes Chapters 10–12 which took place in the third year of Cyrus (537). Therefore, it is clear that the arrangement is not chronological. Nevertheless, in all other cases the logical and chronological arrangements are identical (see Table 15.1.1 which presents the dates of occurrence of the chapters).

The first division of the book has the following logical sequence. The first chapter describes how Daniel and other Jewish boys were brought to Babylon to be educated there for three years so that the more capable of them could serve the king. When the three years had passed, in the second year of Nebuchadnezzar

Table 15.1.1
Dates of Occurrence of the Chapters in the Book of Daniel

Chapter	Date Given in Heading	Year (B.C.E.)
First Division		
1	Third year of Jehoiakim	605
2	Second year of Nebuchadnezzar	603
3	During reign of Nebuchadnezzar	about 600
4	During reign of Nebuchadnezzar	possibly between 568 and 562
5	During reign of Belshazzar, before his death	539
6	During reign of Darius	about 520
Second Division		
7	First year of Belshazzar	553
8	Third year of Belshazzar	551
9	First year of Darius (as counted in the Bible)	517
10–12	Third year of Cyrus	537

(2 1), the king dreamed about a great image, constructed from numerous materials. Daniel was successful in describing and explaining the dream, and as a result Daniel and three of his companions were elevated to high positions. Subsequently, Nebuchadnezzar constructed a great image of gold to be worshipped by the people (3 1,5). The three companions of Daniel refused to worship the image and were thrown into a fiery furnace. Miraculously, the three remained unharmed. In the fourth chapter, Nebuchadnezzar has another dream which again Daniel successfully interprets. Many years later, Belshazzar, the grandson of Nebuchadnezzar (see Section 6.2.2) sees a mysterious hand write on the wall (5 5). Daniel successfully explains the writing to mean that the Babylonian kingdom will be given over to the Medes and Persians. The next event (Chapter 6) occurs many years after the Medes and Persians have conquered Babylon; Daniel is thrown into a den of hungry lions because he worshipped God, but he is saved miraculously.

The second division of the book (Chapters 7–12) is also arranged to form a logical sequence. In the first year of King Belshazzar, Daniel dreamed about four animals (one of them being a lion) representing four kings of different countries (7 1,17). Two years later in the third year of King Belshazzar, Daniel again has a dream about animals, representing the kings of different nations (8 1,20–23). The angel Gabriel explains the meaning of the animals to Daniel. In Chapter 9, Daniel prays to God, and receives a reply from the same angel Gabriel which he saw in the previous chapter (Dan. 9 21). Daniel is told that seventy *shavuim* (שבעים) (periods of forty-nine years) are decreed on the Jewish people (9 24). In Chapter 10 Daniel was mourning for many *shavuim* (periods of forty-nine days), after which time he receives a reply from the angel clothed in linen. This prophecy continues through Chapter 12.

Authorship

The author of the Book of Daniel is Daniel himself, although probably two of the chapters were at least partially written by others. Thus we find that the last six chapters are written in the first person, except for introductory sentences, and were obviously written by Daniel. The first six chapters are somewhat more complicated. Chapter 4 is written in the first person, as if by Nebuchadnezzar; and the main parts of the chapter were probably written by the King and edited by Daniel. The other chapters, namely 1, 2, 3, 5, and 6 are written in the third person and, except for Chapter 3, relate events in the life of Daniel, and were probably written by him. Chapter 3 describes events concerning the three companions of Daniel, and was probably written by one of them and edited by Daniel. In general, the events described in the book are those which were familiar to Daniel. Clearly he was the author of the entire book, although Chapters 3 and 4 may have been written by others and subsequently edited by Daniel.

Language of the Book

The Book of Daniel is written partly in Hebrew and partly in Aramaic. Both of these languages were spoken by Daniel. He was raised in Jerusalem until about ten years of age and, therefore, knew Hebrew. Then, he was brought to Babylon where he was educated in the tongue of the Chaldeans (1 4). The use of the two languages can be easily explained in terms of the best language to describe the occurring events. The first chapter is in Hebrew because the chief officer probably spoke that language to the Jewish captives (1 7,10). Chapter 2, from the fourth sentence on, is in Aramaic because, as stated in Dan. 2 4, the Chaldeans spoke Aramaic to Nebuchadnezzar. Similarly, the third and fourth chapters include conversations with Nebuchadnezzar, and the fifth chapter includes conversations with Belshazzar, and are therefore in Aramaic. The sixth chapter involves conversations with Darius, who spoke Persian. However the chapter is still written in Aramaic to maintain continuity of language. A further possibility is that the conversations with Darius were also in Aramaic, since it was the official language of Persia.

Chapter seven, which is the first chapter of the second division, is written also in Aramaic because that is the language in which the prophecy was conveyed to Daniel. This language was used in this particular case because of unique phrases, such as "עדן ועדנין" which would not mean the same time period if translated into Hebrew (see Section 16.2). The later visions, Chapters 8–12, were conveyed to Daniel in Hebrew, and are therefore written in Hebrew.

15.2 EZRA-NEHEMIAH

Originally the books now known as Ezra and Nehemiah were one work. Thus, the Talmud (*Baba Bathra* 14b), the Septuagint and the old Latin and Syriac versions treated the two books as one. The present discussion will also consider these two books as a single work.

A major difficulty with the book Ezra-Nehemiah has been the correct identification of the mentioned Persian kings. In Chapter Six a detailed analysis has been given clarifying this point and the associated history. As a result the Persian kings can be correctly identified, as presented in Table 15.2.1. Also, in Section 6.2.7 the high priests and the approximate time they ruled is clarified based partly on information supplied in Ezra-Nehemiah.

Organization

Examination of the book Ezra-Nehemiah reveals that there are three separate and distinct divisions; the first two are arranged in chronological order, and the third is arranged in a logical order. The first division, Ezra 1 1–6 22, covers the period from the first year of Cyrus (Ezra 1 1) to the seventh year of Darius I (Ezra 6 15,19), i.e. from 538 to 511 B.C.E.; and describes the history from the time when Cyrus permitted the Jews under the leadership of Sheshbazzar

(Zerubbabel)* to return to Jerusalem and rebuild the Temple, until the first Festival of Matzos was celebrated after completion of the Temple. The chronological order of this division is supported by the specified dates for the events. In the first year of Cyrus—538 (Ezra 1 1) Cyrus gave permission to the Jewish exiles to return to Jerusalem and build the Temple. Zerubbabel thereupon led close to 50,000 people in returning to Judah (2 64,65). By the first day of the seventh month the altar was built and the Feast of Tabernacles was celebrated (3 1,4,6). Then in the second month of 537 the foundations were laid for the Temple (3 8-13). The enemies of the Jews tried to prevent the building of the Temple, and at the beginning of the reign of Ahasuerus—about 531—they wrote accusations against the Jews (4 6). Later, during the reign of Cambyses— about 527—a letter was written by the enemies to Cambyses which led to a halt in the construction (4 7). Then in the second year of the reign of Darius I—516 B.C.E.—(4 24) the construction of the Temple was resumed as a result of prophecies by Haggai and Zechariah (5 1). (From Hag. 1 1 and Zech. 1 1 we know the prophecies were received in the sixth and eighth months of the second year of Darius—516.) By the third day of the twelfth month of the sixth year of Darius—512—the Temple was completed (6 15); and shortly thereafter on the fourteenth of the first month—511—the Passover sacrifice was brought (6 19), and then the Festival of Matzos was celebrated (6 22).

The second division, Ezra 7 1-10 44, covers the period from the seventh year of Artaxerxes II (Ezra 7 7) to the eighth year (Ezra 10 17); i.e. from 398 to 397. This section describes the history of the one-year period from the time when Artaxerxes II permitted the Jews of Babylon, under the leadership of Ezra, to return to Jerusalem, and take considerable gold and silver from the kingdom, until Ezra led the people in eliminating intermarriage. The chronological order is supported by the indicated dates. Thus, the expedition to go to Jerusalem was organized on the first day of the first month of the seventh year of Artaxerxes II (7 7,9). The people were gathered at Ahava till the fourth day (8 15), and it took until the twelfth day of the first month before they departed (8 31). On the first day of the fifth month they reached Jerusalem (7 9); and they gave over the gold and silver to the Temple on the fourth day of the fifth month (8 33). Subsequently a three-day gathering was arranged for the twentieth day of the ninth month (10 8,9) concerning the problem of intermarriage. Between the first day of the tenth month (10 16) and the first day

---

* The identity of Sheshbazzar and Zerubbabel is based on the following evidence:
(A) In Ezra 3 8-10 it is stated that Zerubbabel initiated the laying of the foundations of the Temple, while in Ezra 5 16 it is attributed to Sheshbazzar.
(B) In Ezra 5 14, Sheshbazzar is called the governor (פחה), while in Hag. 1 1 Zerubbabel is called the governor of Judah (פחת).
(C) In Ezra 1 8; 5 14,15; Sheshbazzar is designated as the leader of the returners to Jerusalem, while in Ezra 2 2 it is Zerubbabel.

In general the name Sheshbazzar was used when talking to the kings of Persia, while the name Zerubbabel was used when addressing the Jewish people.

Table 15.2.1
Identification of Persian Kings mentioned in Ezra-Nehemiah

Hebrew Name	Translated Name	Actual Persian King	Reign (B.C.E.)	References
כורש	Cyrus	Cyrus	538–530	Ezr. 1 1,2,7,8; 3 7; 4 3,5; 5 13,14,17; 6 3,14
אחשורוש	Ahasuerus	Hystaspes	531–518	Ezr. 4 6
ארתחששתא	Artaxerxes	Cambyses	529–522	Ezr. 4 7, 8, 11, 23; 6 14
דריוש (המדי)	Darius (the Mede)	Darius I	*(521) 517–486	Ezr. 4 5, 24; 5 5–7; 6 1, 12–15
דריוש הפרסי	Darius the Persian	Darius II	423–405	Neh. 12 22
ארתחשסתא	Artaxerxes	Artaxerxes II	404–359	Ezr. 7 1, 7, 11, 12, 21; 8 1; Neh. 2 1; 5 14; 13 6

* Note that the Bible counts the years of Darius I from 517, that is from the year after the death of his father Hystaspes.

of the first month of the eighth year of Artaxerxes II**(**10** 17) the intermarriage problem was resolved.

The third division, Neh. **1** 1–**13** 31, consists of the entire Book of Nehemiah, and covers the period from the twentieth year (Neh. **1** 1) until the thirty-third year (Neh. **13** 6) of Artaxerxes II, i.e. from 385 to 372, or a period of thirteen

---

**Since the exact calendar system used during the reign of Artaxerxes II is uncertain, the first day of the first month may not have begun the eighth year of Artaxerxes. (See the comments in the next paragraph.)

years. The history describes how Nehemiah was appointed governor of Judah, succeeded in rebuilding the walls around Jerusalem, and initiated a religious revival among the people. The arrangement is in a logical rather than a chronological order, although the first ten chapters until Neh. 11 3 are also in chronological order. The chronological order of the first ten chapters is shown as follows. In the month of Chislev of the twentieth year of Artaxerxes II (385) (1 1) Nehemiah learned that the gates of Jerusalem had recently been burned and many Jews were taken prisoner. This event obviously had occurred after the events described in the Book of Ezra, i.e. after 397, and probably occurred around 385. Later, in the month of Nisan of the twentieth year (2 1; 5 14), Nehemiah was appointed as governor of Judah. (It appears from the text that the years of rule of Artaxerxes II did not begin in the month of Nisan, but sometime between the months of Iyar and Chislev, thus showing a difference in the calendar from that at the time of the early Persian Kings (see Section 5.1).*) Nehemiah went to Jerusalem and organized the rebuilding of the walls of the city. The rebuilding was completed fifty-two days after Nehemiah arrived in Jerusalem, on the twenty-fifth of Elul (Neh. 6 15), which places the arrival of Nehemiah on about the third of Ab. Thus, it took Nehemiah about four months to travel from Shushan to Jerusalem; while it took Ezra about three months and seventeen days to travel from Babylon to Jerusalem (Ezra 8 31; 7 9). This is reasonable since Babylon is slightly closer to Jerusalem than is Shushan. Less than a week after completion of the walls, the people gathered together on the first and second days of the seventh month (Neh. 8 2,13) and numerous portions from different books of the Bible were read publicly. Later the people celebrated the Festival of Tabernacles and the Day of Solemn Assembly (the fifteenth through twenty-second day of the seventh month) (8 17,18). Two days later on the twenty-fourth day of the seventh month (9 1 which continues through 11 2) the people gathered together for reaffirmation of the observance of the Biblical laws. Thus the contents of 1 1–11 2 covers a period of less than eleven months (except for parenthetical remarks such as 5 14).

Examination of subsequent passages reveals serious chronological problems. The contents of 11 3–36 describe the places where particular Jews settled, and refer to succeeding years during the rule of Nehemiah. Also, 12 1–26 gives the genealogies of the priests and Levites, and then in 12 27–30 are specified that the Levites and priests were active at the time of dedication of the rebuilt walls of Jerusalem at the time of Nehemiah (384). Next comes a passage 12 31–13 3

---

* It is impossible to assume that the events of the first chapter followed the second chapter since they offer the background for the decision by Nehemiah to go to Jerusalem. Secondly, Neh. 1 1 states that Nehemiah was in Shushan in the month of Chislev. If this date is after that of Chapter 2, then it is also after the events of Neh. 9 1, where Nehemiah was in Jerusalem in the twenty-fourth of the seventh month. Since it took Nehemiah about four months to travel from Shushan to Jerusalem, it would have been impossible for him to be back in Shushan in Chislev, the ninth month. Hence the events of Chapter 1 must have preceded those of Chapter 2.

where the phrase "on that day" is used three times, with no obvious mention of the date. A simple explanation for the above problems is as follows. The gathering of the Jewish people on the twenty-fourth day of the seventh month is described in 9 1–11 2 and then is continued in 12 31–13 3. To clarify the continuity of these sections the term "on that day" is used. Between 11 2 and 12 31 are inserted relevant passages which refer to events which partly may have occurred in later years. Thus 11 1–2 mentions that people volunteered, or were chosen by lot, at the gathering to settle in Jerusalem. Then in 11 3–36 the particular people who subsequently settled in Jerusalem and in other areas are listed. Similarly the passage of 12 31–47, continuing the description of the gathering on the twenty-fourth of the seventh month, relates the actions of numerous priests and Levites. Therefore the previous passage 12 1–30 concerning the genealogies and background of the priests and Levites is inserted just before, so as to supply relevant information. In this manner, the sections 11 3–36 and 12 1–30, presenting lists of names are placed consecutively. Thus we find here a logical rather than a chronological order.

There is then a jump of thirteen years to the thirty-third year of Artaxerxes II (Neh. 13 6). The introductory sentence 13 4 begins with the phrase "now before this," and indicates that Eliashib the priest was situated in a chamber of the Temple even before the twenty-fourth day of the seventh month (9 1). The remainder of the book (13 4–31) describes events, occurring during or after the thirty-third year of Artaxerxes II, when Nehemiah returned to Jerusalem after a year's absence.

It will be noticed that the above described three sections have in common the return by a leading person to Judah after the Babylonian exile. The first section (Ezra 1 1–6 22) describes the return of Zerubbabel; the second section (Ezra 7 1–10 44) describes the return of Ezra; and the third section (Neh. 1 1–13 31) describes the return of Nehemiah. Furthermore, in the first and third sections we find a list of those who returned with Zerubbabel (Ezra 2 1–70; Neh. 7 6–73). Similarly in the second and third sections we find that Ezra was a key personality (Ezra 7 6 etc.; Neh. 8 1 etc.). It is because of these common elements, that these three sections have been combined into one book.

Authorship

As explained previously, the book Ezra-Nehemiah covers the period from the first year of Cyrus (Ezra 1 1) to after the thirty-third year of Artaxerxes II (Neh. 13 6), which is from 538 to after 372, or a period of over 167 years. This is too long a time for one person to have described, and therefore sections must have been written by different people.

The most probable author for the first division (Ezra 1 1–6 22) is Zerubbabel (also known as Sheshbazzar). He was the governor of Judah (Ezra 5 14; Hag. 1 1), received the Temple vessels to take to Jerusalem (Ezra 1 8), led the people in the return to Judah (Ezra 2 2), was involved in building the altar (Ezra 3 2) and the Temple (Ezra 3 8), and in general was involved in all the incidents described. He was leader of the people not only at the time of Cyrus (538) (Ezra 1 8) but also at the time of Darius I (516) (Ezra 5 2), until the Temple was completed. The fact that the beginning of this section (Ezra 1 1–3), is identical to the end of Chronicles (II Chr. 36 22–23) indicates that Zerubbabel also wrote at least the last few sentences of Chronicles.

The second division (Ezra 7 1–10 44) covers a period of one year from the first day of the first month of the seventh year of Artaxerxes II (398) (Ezra 7 9) until the first day of the first month of the eighth year of Artaxerxes II (397) (Ezra 10 17). The author of this section is clearly Ezra, first because he was involved in all the described incidents, and secondly because the chapters Ezra 7 27–9 15 are written in the first person by Ezra. The remaining parts of the division even though written in the third person, were undoubtedly also by Ezra.

The third division which consists of the entire Book of Nehemiah was obviously written by Nehemiah himself. The book explicitly states (Neh. 1 1) that "these are the words of Nehemiah." He was involved in all the described events; and furthermore the entire book, with the exception of Neh. 8 1–12 30, was written in the first person by Nehemiah.

Since Nehemiah is the author of the last division, he most probably organized the book Ezra-Nehemiah into its present form and did any necessary editing.

It should be noted that for each division, the logical author turns out to be the leader of the group returning to Judah, namely Zerubbabel, Ezra, and Nehemiah respectively.

The passage in Ezra 2 1–70 listing all the people who returned to Jerusalem with Zerubbabel is found repeated, with some variations in the names and numbers, in Neh. 7 6–73. The reason for the repetition may have been the desire by Nehemiah to preserve for the record the variations found in the "book of the genealogy" (Neh. 7 5).

The use of Aramaic in certain sections of the text (Ezra 4 7–6 18; 7 11–26) is simply to give an accurate historical record of the Aramaic letters that were written. Quotations of particular letters are found in Ezra 4 11–16; 4 17–21; 5 7–17; 6 3–12, the division written by Zerubbabel; and in Ezra 7 12–26, the division written by Ezra. Zerubbabel wrote the explanatory comments to the letters in Aramaic to maintain a continuity of language.

15.3 CHRONICLES

In the two Books of Chronicles, which were originally one work, we find mention of the Book of the Kings of Judah and Israel and the Book of [the Chronicles of] the Kings of Israel. Similarly, in the Book of Kings, the Book of the Chronicles of the Kings of Israel and the Book of the Chronicles of the Kings of Judah are mentioned. These three works, as indicated by their titles, are histories of the Kingdoms of Judah and Israel, the Kingdom of Israel only, and the Kingdom of Judah only. Based on the fact that wherever reference is made to the Book of the Kings of Judah and Israel, the corresponding information is found in the Book of Kings, and wherever reference is made to the Book of the Chronicles of the Kings of Judah, the corresponding information is found in the Book of Chronicles, we know that the present Book of Kings is identical to the Book of the Kings of Judah and Israel, and the present Book of Chronicles is identical to the Book of the Chronicles of the Kings of Judah. These cross-references are tabulated in Table 15.3.1. In contrast, where reference is made to the Book of the Chronicles of the Kings of Israel none of the indicated data are found elsewhere in the Bible. Thus in I Kings 14 19; 15 31; 16 5,14,20,27; 22 39 and II Kings 1 18; 10 34; 13 8,12; 14 15,28; 15 11, 15,21,26,31 it is stated that additional information on particular kings of Israel is found in the Book of the Chronicles of the Kings of Israel, and no such additional information is found in the Bible. Similarly, additional information for particular kings of Judah is stated to be found in the Book of the Chronicles of the Kings of Israel (II Chr. 20 34; 33 18;), but no such information is now available. The conclusion therefore follows that the Book of the Chronicles of the Kings of Israel has been lost.

First mention of these three historical works only occurs after split of the monarchy, with respect to Rehoboam (I Kings 14 29), Jeroboam (I Kings 14 19), and Asa (II Chr. 16 11). Thus one would not expect to find events described in these works much prior to the time of Rehoboam and Jeroboam. Nevertheless, the Book of Kings begins with Solomon's reign, while Chronicles goes back to the time of Adam, the first man. That the history of Solomon was included in Kings is not surprising since the events during his reign offer a background for the division of the monarchy. However, the question arises, why does Chronicles go back to Adam? Perhaps the present book contains not only the Book of the Chronicles of the Kings of Judah, but also information added later?

The available data indicate otherwise; in particular, that the genealogies contained in the first nine chapters which go back to Adam, were originally inserted as part of the Book of the Chronicles of the Kings of Judah. Firstly, in I Chr. 9 1 it is stated that genealogies were incorporated in the "Book of the Kings of Israel," which would indicate that genealogies were also incorporated in the parallel work of the Book of the Chronicles of the Kings of Judah. Secondly, in Neh. 12 23 it is stated "The sons of Levi, heads of fathers' houses [i.e. the high priests] were written in the book of Chronicles, and until the days of Johanan the son of Eliashib." This sentence can be explained as meaning that the lineage of the high priests given in I Chr. 5 29-41 until Jehozadak, who was at the time of the Babylonian Exile, is continued in the book Ezra-Nehemiah (Ezra 3 2, Neh. 12 10-11) until the time of Johanan (Jonathan), grandson of Eliashib, who was the high priest at the time of Nehemiah. Thus the statement in Neh. 12 23 supports the contention that genealogies were written in the Book of the Chronicles of the Kings of Judah. Thirdly, the genealogies of the first nine chapters of Chronicles preponderantly emphasize the lineages of (A) the tribe of Judah; (B) the tribes of Simeon and Benjamin who lived in territory immediately adjacent to that of Judah; and (C) the Levites and priests, who served in the Temple located in the Kingdom of Judah. Genealogies of the other tribes are presented in a very condensed form, and are given partly for completeness. As a final reason for concluding that the genealogies are part of the original Book of the Chronicles of the Kings of Judah is the statement in II Chr. 12 15 that the history of Rehoboam is written by Shemaiah the prophet and Iddo the seer, to present genealogies (להתיחש). Thus, at about the time of formulation of the three books on the Kingdoms of Judah and Israel, genealogies were tabulated as background information.

Date of Completion of the Book

From the above discussion it appears that the planning and structure of the Book of the Kings of Judah and Israel, the Book of the Chronicles of the Kings of Israel, and the Book of the Chronicles of the Kings of Judah were formulated at an early time, about the time of Rehoboam and Jeroboam, after split of the monarchy. Naturally material was added to the books as time passed. In particular, some statements in the first nine chapters of Chronicles, show genealogies were added after the time of Rehoboam and Jeroboam: (A) "In the days of Hezekiah King of Judah" (I Chr. 4 41); (B) "The genealogies were prepared in the days of Jotham, King of Judah and in the days of Jeroboam [II] King of Israel" (I Chr. 5 17); (C) "until the exile [by Assyria—719 B.C.E.]" (I Chr. 5 22); (D) at the exile of Judah and Jerusalem by Nebuchadnezzar (586) (I Chr. 5 41); and (E) when Judah was exiled to Babylonia (586) (I Chr. 9 1).

In actuality, there are several cases in Chronicles where dates after the Babylonian Exile are indicated. (A) The first year of Cyrus, King of Persia, (538) (II Chr. 36 22). (B) In I Chr. 3 19–24 ten generations after Zerubbabel are listed (538). These generations can be variously interpreted. One probable lineage is Zerubbabel, Hananiah, Jeshaiah, Rephaiah, Arnan, Obadiah, Shecaniah, Shemaiah, Neariah, Elioenai, and the latter's seven sons. Assuming sixteen years per generation, times ten generations results in 160 years after 538, or approximately 380. (C) The text of I Chr. 9 2–17 is very similar to that of Neh. 11 3–19. In particular I Chr. 9 10–17 is approximately identical to Neh. 11 10–19. This would date Chapter 9 at about 380, the time of Nehemiah.

We thus find that the Book of Chronicles must have been completed about 380, the time of Ezra and Nehemiah. Since great emphasis is placed on genealogies by Nehemiah (Neh. 11 and 12), and because of the great similarity of I Chr. 9 with Neh. 11, and the fact that Chronicles is referred to in Neh. 12 23, the indications are that Nehemiah was the final author of Chronicles rather than Ezra—although Ezra is also a distinct possibility. It should be realized, however, that almost the entire Book of Chronicles was completed by the first year of Cyrus (538), and only the few sections indicated above were added at the time of Nehemiah. Indications as to who authored the individual sections of Chronicles will be given after the discussion of the organization of the book.

Table
References for Additional

King of Judah	Statement in Kings		Corresponding Information Found in Chronicles
	Reference	Statement	
David			
Solomon	I 11 41	The rest of the acts of Solomon, and all that he did, and his wisdom, they are written in the book of the acts of Solomon.	Rest of the acts: II Chr. 1 1–6; 5 11–13; 6 40–7 3; 7 12–16. All that he did: II Chr. 4 1; 8 4,5,11–16. His wisdom: II Chr. 1 7–12.
Rehoboam	I 14 29	The rest of the acts of Rehoboam, and all that he did, they are written in the book of the chronicles of the kings of Judah.	Rest of the acts: II Chr. 11 13–12 1; 12 3–8, 12,14. All that he did: II Chr. 11 5–12
Abijah	I 15 7	The rest of the acts of Abijam, and all that he did, they are written in the book of the chronicles of the kings of Judah.	Rest of the acts: II Chr. 13 3–21 All that he did: II Chr. 13 19
Asa	I 15 23	The rest of all the acts of Asa, and all his might, and all that he did, and the cities which he built, they are written in the book of the chronicles of the kings of Judah.	Rest of the acts: II Chr. 16 7–10 All his might: II Chr. 14 8–15 7 All that he did: II Chr. 15 8–15 Cities which he built: II Chr. 14 5–6.
Jehoshaphat	I 22 46	The rest of the acts of Jehoshaphat, and his might that he showed, and how he warred, they are written in the book of the chronicles of the kings of Judah.	Rest of the acts: II Chr. 17 1–19; 19 1–11; 20 35–37. Might that he showed and how he warred: II Chr. 20 1–30.

15.3.1
Information on the Kings of Judah

Statement in Chronicles		Corresponding Information Found in Kings or Samuel
Reference	Statement	
I 29 29,30	The acts of David the king, first and last, they are written in the words of Samuel the seer, and in the words of Nathan the prophet, and in the words of Gad the seer; with all his reign and his might, and the times that went over him, and over Israel, and over all the kingdoms of the countries.	Words of Samuel the Seer: I Sam. 1 1–19 24 Words of Nathan the prophet: II Sam. 2 1–20,26 Words of Gad the seer: I Sam. 20 1– II Sam. 1 27; 21 1–24 25. With all his reign: II Sam. 2 1–5 5; 7 1–29; II Sam. 23 1–7. And his might: II Sam. 5 6–25; 8 1–18; 10 1–19; 21 15–22 51. And the times: I Sam. 16 1–II Sam. 1 27; II Sam. 6 1–23; 11 1– 20 26; 21 1–14; 23 8–24 25.
II 9 29	The rest of the acts of Solomon, first and last, they are written in the words of Nathan the prophet, and in the prophecy of Ahijah the Shilonite, and in the visions of Jedo the seer concerning Jeroboam the son of Nebat.	Rest of the Acts: I Kings 2 13–33; 6 1–7 12; 3 16–5 5; 7 27–37; 8 50–61; 9 11–16; 11 1–40 Words of Nathan the prophet: I Kings 1–10 Prophecy of Ahijah the Shilonite: I Kings 11 Visions of Jedo the seer concerning Jeroboam: I Kings 12 1–20.
II 12 15	The acts of Rehoboam, first and last, they are written in the histories of Shemaiah the prophet and of Iddo the seer, to present genealogies.	Acts of Rehoboam, first and last: I Kings 14 22–24, 30
II 13 22	The rest of the acts of Abijah, and his ways and sayings, are written in the commentary (midrash) of the prophet Iddo.	Rest of the acts: I Kings 15 3 His ways and sayings: I Kings 15 3
II 16 11	The acts of Asa, first and last, they are written in the book of the kings of Judah and Israel.	Acts of Asa, first and last: I Kings 15 9–24.
II 20 34	The rest of the acts of Jehoshaphat, first and last, they are written in the words of Jehu the son of Hanani, which is inserted in the book of the kings of Israel.	(No reference to book of Kings)

Table 15.3.1

King of Judah	Statement in Kings		Corresponding Information Found in Chronicles
	Reference	Statement	
Jehoram	II **8** 23	The rest of the acts of Joram, and all that he did, they are written in the book of the chronicles of the kings of Judah.	Rest of the acts: II Chr. **21** 2–4, 11–19 All that he did: II Chr. **21** 4,11
Ahaziah	—		
Athaliah	—		
Jehoash	II **12** 20	The rest of the acts of Joash, and all that he did, they are written in the book of the chronicles of the kings of Judah.	Rest of the acts: II Chr. **24** 3, 15–22 All that he did: II Chr. **24** 14,22
Amaziah	II **14** 18	The rest of the acts of Amaziah, they are written in the book of the chronicles of the kings of Judah.	Rest of the acts: II Chr. **25** 5–10, 13–16
Azariah	II **15** 6	The rest of the acts of Azariah, and all that he did, they are written in the book of the chronicles of the kings of Judah.	Rest of the acts: II Chr. **26** 5–20 All that he did: II Chr. **26** 6,9,10,15
Jotham	II **15** 36	The rest of the acts of Jotham, and all that he did, they are written in the book of the chronicles of the kings of Judah.	Rest of the acts: II Chr. **27** 2, 5–6 All that he did: II Chr. **27** 3,4
Ahaz	II **16** 19	The rest of the acts of Ahaz which he did, they are written in the book of the chronicles of the kings of Judah.	Rest of the acts which he did: II Chr. **28** 5–25
Hezekiah	II **20** 20	The rest of the acts of Hezekiah, and all his might, and how he made the pool and the conduit, and brought water into the city, they are written in the book of the chronicles of the kings of Judah.	Rest of the acts: II Chr. **29** 3–31 **21**; **32** 24–29. All his might: II Chr. **32** 1–27. How he made the pool . . . water into the city: II Chr. **32** 30
Manasseh	II **21** 17	The rest of the acts of Manasseh, and all that he did, and his sin that he sinned, they are written in the book of the chronicles of the kings of Judah.	Rest of the acts: II Chr. **33** 10–13 All that he did: II Chr. **33** 14–17 His sin that he sinned: II Chr. **33** 2–9.

DANIEL, EZRA-NEHEMIAH AND CHRONICLES

(continued)

Statement in Chronicles		Corresponding Information
Reference	Statement	Found in Kings or Samuel
II 24 27	Concerning his sons, and the multitude of the burdens (taxes) from him, and the foundation of the house of God, they are written in the commentary (midrash) of the book of kings.	(No reference to book of Kings)
II 25 26	The rest of the acts of Amaziah, first and last, they are written in the book of the kings of Judah and Israel.	Rest of the acts: II Kings 14 4,7
II 26 22	The rest of the acts of Uzziah, first and last, did Isaiah the prophet, son of Amoz, write.	Rest of the acts: II Kings 15 5
II 27 7	The rest of the acts of Jotham, and all his wars and ways, they are written in the book of the the kings of Israel and Judah.	Rest of the acts: II Kings 15 35 All his wars and ways: II Kings 15 37
II 28 26	The rest of his acts, and his ways, first and last, they are written in the book of the kings of Judah and Israel.	Rest of his acts and all his ways: II Kings 16 5, 7–18
II 32 32	The rest of the acts of Hezekiah, and his good deeds, they are written in the vision of Isaiah the prophet the son of Amoz, in the book of the kings of Judah and Israel.	Rest of the acts: II Kings 18 7–19 37; 20 12–19. His good deeds: II Kings 18 4–6; 20 1–11
II 33 18,19	The rest of the acts of Manasseh, and his prayer to his God, and the words of the seers that spoke to him in the name of the Lord, the God of Israel, they are written among the acts of the Kings of Israel. His prayer, and how God was entreated of him, and all his sin and his transgression, and the places wherein he built high places,	His prayer and how ... was entreated: No data in Kings. All his sin and his transgression, and the places wherein ... graven images: II Kings 21 2–17 (Otherwise no reference to Kings)

Table 15.3.1

King of Judah	Statement in Kings		Corresponding Information Found in Chronicles
	Reference	Statement	
Amon	II 21 25	The rest of the acts of Amon which he did, they are written in the book of the chronicles of the kings of Judah.	Rest of the acts: II Chr. 33 22–27
Josiah	II 23 28	The rest of the acts of Josiah, and all that he did, they are written in the book of the chronicles of the kings of Judah.	Rest of the acts: II Chr. 34 3; 35 20–25. All that he did: II Chr. 34 4–13,33; 35 1–19.
Jehoahaz	—		
Jehoiakim	II 24 5	The rest of the acts of Jehoiakim, and all that he did, they are written in the book of the chronicles of the kings of Judah.	Rest of the acts: II Chr. 36 6–7 All that he did: II Chr. 36 5
Jehoiachin	—		
Zedekiah	—		

(continued)

Statement in Chronicles		Corresponding Information
Reference	Statement	Found in Kings or Samuel
	and set up the asherim and the graven images before he humbled himself, they are written in the history of Hozai.	
II 35 26,27	The rest of the acts of Josiah, and his good deeds . . . and his acts, first and last, they are written in the book of the kings of Israel and Judah.	Rest of the acts: II Kings 22 3–7. His good deeds, and his acts: II Kings 23 4–27.
II 36 8	The rest of the acts of Jehoiakim, and his abominations which he did, and that which was found in him, they are written in the book of the kings of Israel and Judah.	Rest of the acts: II Kings 23 36; 24 1–4. His abominations which he did: II Kings 23 37. That which was found in him: II Kings 23 35.

Organization

The Book of Chronicles can be divided into three main sections. The first section (I Chr. 1–9) presents genealogical tables beginning with Adam, and emphasizing the tribe of Judah, and supplies information and lists relative to the Kingdom of Judah. Although any particular genealogical listing is naturally in chronological order, still the arrangement of this first section is according to a logical basis, where the more important people are presented first whenever practical. The first chapter (I Chr. 1) covers the principal personalities from Adam to the Children of Israel; and also supplies detailed listings of the descendants of Ishmael and Esau for completeness. These latter listings are presented before those of the sons of Israel so as not to later interrupt the much lengthier account of the genealogies of Israel (I Chr. 2–8). The descendants of Judah are tabulated first (I Chr. 2 1–4 23) since he is the most important son when considering the Kingdom of Judah, even though Reuben, Simeon, and Levi were older brothers. Similarly the genealogy of David from Hezron is listed first (I Chr. 2 10–15) even though David originated from Ram, the middle son of Hezron. The genealogies of the other sons of Hezron are then listed for completeness (I Chr. 2 18–55). Next, the descendants of David are tabulated (I Chr. 3 1–24) until the time of completion of the Book of Chronicles. The genealogies of the other important personalities of the tribe of Judah are then presented (I Chr. 4 1–23) including such noted people as Othniel, son of Kenaz, and Caleb, the son of Jephunneh. Afterwards, the descendants of the tribe of Simeon are listed (I Chr. 4 24–43). This tribe is emphasized partly because its locality was interwined with that of the tribe of Judah, and also because Simeon was the second oldest son of Israel. Subsequently, the genealogies of the tribes of Reuben (I Chr. 5 1–10), Gad (I Chr. 5 11–22), and half of Manasseh (I Chr. 5 23–26) are given. These three tribes are arranged together because they settled in adjoining territory, and were exiled at the times of Pul and Tillegath-pilneser (Tiglath-Pileser), Kings of Assyria (I Chr. 5 26). These listings were introduced at this point for completeness, since Reuben was the oldest son of Israel. Then the genealogy of Levi is presented (I Chr. 5 27–6 66) to conclude the listings for the three older brothers of Judah, namely Reuben, Simeon, and Levi. Furthermore, the tribe of Levi is of particular importance because its members were the ones who ministered at the Temple, located within the territory of the Kingdom of Judah. In the tabulation of the genealogy of Levi, we again find that the most important people are presented first. Thus, first are given the parentage for Aaron, Moses, and Miriam (I Chr. 5 29) even though they descended from Kohath, the middle son of Levi; followed by the genealogies of the high priests (I Chr. 5 30–41). Next are listed the descendants of Gershon and Merari, the other sons of Levi; relevant information concerning the Temple; and the location of the cities where the priests and Levites resided.

In Chapter 7 are presented for completeness, information concerning the tribes of Issachar, Naphtali, Manasseh, Ephraim, and Asher, who were most probably of some importance relative to the Kingdom of Judah. Information concerning the tribes of Dan and Zebulun is missing, probably since they had little relevance to the Kingdom of Judah. The genealogy of the tribe of Benjamin (I Chr. 8 1–40) was left to the last, even though he was closely associated with the tribe of Judah, so that the lineage of Saul would be given immediately before starting the second section of the book (I Chr. 10) about Saul's kingship. However, subsequently the information in I Chr. 9 2–34, about the resettlers in Jerusalem after the Babylonian Exile, was added by Nehemiah to the Book of Chronicles. Therefore, the genealogy of the tribe of Benjamin, relevant to Saul, was repeated (I Chr. 9 35–44) so as to maintain the proximity with the history of King Saul. Probably a variant manuscript was used when repeating the lineage of Saul, so as to preserve any slight variations which existed.

The second section of the book (I Chr. 10–II Chr. 9) may be considered as the history of the kings before the division of the monarchy into two parts, and refers to the history of Kings Saul, David, and Solomon. This section is arranged chronologically according to the sequence of the kings, although the history of any particular king is not necessarily in strict chronological order. For example, the birth of Solomon, which occurred in the 25th year of David's reign, is mentioned in I Chr. 14 4, although the moving of the Ark of God, mentioned in I Chr. 13 1–14 and continued in I Chr. 15 1–16 43, occurred in the fifteenth year of David's reign.

Because Saul ruled only two years, and was of the tribe of Benjamin, his history is de-emphasized (I Chr. 10). Only the most meager details necessary to understand the beginning of David's rule are presented. For example, Saul is later mentioned in I Chr. 11 2; 12 1,2,19,23,29; in describing the history of David, and these sentences would be unclear without the knowledge that Saul preceded David as king.

The third section of Chronicles (II Chr. 10 1–36 23) covers the history of the kings of Judah from the time of Rehoboam until the destruction of the Temple and the subsequent edict of Cyrus (538). This section is also arranged in chronological order according to the sequence of the kings; and only occasionally, when contemporary events are described, is the narrative for any particular king not in strict chronological order. An example is the sickness of Hezekiah (II Chr. 32 24–26) which is described after the event of Sennacherib although it occurred at about the same time as the threat from Sennacherib's army (II Chr. 32 1–23), as stated in II Chr. 32 24.

In the second and third sections, upon comparing the text to that in the books of Samuel and Kings, it is observed that more emphasis is placed in Chronicles on statitistical matter and Temple worship. This is particularly true of the history of David (I Chr. 11–29) where Chapters 22 to 29 contain additional details not contained in the Book of Samuel.

The history of Solomon is presented in II Chr. 1–9, and corresponds closely to the account in I Kings 3–11, although slight additional material with respect to the Temple service is presented in II Chr. 8 11–16; while the sin of Solomon recorded in I Kings 11 1–40 is not found in Chronicles.

In general, in the second section, for the histories of Saul, David and Solomon, their sins are glided over or completely omitted in the narrative in Chronicles. Thus the detailed account of the reign of Saul, and his many sins (I Sam. 13 1–30 31)— including his not listening to God and the prophet Samuel (I Sam. 13 8–14; 15 1–35); numerous attempts to kill David (I Sam. 18 9–29; 19 1–3, 9–24; etc.); killing of the priests of God (I Sam. 22 17–19); and inquiring of a woman that divined by a ghost (I Sam. 28 7–25); are not given in detail in Chronicles. Also the sin of David with Bathsheba, and having Uriah killed; as well as the consequent punishment of David (II Sam. 11 2–20 22) are not mentioned in Chronicles. Furthermore, the sin of the idol-worship by Solomon (I Kings 11 1–40) is also not referred to in Chronicles. This policy is in sharp contrast to that found subsequently in the third section of the Book of Chronicles (II Chr. 10 1–36 23) about the Kings of Judah, where often sins are mentioned in great detail in Chronicles, while not mentioned, or to a lesser extent, in Kings. This is the case for Rehoboam (II Chr. 11 17; 12 1,14), Asa (II Chr. 16 7–10), Jehoshaphat (II Chr. 19 1–3; 20 35–37), Jehoram (II Chr. 21 2–4, 11–19), Jehoash (II Chr. 24 15–25), Amaziah (II Chr. 25 14–16,20), Azariah (II Chr. 26 16–20), Ahaz (II Chr. 28 19, 24,25), Hezekiah (II Chr. 32 25,26), Amon (II Chr. 33 23), and Zedekiah (II Chr. 36 12–16). Also the repentance of Manasseh is mentioned in II Chr. 33 12–16.

The reason for this difference arises from the different purposes of the second and third sections of Chronicles. The second section was added from existing manuscripts at about the time of Rehoboam or later, to provide a background to the Kingdom of Judah, and to add any previously unreported data. Emphasis is given to additional material concerning the Temple services, while the sins of Saul, David, and Solomon are ignored for conciseness. However, the third section is interested in presenting detailed accounts of the kings of Judah, and therefore the kings' sins are very relevant. The sins of Saul, David and Solomon are however recorded in the books of Samuel and Kings because there the description of the united monarchy is given. In particular, the Book of Kings is called the "Book of the Kings of Judah and Israel" indicating that the emphasis is on the combined monarchy and the interrelationship between the separate kingdoms.

Authorship

It should be realized that numerous parts of the Book of Chronicles are similar, if not almost identical, to the accounts written in other books of the Bible. This correspondence is summarized in Table 15.3.2, and shows that a large portion of the text has only minor verbal variations from accounts given in the books of Genesis, Exodus, Numbers, Joshua, Samuel, Kings, Psalms, Ruth, Ezra and Nehemiah. In Table 15.3.2 we have also listed the probable authors of the passages based on our previous conclusions concerning the authorship of the different books of the Bible. When no parallel passages exist to those in Chronicles, then the probable author, based on the text in Chronicles, is often inserted. Thus, for example, the author of I Chr. 16 4–7 is listed as Asaph, since he plays a prominent role in the story.

Previously we have indicated that Iddo, the prophet, was the originator of the structure of the Book of Chronicles, including the presentation of the genealogical lists at the beginning of the book. It can now also be concluded that the genealogies of the first nine chapters, arose from three different sources: (A) other books of the Bible; (B) other manuscripts of genealogies existing at the time of Iddo, but which are now lost; and (C) genealogies added subsequently to the time of Iddo. Hence the passages in the Bible corresponding to the first nine chapters of Chronicles were one of the main source materials for the genealogies.

Using the same type of reasoning, the second section of Chronicles, i.e. the histories of Saul, David and Solomon, were probably incorporated into the Book of Chronicles by Iddo from (A) the texts in the books of Samuel and Kings, and (B) from historical manuscripts, now lost, written by the Levites and others. Included in these historical manuscripts would be the Book of the History of Solomon mentioned in I Kings 11 41.

When considering how the third section of Chronicles arose, concerning the kings of Judah, we must realize that (A) many of the accounts are almost identical to those presented in Kings, and (B) the two books, the Book of Chronicles and the Book of Kings, evolved simultaneously since they refer to each other throughout (as explained at the end of Section 11.4). Therefore, the identical passages must have been recorded in both books by the same prophets or persons or, what is essentially equivalent, been copied by others from one book to the next. However the differing passages must have been written by different persons, many of whom cannot be ascertained at present. The probable authors of the duplicated sections are tabulated in Table 15.3.2, based on the conclusions reached for the Book of Kings.

The history of the kings of Judah continues until the destruction of the Temple. Mention is then made of the edict of Cyrus (538) (II Chr. 36 22–23), which is essentially identical to the wording in Ezra 1 1–3. As stated in Section 15.2, Zerubbabel probably wrote the first section in Ezra-Nehemiah (Ezra 1 1–6 22). Therefore he was also the concluding author of Chronicles concerning the history of the kings of Judah, and must have done considerable editing of the book. However, Zerubbabel was not the final author, since as stated before, some of the genealogies date from 380, the time of Nehemiah. Genealogical information must have been added by Nehemiah so as to preserve the data for posterity. We may therefore say that both Zerubbabel and Nehemiah were significantly involved in the completion of Chronicles, while Iddo was responsible for providing the initial structure of the book.

A study of Table 15.3.2 reveals that there are many cases for the reigns of David and Solomon where the arrangement of identical passages are different in Chronicles from that in Samuel or Kings. These differences are easily explained once it is realized that logical considerations often modify the chronological arrangement of the events during a king's rule. Since much of the history in Chronicles is not

Table 15.3.2
Parallel Passages to those in Chronicles

General Topic	Passage in I Chronicles	Corresponding Passages in the Bible	Extent of Duplication by Passage in Chronicles	Probable Original Author(s)
I. Genealogies				
A. Pre-Israelite	1 1–4	Gen. 5 3–32	Highly Abridged	Adam, his descendants, and completed by Noah
	1 5–23	Gen. 10 2–4,6–8,13–18, 22–29	Essentially identical	Sons of Noah
	1 24–28	Gen. 11 10–26; 17 5; 16 15; 21 3	Highly abridged	Shem, his descendants, Jacob and Abraham
	1 29–31	Gen. 25 13–16	Essentially identical	Ishmael and his sons
	1 32–33	Gen. 25 1–5	Essentially identical	Isaac
	1 34–42	Gen. 35 10,29; 36 4–5, 10–13, 20–28	Abridged	Jacob, Esau, descendants of Esau
	1 43–54	Gen. 36 31–43	Essentially identical	Descendants of Esau
B. Tribe of Judah	2 1–2	Gen. 35 23–26	Abridged	Jacob
	2 3–5	Gen. 38 2–7,13,16,27,30; 46 12	Abridged	Judah (Jacob, Moses)
	2 6–8	Num. 26 19–21; Josh. 7 1	Expanded	Joshua (and records left by Zerah)
	2 9–12	Num. 2 3; Ruth 4 19–21	Approximately identical	Moses, Boaz

DANIEL, EZRA-NEHEMIAH AND CHRONICLES

2 13–17	I Sam. 16 6–10; 17 12–14;	Additional details	Samuel, Nathan
2 18–20	II Sam. 2 18; 17 25 Ex. 31 2	Additional details	Moses (and records left by Hur)
2 21–55	—		
3 1–9	II Sam. 3 2–5; 5 5, 14–16	Approximately identical	Nathan
3 10–16	I Kings 11 43; 14 31; 15 8,24 II Kings 8 16,24; 11 2; 12 22; 14 21; 15 32, 38; 18 1; 20 21; 21 18, 26; 23 30,34; 24 6,17.	Highly abridged	Numerous Authors; e.g. Ahijah, Iddo, Hanani, Elisha, Jonah, Isaiah, Hozai, Huldah, Jeremiah, Baruch
3 17–4 23	—		

C. Other Tribes

4 24	Gen. 46 10; Ex. 6 15; Num. 26 12,13	Approximately identical	Jacob, Moses
4 25–27	—		
4 28–33	Josh. 19 2–8	Approximately identical	Joshua
4 34–5 2	—		
5 3	Gen. 46 8,9; Ex. 6 14; Num. 26 5,6	Identical	Jacob, Moses
5 4–26	—		
5 27–30	Gen. 46 11; Ex. 6 16,18, 20,23,25;	Approximately identical	Jacob, Moses

Table 15.3.2 (continued)

General Topic	Passage in I Chronicles	Corresponding Passages in the Bible	Extent of Duplication by Passage in Chronicles	Probable Original Author(s)
	5 31–41	Num. 3 2,17,19; 26 57–60.		
	6 1–4	—		
	6 5–10, 14–17, 21–38	Ex. 6 16-19; Num. 3 17–20	Essentially identical	Moses
	6 11–13, 18–20	I Sam. 1 1; 8 2	With variations	Samuel
	6 39–66	Josh. 21 10–19, 5–9, 20–39	Abridged	Joshua
	7 1,6,13, 30,31	Gen. 46 13,17,21,23; Num. 26 23,24,29,35,44,45	Approximately identical	Jacob, Moses
	7 2–5,7–12, 14–29,32–40	—		
	8 1–5	Gen. 46 21; Num. 26 38–40	Approximately identical	Jacob, Moses
	8 6–32	—		
	8 33–34	I Sam. 14 49,51; II Sam. 2 8; 4 4; 9 12	With variations	Samuel, Nathan
	8 35–40	—		

DANIEL, EZRA-NEHEMIAH AND CHRONICLES 347

D. Post-Exilic	9 1-17	Neh. 11 3-19	With variations	Nehemiah
	9 18-38	–		
E. Tribe of Benjamin	9 39-40	I Sam. 14 49,51; II Sam. 2 8; 4 4; 9 12	With variations	Samuel, Nathan
	9 41-44	–		
II. United Monarchy				
A. Saul	10 1-12	I Sam. 31 1-13	Essentially identical	Gad
	10 13-14	–		
B. David	11 1-9	II Sam. 5 1-3, 6-10	Approximately identical	Nathan
	11 10-41	II Sam. 23 8-39	Approximately identical	Nathan
	11 42-12 40	–		
	13 1-5	II Sam. 6 1	Expanded	Nathan
	13 6-14	II Sam. 6 2-11	Approximately identical	Nathan
	14 1-16	II Sam. 5 11-25	Essentially identical	Nathan
	14 17-15 24	–		The Levites
	15 25-16 3	II Sam. 6 12-19	Approximately identical	Nathan
	16 4-7	–	–	Asaph
	16 8-22	Psalms 105 1-15	Essentially identical	Asaph and his brethren
	16 23-33	Psalms 96 1-13	Essentially identical	Asaph and his brethren
	16 34-36	Psalms 106 47,48; 107 1	Essentially identical	Asaph and his brethren
	16 37-42	–	–	Asaph
	16 43	II Sam. 6 19-20	Essentially identical	Nathan

Table 1.3.2 (continued)

General Topic	Passage in I Chronicles	Corresponding Passages in the Bible	Extent of Duplication by Passage in Chronicles	Probable Original Author(s)
	17 1–18 17	II Sam. 7 1–8 18	Essentially identical	Nathan
	19 1–19	II Sam. 10 1–19	Essentially identical	Nathan
	20 1–3	II Sam. 11 1; 12 26,30,31	Essentially identical	Nathan
	20 4–8	II Sam. 21 18–22	Essentially identical	Gad
	21 1–5	II Sam. 24 1–4,8,9	Approximately identical	Gad
	21 6–7			
	21 8–27	II Sam. 24 10–25	Approximately identical	Gad
	21 28–29 26			The Levites
	29 27	I Kings 2 11	Essentially identical	Nathan
	29 28–30			
C. Solomon				
	II 1 1–2			
	1 3	I Kings 3 4	With variations	Nathan
	1 4–6			
	1 7–13	I Kings 3 5–15	With variations	Nathan
	1 14–17	I Kings 10 26–29	Essentially identical	Nathan
	1 18	I Kings 7 1	With variations	Nathan
	2 1	I Kings 5 29,30	Approximately identical	Nathan
	2 2–17	I Kings 5 16–30; 7 14	Significant variations	(Nathan)
	3 1–4	I Kings 6 1–3	With variations	Nathan

DANIEL, EZRA-NEHEMIAH AND CHRONICLES 349

3 5,7	I Kings 6 21,22	With variations	Nathan
3 6,8,9		With variations	Nathan
3 10–13	I Kings 6 23–28		
3 14	—	Abridged with variations	Nathan
3 15–17	I Kings 6 15–21		
4 1		Essentially identical	Nathan
4 2–5	I Kings 7 23–26	With variations	Nathan
4 6–7	I Kings 7 38,39,49		
4 8–9	—	Approximately identical	Nathan
4 10–5 11	I Kings 7 39–8 10	—	The Levites
5 11–13	—	Essentially identical	Nathan
5 14–6 12	I Kings 8 11–22		
6 13	—	Essentially identical	Nathan
6 14–39	I Kings 8 23–50		
6 40	—	Approximately identical	—
6 41,42	Psalms 132 8–10		
7 1–3,6	—	Approximately identical	Nathan
7 4,5,7–12	I Kings 8 62–9 3		
7 13–15	—	Essentially identical	Nathan
7 16–8 1	I Kings 9 3–6		
8 2,3	—	Approximately identical	Nathan
8 4–13	I Kings 9 17–25	—	The Levites
8 14–16	—	Essentially identical	Nathan
8 17–9 24	I Kings 9 26–10 25		

Table 15.3.2 (continued)

General Topic	Passage in II Chronicles	Corresponding Passages in the Bible	Extent of Duplication by Passage in Chronicles	Probable Original Author(s)
	9 25–28	I Kings 10 26–28; 5 1,6	Approximately identical	Nathan
	9 29	—		
	9 30–31	I Kings 11 42,43	Essentially identical	Ahijah
III. Kingdom of Judah				
A. Rehoboam				
	10 1–11 4	I Kings 12 1–19,21–24	Essentially identical	Iddo, Shemaiah
	11 5–12 1	—		
	12 2	I Kings 14 25	Essentially identical	Iddo
	12 3–8,12,15	—		Shemaiah
	12 9–11	I Kings 14 26–28	Essentially identical	Iddo
	12 13–14	I Kings 14 21–22	Approximately identical	Iddo
	12 15–16	I Kings 14 30–31	Essentially identical	Iddo
B. Abijah (Abijam)				
	13 1–2	I Kings 15 1,2,7	Approximately identical	Iddo
	13 3–22	—		
	13 23	I Kings 15 8	Approximately identical	Iddo
C. Asa				
	14 1	I Kings 15 11	Approximately identical	Hanani
	14 2–15 15	—		Azariah son of Oded
	15 16–16 6	I Kings 15 13–22	Approximately identical	Hanani
	16 7–11	—		Hanani

D. Jehoshaphat	16 12–14	I Kings 15 23,24	With variations	Hanani
	17 1	I Kings 15 24	Approximately identical	Hanani
	17 2–18 1	—		
	18 2–3	I Kings 22 2–4	With variations	Micaiah
	18 4–34	I Kings 22 5–35	Essentially identical	Micaiah
	19 1–11	—		Jehu son of Hanani
	20 1–30,34	—		Jahaziel son of Zechariah
	20 31–33	I Kings 22 41–44	Approximately identical	Elijah
	20 35–37	I Kings 22 49–50	Significant variations	(Elijah) Eliezer son of Dodavahu
E. Jehoram	21 1	I Kings 22 51	Essentially identical	Elijah
	21 2–4	—		
	21 5–10	II Kings 8 17–22	Approximately identical	Elisha (Elijah)
	21 11–20	—		
F. Ahaziah	22 1–6	II Kings 8 25–29	With variations	Elisha
	22 7–9	II Kings 8 29; 9 2,6–8,16, 21,27,28; 10 13,14	Abridged with variations	Elisha
G. Athaliah	22 10–23 21	II Kings 11 1–20	Approximately identical, with additions	Elisha
H. Jehoash	24 1–2	II Kings 12 1–3	Essentially identical	Elisha

Table 15.3.2 (continued)

General Topic	Passage in II Chronicles	Corresponding Passages in the Bible	Extent of Duplication by Passage in Chronicles	Probable Original Author(s)
I. Amaziah	24 3	—		
	24 4–14	II Kings 12 5–17	With variations	Elisha
	24 15–22	—		
	24 23–27	II Kings 12 18,19,2?,,22	With variations	Elisha
	24 27	—		
	25 1–4,11	II Kings 14 2–7	Approximately identical	Jonah
	25 5–10, 12–16,26	—		
	25 17–25, 27, 28	II Kings 14 8–14,17,19,20	Approximately identical	Jonah
J. Azariah (Uzziah)	26 1–4	II Kings 14 21–22; 15 2,3	Essentially identical	Jonah, Isaiah Zechariah, the visionary
	26 5–20	—		Azariah, the priest
	26 20–21,23	II Kings 15 5,7	Approximately identical	Isaiah
K. Jotham	27 1–3,8	II Kings 15 33–35	Approximately identical	Isaiah
	27 4–7	—		
	27 9	II Kings 15 38	Essentially identical	Isaiah

DANIEL, EZRA-NEHEMIAH AND CHRONICLES 353

L. Ahaz	28 1–4	II Kings 16 2–4	Approximately identical	Isaiah
	28 5–6	II Kings 16 5–6	With variations	Isaiah
	28 7–15,17–19,25–26	—	—	Oded, the prophet
	28 16,20–21	II Kings 16 7–9	With variations	Isaiah
	28 22–24	II Kings 16 10–18	Abridged	Isaiah
	28 27	II Kings 16 20	Approximately identical	Isaiah
M. Hezekiah	29 1,2	II Kings 18 1–3	Essentially identical	Isaiah
	29 3–30 27; 31 2–19	—	—	The Levites
	31 1,20–21	II Kings 18 4–7	With variations	Isaiah
	32 1,9–23	II Kings 18 13,17–19 36	Abridged with variations	(Isaiah)
	32 2–8,27–32	—	—	
	32 24–26	II Kings 20 1–11	Abridged with variations	Isaiah
	32 33	II Kings 20 21	Approximately identical	Isaiah
N. Manasseh	33 1–10,20	II Kings 21 1–10,18	Essentially identical	Hozai
	33 11–19	—	—	
O. Amon	33 21–25	II Kings 21 19–24	With variations	Hozai
P. Josiah	34 1–2	II Kings 22 1–2	Essentially identical	Huldah

Table 15.3.2 (continued)

General Topic	Passage in II Chronicles	Corresponding Passages in the Bible	Extent of Duplication by Passage in Chronicles	Probable Original Author(s)
	34 3–7,13–14,32–33	—	Approximately identical	Huldah
	34 8–12, 15–32	II Kings 22 3–7,15–23 3	Expanded	Huldah
	35 1–19, 20–24	II Kings 23 21–23,29–30		
	35 25–27	—		
Q. Jehoahaz	36 1–4	II Kings 23 30–31,33–34	Approximately identical	Huldah, Jeremiah
R. Jehoiakim	36 5–8	II Kings 23 36–24 6	Abridged with variations	Jeremiah
S. Jehoiachin	36 9–10	II Kings 24 8–17	Abridged	Baruch
T. Zedekiah	36 11–13, 17–20	II Kings 24 18–25 21	Abridged with variations	Baruch, Zerubbabel
	36 14–16,21	—		Zerubbabel
	36 22–23	Ezra 1 1–3	Essentially identical	Zerubbabel

duplicated in Samuel and Kings, and vice versa, the logical requirements to obtain a continuity of topics are not the same for the different books, resulting in the occasional reversal of the order of the identical passages.

Slight variations in wording in the different books between passages which are otherwise identical may have arisen in several ways. Firstly, the original authors may have varied their wording and emphasis slightly in order to better fit into the purposes of the books; i.e. they may have written two slightly variant accounts. Secondly, the editors of the books (Zerubbabel and Nehemiah for Chronicles; Baruch for Kings) may have modified for clarity some of the wordings and spellings written by others. Thirdly, there may have occasionally been different eyewitness accounts of certain details. To preserve the variant information, one description is presented in Chronicles and a slightly modified description in the parallel account in Kings or Samuels. This third reason is particularly applicable in explaining many of the numerous cases of variant numbers between Chronicles and other parallel passages (Table 15.3.3). For example, one observer may have estimated 7,000 chariot-drivers (I Chr. **19** 18) while a second observer only estimated 700 chariot-drivers (II Sam. **10** 18). In other cases, the different numbers may be reconciled by assuming that they refer to slightly different antecedents. For example, the 600 shekels (I Chr. **21** 25) refer to the gold, and the fifty shekels (II Sam. **24** 24) refer to the silver, that were part of the purchase price for the threshing-floor of Araunah.

Table 15.3.3
Variant Numbers in Parallel Accounts

Reference in Chronicles	Number	Reference of Parallel Account	Number
I **11** 11	300 dead	II Sam. **23** 8	800 dead
I **19** 18	7,000 chariot-drivers	II Sam. **10** 18	700 chariot-drivers
I **21** 5	1,100,000 men 470,000 men	II Sam. **24** 9	800,000 men 500,000 men
I **21** 12	3 years	II Sam. **24** 13	7 years
I **21** 25	600 shekels	II Sam. **24** 24	50 shekels
II **2** 1	3,600 men	I Kings **5** 30	3,300 men
II **4** 5	3,000 baths	I Kings **7** 26	2,000 baths
II **8** 10	250 men	I Kings **9** 23	550 men
II **8** 18	450 talents	I Kings **9** 28	420 talents
II **9** 25	4,000 stalls	I Kings **5** 6	40,000 stalls
II **22** 2	42 years old	II Kings **8** 26	22 years old
II **36** 9	8 years old	II Kings **24** 8	18 years old

PART III

THE REALITY OF PROPHECY

All too often the disbelief in the reality of prophecy has affected the reasoning of Biblical critics. In cases where prophetic passages clearly describe known historical events, the critics claim that the passages were composed after the event, or shortly before the event when the situation clearly pointed to the final outcome. As a result of this approach, it is claimed that many Biblical books were written much after the date specified in the text. For example, the Book of Daniel is often relegated to the time of about 165 B.C.E. because it is recognized that the eleventh chapter gives a precise description of the history of the Seleucid and Ptolemaic empires until at least that time. The critics completely disregard the stated time for the prophecy as the third year of Cyrus (Dan. 10 1), i.e., 536 B.C.E., and the fact that reference was made to the Book of Daniel at the time of Alexander the Great in 332 B.C.E.[1]

In other cases it often is more difficult for the critics to postpone the statement of a prophecy for hundreds of years, and they assume that the historical situation was such that the result of the impending event could easily be predicted. This, of course, is completely contrary to reality. People cannot through logic predict events even a month in advance. For example, who would have predicted the battles of the Six-Day War in June 5–10, 1967 C.E., between Israel and the Arab countries, a month before the fighting, when no clear signs of the impending confrontation were apparent before May 15, 1967?[2]

It is difficult, if not impossible, at the present time to establish the reality of prophetic passages from descriptions of events which occurred 2,500 or more years ago. How can we with certainty establish today that the predictions were made before the occurrence of the events, especially if we realize that, other than the Bible, the main records of those times are rare inscriptions on tablets and stones?

Instead, the approach here taken to prove the reality of prophecy is to show that there are many accurate predictions in the Bible of happenings which occurred, or will occur, long after completion of the Bible. No one could logically say that Biblical descriptions of the history of Mohammad, World War I, World War II, and events of the modern State of Israel could have been written after the event! Accurate Biblical descriptions of these times, as are contained in the Book of Daniel, establish the truth of prophecy. The argument can then be extended to the other prophecies about events which happened about 2,500 years ago, that they are also true prophecies.

There are two main divisions to this Part III concerning the reality of prophecy. The first division is a very detailed explanation of Chapters 2, and 7 to 12 of the Book of Daniel, where many predictions of post-Biblical events are found. Numerous passages which have heretofore never been satisfactorily explained are clarified by literal interpretation. The straightforwardness of the interpretation will verify its basic correctness. In the Book of Daniel there are clear and dated prophecies about Mohammad, World War I, World War II, the United Nations, and establishment of the State of Israel.

The second division will explain the prophetic passages throughout the Bible concerned with events preceding and following "the great and terrifying day of God," which culminate in the construction of the Third Temple. This division will conclude with a summary of the events during the Messianic era based on all the relevant Biblical passages, and the probable dates for the future events. Many of these predictions based on Biblical prophecies will be verified within the next few years, and will be completely carried out by 1996 C.E. More details on these points will unfold as the interpretations are presented.

Chapter Sixteen

COMMENTARY ON PROPHETIC CHAPTERS OF THE BOOK OF DANIEL

A detailed introduction to the Book of Daniel has already been presented in Section 15.1 concerning the authorship and organization of the book. Here we will limit the discussion to those points relevant to the interpretation of the prophetic chapters. Chapters which contain prophecies are Chapters 2, and 7 through 12.

The commentary here presented has been based on the assumption that each phrase has a very precise meaning, and that the understanding of the meaning is dependent on discovering the historical event which is being described. Once the correct historical reference is known, an almost perfect explanation of the text can be achieved.

To help in identifying the historical reference, the text offers numerous time-spans. In several cases these time-spans are clearly stated, such as 2,300 (8 14), 1,290 (12 11), and 1,335 (12 12). In the majority of cases, however, the time-spans are expressed by key words such as ימים (days), שנים (years), and זמן (time). A list of these key words and the durations intended are tabulated in Table 16.0.1. It should be noted that all these key words when used elsewhere in the Bible indicate a somewhat indefinite time period, but when used in the Book of Daniel stand for a very precise duration. Awareness of the time periods meant by these key words enables the clarification of numerous, otherwise inexplicable, passages. It should be furthermore noted that all time-spans, whether expressed in words or numbers, are given in units of years. The only exceptions occur in Chapter 10 and once in Chapter 8 where a few of the key words are given in units of days.

Each place where the key words have been used in the prophetic chapters, they have been interpreted according to the time-spans listed in Table 16.0.1. The specified durations for these key words have been arrived at based on historical correlations given in the text; they can, to some extent, be substantiated from the time lengths meant by the words when used in their usual sense. These substantiations are also presented in the Table.

It should be noted that the Hebrew word עתים, which is the plural of עת, has been reserved for indicating indefinite time periods (see Dan. 9 25; 11 6,13,14). In contrast, the word עת indicates the definite time-span of 25 years.

Another unique feature of the Book of Daniel is the mention of names of angels

Table 16.0.1
Words Used for Specific Time Spans

Hebrew Word	Literal Meaning	Time-Span (Years)	Reason for this Usage of the Hebrew Word	Where So Used in Book of Daniel
זמן	period (night watch; see on 2 16)	1,000	1,000 years is like a night watch in the eyes of God (Ps. 90 4)	7 12
עדן	year (as used in 4 13,20,22,29)	365	365 days in a solar year	7 12,25
שבעים עלם (עלמיא)	years forever (Jubilee year; see Rashi on Deut. 15 17; I Sam. 1 22)	52 50	52 weeks in a solar year 50 years in a Jubilee cycle	11 6,8,13 7 18
שבוע, שבעים	weeks	*49	square of 7; compare שבוע to רבוע, meaning a square.	9 24–27; (Also see 10 2,3)
מועד	festival time	29	29 days in a lunar month	8 19; 11 27,29,35; 12 7
עת	time (a complete day)	25	the beginning of the 25th hour, as used in the expression מעת-לעת	8 17; 9 21; 11 24,35,40; 12 1,4,9,11;
ימים	days	*6	6 workdays in a week	2 28; 4 31; 8 26; 10 14; 11 20,33; 12 11,12; (Also see 8 27; 10 2,3)

* Sometimes used for days rather than years

PROPHETIC CHAPTERS OF THE BOOK OF DANIEL

who represent specific countries. In some instances the country represented by the angel is clearly stated, as is the case for the Prince of the Kingdom of Persia (**10** 13), the Prince of Greece (**10** 20), and Michael the Prince of the Jews (**10** 21; **12** 1). In other instances, the country represented must be assumed based on available information. Gabriel (**8** 16; **9** 21) is the chief angel of the Arabian empire, the man clothed in linen (**10** 5; **12** 6) represents Babylonia, and the two others (**12** 5) are the angels of Germany and England. Knowledge of the countries represented by the angels is required for proper interpretation of the text.

In interpreting the Book of Daniel, the original Hebrew text is given, as well as an English translation. In most cases the translation is based on both the translation issued in 1917 by the Jewish Publication Society of America and that given in *The New English Bible,* Oxford University Press, 1970. However, significant modifications of these translations have been made, according to the requirements of the present commentary. Therefore the translation is largely the original work of the author.

16.1 CHAPTER 2 OF DANIEL

In this second chapter is recounted how Daniel received his first revelation which enabled him to describe and explain the dream of King Nebuchadnezzar. The dream portrays the rise of four successive great nations, followed by the military supremacy of the State of Israel. In many details the prophecy is similar to that described in Chapter 7. In fact, identification of the nations that are sketchily described in this chapter can be obtained by analogy to the more complete description contained in Chapter 7. It should be noted that Rome is *not* considered among the four great nations, neither here nor in subsequent prophecies. This may be because Rome is considered as an outgrowth of Greece. The Roman Empire was thoroughly permeated with Greek civilization, and there were such obvious similarities between the two as kinship of language*, customs, dress, religion, and literature[1].

Numerous details, not particularly relevant to the understanding of the prophecy, are contained within the present chapter, and therefore only selected sentences will be interpreted. One main theory used in the interpretation is that the main events of the second chapter occurred within one night. As a result the word זמן (**2** 16) is used to mean a night watch (see Table 16.0.1).

1. ובשנת שתים למלכות נבוכדנצר חלם נבכדנצר חלמות, ותתפעם
רוחו ושנתו נהיתה עליו.

    In the second year of his reign Nebuchadnezzar had dreams, and his mind was troubled, and his sleep was still upon him.

    Second year—Nebuchadnezzar reigned from 605 to 562 B.C.E. His second year was 603. This was the third year after Daniel was taken captive in the third

---

* Under the Romans many regions, such as Asia Minor, Syria, Mesopotamia, and Egypt, continued to use Greek.

year of Jehoiakim, 605 (Dan. 1 1) (see Section 6.2). During these three years Daniel had matured (Dan. 1 5), and was considered among the wise men of Babylonia.

His sleep was still upon him — Nebuchadnezzar was not completely awake. This is the first indication that the events of the chapter occurred within a single night.
2–7. Nebuchadnezzar realized that he had forgotten the dream. He immediately called together the wise men of Babylonia and asked them to tell him his dream and explain its content. Otherwise, the wise men would be killed and their houses destroyed. But if they were able to interpret the dream they would receive rewards and great honor. The wise men protested that the king must first tell them the dream before they can give an interpretation.

8. ענה מלכא ואמר מן יציב ידע אנא די עדנא אנתון זבנין, כל
קבל די חזיתון די אזדא מני מלתא.
The king answered, "It is clear to me that you are trying to gain time, because you see that I have forgotten the contents."

Trying to gain time — It was the very night of the dream. The wise men hoped that the king's attitude would change by the next morning.
9–11. The wise men answered that nobody on earth can tell the king what he wants to know.

12. כל קבל דנה מלכא בנס וקצף שגיא, ואמר להובדה לכל חכימי בבל.
At this the king in a great rage ordered the death of all the wise men of Babylon.

The death of all the wise men — The order to execute the wise men of Babylon was given the very same night.
13–14. Thereupon all the wise men, including Daniel and his companions were sought out to be slain.

15. ענה ואמר לאריוך שליטא די מלכא על מה דתא מהחצפה מן קדם מלכא, אדין מלתא הודע אריוך לדניאל.
Daniel asked Arioch, the king's captain, "Why has his majesty issued such a hasty decree?" Then Arioch explained everything to Daniel.

Hasty decree — Daniel asks, "For what reason has the hasty decree been issued?" Daniel had not even heard of the king's problem which had only arisen a few hours before.

16. ודניאל על ובעה מן מלכא, די זמן ינתן לה ופשרא להחויה למלכא.
Then Daniel went and requested from the king that he give him time (זמן), and he would tell the interpretation to the king.

Time—Up to this point about one-third of the night had passed. As it subsequently turns out, the amount of time which Daniel needed was another third of the night, i.e., a night watch.

17–18. Daniel then went home, and he and his companions prayed to God that the secret be revealed so they would not be slain.

19. אדין לדניאל בחזוא די ליליא רזא גלי, אדין דניאל ברך לא׳ שמיא.

> Then the secret was revealed to Daniel in a vision of the night. Then Daniel blessed the God of heaven.

Vision of the night—The secret was revealed to Daniel in the middle of the night, probably during the second third of the night.

20–24. After praising God for helping him, Daniel went and told Arioch not to execute the wise men of Babylon, because he could present the interpretation of the dream to the king.

25. אדין אריוך בהתבהלה הנעל לדניאל קדם מלכא, וכן אמר לה די השכחת גבר מן בני גלותא די יהוד די פשרא למלכא יהודע.

> Then Arioch in astonishment brought Daniel before the king and said to him, "I have found among the Jewish exiles a man who will make known to your majesty the interpretation."

In astonishment—Arioch was amazed at the rapidity with which Daniel claimed he had the answer. It was the third watch of the night when Daniel explained the dream to the king.

26–30. Daniel attributes his ability to reveal the dream and its interpretation to God.

28. ברם איתי א׳ בשמיא גלה רזין והודע למלכא נבוכדנצר מה די להוא באחרית יומיא, חלמא וחזוי ראשך על משכבך דנה הוא.

> There is a God in heaven who reveals secrets, and He has told King Nebuchadnezzar what shall be "in the end of the six years." This is your dream and these the visions as you lay on your bed.

In the end of the six years—The term אחרית יומיא refers to the end of the six-year period between the Six-Day War (1967 C.E.) and the War of Gog (1973 C.E.). The word יומיא means six years as explained in Table 16.0.1. Throughout the entire Bible the term אחרית הימים is used in the above sense (compare Section 18.4).

31–36. Now Daniel describes the dream of Nebuchadnezzar: *As you watched, O king, you saw a great image. This image, huge and dazzling, stood before you, and was fearful to behold. The head of the image was of fine gold, its breast and arms of silver, its belly and hips of copper, its thighs of iron, and its feet part iron and part clay. While you watched, a stone was cut out without the use of hands, and it struck the image on its feet of iron and clay, and shattered them. Then the iron, the clay, the copper, the silver, and the gold were shattered into pieces and were carried away by the wind like chaff from the threshing-floor in summer, and no place was found for them; but the stone which struck the image became a great rock and filled the whole land. That was the dream. We shall now tell your majesty the interpretation.*

37-38. אַנְתְּ מַלְכָּא מֶלֶךְ מַלְכַיָּא, דִּי אֱ' שְׁמַיָּא מַלְכוּתָא חִסְנָא וְתָקְפָּא וִיקָרָא יְהַב לָךְ. וּבְכָל דִּי דָיְרִין בְּנֵי אֲנָשָׁא חֵיוַת בָּרָא וְעוֹף שְׁמַיָּא יְהַב בִּידָךְ וְהַשְׁלְטָךְ בְּכָלְּהוֹן, אנְתְּ הוּא רֵאשָׁה דִּי דַהֲבָא.
You, O king, king of kings, to whom the God of heaven has given a powerful, strong and glorious kingdom; and in whose hands He has placed men, beasts of the field, and birds of the heaven, wherever they dwell, and has made you rule over them all—you are the head of gold.

You are the head of gold—The gold represents the Babylonian empire, which prevailed as a mighty nation from the time when Nabopolasser, King of Babylonia, entrusted the command of the army to his son Nebuchadnezzar in 609. The Babylonian empire lasted until 539 B.C.E. when conquered by Persia (see Section 6.4).

39. וּבָתְרָךְ תְּקוּם מַלְכוּ אָחֳרִי אֲרַע מִנָּךְ, וּמַלְכוּ תְלִיתָאָה אָחֳרִי דִּי נְחָשָׁא דִּי תִשְׁלַט בְּכָל אַרְעָא.
After you, shall arise another kingdom inferior to yours; and yet a third kingdom of copper which shall rule over all the land.

Another kingdom—The silver represents the Persian empire, which under the leadership of Cyrus conquered Babylonia in 539. The greatness of Persia lasted until 331 B.C.E.

A third kingdom of copper—The copper represents the Greek empire, which under the leadership of Alexander the Great conquered Persia in 331.

40. וּמַלְכוּ רְבִיעָאָה תֶּהֱוֵא תַקִּיפָה כְּפַרְזְלָא כָּל קֳבֵל דִּי פַרְזְלָא מְהַדֵּק וְחָשֵׁל כֹּלָּא וּכְפַרְזְלָא דִּי מְרַעַע כָּל אִלֵּין תַּדִּק וְתֵרֹעַ.
And a fourth kingdom shall be as strong as iron; as iron shatters and breaks all things, and as iron crushes all these [kingdoms], it shall shatter and crush.

A fourth kingdom—The iron represents the Arabian empire, which under the leadership of Mohammad began a rise to greatness after about 630 C.E. The dominance of the Islamic movement lasted until after World War I (1918 C.E.), when the Ottoman Empire (an outgrowth of the Arabian empire) was broken up.

As iron crushes—The Arab empire conquered and destroyed many nations but rarely built and created. Thus its nature was dominantly destructive rather than constructive.

41. ודי חזיתא רגליא ואצבעתא מנהין חסף די פחר ומנהין פרזל
מלכו פליגה תהוה ומן נצבתא די פרזלא להוא בה, כל קבל די
חזיתה פרזלא מערב בחסף טינא.
And as you saw the feet and toes were part potter's clay and part iron, it shall become a divided kingdom, but there will be in it of the strength of iron; since you saw iron mixed with common clay.

Part potter's clay and part iron—Preceding and subsequent to World War I (1914–1918) the Ottoman Empire was broken up into many parts. Many small Arab countries, such as Syria, Arabia, Lebanon, Egypt, Iraq, Libya, the Sudan, and Jordan were formed or gained independence at about that time[2].

42. ואצבעת רגליא מנהין פרזל ומנהין חסף, מן קצת מלכותא תהוה
תקיפא ומנה תהוא תבירה.
And as the toes were part iron and part clay, the kingdom shall be partly strong and partly brittle.

Part iron and part clay—Some of these Arab countries, such as Egypt, will be militarily strong, while others, such as Lebanon, will be militarily weak.

43. ודי חזית פרזלא מערב בחסף טינא מתערבין להון בזרע אנשא
ולא להון דבקין דנה עם דנה, הא כדי פרזלא לא מתערב עם
חספא.
And as you saw the iron was mixed with common clay, so shall they mix with each other by intermarriage; but they shall not unite one with the other, just like iron does not mix with clay.

Intermarriage—There will be no restraint among the Arabs for a man from one Arab country marrying a woman from another Arab country.

Shall not unite—The individual Arab countries will not unite to form an Arab empire once again.

44. וביומיהון די מלכיא אנון יקים א' שמיא מלכו די לעלמין לא
תתחבל ומלכותה לעם אחרן לא תשתבק, תדק ותסף כל אלין
מלכותא והיא תקום לעלמיא,
And in the period of these rulers the God of heaven will establish a kingdom which shall never be destroyed, nor shall the kingdom pass to another people; it shall shatter and make an end of all these kingdoms, but it shall itself endure for ever.

The period of these rulers—The nation of Israel will be established in 1948 C.E. during the time of the existence of these many Arab countries.

Never be destroyed—The nation of Israel will last forever, and will not be destroyed nor conquered by another nation.

An end of all these kingdoms—At the time of the War of Gog (about 1973) Israel will destroy the attacking Arab countries.

45. כל קבל די חזית די מטורא אתגזרת אבן די לא בידין והדקת
פרזלא נחשא חספא כספא ודהבא א' רב הודע למלכא מה די
להוא אחרי דנה, ויציב חלמא ומהימן פשרה.
For you saw that a stone was hewn from a mountain, without the use of hands, and shattered iron, copper, clay, silver, and gold. The great God has made known to your majesty what is to be hereafter; and the dream is sure, and the interpretation is reliable.

Stone was hewn from a mountain—The stone represents the initial territory of the nation of Israel. The territory was much smaller than the theoretical Biblical boundaries, represented by the mountain.

Without the use of hands—The territory of Israel was designated in 1947, by the United Nations. No military might was involved in cutting up the larger territory of Palestine, and designating only a small portion for Israel. In Sentence 35 it is also stated that the stone that struck the image will become a great mountain and fill the whole land. Implied by the statement is that after the War of Gog, Israel will gain the theoretical Biblical boundaries, and thereby fill the whole land.

Shattered iron, copper, clay, silver and gold—At the time of the War of Gog Israel will be attacked by many nations including the Arab nations (iron and clay), Greece (copper), Iran or Persia (silver), and Iraq or Babylon (gold). All these attacking nations will be destroyed by Israel.

46–49. Then Nebuchadnezzar stated that the God of Daniel was a great God in that He was able to reveal the secrets. Daniel was given many rich gifts; and was made ruler over the whole province of Babylon, and was made the chief prefect over all the wise men. In addition, the companions of Daniel were put in charge of the administration of the province of Babylon.

16.2 CHAPTER 7 OF DANIEL

Daniel experienced a dream in which he saw four different beasts coming out of the Mediterranean Sea. These four beasts represented four countries which were successively to gain control over the territory of Israel. Afterwards the nation of Israel would arise, which is to last forever, and would acquire greatness among the nations of the world.

The beasts as portrayed in this chapter have a triple significance. The type of animal specifies the country. The animal itself symbolizes the king or ruler of the country. The number of parts of the most outstanding feature of the animal represents the number of tribes or groups that aided the ruler in his rise to greatness. Details on these points are given in the comments on the text.

It should be realized that the symbolisms used in different chapters, are not the same. Thus the significance of the animals in this chapter is different from that for the animals described in Chapter 8.

1. בשנת חדה לבלאשצר מלך בבל דניאל חזה חלם וחזוי ראשה
על משכבה, באדין חלמא כתב ראש מלין אמר.
In the first year of Belshazzar, King of Babylon, Daniel saw a dream, and the visions came while he was on his bed; then he wrote down the dream, and he stated the first part.

First year of Belshazzar—Belshazzar reigned from 552 to 539 B.C.E. (see Table 6.1), and his first year of rule was 552.

On his bed—The first sentence of this chapter, which was written by Daniel in the third person, provides the background for the vision. Daniel states that the vision came to him while in bed.

He stated the first part—The first part of the dream, in particular Sentences 2 through 14, was described in words by Daniel when he recorded what he saw. In contrast, the wording of Sentences 17–18 and 23–27, was stated during the dream by an anonymous angel.

2. ענה דניאל ואמר חזה הוית בחזוי עם ליליא, וארו ארבע רוחי שמיא מגיחן לימא רבא.
Daniel said: I saw at the beginning of the night in my vision, and behold, four winds of the heaven broke forth upon the Mediterranean Sea.

Beginning of the night—The night signifies sad times for Israel. The beginning of the night indicates the beginning of these sad times.

Four winds—The four winds are symbolic of four directions. It will be shown presently that the countries of Babylonia, Persia, Greece, and Arabia are meant. If we consider the relative geographical positions of these countries, we find Babylonia to the north, Persia to the east, Greece to the west, and Arabia to the south. These four countries, each at its own turn, conquered practically all the territory surrounding the Mediterranean Sea.

3. וארבע חיון רברבן סלקן מן ימא, שנין דא מן דא.
And four huge beasts coming up out of the sea, each one different from the others.

Beasts—The subsequent sentences will be interpreted on the basis of the following generalizations:

A. The particular type of beast represents the god of war or symbol of strength of the country. Thus the eagle-winged lion is the god of war of Babylonia; the boar (the animal resembling a bear) is the god of war of Persia; the small-winged leopard corresponds to the sphinx, the god of war of Greece; and the ferocious fourth animal corresponds to the unicorn, the symbol of strength of the Moslem countries. The type of animal therefore indicates the specific country being considered.

B. The animal itself refers to the king or ruler of the country. The lion stands for Nebuchadnezzar, King of Babylon; the boar for Cyrus, King of Persia; and the leopard for Alexander the Great, King of Macedon and head of the Greek empire. However, an exception occurs in the case of the fourth animal. The small horn, rather than the animal itself, stands for Mohammad, the main leader of the Arabian empire. This exception is specifically stated in Sentence 23.

C. The number of parts of the most outstanding features of the animals represents the number of groups that aided the leader in his rise to greatness. Thus, the one set of eagle wings on the lion corresponds to the Chaldean people, of the Babylonian empire; the three tusks of the boar represent the three Persian tribes that participated in the uprising of Cyrus against the Medes; the four bird-like wings on the leopard stand for the four groups that assisted Alexander in his conquest of Thebes; and the ten horns on the unicorn correspond to the rulers of the ten Arab tribes around the city of Medina who signed a treaty with Mohammad.

4. קדמיתא כאריה וגפין די נשר לה, חזה הוית עד די מריטו גפה ונטילת מן ארעה ועל רגלין כאנש הקימת, ולבב אנש יהיב לה.
The first was like a lion, and had eagle's wings. I watched until its wings were plucked off, and it was taken away from the land, and made to stand on two feet as a man, and the heart of a man was given to it.

A lion, and had eagle's wings—The idol Nergal of Babylonia and Assyria was a war god. Nergal's emblem was the human-headed and *eagle-winged lion*, which is usually seen as it were on guard at the entrance of royal palaces[3].

Like a lion—The lion represents Nebuchadnezzar, King of Babylon (605–562).

Eagle's wings—The one set of eagle's wings corresponds to the Chaldeans, who were the dominant tribe in Babylonia (compare Ez. 23 23).

Its wings were plucked off—The control of the Bablonian people was taken away from Nebuchadnezzar during the seven years when he acted like an animal (Dan. 4; 5 18–21).

Taken away from the land—Nebuchadnezzar was removed from control of the country during his seven-year sickness.

Stand on two feet as a man and the heart of a man—After the seven years Nebuchadnezzar regained his sanity. Once again he walked as a man and acquired a human heart. No longer did he have his previous arrogance.

5. וארו חיוה אחרי תנינה דמיה לדב ולשטר חד הקמת ותלת עלעין בפמה בין שנה, וכן אמרין לה קומי אכלי בשר שגיא.
And behold another, a second beast which resembled a bear. It was set up on one side, and it had three tusks in its mouth between its teeth. They said thus to it, "Arise, devour much flesh."

Resembled a bear—In many respects, the wild boar resembles a bear. A *boar* is a type of wild pig with coarse, grayish-black hair. It has powerful *tusks* which project from the lower jaw, often extending two or three inches beyond the lip. The boar is capable of killing a man or another animal with its *teeth*[4]. The

Persian deity Verethraghna, god of war, comes in many shapes, one of them being the wild boar[5]. The boar represents Cyrus, King of Persia (559–530).

Set up on one side—Cyrus originally was King of Anshan, a Persian city, subservient to the Median empire. In 553 he began a sucessful revolt which led to his being called king of the Persians[6]. Thus, Cyrus started as ruler of Persia, and later became ruler of both Persia and Media.

Three tusks—In the uprising of Cyrus against the Medes only three of the Persian tribes participated—the Pasargades, Maraphians, and Maspians. It was only after the victory that the whole people became united[7,8].

Devour much flesh—Cyrus eventually conquered Babylonia, Lydia, and other countries[8].

6. באתר דנה חזה חוית וארו אחרי כנמר ולה גפין ארבע די עוף על גבה, וארבעה ראשין לחיותא ושלטן יהיב לה.

After this I watched, and behold another like a leopard, with four bird's wings on its back; the beast had four heads, and a ruler was given to it.

After this—The long pause which occurred in the dream indicates a large time-gap between the events of this and the previous sentence. The previous sentence referred to events up to 530 B.C.E. This sentence refers to happenings about 200 years later, after 336 B.C.E.

Like a leopard with four bird's wings—In Greek mythology the most famous sphinx was that at Thebes, and had the face of a woman, the body of a *lion* and the wings of a *bird*. A falcon-headed sphinx is occasionally found in sculptures representing the king as the war-god[9]. It should be noted that the text mentions a leopard rather than a lion to differentiate this beast from the lion mentioned in Sentence 4.

Like a leopard—The leopard represents Alexander the Great, King of Macedon (336–323).

Four bird's wings—Four groups, the Macedonians, Plataeans, Thespians, and Orchomenians, aided Alexander in his conquest of Thebes. This conquest resulted in the unification of Greece, and the beginning of the rise of Alexander.

Four heads and a ruler—After the death of Alexander the Great, the succession of rulers was arranged as follows: Philip Arrhidacus, who was at Babylon, was proclaimed king. At the same time four regents were appointed—Antipater and Craterus in Europe, Perdiccas and Leonnatus (for whom Meleager was soon substituted) in Asia[10].

7. באתר דנה חזה הוית בחזוי ליליא וארו חיוה רביעאה דחילה ואימתני ותקיפא יתירה ושנין די פרזל לה רברבן אכלה ומדקה ושארא ברגלה רפסה, והיא משניה מן כל חיותא די קדמה וקרנין עשר לה.

After this I saw in the visions of the night, and behold a fourth beast, dreadful and terrifying, and exceedingly strong, with great iron teeth. It devoured and crunched, and trampled the residue with its feet. It differed from all the beasts which preceded it, and it had ten horns.

After this—The pause in the dream again indicates a large time-gap. The previous sentence referred to events up to about 322 B.C.E. This sentence refers to happenings about 940 years later, after 620 C.E.

Visions of the night—These visions were observed during the middle or second third of the night. The beginning of the night was mentioned in Sentence 2, while the end of the night is indicated in Sentence 13. The extended night time is symbolic of a continuation of the sad period for Israel.

Fourth beast, dreadful ....—The fourth beast corresponds to the unicorn, which was regarded as the emblem of strength among the Persians and ancient Egyptians[11]. As early as the thirteenth century C.E. the unicorn is found drawn and described in Moslem literature[12], and probably was adapted from the highly developed art of the conquered nations of Persia and Egypt[13]. The unicorn is a fabulous beast of great strength and fierceness, usually having the head and body of a horse, the hind legs of an antelope, the tail of a lion, and as its chief feature a long sharp twisted *horn* set in the middle of its forehead[14]. The unicorn was described as fighting with its mouth and heels; with the mouth *biting* like a lion, and with the heels *kicking* like a horse[15].

Fourth beast—The fourth beast represents the Arabian empire, rather than a particular ruler, as is specified in Sentence 23.

Ten horns—The horns represent the rulers of the ten Arabian tribes around the city of Medina, who supported Mohammad's rise to greatness. See comments on Sentence 24 for further details.

8. משתכל הוית בקרניא ואלו קרן אחרי זעירה סלקת ביניהן ותלת
מן קרניא קדמיתא אתעקרה מן קדמה, ואלו עינין כעיני אנשא
בקרנא דא ופם ממלל רברבן.

I was observing the horns, and behold, another horn, a little one, was springing up among them, and three of the first horns were uprooted from in front of it; and behold in this horn were eyes like the eyes of a man, and a mouth that spoke great things.

Another horn—The little horn represents Mohammad, who originally led a small group.

Three of the first horns were uprooted—The three Jewish tribes among the ten tribes were destroyed.

Eyes like the eyes of a man, and a mouth—The leader of the small group, Mohammad, had human eyes, and yet spoke marvelous things, such as a new religion and new laws. See comments on Sentences 24 and 25 for further details.

9. חזה הוית עד די כרסון רמיו ועתיק יומין יתב, לבושה כתלג חור ושער ראשה כעמר נקא, כרסיה שביבין די נור גלגלוהי נור דלק.

I beheld, until thrones were set in place, and one that was ancient of days took his seat, his robe was white as snow and the hair of his head like cleanest wool. His throne was fiery flames and its wheels burning fire.

Ancient of days—The Ancient of days represents God, who sits in judgment. A similar representation occurs in Ez. 1 26–28, where God is pictured as a man sitting on a throne, with fire all around.

10. נהר די נור נגד ונפק מן קדמוהי אלף אלפים ישמשונה ורבו רבבן קדמוהי יקומון דינא יתב וספרין פתיחו.

A fiery river flowed and came forth from before him; a thousand thousands served him, and ten thousand times ten thousand stood before him. The judgment was set, and the books were opened.

Thousand thousands—The myriads of persons represent the angels who serve God.

Judgment—God is here pictured as sitting in judgment over the four beasts.

11. חזה הוית באדין מן קל מליא רברבתא די קרנא ממללא, חזה הוית עד די קטילת חיותא והובד גשמה ויהיבת ליקדת אשא.

I was watching at that time because of the sound of the great words which the horn spoke; I watched until the beast was killed and its body destroyed, and it was given to the flames.

Beast was killed—The complete destruction of the fourth beast corresponds to the destruction of the Arab nations by Israel at the time of the War of Gog (1973).

12. ושאר חיותא העדיו שלטנהון, וארכה בחיין יהיבת להון עד זמן ועדן.

And the dominion of the other beasts was taken away; and a length of life of 1,365 years was given to them.

Dominion of the other beasts—The other three empires, namely those of Babylon, Persia and Greece, would be disbanded.

Length of life of 1,365 years—As presented in Table 16.0.1 זמן is 1,000 years, and עדן is 365 years. Thus זמן ועדן is 1,365 years. Notice that the Hebrew letter *vav*, meaning "and", indicates addition.

The 1,365 years refers to the period from the rise of the Babylonian-Assyrian empire until the destruction of the country of Persia. In 729 B.C.E. Tiglath-Pileser III of Assyria conquered the city of Babylon and formed the Assyrian-Babylonian empire, in which Assyria was the dominant country. Eventually, the historical situation changed, and Babylonia under the rulership of Nabopolassar became the dominant nation[16]. It was Nebuchadnezzar, the son of Nabopolassar, who conquered the Jewish nation in 586.

The last of the three nations to be completely destroyed was Persia. In 637 C.E. Omar, head of the Arabian empire, conquered the Persian army and thereby ended the lives of the three other nations.[17]

Thus, from 729 B.C.E.
until 637 C.E.
<u>   </u>
1366
− 1 (no year zero in the dating system)
<u>   </u>
1365 years.

13. חזה הוית בחזוי ליליא וארו עם ענני שמיא כבר אנש אתה הוא,
ועד עתיק יומיא מטה וקדמוהי הקרבוהי.

I saw in the visions of the night, and behold with the clouds of heaven a man had already come. And he approached the Ancient of days, and he was brought near before Him.

Visions of the night—This was the last third of the night.

Clouds of heaven—The appearance of clouds indicates the coming of dawn, and the end of the sad times for Israel.

Man—The man is, in a sense, a type of beast, and therefore represents a nation, rather than a ruler. The man stands for the nation of Israel.

Already come—The nation of Israel, which was established in 1948, was already in existence before the destruction of the Arab countries (in 1973).

Approached the Ancient of days—Initially, when established, the nation of Israel will not be religious. However, before the War of Gog the people will become religious, and they will approach God.

Brought near before Him—God will reciprocate, and will support the State of Israel because of the people's belief in Him.

14. ולה יהב שלטן ויקר ומלכו, וכל עממיא אמיא ולשניא לה יפלחון,
שלטנה שלטן עלם די לא יעדה ומלכותה די לא תתחבל.

And dominion, glory, and kingdom were given to him; and all peoples, nations and languages will serve him. His dominion is an everlasting dominion, and his kingdom shall not be destroyed.

Dominion, glory etc.—After the War of Gog the nation of Israel will attain the theoretical Biblical boundaries, and will eventually be recognized as the greatest nation.

Everlasting—The nation of Israel will last forever and will never be destroyed.

15. אתכרית רוחי אנה דניאל בגוא נדנה, וחזוי ראשי יבהלנני.

As for me Daniel, my spirit was pained in the midst of my body, and the visions bewildered me.

16. קרבת על חד מן קאמיא ויציבא אבעא מנה על כל דנה, ואמר
לי ופשר מליא יהודענני.

> I approached one of those who stood there, and asked him the truth concerning all this. And he told me, and explained the meaning of the words.

One of those who stood there—Daniel approached one of the angels who stood before God.

17. אלין חיותא רברבתא די אנין ארבע, ארבעה מלכין יקומון מן ארעא.

> These great beasts, which are four, represent four kings that shall arise from the land.

Four kings—The four beasts represent the kings, and not the kingdoms or countries. Only when the beast is used to designate the type of animal does it represent the country.

18. ויקבלון מלכותא קדישי עליונין, ויחסנון מלכותא עד עלמא ועד
עלם עלמיא.

> And will receive the kingdom of the Holy Ones of the Most High, and will inherit the kingdom for 50 years and for 2,500 years.

Holy Ones of the Most High—The Hebrew word עליונין, meaning "Most High," refers to the angels. In particular, the Talmud (see e.g., *Sanhedrin* 20b, *Ketubot* 104a) uses the word עליונין to represent angels. The Holy Ones of the angels are those angels, such as Michael (Dan. 12 1), that preside over the Jewish people. The "kingdom of the Holy Ones of the angels" refers to the land of Israel. Similarly the "people of the Holy Ones of the angels," as used in Sentence 27, refers to the Jewish people.

For 50 years and for 2,500 years—The word עלמא, as explained in Table 16.0.1, stands for 50 years. The phrase עלם עלמיא stands for 50 times 50 or 2,500 years. Note that the absence of the Hebrew letter *vav*, meaning "and," between the words עלם and עלמיא indicates that multiplication is to be performed.

Inherit the kingdom for 50 years—The four beasts representing the four rulers Nebuchadnezzar, Cyrus, Alexander, and Omar, will gain control over the land of Israel for a combined total of 50 years. The duration each of these rulers had control over the Jewish land, that is from the time they conquered the territory until their death, is as follows:

Empire	Ruler		Years
Babylonia	Nebuchadnezzar	586–562 B.C.E.	24
Persia	Cyrus	539–529 B.C.E.*	10
Greece	Alexander	331–323 B.C.E.	8
Arabia	Omar	636–644 C.E.	8
		Total	50[18]

*Note that Cyrus died in 529, although he was succeeded by his son Cambyses in 530.

Inherit the kingdom . . . for 2,500 years—The conquests of these four rulers will result in the land of Israel being dominated by the four empires for 2,500 years. In 586 B.C.E. Nebuchadnezzar conquered the Kingdom of Judah, beginning the period of domination. In 1916 C.E. began the attack against the Turkish forces (the outgrowth of the Arabian empire) in Palestine, with the eventual clearing out of their forces from Jerusalem on December 9, 1917[19]. This event marked the end of the domination of the Jewish territory by the four empires of Babylonia, Persia, Greece and Arabia. From 586 B.C.E. until the beginning of, but not including, 1916 C.E.

	2501	
	− 1	(No year zero in this system of counting)
Total years	2500	

19. אֱדַיִן צְבִית לְיַצָּבָא עַל חֵיוְתָא רְבִיעָיְתָא דִּי הֲוָת שָׁנְיָה מִן כָּלְּהֵן דְּחִילָה יַתִּירָה שִׁנַּהּ דִּי פַרְזֶל וְטִפְרַהּ דִּי נְחָשׁ אָכְלָה מַדֲּקָה וּשְׁאָרָא בְּרַגְלַהּ רָפְסָה.

Then I desired to know the truth concerning the fourth beast, which was different from all the others, very terrifying, whose teeth were of iron, and its claws of copper; which devoured and crunched, and trampled the residue with its feet.

Truth concerning the fourth beast—Daniel wanted clarification about the meaning of the fourth beast. The first three beasts clearly signified the kings of the countries, as explained in the comments on Sentence 17. However, the fourth beast did not seem to represent a king or ruler, but rather a kingdom.

Claws of copper—Notice that the feature of claws of copper is added to the previous attributes listed in Sentence 7. This indicates that claws were a definite but minor characteristic of the unicorn. Thus, it has been stated that claws of a lion are occasionally attributed to the unicorn[20].

20. וְעַל קַרְנַיָּא עֲשַׂר דִּי בְרֵאשַׁהּ וְאָחֳרִי דִּי סִלְקַת וּנְפַלָה מִן קֳדָמַהּ תְּלָת, וְקַרְנָא דִּכֵּן וְעַיְנִין לַהּ וּפֻם מְמַלִּל רַבְרְבָן וְחֶזְוַהּ רַב מִן חַבְרָתַהּ.

And concerning the ten horns that were on its head, and the other horn which sprang up, and before which three fell; and this horn had eyes and a mouth that spoke great things, and whose appearance was larger than the others.

Appearance was larger—Initially the additional horn was smaller than the others as stated in Sentence 8. Now we learn that the horn subsequently grew to be larger than the others.

21. חָזֵה הֲוֵית וְקַרְנָא דִכֵּן עָבְדָא קְרָב עִם קַדִּישִׁין, וְיָכְלָה לְהֹן.

I watched, and this horn waged war with the holy ones, and prevailed against them.

Holy Ones—Note that the term "holy ones" (קדישין) refers to the Jews. For example, the Jews are commanded in the Bible (Lev. 11 44) to be holy. On the other hand, the term "Holy Ones of the Most High" (קדישי עליונין) refers to the angels who defend the Jewish people, as explained on Sentence 18.

22. עד די אתה עתיק יומיא ודינא יהב לקדישי עליונין, וזמנא מטה ומלכותא החסנו קדישין.

Until the Ancient of days came, and judgment was given for the Holy Ones of the Most High; and the time came, and the holy ones inherited the kingdom.

Judgment was given for the Holy Ones of the Most High—The angels who defend the Jewish people were found to be in the right.

Holy ones inherited the kingdom—The Jewish people acquired the land of Israel.

23. כן אמר, חיותא רביעיתא מלכו רביעאה תהוא בארעא די תשנא מן כל מלכותא, ותאכל כל ארעא ותדושנה ותדקנה.

Thus he said: The fourth beast signifies a fourth kingdom which shall appear on the land, which shall differ from all kingdoms, and shall devour all the land, tread it down and crush it.

Thus he said—So said the angel who was speaking to Daniel.

Signifies a fourth kingdom—The fourth beast represents a fourth kingdom, the Arabian empire, and does not represent a king or ruler.

Differ from all kingdoms—The country of Arabia differed from the other kingdoms in that it did not have one central ruler, but rather consisted of numerous tribes before the time of Mohammad.

Devour all the land—The Arabs did very little to build and develop the land. They wandered from place to place and fought constantly among themselves. Arabia in the sixth century c.e. differed little from the Arabia of 2,500 years previously[21].

24. וקרניא עשר מנה מלכותא עשרה מלכין יקמון, ואחרן יקום אחריהן והוא ישנא מן קדמיא ותלתה מלכין יהשפל.

And the ten horns signify that ten kings will arise out of this kingdom; and another shall arise after them, and he shall differ from his predecessors; and he shall bring down three kings.

Ten kings will arise—The ten horns represent ten kings. These were the rulers of the ten tribes around the city of Medina, with whom Mohammad made a treaty. The ten tribes were: (A) Banu 'Auf; (B) Al-Harith; (C) Al-Najjar; (D) Sa'idah; (E) Jusham; (F) Al-Aus; (G) Tha'labah; (H) Banu Kuraiza; (I) Al-Nadir; and (J) Kainuka. The last three of these tribes were Jewish tribes[22].

Another shall arise—In the year 622 c.e. Mohammad and his followers migrated from Mecca to Medina. This event, known as the Hegira, marked the beginning of the rapid growth of Mohammedanism (Islam)[23]. The group led by Mohammad corresponds to the little horn.

Shall differ from his predecessors—The group led by Mohammad will be different from the others in that it came from a different city and tried to convert the other tribes to belief in Mohammedanism.

Shall bring down three kings—The three Jewish tribes will be eliminated from Medina because they will refuse to follow the new faith of Mohammad. The Banu Kainuka were besieged in 624 until they surrendered. The tribe was then banished and its property confiscated. The Banu al-Nadir were forced to emigrate in 625, but were allowed to take along their possessions. The third Jewish tribe, the Banu Kuraiza, were forced to surrender in 627, but a more cruel fate befell them. All the men were killed, and the women and children were sold as slaves [24].

25. ומלין לצד עלאה ימלל ולקדישי עליונין יבלא, ויסבר להשניה
זמנין ודת, ויתיהבון בידה עד עדן ועדנין ופלג עדן.
And he shall speak words supporting God, and shall give heed to the Holy Ones of the Most High, and shall think to change the seasons and the religion. And they shall be given into his hand for 1,278 years.

Speak words supporting God—Mohammad professed monotheism and eventually eliminated idol-worship from Arabia.

Shall give heed to the Holy Ones of the Most High—Mohammad attributed his revelations to the angel Gabriel. On occasion he also mentioned the angels Michael and Seraphil[25]. In the Koran, the holy book of Islam, angels of various types are frequently mentioned. Some of the names of the angels are identical with those found in Jewish angelologies[26].

Shall think to change the seasons and the religion—Mohammad introduced a non-intercalary calendar of 12 lunar months, bearing no relation to the seasons. The new calendar began with the time of the Farewell Pilgrimage in 632[27]. He also introduced a new religion, Islam, which was a monotheistic religion[28].

Give into his hand for 1,278 years—The Biblical text reads ועדנין עדן ופלג עדן. According to Table 16.0.1 עדן is 365 years.

Then we get:
$$\text{עדן} = 365 = 365$$
$$\text{עדנין} = 2 \times 365 = 730$$
$$\text{פלג עדן} = \tfrac{1}{2} \times 365 = \underline{182\tfrac{1}{2}}$$
$$1277\tfrac{1}{2} \approx 1278 \text{ years}$$

Note that the Hebrew letter *vav* as used in ועדנין and in ופלג עדן, indicates addition rather than multiplication. (See comments on Dan. 12 7.) The sentence tells us that the land of Israel will be under the domination of the Arabian empire for 1,278 years. Omar, a successor of Mohammad, conquered the territory of Palestine in 636 but Jerusalem was not taken until the end of 637[29]. Palestine remained under Moslem domination, except for occasional short periods, until the end of 1916, when the military campaign was begun to remove Turkish domination from

Palestine (see comments on Sentence 18). Thus, from the completion of the conquest of the land of Israel by Omar in 637, until the beginning of the attack against the Turkish forces in Palestine in 1916, is 1,278 years (the year 1916 is not included).

26. ודינא יתב ושלטנה יהעדון להשמדה ולהובדה עד סופא.

And the judgment will be set, and his dominion shall be removed, to be destroyed and abolished unto the end.

Dominion shall be removed—The Arabian empire* will be destroyed. Around the time of World War I (1914–1918) and thereafter, the Arabian empire was broken into many smaller Arab countries, such as Egypt, Iraq, Jordan, Lebanon, Libya, Saudi Arabia, the Sudan, and Syria. Many of these smaller countries, such as Iraq, Jordan, Lebanon, Saudi Arabia, and Syria will be partially or completely destroyed during the War of Gog in 1973, and much of their territories acquired by the State of Israel.

27. ומלכותא ושלטנא ורבותא די מלכות תחות כל שמיא יהיבת לעם קדישי עליונין, מלכותה מלכות עלם וכל שלטניא לה יפלחון וישתמעון.

And the kingdom, and the dominion, and the greatness of the kingdoms under the whole heaven, shall be given to the people of the Holy Ones of the Most High. Their kingdom is an everlasting kingdom, and all dominions shall serve and obey them.

People of the Holy Ones of the Most High—These are the Jewish people, as explained on Sentence 18.

Greatness of the kingdoms—From the time of the destruction of the Second Temple in 70 C.E. until the re-establishment of the Jewish state in 1948, the Jewish people were a nation without a homeland or a government. Subsequent to 1948, and to an even greater extent after the War of Gog, the Jewish people will be given the greatness and sovereignty typical of all the nations of the world.

Everlasting kingdom—The State of Israel will last forever.

Shall serve and obey them—The State of Israel will become the greatest nation in the world, and therefore all other nations will serve and heed the Israeli people.

28. עד כה סופא די מלתא, אנה דניאל שגיא רעיוני יבהלנני וזיוי ישתנון עלי ומלתא בלבי נטרת.

Up to here is the end of the account. As for me Daniel, my thoughts greatly dismayed me and my appearance was changed in me, and I kept the account in my mind.

Kept the account in my mind—Daniel, upon awakening from the dream, did not forget the details as often happens with people upon waking, but kept the account in his mind to be later written down.

---

*The term Arabian empire as used throughout this chapter includes the Ottoman empire which was a later Islamic outgrowth that controlled approximately the same territory.

16.3 CHAPTER 8 OF DANIEL

Daniel received a prophecy in which was foretold the successive greatness of the Persian, Greek and Arabian empires. Particular emphasis was given to events during the lifetime of Mohammad. Several dates were specified, one of which would be of importance in understanding prophecies that Daniel would receive at a later time (see Dan. 12 11,12).

Just as in the previous chapter, Daniel saw particular animals. However, in Chapter 7 the type of beast indicated the country while the animal itself represented the king. Here the animals represent the king, and the horns specify the country.

1. בשנת שלוש למלכות בלאשצר המלך, חזון נראה אלי אני דניאל
אחרי הנראה אלי בתחלה.
   In the third year of the reign of King Belshazzar, a "vision" appeared to me Daniel, after what appeared to me at the beginning.

Third year . . . of King Belshazzar—Belshazzar reigned from 552 to 539 B.C.E. (see Table 7.1), and his third year of rule was 550.

"Vision" (חזון)—The word "vision," as used in this chapter, has a specific meaning. It refers to the Ka'ba, the sacred shrine of Islam, which contains the Black Stone. This meaning of the word "vision" is not clearly explained because in Sentence 26 Daniel is told to leave the vision unexplained (סתם החזון). The vision of the Ka'ba is described in Sentences 11 through 14.

After what appeared to me at the beginning—Daniel states that the vision of the Ka'ba appeared to him after what he saw at the beginning of the revelation. The part seen at the beginning refers to the descriptions of the animals and the horns given in Sentences 3 through 10.

2. ואראה בחזון, ויהי בראתי ואני בשושן הבירה אשר בעילם
המדינה, ואראה בחזון ואני הייתי על אובל אולי.
   And I saw in the "vision." And when I saw I was in Shushan the citadel which is in the province of Elam. And when I saw in the "vision" I was on the Eulaeus bridge.

And I saw in the "vision"—This phrase properly belongs to the previous sentence. Daniel states that he saw pictures while observing the vision of the Ka'ba.

And when I saw I was in Shushan—When Daniel saw the beginning of the revelation, Sentences 3 to 10, it was as if he were in the citadel of Shushan.

And when I saw in the "vision"—When Daniel saw the vision of the Ka'ba, Sentences 11 to 14, it was as if he were on the bridge over the Eulaeus River. The word אובל is here taken to mean bridge. According to Benjamin of Tudela who lived in the twelfth century C.E. the Eulaeus River divided the city of Shushan into two parts which were connected by a bridge[30].

3. וָאֶשָּׂא עֵינַי וָאֶרְאֶה וְהִנֵּה אַיִל אֶחָד עֹמֵד לִפְנֵי הָאֻבָל וְלוֹ קְרָנָיִם וְהַקְּרָנַיִם גְּבֹהוֹת וְהָאַחַת גְּבֹהָה מִן הַשֵּׁנִית וְהַגְּבֹהָה עֹלָה בָּאַחֲרֹנָה.
And I raised my eyes and I saw, and behold, one ram with two horns standing before the bridge; and the two horns were high, but one was higher than the other, and the higher came up last.

Raised my eyes—Daniel was situated in the citadel of Shushan, and had to raise his eyes to see the Eulaeus bridge.

One ram—The ram represents Cyrus, King of Persia.

Two horns—The two horns indicate that the nation was composed of two smaller kingdoms. In 553 B.C.E. Cyrus, king of several Persian tribes, revolted against the Median empire, and formed the united Persian nation composed of Persia and Media[31].

The two horns were high—Both Persia and Media were powerful countries.

The higher came up last—The higher horn, representing Persia, arose after the lower horn, representing Media.

4. רָאִיתִי אֶת הָאַיִל מְנַגֵּחַ יָמָּה וְצָפוֹנָה וָנֶגְבָּה וְכָל חַיּוֹת לֹא יַעַמְדוּ לְפָנָיו וְאֵין מַצִּיל מִיָּדוֹ, וְעָשָׂה כִרְצֹנוֹ וְהִגְדִּיל.
I saw the ram goring west and north and south; and all beasts could not stand before it, and no one could rescue from its power. It did what it liked, and grew in size.

Goring west and north and south—The Persian empire began from the east and attacked to the west, north, and south. Eventually Cyrus conquered such countries as Lydia to the northwest and Babylonia to the south[32].

All beasts could not stand before it—Soon after the conquest of the Median empire, Cyrus was attacked by a coalition of the kings of Babylon, Egypt, Lydia, and Sparta. In 546 Cyrus took Sardis, thereby making the Lydian kingdom a Persian province[33]. "All beasts" refers to the coalition of kings.

No one could rescue from its power—During the next years the Persians suppressed a rebellion of the Lydians under Pactyas, and subjugated the Ionian cities, the Carians, and the Lycians[34]. Thus other nations and rebellious groups could not stop the spread of the power of Cyrus.

Grew in size—Under Cyrus, the Persian empire greatly increased in size. Cyrus conquered Babylon in 539. Beginning in 538 he dates his years as "king of Babylon and king of the countries" (i.e., of the world).

5. וַאֲנִי הָיִיתִי מֵבִין, וְהִנֵּה צְפִיר הָעִזִּים בָּא מִן הַמַּעֲרָב עַל פְּנֵי כָל הָאָרֶץ, וְאֵין נוֹגֵעַ בָּאָרֶץ, וְהַצָּפִיר קֶרֶן חָזוּת בֵּין עֵינָיו.
And I understood; and behold a young he-goat came from the west over the face of the whole earth, and touched not the ground; and a horn was envisioned between the eyes of the he-goat.

And I understood—Daniel understood what was meant. Daniel saw the revelation in 550, which was a few years after the formation of the Persian-Median empire under the rulership of Cyrus. Thus, Daniel had already experienced the events described at the beginning of the revelation concerning the ram. With his keen insight, he easily understood the remaining references to the ram.

A young he-goat—The young he-goat represents the early years of rule of Alexander the Great, King of Macedon (336–323).

Came from the west over the face of the whole earth—The conquests by Alexander the Great originated in Greece, and spread from west to east around most of what was then the known world[35].

Touched not the ground—Alexander, after his conquests, retained most of the organization of the Persian provinces, appointing new satraps or retaining the former ones. The roads, the ports, and the organization of the empire were still as the Persians had left them. In Egypt he had merely replaced old provincial governors with new ones. In India, Alexander had defeated Porus and then left him in power much as he found him[36].

A horn was envisioned—A horn, representing the Greek empire, was envisioned under the domination of Alexander the Great. He had united under him the separate Greek states, in addition to conquering most of the countries of the known world. The word "envisioned" (חזות) indicates that the empire referred to was not in existence when Daniel saw the revelation. Similarly, the word "envisioned" (חזות) is again used in Sentence 8, where four countries unknown to Daniel are mentioned; though it is not used in Sentence 3 in reference to Persia and Media because these countries were in existence at the time of Daniel.

6. ויבא עד האיל בעל הקרנים אשר ראיתי עמד לפני האבל, וירץ אליו בחמת כחו.

And he came to the two-horned ram which I had seen standing before the bridge, and ran at him with the fury of his power.

Came to the two-horned ram—Alexander the Great, during his eastward march encountered the army of Darius III, King of Persia in 333 B.C.E. This led to the Battle of Issus. The two-horned ram refers to the King of Persia at the time of Alexander, namely Darius III (335–331).

Ran at him with the fury of his power—The Battle of Issus was a fierce battle which started out with Alexander and those around him dashing into the river with a *run*, in order to alarm the Persians by the rapidity of their onset, and to come to close contact sooner, and avoid being greatly injured by the archers.[37]

7. וראיתיו מגיע אצל האיל ויתמרמר אליו ויך את האיל וישבר את שתי קרניו ולא היה כח באיל לעמד לפניו, וישליכהו ארצה וירמסהו ולא היה מציל לאיל מידו.

And I saw him come near the ram and embittered himself against it; and he struck the ram, and broke its two horns; and the ram had no strength to stand before him. He threw it to the land and trampled on it, and there was no one to save the ram from his hand.

Saw him come near the ram—Another encounter between Alexander and Darius III occurred at the Battle of Arbela, which was fought at Gaugamela, sixty miles from Arbela, in October 331[38].

Embittered himself—The fierce struggle which occurred can be fairly acclaimed as one of the greatest battles in antiquity[39].

Struck the ram and broke its two horns—In the battle, Alexander completely vanquished Darius and his army, and conquered the Persian kingdom.

The ram had no strength to stand—Darius III led the retreat when he saw that his army was being defeated[40].

Threw it to the land—Darius fled towards Media[41]. Thus, Alexander threw Darius back to his land in defeat.

There was no one to save the ram—After the Battle of Arbela the generals of Darius III rebelled against him. When Alexander finally caught up to him in 330, Darius had already been murdered by his own generals[42].

8. וצפיר העזים הגדיל עד מאד, וכעצמו נשברה הקרן הגדולה ותעלנה חזות ארבע תחתיה לארבע רוחות השמים.

And the young he-goat became exceedingly great; and when he was at his strongest, the great horn was broken, and four envisioned horns arose in its place, towards the four winds of heaven.

Became exceedingly great—In many ways Alexander became important. In his closing years he became very vain. For example, he decreed that he should be deified in Greece[43], and that his friends should prostrate themselves before him[44]. Furthermore, he became great militarily, in that he conquered most of the known countries of the world. His eminence was such that he subsequently became known as Alexander the Great.

At his strongest the great horn was broken—After his major conquests, Alexander returned to Babylon. In June of 323 he suddenly died of a fever, before he was yet 33 years of age[45]. The Greek empire, represented by the horn, was then broken up.

Four envisioned horns arose ... towards the four winds—After Alexander's death, four smaller states replaced the Greek empire by 300 B.C.E. These were the empires of Ptolemy to the south, Seleucus to the east, Lysimachus to the north, and Cassander to the west[46]. These four empires correspond to the four horns towards the four winds.

9. ומן האחת מהם יצא קרן אחת מצעירה, ותגדל יתר אל הנגב ואל המזרח ואל הצבי.

And from one of them came out a small horn, and it grew more to the south, and to the east and to the desirous land.

From one of them came out a small horn—From one of the four empires was excluded the small Arabian empire, which did not really develop until the time of Mohammad (about 630 c.e.). At the time of Alexander's death, extensive plans had been made to conquer the Arabian territory[47]. Alexander's death from sickness prevented the inclusion of Arabia as part of the Greek empire, and consequently excluded the territory from any of the four smaller empires. Probably, if Arabia had been conquered, its territory would have been included in the Ptolemaic or Seleucid realms.

Grew more to the south and to the east and to the desirous land—Arabia had most of its territory south of the Seleucid realm, another portion southeast; and the smallest portion towards Palestine, the desirous land[48]. See Ez. **20** 6 where Palestine is called "the desirous land for all the countries."

10. ותגדל עד צבא השמים, ותפל ארצה מן הצבא ומן הכוכבים ותרמסם.
And it grew until the "host of heaven," and it cast down to the ground some of the host and some of the stars, and trampled them.

Grew until the "host of heaven"—Arabia grew to the point where it established the worship of heavenly bodies, known as Sabianism. In the Sabian superstitions, the worship of the host of heaven, *Saba* (צבא), formed so conspicuous a part, that from this circumstance it derived its name[49]. The Sabians believed in one God, but also worshipped the stars, on which the angels were supposed to reside[50].

Cast down . . . the host and . . . stars and trampled them—The principles of Sabianism professed belief in one God, but supposed that authority had been delegated to inferior intelligences, whom men were required to worship. This doctrine led, in many cases, to corruptions and idolatry. Temples were eventually erected in Arabia to the seven planets and to the conspicuous stars[51]. Many of the Sabians worshipped only the stars, while others worshipped idols made with the hands to represent the stars[52]. The people by worshipping idols trampled on their own religious beliefs.

11. ועד שר הצבא הגדיל, וממנו הורם התמיד והשלך מכון מקדשו.
And until the chief of Sabianism became great; and from him the permanent [stone] was raised, and the foundations of his temple were thrown back.

Until the chief of Sabianism became great—The condition of disregard of religion existed until Mohammad, who is here called the head of Sabianism, became powerful. Mohammad's followers were frequently called Sabians[53]. It is said, for example, that Islam was born in the desert with Arab Sabianism for its mother, Judaism for its father, and Eastern Christianity for its forster-nurse[54].

And from him—Mohammad.

The permanent [stone]—The Ka'ba, the main shrine of the Moslems, is built about the Black Stone. Legends concerning the stone go back to creation[55]. The Hebrew word תמיד, meaning permanent, refers to the Black Stone, which is supposed to have always existed. The stone is semicircular and measures about six inches in height and eight in breadth; it is reddish-black in color[56].

From him the permanent [stone] was raised—When Mohammad was about 35 years old (605), a violent flood had shattered the Ka'ba. The people of the Koreish tribe began to repair the damage, but many arguments arose concerning which of four groups should put the Black Stone in place. To settle the arguments, it was decided that the first person to enter the court of the Ka'ba by a certain gate should decide the difference, or place the stone himself. By chance it was Mohammad who was first to enter. He immediately thought of a method which would satisfy all those involved. He spread his mantle upon the ground and set the stone thereon. One chief from each of the four groups was to hold a corner of the mantle and help raise the garment. When the stone reached the proper height, Mohammad himself guided it into its proper place[57]. Thus it was by Mohammad's guidance that the permanent stone was raised.

Foundations of his temple were thrown back—The Ka'ba was then rebuilt, though it now occupied somewhat less space than the previous structure. Years later, after the conquest of Mecca under the leadership of Mohammad (630), he is reported to have said, "Verily they have drawn back the foundations of the Ka'ba from their original limit."[58]

12. וצבא תנתן על התמיד בפשע, ותשלך אמת ארצה ועשתה והצליחה.
And Sabianism will be placed on the permanent [stone] rebelliously, and she will spread truth to the land, and she will accomplish and succeed.

Sabianism will be placed on the permanent [stone] rebelliously—In January 630, Mohammad led the inhabitants of Medina in a surprise attack on the city of Mecca[59]. By doing so, Mohammad broke a ten-year truce, signed two years previously, between the inhabitants of the two cities[60]. There was little opposition to the advancing army, and Mecca was soon under Mohammad's control. He then proceeded to the Ka'ba and commanded the destruction of all the idols therein, and the obliteration of paintings of angels on the walls[61]. Thus Islam, a form of Sabianism against idol-worship, was placed in the Ka'ba, the shrine built around the Black Stone. The conquest by Mohammad was a rebellious sin, in that in the process he broke a peace treaty.

She will spread truth to the land—The word צבא (Sabianism), here used for Islam, is feminine because of the feminine qualities that the Arabs saw in the religion. For example, the angels that the Sabians worshipped had female names, and were called goddesses and the daughters of god[62].

At the time when the idols in the Ka'ba were being hewn down Mohammad announced, "Truth has come—truth has come and falsehood gone"[63]. Afterwards, a crier was sent through the city with the proclamation, "Whoever believes in god and in the day of judgment, let him not leave in his house any image that he does not break in pieces." Thus we find that Islam spread the truth of one god to the land.

She will accomplish and succeed—Islam was accepted by the people. Idolatry was eliminated, and the people of Mecca soon fought on the side of Mohammad[64]. The year 631 is called the "year of delegations," because delegations flocked from near and far to offer allegiance to Mohammad and to his faith[65].

13. ואשמעה אחד קדוש מדבר, ויאמר אחד קדוש לפלמוני המדבר
עד מתי החזון התמיד והפשע שמם, תת וקדש וצבא מרמס.
And I heard one who was holy speaking. And one who was holy said to the anonymous person who speaks: "Until when is the vision of the permanent [stone], and the rebellious sin that causes destruction; giving and holiness and Sabianism trampled upon?"

One who was holy—This phrase refers to Jacob. Jacob, in Gen. 42 11,13, is called "one" by his sons. Also in Isa. 29 23, Jacob is called "holy." No other person in the Bible is designated as both "one" and "holy."

Anonymous person who speaks—This phrase refers to Joseph. In Gen. 45 12, Joseph states to his brothers, "It is my mouth that *speaks* to you." In that incident it was the unrecognized Joseph who spoke to his brothers and revealed his identity.

One who was holy said—In Gen. 48, Jacob, shortly before his death, spoke to Joseph. The date of this event is 1668 B.C.E. (see Table 1.5.1). This date is the starting time for the 2,300 years mentioned in Sentence 14.

We here find that Jacob asks Joseph to elucidate the vision. This is understandable since Joseph was a dreamer, able to foresee the future (see Gen. 37 5-11; 40 5-22; 41 17-32). Also, in Moslem literature, in the Koran, Jacob and Joseph are persons of importance. Jacob is pictured in Sura II, 127 as speaking to his sons before his death; and the entire Sura XII describes the history of Joseph. Thus these two persons are common to the Jewish and Moslem religions.

Until when—How long will it take from the time the question is being asked, i.e., from 1668.

Vision of the permanent [stone]—Here we find the only clear indication in the chapter that the "vision," mentioned in Sentence 1, refers to the Ka'ba built about the Black Stone.

Rebellious sin that causes destruction—The "rebellious sin" refers to the breaking of the peace treaty by Mohammad, as explained on Sentence 12. The attack by Mohammad resulted in destruction of the idols in the Ka'ba.

Giving—That is the giving or bringing of sacrifices. Pilgrims who performed the "Greater Pilgrimage" brought animals for sacrificing at Mina[66].

Holiness—The Ka'ba was considered as a holy place.

Giving and holiness and Sabianism trampled upon—Mohammad by attacking the city of Mecca prevented the bringing of sacrifices by pilgrims, and desecrated the holiness of the Ka'ba, and destroyed the idols of Sabianism.

14. ויאמר אלי עד ערב בקר אלפים ושלש מאות, ונצדק קדש.
   And he said to me, "Until evening-morning is 2,300 [years]; then shall holiness be made righteous."

He said to me—Joseph told the answer to Daniel.

Evening-morning—The phrase evening-morning (ערב בקר) refers to the rites performed in the evening and morning during the "Greater Pilgrimage." The pilgrims, starting from Mecca, ascend the hill at Arafat and hasten back the same *evening* three or four miles to Al-Muzdelifa. The next *morning* they go to Mina, where they spend two or three days. The pilgrimage is concluded by the bringing of sacrifices[67].

Made righteous—In March 632, Mohammad performed the Farewell Pilgrimage to Mecca and the Ka'ba. In so doing he reinstituted the Sabian rites of the "Lesser Pilgrimage" and the "Greater Pilgrimage."[68] Upon seeing the Ka'ba, Mohammad is reported to have said, "Add unto this House the dignity and glory, the honor and the reverence . . . ." The reinstitution of the Sabian rites is the event here referred to by the words "holiness be made righteous."

2,300 [years]—From the time of the death of Jacob in 1668 B.C.E., until the evening and morning rites performed by Mohammad in 632 C.E., is 2,300 years (if we include both the initial and final years).

    1668 B.C.E.
     632 C.E.
    ────────
    2301
  − 1 (no year zero in the system of counting)
    2300 years

Hence there are exactly 2,300 years from the time the question was asked by Jacob, until the holiness of the Ka'ba was re-established by Mohammad.

15. ויהי בראתי אני דניאל את החזון ואבקשה בינה והנה עמד לנגדי כמראה גבר.
   When I Daniel was seeing the "vision" I sought understanding; and behold there stood opposing me one with the appearance of a man.

Seeing the "vision"—When Daniel saw the vision of the Ka'ba he wanted further clarification.

Stood opposing me—The Hebrew phrase is עמד לנגדי. The same phrase is used again in Dan. **10** 13,16. In Dan. **10** 13 the phrase clearly means "opposing," rather than the alternative explanation of "opposite."

One with the appearance of a man—The one with the appearance of a man (מראה גבר) represents Mohammad. Henceforth he is simply referred to as "appearance" (מראה). Mohammad knew that his deception would be exposed, and therefore he was against giving any explanation to Daniel.

Alternatively, the one with the appearance of a man could refer to Gabriel, who is mentioned in the next sentence. Then the term עמד לנגדי would be translated "stood opposite me." In fact the angel Gabriel first appeared to Mohammad "in the form of a man."[69] According to this interpretation the word "appearance" (מראה), used in later sentences, would still have to refer to Mohammad.

16. ואשמע קול אדם בין אולי, ויקרא ויאמר גבריאל הבן להלז את המראה.

> And I heard the voice of Adam from the Eulaeus river, and he called and said, "Gabriel, explain the 'appearance' to this person."

He called—Adam called out from the river, so as to prevent Mohammad from not allowing an explanation to be given to Daniel. The Moslems say that Adam, after his expulsion from Paradise, begged of God that he might erect a building like that he had seen there; whereupon God let down a representation of the Ka'ba and set it in Mecca[70]. There are also several traditions which relate Adam to the angel Gabriel[71]. The associations in Moslem tradition of Adam with the Ka'ba and the angel Gabriel, explain why Adam is here the one to desire that Daniel be given an explanation.

Gabriel—According to Arabic tradition, Gabriel is their guardian angel, and is chief of the angels[72]. Gabriel was the messenger who communicated the words of God to Mohammad[73]. Moreover, Moslem legend claims that when Ishmael was rebuilding the Ka'ba, he received the Black Stone from Gabriel[74].

Explain the "appearance"—Explain the significance of the appearance of Mohammad.

17. ויבא אצל עמדי ובבאו נבעתי ואפלה על פני, ויאמר אלי הבן בן אדם כי לעת קץ החזון.

> So he came near where I stood, and when he came I was terrified and fell upon my face; and he said to me, "Understand O son of Adam, because it [the 'appearance'] is for 25 years before the end of the 'vision.'"

He came near—Gabriel came near Daniel.

Son of Adam—Mortal man.

Twenty-five years—The Hebrew word עת is used to represent 25 years, as indicated in Table 16.0.1.

It [the "appearance"] is for 25 years before the end of the "vision"—Gabriel explains the significance of Mohammad with respect to the vision of the Ka'ba. Mohammad's first connection with the Ka'ba was in 605 C.E. which marked the initial hint of his future greatness (see comments on Sentence 11). The end of the "vision" of the Ka'ba is presented in Sentence 12. There it is described how in 630 Mohammad removed all idol-worship from the sacred building. From 605 to 630 is 25 years. See Dan. 12 11 where this same 25-year period is again mentioned.

18. ובדברו עמי נרדמתי על פני ארצה, ויגע בי ויעמידני על עמדי.
When he spoke to me I fell into a deep sleep with my face toward the ground; but he touched me and made me stand up where I was.

19. ויאמר הנני מודיעך את אשר יהיה באחרית הזעם כי למועד קץ.
And he said: Behold, I am making known to you what shall occur in the latter part of the "wrath," that is from 29 years before the end.

"Wrath"—The word "wrath" (זעם) indicates the anger of God against Israel, and refers to the Babylonian Exile (586–516). Thus, in Zech. 1 12 it is stated " . . . that you have vented your wrath (זעמתה) these 70 years"; and the phrase refers to the Babylonian Exile as explained in Section 6.4. The latter part of the "wrath" refers to events after 551 B.C.E.

Twenty-nine years—The Hebrew word מועד designates a period of 29 years (see Table 16.0.1).

Twenty-nine years before the end—The predicted events described in this chapter begin 29 years before the end of the 70-year exile, i.e., 29 years before 516, or 545 B.C.E. Daniel experienced this revelation in 550 (see Sentence 1). The formation of the Persian empire, consisting of Persia and Media (which is described in Sentence 3), had already taken place in 553, and therefore is not a predicted event. Only with the incidents described in Sentence 4, i.e., the conquest by Cyrus of other countries after 546, does the revelation describe future events. Daniel is here told that the predicted events in the revelation begin after 546, i.e., from 545.

20. האיל אשר ראית בעל הקרנים, מלכי מדי ופרס.
The two-horned ram which you saw signifies the kings of Media and Persia.

The two-horned ram—Gabriel now explains to Daniel that the animals represent the kings, while the horns represent the countries. Here the ram represents the king of Persia. The reason that "kings" rather than "king" is stated, is that two kings of Persia have been previously referred to. In Sentences 3 and 4 Cyrus was signified by the ram. In Sentences 6 and 7 Darius III was signified. The two horns correspond to the two small countries from which Persia arose, namely Persia and Media.

21. והצפיר השעיר מלך יון, והקרן הגדולה אשר בין עיניו הוא המלך הראשון.
And the hairy he-goat is the king of Greece; and the great horn that is between his eyes signifies that he is the first king.

The hairy he-goat—The he-goat represents the king of Greece. Here the he-goat is depicted as hairy to signify that before the time of Alexander the Great, Greece was composed of many states and many rulers.

The great horn . . . is the first king—The large horn represents the united kingdom of Greece. At the beginning of Alexander's reign, he was ruler over only one of the states of Greece, namely Macedon[75]. However, by force of arms

Alexander united the separate Greek states. Thus, the horn indicates that Alexander is the first ruler of the united kingdom of Greece.

22. והנשברת ותעמדנה ארבע תחתיה, ארבע מלכיות מגוי יעמדנה ולא בכחו.
And as for the broken [horn] which was replaced by four others, four kingdoms shall rise out of that nation, but not with its power.

Four others, four kingdoms—The four horns represent the empires of Ptolemy, Seleucus, Cassander, and Lysimachus which arose after the disintegration of the Greek empire.

Not with its power—These four kingdoms will not have the power that was exerted by the Greek empire under the leadership of Alexander the Great.

23. ובאחרית מלכותם כהתם הפשעים, יעמד מלך עז פנים ומבין חידות.
And near the end of their kingdoms, when those who commit rebellious sins will have been consumed, there will arise an unyielding king who understands cryptic sayings.

Near the end of their kingdoms—The four kingdoms arose around 300 B.C.E. The text now refers to events more than 900 years later when these four kingdoms and even their outgrowths, such as the Roman Empire, will have crumbled.

Unyielding king—The king referred to is Mohammad, founder of the Arabian empire. He was unyielding in his claim of being a prophet of God, although for many years he had the support of fewer than 100 persons. After gaining the support of a large portion of the people, he was unyielding in requiring conversion to his beliefs or else punishment of death.

Understands cryptic sayings—Messages that Mohammed claimed to have received from God are collected in the Koran. Many of the passages are obscure and difficult to understand. Furthermore, it is recognized that at least 225 verses in the Koran are abrogated by later ones[76].

24. ועצם כחו ולא בכחו ונפלאות ישחית והצליח ועשה, והשחית עצומים ועם קדשים.
And he shall increase his power but not by using his power; and he shall disclaim miracles; and he shall succeed and accomplish. He shall destroy the mighty and the people of the holy ones.

Increase his power—Mohammad will gain the support of the people not primarily because of his physical strength but because of his claim to be the prophet of God.

Shall disclaim miracles—There is no position more satisfactorily established in the Koran than that Mohammad did not in any part of his career perform miracles or lay claim to the power of performing them. In fact he actually disclaims the ability to work miracles[77].

Shall succeed—Mohammad will be successful in convincing the masses that he is a prophet of God.

Shall destroy the mighty and the people of the holy ones—Mohammad conquered many strong tribes and banished and killed many Jews (see e.g. comments on Dan. 7 24). In general, those who would not accept Islam were conquered and often killed.

25. ועל שכלו והצליח מרמה בידו ובלבבו יגדיל ובשלוה ישחית רבים, ועל שר שרים יעמד ובאפס יד ישבר.

And all because of his intelligence; and deceit will prosper in his hand, and he shall become great in his heart, and will destroy many peacefully. He shall rely on the chief of the angels, and will be broken without use of force.

Because of his intelligence—The success of Mohammad was because of his intelligence. He was a master of eloquence. His language was cast in the purest and most persuasive style of Arabian oratory. His poetical genius exhausted the imagery of nature[78].

Deceit will prosper—Mohammad used craft and deception against his foes in many instances. Moreover, in his prophetical career, many supposedly divine revelations were the direct reflection of his own wishes[79].

Become great in his heart—In his early years Mohammad was unsure whether he was receiving divine messages. However, the confidence and support of his wife and his few followers helped him slowly to gain confidence. Eventually, he began to unequivocally assert that he was a prophet, and to believe that he had a divine mission[80].

Will destroy many peacefully—Many peoples did he conquer without battle. Often he gave in to others in many respects until they became loyal followers.

Rely on the chief of the angels—Gabriel, who was considered as the chief of the angels, was the messenger who communicated to Mohammad the word of God. The Koran consists exclusively of revelations which Mohammad professed were told him by Gabriel[81].

Broken without use of force—Mohammad died of a fever in 632[82]. He was not killed in battle, nor did any opposing hand cause his downfall.

26. ומראה הערב והבקר אשר נאמר אמת הוא, ואתה סתם החזון כי לימים רבים.

And the "appearance," involving the evening and the morning which was stated, he is the truth; but you leave the "vision" unexplained for it will occur after many six-year periods.

The "appearance"—The appearance of Mohammad, who was the one involved in the evening and morning rites performed in 632 (as explained on Sentence 14), he is the truth that was sent to the land (see Sentence 12). In other words, when

Mohammad proclaimed "truth has come," he really meant "Mohammedanism has come."

Leave the "vision" unexplained—We therefore do not find in the chapter a clear description as to what the "vision" was about. Only because of the phrase "vision of the permanent [stone]" in Sentence 13, do we determine that the vision is concerned with the Ka'ba, the Moslem shrine in Mecca.

After many six-year periods—The Hebrew word ימים here signifies six years (see Table 16.0.1). Daniel had this revelation in 550. From 550 B.C.E. until 632 C.E., inclusive, (see Sentences 1 and 14) is 1,182 years, or 197 six-year periods.

27. ואני דניאל נהייתי ונחליתי ימים ואקום ואעשה את מלאכת המלך, ואשתומם על המראה ואין מבין.
And I, Daniel, was exhausted and became sick for six days; then I arose and performed the king's business; and I was bewildered by the "appearance," and no one understood it.

Performed the king's business—This statement establishes that Daniel held a high position during the reign of Belshazzar.

Bewildered by the "appearance"—Daniel was bewildered by the description of Mohammad. Daniel could not comprehend what type of person could fit the description of Mohammad as given in this chapter. Note that Daniel was bewildered only by the "appearance" (Mohammad) and not by the "vision."

No one understood it—No one else could comprehend what type of person could fit the description.

16.4 CHAPTER 9 OF DANIEL

Chapter 9 describes events which occurred subsequent to those recounted in the later Chapters 10 through 12. In fact, the revelation received by Daniel in Chapter 9 is the last one he received. The reason this chapter is not placed in chronological order is that reference is made in 9 21 to incidents depicted in Chapter 8 concerning the angel Gabriel. Moreover, the unusual Hebrew word שבעים (Shavuim) is only found in Chapters 9 and 10, and is not used elsewhere in the Bible. For these reasons Chapter 9 was placed between Chapters 8 and 10, rather than subsequent to Chapter 12. Nevertheless, it should be kept in mind that Chapter 9 was the last one to be recorded by Daniel. This explains why the described prophecy skips over the historical details mentioned in the other revelations, and why it predicts happenings of a later date than any of the other prophecies (compare Section 15.1, Organization).

Chapter 9 can be divided into a number of subdivisions. In 9 1,2 is given the historical background to the prayer uttered by Daniel. It was one year before the calculated time for rebuilding the Temple, and yet no indications were apparent that construction would begin. Daniel therefore prepared himself for entreating God for forgiveness (9 3,4). The entreaty itself is divided into two main parts. The first part, prayer (תפלה), also includes confession (ודוי) of sin (9 4–14). Near the end of the prayer (9 11–14) Daniel specifies the punishments that have been inflicted on the nation because of the people's sins. The second part, supplication (תחנה), is where Daniel requests that God's anger against the Temple and Jerusalem be removed (9 15–19). Then in 9 20–23 the angel Gabriel suddenly appears, and answers Daniel's entreaty. Daniel is told that instead of 70 years of anger there are actually 70 × 49 years of anger. Not until the end of this period will the final Temple be completed. The wording of the answer, which contains the detailed prophecy, is written in 9 24–27.

1. בשנת אחת לדריוש בן אחשורוש מזרע מדי, אשר המלך על מלכות כשדים.

    In the first year of Darius son of Ahasuerus, of the seed of the Medes, who was made king over the kingdom of the Chaldeans.

First year of Darius son of Ahasuerus—Darius, son of Ahasuerus, was the same person as Darius I (see Section 6.3.1). His official reign, according to the Bible, began in 517 B.C.E., which is one year before construction began on the Second Temple. Daniel was perplexed because he saw no definite signs that the end of the desolation of Jerusalem had come.

Made king over the kingdom of the Chaldeans—The Babylonian empire was originally conquered by Cyrus, King of Persia, in 539. Darius I was the first Persian king of Median descent to reign over Babylonia.

2. בשנת אחת למלכו אני דניאל בינתי בספרים, מספר השנים אשר היה דבר ד' אל ירמיה הנביא למלאות לחרבות ירושלם שבעים שנה.

    In the first year of his reign I, Daniel, studied in the books; "the number of years that the word of the Lord was told to Jeremiah the prophet" was to complete for the desolations of Jerusalem seventy years.

Studied in the books—The word "books" here refers to the Biblical writings then in existence. In particular, reference is clearly made in this chapter to the Books of Jeremiah (9 2), Numbers (9 11), and Deuteronomy (9 13). Moreover, quotations from the Books of Leviticus (9 7), Kings (9 5), and Psalms (9 17) are presented in the text, as is explained on the specific sentences. In addition, there are probable references in this chapter to the Books of Exodus, Isaiah, Ezekiel, and Chronicles.

It should be realized that the Books of Esther, Haggai, Zechariah, Malachi, Ezra-Nehemiah, and parts of Chronicles were completed after 517, and could therefore not be among the cited Biblical works. The fact that there are similarities in phraseology between this chapter and Ezra 9 6–15, therefore indicates that Ezra was familiar with the Book of Daniel, rather than the reverse.

"Number of years that the word of the . . . to Jeremiah"—This phrase is a modified quotation of the statement in Jer. 25 3, "It is 23 years that the word of the Lord was told to me [Jeremiah]." Daniel states that he calculated that the 23 years mentioned

by Jeremiah will complete 70 years for the desolation of Jerusalem. In performing this calculation Daniel also used the passages in Jer. 25 11,12 and 29 10 where it is stated that upon completion of 70 years for Babylonia, God will remember the Jewish people. The 70-year period for Babylonia, from the start of that nation's conquests until Babylonia was conquered by Persia, is from 609 to 539 (see Section 6.4). By adding 23 years to these dates we get 586 to 516 for the 70-year period for Jerusalem.

It should be emphasized that the concept of 70 years for the desolation of Jerusalem was calculated by Daniel based on passages in the Book of Jeremiah, but was not a direct quotation. The calculation was performed in the first year of Darius (517), one year before the calculated time. Daniel saw no signs of the end of the desolation, and therefore prayed for the forgiveness of the transgressions of the Jewish people. From Sentence 3 to 20 is presented the entreaty of Daniel. Most of the phrases used are based on wording found elsewhere in the Bible. The quoted Biblical statements are cited in the comments on the sentences. In many cases the quoted wording is taken from passages which mention that the Jews will be exiled if they sin. Often, the references also mention that the Jewish people will repent and pray to God, and then the people will return to the land of Israel. Some passages dealing with this theme, from which Daniel has borrowed numerous phrases, are Lev. 26 27–46; Deut. 30 1–10; I Kings 8 44–53; Jer. 29 10–15; and II Chr. 6 34–42.

3. ואתנה את פני אל ד' הא' לבקש תפלה ותחנונים, בצום ושק ואפר.

And I turned my face unto the Lord God to seek prayer and supplication, with fasting and sackcloth and ashes.

To seek prayer and supplication—In I Kings 8 46–53 it is stated that if the people sin and are captured in battle by the enemy, and then pray to God with all their hearts, their prayers will be answered. In particular in I Kings 8 49,50 it is stated "And You will hear in heaven . . . their *prayer* and *supplication* . . . and will forgive Your people who have sinned" ("ושמעת השמים . . . את תפלתם ואת תחנתם . . . וסלחת לעמך"). Daniel therefore sought prayer and supplication so as to be answered by God.

With fasting and sackcloth and ashes—Moreover, Daniel afflicted himself to increase his chance of obtaining a positive reply. The procedure he followed was derived from Isa. 58 5, "Is it a *fast* like this that I desire . . . and to spread *sackcloth* and *ashes?*" ("הכזה יהיה צום אבחרהו . . . ושק ואפר יציע?"), and from Jer. 6 26, "Wrap yourself in *sackcloth* and wallow in *ashes*" ("חגרי שק והתפלשי באפר").

4. ואתפללה לד' א' ואתודה, ואמרה אנא ד' הא' הגדול והנורא שמר הברית והחסד לאהביו ולשמרי מצותיו.

And I prayed to the Lord my God and made confession, and said: O Lord, the great and awe-inspiring God, who keeps the covenant and the kindness with those that love Him and observe His commandments.

I prayed . . . and made confession—Sentences 4 through 14 contain Daniel's prayer. These sentences mainly involve confession of sin, since Daniel considers confession to be a subcategory of prayer.

In Lev. **26** 39–45 it is stated that when the Jewish people are exiled for their sins "they shall *confess* their iniquity . . ." ("והתודו את עונם"). God will then remember the *covenant* ("וזכרתי להם ברית ראשונים"). Similarly in Jer. **29** 12,14 it is stated that the people will "*pray* to Me . . . and I will bring you back . . ." ("והתפללתם אלי . . . והשבתי אתכם"). Therefore, Daniel prayed and confessed so that God would remember the covenant and return the people to the land of Israel.

O Lord—The phrase "O Lord" ("אנא ד'") is the same as that used by Hezekiah (II Kings **20** 2,3) when he prayed to God for his life, and as a result lived for an additional 15 years.

The great and awe-inspiring . . . commandments—Daniel describes the covenant that God will remember by quoting Deut. **7** 9, "the faithful *God, who keeps the covenant and the kindness with those that love Him and observe His commandments*" ("הא' הנאמן שמר הברית והחסד לאהביו ולשמרי מצותיו"). However, Daniel substitutes the words "great and awe-inspiring" for the less appropriate word "faithful," because of the implication from Deut. **7** 21 that you should not fear the enemy since "God is in your midst, a *great and awe-inspiring God*" ("כי ד' א' בקרבך א' גדול ונורא").

There now follows a list of the transgressions that according to the Bible brought about the destruction of the land of Israel.

5. חטאנו ועוינו הרשענו ומרדנו, וסור ממצותך וממשפטיך.
We have sinned, done iniquity, acted wickedly, rebelled, and turned aside from Your commandments and from Your ordinances.

Sinned, done iniquity, acted wickedly—According to I Kings **8** 47 and II Chr. **6** 37 the exiled Jews should pray to God saying "*We have sinned, done iniquity, acted wickedly*" ("חטאנו והעוינו רשענו"). Then God will forgive their transgressions and have compassion on them.

Rebelled—In Num. **14** 9 Caleb and Joshua tell the Jewish people "do not *rebel*" ("אל תמרדו"), otherwise God will not bring the people to the land of Israel.

Turned aside from Your commandments and from Your ordinances—King David tells the leaders of the people that God said to him about his son Solomon (I Chr. **28** 7), "His kingdom will be for ever if he will be strong to do *My commandments and My ordinances*" ("מלכותו עד לעולם, אם יחזק לעשות מצותי ומשפטי"). Daniel here implies that Solomon and the succeeding kings did not always observe the commandments and ordinances, and therefore the nation was exiled.

6. ולא שמענו אל עבדיך הנביאים אשר דברו בשמך אל מלכינו שרינו ואבתינו, ואל כל עם הארץ.

And we have not listened to Your servants the prophets, who spoke in Your name to our kings, princes, and forefathers, and to all the people over the land.

Not listened to Your servants the prophets—It is stated in several places in the Book of Jeremiah (25 4; 26 5; 29 19; 35 15) that the people did not listen to the prophets. For example, in Jer. 26 4-6 it is stated that if the people do not *"listen* to the words of *My servants the prophets"* (ולא...הנביאים עבדי דברי על לשמע" "שמעתם), then the Temple and the city of Jerusalem will be destroyed.

Who spoke ... to all the people over the land—Furthermore, in Jer. 44 16 the people tell Jeremiah, "The word that you have *spoken* to us *in the name of the Lord,* we will *not listen* to you" ("איננו 'ד בשם אלינו דברת אשר הדבר שמעים אליך"). Jeremiah then answers (44 21) that the land is destroyed because of the sins of "you, and your *forefathers,* your *kings* and your *princes* and the *people over the land"* ("אתם ואבותיכם מלכיכם ושריכם ועם הארץ").

7. לך ד' הצדקה ולנו בשת הפנים כיום הזה, לאיש יהודה וליושבי ירושלם ולכל ישראל הקרבים והרחקים בכל הארצות אשר הדחתם שם במעלם אשר מעלו בך.

To you Lord belongs the righteousness, but to us is shamefacedness, as at this day, to the man of Judah and to the inhabitants of Jerusalem, and to all Israelites near and far, in all the countries to which You have driven them for their treachery towards You.

To You ... belongs the righteousness—In Deut. 6 24,25 it is stated that God has commanded us to observe the laws "so that He might preserve us alive *as at this day.* And it shall be *righteousness to us* if we observe..." ("לחיותנו כהיום הזה. וצדקה תהיה לנו כי נשמר"). Daniel implies that since we have not observed the laws therefore the righteousness is not for us but rather for the Lord; instead of life we have evil as at this day.

To us is shamefacedness—The People have sinned, and therefore, as written in Jer. 7 19, God says "Do they anger Me ... ? Is it not themselves [they anger], to make themselves *shamefaced?"* ("האתי הם מכעסים...הלוא אתם למען בשת פניהם"). Daniel confesses that it is true that "to us is shamefacedness."

To the man of Judah and to the inhabitants of Jerusalem—This phrase is repeatedly used by Jeremiah; see for example Jer. 11 2,9,12; 18 11; 25 2; 4 4; 17 25; 32 32; 35 13. Also, the phrase is frequently used in Chronicles (II Chr. 20 15,18,20; 21 13; 32 33; 33 9; 34 30; 35 18). Wherever this phrase is used by Jeremiah it is implied that if the man of Judah and the inhabitants of Jerusalem repent, then good will result; but if they do evil, then destruction will come.

Near and far—The term "near and far" is found in Jer. 25 26 and Deut. 13 8; but it is not used in an analogous manner in either case.

In all the countries to which You have driven them—This phrase is found in several places in the Book of Jeremiah (16 15; 23 3,8; 32 37). In each instance it is indicated that after sending the Israelites into exile, God will subsequently gather them back to the land of Israel. For example in Jer. 16 15 it is stated "By the life of the Lord, who brought the Israelites back from the land of the north and from all the countries to which He had driven them" ("חי ד' אשר העלה את בני ישראל מארץ צפון ומכל הארצות אשר הדיחם שמה").

For their treachery towards You—In Lev. 26 40 God states that the exiled Jews "shall confess their iniquity, and the iniquity of their forefathers, in *their treachery towards Me*" ("והתודו את עונם ואת עון אבתם במעלם אשר מעלו בי"). Then if their repentance is a true repentance, God will not forsake them, but will remember the covenant when He took them out of Egypt.

8.   ד' לנו בשת הפנים למלכינו לשרינו ולאבתינו אשר חטאנו לך.
   O Lord, to us belongs the shamefacedness—to our kings, to our princes, and to our forefathers, who have sinned against You.

This sentence can be considered as a combination of several passages in the Book of Jeremiah, where the sins of the people are specified.

Shamefacedness—to our kings to our princes—In Jer. 2 26 it is stated, "Like the *shame* of a thief when he is found out, so has the house of Israel been shamed; *they, their kings, their princes* . . ." ("כבשת גנב כי ימצא כן הבישו בית ישראל, המה מלכיהם שריהם . . .").

Forefathers who have sinned against You—In Jer. 14 20 it is stated, "We acknowledge, O Lord, our wickedness, the iniquity of *our forefathers*; for we *have sinned against You*" ("ידענו ד' רשענו עון אבותינו כי חטאנו לך"). Also, in Jer. 3 25 it is stated, "Let us lie down in *our shame* . . . for we *have sinned against the Lord* our God, *we and our forefathers*" ("נשכבה בבשתנו . . . כי לד' א' חטאנו אנחנו ואבותינו").

9.   לד' א' הרחמים והסליחות כי מרדנו בו.
   Compassion and forgiveness belong to the Lord our God, for we have rebelled against him.

Passages in the Bible from which this sentence may have been derived are as follows.

Compassion and forgiveness belong to the Lord—In Jer. 16 5 it is stated, "I have *withdrawn* My peace from this people says the *Lord*, even kindness and *compassion*" ("כי אספתי את שלומי מאת העם הזה נאם ד' את החסד ואת הרחמים"). The implication is that God can give or withdraw compassion; and therefore Daniel states "compassion belongs to the Lord." Moreover in Jer. 31 33

God states that when the people recognize Me, then "I will *forgive* their iniquity" ("אסלח לעונם"). Thus Daniel states "forgiveness belongs to God."

We have rebelled against him—The rebellion of the Jews against God is clearly stated in Ez. 2 3, "the Israelites...who *have rebelled against Me*" (בני" "ישראל...אשר מרדו בי).

10. ולא שמענו בקול ד' א׳, ללכת בתורתיו אשר נתן לפנינו ביד עבדיו הנביאים.

And we have not listened to the voice of the Lord our God, to walk in His laws which He set before us by His servants the prophets.

Not listened to the voice of the Lord our God—This exact phrase is found in Jer. 3 25. Also compare Jer. 44 23.

Walk in His laws—In Jer. 26 4-6 God states that the Temple would be destroyed and the city of Jerusalem would be made a curse, "If you *do not listen to Me, to walk in My law, which I have set before you;* to listen to the words of *My servants the prophets*" ("אם לא תשמעו אלי ללכת בתורתי אשר נתתי לפניכם, לשמע" "על דברי עבדי הנביאים).

11. וכל ישראל עברו את תורתך וסור לבלתי שמוע בקלך, ותתך עלינו האלה והשבעה אשר כתובה בתורת משה עבד הא׳ כי חטאנו לו.

All Israel has broken Your law, and has turned aside so as not to listen to Your voice; and You poured out upon us the curse and the oath that is written in the "Law of Moses the Servant of God," for we have sinned against Him.

Broken Your law—A comparable phrase is found in Isa. 24 5-6, "they have broken the laws...therefore a *curse* devoured the land" (כי עברו תורת" "...על כן אלה אכלה ארץ).

So as not to listen to Your voice—In Jer. 42 the Jewish remnant, after the destruction of the Temple, are told that if they reside in the land of Israel God will help them, but if (42 13,18) "you *do not listen to the voice of the Lord*...then My anger shall be *poured out upon you*...and you shall be a curse" ("לבלתי" "שמע בקול ד׳...תתך חמתי עליכם...והייתם לאלה). Daniel partly based the theme of this sentence upon this cited passage in the Book of Jeremiah. Also see Jer. 9 12; 16 11-12; 32 23,40; 40 3 for other cases where variants of the expression "not to listen to Your voice" are used.

Curse and the oath that is written in the "Law of Moses the Servant of God"— As established in Section 10.6, the "Law of Moses the Servant of God" is an early name for the Book of Numbers. The "curse and the oath" mentioned here refer to the same phrase used in Num. 5 21 concerning an unfaithful wife. Daniel makes the analogy between the unfaithfulness of the Jewish people to God, and the unfaithfulness of a wife to her husband. According to Num. 5 27,28, if the wife was in fact unfaithful, then she becomes a curse among her people; but if the wife is innocent, then she conceives and bears children.

Have sinned against Him—In Jer. **40** 3 it is stated that God carried out the evil that He threatened to bring because, "You *have sinned against the Lord*" – ("כי חטאתם לד׳").

12. ויקם את דבריו אשר דבר עלינו ועל שפטינו אשר שפטונו להביא עלינו רעה גדלה, אשר לא נעשתה תחת כל השמים כאשר נעשתה בירושלם.

And He has fulfilled His word that He said about us and about the judges who judged us, to bring upon us a great calamity, such as has not been done under the whole heaven as has been done in Jerusalem.

Great calamity—Implied in this and the following two sentences is the idea that just as God brought about the destruction that he promised, so He will bring about the good that he promised. Thus in Jer. **32** 42 it is stated, "For thus said the Lord: As I have *brought upon* this people all this *great calamity*, so will I bring upon them all the good *which I say about them*"

"כי כה אמר ד׳ כאשר הבאתי אל העם הזה את כל הרעה הגדולה הזאת, כן אנכי מביא עליהם את כל הטובה אשר אנכי דבר עליהם").

13. כאשר כתוב בתורת משה את כל הרעה הזאת באה עלינו, ולא חלינו את פני ד׳ א׳ לשוב מעונינו ולהשכיל באמתך.

As it is written in the "Law of Moses," all this calamity is come upon us, yet we have not entreated the favor of the Lord our God, to repent from our iniquities and to become wise in Your truth.

"Law of Moses"—The "Law of Moses" is an early name for the Book of Deuteronomy (see Section 10.6).

All this calamity is come upon us—Daniel refers to Deut. **28** 15, where it is stated, "If you do not listen to the voice of the Lord your God ... all these curses shall *come upon you* and overtake you" (... אם לא תשמע בקול ד׳ א׳" ובאו עליך כל הקללות האלה והשיגוך"). However, Daniel modifies the quotation slightly by substituting the wording used in Jer. **32** 23, "You have caused *all this calamity* to befall them" ("ותקרא אתם את כל הרעה הזאת"). On the other hand, it is stated in Deut. **28** 1,2, "If you shall listen to the voice of the Lord your God ... all these blessings shall come upon you and overtake you" (אם" שמוע תשמע בקול ד׳ א׳ ... ובאו עליך כל הברכות האלה והשיגך"). Thus, Daniel implies that if the people repent and observe the laws, then blessings will occur.

Not entreated the favor of the Lord—In several instances entreating God resulted in a favorable response. In Ex. **32** 11,14 it is stated, "Moses *entreated the favor of the Lord* his God ... and the Lord relented of the *calamity* He said He would cause to His people" (ויחל משה את פני ד׳ א׳ ... וינחם ד׳ על הרעה").

"לעמו לעשות דבר אשר"). In Jer. 26 19 it is stated that Hezekiah *"entreated the favor of the Lord,* and the Lord relented of the *calamity* He had pronounced against them" ("ויחל את פני ד' וינחם ד' אל הרעה אשר דבר עליהם"). Also in II Kings 13 4 we find "Jehoahaz *entreated the favor of the Lord,* and the Lord listened to him" ("ויחל יהואחז את פני ד' וישמע אליו ד'").

Repent from our iniquities—Compare Jer. 16 10, "Why has the Lord pronounced *upon us all this great calamity,* and what is *our iniquity*" ("על מה דבר ד' עלינו את כל הרעה הגדולה הזאת ומה עוננו").

Become wise in Your truth—Compare Jer. 9 23, *"Become wise* and know Me . . . for these things I desire" ("השכל וידע אותי . . . כי באלה חפצתי").

14. וישקד ד' על הרעה ויביאה עלינו, כי צדיק ד' א' על כל מעשיו אשר עשה ולא שמענו בקלו.

And the Lord was eager concerning the calamity, and brought it upon us; for the Lord our God is justified in all His actions that He did, and we have not listened to His voice.

Was eager—Here again Daniel implies that good will follow the calamity, as stated in Jer. 31 27, "And it will be, that just as I was *eager upon them* to pluck up and to break down, to overthrow and to destroy, and *to cause calamity,* so will I be eager upon them to build and to plant, says the Lord" ("והיה כאשר שקדתי עליהם לנתוש ולנתוץ ולהרס ולהאביד ולהרע, כן אשקד עליהם לבנות ולנטוע נאם ד'").

15. ועתה ד' א' אשר הוצאת את עמך מארץ מצרים ביד חזקה ותעש לך שם כיום הזה חטאנו רשענו.

And now, O Lord our God, who did bring Your people out of Egypt with a strong hand, and made a name for Yourself as at this day, we have sinned, we have acted wickedly.

This sentence begins the supplication (תחנה) (Sentences 15 through 19). Here Daniel uses phrases which were successfully used by others in their requests for help by God.

And now O Lord our God—King Solomon used essentially the same phrase (I Kings 3 7) when he requested a discerning mind. Also King Hezekiah used essentially the same phrase (II Kings 19 19) when he prayed for help against Sennacherib. In both cases they received positive replies.

Did bring Your people out of Egypt . . . as at this day—In Jer. 32 20-21, Jeremiah uses the expressions, *"And made a name for Yourself as at this day, and did bring Your people* Israel *out of* the land of *Egypt* with signs and with wonders and *with a strong hand"* ("ותעשה לך שם כיום הזה, ותצא את עמך את ישראל מארץ מצרים באתות ובמופתים וביד חזקה"). Then God answers Jeremiah (32 26-44) saying that the Jews will be returned to the land after the exile, and good things will come.

16. ד׳ ככל צדקתך ישב נא אפך וחמתך מעירך ירושלם הר קדשך, כי בחטאינו ובעונות אבתינו ירושלם ועמך לחרפה לכל סביבתינו.

> O Lord, according to all Your righteousness, please let Your anger and fury be turned away from Your city Jerusalem, Your holy mountain; because for our sins and the iniquities of our forefathers, Jerusalem and Your people have become a reproach to all that are round about us.

Daniel requests that God should remove His anger from the city of Jerusalem and from the site of the Temple.

Lord according to all your righteousness—Compare Jer. 12 1, "*Righteous are You O Lord*" ("צדיק אתה ד׳").

Your anger and fury be turned away from Your city Jerusalem—Compare Jer. 32 36,37, "Thus says the Lord... concerning this *city*... behold I will gather them from all the countries to which I have driven them in *My anger and fury*... and I will *return* them" ("כה אמר ד׳...אל העיר הזאת...הנני מקבצם מכל הארצות אשר הדחתים שם באפי ובחמתי...והשבתים"). Also compare Jer. 42 18, "As *My anger and fury* has been poured forth upon the inhabitants of *Jerusalem*... you shall be a curse... and a *reproach*" ("כאשר נתך אפי וחמתי על ישבי ירושלם...והייתם לאלה...ולחרפה").

Your holy mountain—Compare Jer. 31 22, "When I shall *return* their settlements... *the holy mountain*" ("בשובי את שבותם...הר הקדש").

Iniquities of our forefathers—Compare Jer. 11 10, "They are *turned* back to the *iniquities of their forefathers*" ("שבו על עונת אבותם").

A reproach to all that are round about us—In several places (Jer. 24 9; 29 18; 42 18) the Jews are told that they will become a reproach among the nations where they are exiled. For example, in Jer. 24 9 it is stated, "I will make them... a *reproach*... in all the places to where I shall drive them" ("ונתתים לחרפה...בכל המקומות אשר אדיחם שם").

17. ועתה שמע א׳ אל תפלת עבדך ואל תחנוניו והאר פניך על מקדשך השמם למען ד׳.

> And now listen, our God, to the prayer of Your servant and to his supplications, and make Your face shine, for the Lord's sake, upon Your temple that is desolate.

Daniel now requests that the Temple be reconstructed.

And now listen—The same phrase was used successfully by Jeremiah (Jer. 37 20) when he presented a supplication for his life to King Zedekiah. Jeremiah said, "*And now listen*... let my *supplication* be presented before you" ("ועתה שמע...תפל נא תחנתי לפניך").

To the prayer of Your servant and to his supplications—King Solomon used similar phraseology in praying that God heed the requests made in the Temple

(I Kings 8 28); and he later received a favorable reply (I Kings 9 3). Solomon stated, "Respond *to the prayer of Your servant and to his supplication* O Lord *my God*" ("ופנית אל תפלת עבדך ואל תחנתו ד׳ א׳").

Make your face shine—In Ps. 80 4,8,20 is found the expression "*Make Your face shine* and we shall be saved" ("האר פניך ונושעה"). This expression "make Your face shine" is used nowhere else in the Bible, and therefore we have a strong indication that Daniel was here quoting the Book of Psalms.

Temple that is desolate—In Lev. 26 31 is found the comparable expression, "I will make your *temples desolate*" ("והשמותי את מקדשיכם").

For the Lord's sake—Similarly we find that Jeremiah prayed to God (Jer. 14 7) saying, "Though our iniquities testify against us, O Lord, accomplish *for Your name's sake*" ("אם עונינו ענו בנו, ד׳ עשה למען שמך").

18. הטה א׳ אזנך ושמע פקח עיניך וראה שממתינו והעיר אשר נקרא שמך עליה, כי לא על צדקתינו אנחנו מפילים תחנונינו לפניך כי על רחמיך הרבים.
O my God, incline Your ear, and hear; open Your eyes and see our desolations and the city upon which Your name is called: for it is not because of our righteousness that we present our supplications before You, but because of Your great mercy.

Daniel once again requests consideration from God concerning the city of Jerusalem, and adds the request for consideration of the desolate cities.

Incline Your ear, and hear; open Your eyes and see—Almost exactly the same phrase was used successfully by King Hezekiah when he prayed to God for help against Sennacherib (see II Kings 19 16, 20; Is. 37 17,21).

Our desolations—The word "desolation" (שממה) is used by Jeremiah to designate the desolation of the cities and of the land (see e.g., Jer. 4 27; 9 10).

The city upon which Your name is called—In Jer. 25 29 it is stated, "With *the city upon which My name is called* I begin calamity" ("כי הנה בעיר אשר נקרא שמי עליה אנכי מחל להרע").

Not because of our righteousness—In Deut. 9 6 it is stated, "And know that it is *not because of your righteousness* that the Lord your God gives you this good land to inherit" ("וידעת כי לא בצדקתך ד׳ א׳ נתן לך את הארץ הטובה הזאת"). Here Daniel, to meet the requirements of the statement in Deuteronomy, admits that "it is not because of righteousness" that he makes the supplication.

Present our supplications before You—Variations of this phrase are found in several places in the Book of Jeremiah (36 7; 38 26; 42 2,9). For example, in Jer. 36 7, Jeremiah expresses the hope that reading from the prophecies will cause the people to "*present their supplication before the Lord*" ("תפל תחנתם לפני ד׳").

Your great mercy—In numerous places in the Bible the mercy of God is mentioned.

For example, in Ps. 119 156 it is stated, "*Great is Your mercy, O Lord*" ("רחמיך רבים ד'").

19. ד' שמעה ד' סלחה ד' הקשיבה ועשה אל תאחר, למענך א' כי
שמך נקרא על עירך ועל עמך.

O Lord hear, O Lord forgive, O Lord listen and act, do not delay; for your own sake my God, because Your name is called upon Your city and Your people.

This sentence concludes the supplication. Daniel makes an impassioned plea that his requests be fulfilled without delay. Some comparable phrases to those used in the sentence are as follows:

Ps. 102 2	"*O Lord hear* my prayer"	("ד' שמעה תפלתי")
Ps. 86 5	"You, Lord, are good, and ready to *forgive*"	("אתה ד' טוב וסלח")
Ps. 86 6	"*Listen* to the voice of my supplications"	("והקשיבה בקול תחנונותי")
Jer. 14 7	"O Lord, *act for Your name's sake*"	("ד' עשה למען שמך")
Ps. 70 6	"O Lord, *do not delay*"	("ד' אל תאחר")
Jer. 25 29	"With *the city upon which My name is called*"	("בעיר אשר נקרא שמי עליה")
Jer. 14 9	"And *Your name is called upon us*"	("ושמך עלינו נקרא")

20. ועוד אני מדבר ומתפלל ומתודה חטאתי וחטאת עמי ישראל
ומפיל תחנתי לפני ד' א' על הר קדש א'.

And while I was speaking and praying and confessing my sin and the sin of my people Israel, and presenting my supplication before the Lord my God on behalf of the holy mountain of my God;

While I was speaking—Daniel, in this and the following sentence, mentions that the angel Gabriel appeared while Daniel was still praying and presenting supplication.

21. ועוד אני מדבר בתפלה, והאיש גבריאל אשר ראיתי בחזון
בתחלה מעף ביעף נגע אלי כעת מנחת ערב.

And while I was speaking in prayer, and here was the man Gabriel—whom I had seen in the vision, at the beginning, exhausted with tiredness, touching me, at about the 25 years before the sacrifice at the evening.

Gabriel—The angel Gabriel, who represents the Arabian empire, is the one to present the revelation to Daniel, because the events described involve the Arab countries (see Sentences 26–27).

Whom I had seen—Daniel now refers back to the revelation described in Chapter 8, where Gabriel had appeared. The ensuing references to that revelation are very condensed, and make sense only when compared to the wording in Chapter 8.

In the vision at the beginning—Refers to Dan. **8** 1, "*vision* appeared to me Daniel, after what appeared to me *at the beginning.*" Daniel here mentioned the first and last key words of that sentence.

Exhausted with tiredness, touching me—Compare Dan. **8** 18 where Daniel states that he "*fell into a deep sleep*," and then Gabriel "*touched me.*"

At about the 25 years before the sacrifice at the evening—The Hebrew word עת is used to mean 25 years (see Table 16.0.1). The 25 years refer to those 25 years mentioned in Dan. **8** 17, which were from 605 to 630, and were approximately up to the time when the sacrifices were brought at the evening-morning rites (632 C.E.) (compare Dan. **8** 14).

22. ויבן, וידבר עמי, ויאמר, דניאל עתה יצאתי להשכילך בינה.
   And he understood; and he spoke to me, and said "Daniel, I have now come forth to make you wise in understanding."

He understood—The angel Gabriel had been quietly standing nearby until Daniel finished praying (see Sentence 20). Daniel realized that Gabriel understood the prayer and supplication.

23. בתחלת תחנוניך יצא דבר ואני באתי להגיד כי חמודות אתה, ובין בדבר והבן במראה.
   At the beginning of your supplications a word went forth, and I have come to tell it, for you are greatly beloved; consider the word and understand the appearance.

At the beginning of your supplications—The prophetic message was released when Daniel began the supplication (Sentences 15 through 19).

A word went forth—The prophecy in Sentences 24–27 was a verbal message.

Understand the appearance—Understand the significance of the appearance of the angel Gabriel. The fact that Gabriel was the one to deliver the message indicates that a prophecy concerning the Arab nations is involved.

24. שבעים שבעים נחתך על עמך ועל עיר קדשך לכלא הפשע ולהתם חטאת ולכפר עון ולהביא צדק עלמים, ולחתם חזון ונביא, ולמשח קדש קדשים.
   Seventy periods of 49 years have been cut off from your people and your holy city, to end the rebellious transgression, and to consume the sin, and to forgive the iniquity, and to bring about everlasting righteousness, and to seal vision and prophecy, and to anoint the most holy items.

It was now implied to Daniel that although he correctly calculated that the Second Temple would be built after 70 years of desolation, yet many of the prophecies in the Bible refer not to the period of the Second Temple but to that of the

Seventy periods of 49 years—The Hebrew word שָׁבֻעִים, which is found only in this and the following chapter, is here used to designate a period of 49 years (see Table 16.0.1). Note that a period of 7 years would have been designated by the word שָׁבֻעוֹת, and a period of 14 years by שְׁבֻעַיִם. The word שָׁבֻעִים is the plural of שָׁבוּעַ (Dan. 9 27), just as the word שָׁבֻעוֹת is the plural of שָׁבֻעַ (Gen. 29 27,28). Seventy periods of 49 years is 70 × 49, which equals 3,430 years.

Cut off from your people and your holy city—The period of 3,430 years will be a time during which the true greatness of the Jewish people and of the holy city of Jerusalem will not be attained. As will be presently shown, the 3,430 years are from Nisan, 1434 B.C.E. (inclusive) through 1996 C.E. Thus

```
   3430
 − 1435
   1995
 +    1    (no year zero in this system
   1996     of counting)
```

To end the rebellious transgression, and to consume the sin, and to forgive the iniquity—Three major misdeeds were committed by the Jewish people before entering the land of Israel under the leadership of Joshua. The first was the selling of Joseph by his brothers, which is denoted by the word פשע (rebellious transgression). Thus, in Gen. 50 17, Joseph's brothers request of Joseph, "Please forgive the rebellious transgression of your brothers ... and now please forgive the rebellious transgression of the servants of the God of your father" (אנא "שא נא פשע אחיך...ועתה שא נא עבדי א' אביך"). (Also compare Amos 2 6, where the misdeed of selling a righteous man is called a "rebellious transgression" [פשע].

The second misdeed was the making of a golden calf, which is denoted by the word חטאת (sin). Thus, in Ex. 32 31,32 Moses requests of God, "This people has sinned a great sin, they made a god of gold; and now if you will excuse their sin..." ("אנא חטא העם הזה חטאה גדלה ויעשו להם אלהי זהב, ועתה" "אם תשא חטאתם"). (Also compare I Kings 12 28,30 where the golden calves set up by Jeroboam are called "sin" [חטאת].

The third misdeed was the lack of faith in God by the spies and the people, which is denoted by the word עון (iniquity). Thus, in connection with this incident Moses pleads to God (Num. 14 19), "Please pardon the iniquity of this people" ("סלח נא לעון העם הזה").

In all these three cases the misdeeds were not entirely forgiven, as indicated in the text (see Gen. 50 15,21; Ex. 32 34; Num. 14 20–23). Also in each of the cases mention is made of punishment of the fourth generation (see Gen. 15 16; Ex. 34 7; Num. 14 18).

Here the angel Gabriel states that it will take 3,430 years to atone completely for these three misdeeds; that is, to end the rebellious transgression, to consume the sin, and to forgive the iniquity.

Bring about everlasting righteousness—After the 3,430 years there will no longer be persecution of Jews; justice will prevail throughout the world; and there will no longer be wars between nations.

To seal vision and prophecy—All the visions and prophecies of the Bible will have been fulfilled after the 3,430 years. The books of the prophets, including the Book of Daniel, will be correctly interpreted by that time.

To anoint the most holy items—One of the final steps in constructing the Tabernacle was the anointing of all the sacred objects to make them most holy, as stated in Ex. 30 25-29. Similarly, the final step in building the Third Temple will be the anointing of the sacred items. Thus, construction of the Third Temple will be completed by the end of the 3,430 years.

25. ותדע ותשכל מן מצא דבר להשיב ולבנות ירושלם עד משיח נגיד שבעים שבעה, ושבעים ששים ושנים תשוב ונבנתה רחוב וחרוץ ובצוק העתים.

And you will know and you will be wise, from the coming forth of the word to return and to build Jerusalem, until the one anointed as a prince, shall be seven times 49 years; and for 62 times 49 years it will return and will be built with streets and cisterns, but in troubled times.

The 70 × 49 years are subdivided in this and the following sentences into three main parts, namely 7, 62 and 1 times 49 years. Moreover the 1 × 49 years are divided into two halves.

You will know and you will be wise—If you will know the historical events that are mentioned, then you will be able to understand the revelation.

From the coming forth of the word to return and to build Jerusalem—Shortly after the Jewish people entered the land of Israel, after the 40 years in the desert, Joshua was confronted by the captain of the army of the Lord (Josh. 5 13-15). This angel said, "I have now come." These words signalled the start of military campaigns by Joshua, where the intent was eventually to conquer Jerusalem. This coming forth of the word by the angel occurred around Nisan, 1434 B.C.E. (see Table 3.1), shortly after observance of the Passover sacrifice (Josh. 5 10).

The use of the word "return" implies that Jerusalem belonged to the Jews prior to the time of Joshua. This is the case, since the territory specified to be given to the offspring of Abraham (Gen. 15 18-21) included the Jebusites, who we know from Josh. 15 63; 18 28; Jud. 1 21; 19 10; and I Chr. 11 4, occupied the city of Jerusalem. Furthermore, in Gen. 33 18,19 Jacob purchased a parcel of ground in Shalem, the city where Shechem lived. Shalem is an early name for the city now known as Jerusalem.

The one anointed as a prince—King Saul was the only ruler (other than

Solomon—see I Chr. **29** 22) who was anointed as a "prince." Thus, God told Samuel (I Sam. **9** 16), "You shall anoint him to be prince" ("ומשחתו לנגיד"). When the anointing of Saul occurred (I Sam. **10** 1), Samuel said, "the Lord has anointed you as a prince over His inheritance" ("משחך ד׳ על נחלתו לנגיד"). The event referred to here, by the angel Gabriel, is the birth of Saul. Saul was anointed in 1041 (see Table 4.1), when he was 52 years old (see Section 4.4). Saul was therefore born in 1093, and his first birthday was Nisan, 1092 B.C.E.

Seven times 49 years—From the coming forth of the word in Nisan 1434, until the first birthday of Saul, in Nisan 1092, is 7 × 49 or 343 years (if we include the initial and final years).

For 62 times 49 years—For 3,038 years after 1092 B.C.E., i.e., through the year 1947 C.E. (since there is no year zero in this system of counting).

Will return—The old city of Jerusalem will be conquered by the Israelites. The actual conquest from the Jebusites (II Sam. **5** 6–8) occurred sometime between the eighth and fourteenth years of David's reign, sometime between 1031 and 1025 (see Tables 4.1 and 11.3.4).

Will be built with streets and cisterns—Paved streets and cisterns for gathering rain water will be built. Because of the scarcity of water in Jerusalem every house was provided with one or more cisterns for gathering rain water[83]. Moreover, a huge underground cistern was built in the city, probably for a water supply[84].

But in troubled times—The old city of Jerusalem, during these 3,038 years, has suffered at the hands of nature and man. She has been rocked by earthquakes and sacked by invaders. She has endured over 20 sieges and blockades, about 18 reconstructions, and two periods of desolation. More than six times she has passed from one religion to another. But Jerusalem still remains[85].

26. ואחרי השבעים ששים ושנים יכרת משיח ואין לו, והעיר והקדש ישחית עם נגיד הבא וקצו בשטף, ועד קץ מלחמה נחרצת שממות.

And after the 62 times 49 years, an anointed ruler, who has no power, shall be cut off; and the city and the holy places will be destroyed by a people of a prince who comes, and his end is sudden; and at the end of a war desolate places shall be cut out.

After the 62 times 49 years—The 3,038 years are completed beginning with Nisan, 1948 C.E.

An anointed ruler, who has no power, shall be cut off—This phrase refers to the termination of the British mandate over Palestine in 1948. The "anointed ruler who has no power" is the King of England who is anointed as king but has no official power to rule his country. Interestingly, at the anointing ceremony the king is supposedly anointed in the same way as was King Solomon. On November 29, 1947 the United Nations Assembly voted for partition of Palestine, and the formation of a Jewish state. Subsequently, the British mandate officially ended May 14, 1948, and on the same day the State of Israel was proclaimed[86].

The city and the holy places will be destroyed—The event referred to is the conquest of the Old City of Jerusalem in 1948 by Transjordan (later known as Jordan), and the subsequent destruction of the Jewish holy places. The day after establishment of the State of Israel, the regular armies of Egypt, Iraq, Transjordan, Syria, and Lebanon invaded. As a result of the fighting Israel gained in territory but lost control over the Old City of Jerusalem. An armistice agreement was signed with Egypt on February 24, 1949; with Lebanon on March 23; with Transjordan on April 3; and with Syria on July 20. The agreement with Transjordan left the Old City of Jerusalem under Arab control[87]. In 1967, after the Six-Day War, during which Israel recaptured the Old City of Jerusalem, it was found that the Jordanians, during their 19 years of occupation, had destroyed all but two of the 58 synagogues, had desecrated Jewish cemeteries, and in general had profaned many holy shrines[88,89].

By a people of a prince who comes—This refers to the country of Jordan (formerly Transjordan). In 1921, Emir Abdullah, a prince of Hejaz was designated by the British as leader of the territory of Transjordan. In March 1946, Transjordan became independent, with Abdullah as king[90,91]. Abdullah is here designated as a "prince who comes" since he was a prince who came from a different country.

His end is sudden—On July 20, 1951 Abdullah was assassinated in Jerusalem[92].

At the end of a war desolate places shall be cut out—The armistice agreements, which concluded the War of Independence between Israel and the neighboring Arab countries, provided for demilitarized zones between Israel and her neighbors[93]. These border regions, often called no-man's-land, were not to be used for military purposes and usually ended up being desolate areas.

27. והגביר ברית לרבים שבוע אחד, וחצי השבוע ישבית זבח ומנחה, ועל כנף שקוצים משומם, ועד כלה ונחרצה תתך על שומם.

And an armistice under the auspices of the "many" will be in force for 49 years; and at half the 49 years slaughter and destruction will cease; and up will rise the wing to cause desolation to those who are detestable; and until an end and an excavation will be poured upon that which causes desolation.

Many of the events described in this sentence are yet to happen or are taking place at the present time, therefore there may be significant inaccuracies in the following interpretations. By 1996 at the latest, when all the described events will have occurred, it will be possible to give a completely accurate explanation.

An armistice under the auspices of the 'many'—The 'many' refers to the United Nations composed of many countries. After the War of Independence in 1948 armistice agreements were signed, under U.N. auspices, between Israel and the neighboring Arab countries. The signing of the armistice agreements with Egypt (February 24, 1949) and with Lebanon (March 23, 1949) occurred before Nisan 1949, and therefore are here considered as having been signed in the year 1948 (based on Nisan as the beginning of the year).

Will be in force for 49 years—The United Nations will consider the armistice agreements as legally binding for 49 years, from 1948 (inclusive) through 1996. For example, even after the Six-Day War in 1967, when significant increases in Israeli territory occurred, Secretary-General U Thant of the United Nations insisted that the original armistice agreements were still fully valid. In fact, the Arab countries continually demand withdrawal of all Israeli forces to the armistice boundaries[94].

At half the 49 years slaughter and destruction will cease—This phrase refers to the cease fire between Israel and Egypt (which indirectly included other Arab countries) that lasted for two years from August 8, 1970[95] until September 8, 1972. Half of 49 years is $24\frac{1}{2}$ years. Based on a Nisan year the exact half point would be September 20, 1971 (the first of Tishri). The cease fire began on August 8, 1970 one year before the half point, shortly before the first of Tishri 1970 (October 1, 1970) and lasted until one year after the half point (September 8, 1972—the day before the first of Tishri 1972). The word זבח here refers to the slaughter of human beings during fighting, and the word מנחה to the destruction of inanimate objects. This is analogous to the usage of the word זבח for animal sacrifices, and the word מנחה for meal offerings, i.e. sacrifices of non-living items[96]. During the period of the cease fire the killing of people and the destruction of property was almost completely stopped.

Up will rise the wing to cause desolation to those who are detestable—The Arab countries, unable to wage a successful military fight against Israel, often resorted to the use of terrorist organizations, officially recognized by their governments, to cause death and destruction in Israel or to Israelis in foreign countries[97]. On September 4,5, 1972, 11 Israeli athletes, participating in the Olympic games in Munich Germany were killed by Arab terrorists. In retaliation for this cold-blooded act, the Israel Air-Force, on September 8, 1972, thoroughly bombed 11 terrorist camps in Lebanon and Syria[98,99], thereby breaking the cease fire arrangements. Numerous attacks by the Israel Air-Force against other terrorist camps followed subsequently. The Israel Air Force is the "wing" and the terrorists are "those who are destestable".

Until an end and an excavation will be poured upon that which causes desolation—A possible interpretation of this passage is that it refers to the destruction of the enemy at the time of the War of Gog in 1973. "That which causes desolation" would be the army of Gog. The "end" and "excavation" would then refer to the destruction and subsequent burial of the people in the army. Numerous other possibilities for this phrase exist, and we have to await the event before we can be certain what was meant.

16.5 CHAPTER 10 OF DANIEL

Chapters 10 to 12 need to be treated as one unit since they describe a single revelation. Chapter 10 contains the introductory passages, Chapter 11 the minute details of the revelation, and Chapter 12 the concluding sections. Daniel knew, from reading of Jer. 25 11,12; 29 10, that the Jewish people would be returned to their land after 539 B.C.E. (see Section 6.4). However in Nisan 539, the beginning of the year when the 70 years to Babylonia were to be completed (i.e., from the start of the conquests by Babylonia until that nation was conquered by Persia), no signs were yet apparent that the Jewish nation would soon regain autonomy. Daniel therefore began a mourning period to ask for the fulfillment of the promise to Jeremiah. Daniel fully expected that an independent Jewish nation would soon be established. Upon completion of the mourning period, the angel dressed in linen appeared. He implies to Daniel that although the 70 years to Babylonia are complete, the Jews would not regain independence immediately. Many different countries would dominate the land of Israel, until eventually at the time of Simon of the Hasmonaean dynasty, in 139 B.C.E., independence would be achieved. However, this independence would not last long. Another, even greater, waiting period would be necessary until finally in 1948 C.E., after two World Wars, and after termination of the British mandate over Palestine, the Jews would become independent forever, with the establishment of the State of Israel.

The background situation in Chapter 10 is parallel to that previously described for Chapter 9. In Chapter 10, Daniel began mourning on the first of Nisan 539 since that date marked the completion of 70 years for Babylonia, and yet no indications were apparent of the reestablishment of the Jewish nation. In Chapter 9, Daniel entreated God in 517 because it was one year before completion of the 70 years for desolation of the Temple, and yet no construction work had begun.

1. בשנת שלוש לכורש מלך פרס דבר נגלה לדניאל אשר נקרא שמו
   בלטאשצר, ואמת הדבר וצבא גדול ובין את הדבר ובינה לו
   במראה.

   In the third year of Cyrus, king of Persia, a word was revealed to Daniel, whose name was called Belteshazzar: and the word was precise; and with a large army; and contemplate the word; and understanding was to him in the vision.

   Third year of Cyrus—Cyrus conquered Babylon in October 539 B.C.E. From the beginning of 538 Cyrus dated his years as king of Babylon and king of the countries[100]. The third year of Cyrus was therefore 536.

   A word—A verbal message.

   Daniel, whose name was called Belteshazzar—The emphasis on the fact that Daniel was also called by the Babylonian name Belteshazzar (see Dan. 1 7) is to establish that it was the same Daniel—the one who was important at the time of the

Babylonian empire—who now during the Persian empire experienced this revelation. Note that the date of the third year of Cyrus is the earliest dating by Daniel of an event during the Persian empire.

The word was precise—Each word or phrase of the verbal message had a precise historical meaning.

With a large army—Within the vision are mentioned a number of war-angels. These are: the man clothed in linen (**10** 5); the prince of the kingdom of Persia (**10** 13); Michael (**10** 13); the prince of Greece (**10** 20); and two others (**12** 5).

Contemplate the word—Analyze the wording carefully.

Understanding was to him in the vision—Objects and persons sighted during the vision helped Daniel to understand the verbal message.

2. בימים ההם, אני דניאל הייתי מתאבל שלשה שבעים ימים.
 In those six years, I Daniel was mourning three times forty-nine times six days.

In this sentence, as well as in all the prophetic chapters of the Book of Daniel, the word ימים (days) is used to indicate the number six, and the word שבעים (weeks) is used to signify the number forty-nine (see Table 16.0.1).

In those six years—Daniel divided the time after the destruction of the Temple into six-year periods. These periods were 586-581; 580-575; 574-569; 568-563; 562-557; 556-551; 550-545; 544-539; and 538-533. The last two six-year periods are those meant by Daniel.

Three times forty-nine times six days—That is, $3 \times 9 \times 6 = 882$ days.

Daniel was mourning 882 days—Let us assume that he period of mourning was begun by Daniel on the first day of the year in which C⋅ us later conquered Babylon, on the first day of Nisan, 539. The mourning period w as completed on the twenty-third day of Nisan 536, the day before Daniel received the revelation, as implied from **10** 3,4. Moreover, assume that none of the three consecutive lunar years (of 354 days) was a leap-year, which is very possible since the calendar was not set at that time. Then the total duration of the mourning period is $3 \times 354 + 23 = 1085$ days. Let us also realize that Daniel did not mourn on major Biblical holidays, namely on the Sabbath, Festival of Matzot, Festival of Weeks, Day of Blowing the Shofar, Festival of Tabernacles, and Atzeret. He did, however, mourn on the Day of Atonement, since that day is prescribed for self-affliction. Now, during the mourning period of slightly more than three years there were:

4×7 days $= 28$ days of Festival of Matzot
3×1 days $= 3$ days of Festival of Weeks
3×1 days $= 3$ days of Day of Blowing the Shofar
3×7 days $= 21$ days of Festival of Tabernalces
3×1 days $= 3$ days of Atzeret

Total $= 58$ days of holidays

Furthermore, during the 1,085 days of the mourning period there were 155

Sabbaths, of which nine occurred on these holidays, and one occurred on the Day of Atonement. Thus, 145 days of Sabbath (155−10) need to be also considered. The sum of 882 + 58 + 145 is 1,085 days, in agreement with the assumption previously made that the mourning period was begun on the first day of Nisan 539.

We may now conjecture as to why Daniel selected a duration of 3 × 49 × 6 days for mourning. Initially Daniel began mourning in Nisan 539 because it was the predicted year for the end of 70 years for Babylonia, and yet no signs of such an event had emerged. When Nisan 538 arrived Daniel realized that it was the beginning of a new 6-year period from the time of destruction of the Temple. When Nisan 537 arrived, he realized it was 49 years after the destruction. Later, Nisan 536 marked the third year of Cyrus. Then, Daniel multiplied the numbers 3, 49 and 6 to arrive at a mourning period of 882 days.

3. לחם חמדות לא אכלתי ובשר ויין לא בא אל פי וסוך לא סכתי, עד מלאת שלשת שבעים ימים.

I ate no choice bread; and meat and wine did not come in my mouth; and I did not anoint myself; until completion of three times forty-nine times six days.

Until completion of three times forty-nine times six days—The type of mourning that Daniel practiced—which involved not eating choice bread, meat, and wine, and not anointing the body with oil—was of a type that could easily be endured for 882 days; especially when the abstentions were not practiced on the Sabbath and holidays.

4. וביום עשרים וארבעה לחדש הראשון, ואני הייתי על יד הנהר הגדול הוא חדקל.

On the twenty-fourth day of the first month, I was on the bank of the great river, that is, the Tigris.

The twenty-fourth day of the first month—This was the day after completion by Daniel of the 882 days of mourning.

5. ואשא את עיני וארא והנה איש אחד לבוש בדים, ומתניו חגרים בכתם אופז.

I raised my eyes and saw, and behold a man clothed in linen, whose loins were girded with pure gold of Uphaz.

Man clothed in linen—The man clothed in linen represents the angel of Babylonia. In Ez. **9** 2–11, the man clothed in linen was the one who selected those Jews worthy of surviving the destruction of the city of Jerusalem; and in Ez. **10** 2–7 he was the one who set fire to the city. Both these acts were accomplished by the Babylonians. The linen garments are representative of the garments worn by the priests (Lev. **6** 3). This type of wearing apparel was necessary for the angel of Babylonia, since he approached the cherubim of the Temple to take burning coals (Ez. **10** 2).

Whose loins were girded with pure gold—The pure gold represents Babylonia, as was the case in Dan. 2 32,38; 3 1.

6. וגויתו כתרשיש ופניו כמראה ברק ועיניו כלפידי אש וזרעתיו ומרגלתיו כעין נחשת קלל, וקול דבריו כקול המון.
His body was like topaz, and his face as the appearance of lightning, and his eyes as torches of fire, and his arms and his feet like polished copper, and the sound of his words was like the sound of a multitude.

His body—The description of the man clothed in linen is similar to that of the cherubim, who represented the Temple. The rare words used here, topaz (תרשיש), lightning (ברק) and torches (לפידי), are used in Ez. 1 13,16 to describe the cherubim; and in particular it is stated (Ez. 1 7) that their feet are like polished copper (כעין נחשת קלל). Moreover, the noise produced by the wings of the cherubim was like the sound of a tumult (Ez. 1 24), which is comparable to the phrase "sound of a multitude" describing the man clothed in linen. The implication of the description of the man clothed in linen is that he had acquired the characteristics of the cherubim. In other words, he represented the Babylonian empire at the time of the destruction of the Temple (586).

7. וראיתי אני דניאל לבדי את המראָה והאנשים אשר היו עמי לא ראו את המראָה אבל חרדה גדלה נפלה עליהם ויברחו בהחבא.
And I, Daniel, alone saw the apparition, while the men who were with me did not see the apparition; but great fear fell upon them, and they fled to hide.

Apparition—The apparition (מראָה) refers to the sight of the man clothed in linen. The word מראָה represents an imaginary sight, that can not be seen by others. In contrast, the word מראֶה (vision), represents an actual sight that can be observed by all. This distinction is indicated by the wording in Num. 12 6-8 (במראָה" (אליו אתודע בחלום אדבר בו . . . לא כן עבדי משה . . . ומראֶה ולא בחידת" "I make myself known to him in an apparition, I speak with him in a dream . . . My servant Moses is not so . . . in a plain vision and not in riddles."

8. ואני נשארתי לבדי ואראה את המראָה הגדלה הזאת ולא נשאר בי כח, והודי נהפך עלי למשחית, ולא עצרתי כח.
And I was left alone, and saw this great apparition, and there remained no strength in me, and my handsomeness turned in me into disfigurement, and I retained no strength.

9. ואשמע את קול דבריו, וכשמעי את קול דבריו ואני הייתי נרדם על פני ופני ארצה.
I heard the sound of his words; and when I heard the sound of his words I was in a deep sleep on my face, with my face toward the ground.

10.   והנה יד נגעה בי, ותניעני על ברכי וכפות ידי.
And behold a hand touched me, and set me on my knees and the palms of my hands.

11.   ויאמר אלי דניאל איש חמדות הבן בדברים אשר אנכי דבר אליך ועמד על עמדך כי עתה שלחתי אליך, ובדברו עמי את הדבר הזה עמדתי מרעיד.
He said to me, "Daniel, man greatly beloved, contemplate the words that I speak to you and stand up where you are, for I am now sent to you." When he spoke this word to me I stood trembling.

12.   ויאמר אלי אל תירא דניאל כי מן היום הראשון אשר נתת את לבך להבין ולהתענות לפני א' נשמעו דבריך, ואני באתי בדבריך.
He said to me, "Do not be afraid, Daniel, for from the first day that you did set your heart to understand and to afflict yourself before your God, your words were heard, and I have come because of your words.

From the first day—Daniel started mourning on the first day of Nisan 539. That very day Daniel's request was already heard.

13.   ושר מלכות פרס עמד לנגדי עשרים ואחד יום, והנה מיכאל אחד השרים הראשונים בא לעזרני, ואני נותרתי שם אצל מלכי פרס.
But the prince of the kingdom of Persia stands opposing me 21 days; and behold Michael, one of the first princes, comes to help me, and I remained there near the kings of Persia.

Prince of the kingdom of Persia—The prince of Persia represents the angel who fights for the Persian empire.

Opposing me—opposing the man clothed in linen, who represents Babylonia.

Opposing me 21 days—The 21 days represents the 21 years during which battles between the Persians and Babylonians will occur. In 539, Cyrus, leader of the Persians, conquered Babylonia. Later, around 520 and 519, Babylon twice rebelled against Darius I, who was then the king of Persia; but the rebellions were put down[101]. From 539 through 519 is 21 years, if we include both the initial and final dates.

Michael, one of the first princes—Michael, as specifically stated in Dan. 10 21; 12 1, was the prince who represented the Israelite nation. Michael is called one of the first princes, since the Israelite nation was among the early nations of the world.

Comes to help me—The Jewish people, in addition to the Babylonians, fought against the Persians. About 520 (see Section 6.3.2) the Jews fought for their lives against the Persians (Est. 9), and in this way Michael came to the aid of the man clothed in linen.

Remained there near the kings of Persia—After the suppression of the rebellions of the Babylonians in 519 B.C.E. Babylonia remained on the side of Persia and no longer rebelled.

14.   ובאתי להבינך את אשר יקרה לעמך באחרית הימים, כי עוד חזון לימים.

And I have come to explain to you what will happen to your people at the end of the six years, for there is another vision concerning the six years."

End of the Six Years—The six years refers to the period from the time of the Six-Day War in 1967 C.E. until the War of Gog in 1973. The end of the six years refers to the last of the six years, i.e. 1973. At the end of the six years the Jewish nation will be firmly established, and will have attained the theoretical Biblical boundaries.

Another vision—Previous visions which involved some events at the time of the six years are given in chapters 2 and 7. In particular see comments on Dan. 2 28, 44,45; 7 11,13,14,26,27. In this revelation, events only go until 1948 C.E. with establishment of the State of Israel. However, the fundamental theme of this revelation is the creation of an independent Jewish nation. At the end of the six years the State of Israel will be firmly established with no future chance of it being destroyed, and it will then be a truly independent country.

15.   ובדברו עמי כדברים האלה נתתי פני ארצה ונאלמתי.

While he spoke to me according to these words, I set my face toward the ground and could not speak.

16.   והנה כדמות בני אדם נגע על שפתי, ואפתח פי ואדברה ואמרה אל העמד לנגדי אדני במראה נהפכו צירי עלי ולא עצרתי כח.

And behold, one in the semblance of humans was touching my lips. Then I opened my mouth and spoke, and said to him that stood opposing me, "Sir, in the apparition, my pains turned upon me, and I retained no strength.

One in the semblance of humans—The man clothed in linen changed his appearance to that of an ordinary person.

17.   והיך יוכל עבד אדני זה לדבר עם אדני זה, ואני מעתה לא יעמד בי כח ונשמה לא נשארה בי.

How can this servant of my master speak with this my master? For I, from now will not have strength within me, and no breath is left in me."

18.   ויסף ויגע בי כמראה אדם ויחזקני.

And he, in the appearance of a man, touched me once again, and strengthened me.

19.   ויאמר אל תירא איש חמדות שלום לך חזק וחזק, וכדברו עמי התחזקתי ואמרה ידבר אדני כי חזקתני.

And he said, "Do not be afraid, man greatly beloved, peace be unto you; be strong, be strong." When he had spoken to me, I was strengthened and said, "Speak, sir, for you have strengthened me."

20. ויאמר הידעת למה באתי אליך ועתה אשוב להלחם עם שר פרס,
ואני יוצא והנה שר יון בא.
He said, "Do you know why I have come to you? Now I will return to fight with the prince of Persia; and when I leave, behold, the prince of Greece shall come.

He said—The man clothed in linen, who now had the appearance of an ordinary man, was the one speaking to Daniel.

Do you know why I have come to you?—I have not come to fight against you, but rather to reveal what will happen in the future.

Return to fight with the prince of Persia—The man clothed in linen, who was the angel representing Babylonia, had to fight against the angel of Persia in the years 520 and 519 B.C.E. Once the rebellion by Babylonia was suppressed, the man clothed in linen would leave, but he would be replaced by the angel of Greece. Thus, after about 499 the main enemy of Persia was Greece. Darius I, King of Persia, made expeditions against Greek states in 492 and in 490. Subsequently, in 466, Persia lost control of the Greek provinces on the Asiatic Coast. Numerous other conflicts occurred between Persia and Greece, until finally, after the unification of the Greek states, Alexander the Great in 331 conquered Darius III and the Persian empire[102].

21. אבל אגיד לך את הרשום בכתב אמת ואין אחד מתחזק עמי על
אלה כי אם מיכאל שרכם.
However, I will tell you what has been written in a precise writing; And no one strengthens me against these except Michael your prince."

Written in a precise writing—The message concerning the future is written with precise wording, where each word has significance, as already stated in Sentence 1.

Against these—Against the prince of Persia and the prince of Greece.

Michael your prince—The Jews, represented by the angel Michael, fought not only against the Persian empire, as mentioned in Sentence 13, but subsequently also against the subdivisions of the Greek empire, namely the Ptolemaic and Seleucid empires. Between 320 and about 142 numerous conflicts occurred between the Ptolemaic and Seleucid empires over the territory of Palestine. In a number of cases the Jews fought against one or the other of these empires. The situations are described in detail in Dan. 11 4-35. The fighting of the Jews against the Persians and Greeks is the way the angel Michael helped the man clothed in linen, the angel of Babylonia.

16.6 CHAPTER 11 OF DANIEL

Chapter 11 continues the revelation begun in Chapter 10. Daniel is here told the exact details of how the Jewish state, during two periods of history, will become independent. The background for the achievement of the first period of independence in 142 B.C.E., during the time of the Second Temple, is given in Sentences 2 to 35. Then there is a skip in time of over 2,000 years, to present the background for the achievement of the second period of independence in 1948 C.E. The details of the background for the second period are given from 11 36 to 12 4.

From Sentences 4 to 35, precise history is given of the Ptolemaic and Seleucid empires. In fact the happenings described are so exact, that historians of this period, on occasion, use the statements in this chapter to supplement the extra-Biblical records[103].

Lists of the rulers of the Ptolemaic and Seleucid empires are presented in Table 16.6.1, to facilitate following the complicated and very condensed histories of these empires as presented in Sentences 2 to 35. The specified dates for the reigns are accurate in most cases to within two years.

1. ואני בשנת אחת לדריוש המדי, עמדי למחזיק ולמעוז לו.
As for me, in the first year of Darius the Mede, my task is to strengthen and fortify him.

As for me—The angel representing Babylonia is continuing his narrative.
First year of Darius the Mede—Darius the Mede is the same ruler as Darius I (see Section 6.3.1). According to the Bible, the first year of Darius I is 517 (see Section 6.4).
My task is to strengthen and fortify him—In 520 and 519 Babylonia rebelled against Persia, but the rebellion was suppressed (see comments on Dan. 10 13). In other words, at that time the angel of Babylonia fought against Darius I. However, after the rebellion was over Babylonia no longer opposed Persia, and therefore the angel of Babylonia was required to support Darius I in 517.

2. ועתה אמת אגיד לך, הנה עוד שלשה מלכים עמדים לפרס והרביעי יעשיר עשר גדול מכל וכחזקתו בעשרו יעיר הכל את מלכות יון.
And now I will tell you the precise message. Behold, another three kings will stand up for Persia; and the fourth shall amass greater riches than all; and when he becomes strong with his riches, everything will awaken the kingdom of Greece.

The precise message—From this sentence through 12 4, the angel of Babylonia presents the precise wording, which has to be analyzed carefully.
Another three kings will stand up for Persia—This revelation was being revealed

to Daniel in the third year of Cyrus, as stated in Dan. 10 1. The three kings after Cyrus (see Table 6.1) were (A) Cambyses (529–522), (B) Pseudo-Smerdis (522), and (C) Darius I (521–486). These three kings were successful in maintaining and increasing the Persian empire of Cyrus[104].

The fourth—The fourth king after Cyrus was Xerxes I (485–465). Under Xerxes the Persians were successfully beaten by Greek states, thus bringing to an end the great fear of Persia[105]. Since the power of Persia declined under the rulership of Xerxes he is mentioned in the text separately from the three previous kings.

Shall amass greater riches than all—Xerxes spent much time in his early years of rule amassing his wealth and strengthening the empire.

When he becomes strong with his riches—When Xerxes felt strong enough he decided to attack the Greeks.

Everything will awaken the kingdom of Greece—Xerxes gathered an immense military force to fight against Greece. In the army were about two million fighting men,

Table 16.6.1
Rulers of the Houses of Seleucus and Ptolemy

Seleucid Dynasty	*Date* (B.C.E.)	*Ptolemaic Empire*	*Date* (B.C.E.)
Seleucus I, Nicator	(312)–305–281	Ptolemy I, Soter or Lagi	(323)–306–285
Antiochus I, Soter	281–260	Ptolemy II, Philadelphus	285–246
Antiochus II, Theos	260–246		
Seleucus II, Callinicus	245–226	Ptolemy III, Euergetes I	246–221
Seleucus III, Soter	225–223		
Antiochus III, the Great	222–187	Ptolemy IV, Philopator	221–203
Seleucus IV, Philopator	187–175	Ptolemy V, Epiphanes	203–181
Antiochus IV, Epiphanes	175–163	Ptolemy VI, Philometer	181–145
Antiochus V, Eupator	163–162	(Ptolemy VI, cojoint with Ptolemy VII	169–164)
Demetrius I, Soter	162–150		
Alexander Balas	150–145	Ptolemy VII, Euergetes II	145–116

and altogether five million men of 46 nationalities. Weapons consisted of shields, bows, spears, helmets, clubs, lances, swords, and axes, and there were 1,200 warships, and 3,000 smaller vessels[106,107]. The Greek states then united to defend themselves against Persia, and in the Battle of Salamis defeated the Persian Forces (480). Subsequently the Greek states formed the Delian League (477). These events marked the awakening of the Greek states as a united power[108].

3.   ועמד מלך גבור, ומשל ממשל רב ועשה כרצונו.
And a mighty king shall stand up, and he shall rule over a great dominion, and shall do as he desires.

A mighty king—In 336 Alexander the Great became ruler over Macedon. He ruled from 336 to 323.

Rule over a great dominion—Alexander the Great will conquer and rule much of the known world.

Shall do as he desires—Alexander was an absolute monarch. In his later years he acted with vanity, and performed numerous acts of violence; yet no one could restrain his actions. Alexander even killed his friend Clitus, because Clitus reproached him[109].

4.   וכעמדו תשבר מלכותו ותחץ לארבע רוחות השמים, ולא לאחריתו ולא כמשלו אשר משל כי תנתש מלכותו ולאחרים מלבד אלה.
And when he shall stand up, his kingdom shall be broken, and shall be divided toward the four winds of heaven; but not to his successor, nor according to the rulership with which he ruled; for his kingdom shall be broken up, even to others besides these.

When he shall stand up his kingdom shall be broken—Just as Alexander was beginning his career as ruler over his empire he died of a fever in 323 at the age of 33.

Divided toward the four winds of heaven—After Alexander's death the kingdom was divided into four parts. Four regents were appointed to rule the empire—Antipater and Craterus in Europe, Perdiccas and Leonnatus in Asia[110].

Not to his successor—Alexander left an illegitimate son named Hercules, who was ten or twelve years old at his father's death. In dividing the empire, the claims of Hercules were ignored[111]. Moreover, Alexander's posthumous son, also named Alexander, never succeeded his father.

Nor according to the rulership with which he ruled—The four regents lacked the authority that Alexander had. Leonnatus was soon replaced by Meleager. Subsequently Meleager was murdered, and Perdiccas assumed command of the great army of Asia[112]. Moreover, many rivalries existed in trying to gain control of portions of the empire.

For his kingdom shall be broken up—Perdiccas broke up the unity of the Greek empire by distributing satrapies to many of the military chiefs[113].

Even to others besides these—Other persons prominently involved in trying to gain control of the empire included Eumenes, Ptolemy Lagi, Antigonus, and others[114].

5. ויחזק מלך הנגב ומן שריו, ויחזק עליו ומשל, ממשל רב ממשלתו.

The king of the south shall become strong, and from his officers. And one will become strong by depending on him, and shall rule; his dominion shall be a great dominion.

The king of the south—That is, Ptolemy Lagi who ruled over Egypt, which was the south most division of the Greek empire. Ptolemy obtained control of Palestine in 301[115].

Shall become strong, and from his officers—The strength of Ptolemy Lagi was derived from the Council of Generals, which gave him control of Egypt[116].

One will become strong by depending on him and shall rule—This statement refers to Seleucus I who became strong because of his reliance on Ptolemy. During the battles which took place after the death of Alexander, Seleucus was driven from Babylonia and found refuge at the court of Ptolemy Lagi. In 312, Seleucus gained control over Babylonia and Persia. Later, in 310, Ptolemy initiated a war which resulted in Seleucus receiving the territory of Cappadocia, part of Phrygia, Upper Syria, Mesopotamia, and the valley of the Euphrates[117].

His dominion shall be a great dominion—The Seleucid empire will become very large. Seleucus soon spread his control over more territory, until by 305 he was master of all the countries lying between the Indus and Euphrates, and between the Jaxartes and the Indian Ocean[118]. After the Battle of Ipsus in 301, Seleucus gained even more territory. The Battle of Ipsus marked the completion of the break-up of the Greek empire[119]. Of all the segments of Alexander's empire, the Seleucid dominion occupied the greatest area. In the next sentence the Seleucid empire is considered as the northern empire since it was situated in the north.

6. ולקץ שנים יתחברו ובת מלך הנגב תבא אל מלך הצפון לעשות מישרים, ולא תעצר כוח הזרוע ולא יעמד וזרעו ותנתן היא ומביאיה והילדה ומחזקה בעתים.

At the end of 52 years they will unite; and the daughter of the king of the south shall come to the king of the north to make an agreement; but she shall not retain the strength of the arm, and he shall not stand and his arm; and she, and those that brought her, and her child, and the one who supports her will be given over during those "times."

At the end of 52 years—The word שנים is used to mean 52 years corresponding to the 52 weeks in a solar year (see Table 16.0.1). In 301 Ptolemy I gained control of Palestine. Fifty-two years later, in 249, an agreement was made between Ptolemy II and Antiochus II in which the rights to Palestine were transferred to Antiochus II[120].

Will unite—The Ptolemaic and Seleucid empires will form a bond by marriage.

Daughter of the king of the south shall come to the king of the north to make an agreement—Ptolemy II gave his daughter Berenice in marriage to Antiochus II, to bring about peace between the countries. Thereupon Antiochus divorced his first wife Laodice[121].

She shall not retain the strength of the arm—Berenice will not be able to uphold the bond between the rulers. By 246 Laodice was reinstated as wife of Antiochus II[122].

He shall not stand and his arm—Ptolemy II and his bond between the countries will not last. Ptolemy II died in 246.

And she—Berenice.

Those that brought her—Antiochus II and his assistants.

Her child—The son born to Berenice from her marriage to Antiochus II.

One who supports her—Historically it is not clear who the "one who supports her" is.

Will be given over during those "times"—In 246, Laodice caused the death of Berenice, the infant son, and Antiochus II[123]. Thus within a few years from the time of the agreement, practically all the people involved were killed. Note that the Hebrew word עתים (times) does not have a particular time length. In contrast עת, the singular of עתים, signifies 25 years.

7. ועמד מנצר שרשיה כנו, ויבא אל החיל ויבֹא במעוז מלך הצפון, ועשו‎ בהם והחזיק.

And his throne shall stand up from one of the shoots of her roots, and he shall come to the army, and shall enter into the stronghold of the king of the north, and shall deal with them, and shall retain control.

His throne shall stand up—The occupant of the Ptolemaic throne, formerly held by Ptolemy II, shall stand up to protect Berenice.

One of the shoots of her roots—Ptolemy III, brother of Berenice. This and the following sentence refer to Ptolemy III who invaded the Seleucid realm and carried home an immense quantity of spoil.

He shall come to the army—Upon hearing of the difficulty of his sister Berenice, Ptolemy III rushed to her aid, but was too late. He then advanced into Syria at the head of a powerful army and took possession of the greater part of the country, which seems not to have been protected[124].

Shall enter into the stronghold of the king of the north and shall deal with them, and shall retain control—In the city of Antioch, the chief city of Seleucid Syria, there was a considerable military force, and the district officers and satraps gathered within its walls. The sight of the Ptolemaic forces convinced Antioch that to resist is hopeless, and Antioch received the invading forces of Ptolemy III[125].

8. וגם אלהיהם עם נסכיהם עם כלי חמדתם כסף וזהב בשבי יבא
מצרים, והוא שנים יעמד ממלך הצפון.
Also their gods with their molten images, and with their precious vessels, silver and gold, he shall bring as booty to Egypt. And he shall withstand the king of the north for 52 years.

Their gods . . . silver and gold, he shall bring as booty to Egypt—After plundering in Asia, Ptolemy III returned to Egypt laden with an immense booty comprising among other objects all the statues of the Egyptian deities which had been carried off by Cambyses to Persia or Babylon. He brought back a vast number of other works of art. In addition, Ptolemy III levied immense contributions from the Asiatics, and is said to have raised over 40,000 talents of silver[126].

He shall withstand the king of the north for 52 years—The word שנים is here used to mean 52 years (see Table 16.0.1). The text states that the Ptolemaic king will be able to withstand the Seleucid king for 52 years. From 249 when a temporary transfer was made of Palestine from Ptolemy II to Antiochus II (see Sentence 6), until 198 when Antiochus III defeated Scopas, a general of Ptolemy V, and finally ended the Ptolemaic rule over Palestine (see Sentence 13), is 52 years.

9. ובא במלכות מלך הנגב ושב אל אדמתו.
And he shall come into the kingdom of the king of the south, but he shall return to his own land.

He shall come into the kingdom of the king of the south—About 242 Seleucus II marched south. Seleucus II was able to deliver Damascus and Orthosia, which were being besieged by Egyptian forces. But an attempt of Seleucus II to penetrate farther south into Palestine itself led to his meeting with a disastrous defeat.

He shall return to his own land—Seleucus II then withdrew the shattered remnant of his army of invasion to Antioch. Soon after this the two powers signed a peace treaty (about 240)[127].

10. ובניו יתגרו ואספו המון חילים רבים ובא בוא ושטף ועבר, וישב
ויתגרה עד מעזו.
And his sons shall prepare for war, and shall gather a multitude of many soldiers, and he shall come and overwhelm on sea and land; and he shall return and wage war up to his stronghold.

His sons shall prepare for war—The sons of Seleucus II, namely Seleucus III and Antiochus III, will prepare for war. After the death of Seleucus II, Seleucus III ascended the throne in 225. Two years later he was assassinated during a campaign in Asia Minor, but his general, Epigenes, got the large army home safely[128]. Antiochus III (the Great) succeeded his brother in 223, and resumed the war with Egypt.

He shall come and overwhelm on sea and land—"He" refers to Antiochus

III. When Antiochus III reached the cities of Tyre and Ptolemais in 219, the gates were opened to him and he took possession of their naval arsenals and considerable stores. Among the booty were no less than 40 vessels, half of which were decked ships of war. Antiochus III then began a slow conquest of Coele-Syria (Palestine). A four-month armistice was then arranged because of the approaching winter[129].

He shall return and wage war up to his stronghold—Antiochus III shall return and wage war up to Sidon, the stronghold of Ptolemy IV. In the spring of 218, Antiochus III returned and waged war against Nicolaus, the general of Ptolemy IV. Nicolaus suffered heavy losses, and retreated to the fortress of Sidon. Antiochus left the Egyptian enemy in Sidon, which seemed too strong to take, but conquered almost all Coele-Syria, part of Phoenicia, and Northern Palestine[130] [131].

11. ויתמרמר מלך הנגב ויצא ונלחם עמו עם מלך הצפון, והעמיד המון רב ונתן ההמון בידו.

And the king of the south shall become very embittered, and he shall go out and fight with him, the king of the north; and he shall set up a great multitude, but the multitude shall be given into his hand.

The king of the south shall become very embittered—All this time Egypt had not brought out her whole forces. The Egyptian army was secretly being prepared in Alexandria, and was to take the field in spring 217[132].

He shall go out and fight with him—In the spring of 217, the army of Ptolemy IV moved across the desert to Palestine, to fight Antiochus III.

He shall set up a great multitude—Ptolemy's army consisted of 70,000 foot-soldiers and 5,000 horsemen.

The multitude shall be given into his hand—The multitude, that is the army of Ptolemy, shall be practically given over to the power of Antiochus III. The term "his hand" refers to Antiochus III, just as did the term "with him" in the previous part of the sentence. The two armies met near the town of Raphia. The cavalry charge led by Antiochus broke and routed the cavalry on the Ptolemaic left. If not for the characteristic impetuosity of Antiochus III, he would have won the battle[133].

12. ונשא ההמון ורם לבבו, והפיל רבאות ולא יעוז.

Then the multitude will rule, and his heart shall be elated; and he shall cast down tens of thousands, but he shall not be strong.

Then the multitude will rule—Then the army of Ptolemy IV will win. Antiochus III in the exhilaration of the pursuit failed to keep in touch with the rest of the field, and on the other wing the Ptolemaic horse drove in the Seleucid. The phalanxes in the center were left to decide the battle. The Seleucid phalanx gave way, and by the end of the day the entire Seleucid army was in flight[134].

His heart shall be elated—Ptolemy IV was completely satisfied with the withdrawal of the Seleucid army, the reacquisition of Palestine, and the restoration of the *status quo*[135].

He shall cast down tens of thousands—Ptolemy IV had killed about 10,000 men of the army of Antiochus III.

He shall not be strong—Ptolemy IV will not act as a victor. The Alexandrine court, having recovered Palestine, had all it wanted. It let Antiochus III off easily, not even demanding an indemnity. A peace treaty was signed between Antiochus and Ptolemy[136].

13. ושב מלך הצפון והעמיד המון רב מן הראשון, ולקץ העתים שנים יבוא בוא בחיל גדול וברכוש רב.

And the king of the north shall return, and will establish a multitude greater than the former; and 52 years after the "times" he will come with a great army and with much wealth.

The king of the north shall return—About 202, or shortly thereafter, Antiochus III invaded Coele-Syria and pushed back the forces of Ptolemy V to the desert between Palestine and Egypt. The city of Gaza did not fall until after a famous siege, around the autumn of 201[137]. (Shortly thereafter, in 199, Scopas, a general of Ptolemy V, recovered the territory of Palestine for the Egyptians[138].)

Will establish a multitude greater than the former—Details of the battles which took place between 202 and 200, and the size of the armies, have not been preserved in the historical sources[139]. It is therefore not possible to verify this statement of the text from extra-Biblical records.

Fifty-two years after the "times"—The word "times" (עתים) refers back to its use in Sentence 6, when an agreement between Ptolemy II and Antiochus II was made in 249. Fifty-two years after 249 is 198.

He will come with a great army and with much wealth—Antiochus III came south again in 198, and defeated Scopas at Panium. Then Antiochus invested Sidon where Scopas made a last stand. The battle of Panium marks the final and definite substitution of Seleucid for Ptolemaic rule in Palestine[140].

14. ובעתים ההם רבים יעמדו על מלך הנגב, ובני פריצי עמך ינשאו להעמיד חזון ונכשלו.

In those times many shall stand up against the king of the south; and the impetuous sons of your people will rule, to establish a vision, but will fail.

In those times—At about 200—the time of the events of the previous sentence.

Many shall stand up against the king of the south—Ptolemy V was not more than five years old when he became king in 203, and under a series of regents the kingdom was paralyzed. Antiochus III and Philip V of Macedonia made a compact to divide the Ptolemaic overseas possessions[141]. In 200, Philip V robbed Egypt of her possessions in Thrace and on the Hellespont. Antiochus III took Coele-Syria, Palestine, and all Egyptian possessions in Asia Minor. Moreover, Egypt was weakened by internal strife, and there were many revolts against Ptolemy V. As a result Egypt lost almost its entire empire[142].

The impetuous sons of your people will rule—The family of Tobias, in particular his son Joseph and his grandson Hyrcanus, placed themselves with the consent of Ptolemy V as tax collectors and ambassadors of the Jews. By means of audacity, cruelty, and strict enforcement, the tax collectors were successful in supplying the required amounts to Ptolemy V. Joseph, during his 22 years of control over the taxes, had brought the Jews from a state of poverty to a more splendid condition. During this time, he collected the taxes of Syria, Phoenicia and Samaria, and saved the Jews from disfavor in the eyes of Ptolemy V[143,144].

To establish a vision but will fail—Joseph and Hyrcanus attempted to achieve the vision of independence and greatness for the Jewish nation, but they did not succeed.

15. ויבא מלך הצפון וישפך סוללה ולכד עיר מבצרות, וזרעות הנגב לא יעמדו ועם מבחריו ואין כח לעמד.

And the king of the north shall come and throw up siege-ramps and capture a fortified city, and the forces of the south will not stand up, nor his select people, and there will be no strength to oppose.

King of the north—Antiochus III.

Shall come and throw up siege-ramps and capture a fortified city—In the spring of 197, Antiochus III launched his forces upon the coast of Asia Minor, with the intent to seize the possessions of the house of Ptolemy. As he passed along the coast of Cilicia, one after another of the towns and fortresses surrendered, including Soli, Corycus, Zephyrium, Aphrodisias, Anemurium, and Selinus. Antiochus met with no check till he reached Coracesium, the strongest place along that rugged coast. The steep isolated hill of Alaya, which reminds one of the Rock of Gibraltar, was constructed so as to be impregnable. The determination to conquer it brought Antiochus III to a halt. Historical records, however, do not state whether Coracesium was conquered[145]. If we assume that Caracesium is the fortified city mentioned in the Biblical text, then it is clear that Antiochus III was successful in conquering the city.

The forces of the south will not stand up nor his select people—Antiochus III then continued with the conquest of the southern coast of Asia Minor. He occupied Pamphylia, Lycia, and Caria, among others[146].

There will be no strength to oppose—Ptolemy V was not able to offer any opposition to the advancing army of Antiochus III[147].

16. ויעש הבא אליו כרצונו ואין עומד לפניו, ויעמד בארץ הצבי וכלה בידו.

And the one who comes to him shall do as he wants, and no one will stand before him, and he shall stand in the desirous land, and destruction will be in his power.

And the one who comes to him shall do as he wants, and no one will stand before him—When Antiochus III was stopped near Coracesium, an embassy from the Rhodian Republic presented itself. The embassy declared that should he attempt to pass the Chelidonian promontory, the Rhodians would oppose his advance with an armed squadron. They justified this action by accusing Antiochus III of a design to join Philip V of Macedonia. Antiochus III assured them that their insinuation was groundless. The embassy then went; and at the moment when its spokesman was addressing the Rhodian assembly, news arrived that Philip of Macedonia met with a final defeat. The Rhodians, then, had no further basis for opposing the advance of Antiochus III[148].

He shall stand in the desirous land and destruction will be in his power—The "desirous land" (ארץ הצבי) here refers to the city of Ephesus which was the greatest of the Ionian cities. Ephesus was the splendid prize towards which the thoughts of Antiochus III were directed. It was the citadel which commanded, both by land and sea, Ionia and cities of the Hellespont; the most convenient base from which the master of Asia could direct military operations against Europe. By the close of 197, Ephesus was captured, and was made the new capital of Antiochus III[149].

17. וישם פניו לבוא בתקף כל מלכותו וישרים עמו ועשה, ובת הנשים יתן לו להשחיתה ולא תעמד ולא לו תהיה.

He will set his face to enter the strong places of his entire kingdom, and righteousness is with him and he will do. And the daughter, of the wives, he will give him to destroy her, and she will not stand, nor will she be for him.

He will set his face to enter ... of his entire kingdom—Antiochus III will plan to conquer all the strongholds of his kingdom, the cities which were formerly under Seleucid rule. From Ephesus, Antiochus III undertook during the winter of 197 to restore Seleucid rule over the free cities of northern Ionia and the Hellespont. Smyrna was the most pre-eminent of these cities in Ionia, and Lampsacus the most pre-eminent on the Hellespont. Unfortunately for Antiochus III, he could not conquer them either by force or persuasion. Other cities of Asia Minor, with the exception of Alexandria Troas, were too weak to resist, and yielded with little difficulty to Antiochus[150].

Righteousness is with him and he will do—The policy of Antiochus was to champion the liberty and autonomy of the conquered states. In each city the party favorable to Antiochus was elevated to power, and the opposition party was crushed. Repeatedly, Antiochus III declared his devotion to the great principles of democracy and autonomy. He also tried to gratify the cities in ways which did not affect his supremacy. By these means, Seleucid rule was restored to the coastal regions of Asia Minor[151].

The daughter, of the wives, he will give him to destroy her—Antiochus III will give his daughter Cleopatra as a wife to Ptolemy V in order to conquer Egypt. Cleopatra was henceforth the characteristic name of the Ptolemaic queens and is therefore called "of the wives." In the winter of 193 the marriage took place[152]. It appears from the text that Antiochus wanted Cleopatra to help in conquering Egypt.

She will not stand, nor will she be for him—Cleopatra did not stand up for the plan of Antiochus III, nor did she support Ptolemy V. After the death of Ptolemy V, we find that Cleopatra was regent for her young son Ptolemy VI, until her death in 173[153]. Insufficient historical details are available concerning Cleopatra to make possible a clear understanding of her role, as expressed here in the text of Daniel.

18. וישם פניו לאיים ולכד רבים, והשבית קצין חרפתו לו, בלתי חרפתו ישיב לו.

And he will set his face to the islands, and shall capture many. But a general, to whom he gives his shame, will stop him; only his shame will he return to him.

He will set his face to the islands, and shall capture many—About 191, Antiochus III decided to extend his control over the "island states." But Rome had gained these islands as friends, and was able to use the islands as points of support in operating on the coast of Asia[154]. Antiochus, in his preparation for struggle against Rome, managed to gain control of several Aeolian towns including Cyme[155].

A general, to whom he gives his shame, will stop him—In 190, after the Battle of Magnesia between the Seleucid army and Rome, Antiochus III was forced to admit defeat. The Roman general, Lucius Scipio, imposed the following terms on Antiochus III: (A) Limitations on the frontiers of the Seleucid empire; (B) the cost of the war, plus additional indemnities, were to be paid to Rome; and (C) twenty hostages and several other individuals to be delivered to Rome[156].

Only his shame will he return to him—Despite the severity of the terms which the Romans imposed upon Antiochus III, they allowed the Seleucid empire to retain its autonomy, and kept none of Antiochus' territory for themselves. Thus only the shame of Antiochus III was given to the Roman general.

These incidents mark the end of the hundred years' struggle of the house of Seleucus for Asia Minor[157].

19. וישב פניו למעוזי ארצו, ונכשל ונפל ולא ימצא.

Then he shall turn his face toward the strongholds of his own land; but he shall stumble and fall, and shall not be found.

Shall turn his face towards the strongholds of his own land—Antiochus III, hurled back from Asia Minor, turned his thoughts once more to the field of his old glories, the east. In the summer of 188, Antiochus III left Seleucus IV in Syria as joint king, and plunged into the east.

Shall stumble and fall, and shall not be found—The Mediterranean lands never saw Antiochus III again. The generally received version of his end was that he had ventured himself with a body of troops in the Elymaean hills, and had been overwhelmed by the fierce tribesmen[158].

20. ועמד על כנו מעביר נוגש הדר מלכות, ובימים אחדים ישבר ולא באפים ולא במלחמה.

And will be established on his throne one who will remove the oppressor, the glory of the kingdom. In 12 years he shall be broken, but not in anger nor in battle.

Will be established on his throne—Seleucus IV became established on the throne formerly occupied by Antiochus III.

One who will remove the oppressor—According to the peace agreement made in 190 after the war of Magnesia (see Sentence 18), the Seleucid empire had to make 12 annual payments to the Romans[159]. These payments were mainly made by Seleucus IV[160], and should have been completed by about 177. Completion of the annual payments would have removed Rome from being an oppressor of the Seleucid empire. Nevertheless some payments to Rome were made by Antiochus IV as late as 173[161].

The glory of the kingdom—The military inaction during the reign of Seleucus IV has led to his being regarded as a weak ruler. However, the political situation was such that an ambitious policy would have been madness[162]. For the first time the inhabitants of Syria saw the Seleucid king sitting year in and year out at home[163]. In this respect Seleucus IV was the glory of the kingdom.

In 12 years—The Hebrew term is ימים אחדים, i.e., two ימים. According to Table 16.0.1, ימים indicates six years. Therefore two ימים specifies 12 years.

In 12 years he shall be broken—Seleucus IV ruled for 12 years, from 187 to 175. In 175, Heliodorus formed a conspiracy against the king, and had Seleucus IV murdered in the quiet of his kingdom[164].

Not in anger nor in battle—The murder of Seleucus was accomplished not because of anger, but because of the desire of Heliodorus to become regent for the infant son of Seleucus, and eventually to become king[165].

21. ועמד על כנו נבזה ולא נתנו עליו הוד מלכות, ובא בשלוה והחזיק מלכות בחלקלקות.

And will be established on his throne a contemptible person, upon whom had not been conferred the majesty of the kingdom. He shall come in peace, and shall secure the kingdom by smooth talk.

Established on his throne a contemptible person—Antiochus IV became established on the throne formerly occupied by Seleucus IV. Antiochus IV, Epiphanes, was nicknamed Epimanes, meaning half-crazed. He loved to do the unexpected, and his caprices ran near insanity. His incalculable nature had its sinister aspect. There was something horribly dangerous and pantherlike in his caresses[166].

Upon whom had not been conferred the majesty of the kingdom—Antiochus IV had been a former hostage in Rome, and afterwards resided in Athens. Upon hearing of the death of his brother Seleucus IV, Antiochus appeared in Syria supported by forces lent by the King of Pergamos, and placed himself upon the Seleucid throne[167].

Shall come in peace, and shall secure the kingdom by smooth talk—The scanty historical data available indicate that it required much dexterity and intrigue on the part of Antiochus IV for him to establish his rule[168].

22. וזרעות השטף ישטפו מלפניו וישברו, וגם נגיד ברית.
    And the opposition forces will be swept away from before him, and shall be broken; and he will also be the leader of an alliance.

Opposition forces ... shall be broken—The initial opposition to Antiochus IV melted away. Heliodorus is no longer heard of. Apollonius, one of the persons of greatest influence with Seleucus IV, retired to Miletus. The Jew Hyrcanus, who had made himself a petty prince in the country east of Jordan, committed suicide. The infant son of Seleucus was assassinated at Antiochus' word by Andronicus, who in turn was put to death[169].

Leader of an alliance—During the early years of the rule of Antiochus IV, a sort of triple alliance was formed by Pergamos, Cappadocia, and Syria. The alliance put a certain check upon Rome[170].

23. ומן התחברות אליו יעשה מרמה ועלה ועצם במעט גוי.
    And one from an association with him will act deceitfully, and shall come up and become strong with a small force.

One from an association with him—When Antiochus IV had established himself in Syria, Egypt was being governed by his sister Cleopatra, the widow of Ptolemy V. She was then regent for her young son Ptolemy VI. In 173 Cleopatra died. Then the anti-Seleucid party, represented by Eulaeus and Lenaeus came to the helm[171].

Will act deceitfully—Egypt under the nominal leadership of Ptolemy VI will act deceitfully in that it will prepare an army for recovering Coele-Syria (Palestine) from the Seleucid empire[172].

Shall come up ... with a small force—The Egyptian army will not be particularly large.

24. בשלוה ובמשמני מדינה יבוא ועשה אשר לא עשו אבתיו ואבות
אבתיו בזה ושלל ורכוש להם יבזור ועל מבצרים יחשב
מחשבתיו ועד עת.

In time of peace shall he come upon the richest places of the country; and he shall do that which his fathers and forefathers did not do, scattering among them spoil, booty and wealth; and will have ambitions against the strongholds, but only for 25 years.

In time of peace shall he come—The Egyptian army, under the nominal leadership of Ptolemy VI, shall take the offensive in late 170 [173] thereby breaking a period of peace between Egypt and Syria.

Upon the richest places of the country—Before the regents Eulaeus and Lenaeus marched out with the army they delivered a harangue to the populace. They claimed they would defeat the enemy, and would make the whole Seleucid realm an appendage of Egypt[174].

Scattering among them spoil, booty and wealth—A strange accompaniment to the Egyptian army were wagons of bullion, of gold and silver plate, of jewels and rich feminine attire, and even furniture from the palace[175]. These items were left behind when the Egyptian army fled before the Seleucid forces.

Will have ambitions against the strongholds—The regents explained that the wealth they were taking along was the means by which they would prevail over the constancy of the Seleucid cities and strongholds[176].

But only for 25 years—Ptolemy VI, the nominal head of Egypt, will remain as leader for an additional 25 years. From the time of the Egyptian offensive in 170 until the end of the reign of Ptolemy VI in 145 is 25 years. The Hebrew word עת is here used to indicate a period of 25 years (see Table 16.0.1).

25. ויער כחו ולבבו על מלך הנגב בחיל גדול ומלך הנגב יתגרה
למלחמה בחיל גדול ועצום עד מאד, ולא יעמד כי יחשבו עליו
מחשבות.

And he will awaken his strength and desire against the king of the south with a large army; and the king of the south shall prepare for war with a large and exceedingly powerful army; but he shall not stand because they will have plans for him.

Will awaken his strength and desire against the king of the south—The attack by Egypt against Syria, described in the previous sentence, awakened the Seleucid power against Ptolemy VI. Antiochus IV gathered a large army and marched until Pelusium, the frontier fortress of Egypt[177].

King of the south shall prepare for war—At Pelusium, Antiochus IV encountered the Egyptian army, led by Eulaeus and Lenaeus. The generals of Ptolemy VI were crushingly defeated. News of the defeat threw Alexandria into unreasoning panic[178].

He shall not stand because they will have plans for him—The young king, Ptolemy VI, was packed on board ship to escape from the Seleucid army. However, the ship was intercepted by the Syrian vessels, and Ptolemy VI fell into the hands of Antiochus IV[179].

26. ואכלי פת בגו ישברוהו וחילו ישטוף, ונפלו חללים רבים.
    Those who eat from his choice food will break him; and his army will go to sea; and many shall fall down slain.

Who eat from his choice food will break him—The people of Alexandria decided to continue their resistance, even though Ptolemy VI had deserted them. They made his younger brother, Ptolemy Euergetes, a boy of about 15, the new king[180]. By replacing Ptolemy VI the Alexandrian people effectively "broke" his leadership.

His army will go to sea—The new government in Alexandria, alive to the danger from Antiochus IV, sent a fleet to secure the frontier city of Pelusium. The fleet, however, was met by the Seleucid ships, and the battle went against the Egyptians[181].

Many shall fall down slain—Antiochus IV then seized the city of Pelusium. Lower Egypt was soon in the hands of Antiochus, except for Alexandria which still supported the new king, Ptolemy Euergetes. Antiochus then fixed the seat of the rival government of Ptolemy VI at Memphis[182].

27. ושניהם המלכים לבבם למרע ועל שלחן אחד כזב ידברו, ולא תצלח כי עוד קץ למועד.
    And the intents of the two kings will be for treachery, and they shall speak lies at one table, and it shall not succeed; since there is another ending to this 29-year period.

The intents of the two kings will be for treachery . . . it shall not succeed—When Antiochus IV returned to Syria in 169 (see next sentence), the two Ptolemy brothers reconciled, and it was agreed that they should reign jointly. But the five years of double reign were anything but years of harmony. In the latter part of 164 Ptolemy VI was forced to flee from Alexandria because of contrivance of his brother[183].

Another ending to this 29-year period—The word מועד is used with the meaning of 29 years (see Table 16.0.1). The 29-year period is from 198 (see Sentence 13), when Seleucid rule definitely replaced Ptolemaic rule over Palestine, through the year 169 (see Sentence 29). The text warns us not to believe that the end of the Seleucid threat against Egypt ends with the departure of Antiochus IV in 169, as mentioned in Sentence 28, but rather with the forced withdrawal in 168 by Antiochus IV, under threat from Rome, as mentioned in sentence 30.

28. וישב ארצו ברכוש גדול ולבבו על ברית קדש, ועשה ושב לארצו.
And he shall return to his own land with great wealth, and his heart shall be against the holy covenant, and he shall do, and return to his own land.

Return to his own land with great wealth—Antiochus IV, when he returned to Syria in 169, was covered with glory and laden with much spoils and wealth[184].

Shall be against the holy covenant, and he shall do—The phrase "holy covenant" refers to the Temple. On his return from his first Egyptian expedition, Antiochus IV entered Jerusalem with a large suite. He entered the Temple and carried off the golden altar, the lamp stand, the table for the bread, the sacred cups, and other holy vessels. He seized whatever secret treasures he found and took them with him when he left for his own country[185].

29. למועד ישוב ובא בנגב ולא תהיה כראשנה וכאחרונה.
At the completion of the 29-year period he shall return and come into the south, but it shall not be like the first and like the latter incidents.

Completion of the 29-year period—The word מועד is used to indicate 29 years (see Table 16.0.1). The 29-year period is from 198 (see Sentence 13) when Seleucid rule definitely replaced Ptolemaic rule over Palestine, until early in 168 (see Sentence 30) when Rome forced Antiochus IV to withdraw completely from Egypt.

He shall return and come into the south—Early in 168 Antiochus IV again marched south against Egypt. His army once more crossed the Egyptian frontier and entered Memphis. Antiochus then turned north heading toward Alexandria[186].

Shall not be like the first and like the latter incidents—The first incident is described in Sentences 23–24, where the army of Egypt attacked the Seleucid cities, and was defeated. The second (the latter) incident is described in Sentences 25–26, where Antiochus IV successfully attacked the Egyptian realm. In both instances the Egyptian army was no match for the Seleucid forces. In this third incident, the situation was different. Roman ambassadors intervened, as stated in the next sentence.

30. ובאו בו ציים כתים ונכאה ושב וזעם על ברית קודש ועשה, ושב ויבן על עזבי ברית קדש.
Roman ships will come to him and he shall despair. He shall return and vent his fury against the holy covenant, and he shall do. And he shall return and show understanding to those who forsake the holy covenant.

Roman ships will come to him and he shall despair—While Antiochus IV in 168 was moving among the ancient cities of Egypt, Gaius Popillius Laenas, the Roman ambassador, set sail for Egypt. Popillius demanded that

Antiochus IV evacuate his forces from Egypt. The ambassador drew a circle in the sand all around Antiochus, and demanded an answer before the king step outside the circle. Antiochus IV then agreed to evacuate, and within a short time withdrew all his forces from Egypt[187].

He shall return and vent his fury against the holy covenant—The "holy covenant," as in Sentence 28, refers to the Temple. In 168 Antiochus IV set out from Egypt in a savage mood, took Jerusalem by storm, and ordered his troops to slaughter everyone they encountered. At the end of three days, the casualties amounted to 80,000 people. Moreover, Antiochus IV, guided by the high priest Menelaus, entered the Temple, and impiously touched the sacred vessels[188].

He shall return and show understanding to those who forsake the holy covenant— "Those who forsake the holy covenant" are those who forsake the Temple and the fundamentals of Judaism. In 167, Antiochus IV sent a high revenue official to Jerusalem with a powerful force. He killed many Israelites, and plundered the city. The city of Jerusalem was made into a citadel, and in there were garrisoned foreigners and Jewish apostates[189]. In this manner support was given to those who forsook the Jewish religion.

31. וזרעים ממנו יעמדו, וחללו המקדש המעוז והסירו התמיד ונתנו השקוץ משמם.
Forces from him will stand up, and they shall profane the fortified Temple and shall remove the permanent and shall set up the detestable thing that causes desolation.

Forces from him will stand up—Antiochus IV issued a decree that all his subjects were to abandon their own laws and religions, and accept the laws and religion of the Seleucid government. Men were appointed to see that these edicts were carried out[190].

Shall profane the fortified Temple—The Temple area had been built up by the Seleucid forces into a fortified position[191]. The Temple was profaned by prohibiting sacrifices, placing of idols, and bringing unclean beasts as offerings[192].

Shall remove the permanent—The word תמיד meaning "permanent" is used in the Pentateuch to refer to the showbread (Ex. 25 30), the daily burnt-offerings (Ex. 29 38,42), the incense (Ex. 30 8), the light in the lampstand (Ex. 27 20), and the fire on the altar (Lev. 6 6). All these items were discontinued as a result of the presence of the Seleucid forces.

Shall set up the detestable thing that causes desolation—On the fifteenth day of the month of Kislev, 167, a statue of Jupiter, which is called in I Macc. 1 54 the detestable thing that causes desolation, was set up on the altar of the Temple[193].

32. ומרשיעי ברית יחניף בחלקות, ועם ידעי א' יחזקו ועשו.
Those that are disloyal to the covenant he shall corrupt with flattery; but the people who know their God shall show strength and prevail.

Those that are disloyal to the covenant he shall corrupt with flattery—Antiochus IV did not omit to have the reasonableness of Hellenism put in a friendly way to those who would hear, and he punished without mercy those who would not. Under the threat of death many of the Jews conformed[194]. The term "covenant" (ברית) may here also be used in the more limited sense of "circumcision." Women who had their children circumcised, and their families, were put to death[195], while those who did not circumcize their sons were left alone.

The people who know their God shall show strength and prevail—Those who held fast to the Jewish religion generally forsook their homes and gathered in wandering groups in desolate places. The uncompromising fidelity to an ideal shone out at that time. At first the resistance was passive. When one band was overtaken on the Sabbath, they allowed themselves to be killed without resistance so they would not profane the holy day[196].

33. ומשכילי עם יבינו לרבים, ונכשלו בחרב ובלהבה בשבי ובבזה ימים.
They who are wise among the people shall cause the many to understand. And they shall stumble by the sword and by flame, by captivity and by pillage for six years.

They who are wise ... shall cause the many to understand—The Hasmonaean family, from the town of Modin, formed a nucleus around which the scattered bands drew together. It was declared permissible to fight for one's life on the Sabbath. Soon the towns and villages which had resigned themselves to a Hellenistic regime found themselves visited by bands of fierce zealots who repaid massacre for massacre, circumcised the children by force, and destroyed the emblems of Hellenistic religion[197].

Shall stumble by the sword ... for six years—The word ימים is used with the meaning of six years (see Table 16.0.1). As a result of the attacks by the Hasmonaeans the Syrian forces will lose in battle for six years. Thus from 166, when Judah became leader of the Hasmonaeans, until 160, when he was killed in battle[198], the Jewish forces were successful.

Judah routed the enemy in night attacks at Beth-Horon, and from the spoils the Jews were supplied with weapons. At Mizpah an army of 40,000 was defeated. In numerous other battles, described in I Maccabees, Judah scored victories against the Syrian army[199].

34. ובהכשלם יעזרו עזר מעט, ונלוו עליהם רבים בחלקלקות.
When they stumble they shall be helped with a little help; and many shall join themselves to them with smooth talk.

Shall be helped with a little help—The Syrians upon failing in battle received support, though very meager, from numerous sources. Many of the neighboring gentiles upon hearing that the Temple had been rededicated decided to massacre the Jews who lived among them. Judah and his brother Simon thereupon made war on these nations, and won in all cases. Battles occurred, for example, with the Idumaeans, the Baeanites, the Ammonites, and the gentiles in Galilee and Gilead. Those Jews who were rescued were brought back to Judaea[200].

Many shall join themselves to them with smooth talk—Many renegade Israelites reported to the Seleucid kings about the successes of Judah, and thereby brought fresh attacks on the Hasmonaeans. This happened, for example, in 162[201] and 161[202], when the renegades used smooth talk to present a one-sided picture of the actions of the Hasmonaeans.

35. ומן המשכילים יכשלו לצרוף בהם ולברר וללבן עד עת קץ כי עוד למועד.

And some of the wise shall stumble to refine themselves and to purify, and to make white until the time of the end, because there is yet more time until the 29 years.

Some of the wise shall stumble—In Sentence 33 the term "wise" was used to describe the Hasmonaean family and their followers. These wise shall stumble, in that they will err in their calculations concerning the date of achieving national independence.

To refine themselves... until the time of the end—A similar phraseology is found in Dan. 12 9–10, concerning persons who believe that by pious acts they can achieve an independent Jewish state. Some of the Hasmonaeans will err in believing that the prophecies concerning "the time of the end" refer to their time. The erroneous calculations are as follows:[203]

A. In Dan. 7 are described four world empires that will hold sway over the Jewish people, followed by the Messianic era. The Hasmonaeans interpreted these four kingdoms as the Babylonian, the Median, the Persian, and the Greek. Now was the "time of the end" when the Messianic kingdom would be established.

B. In Jer. 29 10 it is stated that after 70 years the nation of Israel would be restored. The Hasmonaeans interpreted these 70 years to mean 70 weeks of years, or 490 years. Six days of each of the weeks had already passed, i.e., $70 \times 6 = 420$ years from the destruction of the Temple in 586. (From 586 to 166 is 420 years.) Now was the seventh day of the weeks, which would usher in the Messianic era.

Yet more time until the 29 years—The word מועד, here means 29 years (see Table 16.0.1). The 29 years which are meant are those after 168 (see Sentence 29), i.e., until 139. Historically, practical independence was achieved for the Jewish state in 142; official recognition by Rome of the state's independence occurred in 139[204]. This independence, however, only lasted until 63[205].

The text has now finished its presentation of the background history for the attainment of independence of the Jewish state during the period of the Second Temple. There is now a skip of over 2,026 years until the time of Kaiser Wilhelm II. His history begins the background for the attainment of the final independence of the Jewish state. All commentaries have missed this time-gap in the text, and have therefore found it impossible to interpret the remainder of the chapter satisfactorily.

36. ועשה כרצנו המלך ויתרומם ויתגדל על כל אל ועל אל אלים ידבר
נפלאות, והצליח עד כלה זעם כי נחרצה נעשתה.

The king will do what he chooses, and will exalt and magnify himself above every god, and against the God of gods he will speak miracles. He will succeed until the end of the wrath, because a cutting-off was done.

The king—The word "king" is a substitute for "kaiser." This and the following three sentences refer to Kaiser Wilhelm II of Germany (1888–1918 c.e.).

Will do what he chooses—Kaiser Wilhelm was an absolute monarch who did as he wanted.

Will exalt and magnify himself above every god—The Kaiser believed that he was the anointed of God and therefore could do no wrong; and that any crimes were permissible because they were ordered by Wilhelm II who ruled by the grace of God[106].

Against the God of gods he will speak miracles—Two typical cases where the Kaiser spoke as if he could perform miracles against God are as follows:
A. The Kaiser condescendingly enlisted God as a private in the German army[207].
B. The Kaiser took God for his trusty henchman. "Our old god," he said[208].

He will succeed until the end of the wrath—The "wrath" refers to World War I. At the end of World War I, Wilhelm II was forced to abdicate in order to allow the peace negotiations to proceed[209].

Because a cutting-off was done—In November 1918, the German Socialist party announced the termination (cutting-off) of the monarchy and its replacement by a republic. Instead of fighting the decision, Kaiser Wilhelm II abandoned the army and stole quietly away to Holland[219].

37. ועל אלהי אבתיו לא יבין ועל חמדת נשים ועל כל אלוה לא יבין
כי על כל יתגדל.

He shall not understand the god of his fathers, nor the attraction of women, neither shall he understand any god; for he shall exalt himself above everybody.

Not understand the god of his fathers—When the Kaiser spoke of "our old German god," he did not mean the divinity of Christianity, but rather a barbaric god[211].

Nor the attraction of women—The Kaiser's idea of women was that they were entirely for purposes of amusement or propagation[212]. Moreover, he showed little respect for his wife, and was incapable of loving anyone but himself[213]. He considered his boasting about mistresses in his wife's presence an indication of his complete independence of domestic fetters[214].

Neither shall he understand any god—The Kaiser did not understand the concept of God. At one occasion he claimed to be the anointed of God; other times even god himself; and still other times he berated God.

He shall exalt himself over everybody—The Kaiser in his own "All-Highest" estimation still believed he was the greatest "I Am" even at the time of the armistice agreement[215]. Moreover, in a proclamation to his army September 13, 1914, Kaiser Wilhelm said:

> The spirit of God has descended upon me because I am the German Emperor! I am the instrument of the Most High! I am His sword and His representative upon earth! Woe and death to those who dare oppose my will! Death to the infidel who denies my mission! Let all the enemies of the German nation perish, for God demands their destruction; God who through my mouth summons you to carry out His decrees[216].

38. ולאלה מעזים על כנו יכבד, ולאלוה אשר לא ידעהו אבתיו יכבד בזהב ובכסף ובאבן יקרה ובחמדות.

He shall honor on his throne the god of strongholds; and a god unknown to his ancestors he will honor with gold, silver, precious stones, and costly items.

Shall honor on his throne the god of strongholds—The Kaiser used to offer his 50 million Prussians to the "god of war."[217] Furthermore, the Kaiser was called "Supreme War Lord" by his officers[218].

A god unknown to his ancestors he will honor with . . . costly items—The Kaiser considered himself "Lord of the Sea" of Germany, Great Britain, Russia, and Sweden, and because of this had a collection of hundreds of uniforms of regiments of many countries. This included cocked hats, broadswords, daggers, blue cloth, and silver and gold lace; also ornaments, badges, sashes, sidearms, caps, helmets, silver cords, etc.[219]

39. ועשה למבצרי מעזים עם אלוה נכר אשר יכיר ירבה כבוד והמשילם ברבים ואדמה יחלק במחיר.

He shall make into the strongest fortress that which is with a foreign god, who when recognized provides much honor; and he will make them to rule over many; and territory will be given as its price.

This sentence refers to the island of Helgoland, in the North Sea, which was strongly fortified by the Kaiser.

Make into the strongest fortress—The Germans introduced many changes into the island of Helgoland. In particular, the island was strongly fortified. The old English batteries were superseded by strongly armored towers and mortar batteries, with subterranean casemates. The lower and upper defences were connected by a tunnel[220].

That which is with a foreign god—The island of Helgoland was originally named Fositesland after a god called Fosite or Forseti[221].

Who when recognized provides much honor—The god Forseti possesses the heavenly mansion called Glitner; all disputants at law who bring their cases before him go away perfectly reconciled. His tribunal is supposedly the best that is to be found among gods and men[222].

He will make them to rule over many—Helgoland consists of two islets, the main or Rock Island, and the small Dunen-Insel, a quarter-mile to the east[223]. Therefore, Helgoland is spoken of in the plural. The fortifications on the island made possible control over the waters of the North Sea. On August 28, 1914, the first serious naval encounter between the English and the German forces occurred at Helgoland bight[224].

Territory will be given as its price—The island of Helgoland was ceded to the Germans under the Anglo-German agreement of July 1, 1890 in exchange for the territory of Zanzibar in East Africa[225].

40. ובעת קץ יתנגח עמו מלך הנגב וישתער עליו מלך הצפון ברכב ובפרשים ובאניות רבות, ובא בארצות ושטף ועבר.

Twenty-five years before the end, the king of the south will fight along with him; and the king of the north will storm against him with chariots, horsemen, and many ships; and he will enter countries and will succeed on land and sea.

Twenty-five years before the end—The word עת is used to mean 25 years (see Table 16.0.1). The 25-year period referred to is from 1914, the time of the beginning of World War I, until 1939, the time of the beginning of World War II. The year 1939 is here considered the "end" (קץ), as later specified in Dan. 12 7.

King of the south—At the time of World War I, Austria-Hungary was mostly south of Germany; and Francis Joseph was the emperor-king. Therefore Austria-Hungary is called king of the south.

King of the north—England is northwest of Germany. In 1914 the king of England was George V. Therefore England is called king of the north.

King of the south will fight along with him ... storm against him—Within a few months after June 28, 1914, when Archduke Francis Ferdinand was assassinated, Germany and Austria-Hungary on one side were fighting against England, Russia, Serbia, France, and Belgium on the other side[226]. Additional countries soon became involved in the fighting.

With chariots, horsemen and many ships—During World War I England introduced three new types of weapons—tanks, airplanes, and anti-submarine ships[227].

The names for these three weapons were not in existence in ancient times, and instead the closest equivalent words are used in the text. The underlying idea of the tank—protected mobile striking power—has been used throughout the history of warfare. The Assyrian war chariots and the Chinese armored war-carts represented early exploitation of this concept[228]. Therefore, "chariots" is the best word equivalent to "tanks."

During World War I the airplane was initially used for observation, and only later for other purposes such as support of ground troops and bombing[229]. Analogously, horsemen would ride quickly into enemy territory to observe enemy movements, and then rapidly ride away. Thus "horsemen" is the best word equivalent to "airplane."

The submarine first became a major factor in naval warfare during World War I when Germany demonstrated its full potentialities[230]. England countered the submarine with anti-submarine devices under water, upon the surface, and in the air[231]. These anti-submarine devices and ships are here called "many ships."

He will enter countries and will succeed on land and sea—During World War I, Germany and its allies entered France, Belgium, Poland, Rumania, and Serbia, and were also dominant in the Baltic Sea, and partially successful in blockading England[232].

41. ובא בארץ הצבי ורבות יכשלו, ואלה ימלטו מידו אדום ומואב
וראשית בני עמון.

And he shall enter the desirous land, and many countries shall stumble; but these shall be delivered out of his hand, Edom, and Moab, and the first part of the Children of Ammon.

He shall enter the desirous land—On August 2, 1914, Germany and Turkey signed a secret treaty. Under the terms of the treaty Turkey was to help Germany in return for a guarantee of territorial integrity[233]. Palestine, here called the desirous land, was part of the Turkish empire. Therefore, the alliance between Germany and Turkey in effect allowed Germany to enter the desirous land.

Many countries shall stumble—Early campaigns involving Turkey caused many of its opponent countries to stumble. In particular, the Gallipoli campaign against Turkey in 1915 was an offensive where the English and French attackers were unsuccessful[234]. Moreover, the English campaigns against Turkey in the area of Gaza, in early 1916, were failures because of poor leadership[235]. Attacks by Turkey against the Russians in the Caucasus and against England at the Suez Canal were not military successes, but did serve the strategic purpose of pinning down large Russian and English forces[236].

These shall be delivered out of his hand, Edom . . . Children of Ammon—In one battle area, success was achieved in the fight against Turkey. The success was attained under the guidance of the British Colonel T. E. Lawrence and the leadership of Emir Feisal of Arabia. Under their direction, a slow Arab revolt proceeded which cleared the Turkish forces from Arabia, the low hills of Edom, the deserts of Moab, and finally from the beginning of the territory of Ammon. The names Edom and Moab were often used in describing the regions[237], because the territory involved was where these Biblical countries once existed.

42. וישלח ידו בארצות, וארץ מצרים לא תהיה לפליטה.
And he shall extend his might to countries, and the land of Egypt shall not escape.

Extend his might to countries—With this sentence begins a description of events at the time of, and immediately preceding, World War II (1939-1945). Previous to World War II Germany acquired Austria in March 1938, and Czechoslovakia in March 1939[238]. Then on September 1, 1939, Germany began World War II by invading Poland. Soon Denmark, Norway, the Netherlands, Belgium, Luxemburg, and France were invaded. By June 1940 France had fallen[239].

The land of Egypt shall not escape—In September 1940 Italy, an ally of Germany, began its first offensive directed against Egypt. Some inroads were made, but counterattacking English forces soon drove the Italians back. March 1941 saw the Axis (Italian and German) forces again advancing towards Egypt. However, they were stopped at Tobruk outside Egypt. The third offensive by the Axis forces began in June 1942, and by July they had reached El Alamein about half way into Egyptian territory. In October 1942 the English began a counteroffensive, and by November had ousted the Axis from Egypt[240]. Thus although after the first two campaigns it looked as if Egypt would escape the power of Germany, eventually about half of Egypt was under Axis control.

43. ומשל במכמני הזהב והכסף ובכל חמדות מצרים, ולבים וכשים במצעדיו.
He shall rule over the treasures of gold and silver, and over all the precious things of Egypt; and the Libyans and the Ethiopians shall be in his steps.

Shall rule over the treasures . . . the precious things of Egypt—Hitler, the fuehrer of Germany, having been a painter, decided to make Germany rule over all art. With brute force and conquest he removed to Germany a vast collection of art treasures of all types from the many conquered countries. A special battalion was organized in May 1943 by the German Foreign Ministry to superintend the removal to Germany of articles of artistic value seized in occupied territories[241]. After World War II a survey of the art collected showed it included such items as gems, ivories, paintings, sculptures, jewelry, tombs, bronzes, etc.²⁴² The phrase "precious things of Egypt" means all types of art, such as those originally developed by Egypt. Thus, in Egypt we find the most ancient examples and origins of art. Included among Egyptian art is its architecture such as tombs and temples, sculpture, and painting, and the industrial arts including ceramics, metal work, jewelry and wood carving²⁴³.

The Libyans and the Ethiopians shall be in his steps—In October 1935 Italy, the ally of Germany during World War II, conquered Ethiopia, and the country remained under Axis domination until late 1941 when completely reconquered by England. Italy became ruler over the colony of Libya in January 1939, and remained in control until chased out in early 1943²⁴⁴.

44. ושמעות יבהלהו ממזרח ומצפון, ויצא בחמא גדלה להשמיד ולהחרים רבים.

But news from the east and the north will bewilder him, and he shall come out with great fury to destroy and exterminate many.

News from the east and the north will bewilder him—Germany will hear the news of the military setbacks in the eastern front against Russia and in the north African campaign against the British. The first major defeat of Germany occurred before Moscow (eastern front) in the autumn of 1941. The two turning points of the Second World War occurred in the autumn of 1942, and were the retreat of the Afrika Korps which followed the Battle of El Alamein (in North Africa), and the Battle of Stalingrad (eastern front)²⁴⁵,²⁴⁶.

Come out . . . to destroy and exterminate many—The extermination of the Jews was ordered at a moment when it had become evident to Germany that contrary to the Nazi dreams of 1939–1940, the war they had started would last a long time, whatever its outcome. The decision to eliminate European Jewry was made about early 1941. For practical and other reasons the extermination plan was carried out in stages; the dates of which were June 1941, April 1942, and October 1942. Not until the spring of 1942 did the extermination program, set up during the second half of 1941, begin to go full blast²⁴⁷.

45. ויטע אהלי אפדנו בין ימים להר צבי קדש ובא עד קצו ואין עוזר לו.

And he shall set up the tents of his throne room between seas leading to the holy desirous mountain; and he shall come to his end, with no one to help him.

Set up the tents of his throne room—The Hebrew word used for throne room is *apadna* (אפדן). The *apadna* in Shushan was the king's throne room or great hypostyle hall which covered nearly an acre of ground. It was supported by 36 noble columns—six rows of six each²⁴⁸. The tents of the *apadna* correspond to modern airfield hangers which are also enormous rooms.

Between seas leading to the holy desirous mountain—The "holy desirous mountain" here refers to Mount Etna on the island of Sicily. Mount Etna is often spoken of distinctively as *Il Monte*—the mountain *par excellence*; a name which, in its capacity of the loftiest volcano in Europe, is fully justified. The poets had invested Mount Etna with various supernatural attributes, and had made it the prison house of a chained giant, and the workshop of a swart god. Many myths have been developed by the earlier poets about this mountain to explain its volcanic properties[249].

The term "between seas" refers to the island of Sicily. This island is surrounded by the Tyrrhenian Sea, Ionian Sea, Mediterranean Sea, Straits of Messina, and the Malta Channel[250].

The German plan of defence for Sicily was based on Mount Etna. Its eastern slopes fell down to the Mediterranean and commanded fifty miles of the coastal highway. Its southern slopes looked upon the broad Catania plain. Here the Germans could apply every lesson of defensive warfare[251].

In May 1943, the allies decided to clear the Mediterranean for allied shipping, and also to provide a suitable springboard for the invasion of Italy. It became apparent that the early capture of the airfields in the southeastern corner of Sicily was vital to the future success of the operation[252].

He shall come to his end with no one to help him—The axis airfields were occupied on July 10, and from these the Allied air force was able to maintain effective close support. By August 17, 1943 the island of Sicily was captured. The coast of Italy was then invaded and by September 3, 1943 Italy surrendered unconditionally. This left the Germans *alone* in the battle against the allies[253]. After two more years, in May 1945, Germany surrendered unconditionally.

16.7   CHAPTER 12 OF DANIEL

Chapter 12 is the concluding section of the revelation begun with Chapter 10. In actuality, a more fitting beginning for this chapter would be 11 36. Then Chapter 11 would contain the historical background for the independent Jewish state achieved during the period of the Second Temple; and Chapter 12 (beginning with what is now 11 36) would contain the historical background to the establishment of the modern State of Israel.

Chapter 12 is one of the most misinterpreted chapters of the prophetic section of the Book of Daniel. Not only have the specified dates not been understood, but even the historical events described have been completely missed. In particular, Sentences 2 and 13 are always explained as referring to resurrection of the dead in the Messianic era, when in actuality these sentences have no connection with this concept.

1. ובעת ההיא יעמד מיכאל השר הגדול העמד על בני עמך והיתה

עת צרה אשר לא נהיתה מהיות גוי עד העת ההיא, ובעת ההיא
ימלט עמך כל הנמצא כתוב בספר.

And in that 25-year period shall stand up Michael, the great prince who stands for the children of your people; and there shall be 25 years of trouble, such as never was since there was a nation until that 25-year period. During those 25 years your people shall escape; everything that will happen is written in the book.

In that 25-year period—The Hebrew word עת, used four times in this sentence, indicates a 25-year period (see Table 16.0.1). The 25-year period is that mentioned in 11 40, namely from 1914 to 1939.

Stand up Michael—The prince, Michael, who is the guardian angel of the Jewish people, will stand up to fight.

Twenty-five years of trouble such as never was—The time from 1914 through 1939 was a period of unparalleled worldwide trouble, such as never was since the formation of nations after the Deluge. The battles of World War I raged between 1914 and 1918, and resulted in more casualties than any previous conflict. The unrealistic terms of the subsequent peace settlements led to a very slow and painful recovery period. Each of the major nations of the world suffered internal crises. A worldwide economic emergency was aggravated by the monetary collapse in the United States in 1929. Nearly twenty million persons in the United States were facing starvation in 1933, and the condition of the poorer countries was considerably worse. The economic emergency did not really end until the time of the preparations for World War II around 1939[254].

During those 25 years your people shall escape—During these years the Jews in the countries suffered badly. In Poland, Germany, Lithuania, Rumania, Hungary, Austria, Russia, and other countries, severe anti-Semitism and restrictions against Jews were practiced at various times. Many of the Jews escaped from their countries of restrictions to other nations where greater freedom existed. Thus, 125,000 Polish Jews escaped to Palestine between 1920 and 1939; 100,000 Jewish refugees from Germany and Poland went to France; and thousands of fugitives from Nazi terror found asylum in Canada and the countries of Central and South America, and others found havens in the United States and Palestine. Although the Jews were subjected to suffering, they were able to escape during these 25 years. However, in 1939 many of the escape routes were closed. England prevented further immigration into Palestine by enactment of the White Paper of May 1939. Germany conquered many countries of refuge, such as France. Few escape routes were then left from the extermination policy of the Germans[255,256].

Everything ... is written in the book—The key events for the 25 years are written in the Book of Daniel, especially in the part containing the words of the present revelation (Chapters 10–12). Thus a description of World War I, and some events preceding World War II, are found in **11** 40–43. In addition, some major happenings between 1914 and 1939 are described in **12** 1–3.

2. ורבים מישני אדמת עפר יקיצו, אלה לחיי עולם ואלה לחרפות לדראון עולם.

And many of those sleeping in the continent of earth will awaken, some to the life of the world, and some to reproaches and the disgust of the world.

Many of those sleeping in the continent of earth will awaken—The "continent of earth" refers to the continent of Europe, probably because of the underdeveloped condition of the nations of Europe in the early part of the twentieth century. "Those sleeping in the continent" refers to the underdeveloped countries. It has, for example, been stated, "The First World War brought sweeping changes ... states long dead came to life and new ones were born."[257]

New European frontiers were established by the treaties of Versailles, St. Germain, Sèvres, and Neuilly after World War I. Poland, Czechoslovakia, Estonia, Latvia, Lithuania, and the Free Territory of Danzig emerged as new states. Serbia became part of Yugoslavia. Finland became independent from Russia. Moreover, the boundaries of Germany, Hungary, Turkey, Italy, Bulgaria, France, Belgium, Denmark, Austria, Russia, and Rumania were modified[258]. Previous to World War I, Spain and Portugal were economically and educationally backward, and vegetated outside the mainstream of European events. Equally backward were Greece, Bulgaria, Serbia, Montenegro, and Rumania, although not isolated from European politics. Russia in the early twentieth century was only a half-awakened giant[259].

Some to the life of the world—Many of these new or modified countries were successful in becoming members of the nations of the world, and to exist as nations. Finland, Yugoslavia, Rumania, Bulgaria, Belgium, France, Denmark, Italy, Czechoslovakia, Poland, and others, exist to the present time.

Some to reproaches and the disgust of the world—Other countries, especially Germany and Italy, developed fascist regimes which initiated the Second World War in 1939. These countries, during the war, perpetrated some of the gravest atrocities the world has ever encountered, and therefore have become the permanent reproach and disgust of other nations. The atrocities which they committed will be remembered forever in history.

3. והמשכילים יזהירו כזהר הרקיע, ומצדיקי הרבים ככוכבים לעולם ועד.

They that are wise shall shine as the shine of the sky; and they that make justice for the many, as the stars for the entire world.

They that are wise—The enlightened countries will unite to attain peace, and will form the United Nations. The charter of the United Nations was formulated from April to June 1945, and the first session was held January 10, 1946.

Shall shine as the shine of the sky—The most outstanding building of the United Nations is the Secretariat Building. This 39-story structure stands out in the New York area, and reflects the shine of the sky. The east-west facade of the building is surfaced with blue-green glass, and aluminum. The windows absorb heat and reduce the solar radiation for the interior offices. The north-south ends of the structure are solid grey Vermont marble[260,261].

They that make justice for the many—Connected with the United Nations is the International Court of Justice, the name of which is almost equivalent to the phrase "they that make justice for the many." This group, established in 1946, is the principal judicial organ of the United Nations. Although the International Court of Justice was a separate creation from the Permanent Court of International Justice, established in 1900, the two instruments are essentially identical, except that necessary changes in terminology have been made[262].

As the stars for the entire world—The International Court of Justice is housed in the Peace Palace in The Hague, Holland. The building has numerous starlike spires on the outside, and therefore shines as the stars[263].

4. ואתה, דניאל סתם הדברים וחתם הספר עד עת קץ, ישטטו רבים ותרבה הדעת.

And you Daniel, leave the words unexplained, and seal the book until "25 years before the end." Many will roam, and knowledge will be increased.

Leave the words unexplained and seal the book until "25 years before the end"—The wording of the revelation presented in Chapter 11 is extremely concise. Without use of historical knowledge from extra-Biblical sources it would be impossible to know exactly what is meant. Many of the phrases can be interpreted in more than one way, and often the antecedents are not clearly specified. Moreover, the time-spans of certain key words (see Table 16.0.1) are not defined. This extreme lack of clarity is not by chance, or because of the author's inability to express himself, but because Daniel was commanded to "leave the words unexplained and seal the book" until the phrase "25 years before the end" (11 40). From that sentence on, the description is given of World War I and subsequent events, and the wording is somewhat clearer.

Many will roam and knowledge will be increased—Many nations will come and go, and their locations may change, thereby enabling people in later times to better comprehend the presented descriptions. Moreover, historical knowledge will be increased. These factors will eventually enable the understanding of the revelation, even though it is to be left unexplained by Daniel.

5. וראיתי אני דניאל והנה שנים אחרים עמדים, אחד הנה לשפת
   היאר ואחד הנה לשפת היאר.
   *And I, Daniel, saw, and behold, two others were standing, one on this bank
   of the Nile, and one on the other bank of the Nile.*

   Two others were standing—Daniel sees two other angels representing two
   other nations. The angels were "standing," i.e., they were fighting with each
   other.
   On this bank of the Nile—Throughout the Bible the Hebrew word יאר
   refers to the Nile River in Egypt. For example, see Gen. **41** 1, Ex. **2** 5, Is. **19** 8,
   Jer. **46** 8, Ez. **29** 3, and Am. **9** 5 where the word יאר is connected with
   Egypt. Although Daniel was near the Tigris River (**10** 4), he saw the Nile
   River in the revelation. The two other angels represent the nations of England
   and Germany, who during World War II were fighting in the vicinity of the Nile.
   Looking at a globe, English forces were on the right side and German forces on
   the left side of the Nile. The history of that period is as follows: In February
   1941 the Germans sent troops to assist the Italians in their fight against the
   English in North Africa. The Germans aimed for the Suez Canal, and in June
   1942 reached El Alamein, which is within 100 miles of the Nile. In November
   1942 the English succeeded in repulsing the German forces at El Alamein,
   which eventually led to the clearing of all German forces from North Africa in
   May 1943[264].

6. ויאמר לאיש לבוש הבדים אשר ממעל למימי היאר, עד מתי קץ
   הפלאות.
   *And he said to the man clothed in linen who was above the waters of the
   Nile "until when is the end involving incredible events?"*

   He said—The angel representing England was the one speaking.
   The man clothed in linen who was above the waters of the Nile—The man
   clothed in linen, the angel of Babylonia, was the one telling the revelation to
   Daniel. Here he is pictured as being above the waters of the Nile, since Babylonia was in no way involved in the battles between England and Germany.
   Until when is the end involving incredible events—When will be the "end,"
   referred to previously in **11** 40, involving incredible events?

7. ואשמע את האיש לבוש הבדים אשר ממעל למימי היאר וירם
   ימינו ושמאלו אל השמים וישבע בחי העולם, כי למועד מועדים
   וחצי, וככלות נפץ יד עם קדש תכלינה כל אלה.
   *And I heard the man clothed in linen who was above the waters of the
   Nile; and he raised the one on his right and the one on his left to heaven;
   and he swore by the life of the world; that it will be in 2,523 years; and when
   the shattering of the power of the holy people is stopped, then will all these
   be finished.*

He raised the one on his right and the one on his left to heaven—The angel clothed in linen raised up to heaven the angel on his right side representing England, and the angel on his left side representing Germany. It is thus indicated that just as the greatness of Babylonia has gone, since the man clothed in linen was above the waters, so too the greatness of England and Germany will pass.

He swore by the life of the world—The reassurance is here given that the world will survive despite terrifying calamities, such as World War II. Moreover, the reassurance is given that predictions of events to take place about 2,500 years in the future are meaningful.

It will be in 2,523 years—The Hebrew phrase is מועד מועדים וחצי. As given in Table 16.0.1, מועד represents 29 years. The word מועדים, the plural of מועד, represents $2 \times 29 = 58$ years. Then מועד מועדים is equal to $29 \times 58 = 1,682$ years. To this must be added one-half (חצי) of the 1,682, or 841 years, for a total of 2,523 years. Note that the presence of the Hebrew letter *vav* meaning "and" indicates addition, while the absence of the *vav* indicates multiplication.

The angel clothed in linen states that the "end" (קץ) will occur in 2,523 years. From 586 B.C.E. (see 10 6), the time represented by the angel clothed in linen, through the year 1938 C.E., is 2,523 years.

```
 2523
 -586
 1937
    1   (no year zero in the counting system)
 1938
```

Thus the "end" involving incredible events will begin in 1939 with the start of World War II.

When the shattering of the power... will all these be finished—"All these" refers to the two angels, the ones representing England and Germany, raised up to heaven by the man clothed in linen. During World War II Germany caused the death of six million Jews, mainly on the European continent[265]. England, meanwhile, prevented sizeable immigration into Palestine, according to the policy stated in the White Paper issued on May 17, 1939[266]. This policy contributed to the death of hundreds of thousands of Jews who might have otherwise escaped Nazi persecution. Thus, the warlike activities of both Germany and England were shattering the power of the Jewish people. Subsequent to World War II, England continued its oppressive policies in Palestine until evacuation of its troops in May 1948. Thus, the termination of the angels of Germany and England brings us to the time of the establishment of the State of Israel.

This sentence marks the second period since the Babylonian Exile when the Jewish nation attained independence. The second period of independence, unlike the first at the time of the Hasmonaeans, will last forever.

8. ואני שמעתי ולא אבין ואמרה אדני מה אחרית אלה.
And I heard but I did not understand, and I said "Sir, what is the ending of these?"

Did not understand—Daniel did not understand the part concerning the ending of the war angels of Germany and England. Did their end, e.g., indicate that the countries of Germany and England would be destroyed? The rest of the revelation, however, was understood by Daniel.

9. ויאמר לך דניאל, כי סתמים וחתמים הדברים עד עת קץ.
He said, "Go your way Daniel, for the words are left unexplained and sealed until 'the 25 years before the end.'"

He said—The angel clothed in linen answered Daniel.
Go your way Daniel—Leave your question unanswered.
The words are left unexplained . . . until "the 25 years before the end"—As stated in 12 4, the revelation is to be left unexplained until the phrase found in 11 40 "the 25 years before the end." To answer Daniel's question concerning the ending of the angels of Germany and England would involve supplying sufficient clues so that the early parts of the revelation (11 2–39) could be too easily understood. Therefore, Daniel's question could not be answered.

10. יתבררו ויתלבנו ויצרפו רבים והרשיעו רשעים ולא יבינו כל רשעים, והמשכילים יבינו.
Many shall purify themselves, and make themselves white, and become refined; and the wicked shall act wickedly; but none of the wicked shall understand; but they that are wise shall understand.

Many shall purify themselves—Many people will try to bring about an independent Jewish state by purifying themselves and acting with great refinement.

Wicked shall act wickedly—Many others will act wickedly to try to bring about an independent Jewish state, but they will completely misunderstand the way to achieve this goal. Referred to here in this sentence are the false messiahs who have arisen over the centuries. Some were imposters seeking to exploit the credulity of the people for selfish purposes. Others were victims of their own delusions. Some false messiahs sought to achieve the restoration of an independent Jewish state by penitence, fasting and prayer, and expected the occurrence of miracles to help them. Others tried to achieve their goal by military means. Many of the false messiahs lost their own lives and deluded the people with false hopes. Pseudo-messiahs have arisen from the time of the Hasmonaean dynasty until as late as the eighteenth century[267].

They that are wise shall understand—The Hebrew word משכילים, meaning "wise" or "enlightened," is the same word used in 12 3 to denote the enlightened countries which formed the United Nations. It is through the workings of the United Nations that the independent state of Israel was established. In February 1947 the British government decided to submit the problem of Palestine to the United Nations. On November 29, 1947 the General Assembly voted for the partition of Palestine, and the establishment of a Jewish state. The Jewish state was established on May 14, 1948[268].

In the next two sentences are given the dates for the formation of the United Nations and the Permanent Court of Arbitration.

11. ומעת הוסר התמיד ולתת שקוץ שמם ימים אלף מאתים ותשעים.
And from the 25-year period when the permanent [stone] was removed and the detestable was made desolate, a six-year period 1,290 [years later].

From the 25-year period—The word עת here means a 25-year period (see Table 16.0.1). The time referred to is from 605 to 630 C.E.

When the permanent [stone] was removed—This refers to the event described in 8 11, when the Black Stone around which the Ka'ba is built, was removed temporarily because of a flood (605). The Black Stone is here called "the permanent" because there are Moslem legends that claim it existed at the time of Creation.

The detestable was made desolate—Twenty-five years after the Black Stone was removed, Mohammad, by military conquest, gained control of the Ka'ba, and had the idols within that temple destroyed (see 8 12). Thus in 630 the detestable idols were made desolate.

A six-year period—The Hebrew word ימים is used to denote a six-year period (see Table 16.0.1).

1,290 [years later]—1,290 years after 605 is 1895. The six-year period is from 1895 through 1900, the time when the Permanent Court of Arbitration was established. The history of the formation of this court is as follows. The Interparliamentary Union, a voluntary organization of members of the national legislative bodies of the nations, at its meeting in Holland in 1894, adopted a declaration in favor of a permanent court of arbitration. In 1895, at the first meeting of the Mohonk Conference on international arbitration, a resolution in favor of the establishment of a permanent international court of arbitration was introduced; and the resolution was unanimously adopted at the next annual meeting of the conference[269]. On August 24, 1898, Czar Nicholas II of Russia called the first Hague Conference, which met in The Hague between May 18 and July 29, 1899. The basis for the Permanent Court of Arbitration was set at this meeting, and the court was organized in 1900[270].

Subsequently the Permanent Court of International Arbitration was established in 1920 by the League of Nations; and the International Court of Justice by the United Nations in 1946. In effect, the international Court of Justice is a continuation of the Permanent Court of Arbitration established in 1900. All these courts have located their seats at the Peace Palace (built in 1907) in The Hague[271]. Mention of the International Court of Justice was already made in 12 3.

12. אשרי המחכה ויגיע לימים אלף שלש מאות שלשים וחמשה.
Fortunate is he who waits and reaches the six-year period 1,335 [years later].

Fortunate is he who waits and reaches the six-year period—The dates given here are for the establishment of the United Nations. However, during the same six-year period World War II occurred, when six million Jews were murdered. Therefore, the one who reaches the end of this six-year period is very fortunate.

1335 [years later]—1,335 years after 605 is 1940. The six-year period is from 1940 through 1945. Note that in this sentence as well as the previous sentence the years are considered to begin with the month of Nisan (March or April). The dates concerning establishment of the United Nations are as follows: From the beginning of World War II plans began to be developed for an international organization to prevent further wars. Thus, on September 3, 1939 President Roosevelt stated " . . . the influence of America should be consistent in seeking . . . a final peace which will eliminate . . . the continued use of force between nations"[272]. On October 20, 1939 Pope Piux XII advocated founding a stable international organization after the war. Cordell Hull, Secretary of State of the United States publicly announced on January 8, 1940 the creation of a committee for postwar planning, and during the war directed much effort for development of a United Nations[273].

Some of the more important steps which eventually led to the establishment of the United Nations were: (A) An inter-Allied declaration, June 12, 1941, stating "the only true basis of enduring peace is the willing cooperation of free people." (B) The Atlantic Charter, signed by President Roosevelt of the United States, and Prime Minister Churchill of England, which expressed hopes for a world free of fear and want, and which endorsed disarmament. (C) Representatives of 26 nations in the "Declaration by United Nations" on January 1, 1942 endorsed the objectives of freedom and disarmament. (D) On October 30, 1943, representatives of the four great powers declared that they "recognized the necessity of establishing at the earliest possible date a general international organization." (E) On December 1, 1943 President Roosevelt, Prime Minister Churchill, and Premier Stalin agreed that they had the responsibility "to make a peace which would banish war for many generations." (F) At Dumbarton Oaks, in Washington, D.C. specific proposals for a United Nations were formulated (August 21–September 28, 1944). (G) At Yalta, February 11, 1945, the leaders of the United States, England, and Russia agreed on a conference of United Nations on April 25, 1945 in San Francisco. (H) At the San Francisco meeting (April 25–June 26, 1945) the charter of the United Nations was prepared[274]. (I) The first session of the General Assembly of the United Nations opened in London on January 10, 1946.

13. ואתה לך לקץ ותנוח ותעמד לגרלך לקץ הימין.
And you leave the "end" alone; and she shall rest, and stand up according to your prediction at the end of [the angel on] the right.

Leave the "end" alone—The Hebrew phrase לך לקץ is here used with the same general meaning as לך דניאל found in Sentence 9; i.e., not to bother to gain clarification. Thus, Daniel is told not to try to gain a clear understanding of the "end" referred to in Sentence 6.

She shall rest and stand . . . at the end of [the angel on] the right—She—the Jewish state—shall remain dormant and non-existent until the time of your prediction. At the end of the angel on the right (see Sentence 7), i.e., when the English troops leave Palestine in 1948, the independent State of Israel shall then be established.

16.8 MODERN EVENTS PROPHESIED IN BOOK OF DANIEL

For the convenience of the reader, the main prophecies in the Book of Daniel concerning modern times, i.e., concerning events after the late nineteenth century C.E., are tabulated below.

9 24 The suffering endured by the Jewish people over the past few thousand years can be at least partially attributed to three major sins committed before entering into the land of Israel at the time of Joshua. These sins are (A) the selling of Joseph as a slave by his brothers; (B) the worshipping of a golden calf by the Israelites shortly after hearing the Ten Commandments at Mount Sinai; and (C) the lack of faith by the spies and the Jewish people that God would enable them to conquer the idol-worshipping inhabitants of the land of Israel.

11 36–41 Kaiser Wilhelm II of Germany will in 1914 be one of the initiators of World War I. Germany, Austria-Hungary, and Turkey will fight on one side against England and other countries. Palestine will be under Turkish control, but the territory of Edom, Moab, and the beginning of Ammon (i.e., modern Jordan) will slowly escape Turkish domination.

7 18,25 Palestine will be under the control of the Arab and succeeding Moslem empires until about 1916.

2 41,42 Around the time of World War I the Ottoman empire (the outgrowth of the Arabian empire) will be broken up into many smaller Arab countries. Some of these smaller Arab countries will be strong militarily, while others will be weak.

12 1–2 The 25-year period from 1914 to 1939 will be a time of un-

paralleled worldwide trouble. During this period the Jewish people will escape serious catastrophy. At the same time, many of the underdeveloped countries of Europe will awaken to modern times. Some of these countries, however, such as Germany and Italy, will become the disgust of the world.

11 42–45   Germany will initiate World War II in 1939, and will conquer many countries. Libya, Ethiopia, and part of Egypt will come under German (and Italian) domination. During the war Germany will exterminate many Jews, and will amass art treasures. The downfall of Germany will begin after the conquest of Sicily and the defeat of Italy.

12 5–7,13   During World War II England and Germany will be opposing each other from opposite sides of the Nile. The State of Israel will be established subsequent to the end of the persecutions of the Jews by Germany and England.

12 3,10–12   The United Nations will be founded in 1945. The International Court of Justice, which is part of the United Nations, will owe its origins to the Permanent Court of Arbitration which was organized in 1900. It is through the United Nations that the State of Israel will be established.

9 26   The English mandate over Palestine will end in 1948. There will then follow a war between Israel and the Arabs. At the completion of the fighting, desolate areas (no-man's-land) will be designated as boundaries of the State of Israel. Transjordan will gain control of the Old City of Jerusalem, and will destroy the holy places. Abdullah, the king of Jordan at that time, will be assassinated.

9 27   An armistice agreement will be concluded between Israel and the Arabs, under the supervision of the United Nations. The armistice agreement will be officially in effect for 49 years, i.e., from 1948 to 1996. During the middle of these 49 years, from August 1970 until September 1972, a temporary cease-fire will be arranged to stop existing hostilities. In September 1972 the cease fire will be broken by Israeli bombing of the detestable Arab terrorist camps in Lebanon and Syria.

7 13   The Jews will become religious shortly before the War of Gog.

2 44   The modern State of Israel will never be destroyed, nor will it lose its independence. At the time of the War of Gog, Israel will destroy the attacking Arab countries, as well as Persia (Iran), Greece, and Babylonia (Iraq).

2 45   Israel will attain the theoretical Biblical boundaries after the War of Gog.

9 24   By 1996 the Third Temple will be completed, all predictions in the Bible will have been fulfilled, and eternal justice will be achieved.

7 14,27   The State of Israel will eventually become the greatest nation in the world, and will last forever.

Chapter Seventeen

COMMENTARY ON MESSIANIC CHAPTERS OF EZEKIEL

The Book of Daniel, as interpreted in Chapter Sixteen, supplies a chronological outline of the events to occur in the Messianic era. In particular, the State of Israel is to be established in 1948, by 1996 the Third Temple is to be completed, and midway in-between (around 1971—more exactly from 1970 to 1972) a cease-fire will take place between Israel and her neighbors. However, very meager accounts of the happenings are given. To gain a more complete description of Messianic events it is necessary to use supplemental information from the other prophetic works. One of the clearest and most detailed accounts of the time of redemption is presented in the Book of Ezekiel, Chapters 34–48. Chapters 34 through 39 describe in general terms the re-establishment of the State of Israel, the ingathering of the exiles, and the War of Gog. Chapters 40 through 48, however, give precise dimensions of the Third Temple and the altar, lists of sacrifices to be instituted, method of distribution of the land to the people, and special laws that will be followed in the future.

In interpreting the prophecies, consideration will be given to the exactness of the accounts. When the prophecies are described in general terms, then the explanation will only provide the over-all intent of the passages, without worrying about the meaning of each phrase. In contrast, when precise details are given, as for example concerning the design of the Temple, numerous Hebrew words will be carefully defined and drawings will be provided. For convenience, the chapters in the Book of Ezekiel will not be interpreted in the order of the text, but rather according to a logical, although somewhat arbitrary, arrangement.

17.1 WAR OF GOG (CHAPTERS 38–39)

In Chapters 38 and 39 of Ezekiel is presented a description of a war against Israel led by a leader named Gog. Gog, the head of Magog, a federation of the countries Rosh, Meshech, and Tubal, will be joined by many other nations in the attack against the newly formed State of Israel. The war will take place (**38 16**) in the "latter part of the Six Years" (באחרית הימים), i.e., sometime between April 3, 1973 and March 24, 1974.[1]

The names of the ancient nations listed in Ezekiel as among those attacking Israel can be interpreted in terms of their modern equivalents. Persia (**38 5**) corresponds to Iran. Cush (38 5) is commonly identified as Ethiopia. Put (38 5) is assumed to be identical with Punt, which lay near the Red Sea, and would therefore correspond to the Sudan. The country of Gomer, and all its satellites (38 6), has not been definitely identified, but may possibly be equivalent to China and her satellites, and would then include North Korea, Mongolia, and North Vietnam. The House of Togarmah (38 6) is usually associated with territory in the area of present-day Turkey, and has been translated as Turkey.[2] The Ends of the North and all its satellites is geographically the same as Russia. The Russian satellites include Poland, Rumania, Bulgaria, Yugoslavia, Hungary, Czechoslovakia, and East Germany.

In addition, mention is made (38 13) of Sheba, Dedan, and the traders with Tarshish and all her substates. These countries will ask Gog, "Have you come to acquire spoil; is it for plunder that you gathered your army?" The implication is that these three countries will hesitate, and finally decide not to join the attack. Sheba is commonly known as modern Yemen. Dedan is believed to have occupied either north or south Arabia, and in the present context would fit in nicely to refer to Aden, on the southern tip of the Arabian peninsula. The term "traders with Tarshish" and all her substates, implies a coastal country, with many subdivisions. Probably the country of Trucial Oman is meant, including its numerous substates. The country of Oman may also be included as one of the traders with Tarshish.

The remaining country to be identified is Magog, consisting of a federation of Rosh, Meshech, and Tubal (38 2). Based on present-day political considerations, it appears that Magog will be a federation formed shortly before the attack on Israel, and will consist of many of the Arab countries surrounding Israel, which would otherwise be left unmentioned in the text. The Arab countries include Egypt, Syria, Lebanon, Iraq, Kuwait, Saudi Arabia, and Jordan. Other possible participating countries are Libya, Tunisia, Algeria, and Morocco. Which of these Arab countries will actually participate is uncertain, and awaits the actual war for clarification. From other prophetic works it is clear that Egypt, Jordan, Lebanon (Joel 4 4, 19), Syria (Zech. 11 1–3), and Iraq (Mic. 5 4) will definitely be among the attackers.

The following general description of the War of Gog can now be given. Gog, the leader of united Arab countries surrounding Israel, will be joined by most of the countries of Asia, and many of the nations of Europe (mainly countries north of Israel), and North Africa in a military attack on the re-established State of Israel. The war will take place sometime between April 3, 1973 and March 24, 1974. The enemy will come well armed (38 4), with planes (horsemen), cars (horses), guns (swords), and tanks (shields). The countries of Yemen, Aden, Trucial Oman, and Oman will, however, not join in the attack and will ask, "What is the purpose of the war?" On the day that the military might of Gog will come onto the land of Israel there will be a tremendous noise, probably an atomic bomb followed by a major earthquake. Mountains will be destroyed and every wall will fall to the ground. God will fight against the enemy with disease, blood, overwhelming rain, hailstones, fire and brimstone; and the army of Gog will be annihilated. Moreover, destruction will be sent against the Arab countries of the Magog federation, and against participating islands. Then the holiness of God will be recognized by the Jewish people. It will take seven years to dispose productively of the military weapons of the army of Gog, and seven months to bury the dead in the Valley of Hamon-Gog. The complete ingathering of the exiles from all over the world will then take place, to the extent that practically no Jews will remain outside of Israel.

17.2 DEVELOPMENT OF THE LAND OF ISRAEL (CHAPTERS 34–37)

Chapters 38 and 39 contained a description of the War of Gog against Israel. Although Chapters 34 and 37 are placed earlier in the Book of Ezekiel, they contain prophecies concerning events which will occur both prior and subsequent to the War of Gog. In particular, Chapters 34 to 37 portray the development of the land of Israel and the ingathering of the exiled Jews during the early period of growth of the State of Israel. Below are presented short summaries of the key points of the chapters.

34 11–31 The Jewish people are compared to sheep, and their leaders to shepherds. God will gather His sheep, the Jewish people, back to Israel from wherever they reside. A shepherd named David will rule over the State of Israel. The people will worship God, peace will be in the land, and the ground will be fruitful. No longer will the Jews be a despised people, and no longer will there be hunger in the land.

35 1–15 By the terms Mount Seir and Edom are meant the territory of modern Jordan. The southern part of Jordan is the exact territory formerly occupied by Edom.

Jordan, at the time of the War of Gog, has claimed that the two countries—Israel and Judaea-Samaria (conquered by Israel in 1967)—belong to her. She has stated that Israel will be desolate and shall be given to the sword. Therefore, God says, the nation of Jordan will be made desolate and its territory filled with its dead. The cities of Jordan will no longer be returned to her.

36 1–15 The surrounding nations and Jordan have, prior to the War of Gog, considered the land of Israel as if already in their possession. Instead, Israel will flourish and the land will be developed, but the enemy countries will be destroyed.

36 16–38 The Jewish people will be gathered back to Israel from all over the world and purified from all their sins. They will believe in God and observe His commandments. The land will be rebuilt and the soil will flourish. It will be such a spectacular rebuilding of the land that the nations will say, "This desolate country has become like a garden of Eden."

37 1–14 The Jewish people in exile, who have lost all strength and hope, are compared to dry bones having no flesh or soul. God will open the way for the exiled Jews to come to Israel and regain the spirit of God, just as if graves were opened and the dried bones within were made to live again.

37 15–28 God will gather back to Israel the Jews in exile, and make them into

one nation under the leadership of a ruler named David. The people will believe in God and observe His laws forever. Their leader, David, will be an example for future generations of the ideal ruler. Peace will be everlasting, the population will increase, and the Temple will be built. The nations of the world will recognize that it is God who sanctifies Israel.

17.3 DESIGN OF THE THIRD TEMPLE (CHAPTERS 40 1–43 17; 46 19–47 12)

Ezekiel gives a very detailed description of the design of the Third Temple. Unfortunately, great difficulty has been encountered by the commentators in properly interpreting the details. Each commentator has to resort to forced explanations, for at least a few sentences, in order to obtain a self-consistent design. Moreover, no two commentators would build the Temple according to the same blueprint. It has therefore been necessary to present here a precise explanation of the dimensions of the Temple, and to clarify otherwise obscure passages. For simplicity, drawings are presented, which allow easy perception of the appearance of the Temple area.

One major problem, which has caused the commentators untold difficulties, has been the positioning of the Temple and the altar within the courts. In most cases, the Temple has been placed in the outer court, and the altar in the inner court. A more satisfactory result has here been obtained by placing the Temple in the inner court and the altar in the outer court.

17.3.1 Introductory and Explanatory Statements

40 1–4   In a vision, Ezekiel is transported to the Temple Mount in the land of Israel. An angel, who appears as a man made from copper, guides Ezekiel through the Temple area, and makes measurements for Ezekiel to record. The main building construction was in the southern part of the mountain top.

43 1–12   Ezekiel is shown how the glory of the Lord enters the Temple through the eastern entryway. Then the Temple, which is within the inner court, is filled with God's glory. God tells Ezekiel that the Temple is where He resides among the Jewish people, and this time He will dwell there forever. Ezekiel is told to write down the dimensions so the Temple can be constructed, and so that the top of the mountain will be sanctified.

40 5; 43 13   The unit of measurement is the larger cubit, which is equal to the standard cubit plus a handbreadth. As a rough approximation, the standard cubit is 17.5 inches, the handbreadth 3.5 inches, and the larger cubit 21 inches. Also mentioned (43 13) is the span (זרת), which is equal to one-half cubit.

17.3.2 The Outermost Wall

40 5; 42 15–20   The term "outermost wall" is here used in distinction to the outer and inner walls. The dimensions in cubits of the outermost wall around the Temple area are: length 3,000; width 3,000; thickness 6; height 6.

In **40 5** the word בית refers to the entire Temple area, and the word בנין refers to the outermost wall. This outermost wall encloses an area somewhat larger than the old city of Jerusalem, which indicates that the old city will be enlarged when the Temple is constructed.

17.3.3 Entryways to the Outer and Inner Courts

40 6-16 The arrangement of the entryway to the outer gate, is pictured in Figure 17.3.3.1, based on the description in **40 6-16**. To understand the text properly it is necessary to define a number of words. These are: מעלות = steps; סף = threshold; תא = guardhouse; אלם = entrance hallway; אילים = decorative posts; בית = gateway directly between the walls; מהבית = away from the gateway; שער = wall, mainly around the entryway; גבול = dividing barrier; איתון = entire entryway beyond the wall; חלונות אטמות = windows sealed with glass; פתח = doorway; תמורים = decorations shaped like palm trees. With these definitions, in conjunction with Figure 17.3.3.1, the Hebrew text is easily understood.

40 14 Next to the decorative post, which was 60 cubits long, the wall continued all around the court yard.

40 16 Glass windows were on the three sides of the guardhouses inside the entryway, as well as on the decorative posts.

The entrance hallway (אלם) is often mentioned in the plural (see **40 16**) because it is divided into two parts by the cubit-wide dividing barrier. Similarly, there is a cubit-wide railing for holding on while ascending the steps, and this railing separates the thresholds into two sections.

In general, the entryways for all three locations along the outer wall are of identical dimensions (**40 20-27**). Also, the entryways along the inner wall (**40 28-37**) are of the same dimensions as along the outer walls, except that there are eight steps instead of seven. The entryway along the north inner wall has additional variations, as shown in Figure 17.3.3.2. There are eight tables for slaughtering the sacrificial animals, four tables for holding necessary tools, and two rooms for washing the burnt-offerings (**40 38-42**). Moreover, shelves (שפתים), one handbreadth wide, are attached to the walls (בית) for laying down the slaughtered animals. The meat to be brought as a sacrifice is placed in a container next to the slaughtering tables (**40 43**).

17.3.4 The Inner Court and the Temple

The arrangement of the Temple within the inner court is shown in Figure 17.3.4.1, based on the description presented in Ez. **40 44-41 26**.

40 44-47 Outside the entryway of the inner wall, within the inner court, along the north wall, are singers' chambers (לשכות שרים). The doors to these chambers face south. One of these chambers touches the north corner of the east inner wall, and is designated for the priests who are in charge of the Temple. Opposite these chambers are other chambers on the south inner wall. The doors to these other chambers face north.

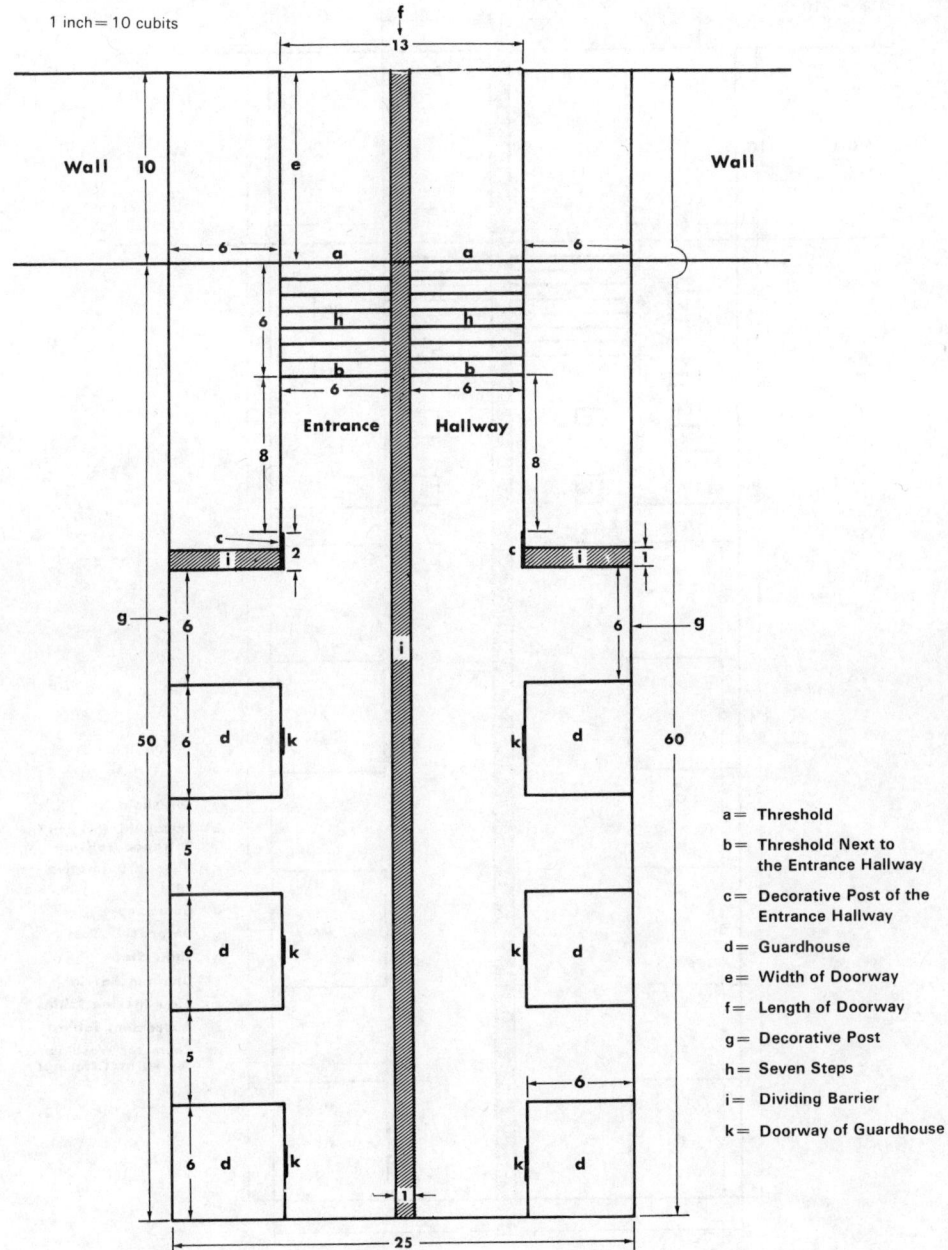

FIGURE 17.3.3.1—Dimensions of Entryway Along Outer Wall (Ez. **40** 6 - 16)

456 PROOF OF THE ACCURACY OF THE BIBLE

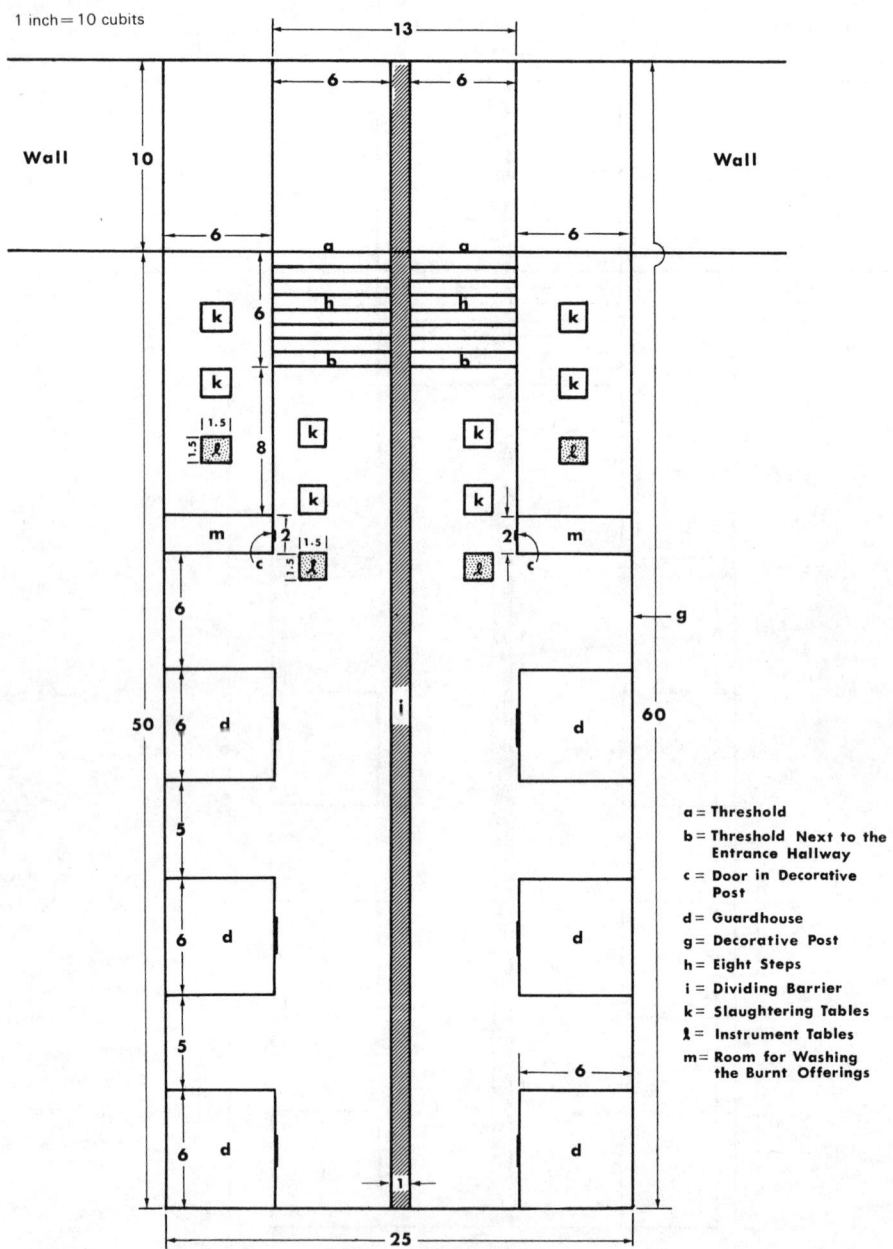

FIGURE 17.3.3.2—Dimensions of Entryway Along North Inner Wall (Ez. 40 6 - 16; 38 - 43)

MESSIANIC CHAPTERS OF EZEKIEL   457

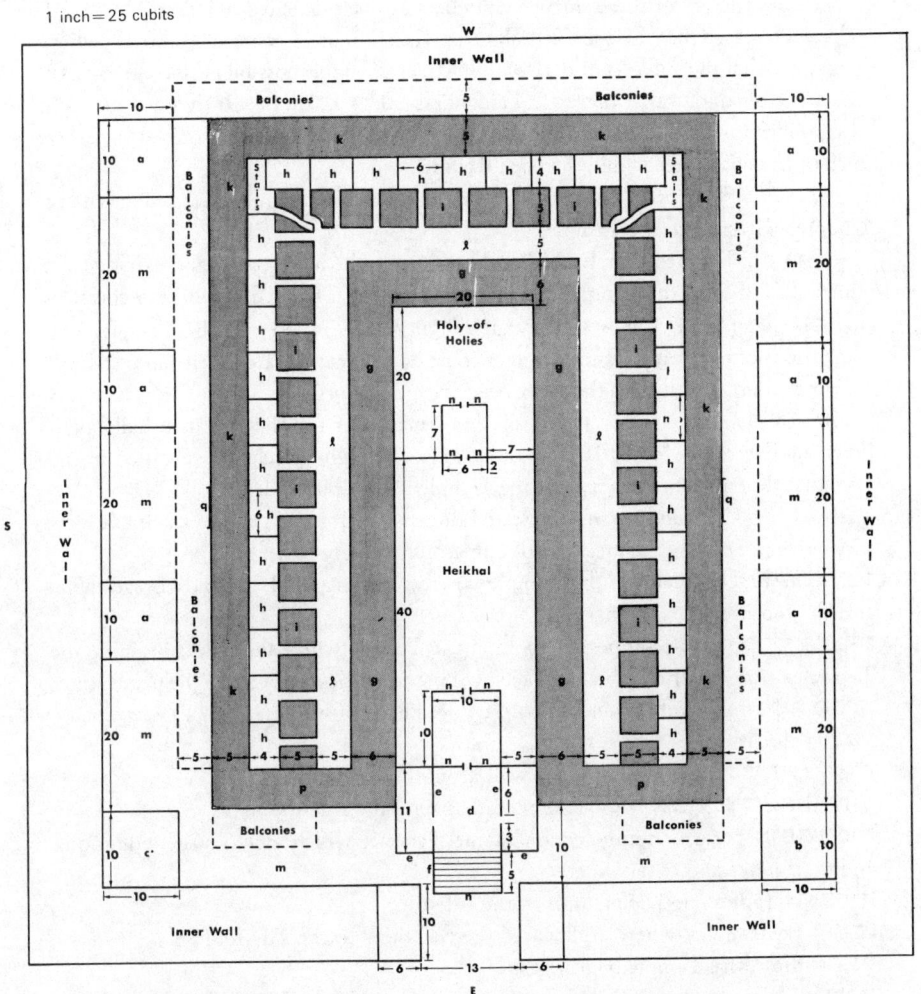

FIGURE 17.3.4.1—Design of the Inner Court and the Temple.

a Singers - Chambers
b Singers - Chambers for the Priests in Charge of the Temple
c Singers - Chambers for the Priests in Charge of the Altar
d Entrance Hallway
e Decorative Posts
f Pillar
g Wall Around the Heikhal and Holy-of-Holies
h Side-Room
i Inner Wall Around the Side-Rooms
k Outer Wall Around the Side-Rooms
ℓ Passageway
m Inner-Courtyard
n Thick Wooden Door
p Outer Wall of the Temple
q Entrance to the Passageway

The dimensions of these singers' chambers can be calculated based on (A) **41 10**, where it is stated that there are 20 cubits between the chambers, and (B) **40 47**, where it is stated that the inner court is 100 by 100. A reasonable possibility that agrees with the available data is that there are 4 chambers 10 by 10 on the north inner wall, and 4 chambers of the same size on the south inner wall. Between the four chambers on each of the sides there would then be 20 cubits.

40 47 The word בית, as used in this and subsequent sentences, until the end of Chapter 41 refers to the Temple.

In **43 5** it is stated that Ezekiel was brought to the inner court, and saw that the glory of God filled the Temple. Hence the Temple was located in the inner court. In this sentence (**40 47**), it is stated that the altar was in front of the Temple. The dimensions of the Temple and the inner court do not leave space for the altar to be in the inner court, and it must therefore be in the outer court.

40 48-49 The interpretation of the dimensions for the entrance hallway is given in Figure 17.3.4.1. It is apparent, even though not clearly specified in the text, that the entrance hallway into the Temple is 10 cubits wide.

41 1-26 To understand the stated dimensions for the Temple it is first necessary to define clearly the meaning of numerous Hebrew words.

היכל *(heikhal)* = room in the Temple where the lampstand, the showbread-table, and the incense-altar are placed;

קדש קדשים (holy-of-holies) = room in the Temple where the Ark containing the Tablets is stored—the original Tablets will probably be recovered in the near future;

קיר הבית = the wall around the *heikhal* and holy-of-holies;

צלע = side-room;

קיר אשר לבית לצלעות = inner wall around the side-rooms;

קיר אשר לצלע אל החוץ = outer wall around the side-rooms;

מוסב הבית = surrounding section of the Temple, which includes the side-rooms and their inner and outer walls;

אצילה = (adjoining unit) length of the side-rooms;

מנח = passageway where are located the entrances to the side-rooms;

בנין = the entire Temple building;

גזרה = the courtyard within the inner walls, on which nothing is built;

קיר הבנין = outer wall of the Temple, which is identical in many places with the outer wall around the side rooms;

אתיק = balcony, attached to the upper part of the Temple;

שחיף עץ = wooden fence for the balconies;

מדות = artwork made to scale;

עב (עבים) = thick wooden doors.

41 2 The dimensions of the *heikhal* are 20 by 40.

41 4 The dimensions of the holy-of-holies are 20 by 20. The total size of the *heikhal* plus the holy-of-holies is 20 by 60. These dimensions are the same as for the First Temple built by Solomon (I Kings 6 2). Moreover the entrance hallway of the

First Temple (I Kings **6** 3) was 20 by 10, which is essentially identical to the 20 by 11 specified here for the entrance hallway (Ez. **40** 49). Hence the height of this Temple, although not specified, is 30 cubits, as was the case for Solomon's Temple.

41 5-6   The side-rooms (צלעות) are 4 by 6. The width of 4 cubits is stated in **41** 5, and the 6 cubits is stated in **41** 8. There are 3 floors of 33 side-rooms, for a total of 99 side-rooms.

41 7   The translation of the sentence should be as follows: the width and turning (i.e., the going around the building) of the side-rooms is the same for the upper stories because the outer section of the Temple (מוסב־הבית) continues upward around the Temple; therefore the width of the Temple is the same at the upper levels; in this manner the bottom floor continues to the top floor via the middle floor.

41 8   There is a raised foundation 6 cubits high for the side-rooms. Also the adjoining unit (or length) of the side-rooms is 6 cubits.

Since the height of the building is 30 cubits, and 6 cubits are occupied by the foundation of the side-rooms, this leaves 24 cubits for the three stories of the side-rooms, or 8 cubits per story. From these stories there extends all around the Temple 3 levels of balconies, as indicated in **41** 16 and **42** 3.

41 9   The width of the outer wall around the side-rooms (קיר אשר לצלע אל החוץ) is 5 cubits; and the wall, next to the passageway, which supports the side-rooms of the Temple, is also 5 cubits.

41 11   The door to each side-room faces the passageway. There are two outside doors to the passageway, one from the north and one from the south. These outside entrances are in the middle of the sides of the Temple, and pass under the lower level of the side rooms.

41 12   Now are given the total dimensions for the Temple. The main part of the building is 70 cubits wide and 90 cubits long. The 70 cubits width consists of 20 for the *heikhal*, two walls around the *heikhal* of 6 cubits each, two passageways of 5 cubits each, two inner walls around the side-rooms of 5 cubits each, two side-rooms of 4 cubits each, and two outer walls around the side-rooms of 5 cubits each. Thus $20 + 12 + 10 + 10 + 8 + 10 = 70$. The 90 cubits length consists of 5 for the outer wall of the Temple, 40 for the *heikhal*, 20 for the holy-of-holies, 6 for the wall around the *heikhal* and the holy-of-holies, 5 for the passageway, 5 for the inner wall around the side-rooms, 4 for the side-rooms, and 5 for the outer wall around the side-rooms. Thus, $5 + 40 + 20 + 6 + 5 + 5 + 4 + 5 = 90$.

41 13   The center of the building is 100 cubits long. This includes the 90 cubits of the main part of the building (בנין) plus the 11 cubits of the entrance hallway, minus 5 of these 11 which are included in the outer wall of the Temple, plus 5 for the pillar and steps, minus 1 of these 5 which protrudes into the entryway of the inner wall. Thus, $90 + 11 - 5 + 5 - 1 = 100$. Moreover, the building and its walls, plus the courtyard is 100 cubits long. Thus, $90 + 10$ cubits for the courtyard equals 100.

41 14 The width of the building, including the courtyard, is 100 cubits. Thus, 70 for the building, plus 2 × 15 for the courtyard is 100.

41 15 The length of the building, on either side of the center, along where the courtyard is located, plus the balconies on the front and back of the building is 100 cubits. Since the building itself is 90 cubits long, it can be concluded that the balconies extend 5 cubits from the building at both ends. The sentence emphasizes that the measurements are not made in the center of the building, by stating that the *heikhal* and the entryways of the court are in the center.

41 16 Now is given information on the balconies. The thresholds (of the doors leading to the balconies), the glass windows, and the balconies surround all three stories containing the side-rooms. Opposite each threshold is a wooden fence all around the balcony to prevent anyone from falling off. The floors of the side-rooms are at the same level as the windows, and the windows are covered with drapes. It can be assumed that there is one door and one threshold from each side-room to each balcony, all around the building.

41 17 Above the top of the entrance (of the Temple) until the top of the building, the interior and the exterior, and all the walls all around, within and without, are covered with artwork made to scale (מדות).

41 18 The artwork consists of cherubim and palm trees. A palm tree is between two cherubs; and every cherub has two faces (one of a man and one of a young lion).

41 19 The face of a man is toward a palm tree on one side, and the face of a young lion toward a palm tree on the other side. In this manner is the artwork made for the entire building all around (above the height of the top of the entrance).

41 20 From the ground until the top of the entrance, cherubim and palm trees are made. This, however, is done only in front of the building and for the wall of the *heikhal;* but not all around the building as in the case for the artwork above the height of the top of the entrance.

41 21 The doorposts of the *heikhal* are square. Since they are 10 cubits wide (**41 2**), the doorposts must be 10 cubits high.

The artwork in the holy-of-holies is like the visions that Ezekiel saw and described in Chapters 1 and 10, with respect to the animals, wheels, firmament, and other details. The phrase המראה כמראה, is again used in **43 3** to refer to those revelations.

41 22 The incense-altar is 3 cubits high and 2 cubits long; its horns are part of the altar (rather than attached to the altar).

The dimensions are best understood in terms of those given in Ex. **30 1–10**. There, the dimensions of the altar for incense are given as 2 cubits high, and a square top one cubit by one cubit. Since the *heikhal* of the Temple is four times the area of the corresponding room in the Tabernacle, the altar for incense must have four times the area for burning four times as much incense. Thus, just as the dimensions of the *heikhal* have been increased from 10 by 20 to 20 by 40, so the top of the altar has been increased in size from 1 by 1 to 2 by 2.

41 23-24 Double doors are used at the entrance to the *heikhal* and holy-of-holies to minimize the chance of someone entering these rooms inadvertently.

41 25 The doors of the *heikhal* are embellished with cherubim and palm trees, as is the case for the walls. Also, a thick wooden door is placed at the front of the entrance hallway to the Temple.

41 26 Glass windows and palm trees are placed on both sides of the entrance hallway, and on the side-rooms, and on the thick wooden doors.

17.3.5 The Outer Court and Its Relation to the Inner Court and the Temple

Descriptions of the outer court, and its relation to the inner court, are found in **40** 17-19, 23, 27, 30, 31, 34, 37; **42** 1-14; **46** 19-24. An over-all view of the outer and inner courts is shown in Figure 17.3.5.1.

40 17, 19, 23,27; 46 21-24: Chambers Along the Outer Wall

The outer court contains 30 chambers (לשכות) along the outer wall (**40 17**). The size of these chambers, although not specified, can be arrived at by calculations. In performing the calculations consideration needs to be given to the presence of the cooking-yards (חצרות קטרות) in each of the four corners of the outer court (**46 21-24**), for cooking the peace-offerings. These cooking-yards are rectangular in shape (מהקצעות), 40 cubits by 30 cubits, with stoves (מבשלות) all around for cooking.

Let us assume that the 30 chambers are distributed fairly uniformly along the four outer walls of the outer court. A satisfactory distribution would be eight chambers along three walls, and six chambers on the fourth wall. There needs to be an even number of chambers on each wall for symmetry. The inside length of each outer wall is 320 cubits. This value is composed of the 100 cubits for the inner court, 2×10 cubits for the thicknesses of the inner walls, and 100 cubits on each side between the outer wall and the inner wall (**40 19, 23, 27**). Of these 320 cubits, 25 cubits (on three sides) are used for entryways, 2×5 cubits for the narrow passages within the outer court, and 2×30 (or 2×40) cubits for the cooking-yards. If, for example, we consider the north side, there is a distance of $320 - 25 - 10 - 60 = 225$ cubits for eight chambers. Consideration has also to be given to the spacing between (A) the chambers, (B) the chambers and the cooking-yards, and (C) the chambers and the narrow passages; for a total of ten spaces. If the length of the spaces is assumed approximately equal to the length of the chambers, then there is available less than 13 cubits per chamber. Based on the above considerations, a size for the chambers of 10 cubits by 10 cubits was selected as a practical size, and identical to that for the chambers in the inner court. Moreover, spaces of 10 cubits

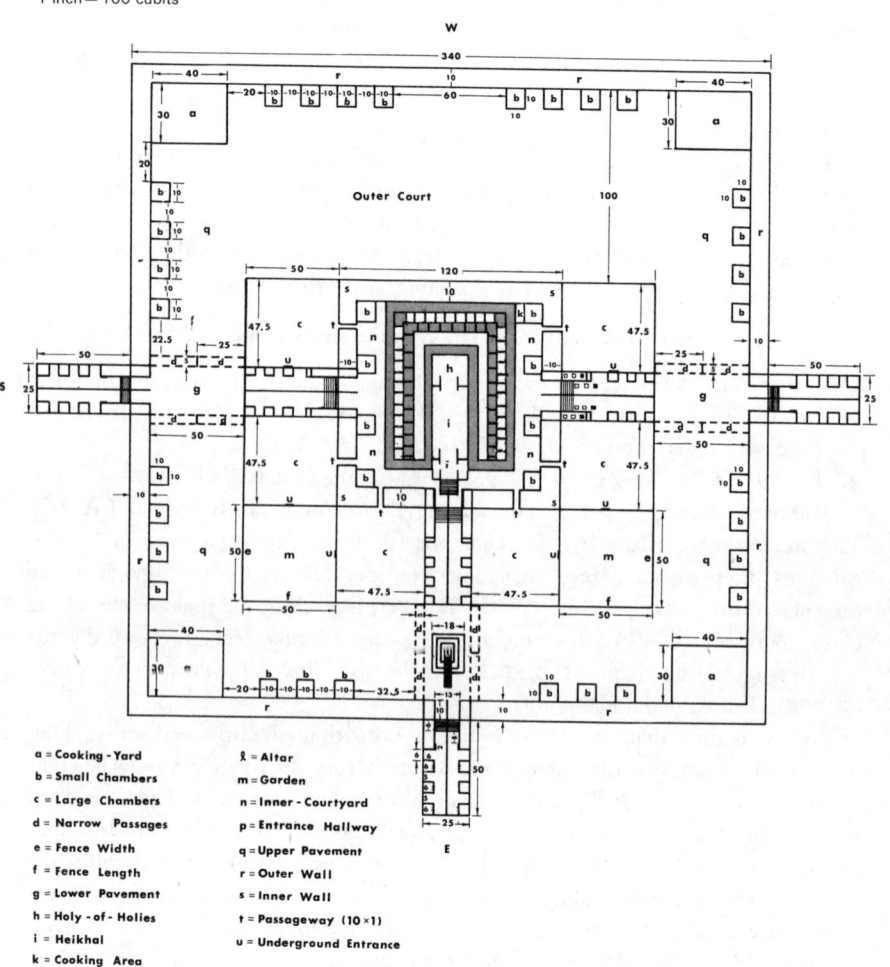

FIGURE 17.3.5.1—The Temple and the Outer and Inner Courts

between chambers, 20 cubits between cooking-yards and chambers, and 22.5 (or 32.5) cubits between chambers and the narrow passages, have been selected. The eastern wall was chosen as the one to have six rather than eight chambers, because it is desirable to have additional space between the altar and its nearest chamber to allow free access to the altar.

40 17–18: Pavement

A paved walk (רצפה) is provided in the outer court near the small chambers. A paved walk is also provided near the entryways, but this walk is at a slightly lower level, and is therefore called the lower pavement (רצפה התחתונה).

40 30, 31, 34, 37: Narrow Passages

Between the entryways to the outer and inner walls are narrow passages leading to the outer court. Their dimensions are 25 cubits by 5 cubits. Since the distance between the entryways is 50 cubits, there is room for two narrow passages on each side, for a total of four narrow passages at each of the three entryways. One narrow passage of each pair could be used for people walking in one direction, and the other narrow passage for people going in the opposite direction. Note that the word ואילִיו (meaning its decorative pillars) (**40 37**) should be replaced by ואילמיו (meaning its narrow passages), as is found in the comparable sentences, **40 31, 34**.

42 1–14: Large Chambers and Gardens

The positions of the large chambers are given in great detail (**42 1–3**). A large chamber is located towards the north, opposite the inner courtyard (גזרה); and opposite the main part of the Temple building (בנין) towards the north; facing the 100-cubit distance between the outer and inner walls towards the north; opposite the 50-cubit entryway; opposite the 20-cubit distance between chambers in the inner court; opposite the pavement in the outer court; with the balconies facing the three stories of balconies of the Temple. This identification of the location is not unique, and fits both of the large chambers on the north side (see Figure 17.3.5.1), and in fact both are meant. Therefore in the following sentence (**42 4**) the word chambers, in the plural, rather than chamber in the singular, is used.

In front of the large chambers are passageways ten cubits by one cubit leading to the inner court (**42 4**). The entrances to the passageways face the north. The reason the ten cubit dimension is called the width rather than the length is that the passageway passes through the 10-cubit width of the inner wall.

The upper floors of the large chambers are smaller than the bottom floor because the balconies impinge on the total area (**42 5, 6**). For example, if the balconies are 5 cubits wide, as is the case with the balconies of the Temple, then the dimensions of the bottom floor are 50 by 47.5 (as explained on **42 8**), of the second floor 40 by 37.5, of the third floor 30 by 27.5, and of the top floor 20 by 17.5. It has here been assumed that the balconies of the large chambers encircle the building. Note that the balconies of the chambers are not supported by pillars, in contrast to the balconies of the Temple which are mainly supported by pillars.

In **42 7, 10, 12**, reference is made to fences enclosing garden areas. From **42 7** we learn that the fence is outside the large chambers, in the outer court, and the 50-cubit length of the fence faces the front of the two northern large chambers. As will be explained on **42 9**, the front entrance for both chambers is from the east. Therefore the 50-cubit length of the fence runs from south to north. From **42 10** we determine that the width of the fenced area is along the east path, i.e., the fence width runs from east to west. The purpose of the fence is indicated in **42 12**, where is used the term הגדרת הגינה, which means the fence of the garden. Thus, the fenced-in areas enclosed gardens. Also from **42 10**, we learn that there was a fenced area towards the south. The two fenced gardens are shown in Figure 17.3.5.1. These garden areas are 50 by 50. The 50-cubit length is specified in **42 7**, while the 50-cubit width is based on the available space.

The dimensions of the large chambers are 50 cubits long by 47.5 cubits wide by 30 cubits high, based on the following reasoning. The length is explicitly stated to be 50 cubits (**42 8**). Also stated in the same sentence is that there are a total of 100 cubits opposite the *heikhal*. In other words, there are two large chambers, each 50 cubits long, one to the north and one to the south of the Temple front. The width of the chambers is 47.5 cubits to fit into the available space. Thus, the total length of the outside of the inner wall is 120 cubits (100 +2 × 10 for the wall thickness). Of these 120, 25 cubits are occupied by the entryway, leaving 95 cubits for two large chambers, or 47.5 per chamber. The height of the chambers is assumed to be the same as that of the Temple, i.e., 30 cubits, since the balconies of the chambers are at the same height as the balconies of the Temple (**42 3**).

Under the large chambers are entrances on the east side, from the outer court (**42 9**). These underground entrances are especially necessary for reaching the chambers situated in the northwest and southwest of the Temple, and are needed to bypass the fenced garden. These underground entrances pass under the gardens to reach the northeast and southeast large chambers, and under the entryways to reach the western chambers.

In **42 10** are delimited the positions of the two large chambers in front of the Temple. They are along the fence width, facing the inner courtyard, and facing the main part of the Temple building.

Passageways 10 cubits by one cubit lead from these eastern chambers into the inner court, just as is the case for the large chambers on the northern side (**42 11**). The sentence also states that the width of the east large chambers is the same as the length of the north large chambers. Thus, the east chambers are identical to the north chambers, except that the buildings are turned by an angle of 90 degrees.

Mention is now made of large chambers on the southern side (**42 12, 13**). Similar to the case for the north large chambers, an underground entrance is constructed to permit entering from in front of the fenced garden.

There are a total of six large chambers—three towards the north, and three towards the south. These six chambers are to be used by the priests for eating of the holy sacrifices (**42 13**).

When the priests enter these large chambers from the inner court through the 10-by-1 passageways, they should not go into the outer court until they remove their priestly garments and put on regular clothes (**42 14; 44 19**). Thus, these large chambers also serve as dressing rooms for the priests.

46 19-20: Cooking Area

In **46** 19-20 is described how Ezekiel was brought to the northwest 10 by 1 passageway leading to the large chambers. Nearby, along the western side of the inner court, was an area to be used by the priests for cooking the guilt-offerings and sin-offerings, and for baking the meal-offerings; so that these portions need not be removed to the outer court. A suitable size for the cooking area is 5 cubits by 10 cubits, since this is the available space.

17.3.6 Heights of Buildings

Extensive details are given in the Book of Ezekiel concerning the length and width of the buildings and structures in the Temple area, but very meager information is given as to the heights of these structures. However, sufficient data are supplied to allow reasonable assumptions to be made concerning the heights.

The height of the outermost wall is specified as 6 cubits (**40** 5). The heights of the outer wall, the inner wall, the small chambers, the guardhouses and the entryways are not mentioned, and are likewise assumed to be 6 cubits. The Temple is assumed to be 30 cubits high, based on the height for the Temple of Solomon, as explained on Ez. **40** 48-49. The side-rooms of the Temple begin 6 cubits above the ground, and are on three levels of 8 cubits each (see on **41** 8). The passageways (מנח) within the Temple are at the same levels as the side-rooms to enable easy access from the passageways to the side-rooms. Similarly, balconies protrude from the building at the same levels as the side rooms. The holy-of-holies and the *heikhal* are only 20 cubits high, as in the Temple of Solomon, thereby leaving room for a storage chamber above. The heights of the large chambers are the same as for the Temple, so that the balconies of the buildings are on the same level (**42** 3).

17.3.7 The Altar

The altar, to be built for the Third Temple, is described in **43** 13-17. A detailed side view of the altar is shown in Figure 17.3.7.1 based on the verbal description. Specific names are given in the text to the diffirent sections of the altar. The base is called Hake (חיק), the next platforms are called small Azarah and large Azarah respectively, and the top platform is called Ariel. Four horns are at the corners of the top platform. All of the platforms are square, the lowest being 18 cubits by 18 cubits, and the top 12 cubits by 12 cubits.

The dimensions of the altar are much larger that the 5-cubit by 5-cubit altar used for the Tabernacle (Ex. **27** 1). The larger dimensions are necessary to accommodate the greater amount of sacrifices that are brought once the people are settled on the land. Similar dimensions to those here specified were used for the altar in Solomon's Temple. There the altar was 20 cubits by 20 cubits, and 10 cubits high (II Chr. **4** 1). Here the altar is 18 cubits by 18 cubits, and 11 cubits high.

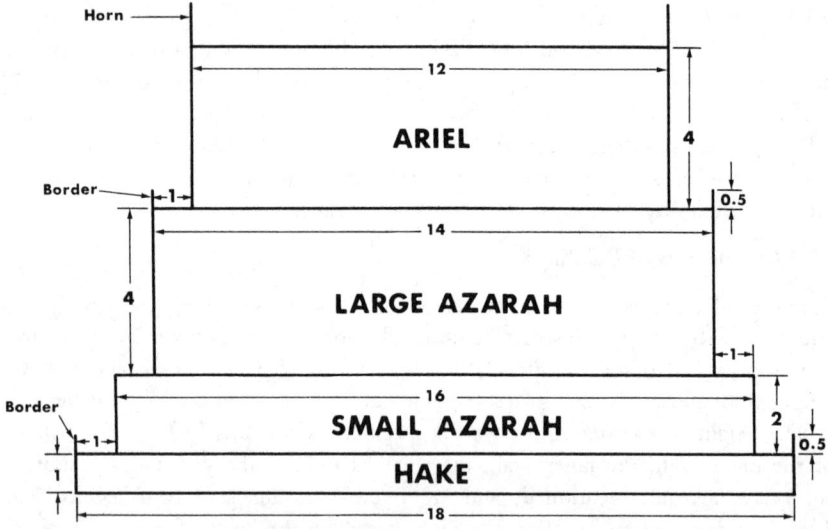

FIGURE 17.3.7.1—Side View of the Altar

Since the altar is 11 cubits high it is necessary for the priest to go up an incline on its eastern side to reach the top (43 17). An incline rather than steps has to be used according to the requirement of Ex. 20 26 that one should not use steps to go up on the altar.

The only available spot in front of the Temple (40 47) large enough to accommodate the 18-cubit by 18-cubit base is between the entryways of the outer and inner walls (see Figure 17.3.5.1). The available space is 25 cubits by 50 cubits, which is sufficiently large so no fire hazard results. This position of the altar explains the requirements that the eastern entryway to the outer wall always be closed (44 1,2), and that the eastern entryway to the inner wall be open only on Saturday and on the New Moon (46 1, 2). These entryways are kept closed to shield the altar from unauthorized visitors.

17.3.8 Water Source from Jerusalem (47 1–12)

Ezekiel is shown water flowing eastward from under the threshold of the front of the Temple, and passing to the south of the altar (47 1). Then he is taken past the outermost wall (שער החוץ) and shown the water trickling to the east (47 2). The water depth increases with increasing distance from the outermost wall, until after 4,000 cubits the water is over a person's head (47 3, 4). On both sides of the river very large boards are to be found (47 7), perhaps to direct the water flow. Ezekiel is then told (47 8) that the water goes towards the Dead

Sea (ימה), to subsitute fresh water for the salt water which has been removed (ימה המוצאים). By this means (47 9,10), fish will be able to thrive in the Dead Sea, and a great fishing industry will be created in the region. Moreover, parts of the sea will be set aside for salt recovery and mineral production (47 11). In addition, fruit trees will be grown and will flourish all along the banks of the river (47 12).

This prophecy of fresh water flowing from Jerusalem seems all the more astounding in that until early 1969 C.E. no water source had ever been discovered in the walled city. Moreover, the surrounding banks of the Dead Sea are devoid of vegetation, and deathlike in appearance.[3] However, in 1969, exceptionally sweet water was found in the old city of Jerusalem by drilling.[4] Undoubtedly, it is only a matter of time until the details of the prophecy will be fulfilled.

17.4 SUPPLEMENTARY REGULATIONS

The Book of Ezekiel specifies numerous regulations to be followed at the time of the restored Jewish nation. These regulations involve bringing of sacrifices, laws for the priests and for the ruler (נשיא), and division of the land among the people. Many of the stated regulations are not found in the Pentateuch and have caused considerable problems in interpretation. Here the regulations will be explained on the basis that they are required (A) for clarification of incorrectly interpreted Biblical laws, (B) for supplying needed methods to reinstitute many unpracticed Biblical procedures, and (C) to introduce supplementary practices.

17.4.1 Sacrifices (43 18–27; 45 18–46 15)

The sacrifices described in the Book of Ezekiel are different in many respects from those specified in the Bible, for what appear to be comparable circumstances. In reality most of the situations are different, and therefore no contradictions arise.

PURIFICATION OF THE ALTAR

In 43 18–27 are specified the sacrifices to be offered by the priests for purification of the altar of the Third Temple, to make it suitable for bringing all types of sacrifices. On the first day, a young bull is brought as a sin-offering, and its blood is spread on the altar. On the second day through the seventh day, a he-goat is brought as a sin-offering according to the same procedure, and a young bull and a ram are brought as burnt-offerings. On the eighth day the altar is ready for the burning of all types of sacrifices.

This procedure is in sharp contrast to that described in Ex. 29 1–37 and Lev. 8 1–36 for initiation of the priests and purification of the altar (see Table 28.1.5). There, for each of seven days, a young bull is brought as a sin-offering, a ram as a burnt-offering, a second ram as an installation-offering, and various types of unleavened cakes as installation meal-offerings. Then on the eighth day (Lev. 9 1–24) the priests bring a bull-calf as a sin-offering and a ram as a burnt-offering; and the people bring a he-goat as a sin-offering, a calf and a lamb as burnt-offerings, a bull and ram as peace-offerings, and a meal-offering.

The apparent discrepancies may be explained as follows. Prior to the War of Gog an altar will be built according to the Biblical dimensions (Ex. 27 1–8). The priests who can establish their descent from Zadok and who observed the Jewish regulations will then be selected to bring sacrifices (Ez. 44 15). They will be initiated as prescribed in Ex. 29 1–37 and Lev. 8 1–9 24. Sacrifices will then be brought on a regular basis until completion of the altar described in Ez. 43 13–17. The new altar will be purified according to the procedure in 43 18–27. It will not then be necessary to initiate the priests since they will have already been consecrated many years previously.

UNIQUE SACRIFICES

There are a few unique sacrifices which are to be brought by the priests, but which are not mentioned in the Pentateuch. On the first and seventh days of the first month a young bull is brought as a sin-offering to purify the Temple area (45 18, 19). The blood of the animals is placed on the doorposts of the Temple and of the inner wall, and on the altar, to remove any disease microorganisms that may happen to lodge in the Temple area. These sacrifices are not prescribed in the Pentateuch because if all Biblical procedures are correctly followed then no disease microorganisms would grow in the area. However, because people do make mistakes, and simple-minded individuals exist who do not know any better (45 20), impure persons will enter and contaminate the Temple area (see Section 28.1). Therefore, particularly before the large influx of visitors at the time of the Passover sacrifice, purification procedures are carried out by placing the blood of a young bull on the specified doorposts. In this way the spread of disease is avoided.

Another unique sacrifice is the extra-large meal-offering to be brought with the daily morning burnt-offering of a he-lamb (Ez. 46 13–15). The usual meal-offering prescribed in the Pentateuch (Ex. 29 40) is one-tenth of an ephah of fine flour and one-fourth of a hin of oil. Here (Ez. 46 14) is stated that an additional meal-offering consisting of one-sixth of an ephah of fine flour and one-third of a hin of oil is to be brought. The reason for this additional meal-offering is not clear, but may be needed to help in controlling the weather (see Section 28.1), since environmental conditions may be somewhat modified at the time of the Third Temple.

SACRIFICES BROUGHT BY THE LEADER

An additional group of sacrifices are prescribed in the Book of Ezekiel which are to be brought by the leader (נשיא) of the Jewish state. The word נשיא is specifically used in **34** 24 and **37** 25 to refer to the ruler of the newly established state. According to **45** 17 the leader is responsible for specific sacrifices to atone for the sins of the people of Israel. These special sacrifices (**45** 21-25; **46** 4-7) are listed in Table 17.4.1.1, and are different from and supplementary to those prescribed in the Pentateuch for the same occasions (compare with Table 28.1.4). The fact that the leader of the nation is directly involved in bringing animals for sacrifices at special occasions ensures that he will be interested in guaranteeing that sacrifices are brought on a regular basis. These additional sacrifices may have the benefit of aiding in weather control. Moreover, the sin-offerings have psychological benefits, in that they atone for inadvertent transgressions. Also, the meal-offerings supply food for the priests, which would not be the case if brought by priests; for then the entire meal-offering would be burned on the altar (see Section 28.1).

17.4.2 Laws for the Leader of the Nation

Included in the class of "laws for the leader" are regulations concerning the nation as well as the ruler himself.

45 9-10 The rulers of the State of Irael are told to maintain justice and righteousness. There should be accurate scales, an accurate dry measure (ephah), and an accurate liquid measure (bath). These regulations are, in effect, a repetition of Lev. **19** 35, 36; but they are mentioned here to introduce the requirement of establishing new and accurate units of weight and measurement.

45 11 The unit of dry measure, the ephah, shall be equal in volume to the unit of liquid measure, the bath. Both the ephah and the bath are to be equal to one-tenth homer.

45 12 Also, a precise monetary system needs to be instituted. The shekel shall equal 20 gerahs; and currency of 5, 10, 20, and 25 shekels shall be established. Note that in 1969 the Knesset passed a law providing that the unit of Israeli currency would be the shekel, but no effective date was set for the change.[5]

45 13-17 Tax (תרומה) is to be given by the legislators (עם הארץ), to supply the items needed by the leader of the nation (נשיא) for the regular and special holiday sacrifices (**45** 16, 17). Only items suitable for sacrifices, such as wheat, barley, oil, and sheep, are involved. One part in 60 of the wheat and barley, one part in 100 of oil, and one part in 200 from the sheep shall be given as tax. Note that the term עם הארץ (people of the land) does not refer to the population in general, but to the leaders of the nation, such as the legislators, who represent the people.[6]

44 1-3 The external part of the eastern entryway through the outer wall is always kept closed, and no one is to enter through it. The leader of the nation, however, may come into the outer court from the north or south entryway, and from there go into the eastern entryway and dine there when partaking of the sacrificial meal. After completion of his meal the leader must leave

Table 17.4.1.1
Sacrifices Brought by the Leader

Time of Year	Animals for Burnt-Offering*			Animals for Sin-Offering		Reference in Ezekiel
	young bulls	rams	he-lambs	bulls	he-goats	
Saturday		1	6			46 4–5
New Moon	1	1	6			46 6–7
14th day of 1st month				1		45 21–22
15th to 21st of 1st month	7	7			1	45 23–24
15th to 21st of 7th month	7	7			1	45 25

* Accompanying the burnt-offerings was a meal-offering consisting of one ephah of fine flour for a bull or a ram, and a hin of oil for each ephah. In the case of a he-lamb the amount of fine flour can vary, and is left to the decision of the leader (**45** 24; **46** 5,7).

the eastern entryway by going back into the outer court. The eastern entryway of the outer wall is kept closed to prevent an excessive number of persons from passing near the altar and distracting the priests.

46 1-3 The eastern entryway through the inner wall is to be kept closed most, but not all, of the time. In general, during the six days of the week the entryway is kept closed. However, on Saturdays and on the day of the New Moon the entryway is kept open all day. On those days the leader of the nation comes from the outer court, past the altar, up to the doorposts of the eastern entryway. The priests then prepare his burnt-offerings and peace-offerings, while he bows down towards the Temple. Similarly, the legislators (עם הארץ) shall bow down at the eastern entryway to the inner wall on Saturdays and on New Moons.

46 8-10, 12 After bowing down, the leader of the nation leaves by the same route that he came. However, on festivals, the leader and the legislators come at the same time to bow down before the Temple, and leave the outer court by the opposite entryway through which they came. Thus, if they come from the south entryway they leave by the north entryway, and vice versa. Moreover, any weekday that the leader of the nation brings a voluntary burnt-offering or peace-offering, the eastern entryway through the inner wall is opened for him, as on Saturday. However, the eastern entryway is closed immediately after he leaves, and not as on Saturdays when the entryway is left open all day.

These regulations allow the leader of the nation and the legislators to have a special closeness to the Temple, thereby increasing their fear and respect for God. On Saturdays and New Moons there is a limited number of visitors in the Temple area. There is then sufficient room along the path from either the north or south entryway for all the visitors to watch the leaders come to pay their respects to the Temple. Therefore on Saturday and the New Moon the leaders return along the same path that they came. However, on festivals the Temple area is thronged with visitors. It is then necessary for the leaders to leave by the opposite route so that they can be observed by all persons present in the Temple courts.

The eastern entryway through the inner wall is kept closed during weekdays, to reduce the number of possible paths to the Temple, and the number of required guards, since there are few visitors to the Temple area on weekdays. On Saturdays and New Moons the eastern entryway is kept open as a special attraction to visitors. However, during festivals, because of the excessively large number of visitors, the eastern entryway is kept closed so as to enable the crowd to proceed in an orderly fashion.

46 16-18 The leader of the nation is in control of two types of estates. The first type is his inheritable land. The regulations regarding the inheritable land of the ruler of the nation are the same as for that of any other person's. Thus, if the leader desires he can give all or part of his inherited land as a permanent gift to his sons during his lifetime. In doing so, he must follow the regulations stated in Deut. 21 15-17, where each son receives an equal portion, except for the oldest who receives a double share. It is to be understood that the leader, or whoever transmits the inheritable land to his sons during his lifetime, does not expect to father any more children, for otherwise an equitable distribution could not be made. Ezekiel here states (**46** 16) that the leader can give from the inheritable land to his sons since the land is destined for them according to the inheritance laws. However, if the land be given as a gift to one of his servants, then the land returns to the ruler on the Jubilee year (**46** 17), in agreement with the laws in Lev. 25 25-28 concerning selling of one's estate. Note that the statements in Ezekiel extend the Biblical laws concerning inheritance and selling of land to the giving of the land as a gift.

The second type of estate under the control of the leader is the property that belongs to the people but is supervised by the ruler because of his office (**45** 7-8; **48** 21). This public property can not be taken away from the people, or passed on to the leader's sons as inheritable land (**46** 18).

17.4.3 Laws for the Priests (44 6-31)

Ezekiel presents the regulations needed to reestablish the services of the priests at the time of the newly formed State of Israel, and emphasizes laws which might be or have been misinterpreted.

44   6-9   In the past uncircumcized non-Jews have served in the Temple area, and profaned the covenant with God. Make certain that no uncircumcized persons come near the Temple.

44   10-14   The ones to serve in the Temple area are only the Levites and priests. Levites, and priests who have been nonobservant of priestly laws during the long period of exile, shall serve as assistants, guards, and slaughterers of the sacrifices; but they shall not come near the most holy objects nor perform priestly functions.

44   15-16 (40 46; 43 19; 48 11)   But the priests, the descendants of Zadok, who have observed the priestly laws during the long period of exile shall offer sacrifices and enter the Temple. Zadok was the high priest at the time of King David (II Sam. 8 17) and King Solomon (I Kings 2 35). Practically all present-day observant Jews who claim to be of priestly descent are in fact descendants of Zadok.

44   17-18   The priests when entering the inner court shall wear priestly garments made only of linen. No woolen clothing shall be worn by the priests when officiating. The hats, pants, and belts shall all be of linen.

This law requiring the wearing of linen is here emphasized to prevent misinterpretation of the phrase "blue, purple, and scarlet" (see e.g., Ex. 25 4; 28 6) as meaning wool-thread dyed these colors (see Section 28.4). Such an interpretation, which is the usual one, results in the high priest wearing prohibited clothing made of *shatnez* (i.e., a mixture of wool and linen threads). Also, the belt of the ordinary priest would then be made of *shatnez*. Actually the Biblical phrase "blue, puple, and scarlet" refers to linen threads dyed these colors, and accordingly the priestly garments are made only of linen.

44 19 Before the priests leave the inner court to mingle with the people in the outer court, they shall remove their linen garments so that no disease microorganisms shall be spread to their priestly clothes. However, if the priests go into the outer court to minister at the altar they retain their priestly garments.

44 20 The priests shall not shave their heads, nor let their hair grow excessively. They shall trim their hair.

In modern times it has become quite common for people to shave their faces. It is therefore emphasized that the priests should not shave their heads. However, the priests have to trim their hair so they not appear unusual. These laws are an elaboration on the regulations in Lev. 21 5, 10, where the priests are commanded not to shave their beards, and the high priest is required not to let his hair grow excessively.

44 21 No priest should drink wine before entering the inner court. This law is a clarification of the restriction in Lev. 10 8 where the priests are prohibited from drinking wine and intoxicating beverages prior to going near the Tabernacle. Here we learn that the inner court, where the Third Temple is located, is comparable in holiness to the Tabernacle. It would otherwise be unclear as to where in the Temple area the priests are prohibited from drinking wine.

44 22 Priests shall marry only virgins of Jewish descent or widows of priests. They shall not marry widows of non-priests or divorced women.

These regulations are a slight extension of those found in Lev. 21 7, 13–14. There, ordinary priests are prohibited from marrying divorcees; and high priests are prohibited from marrying widows and divorcees. The prohibitions are to prevent the possible spread of venereal disease to the priests (see Section 25.5.3). As additional safeguards the ordinary priest is here restricted from marrying non-Jewish virgins and widows of non-priests. Non-Jewish virgins may have contracted venereal disease from their mothers before or during the birth process. Widows of non-priests may have contracted venereal disease from their husbands, who could have become infected by having extra-marital relations. Venereal disease is much less likely to be present in widows of priests, since a priest because of his high office will be restrained in his actions.

44 23–24 The priests shall act as teachers, judges, and guardians of the laws and holidays.

These regulations emphasize that the priests are to act as judges and leaders of the people. Laws to this effect are scattered in many places in the Pentateuch (Lev. 10 10–11; 13; Deut 17 9–12; 19 17; 21 5), but might easily be overlooked. Therefore, a very explicit statement of the authority of the priests is given here.

44 25-27 A priest shall not come near a dead person except for his father, mother, children, brother, and unmarried sister. After contact with a dead body the priest must wait seven days to become purified. When the priest returns to officiate at the inner court, he shall bring a sin-offering.

The limitations here stated concerning contact with a dead body are the same as those specified in Lev. **21** 1-3. Also the requirement of seven days for purification is the same as prescribed in Num. **19** 14, 16, 19. These laws are stated mainly to introduce the requirement that the priest bring a sin-offering after the seven day purification period. The sin-offering adds an extra means of removing disease microorganisms from the priest, and thereby prevents him from becoming a disease carrier. (See Sections 25.5.3 and 28.1.)

44 28 The priests are not to be given any possession upon distribution of the nation's land. This statement in Ezekiel is somewhat clearer that that in Num. **18** 20. There the term חלק is used, meaning a "portion." Here the word אחזה is used, meaning a "possession" or property.

44 29-30 In place of a land possession, the priests are given to eat from the meal-offerings, sin-offerings, and guilt-offerings. Moreover they are to receive all *harem*, the choicest first-fruits, all holy gifts, and the first of the dough.

Here are concisely summarized those portions which are designated for the priests (see Section 27.2.2). These portions include meat from the sacrifices, all sanctified items including *harem* (see Section 27.5), the first-fruits, the first-born animals, and the first of the dough. These regulations are stated here as a background for the next sentence.

44 31 The priests shall not eat bird or beast if it died by itself or was torn by a wild animal.

This law is to emphasize that, even though the priests receive many animals and birds from the people, they should take special care to avoid eating what died of itself or is torn by wild animals. The present regulation clearly explains that it applies to both bird and beast. In contrast, the comparable statement in Lev. **22** 8 is expressed more generally, and does not specify the type of creature to which it applies.

17.4.4 Distribution of the Land (45 1-8; 47 13-48 35)

The territory of Israel, within the boundaries specified in **47** 13-20, is to be distributed among the Jewish people. The specific boundaries, especially in the north, are defined in terms of several locations which are uncertain. These boundaries will be clarified by the time the land of Israel is to be divided among its inhabitants. Approximately the same territory (Num. **34** 1-13) was distributed among $9\frac{1}{2}$ tribes at the time of Joshua.

As a rough approximation the specified boundaries extend from about 30° 30′ to 35° north latitude (a distance of about 300 miles from south to north), and from the Mediterranean to the Jordan River (a distance of very roughly 40 to 60 miles, from east to west).

It should be noted that the State of Israel, after the War of Gog, will acquire much more territory than that actually to be distributed. According to Gen. 15 18; Ex. 23 31; Deut. 1 7; 11 24; Josh. 1 4 the territory controlled by the State of Israel will extend from the Sinai peninsula to the Euphrates River, and from the Red Sea to the Mediterranean. In these Biblical passages the "desert" refers to the Sinai peninsula or perhaps the desert in Saudi Arabia, the "River of Egypt" refers to the Gulf of Suez including the channel which in ancient times crossed the Isthmus of Suez, the "river" refers to the Euphrates, and the "Reed Sea" (ים סוף) refers to the Red Sea. Moreover, the Sea of the Philistines, the Last Sea, and the Great Sea all refer to the Mediterranean. These theoretical boundaries include an area many times larger than the land to be distributed among the people.

Many of the Biblical laws are dependent on the land being divided among 12 tribes, exclusive of the tribe of Levi. However, during the extended period of exile of the Jewish people, only the Levites and priests still truly know from which tribes they originate. Moreover, most other Jews are probably descendants of the tribe of Judah or possibly the tribe of Benjamin, since the other ten tribes were exiled at a much earlier stage in history (II Kings 17 6) and probably intermingled with the Assyrians, and other nations. Therefore, it is impossible to distribute the land according to the tribes from which the Jews have descended. Instead, an arbitrary division of the land into twelve tribes will be made based on where the people settle in the land. Converts to Judaism will also be among those included in the land distribution (47 22, 23). The actual apportionment will be as shown schematically in Figure 17.4.4.1. The diagram is sufficiently clear to enable the understanding of most of the relevant text in Ezekiel (45 1-8; 48 1-35), with the need for only a few additional explanatory comments.

In the Figure the specified dimensions are in units of 6 cubits (about 10.5 feet) (40 5) although not explicitly stated in the text. Accordingly, a distance of 25,000 equals 50 miles, a distance of 10,000 equals 20 miles, and a distance of 5,000 equals 10 miles. It is clear that the unit is 6 cubits since the total Temple area is 500 by 500 in units of 6 cubits (42 16-20). The same value of 500 by 500 is given (45 2) along with the other related dimensions (45 1-6; 48 8-21), such as 25,000, 10,000, 5,000 and 250. The only exception is the open land (מגרש) which is explicitly stated to be 50 cubits wide (45 2), in units of cubits. It should be noted that in the region of Jerusalem the distance from the Mediterranean to the Dead Sea is about 52 miles, which is only slightly greater that the 50-mile distance (25,000 6-cubits) specified in the text for the length of the region reserved for the priests and Levites. Moreover, since the total distance from north to south is about 300 miles, of which 50 miles are set

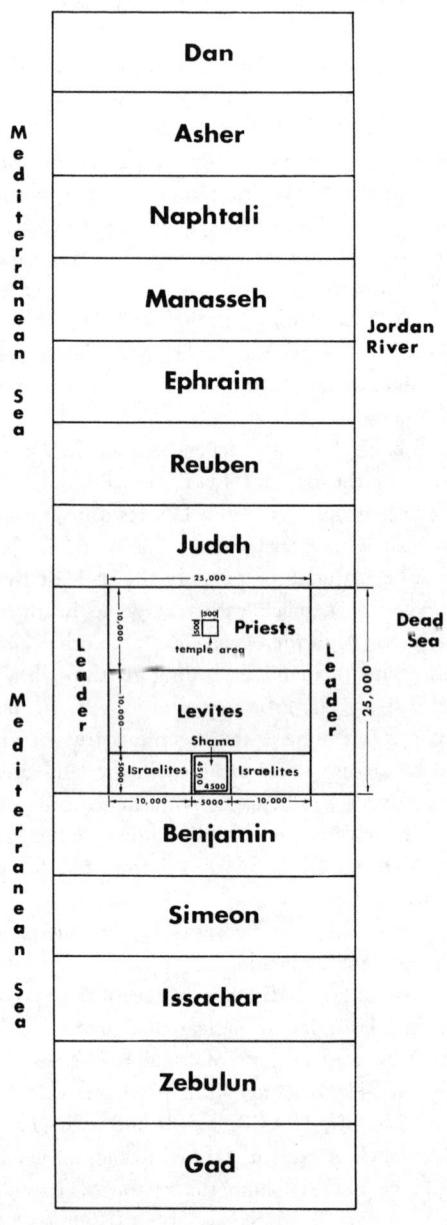

FIGURE 17.4.4.1—Schematic Diagram of Apportionment of Land of Israel Among the Tribes.

aside for others than the tribes, the average width of the land given to a tribe would be about 20 miles (i.e., 10,000 6-cubits). This distance of 10,000 is the same as the width reserved for the priests and for the Levites. In general, the tribes toward the north will receive strips of land narrower than 20 miles, since the length of the strips is longer toward the south. By this means the area provided for each of the twelve tribes will be the same.

No specifications are given for the size and location of the 20 chambers for the Levites, mentioned in **45** 5, and therefore any practical size and location would be suitable.

The special city, which is to be 4,500 by 4,500 (6-cubits), (**48** 16, 30–35) is to be named *Shama* meaning "there," after the Day of the Lord, i.e., after the War of Gog. Naturally, the name of Jerusalem will still be retained for the location now known as Jerusalem. The name *Shama* only applies to a new city that will be formed. This new city will have three gates on each of its four sides for a total of 12 gates. Each gate will be named after one of the 12 tribes (**48** 30–34).

17.5 SUMMARY OF MESSIANIC PROPHECIES IN BOOK OF EZEKIEL

The following outline of the Messianic era is evolved based on the prophecies in the Book of Ezekiel, and a few dates from the Book of Daniel.

Sometime between April 3, 1973 and March 24, 1974 a person named Gog will lead a mighty army against the State of Israel. The army will contain well-armed soldiers from such contries as Egypt, Syria, Jordan, Iran, Ethiopia, Sudan, Turkey, Russia and its satellites, China and its satellites, and other Arab countries. Practically all the nations of Asia, and many of the countries of Europe and North Africa will be among the attacking nations. Miraculously the State of Israel will win a very decisive victory. Probably atomic weapons will be used by Israel in annihilating the army of Gog. It will then take seven years to dispose of the enemy's weapons and seven months to bury the enormous number of dead (**38–39**).

A leader named David will rule over the State of Israel at the time of the War of Gog. The Jewish people will then recognize and worship God. After the War of Gog all Jews, from wherever they reside, will be gathered back to Israel. The land will be rebuilt and the soil will be fruitful. It will be a spectacular rebuilding of the land and peace will prevail (**34** 11–31; **36** 16–**37** 28). By 1996 the Temple will be rebuilt according to the detailed design provided in the Book of Ezekiel (**40** 1–**43** 17; **46** 19–**47** 12).

Many years prior to the rebuilding of the Temple (about 1973) sacrifices will be reinstituted. Priests and Levites will be selected for officiating (**44** 6–31). Subsequently, when the Temple altar is built, special sacrifices will be brought for purifying the new altar (**43** 18–27).

The territory of Israel between the Mediterranean Sea and the Jordan River will be divided into 12 tribal areas in addition to an area reserved for the Temple and other governmental departments. The area for the 12 tribes will be distributed equally among the population (**45** 1–8; **47** 13–**48** 35).

A major water irrigation project will be constructed to purify the salty waters of the Dead Sea. The source of fresh water will be a spring under the Temple area. A great fishing industry will be developed in the Dead Sea, and fruit trees will be grown and flourish along the banks of the river leading from the Temple area to the Dead Sea (**47** 1–12).

Special sacrifices, in addition to those specified in the Pentateuch, will be brought on regular occasions by the leader of the nation (**45** 21–**46** 7). New units of measurement and a new monetary system will be introduced, using Biblical units, such as the ephah, bath, homer, shekel, and gerah (**45** 9–12). The priests will be of special importance not only with respect to Temple rites, but also as teachers, judges, and guardians of the laws (**44** 6–31).

Chapter Eighteen

COMMENTARY ON MESSIANIC PORTIONS OF THE TWELVE PROPHETS

Eight of the books of the Twelve Prophets, namely Joel, Malachi, Obadiah, Micah, Amos, Hosea, Zephaniah, and Zechariah, contain prophecies relevant to the War of Gog and the Messianic era. Explanations of the Messianic passages from these books will be presented in the ensuing sections in the above-listed order. This order is based on the relevancy and clarity of the prophetic passages rather than on the arrangement of the books within the Twelve Prophets. No revelations concerning the Messianic era are found in the Books of Jonah, Nahum, Habakkuk, and Haggai—and these books are therefore not considered in this chapter.

18.1 BOOK OF JOEL

Several factors indicate that the entire Book of Joel is concerned with the Messianic era. First, no date is given as to when the prophecy was received, establishing that the date of the revelation is unrelated to understanding the contents (see Section 12.4). Second, in 1 3 is stated that the prophecy should be passed on from generation to generation, indicating that it refers to a time much after that of Joel. Third, the term "Day of the Lord," which often designates the War of Gog (see e.g., Mal. 3 23; Zech. 14 1) is used frequently in the book (1 15; 2 1, 11; 4 14).

The army of Gog (see Ez. 38–39), which will invade the re-established State of Israel is compared to a plague of locusts (1 4). The allegory of locusts refers to an actual military attack by an army, as clearly indicated by the following points: (A) In 1 6 and 2 2 it is stated that a nation comes against the land of Israel. (B) In 1 19 and 2 3 it is stated that that fire destroys the pastures and trees. (C) In 2 4–7 it is stated that the invading army is prepared for war and supplied with horses (i.e., vehicles), horsemen (i.e., airplanes) and chariots (i.e., tanks). (D) Chapter 4 of Joel, which explains the allusions of the previous three chapters, explicitly states (4 2, 3) that all the nations will attack Israel.

At first thought, the mention in the Book of Joel of the House of the Lord, and priests offering sacrifices (1 9, 13, 14, 16; 2 14, 17; 4 18), would indicate that the events described could not refer to the War of Gog, since construction of the Temple is to occur after the War of Gog (see Ez. 38–42). However, the term House of the Lord does not necessarily mean the Temple, but could also denote the site on which the Temple is to be built. Thus, David, who lived before construction of the First Temple, calls the site of the threshing-floor of Ornan the House of the Lord (I Chr. 22 1). (Several other examples of such usage of the term House of the Lord are mentioned in Section 13.1 under Authorship.) Here, too, the term House of the Lord refers to the site of the Temple, i.e., the Temple Mount. The mention of priests offering sacrifices establishes that sacrifices will be reinstituted prior to the War of Gog. This is in agreement with what was concluded from Ez. 43 18–27 (Section 17.4.1).

Based on the above discussion, the following understanding of the first three chapters of Joel can be attained. An enemy army, so numerous that it cannot be counted, is to come against the land of Israel (1 6). It is as if a plague of locusts will come and devour all the produce of the land (1 4, 5, 7, 10–12, 16–18). As a result, all sacrifices at the site of the Temple will be stopped, and the officiating priests will mourn (1 9, 13, 16). A fast day is to be declared, when the entire population will gather on the Temple Mount to pray to God (1 14, 19, 20; 2 12–17). The Day of the Lord is approaching when God will take revenge on the enemies of the Jewish people (1 15; 2 1, 11). It is a day of darkness— the largest military force ever assembled will come against Israel (2 2, 10; 3 3, 4). In front and in back of the enemy is fire which destroys the land (1 19; 2 3, 5). The enemy is armed with land vehicles, airplanes, and tanks (2 4, 5), and is a mighty force of destruction (2 6–9). God will then have pity on His people (2 18), and will answer their prayers (2 19). He will say to His people that He will save them from the invading army originating in the north, and will drive the enemy to the desert, to the Dead Sea, and to the Mediterranean (2 20). All those who assembled on the Temple Mount and in Jerusalem, and all who called upon God for help will be saved (3 5). The land will once again become productive (2 21–26), and the Israelite people will know that God is in their midst. The Jewish people will never afterwards be ashamed (2 27). Subsequently the spirit of prophecy will descend on the young and the old (3 1, 2).

In the fourth chapter of Joel is given a more detailed account of the events described in the previous three chapters. At the time of re-establishment of the settlement of Judah and Jerusalem, all the nations will gather against Israel (4 1, 2). Among the attacking nations will be the cities of Tyre and Sidon (within Lebanon), and the regions of Philistia (the Gaza Strip) (4 4). The enemy will go down into the Valley of Jehoshaphat (4 2, 12), which is the part of the Valley of Kidron east of Jerusalem between the Temple Mount and the Mount of Olives. The attacking nations will cast lots, and sell the Jewish people in expectation of an easy victory (4 3, 6). The people in Judah and Jerusalem will have been sold to the descendants of Greece even before the fight (4 6)! But miraculously, it will be the attacking enemy who will be defeated, and they will be the ones to be sold to distant nations (4 8). God will judge and destroy the enemy in the Valley of Jehoshaphat on the Day of the Lord. The sun, moon, and stars will become dark (4 15), and the heavens and earth will tremble (4 16), as God roars from Zion and Jerusalem to protect His people. The Israelites will then know that God resides on Mount Zion (4 17). Jerusalem will become holy, and invading armies will no longer go there (4 17). Egypt and Edom (Jordan) will be made desolate (4 19); while Judah and Jerusalem will last forever (4 20). God will have avenged the unavenged blood of the Israelites. Moreover, the land of Israel shall be prosperous, and water will flow throughout the country. A fountain will spring from the site of the Temple (compare Ez. 47 1-12; Zech. 14 8) and water the Wadi of Shittim (4 18).

18.2 MALACHI (CHAPTER 3)

The third chapter of the Book of Malachi describes events preceding the War of Gog. Eliyah (Elijah), the messenger of God, will come shortly before the great and terrifying Day of the Lord, and will reinstitute sacrifices, purify the priests and Levites, initiate the collection of tithes, and cause the hearts of the Jewish people to believe in God.

3 1 The messenger of God, Eliyah, will clear the way for the coming of God to perform miracles. Unexpectedly, Eliyah will arrive, and go to a building reserved for his use (היכלו). He will be the leader for whom the Jewish people are awaiting, and will be the one to re-establish the covenant between God and Israel.

In 3 23 is stated that Eliyah the prophet will come before the Day of the Lord, i.e., before the War of Gog. Furthermore, in II Kings 2 11, is described how Eliyahu (Elijah), the prophet, at the time of the First Temple, died by being carried to the heavens in a fiery chariot. Based on the essential identity of the names of the two prophets, and the fact that the death of Eliyahu of the Book of Kings is not clearly stated, there have arisen many fabulous tales in which the Eliyah at the time of the War of Gog is identified with the earlier Eliyahu. In actuality, the Eliyahu of the Book of Kings died when taken to the heavens. The Eliyah of the Book of Malachi is simply someone with a similar name, who will live at the time of the War of Gog. Nonetheless, it has developed, partly because of the coincidence of the names, that every orthodox Jew anxiously awaits the advent of Eliyah, the prophet.

3 2-4 Eliyah the prophet will initiate the purification of the priests and Levites so that meal-offerings and other sacrifices can be offered again as in ancient times.

Until the advent of Eliyah all people, including the priests, will be considered impure and unable to bring sacrifices. Eliyah will then explain how to proceed. This passage is in agreement with the conclusion reached from the Books of Ezekiel (43 18-27) and Joel (1 9), that sacrifices will be reintroduced before the War of Gog.

3 5   God will ensure that the Biblical laws are enforced. Judgments will be made against sorcerers, adulterers, false-swearers, and those who oppress the hired workers, widows, orphans, and strangers.

3 6   God has not changed nor has He changed the Biblical laws. Although the Biblical laws were given more than 3,400 years ago they are as applicable now as when originally given. Proof of the correctness of the Bible is gained from the fact that, as promised in Lev. 26 44, the Jewish people are still in existence.

3 7–12   Once the priests and Levites are purified, and the sacrifices reinstituted, it will be necessary to initiate the bringing of tithes and terumot (portions for the priests). Bring the tithes to a storehouse so that food will be available for the Levites and priests. As a result there will be plentiful rain, insects will not destroy the crops, and disease will not ruin the agricultural produce.

3 13–21   Despite the coming of Eliyah and the revitalization of belief in God, there will be many who will say, "There is no purpose for worshipping God; the wicked are successful and escape punishment." Therefore God will record those who fear Him, and He will protect and have mercy for them on the Day of the Lord. The wicked will be burned and punished, while the sun of righteousness will shine for those who fear God.

3 22   Remember the Book of Deuteronomy (see Table 10.6.1) where it is stated (Deut. 4 8–10) that the statutes and ordinances received at Horeb should be observed by the Jewish people and their descendants. It is thus here implied that the laws given to Moses over 3,400 years ago are still applicable today.

3 23–24   Eliyah the prophet will arrive shortly before the great and terrifying Day of the Lord. He will turn the hearts of the traditional parents to the modern technology taught the children, and will turn the hearts of the non-believing children to the belief in God of their ancestors, lest God comes and utterly destroys the land of Israel at the time of the War of Gog.

In Section 18.4 it will be concluded that the War of Gog will occur sometime between April 3, 1973 and March 24, 1974. The advent of Eliyah the prophet, who comes before the War of Gog, will then be in 1973.

18.3   BOOK OF OBADIAH

The prophecy presented in the Book of Obadiah describes the destruction of Jordan by Israel at the time of the War of Gog. The name Edom is here used to refer to the country of Jordan, since the southern part of Jordan is identical with the territory once occupied by Edom. The contents of the prophecy should be compared to Ez. 35 and Jer. 49 7–22.

1 1   The Jordanians claim that they have received a message from the Lord to rise up in battle against Israel, and this message has been sent to the nations.

1   2-4   However, Jordan is one of the poorest and despised countries among the attacking nations. It is her own arrogance that has deceived her. She believes that no one can conquer her. However, God states that even if Jordan were among the stars, He would destroy her.
1   5-7   Ordinarily a nation would not be completely destroyed. However, Jordan will be destroyed. Even her fellow Arab countries have deceived her.
1   8-10   At the time of the War of Gog the wise men of Jordan will disappear and the strong men will tremble. All the inhabitants will be killed by the anger of Israel; and Jordan will no longer exist.
1   11   Jordan will be among the attacking nations against Israel at the time of the War of Gog, when the nations will cast lots as to which part of the booty of Jerusalem each will receive.
1   12-14   But Jordan will not survive to see the planned, but unsuccessful destruction of Israel.
1   15   The Day of the Lord is nearing with its destruction of the attacking nations. As Jordan has done, so will be done to her.
1   16   As Jordan, which had controlled the Temple Mount (1948-1967), was vanquished in 1967 by Israel in the Six-Day War, so will all the attacking nations be conquered.
1   17-18   The people on the Temple Mount will survive, and the mountain will become holy. The Jews will inherit the land promised to them by God, i.e., the nation of Jordan and other territory. No remnant of the country of Jordan will remain. Compare 1 17 with Joel 3 5, where it is also stated that the Jews who gather on the Temple Mount will survive.
1   19   The districts of Israel will acquire permanent possession of the nearby territories belonging to the Arab countries. The Negeb, the southern part of Israel, will inherit Mount Esau, i.e., the adjacent southern part of Jordan. The Shephela, the territory of Israel near the Mediterranean and south of Jaffa, will acquire control of the nearby territory of the Philistines, i.e., the Gaza strip. Moreover, the fields of Ephraim and Samaria, now known as Judaea-Samaria, will become part of Israel. The area of the tribe of Benjamin, which was located northwest of the Dead Sea, will inherit Gilead which is the northern part of Jordan right across the Jordan River.
1   20   Now is stated where persons will be found to occupy some of the newly gained territory. The exiles—the existence of whom profanes the Jewish nation—who reside among the Canaanites even unto France (צרפת), and the exiles of Jerusalem who reside in Spain (ספרד), will inherit the cities of the south. The fact that there are many Jews living in exile is here considered as a profanation of the Israeli people.
1   21   Saviors shall come up the Temple Mount to judge Mount Esau. After the War of Gog, judgments will be made. As a result the Temple Mount will be affirmed as part of Israel, and God will be the established ruler.

18.4 MICAH (CHAPTERS 4-7)

The Book of Micah contains two Messianic prophecies. The first, Chapters 4-5, provides many supplemental details concerning the time of the War of Gog. The second, Chapters 6-7, is only partially concerned with the Messianic era.

18.4.1 Chapters 4-5

4 1 At the last part of the six years (באחרית הימים) the mountain containing the site of the Temple shall be established as the leader of the mountains, and peoples shall come streaming to it.

The word ימים (days) is here used to mean six years, just as is frequently the case in the Book of Daniel (see Table 16.0.1). We learn here that the last part of the six years is when the Temple Mount will be recognized as a leader among mountains. Moreover, we know from Ez. 38 16 that the War of Gog will occur at the end of the six years. The implication therefore exists that the beginning of the six years would be the time when Israel gained control of the Temple Mount during the Six-Day War (June 5-10, 1967). The six-year period is then from 1967 through early 1974 (1967 is not included since the Six-Day War occurred after Nisan). Based on Nisan as the first month of the year, the last year of the six years is from April 3, 1973 to March 24, 1974.

The term House of the Lord, as used in the Biblical text, refers to the site of the Temple, and does not indicate that the Temple will be rebuilt by 1973 (see Section 18.1).

4 2 Many nations will visit the Temple Mount to learn the teachings of God. The indication is that the Jewish people will all be religious and believe in God by 1973.

4 3 Israel will judge between many nations, and they shall beat their swords into plowshares and their lances into pruninghooks. Nation shall not lift up sword against nation, neither shall they learn war any more.

After the War of Gog Israel will be recognized as the proper country to act as judge over other nations, and to initiate procedures for attaining permanent peace throughout the world. In modern times the word "plowshare" is the title of a project sponsored by the United States Atomic Energy Commission for constructive excavation uses for nuclear weapons;[1] the word "lance" is the name of a ground-to-ground missile developed by the United States. Therefore the sentence states that "swords," i.e., destructive atomic weapons, will be converted to peaceful constructive uses (plowshares), and "lances," i.e., destructive ground-to-ground atomic missiles, will be converted to peaceful uses of missiles (pruning-forks).

4 4 The people of the world will dwell in peace.

4 5 All the peoples will worship their own god, and the Jewish nation will serve the Lord our God for ever.

We thus learn that in the Messianic era many religions will exist throughout the world.

4 6–7 At that time the Jewish exiles will be gathered together to Israel, and God will rule over them from Mount Zion.

4 8 The new government of Israel, subsequent to the War of Gog, shall meet at Migdal-eder (see Gen. 35 21), a hill in the region of the old city of Jerusalem.

Now is described the situation prior to the War of Gog. The Jewish people are worried because of the size of the attacking army. Therefore Micah states:

4 9–10 Why do you cry out loud? Do you not have a leader? Have you no counsellor that you are seized with pangs like a woman in childbirth? Have pain and burst forth as a woman in childbirth, because you will come even up to Babylon. There you will be saved from your enemies.

Babylon is only slightly further than the Euphrates River, one of the theoretical boundaries of the land of Israel. Thus, the Jewish nation will have to fight even past the Euphrates River to defeat her enemies during the War of Gog.

4 11 Now, before the War of Gog, many nations are gathered against Israel, and they say, "Let Israel be defiled, and she shall see our eyes in Zion."

4 12–14 But the enemy armies do not know the intentions of God, because He has gathered them to be destroyed. Arise Israel and destroy the attacking nations. Israel, gather together your troops because the attacking armies besiege us, and it is as if they smite the cheek of the leader of Israel.

Now are described the characteristics of the leader of Israel.

5 1 And you, the city of Bethlehem, known also as Ephrath (Gen. 35 19; 48 7)—one of the younger developed areas in the territory of Judaea—from you will come the ruler of Israel, and his origins go back to ancient times.

During the Six-Day War in 1967, Israel gained control of Judaea-Samaria from Jordan. Within Judaea is the city of Bethlehem. Subsequent to the Six-Day War a loan by Israel enabled construction in Bethlehem of a large commercial center.[2] Therefore, Bethlehem is considered as one of the younger developed areas in Judaea.

It was in Bethlehem that David was brought up and anointed as king (I Sam. 16 1, 13; 17 12). Thus the name David owes its origin to ancient times. From Ez. 34 23; 37 24 we learn that the name of the ruler of the newly established state is also David, in agreement with what is implied in the present sentence.

5 2 Therefore, the leader of Israel will give the enemy time until the woman in childbirth, i.e., Israel, is ready to give birth, i.e., to fight.

The implication is, that when the enemy gathers against Israel, some time will be needed by the ruler to prepare the army to fight. The leader will therefore delay until all the military preparations have been made. After the defeat of the enemy, the remainder of the Jews in exile will return to the land of Israel.

5 3 The ruler named David will lead the nation with strength from God, and Israel will be settled. The country will expand to the boundaries promised by God.

After the War of Gog a temporary peace will exist until 1996 (see comments on Dan. 9 27).

5 4   This shall be the peace: When Assyria enters the territory of Israel, then seven leaders and eight princes will be set against her.

Assyria corresponds to the modern country of Iraq. Iraq occupies a considerable portion of the territory formerly occupied by ancient Assyria. Moreover, Iraq includes the key ancient Assyrian cities of Nineveh and Babylon. After the War of Gog Israel will border on the remaining territory of Iraq.

5 5   The appointed leaders will waste the land of Assyria with the sword, and save the territory of Israel from her.

5 6-8   The nation of Israel will be an unassuming country among the other nations, and will not want to conquer other peoples. If necessary, however, Israel will be as a lion among other animals, able to conquer any other country.

Thus, at the time of the War of Gog Israel will want peace. But when attacked by other nations she will completely destroy them.

5 9-13   At that time, when Assyria (Iraq) enters the territory of Israel, God will destroy the cars, tanks, cities and fortifications of Iraq. Also, their witchcraft and idols will be eliminated.

5 14   God will take vengeance against the nations that do not observe the peace.

18.4.2   Chapters 6-7

The main part of the prophecy (6 1-7 6) refers to the sins of the Jewish people at the time of Micah. God complains against the Israelites saying that they have not remembered the good He has done for them. The prophet then states that all God wants is for the people to do justice and act properly towards God (6 8). Because of the sins of the nation the people are punished (6 9-16). The prophet then describes the extent of the corruption among the nation's inhabitants (7 1-6). In contrast, the prophet has faith in God and awaits the Messianic era when the enemies of Israel will be destroyed (7 7-10).

7 11   The day will come to build the fences, i.e., to strengthen the nation of Israel. At that time the bad fate of the Jewish people will be set aside.

7 12   At that time (the time of the War of Gog) the attacking enemy will come against Israel from Assyria (Iraq) until Egypt, and from Egypt until the Euphrates, and from sea (the Mediterranean) until sea (the Red Sea), and from Mount Hor (in Jordan).

These are essentially the boundaries promised to the Jewish people (Gen. 15 18; Ex. 23 31; Deut. 1 7; 11 24; Josh. 1 4), namely from the Red Sea to the Mediterranean, and from the desert to the Euphrates River.

7 13   The land shall be desolate for its inhabitants because of their deeds.

The land of the above specified attacking nations, those occupying the theoretical boundaries of the state of Israel will be made desolate during the War of Gog.

7 14   Then God will take care of His people, who dwell alone. They will be as a forest within a fruitful field; i.e., there will be so many people, like the trees in a forest, dwelling in the fruitful land of Israel. The people will feed even in Bashan and Gilead, as in days of old.

The territory of Gilead is within the country of Jordan, while the territory of Bashan is within the country of Syria. Thus, Israel will gain control of Jordanian and Syrian territory.

7 15   God will perform miracles, at the time of the War of Gog, as He performed at the time of the Exodus from Egypt.

7 16–17   Nations shall see the miracles and will, by comparison, be ashamed of their own strength. They will be frightened, and shall fear God.

7 18–20   Who is like unto God, that pardons the sins of His people and does not retain His anger for ever! He will show faithfulness to Jacob and mercy to Abraham, according to His promises to them in ancient times that they would become ancestors of a great nation.

18.5   AMOS (CHAPTER 9 7–15)

The few sentences in the Book of Amos referring to the Messianic era reinforce passages from the other prophets. David will be the ruler of the State of Israel at the time of the War of Gog, and Israel will inherit the theoretical Biblical boundaries.

9   7   The people of Israel, when they sin, are in the eyes of God just as the Ethiopians. Yes, God did take the Israelites out from Egypt, but He also took the Philistines from Caphtor and Aram from Kir.

9   8   God destroys the sinful kingdom from the face of the earth, except that He will not completely destroy the Jewish people.

9   9   God will sift out the Jewish people from among the nations as if they are in a sieve, and no pebble (good person) will fall to the ground.

9   10   The sinning Jews—those who say that evil will not overtake or confront them—will die by the sword.

9   11   At that time, the time of the War of Gog, God will support the faltering country of Israel (which is compared to a temporary structure) ruled by David. The ruins will be repaired and rebuilt so the nation will be as it was in ancient times.

9   12   The Jewish people will gain possession of the remains of the territory of Edom (Jordan), and of all the nations which occupy the territory supervised by God; territory that is promised in the Bible for the State of Israel.

9   13   The time will come when the agricultural produce of Israel will be exceptional, and even the mountains will supply abundant yields.

9   14   The settlement of the Jewish people will be re-established, desolate cities will be rebuilt, and vineyards and gardens will be plentiful.

9 15   The Jewish people will be implanted on their land, and will never again be removed from their territory.

18.6   HOSEA (CHAPTERS 2 15–3 5)

The Messianic prophecies of the Book of Hosea go back to the 1870s when Petah Tikvah, the first major colony, was established. This event can be considered as the beginning of the agricultural development of the land of Israel after centuries of neglect.

2 15   The Jewish people sinned and were punished; and they had forgotten God.

2 16   Therefore God will entice the Jewish people to return to the land of Israel, which had become like a desert, and He will speak tenderly to them.

During the centuries of neglect, while the Jews were in exile, the land of Israel turned into a desert.[3]

2 17   God will give the people vineyards from the former desert, and the colony of Petah Tikvah from the Valley of Achor. The people will respond as in former times, such as upon entering the land after the Exodus from Egypt.

The first major colony established in recent times in the land of Israel was Petah Tikvah. In 1872 a group of Jerusalem Jews attempted to purchase land in the Jericho area, corresponding to the Valley of Achor specified in Josh. 7 26.[4] They adopted as their slogan the words of Hos. 2 17, "Petah Tikvah from the Valley of Achor." However the Turkish authorities voided the land sale. In 1878 a group of orthodox Jews from Jerusalem, including some who had participated in the land purchase six years earlier, established the settlement of Petah Tikvah near the sources of the Yarkon River. Because of malaria, collapse of buildings in the rainy season, and Arab harassment, the settlement was abandoned by 1881. In 1882 the settlement was begun again in a nearby area. In 1887 Baron Edmond de Rothschild came to the aid of the struggling settlement. Vineyards were planted, and the settlers obtained employment in them.[5]

At the very outset of Jewish settlement in the nineteenth century, a vineyard was planted at the agricultural school of Mikve Yisrael. Numerous other vineyards were planted before 1900 in many of the settlements supported by Baron de Rothschild.[6]

2 18   At that time (the time of the War of Gog) the Jewish people will recognize God as the true God, and no longer consider Him as a strange god (Baal).

2 19   Names of strange gods will no longer be mentioned.

2 20   A covenant will then be made with the wild animals, the birds of the heaven, and the creeping things of the ground. War weapons such as the bow and sword will be eliminated, and the people will rest in security.

The animals, birds, and creeping things are symbolic of the mighty nations of the world. For example, Russia is known as the bear, England as the lion, and China as the dragon.

2 21-22   God will betroth the Jewish people for ever—with righteousness, justice, lovingkindness, compassion, and faithfulness—and the Jewish people will recognize God.

2 23-24   At that time the sky and earth will respond, so that grain, wine, and oil will be produced.

2 25   God will implant the Jewish people on the land of Israel, and will treat them with compassion. God will recognize the Jewish people, and they will believe in Him.

3 1-3   Hosea is commanded by God to love a woman whose desires are for others. Hosea acquired such a woman, and told her not to play the harlot, and he would be faithful to her.

3 4   The analogy is to the covenant between God and the Jewish people. When the people forsake God they are punished by being deprived for a long time of a ruler, sacrifices, priestly garments, and also idols of any type.

3 5   Afterwards, when the people once again seek God, then they will have David as their ruler. They will fear God, and receive His goodness at the last part of the six years (in 1973) (see Section 18.4).

18.7   ZEPHANIAH (CHAPTER 3 8-20)

The Messianic verses in the Book of Zephaniah describe the destruction of the attacking nations at the time of the War of Gog, the subsequent serving of God by these nations, and the eventual greatness of the State of Israel.

3 8   Wait for the day when God rises up to the prey, because His determination is to gather the nations together at the time of the War of Gog, and pour out His anger against them.

3 9   Afterwards the nations will call on and serve God.

3 10   From beyond the rivers of Ethiopia the suppliants of the scattered enemy will bring offerings to God.

3 11   At that time the Jewish people will no longer sin on the holy mountain.

3 12   Within the midst of the Jewish nation will be an afflicted and poor people who will take refuge in the name of the Lord.

3 13   The remnant of Israel shall not sin; they shall work and rest and no one shall make them afraid.

3 14-17   Israel be happy, your enemy has been cleared away. God is in your midst. There is no reason to fear evil any more.

3 18   God will gather back to Israel those who were pained by waiting for the appointed time when God would reveal Himself. These people who have strayed from Judaism are descendants of the Jewish people, and have borne a burden of shame for Israel.

3 19   God will remove those who afflict the Jews, and He will gather back

to Israel the lame and those who have gone astray. They will become praiseworthy, even in all the lands of exile where they have been a shame.

3   20   At that time—when God re-establishes the settlement of Israel—He will gather the Jews back to the land, and make them renown among all the peoples of the earth.

18.8   ZECHARIAH (CHAPTERS 9-14)

The Book of Zehariah presents two detailed prophecies concerning the Messianic era. The first prophecy (Chapters 9-11) describes the defeat of Turkey near the end of World War I, the defeat of the armies of Gog by Israel, and the re-etablishment of the greatness of Israel. The second prophecy (Chapters 12-14) presents numerous details about the War of Gog. Many of the details, such as the enemy's conquest of half the old city of Jerusalem, and the splitting of the Mount of Olives are not contained elsewhere in the Bible.

18.8.1   Chapters 9-11

The prophecy begins with a description of the conquest during World War I of the territory held by Turkey in and around Palestine. This territory is here called Hadrach. The conquest of the territory marks the end of the Moslem domination of Palestine.

9   1   Prophecy to the land of Hadrach; and Damascus is where its strength lies. From God's point of view this land is as the eyes of man, that is it is an extremely important part of the world since it includes the land of all the tribes of Israel.

The chief strong point of the territory of Hadrach, and a major goal of the attacking English forces during World War I, was the well-defended city of Damascus. On October 1, 1918 the city was taken. By October 31, an armistice was concluded.[7]

9   2   Homs (חמת) will also be within the boundaries of Hadrach, as well as Tyre and Sidon.

Homs was conquered on October 16, 1918,[8] a little over two weeks after Damascus was defeated. Moreover, Tyre was reached on October 4, and at the same time supplies were brought in from the sea at Sidon.[9]

9   3   Tyre did build herself a stronghold, and gathered much silver and gold.

The access to Tyre involved a mile-long road of huge steps hewn out of rock. Using explosives, this cliff road was opened to wheeled vehicles within three days.[10]

9   4   God will cause Hadrach to be conquered, its army to be smitten at the sea, and the country consumed by fire (i.e., defeated in battle).

On October 30, 1918, the day before the armistice with Turkey was to take effect, over 11,000 Turkish soldiers surrendered near the Tigris river.[11]

9   5-6   The main cities of the Philistines (all within the territory of

Hadrach), namely Ashkelon, Gaza, Ekron, and Ashdod will be conquered. A mean ruler (ממזר) will rule over Ashdod.

All these Philistine cities were conquered by General Sir Edmund Allenby during World War I. A particular goal during the fighting was Gaza, which was finally conquered on November 6, 1917.[12] Allenby is here called a mean ruler because of his violent temper. In fact, his formidable appearance and his even more formidable temper led to his being nicknamed "the Bull."[13]

9 7   God will remove bloody and disgusting statements from the mouths of the English conquerors. The government of England will declare that it is in favor of establishing the land of Palestine for the Jewish People. England will be as a leader of Judah, and both Ekron and Jerusalem (the territory of the Jebusites) will be included in the land designated for the Jewish people.

On November 9, 1917, the English government came out with a proclamation, later known as the Balfour Declaration, which expressed the desire of the English government to establish in Palestine a national home for the Jewish people.[14]

9 8   God will protect the land of Israel from invading armies, and no oppressor shall dominate the land.

The conquest by England of the Turkish army marked the end of Moslem control over Palestine. This event subsequently led to the establishment of the State of Israel in 1948.

9 9   Be happy Zion and Jerusalem. Behold your ruler (David) will come at about the time of the War of Gog (1973). He will be a righteous and victorious man, and will ride on peaceful vehicles.

9 10   Tanks (chariots), warplanes (horses), and missiles (bows), shall be eliminated from Jerusalem. The leader shall speak peace unto the nations, and he shall rule from the (Mediterranean) Sea to the (Red) Sea, and from the Euphrates River until the ends of the land. Thus, Israel will gain the theoretical Biblical boundaries as a result of the War of Gog.

Now is described the ingathering of the exiled Jews.

9 11-12   God, because of His covenant with the Jewish people, will send the Jews out from their imprisonment in exile (from a cistern without water). You, who have been hoping for redemption, return to your fortified land. A great leader will be given to the Jewish people.

Verses 13 through 16 describes the victory of Israel in the War of Gog. Subsequent verses are concerned with events at about this time.

9 13   Judah will be like the bow, Ephraim like the arrows, and Zion like the sword, when Israel fights against Greece.

From Dan. 2 45 we learned that Greece is part of the attacking enemy at the time of the War of Gog.

9 14-16   God will be like lightning in helping Israel fight the enemy. He will protect the Israelites, and they shall defeat the attackers.

9 17   After the victory, how wonderful will be the flourishing of young men and women from the fruits of the land.

10   1   God will supply rain at the proper time so that the vegetation will grow successfully.

10   2   The diviners of the enemy, who predicted the downfall of Israel, have prophesied falsely; therefore the enemy flees like sheep, and are afflicted because of lack of a leader.

10   3–7   God is angry at the leaders of the enemy, and has remembered His own flock. The Israelites will be strong in battle and will succeed. It will be as if the Jewish people were never forsaken, and they will believe in God.

10   8   God will gather the Jews back to Israel, and the people will multiply.

10   9   The people of the nation of Israel will grow and become great among the nations of the world, and the exiled Jews will return to their land.

10   10   The exiled Jews will return from Egypt and Assyria (Iraq). They will settle in Gilead (North Jordan) and Lebanon. So many will return that there will not be sufficient space for the returnees.

10   11   The waters of the Nile will be dried up, and the pride of Assyria (Iraq) and Egypt will diminish.

10   12   The people of Israel will believe in God.

11   1–3   Lebanon, Bashan (Syria), and Jordan will be conquered at the time of the War of Gog.

Now is presented a parable where the inhabitants of the enemy countries are compared to sheep led to slaughter.

11   4–5   The sheep of slaughter are the enemy people in the countries of the attacking nations. The leaders of the enemy countries do not care about their population; only about becoming rich.

11   6   God will no longer have pity on the inhabitants of these countries, and their land shall be ruined.

11   7   The Prophet Zechariah tends the sheep of slaughter. He takes two sticks, one called "pleasantness" and the other called "uniter," to tend the sheep.

11   8   The three leaders—of Lebanon, Syria and Jordan—are loathed by Zechariah.

11   9   The prophet then refuses to tend the sheep of slaughter. He says, "Let them die."

11   10–11   The stick called "pleasantness" is broken as a symbol that God's covenant with the enemy countries is abrogated.

11   12–13   The prophet is paid 30 pieces of silver for his work as a shepherd, but he throws them away to the artisan as further proof of abrogation of the covenant.

11   14   Next the stick called "uniter" is broken, as a symbol that the bond between Israel and the territory of Judaea is cut apart. Perhaps this act indicates

that the Arabs in Judaea will not completely support Israel at the time of the War of Gog.

11 15   Zechariah then takes the tools of a foolish shepherd. These tools are symbolic of a new leader (Gog) of the enemy who will not care for the people and will forsake them. The military might of the foolish shepherd will become useless.

18.8.2   Chapters 12-14

In these chapters are presented numerous details concerning the War of Gog and the startling consequences of the battle. In addition to many details which agree with the descriptions given in the Book of Ezekiel (especially Ez. 38-39), there are also given such supplementary information as the following: (A) The enemy will be partially successful in an attack on Jerusalem. (B) There will be some loss of Jewish life, with extensive mourning for those killed. (C) The territory of Judaea, now mainly occupied by Arabs, will be fighting on the side of Israel. (D) The Mount of Olives will be split in half. (E) Much of the land of Israel will become flattened, while the city of Jerusalem will be raised up. (F) No longer will non-Jews occupy the site of the Temple.

12 1   A prophecy from God concerning Israel.

12 2   God will make Jerusalem into a poisonous threshold for the attacking surrounding nations. The territory of Judaea will be included in the enemy's siege of the Jerusalem area.

12 3   All the nations will gather together to attack Jerusalem.

12 4   At that time God will afflict every horse (airplane) and rider (the pilot) with madness and blindness, but He will help the territory of Judaea.

12 5   Each military leader of Judaea will say to himself, "The dwellers in Jerusalem will strengthen me by their faith in God."

12 6   The military leaders of Judaea will be like fire which devours the surrounding enemy; and Jerusalem will remain settled as she was.

12 7   God will first save the territory of Judaea so that the House of David (the leaders) and the inhabitants of Jerusalem will not have greater glory than that for Judaea.

12 8-9   God will protect the Jewish people in Jerusalem, and will destroy the enemy nations attacking the city.

12 10   The House of David (the leaders) and the resident of Jerusalem will have a spirit of grace and supplication; and they will mourn over the Jewish people who were killed as if the dead were their only sons, or their first-born.

12 11   At that time the mourning in Jerusalem will be as great as at the time of the mourning (in the place known as Hadadrimmon) for King Josiah who was killed in the valley of Megiddo (II Kings 23 29; II Chr. 35 22, 25).

12 12-14   Each bereaved family will mourn separately; also the men and women will mourn separately. Moreover, the families of the leaders, in particular David, Nathan, Levi, and Shimei, will mourn.

13   1   At the time of the War of Gog a fountain will be opened for the House of David and for the residents of Jerusalem to serve as purification waters to be used with the ashes of the red heifer (Num. 19 17) and for recovery of the menstruating woman (Lev. 15 13, 19–22). Both these categories require fresh "living" water for purification.

13   2–6   At that time there will no longer be mention of the names of idols, nor will there be false prophets, nor the persistence of impurity.

13   7   Awaken the sword against both the leaders and followers of the attacking nations.

13   8   As a result, two out of three of the inhabitants of the countries of the enemy, which are within the theoretical Biblical boundaries, will be killed. Only one-third of the population will survive.

13   9   A selected group of the surviving third of the enemy will embrace Judaism and recognize God.

Now in Chapter 14 is given a clearer statement of many of the symbolic and poetical descriptions contained in Chapters 9 through 13. The time described is that of the War of Gog (1973).

14   1   A day will come when the spoils of Jerusalem, captured by the enemy, will be divided among them within the city.

14   2   All the attacking nations will come against Jerusalem. The city will be captured, the houses looted, and the women raped. Half the city shall go into exile, but the remainder of the people shall not be cut off from the city.

14   3   God will then go forth and fight against the attacking nations.

14   4   The Mount of Olives, which lies to the east of Jerusalem, will be split in half. Part of the mountain will move north and part south to form an enormous valley running from east to west.

14   5   The Jewish people will run to this valley with all speed. God and His holy angels will then go forth to fight.

14   6   That day there will be no light—neither precious light, i.e., radiant bright light, nor frozen light, i.e., reflected weak light.

14   7   Then towards the evening of a certain day there will be light.

14   8   As a result, pure living water shall issue from Jerusalem, half flowing to the eastern or Dead Sea, and half to the Mediterranean Sea. The water will flow all year round, both in summer and winter.

14   9   God will then be ruler over the entire land, i.e., the territory within the theoretical Biblical boundaries of the State of Israel.

14   10   The land will become flattened from Geba (II Kings 23 8) to Rimmon (Josh 15 32), i.e., from the north end of the ancient tribe of Judah to the south (possibly from 31° 50 to about 31° north latitude). In contrast, the city of Jerusalem will be raised in height.

14   11   Jerusalem will be settled, and will be secure.

14   12, 15   The persons and animals of the nations attacking Jerusalem will

be afflicted with a sudden unusual illness, where the flesh, eyes, and tongue will rot while the individual still stands on his feet.

14 13   The resultant confusion will cause the enemy to rise up each man against his neighbor.

14 14   Also the people from Judaea will fight against the enemy in Jerusalem. The great wealth of the attackers will be gathered together as spoils.

14 16   The surviving inhabitants of the attacking nations will come each year to serve God and to celebrate the Festival of Tabernacles.

14 17–19   Those nations not coming to Jerusalem to worship God will not receive rain. This includes the Egyptians. This lack of water will be the plague which will afflict those nations who do not come to celebrate the Festival of Tabernacles.

14 20–21   There will be a need for so many pots for Temple purposes that all pots in Jerusalem will be holy and used for cooking the sacrifices. No longer will non-Jews (כנעני) occupy the site of the Temple; i.e., the Mosque of Omar will be removed from its location.

18.9   MESSIANIC PREDICTIONS DERIVED FROM BOOK OF TWELVE PROPHETS

Summarized here will be only the main Messianic predictions found in the Twelve Prophets which are additional to what was already derived from Daniel and Ezekiel.

The initial development of the land of Israel will begin with establishment of the colony of Petah Tikvah (1878). Vineyards will be planted in areas which were formerly desert (Hos. 2 17).

During World War I the territory of Palestine and the surrounding area will be conquered from the Turkish empire. Such locations as Damascus, Tyre, Sidon, Gaza, and Jerusalem will be among the conquests (Zech. 9 1–6).

Eliyah (Elijah) the prophet will come to the land of Israel shortly before the War of Gog (1973). He will reinstitute sacrifices, purify the Levites and priests, initiate the collection of tithes, and cause the Jewish people to believe in God (Mal. 3). Sacrifices will be brought prior to the War of Gog (Joel 1 9).

The term "latter part of the six years" (אחרית הימים) (usually translated "end of days") refers to the end of the six-year period between the Six-Day War in 1967 and the War of Gog in 1973 (Mic. 4 1).

Nations attacking Israel during the War of Gog, in addition to those specifically mentioned in the Book of Ezekiel, include Syria (Zech. 11 1–3), Lebanon (Zech. 10 10), Greece (Joel 4 6; Hos. 9 13; Dan. 2 45), Egypt, Jordan (Joel 4 19; Obad. 1 1), and Iraq (Mic. 5 4).

The army of Gog will achieve initial success against the old city of Jerusalem. The enemy will conquer half of the city before they will feel the vengeance of God. The Mount of Olives will be split in half and form a valley in between, to which the Jews will flee for safety. At the time of the war there will be a day or more when there will be no light of any type. The land around Jerusalem will be flattened, while the city of Jerusalem will be raised in height. The attacking nations will be afflicted with a sudden illness which will cause their people to rot while still standing (Zech. 14 1–15).

The territory of Judaea will support and help Israel in the fight against the enemy (Zech. 12 6; 14 14).

The attacking enemy will be destroyed in the Valley of Jehoshaphat (Joel 4 2, 12). Also, the countries of Egypt and Jordan will be made desolate (Joel 4 19).

The Jewish people who assemble on the Temple Mount will be saved (Joel 3 5; Obad. 1 17). However many Jews will be killed, and there will be a great mourning period (Zech. 12 11–14).

As a result of the battle, Israel will gain the theoretical Biblical boundaries from the Mediterranean Sea to the Euphrates River (Zech. 9 10; Amos 9 12).

After the war, atomic weapons will be discontinued and permanent peace will be established (Mic. 4 3). Each country will worship its own god, and the Jewish nation will serve the Lord our God for ever (Mic. 4 5). Moreover, many of the surviving enemy will embrace Judaism (Zech. 13 9).

Subsequent to the War of Gog, Iraq will attempt an attack on Israel, but will be thoroughly defeated (Mic. 5 4–13).

Chapter Nineteen

COMMENTARY ON MESSIANIC CHAPTERS OF ISAIAH

There are numerous chapters in the Book of Isaiah concerned with Messianic times. These prophecies are found in **2** 2-4; **11** 1-**12** 6; **19** 1-25; **24** 1-**27** 13; **32** 1-**35** 10; and **49** 1-**66** 24. In general, the Messianic predictions are presented in beautiful and imaginative poetry, but do not contain a great deal of concrete information. Therefore, despite the large number of chapters concerned with the Messianic era, only very few details, supplementary to the Books of Ezekiel and the Twelve Prophets, can be gleaned. In this connection, it should be realized that Isaiah was among the first prophets to prophesy about the Messianic era. Hence, one should really expect the subsequent prophets, namely Jeremiah, Ezekiel, and the Twelve Prophets, to supplement the Messianic predictions of Isaiah, rather than the reverse.

19.1 CHAPTER 2 2-4

The prophecy in Isa. **2** 2-4 concerning the "latter part of the six-year period" (אחרית הימים), is identical almost word for word with that prophesied by Micah (**4** 1-3). In the case of Micah's prophecy, these three sentences are part of a long section of two chapters referring to the Messianic era. On the other hand, in the Book of Isaiah, there is a sharp change in tone after statement of these sentences. The prediction is used to illustrate what good results could be achieved if the Jewish people observed the Biblical laws. Instead, the people have sinned and will be severely punished.

Compare the comments on Mic. **4** 1-3 (Section 18.4.1) for an explanation of this passage in Isaiah.

19.2 CHAPTERS 11 1-12 6

Chapters 11 and 12 of Isaiah describe the situation arising from the defeat of the army of Gog (after 1973).

11 1   A branch will grow from the trunk of Jesse.

The well-known offshoot from Jesse was David, King of Israel (I Sam. **16** 13). Here is meant that in the Messianic era, a ruler will arise having the name David. It should be noted that the first use of the name David in the Bible was by the son of Jesse.

11 2–5   The David of Messianic times will be a wise man who will go in the way of the Lord, will judge fairly, be a strong ruler, and act righteously.

11 6–9   At that time wild animals—symbolic of powerful countries—and domesticated animals—symbolic of weak nations—will no longer fight each other. Neither will these countries cause damage on the Temple Mount, since the entire world will be filled with knowledge of the Lord.

The specific animals mentioned are the wolf, sheep, leopard, kid, calf, fatling, cow, bear, lion, cattle, infant, snake, dragon, and young child. Commonly, in cartoons, on flags, and elsewhere, the bear is associated with Russia, the lion with England, the dragon with China, and the young child, who leads some of the animals, represents Israel. The actual countries symbolized by the other animals are not clearly known. Perhaps the snake represents the United States, since in the early history of the United States (around 1775) the rattlesnake commonly appeared on many of the banners.[1]

11 10   At that time, the nation of Israel led by David—the name originated by Jesse—will be sought out by the countries of the world.

11 11–12   God will then gather back the Israelite exiles from the four corners of the earth, including those Jews who remained in Assyria (Northern Iraq), Egypt, Pathros (Southern Egypt), Cush (Ethiopia), Elam (Iran), Shinar (Southern Iraq), Hamath (Syria), and the islands of the sea (Cyprus and Crete).

The names of the ancient countries have here been identified with their modern equivalents (the country in parenthesis) based on the approximate geographical locations.

11 13   There will no longer be two competitive kingdoms, Ephraim (i.e. Israel) and Judah, but one unified nation, Israel.

11 14–16   Israel will gain firm control of the shoulder of the Philistines (Gaza Strip), the Children of the East (parts of Saudi Arabia), and Edom, Moab, and Ammon (Jordan). Moreover, the tongue of the Sea of Egypt (Suez Canal) will be destroyed, and the Euphrates River will be separated into seven wadis. There will then be a dry path from Assyria (Iraq) to Israel, as was the case at the Red Sea when the Israelites came out of Egypt.

12 1–2   At that time the Jewish people will thank God for His being their salvation.

12 3   The people will draw water from the wells of salvation. Compare Ez. 47 1–12; Zech. 13 1; 14 8; and Joel 4 18, describing the fountain, originating from Jerusalem, formed as a result of the War of Gog.

12 4–6   The Jews will give thanks to God and sing praises to Him. In particular, will be used the wording found in Ps. 105 1 and I Chr. 16 8, "Give thanks to the Lord, proclaim His name; declare His doings among the nations."

19.3 CHAPTER 19 1-25

In Chapter 19 is presented a prophecy concerning Egypt at the time of the Messianic era. Prior to the War of Gog there will be poor leadership, internal dissent, and unsuccessful projects in Egypt. Then at the time of the War of Gog Egypt will be utterly defeated by Israel. Subsequently, the Egyptians will fear and serve God.

19   1-4   Prior to the War of Gog, God will come to Egypt and cause great confusion. There will be internal dissent, and the people will be ruled by a cruel ruler.

19   5-10   Many of the waters and rivers of Egypt will either dry up or become contaminated. As a result, crops near the water sources will fail, the fishing industry will suffer, and all types of industry will be unsuccessful.

It is noteworthy that the Aswan Dam built by Egypt to help reclaim desert land has been sharply disappointing. Instead of helping agriculture, the dam has eroded the Nile's banks, decreased the available amount of water, lowered the fertility of the soil, and caused the spread of disease. Moreover, the dam has caused a rise in soil salinity and the decline of marine life in the eastern Mediterranean.[2]

19   11-15   The leaders of Egypt act foolishly and receive poor advice.

19   16-17   After the defeat of Egypt by Israel during the War of Gog, the Egyptian people will be so terrified that even mention of Israel will cause fear.

19   18   At that time there will be five cities in Egypt which will speak Hebrew and swear allegiance to God. One of these cities will be called the city of destruction (הרס), because it will have been almost completely demolished during the War of Gog.

19   19-22   The Egyptians will, to some extent, serve God. An altar to the Lord and a sacred pillar will be set up. The people will be saved from an oppressor or from disease if they appeal to God.

19   23   At that time there will be a road from Assyria (Iraq) to Egypt; and Egypt will serve Assyria. Compare Isa. 11 16 where it is stated that there will be a road from Assyria to Israel.

19   24-25   The three countries, Israel, Egypt, and Assyria, will cooperate and will all be blessed by God.

It should be noted that after the War of Gog, the territory of Israel will be expanded so that Egypt will be the southwest neighbor and Iraq will be the northeast neighbor of Israel. The countries of Jordan and probably Lebanon will no longer exist.

19.4 CHAPTERS 24 1-27 13

Presented in these four chapters is a poetic description of the War of Gog, and the thankfulness to God by the Jewish people for their salvation.

24   1-4   At the time of the War of Gog, God will empty the land (the territory

within the theoretical boundaries promised to Israel, which will be occupied by other nations), scatter the inhabitants, and change the appearance of the land. All persons will be affected irrespective of occupation or wealth.

24   5   The reason for the devastation is that the land has become defiled by its inhabitants. They have violated the armistice agreement which was negotiated under the supervision of the world's nations (the United Nations); i.e., they have attacked the State of Israel.

24   6   Therefore the inhabitants of the land (the enemy nations) have been found guilty, and only a few remain.

24   7-12   All happiness has stopped, including the enjoyment of wine and music. Desolation is found in the cities.

24   13   Only a few persons survive, just as only a few olives remain after beating on the olive-tree.

24   14-15   The survivors, even those in far away countries, will praise God.

24   16   Before the actual battle of the War of Gog we in Israel heard the enemy singing praises to themselves as victors. Each individual in Israel would say, "I am wasting away. Woe is unto me." The rebelling enemy has rebelled, and the "clothing" of the rebelling enemy (i.e., the secondary countries associated with the leading attacking nations) have also rebelled. All these countries are coming against Israel.

24   17-20   Terror, traps, and earth tremors will befall the inhabitants of the enemy countries. The land will be completely destroyed, and the enemy will not again arise in battle.

24   21   At that time God will destroy the enemy airforce in the skies, and the enemy army on the ground.

24   22   The enemy armies will be gathered into a pit, imprisoned, and punished.

Compare Joel 4 2, 12, 14 where it is stated that the army of Gog will be gathered into the Valley of Jehoshaphat and there annihilated.

24   23   The moon and sun will be ashamed. Then God will rule from Zion and Jerusalem, and there will be respect for the elders of Israel.

Compare Zech. 14 6, 7 where it is stated that there will be a day at the time of the War of Gog when there will be no light.

The people of Israel will praise God for destroying the enemy army (25 1-5).

25   1   Praise God because of the miracles He performed. He carried out his promises.

25   2   God destroyed the cities of the enemy, and they will not be rebuilt.

25   3   The mighty enemy nations do therefore fear God.

25   4   God was a stronghold for the poor (Israel) when in distress from the storm of the attacking army of Gog.

25   5   God did subdue the song of imagined victory by the enemy, as the heat of the day is abated by the shadow of a cloud.

Now the text continues with the events that will happen after the War of Gog.

25 6–7 God will make a feast on the Temple Mount for the representatives of the nations, and will remove the veil of sorrow.

25 8 Death in warfare will be eliminated forever; i.e., permanent peace will be established. Moreover, the shame of the Jewish people will be removed, i.e., the exiled Jews will be gathered back to Israel.

25 9 At that time the Jewish people will recognize God who was their salvation.

25 10 The strength of God will reside on the Temple Mount, and Moab (i.e., Jordan) will be destroyed.

25 11–12 Jordan will struggle to survive as a swimmer thrashes with his hands; but Jordan and its fortifications will be brought down.

26 1 At that time the following song will be sung in Israel: Jerusalem is a strong city. God makes its walls a salvation.

26 2 Open the gates so that the Jewish people may enter.

26 3 The Jewish people are a creation dependent on God, who will ensure peace.

26 4 Depend on God forever, for He is an everlasting rock.

26 5–6 God has brought down a strong city so that it can be trampled upon even by the poor.

26 7 The path of the righteous is straight.

26 8–9 Also the paths of God's judgment are straight. We wait for God's help so that the people of the world will learn justice.

26 10–11 The wicked, who will not learn righteousness, shall not see the majesty of God, and will be devoured by fire.

26 12 God will establish peace for the Jewish people; and everything we do is done for us by God.

26 13 Although numerous foreign rulers have ruled over us, only God do we consider as our leader.

26 14 The foreign rulers have been killed, and they will not live again.

26 15 God, you have increased the territory of the State of Israel, and You have therefore been honored.

26 16 Israel prayed to You God when they were in trouble.

26 17 Israel suffered when in exile as a woman in labor.

26 18 Then she gave birth, but not to a live baby; no salvation resulted, nor was the enemy defeated.

26 19 Then suddenly the still-born child will live (after the War of Gog). The enemy is defeated, and the reawakening of Israel results.

26 20 Israel, hide, until the anger of God (against the enemy nations) is spent.

26 21 Behold, God will punish the enemy, and He will take revenge for the innocent Jews who have been murdered.

27 1 At that time God will destroy the great ships of the enemy, which are compared to sea monsters.

27 2   Israel will be called a vineyard of excellent wine.

27 3   God continually watches over His vineyard, Israel, lest trouble be visited upon her.

27 4   God states that He has no anger towards Israel. However, when the people sin, God will be as thorns which will be used to burn up Israel.

27 5   Or if Israel takes strength in God's stronghold (i.e., recognizes God), and tries to make peace with God, then God will allow peace to result.

27 6   After the War of Gog the returning exiled Jews will take root and blossom in Israel, and will fill the world with good fruit.

27 7   Was Israel smitten and killed by God as were the enemies of Israel smitten and killed?

27 8   God punishes Israel with exile. He drives her away from the land with a strong wind, but the nation is not destroyed.

27 9   As a result, the sins of Israel can be atoned for. Remove the iniquity by destroying idols and altars to other gods.

27 10 Then the land of Israel, which was like a forsaken city and an abandoned field, will be repopulated, thereby ending the split of the people from the land.

27 11 However, when the harvest fails (in 1973) the land will be partially broken by the enemy (who is compared to women), who comes to burn the land. But the enemy is not a people of understanding; therefore God will not take pity on them.

27 12 At that time, God will beat the enemy from the Euphrates to the Gulf of Suez, i.e., Israel will gain the theoretical boundaries. Then the Jews will be gathered back into the one nation of Israel.

27 13 At that time a great horn will be blown (perhaps over radio and television), and the exiled Jews in Assyria (Iraq and Syria) and Egypt will be gathered back, and shall worship God on the Temple Mount in Jerusalem.

19.5   CHAPTERS 32–35

These four chapters (Isa. 32–35) describe events which will occur in the Messianic era. A righteous ruler will arise, and shortly thereafter the army of Gog will prepare to attack Israel. As a result the crops in Israel will not be tended and the cities will be deserted. The attacking armies will then be destroyed. Moreover, the territory of Edom (Jordan) will be completely demolished. The State of Israel will flourish and the exiled Jews will return to the land.

32 1   A righteous ruler shall lead Israel, and his officers shall also act justly. The righteous ruler is David, mentioned in Ez. 34 23 and in numerous other passages.

32 2   Each person will be secure, as if protected from the wind, rain, drought, and sun.

32 3–4 People will see and hear properly. They shall understand knowledge and speak clearly.

32 5 People will be evaluated correctly. The vile person will not be considered honorable.

32 6–8 The vile person is defined as one who speaks and performs evil, while the honorable person speaks and performs good.

Shortly after the start of David's rule, trouble will arise from the enemy led by Gog.

32 9 Even the confident women should be aware of the problem.

32 10 A number of days after the beginning of David's reign the crops will fail.

32 11–14 The women should become upset because the crops are not successful and the buildings and cities are deserted.

The cities will be deserted in expectation of the attack by the army of Gog.

32 15–16 The difficult situation will last until God will destroy the attacking enemy. Then the desert will become a fruitful field, and the fruitful field will produce dense growth like a forest.

32 17–18 Permanent peace will be established for Israel.

32 19 It will hail (i.e., rain) on the lower extensions of the fruitful forest, and the city will extend into the valley.

Thus, the land will prosper, and the cities will grow in size.

32 20 Happy will be those who sow on all types of waters and feed their cattle on rich pastures.

Now is described the destruction of the army of Gog.

33 1 Woe to the attacking army of Gog that plunders without cause. As a result the army of Gog will be destroyed and plundered.

33 2 The people of Israel pray that God should have mercy. Let the strength of the enemy be as cattle, ready for the slaughter. Let God be our salvation in the time of trouble.

33 3 The attacking nations will be scattered by the noise and power of God.

33 4 The spoil of the enemy will be gathered as if by locusts; like the rushing of locusts yearning for spoil.

33 5 Then God will be exalted for He filled Zion with justice and righteousness.

33 6 He will be the faith of your times; a hoard of salvation, wisdom and knowledge. The fear of the Lord is His treasure.

33 7 The leaders of the enemy have yelled to signal the beginning of the attack. Messengers who were sent to bring peace between Israel and the enemy cry bitterly.

33 8 The highways are desolate without any users. The enemy has broken the truce agreements. He has despised the cities and the people of Israel.

33 9 The land of Israel mourns. The fertile places of Lebanon, Sharon, Bashan, and Carmel are like a wilderness and are barren.

33 10 God now says, "I will arise and be exalted."

33 11-12 The enemy nations shall be burned as straw.

33 13 God says, "Those who are far off and those who are near, recognize the might of the Lord."

33 14 The sinners in Zion will be afraid, and shall wonder if they will survive the devouring fire of God.

33 15-16 In contrast, the righteous persons will feel secure because of the protection by God.

33 17 The righteous will see their ruler in his glory, ruling over much formerly distant territory.

33 18 You will consider the past terror. What happened to those who counted and weighed the military might of the enemy nations versus that of Israel?

33 19 You will not see the foreign enemy come into Israel, since he will be destroyed.

33 20 You shall see Zion and Jerusalem firmly established.

33 21-22 Jerusalem will be like a place of rivers and streams, over which no enemy ships will pass; because God, who is our judge, lawgiver and king, will save us.

33 23 The enemy ships will not function properly. The spoils of the enemy will then be divided among the people of Israel; even the lame will take spoils.

33 24 The dwellers in Jerusalem will not say they are sick, since they will be pardoned for their sins.

Now is described the defeat of the attacking nations, with special emphasis on the desolation that will occur in Edom. Edom occupied the territory corresponding to the southern half of the modern country of Jordan. It is in the country of Jordan that the army of Gog will congregate to launch the attack on Jerusalem.

34 1 All the nations and the entire world should listen to this prophecy.

34 2-3 God is angry at the attacking nations and their armies. Their soldiers will be killed.

34 4 Their army of the sky (the warplanes) as well as their foot-soldiers will be destroyed.

34 5-7 God will destroy Edom (Jordan) and its city Bozrah (believed to be the modern Busaire, south of the Dead Sea).

34 8 It will be a day of vengeance for the Lord.

34 9-10 The streams of Jordan will be turned into pitch, and its soil into brimstone. The land will be as blazing pitch which shall burn forever.

34 11 The territory of Jordan will be chaotic, inhabited by numerous birds.

34 12 The rulers of Jordan will not provide any leadership.

34 13-15 The country will be inhabited by all types of wild animals and birds, such as jackals, ostriches, and kites.

34 16-17 None of the wild animals and birds specified in the Pentateuch (see e.g., Lev. 11; Deut. 14 3-21) will be missing from the devastated land—and they shall dwell there forever.

After the destruction of the attacking army of Gog, the soil of Israel will become fruitful and the Jews in exile will return to the land.

35 1-2   In contrast to the destruction of the territory of Jordan, the State of Israel will thrive. The deserts will blossom, and the territories of Lebanon, Carmel and Sharon will be very productive (confer **33 9**).

35 3-4   The people in Israel who are afraid will be given confidence, because God will take vengeance from the enemy and will save the Israelites.

35 5-7   Even the blind, deaf, lame and dumb will be as healthy people, because water will be available in the deserts for growth of reeds and rushes.

35 8-9   A sacred highway will be formed for the exiled Jews to safely travel over it to Israel.

35 10   The redeemed Jews will return to Zion with everlasting joy and happiness.

19.6 CHAPTERS 49–66

Chapters 49 through 66 of the Book of Isaiah present numerous prophecies concerning the Messianic era. Here these prophecies are clarified as to the particular times and events being mentioned.

It should be noted that in **49 1-6, 50 4-11**, and **52 13-15** the one who speaks or the one being referred to is denoted as the "servant." In all these cases the "servant" refers to the nation of Israel, as is clearly indicated in **41 8; 44 1, 2, 21; 45 4; 48 20;** and **49 3**.

19.6.1 Chapter 49 1-13

49 1   The exiled people of Israel speak (**49 1-6**): God selected the nation of Israel before it was born, and gave it a name (Jacob) while in the womb (see Gen. **25 26**).

49 2-3   He gave strength to the nation and called it Israel (compare Gen. **32 29**), so it would be a glorious nation.

49 4   We have been exiled, therefore it is as if all the effort and labor have been for nought. Let us have judgment with God to convince Him to carry out his promise to Israel.

49 5   Now God says He will restore the nation of Israel, the country will be honored, and God will be its strength.

49 6   He states that He will accomplish not only the simple task of restoring the nation and bringing back the exiles, but He will also make Israel as a light for the other nations and as an example of the salvation from God.

49 7   The following verses (7-13) are stated by the Prophet Isaiah in the name of God:

The country of Israel which was despised, will become respected by the rulers and princes of other nations.

49 8   Israel will be established as a nation, and the desolate land will be made into inherited portions.

49 9-12   The exiled people from all over the world will return to the land, using well-built highways so they shall not suffer on the way.

49 13   Let the heavens and earth be joyful because God has had compassion for His people.

19.6.2 Chapters 49 14–50 11

49 14   Before the War of Gog Zion will say that the Lord has forsaken her.

49 15–16   God answers that just as a mother does not usually forget her child, He will definitely not forget the Jewish people.

49 17–22   Exiled Jews, hurry and return to Israel, because those enemies who desire to destroy the nation will disappear. The exiles will be as ornaments to the country, and there will be so many returnees that there will be a shortage of space for settlement.

49 23   The leaders of other nations shall respect you. Israel will know that God does not forsake those who have faith in Him.

49 24–26   God will fight the battles of Israel, capture the booty from the strong enemy, and make them drunk from their own blood. Everyone will then know that God has saved Israel from the army of Gog.

50 1   The people of Israel were exiled temporarily because of their sins, but no permanent divorce was given by God.

50 2–3   When God comes to fight against the army of Gog, it is as if there is none in Israel to help in the battle. God will destroy the enemy, dry up the seas and rivers, and make the skies dark at the time when He fights against Gog.

50 4   Israel now responds: God has given me, Israel, an educated tongue with which to speak and an aroused ear with which to hear.

50 5   I have not rebelled nor turned backward.

50 6–8   Even though the enemy nations hit me and pluck my hair, I am not ashamed because God is with me.

50 9   God will help me; and the enemy nations will be consumed as if a garment eaten by moths.

50 10   Who among the enemy nations fears God and listens to Israel, His servant—Israel, who previously walked in darkness. Israel will now rely on the name of God.

50 11   All you enemy nations who attack Israel with fire, be burned with your own flames. This will happen because of my (Israel's) strength. As a result you nations will lie in pain.

19.6.3 Chapter 51 1–11

51 1–2   God is speaking: Those who seek the Lord, remember that the origin of the Jewish people is from Abraham; and he was blessed by God.

51 3   Therefore God will comfort the waste places of Zion, and make the

desert into a Garden of Eden. Happiness, thanksgiving, and song will be found in the land.

51   4   Teaching and judgment will go forth from the Lord to all the nations.

51   5   The might of God will judge the nations, and then they will trust in Him.

51   6   The skies will be darkened with smoke, the ground ruined, and the inhabitants killed, when God saves His people (at the time of the War of Gog).

51   7-8   People of Israel, do not fear the taunts of men because they will be destroyed as a moth destroys a woolen garment. In contrast, the justice and salvation of God will last forever.

51   9-10   The people of Israel request God to show His strength—the strength which destroys monsters, dries up the waters, and makes the depths of the sea for a path over which the redeemed Jews can travel.

51   11   (After the War of Gog) the exiled Jews will return to Israel with gladness and joy.

19.6.4   Chapters 51 12-52 12

In this prophecy is emphasized the conquest of Jerusalem during the War of Gog.

51   12-13   God comforts the Jewish people. Why are you afraid of mortal man (the enemy army of Gog), and have forgotten God who created the world? Where is the fury of the oppressor (now that the enemy army is destroyed)?

51   14   The Jewish exiles will be quickly allowed to return to Israel, and they will not die nor starve.

51   15-16   It is God who has protected Israel, and told Zion that it is His people.

51   17   Awaken Jerusalem, the city which received the anger of God (during the War of Gog).

Compare Zech. 14 2 where it is described how the enemy will initially manage to conquer half the city of Jerusalem.

51   18   There will be no leader of Jerusalem from among the Jewish people reared in the city (when the enemy gains control).

51   19   Twice it will happen that Jerusalem will be conquered. The first time will be during the War of Independence (1948), and the second time during the War of Gog (1973). Who can comfort you for the desolation, destruction, famine, and killing?

51   20   The residents of Jerusalem have been caught as an antelope in a net because of the anger of God.

51   21-22   Therefore God says He will fight for His people. No longer will Jerusalem drink the cup of God's anger.

51   23   Instead the enemy nations who attacked Jerusalem will receive God's anger.

52 1-2 Awaken Jerusalem! Put on your beautiful garments you holy city. Never again will the enemy conquer you.

52 3 You were sold to the enemy but no price was paid, and therefore you will not be redeemed with money (but by military force).

52 4 Originally (at the time of Jacob) My people went down to Egypt, and later Assyria oppressed My people without cause.

52 5 And now (during the War of Gog) what nations are attacking Israel that she is being conquered for nought?

It is here implied that Egypt and Assyria (Iraq) will be among the attacking nations.

The leaders of the enemy are exulting, and they despise God's name.

52 6 The Jewish people will therefore know God's name on that day (when He destroys the army of Gog).

52 7 How wonderful it is to hear the messenger of good tidings announcing peace, salvation, and that God reigns!

52 8 The watchmen will raise their voices in song when they see the return of God to Zion.

52 9 The ruins of Jerusalem shall sing because God has comforted His people and redeemed the city.

52 10 All the nations will see the great victory by God.

52 11 The Jewish exiles shall go out from the devastated enemy nations. They shall not touch any of the impure dead bodies of the enemy. Those who carry the vessels of the Lord (such as Torahs) shall cleanse themselves.

52 12 But they shall not run out hastily. God will lead the way and protect the rear.

19.6.5 Chapters 52 13–53 12

This prophecy describes the fate of the servant—who represents the nation of Israel—after the War of Gog.

52 13 The nation of Israel shall be very wise and great.

52 14-15 Just as other nations were previously appalled at the desolation of Israel, so now nations and their leaders shall be astonished at the unbelievable development of Israel.

53 1 The other nations now speak: Who would have believed what we heard, that the strength of God revealed itself for Israel?

53 2-3 Israel was like a sapling in waterless soil, who suffered from sickness, and was not worthy of consideration.

53 4-9 In reality, the people of Israel did bear the sicknesses, the pains, and the sins of the other nations. Israel was like a lamb led to slaughter and did not speak up. Although there was no violence and deceit among the Jews, they were buried with the criminals.

53 10 The reason for Israel's sufferings was that God desired it. If Israel

recognizes his own guilt then his life will be prolonged, and God will successfully carry out His good intentions through him.

53 11-12   God now states that Israel will be rewarded because of his past afflictions. With his knowledge he will make the other nations righteous, he will be a servant to help the many countries, and will tolerate their iniquities.

To accomplish these tasks, God will give Israel territory among the nations of the world.

19.6.6 Chapter 54 1-17

54   1   The country of Israel with her people in exile is compared to a woman without children. There will be a larger population in the re-established State of Israel than in many other countries whose people have never been exiled.

54   2-3   Israel will extend her territory, inherit the land of other nations, and inhabit formerly desolate cities.

54   4   Israel will forget the shame experienced when her population was in exile.

54   5   These things will happen because God will redeem Israel.

54   6-8   God forsook Israel for a short time. But He will redeem her forever with great mercy.

54   9-10   God has promised to never again be angry and rebuke Israel, just as He promised never again to bring a deluge. The covenant of peace which will be established shall last forever.

54   11-12   God will fill the land of Israel with precious stones; i.e., the land and buildings will be well and artistically constructed.

54   13   The entire population will be well educated in the ways of God, and there will be peace.

54   14   There will be righteousness, no oppression, and no fear.

54   15   Anyone who attacks Israel will be defeated.

54   16-17   Any weapon that is used against Israel will not function, and anyone who speaks against the country will be judged guilty. These are the rewards from God to His servants, the people of Israel.

19.6.7 Chapters 55 1-56 8

55   1-2   If the people listen to God they will have such a large food supply that water, wine, and milk will be available free.

55   3   Listen to God and He will make an everlasting covenant and will provide the faithful mercies of David to the Jewish people.

55   4   Behold, David (the leader of the Jewish nation) will be a witness, leader, and commander to the nations of the world.

55   5   Nations which did not know Israel will be called, or will come by themselves, to learn about Israel, because God has glorified the country.

55 6-9 Now at the time of redemption everyone should seek God. Forsake your sinning ways, and God will pardon you. God's ways are much superior to those of man.

55 10-11 God will carry out His prophecies, just as rain must water the ground.

55 12 The Jewish exiles will with joy return to Israel.

55 13 The land of Israel will change from a place of thorns to one of useful trees. These trees will be an eternal memorial of God's deeds.

56 1 (Before the War of Gog) God says be righteous because the salvation by God will soon occur.

56 2 Happy is the righteous man who observes the Sabbath and does no evil.

56 3-7 Also the converts to Judaism and the eunuchs should observe the laws. Eunuchs who follow the commandments will be rewarded with eternal fame, and converts will joyfully bring sacrifices to the Temple. The Temple will be called a house of prayer for all the nations.

56 8 God will gather back to Israel not only the Jews in exile but also others, such as converts.

19.6.8 Chapters 56 9-57 21

56 9 All the animals of My field come and eat all the animals of the forest.

The animals of My field are the military might of Israel. The animals of the forest represent the army of Gog. Israel is told to destroy the army of Gog.

In verses 56 9 to 57 1 are described the animals of the forest, i.e., the army of Gog.

56 10 Their watchmen are all blind and without knowledge. They are dumb dogs unable to bark and warn the soldiers. They are raving watchmen who love to sleep.

56 11 The dogs, i.e., the leaders of the army of Gog, are greedy and never satiated. They are all interested in their own personal gain.

56 12 The leaders say to each other, "Come let us drink wine and strong drink. Tomorrow we will do the same to an even greater extent."

57 1 The righteous among the army of Gog perish, and no one cares.

57 2 Now the prophet Isaiah states: When peace comes, after the defeat of the army of Gog, the righteous will rest in their beds without any fear.

57 3 The soldiers in the army of Gog are adulterers.

57 4 Against whom are they making sport, these persons of transgression and falsehood.

57 5-10 They commit all types of atrocities, such as killing children, immorality, and bringing false sacrifices.

57 11 The army of Gog has not feared the eternal God.

57 12 Even if God considers all your righteous acts it will not help.

57 13 When you cry for help, your gathered number will not help you. The

entire army of Gog will be carried away by the wind and destroyed. In contrast, Israel who believes in God shall inherit the land and the holy mountain.

57 14   Pave a way and clear a path so that there will be no stumbling block for the Jewish people when returning to Israel from exile.

57 15–16   For God, who dwells on high and yet cares for the humbled Jews in exile, says that He will not be angry forever.

57 17   God was angry because of the sins of the Jews.

57 18–19   God will heal the ways of the Jewish people, comfort them, and give them peace.

57 20–21   However, the wicked will not obtain peace, and will be troubled like the rough seas.

19.6.9   Chapters 58 1–59 21

58 1   Tell the Jewish people their sins.

58 2   Yet the Jewish people act as if they were righteous and did not forsake God; and they desire God's help.

58 3–5   The people complain, "Why do we fast and afflict ourselves, and yet God does not acknowledge our efforts?" The answer is that your fast-days are filled with strife and wickedness, and therefore are not acceptable.

58 6–7   Instead, stop your wickedness, free the oppressed, give food to the hungry, clothe the naked, and do not forsake needy relatives.

58 8–9   Then you will be healed and God will answer your cries.

58 10–12   If you give food to the hungry then your light will shine even in the dark. God will lead you and you shall be like a watered garden. The waste places will be rebuilt and the breaches repaired.

58 13–14   If you observe the Sabbath, then you will delight in the Lord, and will feed in the heritage of Jacob.

59 1   It is not difficult for God to save the Jewish people.

59 2   However your sins remove you from God's help.

59 3–8   You have lied, killed unjustly, and committed all types of iniquities.

59 9–11   Therefore all sorts of troubles have occurred to the Jewish people.

59 12–15   These troubles have come about because we have sinned. God saw our actions and He was displeased.

59 16   God saw that there was no leader who would stop the transgressions. Therefore God's own righteousness and strength were necessary to bring salvation.

59 17–18   God acted as a warrior and punished the enemy (the army of Gog) according to their deeds.

59 19   Peoples in the East and West will fear the name of the Lord, because God will drive away the enemy.

59 20   A redeemer will come to Zion, and unto those Jews who renounce transgression.

The redeemer is the Prophet Eliyah (Elijah) who will arrive shortly before the War of Gog (Mal. 3 23-24).

59 21 This is the covenant that God will make with the Jewish people: "The spirit of God and His teachings will not be removed from the mouths of the Jewish people and their descendants, from now onward and for ever."

19.6.10 Chapter 60 1-22

60 1 Awaken, Israel, because God's light will shine upon you.

60 2 Darkness will cover the enemy nations (at the time of the War of Gog) but the glory of the Lord will shine upon Israel.

60 3 Afterwards other nations and their leaders will walk in the light from Israel.

60 4 The exiled Jews will be gathered back to Israel.

60 5-7 Then the wealth of other nations, including camels, gold, and spice from Sheba (Yemen), sheep of Kedar, and rams of Nebaioth (Arabian countries), will be brought to Israel.

60 8 Many of the exiled Jews will return by airplane to Israel.

60 9 Others will return in strong ships, bringing with them their wealth.

Here is given a clear statement that during the ingathering of the exiles, the Jews will be allowed to bring their possessions, and will not have their property confiscated.

60 10 Foreign workers and their rulers will help in the rebuilding of Israel.

60 11 Day and night the wealth and leaders of other nations will arrive.

60 12 Any nation which will not serve Israel shall perish.

60 13 The great trees of Lebanon will beautify the site of the Temple.

60 14 The children of those who afflicted you will bow down, and they will call Zion the city of God.

60 15 Instead of being forsaken and hated, the Israelites will be the joy of all generations.

60 16 You will obtain supplies from many nations, and shall know that the Lord is the redeemer of Israel.

60 17 You will have superior quality materials, gold instead of copper, silver instead of iron, copper instead of wood, and iron instead of stone. Moreover, in place of punishment you will have peace, and in place of oppression you will have righteousness.

60 18 Violence, destruction, and desolation will disappear from within your boundaries.

60 19-20 God will be a light unto Israel.

60 21 The Jewish people will all be righteous, and shall inherit the land of Israel forever.

60 22 The people of Israel will multiply exceedingly. God will speed the occurrence of these events at the proper time.

19.6.11 Chapters 61 1–62 12

Described here are the benefits to Israel occurring after the War of Gog.

61   1–3   Isaiah was appointed to bring good news: to proclaim freedom for the exiles to return; to announce the day of vengeance of God; to inform the mourners of Zion concerning their coming happiness.

61   4   The Jewish people will rebuild the desolate places.

61   5   People from other countries will assist Israel in her agricultural tasks.

61   6–7   The people of Israel will be considered as the priests of God. They will receive the wealth of the nations, and achieve everlasting joy.

61   8–9   God will make an everlasting covenant with the Jewish people. They will be recognized as the offspring blessed by the Lord.

61   10   The Prophet Isaiah is joyful because he brings good news to the Jewish nation.

61   11   Just as the earth brings forth her produce, so God will cause righteousness and praise to spring forth before all the nations.

62   1   The Prophet Isaiah now says that he will not stop his activities until the salvation of Jerusalem goes forth as a bright light.

62   2–4   Jerusalem will then be called "desirous," and the land of Israel will be called "espoused."

62   5   Just as a young man enthusiastically marries a virgin, so the Jewish people will take possession of Israel.

62   6–7   God watches over Jerusalem so that the city shall become praiseworthy.

62   8–9   God swears that never again will the grain and wine of Jerusalem be given over to the enemy. Those who gathered the agricultural produce will be the ones to use it.

62   10–12   Prepare the highway for the returning exiles to return to the land. Jerusalem will then be called "desirous," a city not forsaken; and the returnees will be called "the holy people."

19.6.12 Chapter 63 1–6

Here is described the destruction of Edom (Jordan) during the War of Gog.

63   1   An oratorical question is posed: Who comes from Edom (Jordan) proudly, but with stained clothes? God answers: I, the one who speaks righteously, and acts victoriously.

63   2   Another oratorical question: Why are your clothes red?

63   3   God answers: I (representing the State of Israel), without assistance from any other nation, have trampled the people of Edom in My anger, and their blood has stained My clothes.

63   4   For the day of vengeance of the Lord, and the year of redemption, have come.

63 5   And God saw that there was no nation to help Israel (in the fight against the army of Gog). Therefore, My own strength and anger saved Me (i.e., God represented the nation of Israel).

63 6   God trampled the enemy nations, and poured out their life-blood on the ground.

19.6.13   Chapters 63 7–65 25

Described here is the prayer of Israel before the time of redemption, followed by the answer from God stating that redemption is near.

63 7–9   Israel prays to God: God was good to the Israelites, and He selected them as His people. He saved them from all types of adversity.

63 10   However, the Jewish people rebelled against Him, and God then became their enemy.

63 11–14   Then God remembered Moses and His people. The suffering Jews ask: Where is God who performed many miracles for the Jewish people in the past?

63 15   The people now pray to God. God look down from the heavens. Where is Your zeal and where are Your mighty acts?

63 16   You, our God, are our father. Abraham and Israel are historical persons who have never met us; but you God are our redeemer forever.

63 17   Why do You make us err from Your ways? God return to us.

63 18   Our enemies may soon destroy the Jewish people, and they have already destroyed the Temple (in past history).

63 19–64 2   It is as if you, God, never ruled over us. If You wanted, You could make mountains melt and nations tremble.

64 3   No one has ever seen any false god perform the miracles You have done for the Jewish people.

64 4   You have punished those that act righteously. As a result we have sinned. Upon these same people You could build the world, and then we would be saved.

64 5   We were as unclean people, and we withered from our sins.

64 6   None called upon God because You hid from us, and we were consumed by our sins.

64 7–8   Now God do not be angry forever. Look, we all are Your people.

64 9   The holy cities, Zion and Jerusalem have become deserts and desolate.

64 10   The Temple was burned, and all our prized possessions have been laid waste.

64 11   After all this, will God continue to hold Himself back from helping us, and continue to afflict us?

65 1   God now answers the prayer of Israel. I was available to help, but the people did not seek Me.

65 2–4   The Jewish people rebelled and went in evil ways. They angered

Me and brought illegal sacrifices. They sit among the graves and eat pig's meat.

65 5 They say, "Do not come near me. I am holier than you." These actions make Me exceedingly angry.

65 6-7 I will not rest until I have punished them for their sins and those of their ancestors.

65 8 However, just as the poor quality grapes are preserved for the little wine within, so I will not destroy the entire Jewish people because of the few who are righteous.

65 9 I will take from the Jewish people those who shall inherit My mountains and shall dwell within the land of Israel.

In 1862, Zevi Hirsch Kalischer and Moses Hess each wrote a book advocating the colonizing of Palestine to initiate the establishment of a Jewish state.[3] These publications eventually led to the formation of colonies, starting with the agricultural school Mikveh Yisrael in 1870.

65 10 And the Sharon shall be a place for sheep, and the Valley of Achor a place for herds, for My people that have sought Me.

In 1890 the agricultural settlement of Hadera was established in the northern Sharon Plain. Later, after World War I, the entire land in the Sharon region became available for further Jewish settlement. This region soon became the most densely settled Jewish area in Palestine.[4]

The first modern agricultural settlement in Palestine was Petah Tikvah,[5] founded in 1878. The origin of the settlement goes back to 1872, when a group of Jerusalem Jews attempted to buy land in the Valley of Achor, based on the statement in Hos. 2 17 "Petah Tikvah from the Valley of Achor."

The text here emphasizes that these early settlements in Palestine will be established by those Jews who seek God.

65 11-12 But those who have forsaken God and the holy mountain (Zion), and have depended on fate, will be slaughtered; because God called and you did not listen, and you chose that which God did not want.

Beginning with the writings of Kalischer, the call back to Zion slowly developed and gained momentum. Eventually Theodor Herzl brought about the formation of the Zionist movement with the convening in 1897 of the First Zionist Congress. However, many Jews strongly opposed the call of Zion. Numerous Orthodox Jews believed that the restoration of the nation had to be accomplished miraculously by the Messiah. At the other extreme were the assimilationists, who were convinced that there was no longer any purpose in the revival of a Jewish nation.[6] Unfortunately, as history well attests, six million of those Jews who remained in Europe and did not emigrate to Israel were slaughtered during World War II.

65 13-15 Therefore God says: My servants (the ones who settled in Israel) shall eat, drink and be happy; but those who forsook the call to Zion shall starve, scream, and be killed.

65 16-17 Those who bless and swear by the land of Israel will bless and swear

by the true God. All former troubles will be forgotten with the development of the State of Israel.

65 18-19 God will make Jerusalem into a happy city (after the War of Gog), and there will no longer be heard within the city sounds of crying and weeping.

65 20 People will live to more than 100 years of age, and only the foolish and sinners will die at 100.

65 21 The Jewish people will erect buildings, plant vineyards, and eat the fruit thereof.

65 22 The Jewish nation shall last as long as the lifetime of a tree, which has the potential to live forever.

65 23 The people will not labor in vain, and they shall have blessed children.

65 24 Before they can express their needs, God will answer.

65 25 Warring nations, symbolized by animals such as the wolf, lion, and snake, will not attack Israel and will not cause destruction on the holy mountain.

19.6.14 Chapter 66 1-24

66 1 God says: I fill the skies and earth. Where is there a house suitable for Me?

66 2 The entire world was created by God at His verbal command. In spite of His greatness He listens to the poor and the God-fearing.

66 3 However, those who bring sacrifices and also commit crimes—for example, those who offer an ox as a sacrifice and also commit murder—have chosen disgusting practices.

66 4 Therefore, God will punish the evil-doers according to their actions.

66 5 Listen to the message of the Lord you who fear Him. Your sinning brethren, who hate you the righteous, say "God will be glorified because of me (the sinner), and then we sinners will see how happy you righteous people will be." The truth however is that they, the sinners, shall be ashamed.

66 6 At the time of the War of Gog, God will punish His enemies.

66 7-8 Afterwards, the territory of Israel will be quickly repopulated, much quicker than would be expected because of the natural increase by giving birth.

66 9 The reason for this rapid increase is that God desires it. Would God arrange for the territory belonging to Israel to be returned without providing for the population to fill it?

66 10-11 Rejoice with Jerusalem, all those who love the city and have mourned over her desolation. As a result you will derive pleasure from the glory of Jerusalem.

66 12-13 God will supply peace and the respect of nations to the city; and the people will be comforted in Jerusalem.

66 14 You will see the happenings and will be happy. The strength of God will be known to His adherents, and His anger will be vented against His enemies.

COMMENTARY ON MESSIANIC CHAPTERS OF ISAIAH

66 15-17 God will fight against the army of Gog with fire and sword (guns). Many will be the slain of the enemy.

66 18 God will direct the actions and thoughts of all the nations (in the army of Gog) to come and see the glory of God (when He destroys them).

66 19 The survivors from the enemy will be sent as a sign of God's glory back to their nations—to such countries as Tarshish, Pul, Lud, Moshchei Keshet, Tubal, and Javan.

The actual countries referred to are not clear in each case. However, Magog is known to consist of Meshech and Tubal (Ez. 38 2), and Javan corresponds to modern Greece.

66 20 Afterwards, the Jews in exile among all the nations will be sent back to Israel and the holy mountain by means of all types of transportation vehicles; just as the Jews in Israel will bring their offerings in all types of pure vessels.

66 21 God will select priests and Levites not only from the Jews residing in Israel but also from the returning Jewish exiles.

66 22 Just as God will make a new heaven and earth in the land of Israel, so the Jewish people and their fame will survive.

After the War of Gog the contour of the land and mountains will be changed (see Zech. 14 10), and it will therefore be as if a new heaven and earth will be made.

66 23 Subsequently, on every Sabbath and New Moon, people from all the nations will come to worship before God.

66 24 And they will go forth and see the graves of the soldiers of the army of Gog, located in the Valley of Hinnom; for the hideousness of the acts of the army of Gog will remain in history, and it shall be an abhorrence to all people.

19.7 MESSIANIC PREDICTIONS DERIVED FROM BOOK OF ISAIAH

Here will be emphasized only those prophecies of Isaiah concerning the Messianic era which supplement the information already derived from the Books of Ezekiel and the Twelve Prophets. Although there are numerous prophecies in Isaiah concerning the Messianic era, very few of them have sufficient details to supply information additional to those given by Ezekiel and the Twelve Prophets. As a result only very few new points are here described.

The early colonizing of Palestine, beginning in the 1870s, is predicted in the Book of Isaiah (65 9-10). Such key colonies as Hadera and Petah Tikvah will be established before 1900. Those European Jews who do not respond in a positive manner to the call to resettle Palestine will be slaughtered during World War II (65 11-12). In contrast, those Jews who settle in Palestine will thrive and succeed (65 13-15). This prophecy in Isaiah explains the true reason for the death of six million Jews during World War II. It was because of the sin of the people in refusing to return to the land of Israel.

Before the War of Gog the harvest will fail in the land of Israel (**27** 11; **32** 10; **33** 9).

The battle during the War of Gog will result in the destruction of the Suez Canal, and the separation of the Euphrates River into seven wadis (**11** 15).

After the War of Gog, a highway will be constructed from Assyria (Iraq) leading to Israel and to Egypt (**11** 16; **19** 23; **35** 8–9). The three countries, Israel, Egypt, and Assyria (Iraq) will cooperate with each other (**19** 24–25). There will be five cities in Egypt that will speak Hebrew and swear allegiance to God (**19** 18), and there will be in Egypt an altar to the Lord (**19** 19).

Subsequent to the War of Gog much wealth from the nations of the world will be given to Israel (**60** 5–7). People from all the nations will come to worship before God (**66** 23). People will eventually all live to ages over 100 years; and only the foolish and the sinners will die at as young an age as 100 (**65** 20).

Chapter Twenty

MESSIANIC PASSAGES IN JEREMIAH AND THE PENTATEUCH

Thus far we have interpreted the Messianic passages found in the Books of Daniel, Ezekiel, the Twelve Prophets, and Isaiah. Remaining to be explained are the predictions found in Jeremiah and the Pentateuch. In actuality, only a very few Messianic passages are found in either of these works, and for convenience these books are here considered in the same chapter.

20.1 COMMENTARY ON MESSIANIC CHAPTERS OF JEREMIAH

Most of the redemption prophecies in the Book of Jeremiah refer to events involving the restoration of the Jewish nation after the Babylonian Exile. Only a few prophecies clearly refer to the Messianic era to any significant extent. These Messianic passages are Jer. **30** 4–**31** 39; **48** 47; and **49** 2, 7–22, 39.

20.1.1   Chapters 30 4–31 39

30   4   These are the words that the Lord spoke concerning Israel and Judah.
30   5   For thus says God: We have heard the sound of trembling; of fear and not of peace.
 The fear is that of the people of Israel prior to the attack by the army of Gog.
30   6   The men are in such pain that it is comparable to their enduring the pangs of childbirth. Every face has turned pale.
30   7   The War of Gog will be a great and unparalleled day of trouble for Israel; but Israel will be saved.
30   8   At that time God will break the yoke of the enemy off of Israel's neck, and no longer will foreign nations dominate Israel.
30   9   The Jewish people will serve God, and their ruler David.
30   10   Israel do not be afraid, because God will save your people from the distant countries where they are captive, and then there will be peace.
30   11   God is with the Jewish people to save them. He will destroy the nations to which the Jews have been exiled; but the Jewish people shall survive, even though they shall be punished.
30   12–15   Thus says God: You Israel are severely punished because of your sins.

30 16-17 However, all those who afflict you will themselves be punished, but Israel will be healed from her wounds; because those who afflict you have claimed that there is none who cares for Zion.

30 18 God will restore the settlement of Israel, reconstruct the buildings, and rebuild the cities.

30 19 Thanksgiving and happiness will come from these places, and the population will increase.

30 20-21 The people will be firmly established as in ancient times, the leaders will be from their midst, and all who oppress the nation will be punished.

30 22 The people will be faithful to the Lord, and He will be their God.

30 23 The fury of God shall descend upon the wicked.

30 24 The anger of God shall not be quieted until he carries out His plans, at the end of the six years (i.e., in 1973).

The six years refers to the time between the Six-Day War in 1967 and the War of Gog in 1973.

30 25 At that time God will be recognized by all the families of Israel, and they will be His people.

31 1 Thus says the Lord: The Jewish people who are remnants from the sword (the persecution of the enemy) have found the favor of God in the land of Israel, which is like a desert. God will calm the people of Israel.

This sentence refers to the early colonizing of the land of Israel in the 1870s, at the time when the country was like a desert.

31 2 God will appear to the Jewish people when they are in exile far away from the land, and He will love them and draw them to Israel with kindness.

31 3 Once again God will build the land, and the people will be happy.

31 4 Again vineyards will be planted on the mountains of Samaria, and the fruit will become suitable for eating in the fifth year after planting (compare Lev. 19 23-25).

Control of the mountains of Samaria was achieved by Israel only after the Six-Day War in June 1967.[1]

31 5 There will be the day when the watchmen shall call to Mount Ephraim: Let us go up to Zion, to the Lord our God.

31 6 For thus says the Lord: Be happy Israel, for God has saved the remnant of the Jewish people.

31 7 God will gather the exiles back to Israel from distant lands, including the blind, lame, pregnant, and recent mothers. A large group shall return to Israel.

31 8 They will come with tears of joy, and praying to God. God will lead them in a straight path to sources of water.

31 9 Listen to the word of the Lord you nations, and tell in distant places that God gathers the scattered Jewish people to Israel, and cares for them.

31 10 For God has redeemed the Jewish people from a much greater military power (namely the army of Gog).

31 11 The returning exiles will come to the goodness of the land, to items such as grain, wine, oil, sheep, and cattle. They will no longer be troubled.

31 12 The young and old will be happy, and forget their sorrows.

31 13 The priests will be satiated with their portions of the sacrifices; and the people will be satisfied with the goodness of the land.

31 14 These are the words of the Lord: In Ramah (near Jerusalem) is heard the bitter cry of Rachel, the ancestress of a section of the Jewish people (especially Ephraim), crying for her children because they are not in the land of Israel.

31 15–16 So says the Lord: Do not cry, because the exiled Jews will return to Israel from the enemy countries.

31 17–18 Ephraim, representing the people of Israel, now states that he has been punished, is repentant, and wants to return to God.

31 19 God answers: Ephraim is a darling son if he wants to be a delight to Me (i.e., to follow in the righteous path). Whenever I speak of him, My heart yearns for him; I will surely have compassion upon him.

31 20 You Jewish exiles, set up markers to denote the road back to the cities of Israel.

31 21 How long will you foolish girl (the people of Israel) be indecisive. God will cause you to change from a weak girl to a powerful man (i.e., from a poor people to a powerful nation).

31 22 So says God: Again it will be said in the land of Judah and its cities, when their settlement is re-established, "God bless this place of righteousness, the holy mountain."

31 23 The land of Judah will be settled with farmers who will travel with their flocks.

31 24 For God has satisfied the weary and troubled souls.

31 25 The prophet states: I awoke and my sleep was a pleasant one (since I received a comforting message).

31 26–27 The time will come when Israel will be filled with people and cattle; and the people will build and plant with diligence.

31 28–29 At that time each man shall die not for his parents' sins, but only for his own.

During the period of exile, Jews often died for their parents' sins, since the people suffered the effects of exile because of the transgressions of their ancestors.

31 30–32 God will make a new covenant with the people of Israel, wherein the teachings of the Lord will be accepted; He will be their God and they will be His people.

31 33 Everyone, young and old, will believe in God; and the sins of the people will be forgiven and forgotten.

31 34–36 God, who makes the world function for ever, promises that the Jewish people will remain His nation for ever.

31 37–38 The time will come when the old city of Jerusalem will be built from

the Tower of Hananel in the northeast, to the Gate of the Corner in the northwest, to the Hill of Gareb in the southwest, to Goah in the southeast.

The locations of all these places are not exactly known. Compare Zech. **14 10** where the Gate of the Corner and the Tower of Hananel are mentioned as forming some of the boundaries of Jerusalem, after the city is raised in height during the War of Gog. Also compare Ez. **42 15-20** (Section 17.3.2) where the lengths of the four boundaries of Jerusalem will each be 3,000 cubits, somewhat larger than at present. All these prophecies indicate that some changes will occur in the boundaries of the old city of Jerusalem after the War of Gog.

31 39 Included in the city of Jerusalem will be the Valley of the Dead Bodies, and of the Ashes, and all the fields until the Brook of Kidron, until the corner of the Horse Gate toward the east. These places shall be holy to the Lord and shall never again be destroyed.

Implied here is that some, if not all, of these locations will be destroyed during the War of Gog.

20.1.2 Prophecies by Jeremiah Against the Nations

Several prophecies in the Book of Jeremiah are concerned with events to happen in Messianic times to the nations of Moab (**48 47**), Ammon (**49 1-6**), Edom (**49 7-22**), and Elam (**49 39**). The respective passages refer not to the actual ancient nations but to the territory that these countries once occupied.

20.1.2.1 Prophecy to Moab

Chapter 48 of Jeremiah describes how the land of Moab will be destroyed and its inhabitants sent into captivity. The passage concludes with the statement (**48 47**) that God will re-establish the settlement of Moab at the end of the six year period (באחרית הימים). What is meant is that Israel will acquire the territory of Moab (the middle part of Jordan) after the War of Gog (1973), and will develop the land and form settlements therein.

20.1.2.2 Prophecy to the Children of Ammon

The Children of Ammon occupied the territory which is now the northern part of Jordan. The prophecy in Jer. **49 1-6** mainly refers to Jordan, especially from Verses 2 to 6.

49 1 Thus says the Lord to the Children of Ammon: Does Israel have no sons, to be heirs and repossess the land? Why then have the Children of Ammon inherited the land occupied by the tribe of Gad?

49 2 Therefore the time will come (during the War of Gog) when Rabbah (the city of Amman, capital of Jordan) will become a desolate mound, and its villages shall be burned with fire. Then Israel will inherit the territory which was previously inherited by the Jordanians.

49 3 Wail and mourn you inhabitants of Rabbah, because the leaders of Jordan shall go into exile.

49 4 Why do you boast in the valleys you wayward people, you who trust in your arsenals and say "Who shall dare attack me?"

49 5 Behold God will bring fear upon you from every side, and you will be driven out in every direction.

49 6 Afterwards God will re-establish the settlement (of the Jews) in the territory of the Children of Ammon.

20.1.2.3 Prophecy to Edom

The similarity of many of the sentences of Jer. 49 7–22 to those in Obadiah, indicates that Jeremiah's prophecy to Edom refers to the Messianic era. Here Edom refers to Jordan in general, and in particular to the southern half of Jordan.

49 7 Thus says the Lord to Edom: Is there no longer any wisdom in Teman (a district in Edom), i.e., in Jordan?

49 8 Flee you inhabitants of Dedan because Esau (i.e., Jordan) will be severely punished.

Dedan is a country south of Jordan, possibly modern Aden (see Section 17.1).

49 9 Grape gatherers leave some grapes behind. Thieves leave behind what they do not need.

49 10 But God will make Esau bare, and all its people will be destroyed.

49 11 Only the orphans and widows will remain alive, and they shall believe in God.

49 12 For thus says the Lord: Other nations, among the army of Gog, who are not very guilty, shall drink of the cup of God's anger. Surely Edom, which is very guilty, shall also drink of the cup, and be destroyed.

49 13 For Bozrah (the modern Busaire, 20 miles southeast of the Dead Sea), and all the cities of Edom shall be completely destroyed forever.

49 14 The Jordanians claim that they have received a message from God to rise up in battle against Israel, and this message has been sent to the nations.

49 15 However, Jordan is one of the poorest and despised nations.

49 16 Your pride has deceived you. Even if you were in a high and fortified place, God would lower you down.

49 17–18 Edom (the southern half of Jordan) will be so completely destroyed that no person will be able to live there.

49 19 Behold, Israel will fight against Edom, as a lion comes from the Jordan River against good pastures. For I, God, will quiet the military might of Edom, and make Israel escape from Edom's fury. I will appoint select soldiers against Edom; for who can fight against Me.

49 20   The young sheep (i.e., Israel) will be the ones to destroy the land of Edom.

49 21   The earth will tremble at the destruction. The noise will be heard in the Red Sea.

49 22   Israel will come against Edom and Bozrah like a vulture. At that time the strong ones of Edom will be afraid like a woman during childbirth.

20.1.2.4   Prophecy to Elam

In Jer. **49 34–38** it is prophesied how the country of Elam will be destroyed and its people exiled. Then in Jer. **49 39** it is stated that at the end of the six years (i.e., in 1973) the settlement of Elam will be re-established. Since Elam was situated east of Babylon past the Tigris River, outside the theoretical Biblical boundaries for the State of Israel, it is unlikely that settlement of Elam by Israel is meant. Possibly a new country will be formed after the War of Gog, in the area formerly occupied by Elam.

20.2   MESSIANIC PASSAGES IN THE PENTATEUCH

A number of passages in the Books of Leviticus, Numbers, and Deuteronomy supply information concerning the Messianic era. The most remarkable aspect of these prophecies is that many of them, even before the initial establishment of the Jewish nation in the land at the time of Joshua, predict events relative to the permanent settlement of the Jews in Israel after a long period in exile.

20.2.1   Leviticus 26 44–45

In Leviticus **26 14–43** are described the dire consequences that will happen if the Israelites do not observe the Biblical laws. Not only will they suffer from disease and hunger, but they will be defeated by the enemy and sent into exile. However, God promises (Lev. **26 44–45**) that when the Israelites are in exile in the land of their enemies, He will not reject them to break the covenant with them. He will still remember the covenant to be their God, made with the Israelites at the time of the Exodus from Egypt.

20.2.2   Numbers 24 14–19

Among the statements made by Balaam is one which predicts what will happen to Moab and Edom at the time of the War of Gog.

24 14   Balaam tells Balak, King of Moab, what the Israelites will do to the territory of Moab (the middle part of Jordan) at the end of the six years, i.e., in 1973 during the War of Gog.

24 15–16   The prophecy is spoken by Balaam who receives messages from God.

24 17   The described events will happen in the distant future, i.e., in 1973. A star (a missile) shall travel from Jacob, and a comet (שבט) shall rise out of Israel, to destroy the ends of Moab. All the descendants of Seth (i.e., all the people of the world) will tremble in fear.

24 18   Also Edom (the southern part of Jordan), the enemy of Israel, shall become a possession of Israel.

24 19   And (a missile) shall come down from Jacob and destroy the remnant from the cities of Edom.

20.2.3   Deuteronomy 4 25-31

Moses speaks to the Israelites and warns them that when they do not observe the Biblical regulations they will be exiled from the land of Israel (4 25-28). Eventually they will seek out God with all their hearts, and they will find Him (4 29). These events will have happened by the time of the end of the six years (1973). The Jewish people will then be in distress (at the time of the War of Gog) and will return to God and observe His commandments (4 30). God will have mercy on His people and not forsake nor destroy them; neither will He forget the covenant made with their forefathers.

20.2.4   Deuteronomy 30 1-10

Moses, in concluding his lecture to the Jewish people, tells them:

30   1   When it happens that both the blessings and curses, which are specified in the Bible (Deut. 28 1-68), have occurred; then consider it in your heart, in whichever countries of exile you may dwell.

30   2   Return to God and observe His laws with all your soul.

30   3-4   Then God will re-establish your settlement, and gather the Jewish people back to Israel from all the countries to which they have been scattered.

30   5-6   God will bring you prosperity and make you more numerous than your forefathers were; and He will open your hearts to love God with all your soul.

30   7   All the curses specified in the Bible will be inflicted on your enemies and persecutors.

30   8   The Jewish nation will then observe all the Biblical commandments.

30   9-10   As a result God will reward you with excellent children, cattle, and agricultural produce; and He will rejoice over your success as He rejoiced over the success of your forefathers.

20.2.5   Deuteronomy 31 29

Moses mentions to the Levites that he knows that after his death the Israelites will turn away from the laws of God. Then at the end of the six years (1973) evil will call upon (threaten) the Jewish people (with the approach of the War of Gog) because the people have angered God by their evil ways (Deut. 31 29).

20.2.6   Deuteronomy 32 34-43

Moses teaches the Jewish people a special song (האזינו) which will serve as a witness to the evil actions that the people will perform (Deut. 31 19-22). Near the end of the song are references to the destruction of the army of Gog, when God will relent over punishing the Jewish people.

32 34-36   God will (at the time of the War of Gog) take vengeance against the enemies of Israel, because He will have compassion for the Jewish people.

32 37-38   The enemy will say of Israel: Where is their God in whom they trust; to whom they offer sacrifices? Let Him rise up and help you; let Him be your protection!

32 39-40   God will then speak up: See now, that I am the true God, and there is no one who can be saved from My might.

32 41-42   I will take vengeance from My adversaries. My arrows and sword will become drunk with the blood of the slain enemy (of the army of Gog).

32 43   Nations of the world rejoice with the Jewish people, because God will avenge the blood of His servants, and take vengeance on His adversaries; and the land of Israel will be appeased for the blood that was shed of the Jewish people.

Chapter Twenty-One

DETAILED PICTURE OF THE MESSIANIC ERA

By the Messianic era is here meant that period of time beginning after 1860 C.E. during which will occur such events as the permanent establishment of the State of Israel, the building of the Third Temple, and the attainment of peace throughout the world. Many predicted events of the Messianic era have already occurred, and these events show the correctness of the corresponding Biblical prophetic passages. However, the majority of the Messianic predictions have yet to be fulfilled. When these predictions will happen, then the reality of Biblical prophecy will be confirmed. No skepticism will then remain that God has, in numerous instances, revealed future happenings through His prophets.

In this chapter will be presented a summary of those Messianic events described in the previously interpreted passages. It should be realized that the resultant picture is dependent on the manner of interpretation of the passages. A modified picture could result if variant explanations were used. Needless to say there are undoubtedly imperfections—hopefully minor ones—in the Messianic picture to be presented. Therefore if not every prediction to be given here turns out exactly as stated, it does not invalidate the conclusion that prophecy exists. All that can be inferred is that errors in interpretation have been made.

The author feels that there is a high likelihood that most of the details and dates are reasonably correct, and that future events will turn out as predicted. Should this not happen, then a reinterpretation of the relevant passages will be necessary.

One underlying prediction that is found in numerous places in the Bible involves the fact that the Jewish people will sin and God will punish them. As a result the Jewish people will be exiled and they will suffer greatly. Nonetheless, God will not utterly destroy His people. Eventually the State of Israel will be re-established and the Jews will be gathered back to the land. (See e.g., Lev. **26** 44; Deut. **4** 25–31; **32** 26–27; Jer. **30** 11; **46** 28; Amos **9** 8.)

21.1 EARLY EVENTS LEADING TO ESTABLISHMENT OF THE STATE OF ISRAEL

During the long period of exile of the Jewish people, the land of Israel will become like a desert. Then in 1862 the call will arise for the Jews to return to Palestine. The colony of Petah Tikvah will be established in 1878, and colonies will be founded in the Sharon plain, beginning in 1890 with the formation of the colony of Hadera. Vineyards will be grown in the early colonies (Isa. 65 9–10; Hos. 2 16–17; Jer. 31 1). Those European Jews who sin by not responding in a positive manner to the call for resettlement of Palestine will be slaughtered during World War II, while those who settle in the land of Israel will thrive and succeed (Isa. 65 11–15).

Kaiser Wilhelm II of Germany will have peculiar concepts of God, and will consider himself above God. The Kaiser will be one of the initiators of World War I in 1914. Germany and Austria-Hungary will begin fighting against England, Russia, Serbia, Belgium, and other countries. Turkey will be an ally of Germany, and will be in control of the territory of Palestine. During World War I the territory of modern Jordan (Edom, Moab, and Ammon) will slowly escape from Turkish domination (Dan. 11 36–41).

The beginning of the removal of Moslem domination over Palestine will occur in 1916 (Dan. 7 18,25). The Turkish empire (Hadrach), which includes the cities of Damascus, Tyre, Sidon, Homs, Ashkelon, Gaza, Ekron, and Ashdod, will be conquered by England during World War I. On November 9, 1917 the Balfour Declaration will be proclaimed by England favoring the establishment in Palestine of a national home for the Jewish people (Zech. 9 1–7). Subsequently the Turkish empire will be broken up into many small countries (Dan. 2 41–42).

The period between 1914 and 1939 will be a time of worldwide troubles, greater than any that ever occurred since the formation of nations. However, the Jewish people will escape from excessive persecution. At that time, many new countries will be formed in Europe. The nations of Germany and Italy will become the disgust of the entire world because they will, in 1939, initiate World War II and commit many atrocities (Dan. 12 1–2).

During World War II Germany will invade Poland, Denmark, Norway, the Netherlands, Belgium, Luxemburg, and France. Similarly, Italy, the ally of Germany, will invade Egypt, Libya, and Ethiopia. During the war Germany will exterminate millions of persons, including six million European Jews. Eventually the Italians will be defeated in Sicily, and then Germany will fight alone until defeated in 1945 (Dan. 11 42–45).

During World War II the armies of Germany and England will oppose each other from opposite sides of the Nile River in Egypt. When these two countries, each in its own way, stop crushing the Jewish people, then the State of Israel will be established (Dan. 12 5–7,13).

The United Nations will be founded in 1945. It will be as a result of a decision of the United Nations, calling for the partition of Palestine, that the State of Israel will be formed on May 14, 1948 (Dan. 12 3,10–12).

In 1948, English troops will leave Palestine, and Arab forces will attack the newly formed nation of Israel. During this War of Independence the old city of Jerusalem will come under control of Jordan. At the end of the fighting, armistice agreements will be signed under the direction of the United Nations. Desolate places, known as "no-man's-land" will be designated at the boundaries of Israel. The armistice agreement will last, in one form or another, for 49 years until 1996. During Jordanian control over Jerusalem the holy places will be destroyed. Abdullah, the leader of Transjordan at the time of establishment of Israel, will be assassinated (Dan. 9 26–27).

The State of Israel will be a united country, and will not be divided into two or more parts as was the case during the period of the kings (Isa. 11 13; Ez. 37 15–22).

21.2 THE SITUATION PRIOR TO THE WAR OF GOG

In 1973, prior to the War of Gog, a number of important events will happen. The Prophet Eliyah (Elijah) will appear, David will become ruler of Israel, and the War of Gog will be imminent.

Before the great and terrifying day during the War of Gog, when God will take vengeance on His enemies, there will arrive in Israel a prophet having the name Eliyah. This person should not be confused with the Prophet Eliyahu of the Book of Kings, who died over 2,800 years ago. Eliyah will go to a building reserved for his use, and will re-establish the covenant between God and Israel. He will turn the hearts of the traditional parents to the modern technology taught the children, and will turn the hearts of the non-believing children to the belief in God of their ancestors. Eliyah will initiate the selection and purification of the priests and Levites, so that sacrifices can be offered once again. Moreover, the giving of tithes and *terumah* will be begun. The importance of observing the laws of the Pentateuch will be impressed on the Jewish people. Nonetheless, not everyone in Israel will return to the belief in God. Many non-believers will subsequently be punished during the War of Gog. (Compare Mal. 3 1–24; Isa. 59 20–21; Jer. 31 30–33. Also see Joel 1 9,13; 2 17; and Ez. 43 18–27 from which it can be derived that sacrifices will be offered before the War of Gog. Moreover, it is implied in Dan 7 13 that the Jews will become religious before the War of Gog.)

The Jewish people will be ruled by a leader named David, who will forever be the example of the ideal ruler. He will be righteous, and will speak peace to the nations. David will judge fairly, and yet rule with a mighty hand (Isa. 11 1–5; 32 1–8; 55 3–4; Jer. 30 9; Ez. 34 23–24; 37 24–25; Hos. 3 5; Amos 9 11; Mic. 5 1–3; Zech. 9 9; 12 7–12). From Amos 9 11–12; Isa. 32 1–15; and Mic. 5 1–3 it is clear that David will begin ruling prior to the War of Gog. The Biblical references to the ruler David have frequently been misinterpreted as referring to a descendant of King David, the son of Jesse, but this is not stated in the Bible. Instead the Messianic passages clearly state that someone with the name David will be the ruler. It should be noted that the ancient promise by God to King David that subsequent kings would be from his descendants, was conditional on their observance of the Biblical commandments (II Kings 2 4). Since many descendants of King David did not follow in the correct path, that promise by God no longer holds.

Before the War of Gog, when the threat from the enemy will be apparent, the people of Israel, especially the sinners, will show signs of fear (Isa. 51 12–13; Jer. 30 5–7; Mic. 4 9–10). The land of Israel will appear deserted and the harvest will fail (Isa. 27 11; 32 10–14; 33 9; Joel 1 11–14).

Prior to the War of Gog, there will be internal dissent in Egypt, and the Egyptians will be led by a cruel ruler. Many of the waters of Egypt will either dry up or become contaminated. Crops near these waters will fail, the fishing industry will suffer, and all types of industry will be unsuccessful (Isa. 19 1–10).

21.3 THE WAR OF GOG

Before proceeding with a description of the War of Gog, let us first establish the date of the war as closely as possible. Based on the phrase "the last part of the six years" (אחרית הימים), as explained in section 18.4.1, we learn that the War of Gog will occur sometime between April 3, 1973 and March 24, 1974. The six year period refers to the time from the Six-Day War (June 5–10, 1967), when Israel gained control of the Temple Mount, until the year of the War of Gog, when the Temple Mount becomes the rightful possession of Israel. The year 1967 is not included in the calculation since the Six-Day War occurred after Nisan.

The War of Gog will begin with an attack on Israel by one of the largest armies ever amassed. Gog, the name of the leader of the federated Arab countries surrounding Israel, will be joined in the attack by most of the countries of Asia, and many of the nations of Europe and North Africa. The attacking countries will probably include the modern nations of Egypt, Jordan, Lebanon, Syria, Saudi Arabia, Iraq, Iran, Ethiopia, Sudan, Turkey, and Greece. Also included will be China and her associated countries, such as North Korea, Mongolia, and North Vietnam; and Russia and its satellites, such as Poland, Rumania, Bulgaria, Yugoslavia, Hungary, Czechoslovakia, and East Germany. It will be almost as if all the nations of the world were attacking Israel, and no country coming to Israel's defence (Ez. 38 2–16; Joel 2 2–10; 4 2,9–11; Mic. 4 11). The enemy will come well-armed with planes, cars, guns, and tanks (Ez. 38 4). However, the leaders of the army will be ignorant, callous, and deceitful (Isa. 56 9–57 13; Zech. 11 4–17).

The people of Israel will declare a fast-day and pray to God for mercy. They will gather together at the Temple Mount to call for God's help (Isa. 33 2; 50 4–11; Joel 1 14; 2 12–18; 3 5).

The army of Gog will achieve initial success against the old city of Jerusalem. Half the city will be exiled, the buildings will be looted, and the women raped (Isa. 24 16; 51 17; Jer. 31 39; Zech. 12 2–7; 14 1–2; Joel 1 4–20; 2 3). Moreover, the enemy will assemble in the Valley of Jehoshaphat, near Jerusalem; and the territory of Judaea and its inhabitants will be under siege by the attackers (Joel 4 2, 12–14; Isa. 51 17–19; 52 1–2,9; Zech. 12 2–3,7).

Then suddenly and miraculously Israel will win! There will be a tremendous noise in the land of Israel. Probably missiles with atomic warheads will be launched by Israel against the enemy, followed by a major earthquake. The army of Gog will

DETAILED PICTURE OF THE MESSIANIC ERA

be subjected to plague, blood, overwhelming rain, hailstones, fire, and brimstone. Moreover, the enemy airforce will be destroyed in the skies. Many of the attacking enemy will be annihilated in the Valley of Jehoshaphat. The sun will be darkened, the moon will be like blood, and there will be pillars of clouds. All the weapons of the attackers will be useless. The enemy soldiers will be subjected to a disease which shall cause their skin, eyes, and mouth to rot while each individual is still standing. (Compare Deut. 32 41–43; Isa. 24 1–13,17–23; 25 1–5; 33 1–4,10–13,19–23; 34 1–4; 49 24–26; 50 2–3; 51 6; 52 7–10; 59 17–18; 66 15–18,24; Jer. 30 8; Ez. 38 18–23; 39 3–5; Joel 2 1–2,11,20; 3 3–4; 4 14–16; Mic. 4 10–13; 7 15–17; Zeph. 3 8; Zech. 9 13–16; 12 4–6; 14 3–7, 12–15.) The territory of Judaea will be saved first from the enemy, and afterwards the old city of Jerusalem (Zech. 12 7).

It will take seven years to dispose productively of the weapons of the enemy, and seven months to bury the dead in the Valley of Hamon-Gog. The graves of the soldiers of the army of Gog will be an abhorrence to all visitors (Isa. 66 24; Ez. 39 9–16).

Missiles will also be sent by Israel against the nearby territory of the enemy nations and against participating islands, destroying much of the land. In particular Edom (the southern part of Jordan) will be completely destroyed forever. In addition, Egypt will be made desolate, as well as Iraq, Iran, and Greece. The waters of the Nile will be dried up. (Compare Num. 24 17–17; Isa. 11 14–15; 19 16–18; 25 10–12; 34 5–17; 63 1–6; Jer. 49 2,7–22; Ez. 35 1–15; 36 5,7; Joel 4 19; Amos 9 12; Obad. 1 1–21; Mic. 7 12–13; Zech. 9 13; 10 11; 11 1–3; Dan. 2 44).

As a result of the terrible destruction, there will be significant changes in the terrain of the land of Israel. Many mountains will be levelled, and walls will fall to the ground (Ez. 38 20). The Mount of Olives will be split in half; part of the mountain will move north and part south to form an enormous valley running from east to west. (At the time of the war this valley will serve as a place of refuge for the Jewish people.) Furthermore, the land of Israel will become flattened from Geba to Rimmon (possibly from 31° 50' to about 31° north latitude), and the city of Jerusalem will be raised in height (Zech. 14 4–5,10). The Euphrates River will be separated into seven wadis (Isa. 11 15). In general, a new land will be formed for Israel (Isa. 66 22).

Another major change will be the uncovering of an immense spring in Jerusalem near the site of the Temple. The spring will supply sufficient pure water to enable formation of a river leading to the Dead Sea. Fruit trees will be grown and flourish along the banks of the river. Moreover, the fresh water will be used to decrease the salinity of the Dead Sea, so that a fishing industry can be developed. Water will also go toward the Mediterranean Sea, and irrigate the land in its path (Isa. 12 3; 33 21; Ez. 47 1–12; Joel 4 18; Zech. 13 1; 14 8).

Israel, by winning the war, will acquire the entire territory promised by God to Abraham and his descendants, namely from the Red Sea until the Mediterranean, and from the desert until the Euphrates River (see Section 17.4.4). Particular locations within these boundaries, which are specified as being acquired by Israel, are: Edom, Moab and Ammon (Jordan), Gilead (north Jordan), Bashan (Syria), shoulder of the Philistines (Gaza strip), Children of the East (parts of Saudi Arabia), and Lebanon (Num. 24 18; Isa. 11 14; 27 12; 33 17; 54 1–3; Jer. 48 47; 49 6; Amos 9 12; Obad. 1 19; Mic. 5 3; 7 14; Zech. 9 10; 11 1–3). Moreover, the Temple Mount will become firmly established as part of Israel (Isa. 2 2–3; Obad. 1 21; Mic. 4 1–2).

Not all the Jews in Israel will survive the War of Gog. Righteous persons, including those who assemble on the Temple Mount to pray, will survive. However many of the wicked and non-believing Jews will be killed and punished (Isa. 66 6; Jer. 30 23; Joel 3 5; Obad. 1 17; Mal. 3 13–21). Those Jews killed in the war will be mourned. Each family will mourn separately, with the men and women mourning apart. Some leading families that will be mourning include the families of David, Nathan, Levi, and Shimei (Zech. 12 10–14).

After the War of Gog all the Jews will believe in and worship God, and will be His people for ever. The nations of the world will know that God is the holy one of Israel. The Biblical commandments will be observed, and the Lord will dwell in Zion. God will be the glory of the Jewish people. Note, however, that each country will still serve their own particular god. (See Deut. 4 30; Isa. 12 1–6; 25 1,9; 26 1–27 13; 33 5–6; 51 16; 52 6; 60 19–21; 65 24; Jer. 30 22,25; 31 32–33; Ez. 34 30–31; 37 23–24; 39 7,22; Hos. 2 18–22; Joel 2 27; 4 17,21; Mic. 4 5; 7 18–20; Zeph. 3 11–17; Zech. 10 6–7,12; 14 9; Mal. 3 20,22.)

Only one-third of the population of the enemy countries, occupying territory within the theoretical boundaries of Israel, will survive. A selected group of the survivors will embrace Judaism and recognize God (Zech 13 7–9). Moreover, the surviving inhabitants of the attacking countries will come each year to serve God and to celebrate the Festival of Tabernacles. Those nations not coming to Jerusalem to worship God will not receive rain. This includes the Egyptians (Zech. 14 16–19). An altar to the Lord and a sacred pillar will be set up in Egypt. The Egyptians will be saved from an oppressor or from disease if they appeal to God. Furthermore, there will be five cities in Egypt that will swear allegiance to God. (Isa. 19 18–22). Even from beyond the rivers of Ethiopia offerings will be brought to God (Zeph. 3 9–10). Every Sabbath and New Moon people from all the nations will come to worship before God (Isa. 66 23). (Also see Isa. 24 14–15; 25 3; 59 19; Jer. 49 11.)

The greatness of the State of Israel, the nation made holy by God, will be recognized by the other nations of the world. The inhabitants of the other countries will come to Israel to learn the teachings of the Lord. Israel will judge and will be a light to the nations. The leaders of other countries will serve Israel, and bow down. Gifts will be brought from all over the world, and the Jews will be recognized as children blessed by God. The State of Israel will remain forever. (Compare Isa. 2 3–4; 11 10; 25 6–8; 49 6–7,23; 55 5; 60 11–16; 61 5–7; 62 1–4; 66 12; Jer. 31 21; Ez. 37 28; Amos 9 15; Mic. 4 2–3; Dan 7 14,27.)

21.4 CONSEQUENCES OF ISRAEL'S VICTORY

In addition to the numerous immediate benefits for Israel, described in Section 21.3, there are many long-range benefits resulting from victory in the War of Gog.

The government of Israel, subsequent to the War of Gog, shall convene at Migdaleder, a hill in the region of the old city of Jerusalem (Mic. 4 8).

A large shofar (ram's horn) will be blown (probably over radio and television) to announce the ingathering of the exiles. Jews from all corners of the world and from wherever they reside will then be gathered back to Israel, until none is left in exile. Even the lame, blind, pregnant, and recent mothers will come back. The returnees will be transported with compassion, and many will cry with happiness. They will come by airplane, ship, and other transportation vehicles, and will travel along well constructed roads. They will return even from Egypt and Assyria (Iraq and Syria), places where the Jews were persecuted, to settle in Gilead (north Jordan) and Lebanon; and there will be a shortage of space because of the large number of ingathered Jews. Moreover, the Jews from Pathros (southern Egypt), Ethiopia, Elam (Iran), Shinar (Iraq), Hamath (Syria), and the isles of the sea (Cyprus and Crete), will return. Special highways will exist for the returnees from Assyria, and there will also be a highway from Assyria to Egypt. The returnees will not stumble nor err in their return to Israel. They will not have to run out in haste, but will come with their possessions and wealth. The nations of the world will assist in gathering back the exiles to Israel. (Compare Deut. 30 3–4; Isa. 11 11–12,16; 19 23; 27 6,13; 35 8–10; 49 9–13,17–22; 51 11,14; 52 11–12; 55 12; 56 8; 57 14; 60 4,8–9; 66 20; Jer. 30 10; 31 6–11, 14–16,20; Ez. 34 11–16; 36 24; 37 1–14,21; 39 27–28; Obad. 1 20; Mic. 4 6–7; 5 2; Zeph. 3 18–20; Zech. 9 11–12; 10 8–10.)

The section of the land of Israel west of the Jordan River, as delineated in Ez. 47 13–21, will be divided into twelve equal parts, representing twelve tribes, after the setting aside of a prescribed area for the Temple, priests, Levites, and government (see Fig. 17.4.4.1). The actual twelve tribes from which the individual Jews originated are unknown (except for the priests and Levites); therefore the division into tribes will be made according to where the people settle. Included in the tribes and land distribution will be converts to Judaism (Ez. 45 1–8; 47 13–48 35).

Israel will succeed agriculturally and economically. Even the deserts will blossom. The rains will come on time, the trees will bear their fruit, and the ground its produce. The Jewish people will not suffer from hunger. Happiness, thanksgiving, and peace will be found in the country. The land of Israel will be repopulated, the ruins rebuilt, and the cities settled. People and supplies from other countries will aid in the rebuilding. No longer will the land be a shame for the nations of the world. Other nations will be astonished at the unbelievably rapid development of Israel. It will be said, "This desolate land has become a garden of Eden and the destroyed cities have become settled and fortified." (Compare Isa. 32 15–20; 35 1–2,6–7; 51 3; 52 13–15; 54 11–17; 55 13; 60 1–22; 61 4–6, 11; 65 18–19,21; 66 7–9; Jer.

30 18-20; 31 11-13,22-24,26-27; Ez. 34 26-29; 36 8-15,29-30,33-38; Hos. 2 23-35; Joel 2 18,21-26; Amos 9 13-15; Zech. 9 17-10 1.)

The Jewish people will live full lives, to an average age of approximately 120 (Gen. 6 3). Only the foolish and the sinners will die when as young as 100 years (Isa. 65 20).

Numerous regulations, supplementary to those in the Pentateuch, will be instituted based on Ez. 43 18-46 18 (see Section 17.4). These regulations are concerned with such topics as sacrifices, laws for the leader of the nation, and laws for the Priests. Several noteworthy features are as follows:

A. New monetary and measurement units, such as the shekel and the ephah, will be introduced (Ez. 45 11-12).

B. A number of unique sacrifices will be brought by the priests and by the leader of the nation (Ez. 45 17-46 15).

C. Special procedures are to be followed by the leader of the nation in entering the Temple area (Ez. 44 1-3; 46 1-15).

D. The priests will be of special importance not only with respect to Temple rites, but also as teachers, judges, and guardians of the law (Ez. 44 23-24).

Peace will be established throughout the world under the guidance of Israel. Atomic weapons and missiles will be diverted for constructive purposes. Nations will no longer spend effort on the development of military capability. All wild animals, i.e., warlike nations, will become tamed. Should Assyria (Iraq) attack Israel after the War of Gog, then Assyria will be thoroughly destroyed. Eventually, Israel, Egypt, and Assyria will cooperate and work together. Eternal justice will be firmly established by 1996. (Compare Isa. 2 4; 11 6-9; 19 24-25; 25 8; 32 17-18; 60 18; 65 25; 66 12; Jer. 30 10; Ez. 34 25,27; 37 26; Hos. 2 20; Mic. 4 3-4; 5 4-14; Zech. 9 10; Dan. 9 24.)

The Third Temple, including the surrounding walls, will be constructed according to the plans presented in Ez. 40 1-43 17; 46 19-47 12. Sacrifices will then be offered on the Temple altar, instead of on the temporary altar constructed after the coming of Eliyah, the prophet. The Temple will be completed, including the anointing of all the holy vessels, by 1996 (Isa. 56 7; Jer. 31 37-39; Ez. 37 26-28; Zech. 14 20-21; Dan. 9 24).

After the War of Gog (or possibly around the time of the war) numerous persons, old and young, will see true prophetic visions (Joel 3 1,2). In contrast, false prophecy will be eliminated from the land (Zech. 13 2-6).

It should be noted that there is no mention in the Bible of resurrection of the dead in the Messianic era[1,2]. The Biblical passages of Ez. 37 1-14 and Dan. 12 2,13, which have often been used to support this concept, do not in actuality refer to resurrection. In particular, Ez. 37 1-14 refers to the ingathering to Israel of the exiled Jews who had lost all hope (see Section 17.2); Dan. 12 2 refers to the awakening after World War I of the underdeveloped countries; and Dan. 12 13 refers to the establishment of the State of Israel in 1948 (see Section 16.7).

PART IV

RATIONALE FOR THE BIBLICAL LAWS

One method for establishing that the laws in the Pentateuch were developed by God would be to show that observance of the laws would result in innumerable benefits to the Jewish people. Unfortunately the Biblical regulations have not been followed in their entirety since at least the destruction of the Second Temple in 70 C.E., nor have detailed records been kept of the resultant benefits on the occasions when the laws were observed in ancient times, and therefore the benefits can rarely be demonstrated from actual practice. However, it is possible, as done in this Part IV, to explain the beneficial nature of the Biblical regulations on the basis of modern scientific developments. Nonetheless, because of deficiencies in scientific knowledge—which it should be possible to eliminate with additional research—it is not feasible at present to give a perfectly satisfactory reason for every law in the Pentateuch. In many cases it is necessary to resort to conjecture, based on limited scientific data. Whether all the conjectures used in providing rationales turn out correct or not is immaterial. The basic structure here developed establishes that observance of the Biblical laws leads to great benefits for the society. Any imperfections in the explanations just show that the present level of scientific knowledge is deficient. In general, the better the fit obtained to the details of the Biblical law, the more probable that the given explanation is close to the correct reason.

It should not be assumed that the presented explanations are the only reasons for the regulations. As is shown in numerous instances, a law may have many beneficial purposes. Frequently, additional advantages are unknown because of limitations of scientific knowledge, or because they have been overlooked in this presentation. Therefore, if in certain cases the same benefits as those suggested can be achieved by different methods, it does not mean that the Biblical regulations need not be observed. The laws of the Pentateuch must be followed because we as Jews were so commanded by God. The present work only illustrates how observance of the laws leads to the blessings specified in the Bible. The fact that these benefits arise as a direct result of observing the commandments, and not in any mysterious manner, supports the need for strict observance of the regulations in the Pentateuch.

The benefits arising from observing the commandments are specified in numerous places throughout the Pentateuch (see e.g., Ex. **15** 26; **23** 25–30; **34** 11; Lev.

26 3-13; Deut. 4 40; 6 17-19,24-25; 7 12-16; 8 1; 11 8,9,13-15,21-25; 28 1-14; 30 16,19,20; 32 46,47).

Typical of these benefits are the following promises:

Ex. 23 25-30   Your bread and water will be blessed, sickness will be removed from your midst. None shall miscarry or be barren in your land, you shall live full life spans. Your enemies will fear you and run from you.

Lev. 26 3-13   Your rains will be at their proper times, the land shall yield its produce, the trees shall yield their fruit. You shall eat your fill and live secure in your land. There will be peace in the land and you shall lie down to sleep with no one to cause fear; dangerous beasts will be eliminated from the land, and your land will not be ravaged by war. You shall chase your enemies, and they shall fall in battle before you. You shall be fruitful and your numbers shall increase. The Tabernacle will be established in your midst.

Deut. 7 12-16   You will be blessed and will multiply; blessed will be the fruit of your body, the fruit of your land, and the offspring of your cattle. You shall be blessed above all peoples; none among you and your cattle will be barren. All sickness will be removed from you, including the foul diseases of Egypt. You shall devour all the peoples.

Upon converting the Biblical promises into more modern terms we obtain the following Utopian benefits:

A. elimination of all sickness—from man, animal and plant;
B. elimination of all crime from the society;
C. a stable economy—no inflation, no land speculation, few poor people;
D. a full 120-year life-span—achieved by eradicating disease, murder, and accidents;
E. a bountiful agricultural yield—no shortage of healthful food;
F. rain will occur at appropriate times;
G. because of perfect health, a stable economy, and excellent productivity, the people will be stronger than any other nation and will win every battle;
H. the people will be secure in their land.

In contrast to the above blessings which come as a result of observance of the Biblical commandments, there are numerous curses that arise from non-observance of the commandments. These curses are specified in great detail in Lev. 26 14-46 and Deut. 28 15-69, and are paraphrased below:

Lev. 26 14-46   There will be suffering from numerous terrible sicknesses, lack of agricultural produce, no rain, your efforts will be wasted, wild animals will be present in the land, you will be conquered by the enemy, there will be hunger and insufficient food, you will eat your children, your cities will be laid waste, the Temple will be destroyed, the country will be conquered, and you will be sent into exile. Even in exile you will suffer and be afraid.

Deut. 28 15-69   You shall be cursed in the city and in the field; cursed will be your agricultural produce, children and cattle; numerous sicknesses will afflict you, no rain, you shall be defeated by the enemy, you will be killed, oppressed and robbed, your efforts will be futile, you will be crazed by the sights of your eyes, you will be exiled and ridiculed, you will be a slave to your captors, you shall eat your children from hunger, you will be few in number, you will be scattered among the nations and there too you will be afraid.

We know from tragic historical experience that the stated consequences for nonobservance of the Biblical commandments are correct. Twice the Jewish nation has been exiled from its land, and many more times have the Jewish people been cruelly persecuted in the countries where they resided. Now let us examine and show from a scientific viewpoint that the promised results for obedience to the commandments are also correct.

The approach used in interpreting the Biblical laws has been to give a literal interpretation of the text. Not in every case does this interpretation agree identically with the laws as developed by the rabbinical authorities. However, in most cases where exceptions have been taken, the variations are usually slight and often have been suggested by traditional commentaries. This does not mean that on occasion sharp differences from the usual rabbinic explanations do not occur. It should be realized, that any interpretation giving beneficial reasons for the Biblical laws must by logical necessity restrict itself to commandments stated in the Pentateuch, and not include rabbinic restrictions and modifications. The rabbinic additions have been made to prevent transgressing the Biblical regulations and to define the laws, and were not specifically developed for beneficial reasons. In actual practice the rabbinic interpretations and the resultant legal code must be followed. The arguments presented here are for theoretical and not for legal purposes. Only a recognized rabbinic legislative body, of sufficient numbers and capability, could have the power to modify the rabbinic interpretation of the laws.

Naturally the explanations presented are limited by modern scientific knowledge. It would therefore be worthwhile to perform scientific studies and experiments to verify or disprove suggested reasons for the Biblical laws. By this approach, significant scientific advances could be made concerning economic, social, and health factors, and further understanding of the rationale for the Biblical laws could be achieved.

In organizing the Biblical regulations no attempt has here been made to limit the total number to the 613 commandments claimed by tradition. Numerous opinions exist as to which laws are to be included among the 613, and to agree with all the opinions it would be necessary to specify more than 613[1]. Rather, the approach here has been to explain the reasons for all the commandments, regardless of whether or not a particular law is included in a specific listing.

In the present treatment, the laws are arranged logically rather than in the historical order given in the Bible. The following main categories are used:

A. Monotheistic Principles
B. Educational Practices

C. Governmental Restrictions
D. Health Regulations
E. Physical Protection of the Population
F. Economic Policies
G. Ritualistic Procedures

These main categories are further subdivided into numerous subdivisions. For each subcategory the relevant laws are presented first, followed by the rationale for these laws. Usually a paraphrasing, rather than a literal translation, is given for the Biblical regulations. Occasionally the same law may be presented under more than one category because it has several important beneficial purposes. Since the scientific information on which the explanations are based is being constantly developed, citations have been frequently made from recent developments, as summarized in newspapers or popular articles.

During the preparation of this section concerning the rationale of the Biblical laws the following references were frequently consulted for ideas and background information:

A. J. D. Eisenstein, *Ozar Dinim Uminhagim* (in Hebrew), Hebrew Pub. Co., N.Y., 1938.
B. R. J. Z. Werblowsky and G. Wigoder (eds.), *Encyclopedia of the Jewish Religion*, Holt, Rinehart and Winston, Inc., N.Y., 1965.
C. ספר החנוך על תרי"ג מצוות, אהרן הלוי, Eshkol Pub., Jerusalem, 1958.
D. J. H. Hertz (ed.) *Pentateuch and Haftorahs*, 1941 edition.
E. תורה, נביאים כתובים, א. ש. הרטום, Yavneh Pub. House, Tel Aviv, 1962–3.
F. *The Jewish Encyclopedia*, Funk and Wagnalls Co., 1901.

In addition, the English translations of the Bible, as presented in the translation issued in 1917 by the Jewish Publication Society of America and in *The New English Bible* Oxford Univ. Press, 1970, have been frequently consulted in preparing the paraphrasings of the Biblical laws.

Chapter Twenty-Two

MONOTHEISTIC PRINCIPLES

Basic to the observance of the Biblical laws is the belief in the one and only God, who created the world and revealed the laws to His chosen people. In Part I of this book we have established the historical accuracy of the Bible. Therefore, when the Bible repeatedly describes incidents where only one God is involved, we have a definite proof of His existence. As a very striking example is the revelation of God to the entire Israelite nation, of several million people, when the Ten Commandments were spoken on Mount Sinai (Ex. 19 18–20 18).

In addition to the Biblical historical record, there is also logical proof of God's existence. The reality and perfection of the world, and the living forms thereon, attest to a Creator, just as a building attests to an architect. Furthermore, it is inconceivable that there could be more than one God, for then His powers would be limited, which is contrary to the concept of God.

Laws
The Biblical laws relevant to the principles of monotheism, including the stated reasons for these laws, are as follows:

Belief in One God

Ex. 20 2; Deut. 4 35–39; 5 6; 6 4	Believe in the one God who took the people of Israel out of Egypt and who has demonstrated His existence in many ways.
Deut. 6 5; 10 12; 11 1	Love God with all your heart and all your might.
Ex. 23 25; Deut. 6 13; 8 6; 10 12,20; 13 5	Fear and worship God, and swear only in His name.
Ex. 20 7; Lev. 19 12; Deut. 5 11	Do not use the name of God in vain, because He will not excuse the person who does so. Do not swear falsely in God's name, because you will profane His name.
Deut. 6 12;	Do not forget God; because as a result you will not

8 11,19–20;	observe His commandments and will worship other gods.
Deut. 6 16 (Ex. 17 7)	Do not test God, by asking for a miracle to prove that He is in your midst.
Deut. 9 7	Remember how you angered God in the wilderness.
Ex. 22 27 Lev. 24 15,16	Do not curse God. A person who blasphemes the name of the Lord is subject to the death penalty by stoning.

OBSERVANCE OF THE COMMANDMENTS

Lev. 19 37; 20 8; 22 31; Deut. 11 1,32; 13 5; 26 16–19; 27 10.	Observe the Biblical laws because God has so commanded.
Lev. 26 3–13; Deut. 28 1–14; 30 1–10	There are numerous rewards for observing the Biblical commandments.
Lev. 26 14–43; Deut. 27 26; 28 15–68; 29 17–28.	There are numerous punishments for not observing the Biblical commandments.
Deut. 4 2; 13 1	Everything that God commands should be followed exactly. Do not add or subtract anything from the commandments.

IDOL-WORSHIP

Ex. 20 3–6,20; 22 19; 23 24; 34 13–17; Lev. 19 4; 26 1 Deut. 4 16–19, 23–31; 5 7–10; 6 14,15; 11 16,17,28; 27 15; 30 17,18.	Do not make idols, nor worship them or other gods, because God is a jealous God who will punish sins and will reward following His commandments. You will be exiled from the land if you worship idols.
Lev. 18 21; 20 1–5; Deut. 18 10	Do not sacrifice your children to Molech (idol-worship). One who does should be killed by stoning. If not, he will be punished by excision.
Num. 33 52; Deut. 7 5,25,26; 12 2–4.	Destroy the idols and the places of worship of the neighboring nations. Do not desire the precious materials from which the idols may be constructed lest you be snared by them, and because they are an abomination.

Deut. 13 13–19	Completely destroy a wayward city that worships idols; destroy the people, the animals, and the materials; so that God will turn away from His anger and show you mercy.
Deut. 16 21–22	Do not plant a tree near the altar of the Lord, nor set up a pillar which the Lord hates.
Deut. 13 7–12	Kill, by stoning, anybody—even a close relative—who advocates that you worship false gods; because he sought to draw you away from the Lord. All Israel will hear of it and be afraid, and will not continue to do any such wickedness in your midst.
Ex. 23 13	Do not recall the names of other gods, nor let their names be heard from your mouth.
Ex. 23 32–33; 34 12,15 Deut. 7 1–4	Do not make covenants with the neighboring countries which you are to conquer. Their people shall not dwell in your land lest you would worship their gods, and in this way become ensnared.
Ex. 22 17; Lev. 19 26,31; 20 6,27; Deut. 18 9–14	Do not practice witchcraft and similar types of rites. Kill by stoning anyone who does so. Otherwise the person is punished by excision.

False Prophets

Deut. 13 2–6	Kill a false prophet who advocates the worship of strange gods, because God is testing you to determine whether you love God with all your heart.
Deut. 18 15–22	Listen to the true prophets; but kill false prophets who either predict events which do not occur, or speak in the name of other gods.

Rationale

The basic premise for observance of the Biblical commandments is that one God exists who gave the laws for the benefit of the Israelites. To insure that the regulations are continually obeyed it is necessary that we believe in God, love Him, fear Him and worship Him. We should not do anything which would detract from our belief, such as using God's name in vain or swearing falsely by Him. Neither are we permitted to forget God, test Him, or anger Him. We especially should not blaspheme the name of the Lord, for such an act would contradict our belief in God.

The Biblical commandments should be observed because they were given by God. Furthermore, obeying the laws results in numerous benefits, while non-observance of the regulations results in even more numerous calamities. Since the laws were developed by God, they are perfect. Any additions or subtractions from these laws would introduce imperfections which would detract from the benefits that could be expected from their observance.

Making or serving idols, or worshipping strange gods, are practices which undermine the belief in one God, and thereby result in non-observance of the Biblical regulations. Consequently, idol worship eventually leads to sickness, crime, and poverty—factors which result in death, destruction, and exile. Since the consequences of serving strange gods are so terrible, the practice of idol-worship is a capital offense. The sinner is killed by stoning so that the people will witness and participate in the severe punishment.

Not only the idol-worshippers but also the idols themselves need to be destroyed. Saving the precious materials from which the idols are constructed could lead to others turning to idol worship. In addition, the materials may frequently be contaminated with disease-causing microorganisms because of the abominable practices of the idol-worshippers, such as sacrificing children.

For similar reasons a city that turns to idol-worship should be completely destroyed. Nothing in the city should be taken as booty, for otherwise people may be tempted to consider a city as wayward just for the material possessions therein. Even the animals need to be destroyed, because they may be carrying all types of disease.

Moreover, preventive measures need to be taken to avoid the possibility of spread of idol-worship. A tree should not be planted nor a pillar erected in a place where it might be worshipped, such as near the altar of the Lord. Also the names of other gods should not be spoken because it can lead to thinking about, and subsequent worship, of these gods. Most importantly, anybody who advocates worshipping strange gods, whether he be a very close relative or a false prophet, should be killed by stoning. In fact, one way of recognizing a false prophet is by his advocacy of idol-worship. Certainly you should not make covenants with the neighboring nations or allow their people to dwell in your land lest you be ensnared by their ways and turn to idol-worship.

Witchcraft, divination, soothsaying, and similar rites, attest to a non-belief in God, and are therefore equivalent to idol-worship. Furthermore, these practices are often associated with, or may lead to, actual idol-worship.

In all the cases where the required punishment of death by stoning is not carried out, the sinner is eventually punished by excision, that is he dies prematurely. Probably, non-observance of some Biblical commandment will eventually cause the person to contract a disease and die as a result.

Chapter Twenty-Three

EDUCATIONAL PRACTICES

To perpetuate the observance of the Biblical commandments from generation to generation, it is necessary that the laws be known by the population. Children have to be educated; and the entire population has to be reminded of the regulations at frequent intervals.

Laws

The main commandments that emphasize the principles of education are the following:

Deut. 4 1; 5 1; 6 1	Learn the laws so as to observe them.
Deut. 4 9; 6 6-7; 11 19; 32 46.	Teach the laws to your children, and grandchildren; when sitting at home, when walking by the way, when lying down and upon arising.
Ex. 10 2; 12 26,27; 13 8,14; Deut. 6 20-25.	Tell your children and grandchildren the history of the Israelite people in Egypt, and the miracles by which God took us out from there. Afterwards God gave us the commandments, which are for our benefit if we observe them.
Deut. 6 9; 11 20	Write the laws upon the doorposts of your house, and upon your gates.
Ex. 13 9,16; Deut. 6 8; 11 18.	Bind the laws for a sign upon your hand, and as frontlets between your eyes.
Num. 15 37-40; Deut. 22 12	Make fringes on the corners of the garments, and put with the fringe of each corner a blue thread, so that you will see it and remember all the commandments of the Lord.
Deut. 27 1-8. (Josh. 8 30-32)	When you cross the Jordan River into the land of Israel, select huge stones which will later be used for constructing an altar on Mount Ebal. Afterwards, write the contents of the second discourse of Moses (Deut. 4 44-28 69) on the stones.*

---

* See Section 10.5, Organization, where "התורה הזאת" is defined as Moses' second discourse.

Deut. 31 10–13	Every Sabbatical year on the Festival of Tabernacles, assemble the people, men, women, children, and aliens. Read the second discourse of Moses (Deut. 4 44–28 69) to them so they will listen, learn, fear God, and observe the commandments.
Deut. 31 19–23	Teach the Israelites the "Song" (Deut. 32 1–43), so it will be as a witness when they sin and are beset with many troubles.
Deut. 32 7	Within the "Song" (Deut. 32 1–43) is found the statement, "Remember the years of the world, consider the years of each generation, ask your father and he will tell you, your elders and they will say to you."
Deut. 26 1–10	When you bring the first of all the fruit of the ground to the place selected by God, you should recount the history of how your ancestors went down to Egypt, and how God brought them out from there to the land of Israel.
Deut. 8 10	You shall eat and be satisfied, and bless the Lord your God for the good land He gave you.

RATIONALE

Many means are used in the Bible to educate the population. First, the population should study the laws by themselves. Second, parents should teach their children, and even their grandchildren, at suitable occasions, such as when sitting in the house or taking a walk. Note that the text does not require teaching the children, for example, when working in the field, because this is not a practical opportunity. Third, you should teach your children not only the laws, but also the background history as to how it came about that God gave us the laws. In other words, supply the youngsters an incentive for observing the commandments.

In addition to the verbal methods of teaching, also educate the people using the written word and symbolisms. Write individual regulations on the doorposts and gates so that they will be read when people pass by. Similarly, bind the laws in some manner on your hand and between the eyes to constantly remind the person of the commandments. Also, make fringes, having a blue thread, on the corners of the garments. It should be realized that the blue thread of the fringes (ציצית) would remind the individual of the blue thread holding the plate (ציץ), inscribed with the words "Holy to the Lord," on the forehead of the high priest (Ex. 28 36–38). Thus the fringes would indirectly remind people of all the commandments of the Lord.

It is of particular importance that the population be familiar with all the commandments found in the second discourse of Moses (Deut. 4 44–28 69), since the main laws affecting the general public are there summarized. Therefore, a copy of these commandments is to be inscribed on the stones of the altar on Mount Ebal, available for everyone to read. Furthermore, at the beginning of each Sabbatical year, on the Festival of Tabernacles, when the people are freed from agricultural tasks, the entire population including women, children, and aliens, are assembled together to hear the reading of the second discourse. The psychological impact of such a mass gathering would leave a deep impression of the laws on the listeners.

The special requirement that the people learn the "Song" (Deut. 32 1–43), has a double purpose. First, learning the "Song" has an educational value by itself. Second, the contents of the "Song" emphasize the importance of believing in God and not worshipping idols; otherwise the nation will be severely punished. In addition, it is stated in the "Song" that the people should learn the history of the Israelite nation, thus again advocating that the people should educate themselves.

Numerous other laws involve some form of education of the people during their performance, although the main purpose of the law may be for entirely different reasons. For example, each person who brings the first of the fruits of the ground also recounts the history of how his ancestors went down to Egypt and were brought out by God. By making the required statement, the bringer of the first-fruits learns some history, although the main purpose of bringing the fruits is probably for nutritional reasons. Similarly, the commandment that we bless God, after eating to the point of being satiated, may have as its main reason the recognition of the existence of God. However, the learning of a suitable blessing also involves education of the individual.

Chapter Twenty-Four

GOVERNMENTAL RESTRICTIONS

To operate efficiently, the nation of Israel needs to select a person to act as leader. This leader must be interested in the well-being of the people as well as in developing the nation. The extent of the country's success greatly depends on the ruler, his capability, and his motivation. Nevertheless, no matter how capable he is, still numerous restrictions and guidelines need to be imposed upon his power so that he does not make serious errors. Furthermore, numerous requirements need to be demanded from the people so that the government will not be obstructed, and the nation will have confidence in its leadership.

Laws
The Biblical regulations which are concerned with the successful operation of the government are as follows:

Deut. 17 14–20	When the nation is ready for a king or ruler, then select someone from among you, rather than a non-Israelite. The ruler shall not maintain an excessive number of horses, nor should he return the people to Egypt. The ruler shall not have many wives, so his heart should not turn away nor should he have excess silver and gold. When he sits on his throne he should write a copy of the second discourse of Moses (Deut. 4 44–28 69), before the priests. This copy should be with him and he should read it all his life to learn to fear God and to observe the laws, so that he will not be proud and veer from the commandments. Observance of these regulations will prolong his years of rule, as well as those of his children.
Ex. 22 27	Do not curse a ruler of your people.
Ex. 23 20–23	Heed your leader and do not rebel against him; because he will not pardon your sin. If you listen to your leader, then God will help you win against your enemies.

Ex. 30 11-16   When counting the population, each person above 20 years of age should give a half-shekel, so an epidemic will not occur. The money should be used for Temple worship as an atonement for your lives.

Num. 10 1   Make two silver trumpets, to be blown by the priests, for calling together the people and for directing the camps. If a war develops in the land, then sound the alarm with the trumpets.

RATIONALE

The Bible does not prescribe the exact type of government to be formed. It would be equally satisfactory for the people to establish a democracy or a limited, inherited monarchy. Nonetheless, whatever the type of government formed, reliance has to be placed on the personal integrity of the ruler.

In general, the leader of the Israelite nation must have the welfare of the people at heart. A ruler who is not an Israelite would be subject to conflicts because of dual allegiance—allegiance to his own beliefs as well as to the Jewish religion—and, therefore, is not suited to lead the nation and guarantee the welfare of its citizens.

The main restriction on the ruler is that he must follow the Biblical commandments. To attain this goal, he is required, as soon as he becomes the leader, to write a copy of Deut. 4 44-28 69, under the supervision of the priests. The act of writing, coupled with the explanations of the text provided by the priests, enhance the learning process, and assure that a thorough knowledge is achieved. Reinforcement of the acquired knowledge is gained by his reading from the written copy throughout his lifetime. In this manner, the ruler learns to fear God and observe the Biblical laws. By obeying the laws, the country prospers; and the ruler will not become proud, and will do his best for the people. In return, the population will honor and respect him, and no rebellion will occur. Thereby his years of rulership will be prolonged.

Additional restrictions on the leader so as to maintain his efficiency involve limitations on the number of wives and the extent of his wealth. Catering to many wives can turn the ruler's heart away from God, as happened to King Solomon (I Kings 11 4), and can also sap his physical strength and divert his attention from the nation's problems. Similarly, a ruler who is not limited as to the amount of riches he can amass, might acquire personal wealth at the expense of the country's economy. Numerous instances in world history can be cited where the monarchs maintained large harems or acquired enormous fortunes to the detriment of their subjects. The Biblical restrictions forestall just such situations.

The laws prohibiting the ruler from maintaining an excessive number of horses, or from returning the people to Egypt, can be explained on a different basis from that of the preceding restrictions. Horses suffer from numerous diseases, some of which can be transmitted to man. By reducing the number of horses you also reduce the reservoir of these equine maladies. For example, a decrease in the horse population of the

United States from 28 million in 1920 to less than 4 million in 1953 resulted in a marked reduction in numerous horse diseases[1]. Furthermore, there was also a marked decrease in the insects that feed on horses, such as the horsefly. The horsefly, in turn, can transmit disease to animal and man[2]. Thus, the prohibition against having too many horses in the land, even if needed for military purposes, is to protect the population from possible epidemics.

Similarly, the ruler should not return the people to Egypt, temporarily or permanently, because of the possibility of catching the diseases endemic to Egypt. For example, the Bible (Deut. **7** 15; **28** 27,60) implies that there were in ancient times numerous diseases specific to Egypt. Also in modern times, we know that there are certain sicknesses specific to that country. For example, the disease bilharziasis has plagued Egyptians since the days of the Pharaohs, and presently infects 20 million people in the Middle East[3]. The sickness is harbored by tiny snails, and is carried by a water-borne larva which enters directly through the skin of humans washing in river water. It is only recently that a drug has been developed to treat the disease in the human body without producing deleterious side effects. We thus see that the prohibition against returning to Egypt has the practical purpose of preventing the spread of numerous diseases to the people of Israel.

To maintain respect for the ruler it is necessary that no one curses him, and the people do not rebel against him. If the ruler overlooks such behavior he weakens his leadership. By listening to the leader, the people will be united in solving national problems and will be successful in combatting the enemy.

One duty of the government is to plan ahead. Accordingly, it is necessary to know the size of the population. When a census is taken, care must be taken to avoid an epidemic. For example, a plague may be spread throughout the people if they are assembled to be counted. The way to count is by collecting an item, such as a half-shekel, and counting the number of items collected. In this way the people do not have to be gathered together, and an epidemic is avoided. The collected money is appropriately used for purposes related to the Temple.

Another need of the government is for rapid communication with the people. Silver trumpets are used to call the people together. Various signals are used such as one blast, two blasts, and different tones. In this way the people can, for example, be gathered together rapidly in case of an emergency, such as a war. Modern analogies to the silver trumpets are air-raid sirens and fire alarms.

Chapter Twenty-five

HEALTH REGULATIONS

During the past 100 years, extraordinary medical progress has been made in understanding the causes, prevention, and treatment of all types of sickness. Nevertheless, much still remains unknown. Disease is still prevalent, and the causes of numerous ailments, such as cancer, diabetes, and stroke await to be determined. Furthermore the so-called "common cold," which may be caused by any one of over 100 viruses, and is one of the most widespread of man's afflictions, is one of the least known as to its cause and origin.[1] It is therefore evident that although many scientific advances have been achieved, much remains unexplained.

In this chapter consideration is given to those Biblical laws mainly concerned with the prevention of disease and sickness. Attempts are made using modern medical knowledge to clarify the purpose of each of the health regulations. However, because of the imperfect state of our present understanding, it has often been necessary to resort to conjectures and generalizations to explain many of the laws. Obviously, these guesses are not going to be correct in every case, and surely they will frequently be inexact in explaining the fine details of the health regulations. With future discoveries improved clarification will be achievable.

The purpose here is not to say that the presented rationales are the only reasons, but rather to demonstrate that within existing medical limitations, it is possible to present a plausible case to show that strict observance of the Biblical laws would prevent all illness among the population of Israel.

It should be noted that there are numerous additional regulations concerned with health which are explained in other chapters. For example, many of the agricultural ordinances (Section 27.6) and sacrifices (Section 28.1) have health benefits as their main purpose. To attain a complete picture of all the means used by the Bible to prevent disease requires the reading of these other sections.

The health laws are here divided into the following main subdivisions:
A. Dietary Restrictions
B. Psychological Measures
C. Sex Prohibitions
D. Additional Regulations Concerning Disease Prevention
E. Priestly Statutes

25.1 DIETARY RESTRICTIONS

There are numerous foods and items which are not permitted to be eaten according to the regulations in the Pentateuch. Nevertheless, many people throughout the world eat these prohibited foods without apparent harm, and consider them to be valuable sources of nourishment. Here we will show that, despite the fact that the foods are nutritious, they are potential sources of disease and poison. Although in many cases no harm will result to the one who eats the prohibited items, every so often he may contract a disease or may be poisoned. Death or prolonged sickness may occur in a considerable number of instances. The dietary restrictions have as their purpose the elimination of all such sicknesses which may result from eating the prohibited foods.

The questions may then be asked, "Are there not some sicknesses that can be contracted from eating foods permitted by the Bible?" and "Would it not be necessary to prohibit all foods in order to protect the people?" The answer to these questions is straightforward. Sickness that might be contracted by eating from permissible foods are prevented by other Biblical regulations.

In the subsequent development, particular cases will be given to substantiate the generalizations stated above.

Under "dietary restrictions" will mainly be considered animal foods. The few Biblical restrictions on agricultural produce, such as *orlah* (fruit from a tree during the first three years after planting), and *hadash* (new grain before the bringing of the omer) will be treated in Sections 27.6 and 28.2, respectively.

25.1.1 Animal Foods

LAWS
The main Biblical restrictions on eating animals, fish, birds, and insects are listed below. It should be noted that frequently restrictions on handling the carcasses are given, in addition to the dietary regulations. Explanations will therefore be presented for the restrictions on both the consumption and touching of the prohibited carcasses.

Lev. 7 24; 11 1-8; 24-28; 39-40; 17 15-16; 20 25; Deut 14 4-8, 21

Permissible animals—such as the cow, sheep, goat, hart, gazelle, roebuck, deer, and antelope—are those animals which have split hooves and chew their cuds. However, animals which have only one of the two required characteristics, such as the camel, hare, rock badger, and pig, may not be eaten. Naturally, animals which have neither split hooves nor chew their cuds are not permissible.

Do not touch the carcasses of the prohibited animals. If you happen to touch the carcass of a prohibited animal, then you are unclean until the evening. Further-

HEALTH REGULATIONS 551

more, whosoever carries the carcass of a prohibited animal shall wash his clothes and is unclean until the evening. The carcass of a permissible animal which dies by itself may be touched, but whosoever does so shall be unclean until the evening. The carcass may not be eaten by an Israelite, but may be given to a non-Israelite for eating, or sold to a foreigner. Nonetheless, whosoever eats or carries the carcass of the permissible animal which dies by itself, or which is torn of beasts, shall wash his clothes and be unclean until the evening.

Lev. 11 9-12;
Deut. 14 9-10

All water creatures (fish) which have scales and fins may be eaten. Those water creatures which do not have scales and fins should not be eaten, and their carcasses should be detested.

Lev. 11 13-19;
Deut. 14 11-18;

All birds may be eaten; except for the vultures, ospray, kite, falcon, raven, ostrich, hawks, owls, cormorant, pelican, stork, heron, hoopoe, glede, and bat—which are flying creatures to be detested.

Lev. 11 20-23;
Deut. 14 19-20

All flying insects that walk like quadrupeds should not be eaten and are detestable; except for those insects which have jointed legs above their feet for leaping on the ground, such as locusts, crickets, and grasshoppers.

Lev. 11 29-38;
41-45;

All land creatures—whether they crawl on the belly, go on all fours, or have many feet—shall not be eaten, because they are detestable. The carcasses of the mole rat, the mouse, every type of lizard, the gecko, and the chamelion, are particularly unclean. Whosoever touches their dead bodies shall be unclean until the evening. Also vessels made of wood, cloth, skin, or sack, that touch their carcasses, need to be washed, and are unclean until the evening. If their carcasses fall in an earthen vessel, everything in the vessel on which liquid had come becomes unclean, and the vessel should be broken. If their carcasses fall on anything, then the object becomes unclean—if on an oven or a cooking stove, then it should be broken into pieces, and is unclean. However, a spring or a cistern where water collects remains clean, but whatever (or whoever) touches their carcasses in the water becomes unclean. If the carcass falls on dry seed for sowing, the seed remains clean; but on wet seed, the seed becomes impure.

RATIONALE

Animals Animals are the natural hosts for many diseases transmissible to man. Of the approximately 100 animal diseases known also to infect man, the most important are brucellosis, bovine tuberculosis, trichinosis, rabies, tapeworm, plague, tularemia, anthrax, psittacosis, leptospirosis, equine encephalitis, and several types of fungus infections.[2,3] The Biblical restrictions on eating and touching animals were designed to prevent the transmission to man of many of the animal diseases.

In general, eating the meat of properly slaughtered permissible animals, even if they had been diseased, does not transmit sickness to man. For example, bovine tuberculosis is not given to man by eating the meat because tubercle bacilli are rarely found in the muscular tissue, which we call "meat," and because the microorganism is readily destroyed by cooking. In fact the only disease caused in the past by meat is "beef tapeworm," and this illness has become unusual because of better sanitation.[4]

In contrast, a moderate number of animal diseases are known to be contracted upon eating or touching particular non-permissible animals. Undoubtedly, additional sicknesses could be and are being transmitted to man upon consuming or coming in contact with the carcasses of practically all the non-permissible animals, but insufficient medical information is available to correlate which disease originates from which animal. Examples of the diseases known to be transmitted are as follows.

The disease trichinosis is acquired by the human being upon eating insufficiently cooked pig or bear meat.[5] Although thorough cooking of pig meat is known to prevent transmission of trichinosis, still it is prevalent among about 10 percent of the people in the United States. Because of recent legal limitations on the feeding of garbage to pigs, the incidence of the infection has decreased from 16 to 5 percent in the past 20 years;[6] which is still an intolerable level considering that the disease causes severe symptoms in about 1 percent of the population of the United States.[7]

Another disease known to be contracted by eating insufficiently cooked contaminated pig's meat is pork tapeworm.[8]

The fatal disease known as kuru occurs only among the cannabilistic Fore tribe in New Guinea. One probable explanation for the spread of the sickness, is that it is contracted by eating the brain of dead human beings.[9] It should be realized that human corpses are included in the Biblical category of animals not permitted to be eaten.

Other sicknesses are known to be transmitted dominantly by handling or touching infected animals rather than by eating their meat. For example, tularemia, which is a fatal disease in about 5 percent of the cases, is acquired mainly by handling the carcasses of infected rabbits.[10] However, tularemia can be acquired by eating rabbit meat not well-cooked.[11] Also, it has been reported that a death from plague occurred to a person who had killed and skinned a wild rabbit.[12]

Anthrax is another disease worth mentioning here. Anthrax is a rare skin disease in man, resulting from contact with infected cattle, goats, horses, sheep, and swine. The sickness may be contracted by direct contact with contaminated animal parts such as wool, hair, or hides, or by consumption of contaminated meat.[13]

One method of minimizing the chance of contracting disease from the non-permissible animals is for the person who touched the dead animal to wash himself. Washing may frequently remove the disease microorganisms from the skin, preventing the disease from entering the body. If a more prolonged contact occurs, such as carrying the carcass of the animal, then the microorganisms may spread to the person's garments, and it becomes necessary for him to wash not only his body but also his clothes. The person remains impure, however, until the evening because residual microorganisms may linger for a while and may possibly be transmitted to someone else during that time.

A permissible animal, upon being slaughtered, loses a significant portion of its blood, and even if the animal is diseased the meat will not usually become contaminated from the remaining blood. However, if the animal dies by itself, then disease microorganisms can spread more readily from the blood to the flesh, and thereby contaminate the meat. Nevertheless, the degree of impurity of the permissible animal which dies by itself is not as great as for the prohibited animal. The carcass may be touched on condition that the person washes himself afterwards, and may be carried on condition that the person's clothes are also washed. Furthermore the carcass of a permissible animal that dies by itself may be given to a non-Israelite for eating. Since cooking of the meat would readily kill any disease microorganisms, there is little chance of sickness being spread by the carcass. However, to avoid even this slight chance, a Jew may not eat the meat.

It is noteworthy that on occasion poisoning may also occur from eating non-permissible animals. For example, eating of the livers of dogs and polar bears (as well as of whales and seals) may result in hypervitaminosis A because of the extremely high vitamin A content of the livers of these animals.[14, 15]

Water Creatures In the case of water creatures, not only do we find that eating the non-permissible species may result in contracting disease, but also may commonly result in severe poisoning. However, eating of freshly cooked permissible fish is rarely, if ever, a cause of food poisoning.[16] Examples of diseases and poisons spread by non-permissible water creatures are as follows.

Shellfish, such as oysters and clams, pass many gallons of water daily through their systems in order to absorb food particles. In the process, viruses, bacteria, and poisons, are concentrated within the shellfish. Virus counts may, for example, become more than ten times greater than in the surrounding waters.[17] Diseases which have been definitely etablished as being contracted by man by eating steamed or poorly cooked shellfish include typhoid fever[18] and hepatitis.[19] Furthermore, in Japan, cases of infection have been connected with eating raw crabs and oysters contaminated with the bacterium vibrio parahaemolyticus.[20]

Cases of poisoning are also known to be traceable to shellfish. Great quantities of the dinoflagellate plants, which are highly poisonous to animals and man, are ingested and stored within oysters and clams. Sickness, and even death, often results upon human consumption of these contaminated shellfish.[21] Radioactive wastes are also known to be concentrated within oysters, to the point that they show high levels of radioactivity.[22] In the case of shellfish which contain poisons, thorough cooking would not eliminate the hazard.

Mercury contamination of fish has been encountered particularly with prohibited species. Swordfish,[23] seals[24] and whales have all been found to have mercury concentrations far in excess of what are considered to be safe limits, while permissible fish have not been found to have large excesses. For example, typical concentrations of mercury in swordfish are one part per million,[25] sufficient to cause brain damage to someone who eats large portions over a period of a year or two.[26]

Another interesting possibility of poisoning can occur upon eating the liver of whales, seals, and even polar bears. Hypervitaminosis A, i.e., toxic effects resulting from ingesting excess amounts of vitamin A, has been observed in arctic expeditions after consumption of the liver of these prohibited species, because of the extraordinarily high vitamin A content of this organ.[27]

The snail, another non-permissible water creature, has been found to harbor the blood fluke bilharziasis,[28] that results in a disease which has spread to about 200 million people in Africa, Asia, and Latin America.

It should be noted that the carcasses of water creatures may be touched, although handling of the non-permissible species should preferably be avoided since their carcasses are to be detested. The fact is that diseases and poisoning from the prohibited type water creatures usually arise only from actual eating of the flesh, and not merely by physical contact, in agreement with the Biblical regulation.

Birds The prohibited birds all belong to the class denoted as birds of prey, and many live in dark ruins or marshy land.[29] Probably, these birds may become carriers of disease microorganisms harmful to man upon consuming their victims. It should be noted that the actual birds which are prohibited are not specifically known in most cases, since the true meaning of the Hebrew names has often been forgotten. Therefore, there is some uncertainty as to which birds are prohibited and which are permitted.

Only a limited number of examples exist as to diseases which may be transmitted from bird to man, although it is known that birds are subject to the same general types of disease as man.[30] The main case is psittacosis, which is a contagious influenza-like virus disease communicated to man by contact with birds belonging to the psittacus (parrot) family. About one out of three persons who contract the disease die. Also many birds of other species, such as canaries, sparrows, finches, herring gulls, petrels, ducks, turkeys, and pigeons are susceptible.[31]

Another example is the dreaded sickness rabies. Although the virus may be carried by numerous animals, some of the main carriers are dogs and bats. Bites from infected animals and birds spread the disease to man.[32]

Most of the birds eaten by mankind, such as chickens, ducks, turkeys, etc., are permissible fowl, and therefore little information has been accumulated concerning diseases which may possibly be contracted upon eating non-permissible birds. Undoubtedly, just as with the prohibited animals and fish, many serious illnesses may result from eating prohibited birds.

Insects Most persons in modern societies consider insects as repulsive, and take precautionary measures to avoid eating them. However, in many areas of the world insects are regularly consumed.[33] African natives, as well as residents of Arabia and Egypt, eat grasshoppers and locusts. Termites are also commonly eaten in Africa. Many American Indian tribes eat both raw and cooked large carpenter ants. The natives of North Queensland, Australia consume ants. Caterpillars were formerly eaten by the Indians in the Nevada-California region. In many countries people eat flour, bugs and all, even when heavily infested with insects. We thus see that man does not have a natural aversion to insects, and therefore the Biblical restrictions on eating insects are very necessary. Of interest is the fact that locusts and grasshoppers, which are permitted by the Bible, are among the more commonly ingested insects.

Practically no knowledge exists as to diseases contracted by eating insects. This is not because disease cannot be transmitted in this manner, but rather because insects are consumed mainly in backward countries, where no effort is made to correlate disease with diet. Nevertheless, it is almost an obvious fact that sickness can be contracted from insects. Many dozens of diseases are known to be carried and spread by them.[34] Cockroaches can carry typhoid fever, and have been suspected of carrying the bacillus causing leprosy. The body louse is the vector of epidermic typhus, and also carries relapsing fever. Anopheles mosquitoes spread malaria; culex mosquitoes spread yellow fever; and the tsetse fly carries sleeping sickness. The housefly may spread typhoid, dysentry and cholera. Fleas carry plague and endemic typhus. Hard ticks carry various rickettsiae, such as United States Rocky Mountain spotted fever, while soft ticks carry relapsing fever. Mites carry scrub typhus. The World Health Organization estimated in 1955 that 50 percent of all human deaths are caused by insect-borne diseases. It is true, that many of the above illnesses can only be spread through the blood stream by insect bites,[35] but many others probably could enter the human body through other channels, such as from food.

It is also known that numerous biting or stinging insects, such as bees, mosquitoes, hornets, and wasps contain toxic substances in their venoms.[36] Eating such insects might in some cases poison the human being.

Land Creatures Among the land animals, a few types such as the rat, mouse, and lizard, have been specified by the Bible as being especially unclean. Not only do their carcasses impart uncleanness to the person who touches them, but also to materials and utensils with which they come in contact. It is particularly with the rat and mouse that medical information is available as to their potential for carrying and spreading disease.

Rats are known to be carriers of as many as 35 different diseases.[37] Some of the more serious ailments include typhus and bubonic plague, which are then spread to man by fleas, and rat-bite fever. Furthermore, the blood and intestines of the rodent may carry amebic dysentery, tularemia, salmonellosis, jaundice, and rabies. The habit of the rat of urinating and leaving droppings wherever he goes is one means by which sickness is spread to the human being.

Similarly, mice are known to be carriers of many sicknesses, such as tularemia, salmonella, rat-bite fever, lymphocytic choriomeningitis, tape-worm, favus, and rickettsialpox.[38, 39]

We thus see that eating mice or rats exposes the person to numerous possible infections. Furthermore many of the rodent diseases may be contracted by touching their dead bodies. To minimize such a chance, the person who happens to handle the carcasses must wash his body and remains impure until the evening. The fact that their urine and droppings also harbor disease may explain the extreme uncleanness of these rodents. A small amount of moisture may be sufficient to dissolve residual urine on these creatures, thereby spreading infection. Washing the infected articles is usually sufficient to remove the contamination. However earthen vessels, once contaminated, probably retain the disease microorganisms indefinitely, and therefore must be broken. Possibly, ovens and stoves, if contaminated, could spread the disease microorganisms through the air, upon being heated, and therefore they too have to be broken and cannot be cleansed. A spring of water would not become impure from the carcass of one of these prohibited land creatures because of the self-cleansing nature of water, where disease microorganisms slowly die out. However, the carcass even in the water retains the disease microorganisms and can spread them upon direct contact. Dry seed intended for planting does not become infected, and even if the seed becomes contaminated, the disease microorganisms would be neutralized, after sowing, by other microorganisms in the ground. However, wet seed to be used as food becomes impure upon coming in contact with a carcass of one of these land creatures. Moreover, the contaminated wet seed, when planted, may produce diseased plants.

25.1.2 Blood and Fat Avoidance

LAWS

The Biblical restrictions related to eating blood and certain types of fat are as follows:

Lev. 7 26	Do not eat blood from an animal or bird, in any of your dwellings.
Deut. 12 16, 24, 25; 15 23	Do not eat blood; pour it out upon the ground as water. Do not eat blood, so all will be well with you and your children.
Gen. 9 4; Lev. 19 26; Deut. 12 23	Do not eat meat with its lifeblood.

Lev. 17 13	An Israelite or resident alien who hunts permissible beasts or birds, shall pour out the blood and cover it with earth.
Lev. 7 27; 17 10–12, 14	An Israelite or a resident alien who eats any blood will be punished by excision, because the life of flesh is in the blood, and blood is to be used on the altar to make atonement for your souls.
Lev. 3 17; 7 23–25	Do not eat *heleb* (i.e., the fat that covers the inwards, the kidneys, and the loins) of the cow, sheep, or goat, in any of your dwellings. A person who does eat *heleb* will be punished by excision.
Deut. 12 15, 20–22	It is permissible to slaughter animals anywhere in the land. Both the clean and the unclean person may eat from the meat.
Lev. 22 28	A cow or sheep (and goat) shall not be slaughtered on the same day as its young.

RATIONALE

The prohibition against eating blood, or meat containing blood, can be interpreted on the basis that blood is an excellent carrier of microorganisms.[40] Consumption of blood would therefore expose the person to all types of diseases. The Biblical punishment of excision, i.e., premature death, for the one who eats blood is the direct consequence of the contracting of disease from the blood.

Specifically prohibited is the blood from animals or birds. Such blood is well known to harbor pathogens. On the other hand, the blood of fish can be eaten. Probably the blood of permissible fish does not carry pathogens dangerous to man.

It should be realized that in modern civilized nations it is considered abhorrent to consume blood. Therefore, specific information as to which diseases could be contracted by eating blood has not been established.

The blood of animals and birds is to be poured upon the ground. The microorganisms in the soil would counteract any pathogens in the blood,[41] thereby rendering the blood harmless. In the case of wild animals and birds the blood needs to be covered by earth, while for domesticated animals it is only necessary to pour the blood on the ground. Perhaps the pathogens within the blood of domesticated animals are more easily neutralized than are those found in the blood of wild animals and birds.

Probably, just as with blood, pathogens may flourish in the *heleb* of cattle, sheep, and goats. Therefore the *heleb* should not be eaten.

Inferred from the Biblical laws is that animals and birds should be killed in a manner that allows the easy pouring out of their blood on the ground. This is accomplished by slaughtering the animals according to the traditional method, which involves cutting the main blood vessels supplying and draining the head and brain.[42] Most of the blood flows out, resulting in the flesh remaining unspoiled for approximately three times as long as for animals killed by other methods.[43] Little danger exists that properly slaughtered meat will become infected from a diseased person. Therefore, both the clean and unclean person may eat from meat slaughtered outside the Temple area.

A cow, sheep, or goat should not be slaughtered on the same day as its parents because of the mental anguish suffered by the parent or child upon seeing the death of its loved one. This mental stress results in an increased rate of blood clotting for the animal. For example, in human beings it is known that stress accelerates the rate of blood clotting and raises the level of cholesterol, increasing the chance of heart trouble.[44] If the surviving animal is slaughtered on the same day there may be incomplete drainage of blood from the carcass, making the flesh more subject to contamination by disease microorganisms. It is here assumed that the main restriction is in slaughtering the related animals in each other's presence. If the slaughtering is postponed until the next day, the change in the clotting properties of the blood will have reversed, and no contamination of the flesh with disease microorganisms will result from incomplete blood drainage.

25.1.3 Contaminated Meat

Laws

The following Biblical regulations are designed to prevent the eating of contaminated meat.

Ex. 22 30	Do not eat meat found in the field, which was torn by beasts. Throw it to the dogs.
Lev. 7 16–18; 19 5–8	Meat from a vow or freewill offering (types of peace offerings) should be eaten on the day of the offering, and the next day. Meat left over to the third day shall be burned. Anyone who eats of the meat on the third day will be punished by excision, because he has profaned the holy item.
Lev. 7 15; 22 29–30	Meat from a thanksgiving offering (type of peace-offering) shall be eaten on the day of the offering. None of the offering shall be left until the morning.
Lev. 7 19–21	Meat (of a sacrifice) that touches any unclean thing shall not be eaten. It shall be burned. Everyone that is clean may eat of the peace offering. But the unclean person, who eats of the meat, such as one who has touched a dead person or the carcass of an animal, shall be punished with excision.

RATIONALE

Meat torn by beasts that was found in the field has a high probability of being infected. An animal infected by disease may have attacked the carcass. Rabies, for example, is a disease known to be spread by numerous species of biting animals.[45] A person who would eat of the meat in the field may then himself become infected. However, the meat may be used for feeding dogs, since it is remote that the dog would become sick, and if he did it would be even more remote that man would contract the illness from the dog.

The prohibition against eating meat of a sacrifice that stood around for a while is to prevent food poisoning. Staphylococcus and salmonella microorganisms are known to thrive in meat left at room temperature.[46] Eating such infected flesh could result in severe illness. The precaution of not eating unfresh meat is particularly important with respect to sacrifices, where a great many people may partake of the food.

The meat from a vow or freewill offering could be eaten for two days. The sacrifice simply consisted of the flesh of the animal. In contrast the meat from a thanksgiving offering could be eaten for only one day. In this case the sacrifice also included unleavened cakes mingled with oil, unleavened wafers spread with oil, fine flour cakes mingled with oil, and cakes of leavened bread (Lev. 7 12, 13). Probably the presence of these added food items could allow a more rapid growth of microorganisms, thereby speeding up the spoilage process of the meat.

Over 50 percent of the outbreaks of food poisoning involve some form of meat dish. In general, freshly cooked—roasted, boiled, or fried—meats do not cause poisoning. Only meats that have been standing around are sources of food poisoning.[47]

Burning the leftover meat by fire ensures the complete destruction of the potentially contaminated meat, and prevents any disease microorganisms from being spread through the air to any other food.

Meat of a sacrifice that happens to touch an unclean object may become infected. Therefore the meat should not be eaten, and should be burned. Similarly, an impure person may contaminate the meat with pathogens.

It should be noted that the person who eats from sacrificial meat when impure does not follow the Biblical impurity laws. He therefore is subject to numerous diseases, which shorten the lifespan. In contrast, an impure person may eat nonsacrificial meat. This is because holy meat involves food for large numbers of people, and extra precautions need to be taken to prevent epidemics.

25.1.4. Miscellaneous Cases

LAWS

There are several additional dietary restrictions which need to be considered.

Gen. 32 33   The children of Israel will not eat the sinew of the thigh vein which

	is upon the hollow of the thigh, because Jacob was struck in the hollow of the thigh in the sinew of the thigh vein.
Ex. 23 19;	Do not cook a kid in its mother's milk.
34 26;	
Deut. 14 21	
Deut. 14 3	Do not eat any abominable thing.

RATIONALE

The prohibition against eating of the sinew of the thigh vein is only mentioned once in the Bible, and not as a law from God but as a voluntary restriction to commemorate that Jacob was struck in that particular part of the body. It may very well be that the prohibition against eating the sinew of the thigh vein has only a historical basis and is not necessarily a beneficial law. On the other hand, the fact that the statement of the prohibition was allowed by Moses to remain in the Book of Genesis indicates that the law does have a useful purpose. Possibly the sinew of the thigh vein should not be eaten because it may carry disease microorganisms, or because the part is not easily digestible.

The prohibition against cooking a kid in its mother's milk needs to be considered in comparison to the cooking of milk and meat separately. The laws of the Pentateuch are designed to eliminate all diseases from the permissible animals, and thereby prevent any pathogens from being spread to man through the meat or milk. However, if a permissible animal should happen to contract an illness it is unlikely, as discussed in Section 25.1.1, for the sickness to be transmitted to man. Cooking of permissible beef or heating of milk kills the pathogens. For example, contaminated milk has been known to spread typhoid fever, scarlet fever, diptheria, paratyphoid fever, dysentery, food poisoning, gastroenteritis, undulant fever, and tuberculosis.[48] Yet, if milk is heated to 62° C (144° F) for 30 minutes or to 71° C (160° F) for 15 seconds, as is done in pasteurization processes, all disease microorganisms are killed.

Nevertheless, when meat and milk are mixed together, the Biblical law implies that the cooking process, instead of killing the pathogens, may actually cause them to multiply under certain conditions. Possibly the meat-milk mixture acts as a culture medium, and allows a dangerous concentration of disease microorganisms to build up. The pathogens in the cooked meat-milk mixture may then spread through the air, even if not ingested, and cause disease in humans.

The main Biblical prohibition is against cooking the meat and milk together, especially if the meat and milk are from the same species of animal. Logical inferences from the Biblical restrictions are that the cooked meat-milk mixtures should surely not be eaten, and should not be used for any purpose.

The prohibition against eating any abominable thing (Deut. 14 3) is usually interpreted to refer to the non-permissible animals, water creatures, fowl, and insects, the laws of which are stated in the Bible immediately afterwards (Deut. 14 4–21). Here, however, the prohibition is taken to refer to anything disgusting which people may consume. Thus the Bible prohibits eating anything which may be harmful to health even if otherwise permissible. Included in this category would be such items as spoiled foods, poisons, drugs, and even cigarette smoking. Not eating spoiled foods and poisons is almost self evident. Spoiled foods may spread disease, while poisons can kill. A more elaborate explanation is however needed for drugs and smoking.

Drugs are commonly prescribed by physicians to help cure people from many serious illnesses or to alleviate annoying symptoms. Nevertheless many severe adverse reactions result from taking medication. Recent studies have shown that one out of every 100 times a hospital patient swallows a pill or gets some medication, the adverse reaction is serious enough to threaten life or seriously complicate the existing sickness.[49] Approximately 10 to 30 percent of hospital patients suffer some adverse reactions from drugs. In fact, in Britain about 5 percent of all hospital admissions result from the ill effects of medication. Amazingly enough, many medical doctors are unaware of the dangers from drugs, and prescribe medication very freely.[50] Even aspirin, which is considered to be one of the safest drugs, can cause dangerous problems for many individuals.[51]

From the Biblical point of view, drugs could be considered as "abominable things" and would be prohibited. Only in cases of severe illness, where the sickness is potentially more dangerous than the medication, would drugs not be considered as abominable. In this respect it should be realized that many modern medicines are lifesaving, and are perfectly permissible when used to cure sickness, even if adverse reactions are possible. However, strict observance of the Biblical laws would eradicate all illness and thereby would result in the rigid prohibition of taking any medicines. Once no drugs were taken there would be no problem from sickness caused by medication. Unfortunately, many sicknesses are the direct or indirect result of taking medication of one type or another. Undoubtedly many maladies, whose causes are presently unknown, originate from sensitivities to particular drugs.

Smoking of cigarettes can also be considered as eating abominable things. Smoking has been implicated in numerous sicknesses such as lung cancer and heart disease. People who smoke even one cigarette a day decrease their life expectancies by about four years.[52] Clearly, the act of smoking is an abominable thing, and is prohibited by the Bible.

Law
There is one other miscellaneous law worthy of consideration. This involves the voluntary avoidance of alcoholic drinks and grape products by a person who proclaims himself to be a Nazir.

Num. 6 1-21   A man or woman may become a Nazir by vowing to abstain for a definite time from wine, intoxicating liquor, vinegars of strong drink, and any grape product. The Nazir should not cut the hair of his head, and should not become impure from a dead body—

even a close relative such as parent, brother, or sister. If he unexpectedly does become impure by the sudden death of a person, he should purify himself—requiring seven days—and should cut off his hair on the seventh day. On the eighth day he should bring two birds—one as a sin-offering and one as a burnt-offering, and a he-lamb as a guilt-offering. Then he should restart the counting of the period of being a Nazir. Upon completion of the vowed period, the Nazir should bring a burnt-offering of a he-lamb, a sin-offering of a ewe-lamb, and a ram for a peace-offering. Then the Nazir should cut his hair, and have it burned on the fire under the peace-offering. After following the prescribed sacrificial rites, the Nazir may once again drink wine.

RATIONALE

The above laws make sense when interpreted in terms of alcoholism—a sickness manifested by consistently undesirable results following the ingestion of alcohol. The main characteristic is the uncontrollable drinking by the alcoholic. It is estimated that 6 percent of the adult population in the United States is afflicted with alcoholism. Many sufferers display extreme reluctance to abstain from alcohol, as if it is disgraceful not to be able to drink and a sign of weakness of character. The earlier that the person abstains from alcohol, the sooner recovery can be accomplished.

Some characteristics of alcoholics, in chronological sequence are (A) frequent excessive drinking—not necessarily resulting in getting drunk; (B) beginning of addiction—frequent excessive drinking to the point of reproach by family and friends; (C) continued excessive drinking, with loss of friends and often neglect of eating; and (D) complete addiction without any attempt at control. While in most cases addiction occurs only after prolonged use, there are rare situations where a person shows addiction with the very first drink. The only answer for an alcoholic is the complete and total abstinence from alcohol. This is easier for the problem drinker than for the confirmed alcoholic.[53]

The Nazirite laws require the complete abstinence from intoxicating beverages just as with an alcoholic. Furthermore, the Nazir must not eat any grape product, to minimize his desire for similar tasting liquors, such as wine. The Nazir is recognized as a dignified member of the community, giving an incentive to the alcoholic to become a Nazir, and to refrain from drinking. He lets his hair grow long to let people know he is a Nazir thereby acting as a deterrent from taking a drink in a weak moment, since other people would stop him. The psychological effect of involving himself with the body of a near relative might induce him to break his vow. Therefore the Nazir should not become impure even for his father and mother. Moreover, since the Nazir has a large growth of hair, the chance of his contracting a disease by touching a dead body may be greater than usual, since it is more difficult to remove disease germs from the hair. To eliminate this problem he has to cut his hair on the seventh day of impurity. If the potential alcoholic stopped drinking in an early enough stage, he may often resume drinking in moderation after his period of being a Nazir has expired.

25.2 PSYCHOLOGICAL MEASURES

There are numerous Biblical laws whose main purpose is to promote the psychological and mental health of the individual. Most of these laws do not involve concrete actions but are rather concerned with directing a person's thoughts and speech.

Naturally, a great many of the other Biblical regulations, in addition to those to be here listed, promote sound mental health. Regulations against committing crimes, such as prohibitions against stealing and killing, when observed prevent guilt feelings. Statutes which eliminate disease, remove the possibility of mental illness caused by microorganisms, as is known to result for example from syphilis. Laws which guarantee the prosperity of the country increase the self-confidence and emotional stability of the individual. Furthermore, regulations which assist in providing a strong military capability for the nation add to each person's inner security. Therefore, it may be stated in a general sense that the observance of all the Biblical laws, directly or indirectly affects the psychological well-being of all the citizens.

Laws
The laws which are particularly concerned with maintaining the mental health of the population are as follows:

Lev. 19 18	Love your neighbor as yourself.
Lev. 19 33, 34	If an alien settles in your land, you shall not oppress him. He shall be treated as a native born among you, and you shall love him as yourself, because you were aliens in Egypt.
Lev. 19 17	Do not hate your brother in your heart. Rebuke him, so you will not bear sin because of him.
Lev. 19 18	Do not take revenge nor bear a grudge against your kinsfolk.
Ex. 23 1; Lev. 19 16	Do not go about as a talebearer among your people.
Lev. 19 16	Do not stand idly by the blood of your neighbor.
Lev. 19 14; Deut. 27 18	Do not curse the deaf; nor put an obstruction in front of, or mislead the blind.
Ex. 20 14 ; Deut. 5 18	Do not desire your neighbor's house, field, wife, servants, animals, or anything belonging to your neighbor.
Deut. 7 17, 18, 21; 20 1, 3, 8; 31 6	Do not fear the enemy when going forth to battle.
Lev. 19 32	Rise up before and honor the white-haired, elderly person.

Rationale

A high degree of emotional security is essential for physical and mental health. Persistent insecurity may result in both physical and mental disorders.[54] Psychological problems have been known to manifest themselves as motor disorders, such as paralysis and trembling, unconsciousness, loss of sensation, visual and auditory illusions, stuttering, respiratory disorders, ulcers, colitis, and nausea.[55] Many other diseases, such as rheumatoid arthritis, allergies, skin diseases, and heart trouble are influenced negatively by emotional stress.[56] It is thus evident that a person's mental state significantly affects his health. Roughly one out of ten people in the United States suffer from mental illness severe enough to warrant treatment.[57]

Many of the Biblical laws are designed to direct, in a positive manner, the thought processes of the individual so no mental sickness will result. The commandment to love your neighbor as yourself implies that you should not only love your neighbor but should also love yourself. It is well known that a person who likes himself is usually mentally healthy.[58] Sound mental health includes self-respect as well as respect for others. Naturally, loving your neighbor will also lead to good deeds for his benefit, and mutual cooperation. Furthermore, respect for one's fellow man produces a good inward feeling and raises a person's own self-esteem.

Similarly, the commandment to love an alien as yourself promotes a person's mental well-being, and leads to concrete physical benefits for a racial minority. It has been claimed that racism in the United States negatively affects the mental health as well as the physical health of the nation.[59]

One very important regulation is to not hate your fellow man in your heart. Inward hatred often is a result of a misunderstanding. Rebuking of your neighbor frequently clears the air and leads to actual friendship. It has been stated that when somebody is angry and hides it from himself it can be quite self-destructive, both emotionally and physically.[60] In contrast, anger experienced and expressed between people can be a warm emotion, which is often followed by feelings of love. It should be noted that repressed anger may lead to vindictive acts, inappropriate bursts of rage,[61] excessive gain of weight,[62] and high blood pressure.[63]

Taking revenge and bearing a grudge reinforce hatreds between people and never accomplish anything constructive, and are therefore prohibited by the Pentateuch. Not "getting even" for something done to you can lead to cooperation between persons resulting in increased accomplishments and a minimum of dissipated mental energy in unnecessary hatreds. Similarly, a person who goes about as a talebearer often causes unfounded hatreds which can lead to very serious consequences. In addition to the possible negative actions that can occur, there is also the mental anguish which may result from telling tales.

Standing by idly while someone else is suffering leads to physical anguish by your neighbor and subsequent guilt feelings on your part. If, instead, you helped the person in distress, friendships could be made and lives could even be saved.

The commandments prohibiting cursing the deaf or putting an obstruction in front of the blind can be explained in several ways. First of all, the person who does such things loses his own self-respect, since he takes advantage of another person's misfortune. Secondly, cursing the deaf can cause others to dislike the deaf person, while an obstruction in front of a blind man can cause injury. Thus, physical harm can result. Thirdly, the prohibition can be interpreted in a more general sense, namely not to mislead, shame, or cause injury to a fellow human. The person who purposely does cause such results would probably suffer from mental anguish.

The regulation prohibiting a person from desiring his neighbor's possessions, particularly emphasizes items which in most cases can not be obtained legally. The neighbor's wife, servants, and favorite animals are not for sale, nor will the neighbor part with his house or inherited field. As a result, the person desiring such items will have inner feelings of frustrated jealousy which might even lead to criminal actions. Someone having such feelings of jealousy is required by the Bible to channel his thinking to more constructive purposes.

The requirement that the soldier not fear the enemy when going forth to battle has more than one practical purpose. Militarily, fearless soldiers can lead to victory, under the same circumstances where scared soldiers would result in defeat (see Section 26.3). In addition, from a psychological viewpoint, a soldier who is not afraid has less chance of developing war neurosis. Causative factors of such neurosis are physical and emotional depletion and fatigue.[64] Naturally, fear is one major reason for a soldier's emotional fatigue. Thus, it has been found that cowardice and fear during battle are the most common reasons for subsequent consultation with psychiatrists by soldiers.[65] The Bible requires that the soldier not concentrate on fear, but should rather direct his thoughts to other topics.

The commandment to rise up before and honor the white-haired is designed for the mental well-being of elderly people. Thus it is known that aged persons do not have the physical strength and are not as active as they were when younger. If they continue to feel important and secure, they are less likely to develop mental disorders or to deteriorate physically.[66] Rising up and showing respect to the elderly is one important way of making them feel needed and important. The specification of white-haired people is to give persons an easy way of identifying who is to be considered elderly and therefore deserving of extra respect.

In general, most of the previously discussed cases involve numerous mental attitudes such as love, hate, jealousy, fear, and respect. From a medical point of view the emotions of love and pity are not harmful to a person. In contrast uncontrolled anger, hate, jealousy, resentment, frustration, selfishness, fear, insecurity, and worry can lead to serious harm to the body.[67]

It is known that in situations which give rise to feelings of fear, disgust, or dejection, the stomach becomes inactive and secretes relatively little acid.[68] On the other hand, life situations which cause feelings of conflict with anxiety, hostility, and resentment are accompanied by opposite changes, namely engorgement of the mucous membrane with blood, increased motor activity, and accelerated secretion of acid. Changes in the stomach which occur during such emotional states often lead to peptic ulcer. Similarly, changes in the blood flow in the colon which result from situational stress frequently cause various types of colitis. Furthermore headache, cardiac pain, and high blood pressure may be caused by reaction to emotional stress.

The Biblical laws which direct a person's attitudes and thinking have as one of their major purposes the prevention of psychologically caused illnesses.

Law

An extremely fundamental regulation which has as one of its main purposes the mental health of the individual, is the observance of the Sabbath. This regulation has many other beneficial aspects, which will also be considered here.

Gen. 2 1-3;
Ex. 16 22-26, 29-30; 20 8-11;
23 12; 31 12-17;
34 21; 35 2-3;
Lev. 19 3, 30;
23 3; 26 2;
Num. 15 32-36;
Deut. 5 12-15.

Observe the Sabbath to keep it holy. Work six days and rest on the seventh. You, your children, your servants, your animals, and the alien within your territory should rest. Do not do all types of work; do not kindle fire, do not plow, do not harvest, do not gather wood, do not leave your settlement. The penalty for non-observance of the Sabbath is death by stoning; otherwise the person is punished by excision. Observe the Sabbath because it is a sign between you and God that He created the world in six days and rested on the seventh day; and because God took you out from Egypt where you were slaves.

Rationale

A day of rest each week allows recovery from physical and mental strain. Rest is known to hasten repair of wounds and irritated surfaces, as well as to help cure many physical ailments and infections.[69] Furthermore, extra sleep results in less fatigue and tension, and increased efficiency.[70]

The Sabbath is a day when all constructive work is prohibited. As a consequence, the person's thoughts tend to be diverted from the worries and problems encountered during the week, and become channeled on more pleasurable ideas. In this manner is achieved not only physical but also mental relaxation.

People with an inordinate drive to achieve as much as possible in as short a time as possible develop a keen sense of time urgency and inner internal struggle. They become aggressive, ambitious and hurried. Persons of this emotional type tend to have about three times as much coronary heart disease as people who are more relaxed, less competitive and have less of an urge to get things done.[71, 72] Now, a person who observes the Sabbath will be forced to relax one day a week. Such relaxation will significantly reduce aggressive and ambitious tendencies and thereby decrease the possibility of heart disease. A statistical survey in Israel tends to support the above argument. It was found over a five-year period that those who go to the synagogue daily (i.e., very religious Jews) had an incidence of 29 heart attacks per 1,000 individuals; those who go occasionally (i.e., moderately religious Jews) had an incidence of 37 heart attacks per 1,000; and those who go rarely (i.e., non-religious Jews) had an incidence of heart attacks of 56 per 1,000 population.[73] Thus, those who obtained relaxation by observance of the Sabbath had about half the incidence of heart attacks as those who probably did not rest on the Sabbath.

Along with the commandment to rest on the Sabbath, it is also stated that work should be done for six days. In effect, this latter phrase is a commandment to accomplish and to exercise. Modern studies have shown that one of the basic needs of people is to achieve and accomplish, so as to maintain good mental health.[74] Also strong evidence exists that exercise is beneficial to the body, and reduces the incidence of coronary heart disease.[75] Thus, not only is it important to rest on the Sabbath, but it is equally important to work on the other six days.

The fact that the Bible has selected one day out of seven days for relaxation, rather than for example one day out of ten, can be explained by assuming that this ratio results in the optimum combination of work and rest. More frequent rest days than once a week would cause underachievement, and perhaps would diminish a person's ambition. On the other hand, less frequent rest days could harm a person's physical and mental health.

Not only is the head of the household required to rest on the Sabbath, but also his children, servants, and animals, as well as the resident alien. Obviously lack of weekly rest would harm the health of people irrespective of their status, and also would hurt the animals.

A specific Sabbath prohibition emphasized in the Pentateuch is the kindling of fire (Ex. 35 2, 3). Not kindling fire one day a week would significantly decrease the extent of air pollution, since most of the pollutants in the air arise from burning.[76] For example, an experiment in Tokyo, where for one day cars were not allowed in certain parts of the city, resulted in dramatic decreases in the concentrations of carbon monoxide in the air.[77] Air pollutants have been shown to play a major role in such sicknesses as lung cancer,[78] respiratory diseases,[79] asthma, and eczema,[80] as well as harming plants and thereby decreasing agricultural produce.[81] The Biblical restriction against lighting fire one day a week thus helps purify the air, and allows recovery from any air-pollution damage that may have occurred.

The other specific Sabbath prohibitions in the Pentateuch, such as not plowing, harvesting, gathering wood, or leaving one's settlement, were probably mentioned because they clarify what types of work are prohibited.

Although non-observance of the Sabbath hurts only the transgressor, still the willful disobedience of this regulation is punishable by death by stoning. This is because the Sabbath is a special sign that God created the world in seven days (Ex. 31 12–17). Anyone who willfully does work on the Sabbath indicates that he does not believe in God, and denies one of the fundamental principles of the Bible.

The punishment is therefore the same as for someone who worships idols (see Chapter Twenty-two). If the violator of the Sabbath goes unpunished, he will eventually become sick, as explained previously and will die prematurely (i.e., he will be punished by excision).

25.3 SEX PROHIBITIONS

There are over 30 regulations in the Pentateuch concerned with restrictions on possible sexual relations and practices. Despite the large number of regulations, they can be neatly divided into three major categories, namely: (A) laws to prevent disease transmission; (B) laws to eliminate inherited defects: and (C) laws to protect the society. Before considering regulations falling into these categories, it is worthwhile to consider the basic commandment requiring people to be fruitful and multiply.

LAW
Gen. 1 28;   Be fruitful and multiply, fill the land and subdue it. Rule over the
9 1–2, 7;   fish in the sea, the birds of the sky, and every living thing that
35 11.   moves upon the land.

RATIONALE
The requirement "to be fruitful" is a very basic law, and implies that man and woman should have sexual relations, have children, and spread out over the land. The more people born, the greater will be man's control and domination of the world. The more people in existence, the more constructive work that can be accomplished. It should be realized that men and women were designed so that having children would be natural and healthful. Only because of diseases and sicknesses, which would be eliminated by strict observance of the laws in the Pentateuch, are there health problems associated with bearing children.

Much publicity is nowadays given for limiting family size and practicing contraception, in contradiction to the law "to be fruitful." However, many contraceptive methods are not completely free from danger to the woman, and many wives have become sick and died as a result. For example, one of the safest methods involves taking certain oral contraceptives. Yet is has been shown in Great Britain that one in every 2,000 women using oral contraceptives is hospitalized each year with blood clotting in the lungs and legs, compared with one in 20,000 for those not taking the pill.[82] Thus serious blood complications are ten times as frequent among those using contraceptive pills. Furthermore, the argument is often stated that the world is rapidly becoming overpopulated, and the food supply cannot keep pace with the population growth. This argument is fallacious, since each healthy grown person has the physical capability, even without modern machinery, to produce enough food for at least several people, and given an opportunity no food shortage should exist. The main problem, however, is that people are not always given an opportunity to work. The Biblical laws, in general, are designed so that people will be healthy, and have the opportunity to work and accomplish. There is therefore no need for restricting the population and practicing contraception.

Although mankind is commanded to be fruitful and multiply, many restrictions are given as to what unions are permissible. These regulations are to prevent disease, inherited defects, and sociological problems, and will now be elaborated on.

25.3.1 Prevention of Disease Transmission

LAWS

The following regulations are especially designed to eliminate sexually transmitted diseases from the population.

Ex. 20 13; Lev. 18 20; 20 10; Deut. 5 17; 22 22.	If a man has an adulterous relation with a married woman, both he and the woman should be killed.
Lev. 19 29; Deut. 23 18.	Do not profane your daughter to make her a prostitute. There shall be no male or female prostitute from among the Israelites.
Deut. 23 19	Do not bring merchandise or money obtained for prostitution into the Temple for any vow, because it is an abomination unto God.
Lev. 18 22; 20 13	Men who have homosexual relations shall be put to death.
Ex. 22 17; Lev. 18 23; 20 15-16; Deut. 27 21.	A man or woman who has sexual relations with an animal shall be killed, and also the animal shall be killed.
Lev. 18 19; 20 18.	Do not approach a menstrually unclean woman to have sexual intercourse. A man and a menstruating woman who do have relations will both be punished by excision.
Deut. 24 1-4.	If a man marries a woman, and she does not find favor in his eyes, then he should write her a note of divorce, give it to her, and send her from his house. Now if she marries a second man, and he too divorces her, or dies, then the first husband cannot remarry her. Such a procedure would be an abomination to God.

RATIONALE

The regulations prohibiting adultery, prostitution, homosexuality, and intercourse with an animal, can be interpreted in terms of what is known about venereal diseases. These diseases are illnesses which are transmitted dominantly by sexual relations with an infected individual. Infection from non-sexual sources occurs occasionally, such as congenital syphilis and gonorrhea infection of the eyes of a newborn infant during the birth process.[83] However, the main method of transmission is through intercourse.

In fact, venereal diseases could be completely eliminated by preventing contact of uninfected persons with persons of promiscuous sexual behavior and those known to be infected.[84]

The five most common venereal diseases, caused by different microorganisms, are syphilis, gonorrhea, lymphogranuloma, venereum granuloma inguinale, and chancroid. In 1954, syphilis infected about 1.5 percent of the United States population, and gonorrhea about 0.8 percent.[85] In 1970 the ratios had changed somewhat; gonorrhea infected over 1.0 percent of the United States population, and syphilis about 0.04 percent.[86] In fact, venereal diseases now rank as the greatest infectious disease problem in the United States.[87] This is in spite of the availability of penicillin which is used to treat both syphilis and gonorrhea. It should be pointed out that penicillin treatment, even if used in every case, would still not be the complete solution. Many persons get serious adverse reactions from the drug, and also some resistant strains of microorganisms have appeared which are not easily killed by penicillin.

The Biblical prohibitions against adultery, prostitution, and male homosexuality are clearly to prevent the spread of venereal disease. All three types of contacts are known to spread these sicknesses. For example, a statistical survey in Massachusetts showed that 3 percent of the venereal disease results from contact with prostitutes, 12 percent results from homosexual male contacts, and 85 percent from heterosexual free love relations.[88] We may also assume that the prohibition against having sexual relations with animals is to prevent the spread of venereal disease.

It should be pointed out that untreated cases of syphilis frequently result in death, insanity, or blindness, while untreated cases of gonorrhea frequently cause sterility in men and women, and occasionally death.[89] Therefore persons who commit prohibited acts which spread venereal diseases threaten to kill out many people, and are subject to the death penalty. In particular, the Pentateuch prescribes death for those who commit adultery, male homosexuality, or have sexual relations with animals. In the latter case, the animal is also to be killed since it may spread disease to other animals, and even possibly to other people. Note that female homosexuality is not specifically prohibited by the Bible, since venereal disease is not spread in this manner.

Merchandise or money obtained in exchange for prostitution may possibly become contaminated, and should not be brought to the Temple where highest purity must be maintained. Furthermore, the acceptance of such items to pay for Temple expenses could in effect give legal encouragement to promiscuity.

The restriction on having sexual intercourse with a menstrually unclean woman may be interpreted in terms of cancer of the uterus and of the prostate. It has been established that throughout the world Jewish women have only about one-ninth the incidence of cancer of the uterus as compared to non-Jews.[90, 91] Previously this difference was attributed to circumcision of the Jew, but now that most men of all faiths are circumcised the lower risk still exists. It has further been noted that women who have experienced frequent spotting and inter-menstrual bleeding run a 3.5 times greater than average risk of developing uterine cancer.[92] Also, the disease is especially prevalent among women who have many sex partners. These points strongly indicate that the more complete separation of Jewish couples during the wife's menstrual period is the main reason for the lower incidence of cancer of the uterus among Jews. In fact, many gynecologists and obstetricians feel that the Pap smear, a method for testing for cancer of the uterus, does not have to be administered to women who observe the menstrual separation requirements, because of the rarity of this disease among these women.[93] Similarly, it has been found that the incidence of cancer of the prostate is much below the average among Jewish men.[94] Both types of cancer cause premature death, in agreement with the punishment of excision specified in the Bible. It was not necessary for the Bible to prescribe a death penalty for having sexual relations during the wife's period because the resultant cancers are not contagious, and only affect the people involved.

The regulation preventing a husband from remarrying his former wife after she has married a second husband, and then been divorced or widowed, is to prevent legalized adultery. Otherwise, a married couple who wanted to remain married, might for the purpose of momentary pleasure become divorced to allow the woman to marry and have relations with another man. Afterwards the second husband would divorce her, and she would become remarried to her first husband. This practice could than be repeated many times, resulting in the spread of venereal diseases and in utterly destroying the family unit.

Incidental to this regulation is the specification of marriage and divorce procedures. In particular, the Bible indicates that the man is the one who initiates the marriage or the divorce. A written document given to the woman is necessary for a divorce so she can prove that she is no longer married. In contrast, no written record is necessary for proof of marriage, since the fact that the couple lives together in one house is sufficient evidence.

25.3.2 Elimination of Inherited Defects

Bodily defects in a newborn child may arise from many negative influences on its pregnant mother, such as disease, drugs, poor nutrition, and physical disorders. Diseases known to cause birth defects include rubella, scarlet fever, cholera, malaria, smallpox, measles, mumps, and chicken pox.[95, 96] Potentially dangerous drugs are aspirin, antihistamines, thalidomide, and cigarette smoke.[97, 98] Poor nutrition, such as insufficient amounts of vitamins C and D in the diet, are known to cause scurvy and rickets in the newborn.[99] Body disorders in the pregnant mother, which can be of danger to the fetus, include nephritis, certain heart conditions, diabetes, and goiter.[100]

Birth defects from the above causes are prevented by the Biblical laws through the means of eliminating disease, prohibiting the use of drugs, and supplying a nutritious diet and plentiful food for the entire population. Other possible sources of birth abnormalities that the Bible tries to eliminate are inherited abnormalities.

Here will be presented those laws specifically designed to prevent the occurence of such defects.

Laws

The following regulations are designed to prevent the occurrence of inherited defects. It should be noted that the prohibited unions are expressed from a male point of view, since it is usually the male who initiates sexual relations. Undoubtedly the equivalent unions, from a female point of view, are also prohibited. For example, the prohibition against intercourse with your mother's sister also implies that relations with your mother's brother are not permitted.

Lev. 18 7	Do not have intercourse with your mother.
Lev. 18 9, 11; 20 17 Deut. 27 22.	Do not have intercourse with your sister or half-sister—punishment of excision.
Lev. 18 12, 13; 20 19.	Do not have intercourse with your father's sister or your mother's sister.
Lev. 18 10.	Do not have intercourse with your son's daughter or your daughter's daughter.
Lev. 18 8; 20 11; Deut. 23 1; 27 20.	Do not have intercourse with your father's wife—punishment of death.
Lev. 18 14; 20 20	Do not have intercourse with your father's brother's wife—punishment of childlessness.
Lev. 18 16; 20 21.	Do not have intercourse with your brother's wife—punishment of childlessness.
Lev. 18 15; 20 12.	Do not have relations with your son's wife—punishment of death.
Deut. 23 2	A sexually-maimed person should not marry among the Jews.
Deut. 23 3	A bastard (ממזר) should not marry among the Jews, even for ten generations.
Deut. 23 4–7	An Ammonite and Moabite should not intermarry into the Jewish community, even for ten generations, because they have acted improperly to you. Do not seek their welfare or their good.
Deut. 23 8–9	Children of the third generation of the Edomites and Egyptians may intermarry among the Jews.
Ex. 34 16; Deut. 7 1–4.	Do not intermarry with the seven nations occupying territory promised to Israel, namely the Hittites, Girgashites, Amorites, Canaanites, Perizzites, Hivites, and Jebusites, lest they turn away your sons to idol-worship.

Rationale

We will here assume that the Bible prohibits intercourse not only with mother, sister, half-sister, aunt, and granddaughter, but also with their male counterparts, namely father, brother, half-brother, uncle, and grandson.

According to genetic theory, chromosomes and their subdivisions called genes, are the means by which inheritable traits are transmitted. Each person has 46 chromosomes, of which 23 are transmitted to his child. On the average, a brother and sister, and a parent and child have one-half of their chromosomes the same.[101] Similarly, uncle and niece, aunt and nephew, grandparent and grandchild, and half-brother and half-sister have one-fourth of their chromosomes of the same type. Cases where one-eighth of the chromosomes are identical are first cousins, great-uncles and great-nieces, great-aunts and great-nephews, and great-grandparents and great-grandchildren. The Bible has prohibited intercourse between persons having one-half or one-fourth of their chromosomes the same; i.e., relations between parent and child, and sister and brother (one-half identical chromosomes); and relations between aunt and nephew, uncle and niece, grandparent and grandchild, and half-sister and half-brother (one-fourth identical chromosomes). However, according to the Pentateuch, intercourse between persons having one-eighth of their chromosomes the same is permissible.

The reason for these restrictions is that children born from unions between persons having many chromosomes identical often have inherited defects. Thus, a study of father-daughter and brother-sister unions has shown that 11 out of 18 offspring, i.e., more than half, had serious physical or mental abnormalities.[102] This is because of the high probability of the children receiving a double dose of any particular defective recessive genes. For example, for relationships between persons having one-half of their chromosomes the same, the probability of any particular defective genes being paired is one in four.

On the other hand, when first cousins, or others having one-eighth of the chromosomes in common marry, the chances of the children having double doses of any particular defective trait is only one-sixteenth. Now if the family is relatively free of genetic flaws, then instead of having defective offspring, above-average children may result.[103] By following the Biblical laws, factors which lead to defective genes, such as disease or taking of drugs, are eliminated, and therefore the people are relatively free of genetic flaws. Hence, unions between persons having one-eighth of their chromosomes identical should theoretically be permissible, as is the case in the Biblical regulations.

Another group of prohibited marriages involve relationships with the wife of your father, uncle, brother, or son. These are cases of relations with the wife of a relative having one-half or one-fourth of the genes in common. In two cases, for a brother's wife and for an uncle's wife, the Bible states that childlessness will result. Yet, we find from Deut. 25 5, 6 that if the husband dies, and the wife is childless, then the husband's brother should marry the widow in order to have children. It thus appears probable that the penalty of childlessness will only result if the wife has already had children from her previous husband. Scientific knowledge does not provide a clear explanation for these cases. However, an analogous case involves RH incompatibility. This involves incompatibility between the blood of a mother and her fetal child, resulting from inherited differences in some of their blood elements. This condition only occurs after one child has been born, and sometimes results in death or severe injury to the newborn.[104] Similarly, it may happen that once a child is born to the wife of the father, uncle, brother, or son, an incompatibility develops between the close relative and the wife, making such a union dangerous.

Restrictions against marriage by a sexually-maimed person indicate that children from such a person may have defective characteristics. Damaged or improperly developed chromosomes may be supplied by such a maimed person.

Similarly, the restrictions against marriage by a bastard (ממזר), imply that he may have defective characteristics. The meaning of the Hebrew word ממזר is not known for certain, although it is usually translated as "bastard." According to one generally accepted explanation, a ממזר is a child resulting from relationships prohibited by the Bible. If the relationship involved close relatives, then there is a high probability that the bastard child has defective chromosomes which could be transmitted to his children. If the relationship involved a man and, for example, a married woman, then there is a high chance that venereal disease has developed; and as stated previously some common venereal diseases can also be transmitted to the baby either before or during the birth process. The bastard then should not marry because of the chance of spreading venereal disease.

Not intermarrying with Ammonites or Moabites, as well as with the seven ancient nations near Israel, will prevent being influenced by their idol-worshipping cultures; will prevent becoming infected with venereal or other diseases which these peoples are subject to because of their immoral actions; and will prevent inheriting any defective genes that could be transmitted to their offspring. However, the Edomites and Egyptians are probably not as sinful. Therefore they do not have as high an incidence of disease or of defective inheritable traits. By the third generation any such imperfections which remained could easily be avoided, and most probably any such faults would have been eliminated by that time.

25.3.3 Protection of the Society

LAWS

There are a number of regulations related to sex whose main purposes appear to be mainly sociological rather than hygienic.

Lev. 18 17; 20 14; Deut. 27 23.	Do not have intercourse with a woman and her daughter, or her granddaughter; it is lewdness—punishment of death by burning.

Lev. 18 18	Do not marry the sister of your wife, to make them rivals during your wife's lifetime.
Deut. 20 14 21 10–14.	If you see a pretty woman, whom you desire, among the captives of a city, you may take her to your house to become your wife. However, before having intercourse with her, she must shave her head, cut her nails, change her clothes, and mourn for her father and mother a full month. If you no longer find her pleasing, then divorce her, but do not sell her for money. Do not treat her harshly since you afflicted her.
Deut. 22 5	Do not wear clothing of the opposite sex, for it is an abomination to do this.
Deut. 22 13–21	If a husband, after the first intercourse with his new wife, claims she was not a virgin, then the wife's parents should expose their daughter's hymen to the elders of the city. The husband should thereupon be punished for giving a bad name to a virgin of Israel, and he should be fined 100 shekels of silver which he gives to the father of the bride. The husband is then not permitted to divorce the wife for his entire life. If, however, the husband's claim is correct and the bride was not a virgin, then the woman should be stoned to death by the men of her city, because she was a prostitute while residing in her father's house.
Deut. 22 23–27.	If an engaged* girl has intercourse with a man in the city, then both she and the man should be stoned to death. The girl is killed because she did not cry for help, and the man because he had relations with a married woman. But if the man forced intercourse upon the girl in the country, only the man should be killed, because undoubtedly she cried for help, but there was no one to rescue her.
Ex. 22 15–16	If a man entice an unengaged virgin to have intercourse, then he should pay the dowry for her to become his wife. If her father refuses to give her to him, then he should pay money according to the dowry of virgins.
Deut. 22 28–29.	If a man force an unengaged virgin to have intercourse, and they be found, then the man should give to the girl's father 50 shekels of silver, and she shall be his wife. He may not divorce her all his life.

* By "engaged" is meant a girl who is contracted to be married, but has not yet gone to live in her husband's home.

Num. 5 11-31	If a husband has a fit of jealousy and suspects, without any concrete evidence, that his wife had sexual intercourse with another man, then the husband should bring his wife to the priest. She undergoes a trial by ordeal according to the specifications in Num. 5 15-27. Then if she had been unfaithful, the bitter water she drinks will cause her belly to swell and her thigh to fall. However, if she is not guilty, then she shall be proved innocent, and will be able to conceive.
Lev. 19 20-22	If a man has sexual relations with a maidservant who has become disgusting to her master but she has not been redeemed or freed, then an investigation should be made, and the maidservant and man should not be killed just because she was not freed. The man should bring a ram as a guilt-offering to atone for his sin.

RATIONALE

The main reason for not marrying a woman and her daughter, or a woman and her granddaughter, may be sociological. The dependence of the child on her mother, and the respect required of a daughter for her parent, could result in lack of harmony in the family, where the husband is considered the head of the household. Similarly, the prohibition against marrying two sisters is specifically stated to have the purpose of preventing rivalry between the wives. It is difficult to argue that any obvious health problem would result from marrying two sisters, since after the death of one of them it is permissible to marry the other. Nevertheless, the punishment of death by burning, in the analogous case involving marriage to a woman and her daughter, implies that some serious disease or sickness may result.

The procedure for marrying a captive woman has several practical benefits. First of all, the law prohibits intercourse between a soldier and women captives during or immediately after the battle, thereby preventing spread of venereal disease, and birth of children out of wedlock. Secondly, the woman's shaving her head, cutting her nails, and changing her clothes removes probable sites for disease microorganisms, namely the hair, the dirt under the nails, and contaminated clothing. Thirdly, the one month waiting time, before intercourse is permissible, allows the detection of any imperfections or sicknesses which the captive woman may have. Furthermore, the captive woman's anger and shock may wear off during this time, thus allowing the marriage a greater chance of success. If it happens that the soldier loses interest in the woman, then she cannot be sold, but must be given her freedom. In this way, promiscuity with captive women is prevented, and in the process the women are educated, for at least one month, to become useful members of the society.

Wearing clothing of the opposite sex, is not harmful in itself, but it could lead to unhealthy thoughts and actions. Promiscuity, homosexuality, and other vices can result. To prevent such immoral consequences, the Bible prohibits men dressing in women's clothes, and women in men's clothes.

The regulations concerning marriage to a supposedly virgin woman, who turns out not to be a virgin, have been variously interpreted. Here it will be assumed that the legal proceedings must take place within a short time after the first intercourse. In general, if the girl had really been a virgin, then the rupture of the hymen would not be complete, and residual signs recognizable by the elders of the city would exist, proving her innocence. If, however, she is found actually not to have been a virgin, and it can be proved by witnesses that she had been a prostitute prior to marriage, then she is subject to death by stoning, because of the danger of spread of venereal disease.

According to the above interpretation there are many practical aspects to the regulations. First, the procedure given is a way of detecting if the supposedly virgin bride had previous intercourse and was therefore possibly suffering from venereal disease, or already pregnant by another man. Secondly, the law serves as a deterrent on the girl from having promiscuous relations prior to marriage, lest she be found out subsequently and killed. Furthermore, chances of rumors being spread years later that she was not a virgin when married are minimized, since she can always claim that her husband made no such complaint against her. Naturally, limitations have to be set to prevent unscrupulous husbands, for example those who want to take revenge on the woman, from making false accusations. Therefore, if the accusation turns out to be false, the husband has to pay a fine, and is not permitted subsequently to divorce the wife.

If an "engaged" girl, i.e., a woman whose marriage has not yet been consummated, voluntarily has intercourse with another man, then both she and the man should be killed. This law is to plug a loop-hole that would otherwise exist. Suppose, for example, that the girl is engaged to someone who by the nature of his temperament is unlikely to make a complaint if he later finds out that his wife is not a virgin. Then between the time of the girl's engagement and the consummation of the marriage, she and other men would be free to have intercourse without any punishment other than a fine. The man with whom she has relations would not be required to marry her, since she is already engaged to someone else. To avoid this possible legalized prostitution, the Bible prescribes the death penalty for both the man and the woman. This punishment for the woman applies only when she consented to intercourse. If, however, intercourse was forced upon the girl against her will, then she is not punished, because otherwise an innocent person would be killed.

On the other hand, if a man has intercourse with an unengaged virgin, the situation can easily be remedied by the man paying the required dowry and marrying the girl. If the girl's father refuses to allow the marriage, then the man still has to pay the dowry as a punishment for his actions. However, if a man rapes an unengaged virgin, then again the situation can be remedied by his marrying the girl, but in this instance a fine of 50 shekels, much higher than the usual dowry, must be paid to the girl's father. Furthermore, the man may not divorce the girl for his entire life, since he forced intercourse on her against her will.

A husband's suspicion that his wife has been unfaithful, even if he has no evidence to support his belief, can lead to the disruption of an otherwise happy marriage. To prevent such a result, the Bible provides a psychological method by which the wife's guilt or innocence can be determined. The husband brings his wife to the priest so she can undergo a trial by ordeal as described in Num. 5 15-27. She drinks specially prepared bitter water which, if she is guilty, will make her belly to swell and her thigh to fall. These manifestations are very analogous to those symptoms of false pregnancy (pseudocyesis) exhibited by many women.[105] As a result of psychological problems the woman can experience all the symptoms of pregnancy, including enlargement of the abdomen, even though not pregnant. Pseudocyesis is considered to be a form of hysteria, resulting from mental stimulation of the woman's glandular system.[106] If the trial by ordeal gives negative results, then the husband's jealousy is proved to be unfounded, and intercourse between the husband and wife can be resumed. If the woman is proved guilty, then the woman becomes a curse among the people.

The law concerning a maidservant may be explained as follows. According to Ex. 21 7-11, a person's daughter may be sold as a maidservant and married to the master or his son. If she is not liked by her master (or his son) then she must be redeemed or set free. Now in a case where the maidservant is disgusting to her master (Lev. 19 20-22) and she was therefore not married to him, yet he has not had her redeemed nor has he freed her, then if another man has sexual relations with her they are not subject to the death penalty as would be the case for having relations with an engaged* woman (Deut. 22 23-24). The maidservant was entitled to be free, and the master had relinquished all intent of marrying her and therefore her status was not that of an engaged woman. An investigation is made to ensure that she really should be free. If this is found to be the case, then the only penalty is that the man has to bring a ram for a guilt-offering. As a result of this law the maidservant would gain her freedom and could then marry the man with whom she had relations.

25.4 ADDITIONAL REGULATIONS CONCERNING DISEASE PREVENTION

Numerous Biblical laws are designed to prevent disease transmission. Some of the laws eliminate places of growth of pathogens, others control the populations of insects and animals which transmit disease, while others purify the individual who may be a carrier of disease microorganisms. Many of the laws involving disease control have already been listed under other categories, such as dietary restrictions and sex prohibitions. In this section are discussed miscellaneous regulations which do

---

* "Engaged" here means a woman who was married but did not yet have sexual relations.

not conveniently fall into other categories. Particular emphasis is here given to laws relevant to different types of impurity.

LAW

Num. 19 1–22   A perfectly red, unblemished cow, upon which never came a yoke, should be slaughtered and completely burned outside the camp. A priest should add cedar wood, hyssop, and scarlet to the burning cow. The latter priest, as well as the one who burns the cow, the one who gathers the ashes, and the person who touches the subsequently prepared ash-water mixture, must wash their clothes and bodies, and are impure until the evening. A small amount of the ashes are added to a vessel of fresh water to produce an ash-water mixture, which is sprinkled upon objects and persons who became impure by contact with dead human bodies.

Objects and people become impure for seven days from dead humans by contact with the body, or a bone, or a grave, and even by being in the same tent as the dead body. An impure person must have the ash-water sprinkled on him on the third and seventh days of impurity in order to become clean. Then on the seventh day the impure person washes his clothes and himself, and becomes clean in the evening. An impure person who does not have ash-water sprinkled on him is subject to the penalty of excision, because he has defiled the sanctuary.

Anything which touches a person who is impure from a dead human body becomes unclean. Likewise, a person who touches the impure person becomes unclean until the evening.

RATIONALE

From the description of the regulations involving the ash-water mixture, it seems apparent that the mixture is an extremely powerful antiseptic agent which kills numerous pathogens. In fact, it is so effective that only a small amount needs to be sprinkled on the impure person or object. To be certain that the correct chemical results upon burning the cow, it is necessary to select a perfectly red, unblemished animal, upon which a yoke was never placed. The placing of a yoke on the cow could possibly result in changes in the hormonal balance which would modify the nature of the chemical obtained upon burning the animal.

The surprising fact that the ash-water mixture, which is used to purify people and objects from impurity, causes all those who come in contact with the ashes or the mixture to become impure until the evening, can be explained by the potency of the chemical. Probably, adverse drug reactions may occur unless the person who touched the ashes washes his body and clothes. Even the person who is being purified by the ash-water mixture, and only receives a sprinkling of it, must wash his body and clothes on the seventh day to prevent an adverse reaction.

People who have come in contact with a dead human body are impure for seven days and need to have the ash-water mixture sprinkled on them on the third and seventh days. In general, after death of a person there is no longer any prevention of the rapid growth of disease transmitting organisms. Therefore touching of the dead person, as well as being in the tent (or room) in which he died, and even touching a human bone or grave makes a living person impure for seven days. If the person does not purify himself within this time, then often he will succumb to or be a carrier of a disease. The ash-water mixture, however, if sprinkled on the person on the third and seventh days, will kill pathogens, and prevent disease and possible excision. Even if the person does not go to the Temple, he will indirectly defile it, since he will be the cause of the spread of disease, which may eventually be transmitted to someone who will enter the Temple area.

Medical doctors who perform autopsies on humans have, for example, to take extra precautions when the dead person had contracted such sicknesses as venereal disease or tuberculosis. Otherwise, it is known that there is a high probability that the doctor will catch these sicknesses. A famous example where medical doctors have carried disease after contact with dead bodies occurred in the General Hospital at Vienna in the early nineteenth century. It was there established that the infective material that spread puerperal fever among women delivering babies, was carried by physicians who did not thoroughly wash their hands after contact with corpses.[107]

Someone who touches a person who became impure by contact with a dead human body also becomes impure, because of the possibility of the second person contracting a disease from the first person. However, the second person's impurity lasts only until the evening, since the chances of contracting disease microorganisms are greatly reduced.

LAW

Num. 31 20–23 Inanimate objects which come in contact with dead human beings, for example during war time, need to be purified on the third and seventh days with the ash-water mixture from the red cow. In addition, metallic objects, such as those made of gold, silver, copper, iron, tin, and lead, must first be passed through fire. Similarly, items made from materials which cannot withstand fire must first be passed through water.

RATIONALE

Previously in the text (Num. 19 1–22), the Pentateuch specified that persons who came in contact with a dead human being needed to purify themselves with the ash-water mixture. Now we are told that inanimate objects which came in contact with a dead body also need to be purified with the mixture. In addition, the items which can withstand fire without damage must first be passed through fire. It is well known that disease microorganisms are killed by heat from a flame.[108] Similarly, other items need first to be passed through water, because washing is known to remove disease microorganisms. These preliminary cleansing procedures are required so as to ensure that the subsequent use of the ash-water mixture will completely kill any pathogens on the materials.

LAW

Deut. 21 22, 23   The body of a person executed for a crime should be hanged on a tree. However, the body should be buried that same day so as not to defile the land.

RATIONALE

The hanging of an executed person is to make the population aware of the penalty for serious criminal actions. However, once a person is dead the body no longer keeps pathogens in check, and they can multiply rapidly within the body and become a source of infection for the population. If the body is buried the same day, the chance of a disease being spread would be remote. Burial of the body prevents further contamination since the microorganisms in the soil keep the pathogens in check. Thus, it is known that the soil has a purifying action, causing the disappearance of pathogens, such as typhoid and staphylococcus, because of counteracting molds and bacteria.[109]

A logical conclusion that can be deduced from this law is that any dead person, not necessarily someone executed for criminal actions, should be buried on the day of death or as soon as possible thereafter, so as to prevent spread of disease.

LAW

Gen. 17 10–14   All male Israelite children should be circumcised when eight
Ex. 12 44, 48;   days old, as a sign of a covenant between God and the Israelite
Lev. 12 3;   people. Also non-Israelite slaves should be circumcised. A resident alien can become a citizen, i.e., can convert to Judaism, by being circumcised. An uncircumcised male will be punished with excision, and is not permitted to eat from the Passover sacrifice.

RATIONALE

Circumcision involves cutting away the foreskin or prepuce of the penis.[110] Upon the inner layer of foreskin there are situated a number of glands which secrete a cheeselike substance called smegma. Accumulation of smegma may result in great physical and psychological discomfort and may serve as the source of a rather penetrating odor. Balanitis or inflammation of the penis, which to some extent is always present in the uncircumcised, is eliminated by circumcision. Also, the often associated phimosis or narrowing of the external orifice of the penis, is relieved.[111] Circumcision substantially reduces the possibility of cancer of the penis, which causes about 300 deaths in the United States each year.[112] In fact, in India, the Hindus who do not undergo circumcision have a far greater incidence of cancer of the penis than the Moslems who usually are circumcised at about 10 or 12 years of age. Among the Jews, who are circumcised when eight days old, cancer of the penis virtually never occurs.[113] Nowadays, in the western world, circumcision of newborn boys is widely practiced for hygienic reasons.[114] It has also been noted that cancer of the cervix of the uterus is much less common in women whose husbands have been circumcised.[115]

For a baby of eight days of age, the circumcision procedure is relatively painless, and yet the newborn is old enough so that danger to life is minimal. In contrast, circumcision on mature persons is a painful operation. It has been claimed that the possibility exists of psychological harm when a circumcision is performed after the boy is a few months old.[116] Moreover, it has been asserted that the chance of hemorrhage is at a minimum when the baby is eight days old.

The inflammation of the penis which is always present to some extent in the uncircumcised may serve as a source of infection to others. Therefore, to protect those going to the Temple area, the Passover sacrifice cannot be eaten by someone who is not circumcised.

LAW
    Lev. 15 16–18   When a man has emitted semen, he shall bathe his whole body in water and be unclean until the evening. Every piece of clothing or skin on which there is any semen shall be washed and remains unclean until the evening. Also a man and a woman who have had intercourse shall bathe in water and remain unclean until the evening.

RATIONALE
The impurity attributed by the Bible to semen indicates that it can support the growth of disease-causing microorganisms. For example, semen is known to be one of the main means by which venereal diseases are transmitted. Washing the entire body and contaminated clothing removes the semen, and prevents the spread of pathogens. Even after washing, some virulence of the microorganisms may remain, and it is therefore necessary to wait until the evening to ensure that all pathogens have died out. In the case of insects, for example, it has been found that they are most susceptible in the late afternoon to being killed by insecticides.[117]

LAWS
    Lev. 15 19–24   A woman who has a discharge of blood at her regular menstrual period, is impure for seven days. Any bed or chair that she uses becomes unclean. Anyone touching her, her bed, or her chair, shall wash himself and his clothes, and is unclean until the evening. Anyone touching an object on her bed or chair is also unclean until the evening. Anyone having intercourse with her, and getting some of her dis-

Lev. 15 25–30. charge on him, shall be unclean for seven days, and every bed that he uses becomes unclean.
If the discharge of blood occurs not at the time of her menstruation, or continues beyond the period of menstruation, all the days of her discharge she shall be impure just as during her regular menstrual period. When she becomes cleansed from the discharge, she shall count seven days and then be clean. On the eighth day she shall bring two turtledoves or pigeons, one as a burnt-offering and one as a sin-offering.

RATIONALE

The average duration of the menstrual flow is four days but may continue for a week. During this time the basal metabolic rate and temperature fall somewhat, skin secretions and saliva change more or less, and capillary vessels of the skin bleed more readily. A day or more before the external flow has ended, the processes of repair are well under way.[118]

The impurity attributed to the menstrual flow by the Bible corresponds to the changes in skin secretions and saliva in the woman. These secretions, which are transmitted in trace amounts upon contact, can probably support the growth of pathogens. Therefore items with which the woman has prolonged contact, such as a bed or chair, become impure. Also anyone touching the menstruating woman becomes impure. By washing the clothes and the body, a person who has touched the woman can remove sufficient amounts of the secretions, so that disease-causing microorganisms would die by the evening. Especially contaminating is having intercourse with the woman at the time of her period, whereby her discharge gets mixed with the man's semen. The combined effect of these two impure secretions results in the man becoming unclean for seven days, since pathogens can gain a strong foothold.

Intermenstrual flow is not normal and may be the result of such factors as non-malignant tumors of the uterus, cancer of the cervix, inflammation of the uterus or other nearby organs, disorders of some endocrine glands, and many other possibilities.[119] Since bleeding between periods indicates some type of disorder, it is necessary for the woman to continue in her state of impurity seven days after the discharge has stopped before she becomes officially clean. The extra seven days are necessary to ensure that recovery is complete. In contrast, no extra waiting period beyond the seven stipulated days, are required after the menstrual period, since it is a natural process, and repair is essentially complete when the blood discharge has ended.

Of particular relevance to the above laws is the fact that women who report frequent spotting and intermenstrual bleeding run a 3.5 times greater than average risk of developing uterine cancer.[120] (See Section 25.3.1 concerning restrictions against intercourse during menstruation.)

Law
Lev. 12 1–8   A woman after bearing a male child shall be unclean for seven days, as during her menstrual period. For an additional 33 days she shall not touch anything holy nor enter the sanctuary. After bearing a female child, a woman shall be unclean for 14 days, and not be permitted to touch holy items for an additional 66 days. Afterwards she shall bring a burnt-offering and a sin-offering to complete final purification.

Rationale
At the present time obstetricians consider six weeks (i.e., about 40 days) as necessary for complete recovery by the mother after childbirth, irrespective of whether the baby was male or female.[121] This time corresponds to the 40 days for full recovery specified by the Bible after a male child is born, but is only half the 80 days required if a female child is born. However, it is known that there are differences between pregnancies for a boy or a girl. For example, a boy is frequently carried slightly differently by the pregnant woman than a girl. Also, the average time of gestation is slightly shorter for a boy than for a girl. Therefore, there may also be different recovery rates for the two cases, which will eventually be recognized by medical doctors.

The Biblical regulation indicates that a woman after childbirth may readily contract sicknesses. Medical experience has verified this point. For example, in the early nineteenth century in the General Hospital at Vienna, the death from puerperal fever among women delivering babies was between 10 and 30 percent.[122] Subsequently, it was shown that the infective material was conveyed by physicians who did not wash their hands after contact with dead bodies. By enforcing thorough washing of the hands of the physicians, the death rate in 1846 was reduced to only 1 percent.

It is noteworthy that after one or two weeks the new mother is no longer as impure as a menstruating woman. However, she is still not sufficiently clean so that she can touch holy objects or go into the sanctuary. Higher standards of purity are needed for the Temple area because of the large numbers of people that gather there, and the possible chance of starting an epidemic.

Law
Lev. 13 1–46;   Numerous regulations are presented concerning leprosy-type
Num. 5 1–4;   skin diseases. Details are given so that cases which are of the
Deut. 24 8–9   leprosy-type can be differentiated from those which are not. The priests are the ones who have the final say as to the type of skin disease the person has. Often the diagnosis is delayed for one or more weeks to determine the manner in which the disease progresses. The person diagnosed as being a leper

should wear rent clothes, his hair should be dishevelled, his upper lip should be covered, and he should reside outside the settlement.

RATIONALE

The Biblical leprosy regulations are designed to prevent the spread of leprosy-type diseases, and thereby eliminate these types of sicknesses from the community. By leprosy-type diseases are meant those illnesses which require long or repeated exposures to be transmitted from person to person. For such illnesses, the isolation of the sick prevents the transmission of the disease to others. In contrast, quarantine of persons suffering from more easily communicable diseases, such as mumps, scarlet fever, and measles, has proved to be completely ineffective.[123] Frequently these communicable sicknesses have been spread to others even before the ailing person is quarantined.

Leprosy is an example of the leprosy-type diseases. Unlike most communicable illnesses, leprosy requires long continuous or repeated exposures for successful transmission. The disease progresses slowly, and in many cases only a few superficial lesions develop which may persist without change or gradually disappear.[124] The exact means by which leprosy is transmitted is unknown, and the incubation period is usually longer than one year.[125] The prevention of leprosy is effected by removing the patient from the environment in which he may be a menace. In modern times leprosy is negligible as a public health problem in western Europe and North America, perhaps because of isolation of those who are afflicted, while in certain areas of Africa up to one-tenth of the population may suffer from the sickness.

The exact names of the diseases being referred to by the Biblical descriptions are not known. Varying opinions have been expressed, such as leprosy, white leprosy, and variations thereof.[126] However, no matter what the names are for the skin afflictions, the Biblical descriptions of the symptoms are sufficiently precise so that exact diagnoses can be made. It is very probable that some of the described symptoms are common to more than one ailment.

The person diagnosed as a leper is required to dress in an unusual manner, with the apparent purpose of being easily identified as someone to avoid. It may also be that the unusual manner of dress has the benefit of speeding recovery. For example, in the case of leprosy, lesions usually first form in the nose and on the exposed parts of the skin.[127] Also lesions may spread to the hair of the head and the beard (Lev. 13 29). Corresponding to these body areas we find that (A) the upper lip should be covered—perhaps to prevent spread of lesions from the nose; (B) the clothes should be rent—perhaps to allow air circulation to the skin areas; and (C) the hair should be dishevelled or loose—to minimize infection of the skin under the hair.

LAW

Lev. 13 47–59   A garment or thread, of wool or linen, or anything made of skin, which is stained with a green or red leprosylike affliction shall be shown to the priest. If the coloration spreads within seven days, then the afflicted item shall be burned. If the coloration does not spread, then the afflicted item should be washed and stored for another seven days. If the affliction then still has the same appearance as before, the item has to be burned; but if the coloration is dimmed, then the afflicted part is torn out, and the item is washed again and becomes useable. However, if the coloration later reappears, the afflicted item has to be burned.

RATIONALE

The above regulations concerning green or red growths on wool, linen, or skin, indicate that such afflictions can lead to infections in man. To prevent the occurrence of resultant disease, the Bible prescribes the burning or washing of the infected items. Undoubtedly, the cases where the afflicted item can be reused after washing are instances where no danger to the person exists.

Scientifically, the afflictions can be considered as being mold or fungus infections. Molds, for example, can stay alive indefinitely on numerous inanimate objects, such as cloth, fabrics, and leather.[128]

Fungus infections in people are very common. Usually the fungi cause skin diseases, but they can also attack underlying tissues and cause fatal infections. They can lodge in the bones, lungs, and other organs.[129]

LAW

Lev. 19 19;   Do not put on a garment made of wool and linen.
Deut. 22 11

RATIONALE

The prohibition here is not against making or owning a garment made from wool and linen, but against wearing the garment. When worn, it is exposed to the warmth and perspiration from the body. This would probably provide an environment suitable for growth of disease-carrying molds or fungi, as indicated for the previous case. Especially of interest is the fact that the two materials wool and linen are combined, both of which individually could be suitable for growth of dangerous green or red growths, as stated above. The close physical contact between the person and the wool-linen garment would allow the easy transmittance of any disease-causing microorganisms to the skin.

LAW

Lev. 14 1–32   A detailed purification procedure is followed upon recovery of a leper. The priest arranges for the immersion of a live bird in the water-diluted blood of a freshly slaughtered bird, and the sprinkling of the liquid on the recovered person. Afterwards the former leper washes his clothes, shaves off the hair from all parts of his body, bathes in water, and waits for seven days. On the seventh day he again washes his clothes, shaves, and bathes. Then the recovered leper brings a he-lamb as a guilt-offering, and some oil. Some of the blood of the he-lamb is put on the right earlobe, the right thumb, and the right big toe of the leper; and later some oil is placed on the same spots, as well as on his head. A sin-offering, a burnt-offering, and a meal offering are then brought to complete the purification ceremony.

RATIONALE

Even after the lesions of the leper are healed the possibility exists that he may still be a carrier of the disease. For example, the United States Public Health Service requires that the leprosy microorganism not be detected for six months before a patient be considered fully recovered.[130] To speed up recovery and to ensure that any causative microorganism has been removed, the Bible prescribes a detailed purification procedure involving blood from a bird, washing of clothes, shaving, bathing, blood from a he-lamb, and oil. Afterwards the former leper is completely purified and no longer a carrier of leprosy.

From the above description it is evident that the leprosy microorganism could survive on the clothes, skin or hair of the leper. Hair, in particular, has been shown to hold bacteria very tenaciously.[131] For that reason shaving off all the hair of the body is required to enable complete purification. Similarly, bathing helps remove the microorganism from the skin, washing the clothes removes the microorganism from the garments, and the use of the blood and oil provide additional antisepsis.

LAW

Lev. 14 33–57   If green or red leprosy-type depressions are observed growing in the stones of a house, then the building should be emptied and closed for seven days. During this time, anyone entering the house becomes impure until the evening, and anyone eating or sleeping in the house must wash his clothes. If on the seventh day the priest sees that the colorations are spreading, then the infected stones should be removed and the area scraped clean; and new stones should be substituted. If afterwards the colorations reappear, then the entire building must be disassembled. However, if the colorations do not reappear, the house is declared clean by the priest. Final purification of the building is accomplished by sprinkling the house seven times with the water-diluted blood of a freshly slaughtered bird in which was immersed a live bird.

Rationale

Here we see that green or red fungus growths on stones of a house can lead to the spread of disease to man. By removing the infected stone, and substituting new ones, it is often possible to eradicate the fungus from the building. A person who enters an infected building is impure until the evening, and he may contract the disease unless he bathes. Furthermore, if he stays long in the building, for example if he eats or sleeps there, then his clothes may contract the fungus, and need to be washed.

If after substituting new stones for the infected ones, the green and red colorations do not reappear, then the building may be completely purified by sprinkling the house seven times with the water-diluted blood of a freshly slaughtered bird in which a live bird was immersed. This is the same procedure as used in the purification of the recovered leper (Lev. 14 4-7), and supports the contention that the bird's blood, prepared in the prescribed manner, has antiseptic qualities against certain leprosy-type microorganisms.

Law

Lev. 15 1-15   If a person has a discharge from his skin, the discharge as well as the person are unclean. Any bed, chair, or riding seat that he uses becomes unclean. Anyone who touches the impure person's bed or skin, or sits on or carries his seat, or is spit on by the impure person, shall wash himself and his clothes and is unclean until the evening. Furthermore anyone touching the impure person's seat becomes unclean until the evening; and any earthenware vessel touched by the impure person shall be broken. However, a wooden vessel touched by the impure person needs only to be washed, and if the impure person washed his hands then the individual he touches does not become unclean. When the person is cleansed from his discharge he should count seven days, wash himself and his clothes in fresh water, and then becomes clean. On the eighth day, a sin-offering and a burnt-offering are brought to complete the purification process.

Rationale

A discharge or oozing from the skin can result from a skin infection or chemical irritation. Furthermore, disease microorganisms may thrive on the discharge. To prevent spread of disease it is necessary for anyone, who even indirectly comes in contact with the discharge from an impure person, to wash himself and his clothes as prescribed.

Impetigo is a disease which is an example of a skin infection. The dermatitis, which is caused either by staphylococci or streptococci, characteristically develops as small blisters, weeping sores, and crusts. It is transmitted from one person to another by direct or indirect contact.[132]

Another example of dermatitis are boils. These infections are usually caused by a staphylococcus that enters the skin along hair follicles. The disease is spread from one part of the body to another or from person to person by contact, clothing, towels, etc.[133]

Poison ivy is a skin reaction, accompanied by oozing, which is caused by contact with poisonous plants. The toxic chemical is urushiol, which may be carried from the plant on clothing, shoes, tools, soil, and animals. Poisoning may even occur if contaminated clothing is worn a year after contact with poison ivy. Washing of exposed parts of the body with water immediately after contact, or as soon as possible thereafter, can minimize the extent of reaction to the poisonous chemical.[134]

The above examples of skin discharges indicate the variety of causes and symptoms which may occur. The Biblical regulations concerning skin discharges are sufficiently general to prevent the spread of such infections for all these various cases.

LAW

Lev. **19** 27–28; Do not cut yourselves nor make any baldness between your
21 5; eyes in mourning for the dead. Do not round off your hair
Deut. **14** 1–2. on the sides, nor destroy or shave the edges of your beard. Do not tattoo yourselves.

RATIONALE

All these restrictions involve cutting of the skin, or situations where cutting of the skin of the head may occur, such as when shaving the beard with a razor. Not cutting the skin is to prevent infection of the person with any one of numerous diseases. Theoretically, any disease involving a stage of bloodstream invasion could be transmitted through a cut or by injection.[135]

It is only in recent years that use of sterilized razors and implements have been introduced. Nevertheless, many diseases are still transmitted, although accidentally, by cutting through the skin. For example, contaminated hypodermic needles, used during medical procedures, have been responsible for such diseases as tetanus, septic meningitis, malignant malaria, and viral hepatitis.[136]

Tattooing consists of puncturing the skin in the pattern desired and rubbing in coloring material so that the pattern is indelibly fixed.[137] Today the craft is done under fairly antiseptic conditions. Old-time jab artists, however, used to wet the tattooing needle with the lips, and if they had syphilis, it was passed on to the customer.[138]

One might argue, "Why should shaving of the head be forbidden? Cutting of the skin could be avoided if proper care is taken." However, it should be realized that one accidental cut, out of thousands of shaves, might be sufficient to transmit a serious disease. Furthermore, many men have extremely sensitive skin on the face and shaving irritates the skin and causes tiny pimples. In such cases, one solution recommended is to grow a beard.[139] Sycosis of the skin is a staphylococcal infection involving the hair follicles. After shaving, the skin is known to be more susceptible to invasion by these microorganisms.[140]

It is noteworthy that the Bible emphasizes the prohibition of cutting the hair of the head. This may be for several reasons. First, it is most common to cut the hair from the head rather than from other parts of the body, and therefore the danger of accidentally cutting the skin is greatest there. Second, the skin of the face is sensitive and easily irritated. Third, and probably the most important reason, the head is nearest the brain. Any disease microorganisms which may enter through an accidental cut could reach the brain and cause death fairly rapidly, even before the body's defenses could become effective. In contrast, the chance of recovery from disease introduced through cuts in lower parts of the body, is much greater. It is, for example, known that bites by rabid animals on the face and lips are more serious than on the feet because the point of inoculation of the virus is nearer to the brain.[141]

There are also positive reasons for maintaining the hair of the head. Hair offers protection to the head. It keeps off the rays of the sun and cushions against accidental blows.[142] Maintaining the hair therefore minimizes the chance of serious injury to the vital organs of the head.

It is noteworthy that despite the prohibition against shaving the beard and certain other parts of the hair of the head, the Bible requires the recovered leper to shave off all the hair of the body (Lev. 14 8, 9). In the case of the former leper the requirement to shave the hair aids in preventing the recovered person from becoming a carrier of leprosy, and thereby protects the community. Under such a situation, the need for removing all the hair of the body is more important than the general prohibition designed to prevent the possible infection which may be caused if an accidental cut occurs. Similarly, the shaving off of all the hair of the Levites to purify them (Num. 8 7) is for the purpose of eliminating any microorganisms retained in the hair.

25.5 PRIESTLY STATUTES

There are numerous regulations which apply only to the priests, and a few which apply only to the Levites. These regulations reflect the fact that these groups have been assigned special honored tasks relevant to the sanctuary. In particular, the priests are involved in the bringing of sacrifices, while the Levites assist the Priests in many sanctuary-related functions.

In trying to understand the purpose of the priestly statutes, it must be realized that the priests are directly involved in the preparation of food for large numbers of people, and occasionally for almost the entire population. In a sense, they may be considered as running a gigantic public restaurant. Understandably, when preparing food for large numbers of people, great care must be taken to prevent the spread of disease. The presence of pathogens in the meat could result in a major and disastrous epidemic. For this reason certain added limitations are placed on the priests so as to prevent them from contracting diseases and spreading them to the population. The extra requirements for the priests are to safeguard them against illness even in situations where it would be rare for anyone to become sick, even if these extra precautions were not maintained.

The statutes to be considered in this section are subdivided into three parts: (A) responsibilities of the priests and Levites; (B) requirements for officiating; and (C) special prohibitions. Additional regulations involving the priests and Levites will be found in the sections dealing with taxes (Section 27.2), sacrifices (Section 28.1), and priestly garments (Section 28.4).

25.5.1 Responsibilities of the Priests and Levites

LAWS

Num. 3 6–10; 8 19; 18 1–7; Deut. 18 5.	The priests are responsible for the tasks of the sanctuary and the altar. The Levites assist the priests, but are not permitted to bring sacrifices or to use the holy vessels; otherwise death may result. An unqualified person who draws near shall be put to death.
Lev. 21 6	The priests shall be holy to God and not profane His name, because they offer the sacrifices to God.
Num. 6 22–27	The priests shall bless the Israelites according to a specified wording, which includes the statements that God should bless you, watch over you, make you gracious, and give you peace. The priests will put the name of God upon the Israelites, and He will bless them.

RATIONALE

Specific groups, namely the priests and Levites, are responsible for caring for the Temple worship. By having specialization, the chances of errors in the procedures are minimized, and it becomes practical to require higher purity standards for the persons involved than for the rest of the population. The priests have to meet the highest standards since they have direct contact with the sanctuary and the sacrifices; the Levites have lower standards since they only assist the priests, but do not have direct contact with the holy vessels and sacrifices; and the Israelites have even lower requirements of purity. If these high standards of purity were not observed for the Temple area, major epidemics could result which would cause death to many. Therefore, an unqualified person, such as a regular Israelite, who performs tasks reserved for the priests is subject to the death penalty.

Blessing of the people by the priests serves a beneficial psychological purpose. However, the blessings must be stated in a proper way. The recipients must recognize that it is God who is blessing the people, and not believe that the priests cause beneficial results. Therefore a prescribed phraseology must be used by the priests, to show that the blessings really come from God.

25.5.2 Requirements for Officiating

LAWS

Ex. 29 1–37; Lev. 8 1–36	The priests are initiated into office according to an elaborate procedure. They are first washed with water and dressed in their priestly garments; and the high priest is anointed with oil. Then a bull-calf is brought for a sin-offering, a ram for a burnt-offering, and another ram for an installation-offering. In addition variously prepared cakes and unleavened bread, made from fine wheat flour, are brought. The procedure is repeated each day for seven days in order to consecrate the priests and the altar.
Num. 8 5–22	Before being able to serve, the Levites are purified according to the following procedure. Purifying water is sprinkled on them, all their body hair is shaved off, and their clothes are washed. Then two young bulls are brought, one for a sin-offering and one for a burnt-offering. Afterwards the Levites may perform their tasks associated with the sanctuary.
Num. 4 3, 23, 30, 35, 39, 43, 47; 8 23–26	The Levites may perform work for the sanctuary when they are 25 years of age. However the main active work is performed by Levites between 30 and 50 years old. After 50, the Levites shall only assist their colleagues, but shall not perform regular services.
Lev. 21 16–24	A priest with a physical defect shall not offer sacrifices, and thereby profane the sanctuary. Typical defects are blindness, lameness, having a broken foot or a broken hand, and being hunchbacked. The priest with a defect may, however, eat from the holy and most-holy foods.
Lev. 22 1–9	A priest who is unclean shall not approach items which are holy, otherwise he will be punished with excision. A priest who is a leper or has an issue shall not eat from the holy foods until he becomes clean. Also, if he is unclean until the evening from any one of many causes, he should bathe in water and wait until the setting of the sun before eating holy foods.
Lev. 10 8–11	Priests shall not drink wine nor intoxicating drinks before coming to serve at the sanctuary, so that they not die. Also they should not drink before differentiating between holy and non-holy, between clean and unclean, and when teaching the laws of God.
Deut. 18 6–8	A Levite or priest who desires to serve in work associated with the sanctuary, may come from where he dwells to help in the services, in an equal capacity to his fellow Levites or priests.

Lev. 22 10–16   Persons who may eat holy food are the priests, his family, and his slaves. However, a priest's daughter upon marrying a non-priest, can no longer eat holy food. If the daughter becomes widowed or divorced, and has no children, then if she returns to her father's house she may once again eat holy food. A non-priest, including a hired worker, and one who dwells in the priest's home, shall not eat holy food. Anyone who by mistake does so shall pay a one-fifth penalty to the priest, so as not to profane the holy objects.

RATIONALE

The initiation procedure for the priests lasts seven days to ensure that any pathogens which might have been present on their bodies would be completely removed. Each of the seven days the priests bathe with water, put on the clean priestly garments, and have blood from a ram applied to their right earlobes, thumbs and big toes. In addition, blood from the altar and some anointing oil are sprinkled on the priests and their clothes. All these procedures probably kill any disease microorganisms which may have been present, and thereby remove any possibility that the priests would be carriers of disease. Also, the wearing of the priestly garments for seven days enables the priests to become accustomed to the special clothes, and not feel uneasy while wearing them.

In contrast to the seven days for the priests, the purification procedure for the Levites is performed within one day. Purifying water is sprinkled on the Levites, all their body hair is shaved off, and their clothes are washed. In this manner most but not necessarily all, pathogens are removed. It should be noted that microorganisms,[143] and insects such as lice,[144] are not easily removed from the hair of the body by washing, especially when the purification procedure lasts only one day; and therefore shaving of the hair is required. Moreover, hospitals have traced infections to microorganisms in doctor's hair and beards.[145] The lesser degree of purity for the Levites as compared to the priests is satisfactory, since they do not come in direct contact with the sacrifices and the vessels of the sanctuary.

The age limitations on the Levites, namely that the main workers should be between 30 and 50 years old, is to ensure that physically strong and mentally mature persons do the work. By this means the Bible saw to it that the tasks for the Levites were not beyond their physical strength; thereby minimizing the chances of accidents and errors.

Priests who have obvious physical defects would, if they offered sacrifices, lower the respect of the people for the sanctuary. Persons would say, "See, even the disfigured priests may serve in the Temple!" Another reason for the prohibition against their serving is that priests with physical defects would tend to have a higher accident rate and to make more mistakes than physically perfect individuals. Thus, to insure that the Biblical laws are followed exactly, it is necessary that only unblemished priests officiate. Nonetheless, those priests with physical defects may eat from the holy foods, since the presence of a disability has no connection with the possibility of spreading disease.

When a priest is unclean, there is a high likelihood that he is a carrier of disease microorganisms. Upon physical contact with holy items, the microorganisms may spread, thereby resulting in eventual sickness for others. Furthermore, a priest who eats holy food while unclean, obviously does not observe the impurity laws. When these laws are not observed, the person involved may contract a serious illness, which could result in premature death.

The priests should not drink intoxicating beverages before ministering because alcohol impairs a person's ability to make decisions, increases the chance of an accident, and could lead to desecration of the services. Alcohol has the unusual effect that at the same time that it decreases efficiency, slows reaction time and impairs judgment, it also increases a person's self-confidence.[146] Although skills are diminished, self-delusion as to abilities is enhanced. This combination of effects could seriously impair the proper performance of tasks by the priests.

Not all Levites or priests who are entitled to minister actually do so. Some derive their livelihoods from other occupations. However, if a Levite or priest desires to serve at the sanctuary, then he is permitted to serve with the others who are already there. By this regulation, the Bible prevents the practicing Levites and priests from forming a special clique which restricts others from gaining experience. Furthermore, this regulation allows a priest to supplement his outside income, in that he becomes entitled to eat the food from many of the sacrifices he offers.

Persons allowed to eat from the holy food are the priest and all those dependent on him, such as his wife, children, and slaves. However, if his daughter marries a non-priest, she becomes dependent on her husband rather than on her father, and can therefore no longer eat holy food. If she becomes widowed or divorced, but has children, then she is supported from the inheritance received by her children (Num. 27 8), and still can not eat holy food. However, if she has no children and returns to her father's home, she again becomes dependent on her father and can therefore eat holy food. Anyone who is not entitled to eat holy food but does, is required to pay a one-fifth penalty to the priest. This payment is equivalent to the one-fifth penalty required from persons who voluntarily confess that they stole (Num. 5 5–7).

25.5.3 Special Prohibitions

LAWS

Lev. 21 1–4	A priest shall not make himself unclean by contact with a dead body except for close relatives—mother, father, son, daughter, brother, unmarried sister, and wife.

Lev. 21 7	A priest shall not marry a prostitute, a profaned woman, or a divorcee, because he is holy unto God.
Lev. 21 9	When a priest's daughter profanes herself by being a prostitute, she profanes her father. She shall be burned to death.
Lev. 21 10–12	The high priest, the one who has had anointing oil poured on his head and has been consecrated to wear special vestments, shall not leave his hair dishevelled nor tear his clothes. He shall not come in contact with a dead body, not even for his father or mother. Neither shall he go out of the sanctuary for fear that he profane the sanctuary.
Lev. 21 13–15	The high priest shall not marry a widow, divorcee, a profaned woman, or a prostitute. He shall only marry a virgin of his own people, and not profane his children.

RATIONALE

In addition to the benefits derived by the priests from their position, there are a number of prohibitions which only they have to observe. The main purpose of these special regulations is to prevent the spread of disease to the community.

A priest should not become unclean by contact with a dead body, except for that of a close relative who might otherwise not have anyone to take care of his burial. In general, after death, microorganisms grow rapidly since there is no longer any bodily restraint on their multiplication. Therefore contact with a human corpse can frequently lead to the spread of disease. For the average Israelite, subsequent purification with the ash-water mixture from the red cow is sufficient to eliminate the possibility of contracting a disease; but, undoubtedly, every now and then despite following the required purification procedure some sickness may occur. To minimize such a possibility the priests are limited in the number of contacts allowed with dead bodies. Nevertheless, if the priest is not allowed to help bury his close relatives, there may be no one interested in doing so. Therefore, exceptions are made in the case of mother, father, son, daughter, brother, unmarried sister, and wife. In contrast, the burial of a married sister could be handled by her husband or children, and therefore the brother who is a priest need not be involved.

A priest should not marry a prostitute, a profaned woman, or a divorcee because there is at least a moderate probability of the woman having contracted a venereal disease. Prostitutes have had sexual relations with many men, and are the most suspect. A profaned woman, according to one explanation, is someone who was raped; and in the process she may have become infected. A divorcee has had permitted sexual relations, and is least suspect of the three categories. However, the fact that her husband divorced her introduces the possibility that she may have had illicit relations. In contrast, a widow can be married to a priest, since there is little likelihood that she suffers from venereal disease.

A priest's daughter who becomes a prostitute is punished with death by burning.

The probability exists that she may contract a venereal disease which she will spread to her father by non-sexual means. Although most venereal diseases are transmitted by intercourse, sometimes the infections may be spread in other ways. For example, syphilis is occasionally transmitted by kissing.[147] The unusual punishment of death by burning for the priest's daughter is to emphasize the seriousness of her crime in that it may lead to an epidemic, and to prevent spread of venereal disease to her father upon burial of her corpse. The punishment for a prostitute who is not a priest's daughter, is death by stoning as implied in Deut. 22 21.

The high priest is the one who sees to it that the priestly functions are performed correctly, and who performs certain specific rites requiring the utmost in purity. It is therefore necessary that the high priest observe prohibitions even more severe than those for other priests. He should show no signs of mourning, such as dishevelled hair or torn clothes, upon the death of a close relative. In fact, even if his parents die he should not come in contact with their dead bodies, publicly mourn for them, or leave the sanctuary. Contact with the dead bodies could possibly lead to disease, as mentioned previously. Mourning and leaving the sanctuary would interrupt the Temple services.

The high priest must marry only a virgin. He cannot marry a widow, although that is permissible for the other priests. This is to prevent even the remotest chance of the high priest contracting a venereal disease. The danger also exists that if his wife suffers from a venereal disease, such as syphilis or gonorrhea, the sickness may be passed on to the children, either during pregnancy or at the time of birth. Such infections could lead to serious physical defects and thereby profane the children.

Chapter Twenty-six

PHYSICAL PROTECTION OF THE POPULATION

It is incumbent upon the government to make certain that the people within the country receive physical protection. Regulations have to exist on accident prevention, control of crime, and military supremacy. Without such regulations it would be impossible for the country to function efficiently. People would be constantly afraid of physical harm, to the point where the productivity of the individual, as well as of the country, would seriously suffer.

This chapter is concerned with the Biblical laws that deal with the physical protection of the population. Regulations involving accident prevention, crime control, and military requirements are discussed.

26.1 ACCIDENT PREVENTION

Accidents are a major source of death and disability all over the world. For example, in the United States accidents are the most frequent cause of death among all persons from ages one to 25, the second most frequent cause among those from ages 25 to 44, and rank fourth when considering all age groups together. These mishaps cause a greater loss of productive years than any disease. Half of the accidents occur on the highway, one-quarter in the home, and the remaining one-quarter elsewhere[1]. In the United States, about 95,000 deaths a year (i.e., about 1 in 2,000 of the population), and 15 million serious injuries result from accidents[2].

To prevent such tragic statistics the Bible has several laws designed to minimize the chance for the occurrence of accidents.

Laws

Deut. 22 8	When you build a new house, erect a fence around your roof so no one will fall and be killed.
Lev. 19 14	Do not put a stumbling block in front of the blind.

Rationale
The requirement of erecting a fence around the roof is to be interpreted not only literally, but also as a general rule that precautions should be taken to prevent serious accidents. Similarly, the prohibition against placing a stumbling block in front of the

blind can be interpreted as meaning that no positive action should be performed that would probably lead to a mishap. Thus the Bible warns against having dangerous conditions. Everything possible should be done to prevent situations which are potential causes of accidents.

Nowadays, automobile accidents are a serious cause of death and injury. From the Biblical viewpoint it would be necessary to build safer and more reliable cars, design better roads, inspect cars periodically for safety, and license only capable, mature drivers. By following such procedures, amazing reductions in the frequency and severity of automobile accidents could be accomplished.

It should be realized that the Bible also prevents accidents in more subtle ways. The regulations that promote good health and proper mental attitudes for the population would indirectly improve each person's performance, thereby decreasing the occurrence of accidents. Furthermore, not taking drugs or drinking excessively would significantly reduce the number of highway accidents[3].

Law

One additional safety law of extreme importance involves the punishment prescribed for those persons who accidentally cause the death of someone else.

Ex. 21 13; Num. 35 6,9–29,32; Deut. 4 41–43; 19 1–17; Josh 20 1–9.	Set aside, under the supervision of the Levites, six conveniently located cities of refuge for the person who accidentally kills another, and did not previously hate him. The manslayer, whether a citizen or an alien, shall run to a refuge city lest he be murdered by the blood avenger (i.e., the dead man's next-of-kin). The manslayer shall then be judged as to whether the killing was willful or accidental. If the death was accidental, the manslayer must dwell within the refuge city until the death of the high priest, and then returns to his property. If, however, the manslayer leaves the refuge city, he may be murdered by the blood avenger without any penalty. The refuge cities are not to be used as punishment for willful murderers.

Rationale

The purpose of the refuge cities can be understood in terms of the accident-prone individual, i.e., the person who has a disproportionately high share of accidents. Statistical studies have shown that, for example, in industrial plants approximately 65 per cent of the accidents are experienced or caused by about 15 per cent of the work force[4]. Thus, someone who has caused a serious mishap is more likely than others to do the same thing again. If an accident is so severe that death results, then measures must be taken to protect the society. The manslayer is required from then on to live in a refuge city. If he causes another fatal accident, in all probability it will be another manslayer who will be killed. Furthermore, the refuge cities, wherein live numerous accident-prone individuals, would undoubtedly be constructed with the emphasis on safety, thereby minimizing the occurrence of accidents.

A person exiled to a city of refuge may not leave, until the high priest dies, except at risk of death at the hand of the blood avenger. Now the time when the high priest will die, even if he is extremely old, is never known. Therefore the manslayer will resign himself to semipermanent residence in the refuge city, and will work hard in his new location. When the high priest does die, great sadness and mourning will occur throughout the nation, possibly making the blood avenger forget his hatred for the manslayer. Afterwards all the manslayers from all the refuge cities return to their inherited property. In this way, the refuge cities do not become overcrowded, and inherited portions of land do not become desolate.

The regulations concerning manslayers removes the accident-prone person from his immediate surroundings, preventing a subsequent accidental death of an innocent individual. Moreover, once the manslayer is exiled, the blood avenger does not continually see him, thereby quieting the spirit of revenge and eliminating possible resultant psychological illnesses. In this way, needless murder by the blood avenger is also prevented.

Naturally, intentional murderers should be killed, and may not settle in the refuge cities, otherwise the benefits from these cities will be negated.

26.2 CRIME CONTROL

Many of the Biblical laws are designed to minimize the extent of crime. The laws are aimed at providing (A) justice for all citizens, the innocent as well as the guilty; (B) punishing the criminal according to his actions—but not by placing an economic burden on the community; and (C) making the punishment of such a nature that the criminal will avoid repeating the offense.

In addition to the laws discussed in this section which deal directly with crime, many other Biblical laws also tend to minimize misconduct. Laws which prevent poverty, discrimination, economic crises, and illness, and strengthen the family, naturally will prevent many of the major reasons for crime. Nevertheless, felonies will still occur, if only on rare occasions, and then the Biblical regulations dealing with the criminal are needed.

A recent book made an extensive report on the problems of crime in the United States, and supplied recommendations for improvement of existing piteous conditions[5]. Many of the points discussed, which are summarized in an extremely concise manner below, can be interpreted to indicate the effectiveness of the Biblical crime-laws.

The report specifies the following methods to minimize crime:

A. Assure to all people the responsibilities and benefits of the community: eliminate bad social conditions, and improve education. In a sense, social and economic conditions cause crime. Crime flourishes in slums, overcrowded neighborhoods, and places of economic deprivation, social disruption, and racial discrimination. Reducing poverty, discrimination, ignorance, disease, and the anger or despair these conditions can inspire, is one major step towards reducing crime.

B. Criminal justice must eliminate existing injustices to win the respect of all citizens. Improved methods for selecting personnel are needed. Investigative units should be set up to insure complete fairness. Better people must be attracted as policemen, prosecutors, judges, and defense attorneys, having more knowledge and integrity.

C. Develop laws of a far broader nature for dealing with offenders. Often policemen may overlook certain offenses if they believe that the punishment is too severe for the crime. Commitments of offenders to prison can cause more problems than they solve. Prisons isolate people from the society, cutting them off from schools, jobs, and families. In contrast, too lenient punishments can lead to repetition of crimes. Laws commensurate with the offense need to be developed, which the public wants to have enforced[6].

26.2.1 Laws to Promote Justice

The Biblical crime-laws can be separated into two major categories, based on the above discussion: (A) laws to promote justice; and (B) commensurate punishments for criminal actions. First we will consider those laws which promote justice, which mainly involve regulations for judges, and laws concerning witnesses.

26.2.1.1 Regulations for Judges

LAW

Deut. 1 13–15; 16 18   Appoint judges and officers throughout your settlements; and they shall judge the people righteously.

RATIONALE
This law requires that the selected personnel be men of integrity, capable of judging honestly. Not only the judge but also the officer (policeman) has to be an honest individual. This is because law enforcement policy is made by policemen as well as by judges. Every day policemen make policy informally by exercising personal discretion[7].

It is implied by the Biblical law that there be a sufficient number of policemen and judges to handle the situations which occur. Analogously, it has been demonstrated that increasing the police force in a given area, causes a decline in crimes directed against the citizen in the street. A principle purpose of patrol is deterrence, i.e., discouraging people who are inclined to commit crimes from following their inclinations. Street crimes are reduced because of fear of immediate apprehension[8].

Similarly, having a sufficient number of judges allows the rapid trial of individuals, without long delays. In the United States it often takes many years to bring criminals to trial, and by that time witnesses may have died, and what happened may have been forgotten. As a result, many injustices occur.

Laws

Ex. 23 2,3,6–8;
Lev. 19 15;
Deut. 1 16–17;
16 19–20; 27 25.

Judge fairly: do not deviate the judgement; do not show recognition to individuals, such as the poor or the mighty; and do not take bribes since bribes blind the wise and the righteous. Seek justice so you may live and inherit the land. Keep far away from falsehood, and do not kill the innocent. Do not be afraid of any man in making the correct judgement. Do not blindly follow the majority to decide to do evil.

Rationale

It is quite obvious that unfair legal decisions lead to disrespect and non-cooperation by the people. The penalty for a particular crime should be the same whether done by a poor uneducated man or one who is rich and scholarly, whether it is the first time that the person performed such an act or the fifth time, and whether the accused is or is not a friend of the judge, or has or has not done a favor for the judge.

In the United States such is not always the case. A teenager caught stealing may go free with the only punishment being a reprimand, while an older person may, for an identical crime, be sentenced to several years imprisonment. The opposite situation may also happen. Much other unfairness occurs because of bribery, prejudice, or incapable judges.

Law

Lev. 24 22;
Deut. 24 17–18;
27 19.

Do not pervert justice for an alien, orphan, or widow. Remember you were a slave in Egypt. Have the same penaty for the alien and citizen alike.

Rationale

In particular, the alien finds himself bewildered in a strange country, the orphan does not have his father to uphold his rights, and the widow is without the protection of her husband. People in these categories are most subject to possible injustices, and have therefore been singled out by the Bible so that extra care will be used during judgment. The principle of equality of justice naturally extends to other groups, such as racial minorities. By having equal justice for all, such happenings as race riots, which have often occurred in the United States because of prejudice against the Negro, would be prevented.

Law

Deut. 24 16

Do not kill parents for their children's sins nor children for their parents' sins. Each man shall be put to death for his own sin.

RATIONALE

Not only does this law imply that punishment should be just, but also that each person is responsible for his own actions, no matter what his upbringing or the circumstances. You should not say, for example, that if a teenager commits murder, his parents are guilty for not teaching him proper ethics. No matter what the upbringing, the teenager still has final say as to his own actions.

LAW

> Deut. 1 17; 17 8–13.   Have a higher court and a higher priest to decide difficult legal questions, which the lower courts do not know how to judge. The higher court should reside in the place, chosen by God [namely Jerusalem]. Anyone who purposely does not follow the decision of the higher court or the higher priest is subject to the death penalty, so that the people will listen to and fear the court's decisions.

RATIONALE

It should be realized that the higher court was only to decide legal questions which the lower courts were unable to handle; not to overturn or reverse decisions of the lower courts. In contrast, in the United States the higher courts often reverse decisions of the lower courts, so the decisions of the lower courts are not final, and many cases may wait years until the judgment is finalized.

The higher court would reside in Jerusalem to increase the respect held for the court. Psychologically, people will associate the respect for the Temple with the respect for other government agencies located in the same area.

A person who does not obey the rulings of the higher courts is subject to the death penalty. Otherwise, the entire judicial system would suffer, since there would be instances where decisions would not be followed.

26.2.1.2 Laws Concerning Witnesses

LAWS

> Num. 35 30;   A legal decision against a person should be decided on
> Deut. 17 6; 19 15.   the basis of two or three witnesses, never by the testimony of one witness.
>
> Deut. 13 10; 17 7.   In the case of a death penalty, the hands of the witnesses should be first upon the guilty person to put him to death, and afterwards the rest of the people.
>
> Ex. 20 13; 23 1;   Do not be a false witness against your neighbor; do
> Deut. 5 17.   not join with a wicked person as an unrighteous witness.

Deut. 19 16–21   A witness who is found, after careful inquiry by the judges, to be a false witness, should be punished according to his intentions; e.g., an eye for an eye, a tooth for a tooth, and a life for a life. In this way evil will be removed from your midst, and other people will be afraid to do similar deeds.

Lev. 5 1,5–10   A person who was a witness or knows some information that has been requested with threat of a curse, has sinned if he does not tell his information. To remove his sin he must confess, and bring an atonement sacrifice.

RATIONALE

The most productive methods of criminal investigation are, first, questioning a person who has some knowledge of the identity of a criminal and, second, tracing stolen property[9]. Thus, even today where great scientific advances have been made in criminal investigation, the most important method is listening to testimony of witnesses.

The Bible requires a minimum of two witnesses to allow a decision. There are some practical difficulties in relying on the testimony of only one person. First, the person may be mistaken. Secondly, the witness may bear a grudge against someone, and feel he can get revenge by testifying falsely. To prevent such incidents, the Bible requires two witnesses. Furthermore, there may be cases where the judges feel that even relying on two witnesses may lead to injustice. In such cases, the judges can require three witnesses before they are forced to pass judgment.

Even with the requirement for two or three witnesses, still cases may occur where false testimony is given. Therefore the requirement is made in the case of a death penalty (i.e., in a case when after the decision is carried out it can not be reversed upon discovery of new information) that the witnesses themselves be the ones to initiate the execution of the guilty person. In most cases, only witnesses who have testified honestly will be able to carry out the sentence. Often, false witnesses, afraid of having the blood of an innocent man on their consciences, will back down at the last moment.

As a further means to prevent false testimony, the punishment for doing so is very severe. The false witness is to be punished with the same penalty he wanted to inflict on the innocent person. For example, if the penalty would have been death, then the false witness is killed. It has been stated that more effective deterrents against perjury are needed in the United States[10]. Observing the Biblical law of punishing a false witness according to his intentions would be the needed deterrent against perjury.

Since the means for punishing a criminal and bringing justice are limited to the availability of two witnesses, it becomes necessary for witnesses to come forward on their own to ensure that justice is done. Therefore a curse would be publicly proclaimed on whomever did not come forward to tell what he knows about a particular incident. If, subsequently, the person who has sinned by not testifying wants to rid himself of the curse, he must first confess his sin (which in effect results in his finally coming forward with his testimony) and then bring a sin-offering.

These extensive Biblical laws concerning witnesses were made to guarantee justice.

26.2.2 Commensurate Punishments for Criminal Actions

The second major category of crime laws involves punishment of the criminal according to the crime. The punishment should be of such a nature as to make the crime unprofitable, discourage the criminal from repeating the act, and yet not place an economic burden on the community as is the case with the prison system in the United States. It should be noted that crimes falling under other categories, such as sex offenses, are discussed elsewhere (see e.g., Section 25.3).

26.2.2.1 Crimes Punishable by Death

LAW

Gen. 9 5–6;	Do not murder any person. The punishment is death
Ex. 20 13; 21 12–13;	when the murder is intentional, and there are two or
Lev. 24 17,21;	three witnesses. No other punishment, such as money
Num. 35 16–21,	payment, is acceptable. The blood avenger (i.e., the
30–34;	dead man's next-of-kin) has the right to kill the
Deut. 5 17;	murderer. The murderer is cursed if he kills secretly
19 11–13; 27 24.	without witnesses.

RATIONALE

The crime of murder is a clear case where the punishment fits the crime, namely a life for a life. The murderer has to be killed to protect the society from his repeating the crime and killing someone else. Imprisonment of the murderer is not a solution, since it would impose an economic burden on the community, the murderer would be unproductive, and he still might kill again while in prison.

LAW

Deut. 21 1–9	If a murdered person be found in the field, and the killer is unknown, then the leaders of the nearest city will break off the neck of a heifer, that never did any work, near a stream where the land is not cultivated. The priests and city leaders will wash their hands over the heifer and will proclaim: "We have not shed this blood and we did not see. Atone for this innocent blood."

RATIONALE

The purposes of this ritual are several. First, it publicizes the murder, thereby possibly leading to the punishment of the murderer. Secondly, the city leaders are made aware of their responsibility to see to it that everything be done to prevent murder and apprehend the criminal, even outside the city limits. The killing of the unworked heifer is symbolic and represents the death of the innocent person.

LAW

Ex. 21 16; One who kidnaps a person, and either sells him or keeps
Deut. 24 7 him in his possession, shall be put to death.

RATIONALE

This law is to prevent the making of free men into slaves, and profiting from human misery. By kidnapping and selling or making a slave of a person, the kidnapper is ruining the person's life, and puts the kidnapped person in danger of death. Such actions tend to be repeated because of the large personal gain involved. For all these reasons the kidnapper is subject to the death penalty.

LAW

Lev. 18 21; 20 1–5; A person who sacrifices his child for idol-worship is
Deut. 18 9–10. subject to death by stoning. If he is not killed by the community, then God will kill him and all his followers by excision.

RATIONALE

Sacrificing a child is obviously murder and is therefore subject to the death penalty. Furthermore, the person is subject to death for worshipping idols. If the sinning person is not punished by the courts, he will die by excision, i.e., he will contract a disease, since he touched a dead human body and, in all probability, did not purify himself to cleanse himself from disease germs which thrive on a dead body (see also Chapter Twenty-two).

26.2.2.2 Crimes Punishable by Payments

LAWS

Ex. 20 13; 21 37; Do not steal. Do not deny a debt or lie about owing it to
22 1–3,6–8; your fellow man. If someone steals an ox or a sheep
Lev. 19 11; and kills it or sells it, then he should pay five oxen for
Deut. 5 17. an ox, and four sheep for a sheep. If the stolen object be found in the possession of the thief, then the thief should pay double the value of the object (even an ox, donkey or sheep). If the thief cannot pay, then he is

sold as a slave to work off the debt. Someone who kills a thief while he is breaking in, is not to be punished, unless it was clear that the thief would not cause any physical harm.

RATIONALE

Theft is not a crime to be punished by death. Often a person will steal because of poverty. For ordinary stealing, where the stolen object is retained by the thief, the offender has to pay twice the value of the object. This double payment serves several purposes. First it compensates the victim for annoyance and mental disturbance. Secondly, it punishes the thief so he will not find it profitable to steal. For example, if we assume that the average thief is caught roughly about 50 per cent of the time, then by requiring a double payment, any monetary gain is eliminated, even for those cases in which the thief was not apprehended.

However, if the stolen object is sold so it cannot be returned, or slaughtered or damaged so it loses its value, then the penalty is a fourfold payment. In the case of an ox, a fivefold payment is required since the owner is also deprived of the work that the ox could do, and it becomes necessary to train another animal to do the work. In these cases, apprehending the criminal is more difficult because the evidence has been destroyed or sold, therefore the larger penalty. Also, a thief who sells or slaughters the stolen objects is one who steals for monetary gain, rather than for personal need, and should be punished more severely.

Naturally killing a thief while he is breaking in, and where danger to life exists, does not require punishment. The killing of the thief was in self-defense.

If the thief does not have enough money to pay the required penalty, he is sold as a slave to earn the money. The thief thus learns an occupation or trade, so afterwards he will not have to steal to obtain his necessities; and he also learns how much effort it requires to earn the money he stole. In this manner the thief is rehabilitated, and the chance of his repeating the crime of stealing is minimized.

In contrast, stealing in the United States is not punished by payment but by imprisonment. The thief is idle while imprisoned, loses any job he may have had, and his wife often divorces him during this time. Also, he comes in contact with other criminals during his stay in prison. Instead of being rehabilitated he all too frequently becomes a hardened criminal. The idleness results in prisoner unrest and disciplinary problems. Juvenile offenders are often treated differently, since the punishment of prison is too severe. Instead of being imprisoned, they are often not punished nor required to make payment. Since juveniles often go free, the incidence of juvenile crime becomes high. For example, in the United States, one boy in six is referred to juvenile court; and although the 15 to 17-year age group represents 5.4 per cent of the population, it accounts for 12.8 per cent of all arrests[11]. In 1965 a majority of all arrests for major crimes against property were people under 21[12].

Law

Lev. 5 20–26;
Num. 5 5–8.

A person who sinned by denying knowledge of a deposit, a pledge, or a stolen item, or oppressed his neighbor, or denied finding a lost item, or swore falsely—if he confesses his sin, he should return the original object and add on a fifth of its value. If the person against whom he sinned is no longer alive, then the payment should be made to the nearest relative. If no relative exists, then the payment should be made to a priest. Furthermore, a ram should be brought as a guilt-offering so the sinner may be forgiven.

Rationale

In contrast to the double payment required of a person who was caught stealing, a person who confesses pays only one and one-fifth times the original value of the stolen object. This lesser punishment for confession of the crime, gives the criminal a strong incentive to confess. Naturally, return of the stolen object without any fine would not be sufficient punishment. The criminal could then say to himself that if he were being chased by the police he would run to confess and thereby escape any penalty. It is therefore necessary that the fine be paid, even if the person from whom the object was stolen had died, and there were no relatives. Furthermore, recompense needs to be given to the person from whom the object was stolen for the anguish involved.

Confession of the crime implies that the sinner's conscience bothers him. He therefore also brings a ram as a guilt-offering so as to relieve his guilt feelings.

Laws

Lev. 19 13;
Deut. 24 14–15.

Do not oppress your neighbor; do not rob; do not hold the wages of a hired worker until the next morning.

Lev. 19 35,36;
Deut. 25 13–16.

Do not have dishonest measurements, either in length, weight, or volume (dry or liquid volumes). Have true measures, so as to lengthen your lives.

Deut. 19 14; 27 17.

Do not extend your boundary line into your neighbor's field.

Rationale

These cases mainly involve subtle types of stealing. Thus, oppressing your neighbor often leads to monetary gains. Similarly, withholding a worker's wages until the next day can sometimes lead to gain: for example, if the worker should happen not to be able to return, he might lose the entire day's wages. Dishonest measurements involve stealing very small amounts at a time, which could involve very large amounts over a long period. By having honest measurements you have a more honest society, which could prevent retaliatory actions. Extending your boundary line is a hidden way of stealing land.

Punishments for these particular crimes are not specified, perhaps because it would be difficult to establish guilt. The person can usually claim he made a mistake, and then correct the error. However, the penalty for these actions when done wilfully is clear, namely double payment, as with ordinary types of stealing.

26.2.2.3 Crimes Against Parents

Law

Ex. 20;	Respect your parents so as to have a long and good
Lev. 19 3;	life. Fear your parents.
Deut. 5 16.	

Rationale
The family plays an exceptionally important role in determining the behavior patterns which the child will exhibit[13]. If the child is respectful and fearful of his parents, he will carry over the same responses to the society, and will probably become a useful member of the community. In contrast, lack of respect for parents and family often leads to delinquent behavior[14]. The low crime rates among Jews in the United States and Europe has, for example, been attributed to their close family and community ties[15].

There are several ways by which respecting parents can result in long lives. First, if the children respect their parents, this will contribute to a peaceful family environment, resulting in the psychological well-being of the parents and children. Second, the good habits acquired by showing respect for the parents will be carried over to the community, making the society a better environment in which to live. Third, just as you respect your parents and help them in times of need, so in turn your children will help you in case of emergency.

Law

Ex. 21 15,17;	Death penalty for hitting or cursing one's parents.
Lev. 20 9;	
Deut. 27 16.	

Rationale
When a person does not show respect for his parents, to the extent that he openly curses or hits them, then this person will not be respectful of the community and the society. Such a person is most likely to grow up to be a criminal and a detriment to the society, and therefore should be killed before he actually commits a serious crime. In particular, a person who hits his parents may some day kill them. The death penal-

ty for such an individual who strikes his parents is one way of protecting the parents from further harm.

LAW

Deut. 21 18–21   If a son is rebellious and does not listen to his parents even after being warned and punished, then his parents should state to the leaders of the city that their son does not listen to them, and is a glutton and drunkard. The members of the city should stone the son to remove the evil from their midst.

RATIONALE

Here, although the son does not curse or hit his parents, he does not listen to them, and obviously is delinquent by nature. He is so rebellious that his own parents believe society would be better off with him dead. Such a child should be killed by stoning by the community, before he actually commits a serious crime. Observance of this regulation could protect the society from vicious juvenile delinquents.

26.2.2.4 Penalties for Bodily Damages

LAW

Lev. 24 19–20   A person who intentionally maims someone else, should be punished accordingly; a broken limb for a broken limb, an eye for an eye, a tooth for a tooth.

RATIONALE

This law refers to intentional physical damage of a particular organ; for example, the purposeful knocking out of the eye of one's fellow man, with particular intent to destroy the eye. Payment of damages would not be sufficient punishment, since the person who caused the injury might, if wealthy, be easily able to pay, and would still be in good physical health. In contrast, a death penalty would be too severe since no one was killed. A just punishment is the equivalent maiming of the person who caused the injury so he will know how seriously he has hurt someone else, and will not repeat the crime.

LAW

Deut. 25 11   When two men fight against each other, and the wife of one of them comes to the aid of her husband, and grabs the sex organs of his opponent, then cut off her hand.

RATIONALE

In this case the woman intentionally maims the man in his sex organs. Since she is a woman, she can not be punished according to her actions. Instead her hand is to be cut off so she can not repeat such a crime. Naturally we are talking about a case where the two men who are fighting are not trying to injure each other seriously. If it were a case where serious injury or murder was intended, then the woman would be in the right to try to save her husband's life by any means available.

LAW

Ex. 21 18-19, 22-25. A person who injures someone else, but not with full intent—for example, two men are fighting with each other, and one knocks the other one down—if the injured person recovers then the only punishment for the one who hurt the other is payment for medical expenses, and for the time lost from work. Another case is when two men are fighting and they hurt a pregnant woman, who then miscarries. A reasonable amount of money has to be paid for the damage to the fetus according to the evaluation of the husband. However, if an accident occurs, and injury to the mother results, then payment should be made according to the injury; a life for a life, an eye for an eye, a tooth for a tooth, a hand for a hand, and a foot for a foot.

RATIONALE

These are cases where injury results because of serious carelessness, if not criminal negligence, and therefore damages have to be paid. However, there was no premeditated desire to injure anyone seriously. Hence a suitable punishment is payment for the damage according to the extent of the injury.

LAW

Ex. 21 20-21 If a man kills his slave by hitting him with a rod, then the master should be killed. However, if the slave lives for a day or two, the master should not be killed be-because the slave is his property.

RATIONALE

The owner of the slave has the right to hit his slave to get the work accomplished. The master ordinarily does not want the slave injured, because then he defeats his own purpose since the slave cannot then work efficiently. Accidents sometimes will happen where the master will hit the slave harder than he thought, and after a few days the slave dies. Once the master realized that he hit the slave too hard, he probably would not hit him again, and even would try to cure him. Since the master loses by the slave's death, the master is not punished under such a circumstance.

However, if the slave dies on the same day that he is hit, it indicates that it was not a matter of misjudgement by the master in hitting the slave too hard, but rather a case of intentional murder. Then the master is subject to the death penalty.

LAW

Ex. 21 26–27   If the master hits and destroys the eye of his slave, or the tooth, then the slave goes free.

RATIONALE

Some restraint needs to be placed on a master hitting his slave. In general, the master hits the slave to make him work harder. Hitting the slave to such an extent that actual injury occurs, indicates that the master is treating the slave cruelly, and therefore the slave goes free.

LAW

Ex. 21 28–32   If an ox gores and kills a person, then the ox should be stoned to death, its meat should not be eaten, and the owner is not punished. However, if the ox has the habit of goring, and the owners were warned and did not take precautions, then if the ox gores and kills a person, the ox should be stoned to death and its owner killed. If, instead, the court decides that the owner should pay a fine, then he should pay whatever fine is set. The same principles hold true if the ox gores a son or daughter. If the ox gores a slave, then the ox is stoned to death, and payment of thirty shekels is made to the owner of the slave.

RATIONALE

These laws involve death caused by an animal. When the owner of the animal could not expect his animal to cause injury, then the owner is not punished with death. However, the owner should have been more careful, and therefore he loses the value of the flesh of the animal. The animal is naturally killed to prevent the recurrence of such an incident. Furthermore, the animal may have been afflicted with a disease, such as rabies, which makes him go wild. Eating the animal might spread the illness to man, and therefore its meat is not to be eaten even by a foreigner.

If the animal has the disposition to gore, and therefore is potentially dangerous, and the owner was warned and took no precautions, then if the animal kills a person and it is obviously a case of intentional murder by the owner, the owner is killed. However, if it appears that it was a case of negligence, then a fine is imposed on the owner according to the degree of guilt.

No distinction is here made whether the person gored is a child or a mature person. In contrast, we saw previously that death to a fetus is not punishable by the death penalty (Ex. 21 22).

In the case of death to a slave, the owner of the animal pays a set fine of 30 shekels to the owner of the slave.

26.2.2.5 Damages to Animals or Inanimate Objects

LAW

Lev. 24 18,21 — He that intentionally kills an animal shall pay the equivalent of a life for a life.

RATIONALE

In contrast to the killing of a human being, where the murderer is subject to death, a person who intentionally kills an animal need only pay for the value of the animal. This law clearly shows that there is a marked difference between the value of a human life, and that of an animal. An animal is merely considered as an example of a piece of property. A human is a potentially creative individual who is the basis of the society.

LAW

Ex. 21 33–34 — A person who opens a pit or digs a new pit and does not cover it, and an ox or a donkey falls in it and is killed, the opener of the pit pays the value of the animal to the owner; but the value of the dead animal belongs to the opener of the pit.

RATIONALE

This is a case of negligence which brought about the death of the animal. The negligent person is responsible for paying for the damages caused. Here the damages are the value of the live animal minus the value of the dead body. It would be unfair to charge the negligent person with the full value of the live animal, since the owner, if he did not receive payment, would still have the value of the dead body, which could be used, for example, for its skin and meat.

LAW

Ex. 21 35–36 — If one person's ox kills another person's ox, then the value of the two oxen (the live one and the dead one) is divided between the two owners. However, if the live ox was known to be a gorer, and its owner did not watch it, then the owner of the goring ox has to pay an ox for an ox, but he keeps the value of the dead ox.

RATIONALE

In the first case neither owner was more negligent. It could just as well have happened that the other ox would have been killed. Therefore both owners divide the damages between themselves. However, if one of the oxen was a known gorer, then its owner was negligent and he has to pay for the difference in value between the ox when alive and when dead. Note that the negligent owner of the ox pays the same damages as the negligent opener of the pit (See Ex. 21 34).

LAW

Ex. 22 4–5   A man who sends his animal to eat in the field or vineyard of his neighbor should pay on the assumption that his animal ate the best of the produce of his neighbor's field or vineyard. Similarly, someone who starts a fire, and it destroys the produce or the field of someone else, should pay for the damages caused.

RATIONALE

Here we see that even though the person does not himself cause damage to someone else, but indirectly brings about damage, he must pay to compensate for the destruction. If the exact value of the damage is not known, then an estimate is made based on the best quality items still remaining.

LAW

Ex. 22 6–12   If a person watches inanimate objects, and they are stolen, and the thief is found, then the thief pays double to the owner. If the thief is not found, then the one who watched swears that he did not take the object. Similarly, for recognizable lost objects—whether living or inanimate—the one found guilty of trying to steal pays double to his neighbor.

If a man gives an animal to his neighbor to watch, and the animal dies, is injured, or is forcefully taken away, if there are no witnesses, then the person who watched should swear that he was not responsible for the damage. The owner should take back the animal (if available) in its present condition, without any compensatory payment. If the animal was stolen, then the watcher has to pay. If the animal was torn in pieces, the watcher should bring the remains as a proof, and need not pay for the damages.

RATIONALE

The reasons for the numerous distinctions in the law can be explained as follows. A person who watches inanimate objects usually puts them in a safe place until the owner comes. If the object was stolen, the watcher does not have to pay, since he does not have to watch his friend's objects better than he would his own, and his own things could also be stolen. However, the watcher has to swear that the object was stolen, and that he didn't take it himself. The requirement of swearing acts as a deterrent to prevent the watcher from stealing the object. If the thief be found then a double payment is made to the owner.

Another example of watching objects is if a person finds some lost item. In this case, the lost property could be either a living animal or an inanimate object. The finder has to keep the identifiable lost item until the owner is found. If the found item or animal be stolen, then the finder is not guilty and does not pay. However, whoever is found guilty of taking the item—whether a thief or the finder—has to pay double. In this case no distinction is made between living or inanimate property, since the degree of responsibility for lost property is not as great as for a watched object.

One who watches a living animal has the same responsibility as when watching an inanimate object. However, when an animal is stolen it will scream, letting the watcher know that something unusual is happening. Therefore the watcher must pay the owner, if the animal is stolen. However, if the animal is torn in pieces, the watcher is not responsible since he would have to endanger himself to protect the animal from a ferocious beast. Still, he has to bring the torn animal as proof of what happened, otherwise it would be a case of a stolen animal and the watcher would have to pay. In contrast, if the animal dies by itself, injures itself or is forcibly captured, we cannot expect the watcher to protect the animal continuously from such hazards, and therefore he does not have to pay; he just has to swear that he did not cause the damage. Naturally the owner retains possession of the animal, even if, for example, it is injured; and the owner takes back the animal whatever its condition.

It should be noted that no distinction is made in the Bible whether the watcher is paid for caring for the property or not. Thus, once the watcher has assumed responsibility, it does not matter whether he received compensation.

Law

Ex. 22 13–14   If a person borrows a living animal and it is hurt or dies, or if he borrows an inanimate object and it be broken, if the owner is not present then the borrower has to pay for the damage. If the owner is present, then no payment is required. A person who rents an object does not pay if it is damaged, since he paid to be able to use the object.

Rationale

It is only logical that a person who borrows something is required to pay for it if it becomes damaged during use. However, if the owner is present, then the owner would have made sure that the borrowed item was used correctly. Hence no negligence on the part of the borrower occurred, and no payment need be made.

A person who rents an object does not pay for damage during use, since the payment for renting covers the contingency that the borrowed item becomes damaged.

26.2.2.6   Crimes Punishable by Lashes

LAW

Deut. 25 1–4   If two men have a controversy, and the judge rules that one is righteous and the other one wicked, and the wicked person deserves to be beaten, then he should be beaten in a leaning position. The number of lashes should be determined according to his wickedness but should not exceed forty, lest the person be dishonored.

RATIONALE

Previously we have found mention in the Pentateuch of such punishments as death, payments, temporary slavery, and maiming. Here we find that wicked persons can also be punished with lashes. Restrictions are imposed on the number of lashes so that the person being punished does not become seriously injured or dishonored. Implied in the regulation is that lashes can be administered as punishment, according to the judge's opinion, for crimes which do not have any specified penalty. The rabbinic authorities, for example, have specified lashes for numerous transgressions of negative commandments, which otherwise would not have any prescribed punishment.

A guilty person who receives a beating will remember the punishment and try to avoid its repetition. It should be noted that the penalty of lashes does not place a financial burden on the community. No extensive special equipment is needed, and the punishment is over within a short time. After being beaten, the guilty person may return to his work and once again become a contributing member in the development of the nation.

Only under one condition is imprisonment indicated in the Pentateuch, namely for preventing a person from escaping before trial. Twice such a situation arose at the time of Moses. In the first case (Lev. 24 12) the son of an Israelite woman blasphemed the name of God, and in the second case (Num. 15 34) a man was found gathering wood on the Sabbath. Subsequently both persons were killed by stoning. It is noteworthy that imprisonment is never used in the Pentateuch as a prescribed punishment for wrongdoing. The maintenance of people in prison is expensive, and the prisoner, instead of being rehabilitated, all too frequently becomes a hardened criminal.

26.3   MILITARY REQUIREMENTS

There are a number of regulations in the Pentateuch which are specifically designed to ensure the military supremacy of Israel and to minimize the loss of life during battles. These regulations involve such various topics as the boundaries of the country, procedures for waging war, and personnel suited for military service. It should be realized that in addition to the laws specifically related to military matters, observance of practically all the Biblical laws adds to the military might of the country. Thus, regulations which eliminate disease, minimize the incidence of crime, strengthen the economy, and provide excellent agricultural yields will all indirectly add to the physical vigor of the nation.

Law

> Gen. 15 18–20;
> Ex. 23 31;
> Deut. 11 24;
> Josh 1 4.

The boundaries of the nation of Israel are to be from the Red Sea to the Mediterranean Sea, and from the desert to the Euphrates River.

Rationale

The specified boundaries are based on natural barriers such as rivers, seas, and deserts. These natural boundaries are a great protection against invasion by enemy armies, and reduce the required size of the defense forces which would otherwise be needed. Even today, when airplanes and motorized vehicles allow the easy crossing of all types of natural obstacles, still rivers, seas, and deserts offer a considerable degree of security to a nation. For example, after the 1967 Six-Day War, when Israel acquired the Sinai peninsula, with the Red Sea and Suez Canal as natural boundaries, she needed fewer soldiers to defend the boundary with Egypt than previously, although the length of the dividing line had been greatly increased.

Another benefit of having natural boundaries is the prevention of the spread of disease and insects from neighboring countries[16]. Furthermore, as will be demonstrated subsequently (Section 28.1), bringing of sacrifices controls the rainfall in Israel. If the country were to extend beyond the specified boundaries, the rainfall might be insufficient in the outlying areas.

Law

> Num. 33 50–56

Conquer all the nations occupying the territory promised to Israel, and distribute the land to your families. If you do not drive out the inhabitants of the land, then those who remain will be as barbed hooks in your eyes and as thorns in your sides, and they shall harass you.

Rationale

If the Biblical boundaries are not attained, then there will not be natural boundaries of mountains, rivers, and deserts to protect Israel from invasion. Furthermore, the presence of nearby enemies, even if weaker than the Israelites, will allow them to wage guerrilla warfare and perform acts of sabotage, and therefore they will be as thorns. In addition these idol-worshipping peoples in your midst may lead your people astray by their example, and will be a reservoir and a source of disease microorganisms, which can result in many plagues for the nation.

Law

Deut. 7 1–5;
20 16–18

When waging war against the cities of those nations occupying territory promised by God to Israel, do not leave anything alive. Utterly destroy those nations, do not have pity on them—Hittites, Amorites, Canaanites, Perizzites, Hivites, Jebusites—so they will not teach you to do their abominations, resulting in your sinning against God. God will make you succeed against them.

Rationale

The people of these nations, occupying the promised territory, all deserved death. They worshipped idols, sacrificed their children, and frequently performed abominable acts. As a result of their sins they were undoubtedly plagued with sicknesses and diseases of all types, and their possessions were contaminated with disease-causing microorganisms. To protect the people of Israel from such sicknesses, as well as preventing the Israelites from learning the ways of idol worship, it was necessary that these nations be utterly destroyed.

Law

Deut. 20 10–15

When waging war against distant cities, not included in the promised territory for the nation of Israel, first make an offer of peace. If they accept the offer and open up the city to you, then all the people found in the city shall become tributary to you and will serve you. If they do not make peace with you, and wage war against you, then you shall besiege them. When they are finally delivered by God into your hand, then kill all the men with the sword. But the women, children, and animals, as well as all the possessions of the city, will be spoils of war.

Rationale

One main purpose of the above regulation is to minimize loss of Israelite life during war. Therefore, first you call to an enemy city to submit peacefully. If it accepts the offer, it will serve you and become tributary to you. In this way many battles may be averted, and lives saved. If, however, the enemy city refuses to submit and wages war, then you do not try to subdue them by force, but rather by besieging the city. The siege will eventually weaken the city by depriving the people of food and other necessities, and thereby make it submit. The siege will weaken the enemy without any battle in which Israelite life is lost. However, since the persons within the city are of the type who will fight against you, it is necessary to destroy all the mature men so they will not subsequently perform acts of sabotage or take revenge. Moreover, the punishment to the city for resisting has to be significantly greater than for submitting, so as to give the people a strong reason for accepting the offer of peace.

Since the distant enemy nations are not as abominable or as sinful as the nearby nations, their possessions are not seriously contaminated with disease-causing microorganisms, and it is permissible to take spoils of war. The use of the captives as slaves enables teaching them more proper behavior patterns.

LAW

| Ex. 17 14–16; Deut. 25 17–19; (I Sam. 15 2–3). | Remember how the Amalekites ambushed you on your way out of Egypt. Therefore, when God will give you peace from your surrounding enemies, in the land which he is giving you to occupy and transmit as an inheritance, you shall not fail to blot out the memory of the Amalekites from under heaven. |

RATIONALE

The implication of the Biblical passages is that the Amalekites should be completely destroyed so that no memory of the nation should exist. In particular, the commandment is given by the prophet Samuel (I Sam. 15 3) that the Amalekites should be completely killed out, and their property destroyed.

We thus see that the Amalekites are to be utterly destroyed, just as is the punishment for those nations occupying the territory promised by God to Israel. However, the reason given in the case of the Amalekites is their treacherous nature, rather than their abominations. Nonetheless, it is very probable that Amalek performed abominations in addition to acts of treachery, and therefore the danger of spread of disease existed if their people and possessions were not utterly eradicated.

LAW

| Num. 25 6,14–18; 31 1–24,35. | When waging war against the Midianites, kill all the males, and kill all females who have experienced sexual relations. Only virgin girls may be taken captive. In addition, animals and material possessions may be taken as spoils of war. However, all material objects need to be purified before use. |

RATIONALE

The regulations concerning war with Midian were slightly different from those for other distant nations. With distant nations only the mature males had to be killed. However, with Midian all the males, and all females who had experienced sexual relations, had to be killed. The probable reasons for the distinction were the immoral practices of the Midianites (as may be implied from Num. 25 1–8), as well as their trickery aimed at harming the Israelites (Num. 25 16–18). Because of their immoral practices, all Midianites who had sexual relations had probably contracted venereal diseases, and needed to be killed out lest they infect the Israelites. Moreover, young boys of the Midianites also were subject to death because of the trickery which they may have learned. The danger existed that when the Midianite boys matured they might take revenge and harm the Israelites. Thus, the only Midianites whom it was safe to take captive were virgin girls.

The reason why the material objects, taken as spoils of war, had to be purified is explained in Section 25.4.

LAW

> Num. 10 9 — When you go to war in your land against an adversary that oppresses you, then you shall blow the silver trumpets, and you will be remembered before God, and you shall be saved from your enemies.

RATIONALE
The blowing of the silver trumpets is a signal of an emergency. The people will rapidly gather together and prepare to fight. By this means the people are not surprised by the enemy, and they are saved from destruction. The loud noise emitted by the trumpets guarantees that the sound would be heard at great distances.

LAW

> Num. 1 3; 26 2 — The age for military service begins at 20 years.

RATIONALE
A man reaches complete physical maturity at about the age of 20. Below this age many persons are still growing, and therefore have not reached their maximum physical strength.

LAW

> Deut. 7 17–21; 20 1–4,8. — Prior to battle, the priest should speak to the army: "Today you are approaching a military battle with the enemy, do not be afraid because God is with you to save you."
> When going out to fight do not be afraid of the enemy even if they are superior to you in numbers and equipment, because God who saved you from the Egyptians is with you. A soldier who is afraid should return home, lest he impart fear to the other soldiers.

RATIONALE
The psychology of the soldier is very important to success in battle. A soldier who is afraid will run, often when he could have conquered the enemy. Furthermore, fear in battle is contagious. When one soldier shows fear, many others will follow.

Therefore, it is necessary to do everything to minimize this possibility. An exhortation by the priest and the officers, and commands not to be afraid are essential to the success of the army, as well as to the preservation of the individual soldier's life.

A person who is afraid and does go into battle may develop war neurosis with resultant permanent psychological problems. For further details see Section 25.2.

Law

Deut. 20 5–9   After the speech by the priest, before going to battle, the officers should speak to the army saying, "Whoever has built a new house and not dedicated it should return home lest he die and someone else dedicate the house. Whoever planted a vineyard and has not used the fruit should return home lest he die and someone else use the fruit. Whoever has betrothed a woman and not married her should return home lest he die and someone else marry her. Whoever is afraid and fainthearted should return home lest he spread fear among his fellow soldiers." Afterwards officers should be appointed at the head of the army.

Rationale

We find here again the desire to select those soldiers who are best suited psychologically for battle. Soldiers who recently started and partly completed a major project at home, for example, building a new house, planting a vineyard, or betrothing a woman, should return home and complete the project. The reason for this is that people may become anxious over their uncompleted projects and may hesitate to fight as valiantly as they would otherwise. Their minds may be distracted, for example, by love-sickness or by details of completion of the projects. These soldiers are not the best and are more a detriment than a help. Furthermore, by having these exemptions, a person who is afraid and therefore completely unsuited for fighting would be able to return home without having to be ashamed. If there were no other people who were required to return home, a fearful soldier might even be afraid to return home. Instead, he can leave unobtrusively, fully realizing that others will not know the true reason for his returning home.

Only after the persons return home is it possible to appoint the final officers for battle. Otherwise, the officers themselves, since they would be essential, would not be able to go home even if afraid.

Law

Deut. 24 5   A person who has taken a new wife is free from military service for a year, to make his wife happy.

Rationale

During the first year of marriage, a woman does not have any children, and is especially dependent upon her husband for companionship. If during this time the husband goes away for a prolonged period, it can lead to adultery on her part. From the husband's point of view, he may become lovesick for his wife and not perform properly as a soldier. Also he may be reticent about risking his life, if he has no offspring to carry on his name.

Law

Deut. 23·10–15

When you are encamped against the enemy be careful of evil things. A man who has nocturnal emissions shall go out of the camp, shall wash himself before sunset, and return to the camp after sunset. Also a place outside of the camp should be set aside for bathroom needs. After a person squats outside he should cover the excrement with soil, using a trowel which each soldier carries with him. God is in your camp, and should not see unseemly items and turn from supporting you.

Rationale

When encamped against the enemy there are two significant means whereby plagues may be spread among the army. First, if a soldier has a nocturnal emission of semen, he may become a carrier of pathogens. To prevent this eventuality, he should go out of the camp, bathe himself before sunset, and then after sunset he may return to the camp. Perhaps washing before sunset results in a thorough removal of disease microorganisms. For example, it has been found that insects are most easily killed by insecticides in the late afternoon[17]. (See also Section 25.4, concerning Lev. 15 16–18.)

Second, leaving excrement uncovered can result in the spread of disease. In particular, it is known that typhoid fever is spread by the fecal discharges of infected persons. In the past, typhoid fever was one of the greatest hazards in military campaigns. In the Boer War, for example, one in seven of the million men in the British army contracted typhoid[18]. It is therefore necessary for soldiers camping out to have a separate area for bathroom needs, and to cover excrement with soil. Soil is known to have a purifying action on buried organic matter because of the soil's content of counteracting molds and bacteria, which result in the disappearance of pathogens such as typhoid and staphylococcus[19].

The above regulations prevent the spread of disease during military campaigns, and thereby increase the national strength.

Law

Deut. 20 19–20   When you besiege a city for a long time in order to capture the city, do not destroy the fruit trees by cutting them down with an axe. The fruit trees are needed for you to eat from, since man is dependent on the tree. Only trees that are known not to be fruit trees may be chopped down for use in siegeworks against the enemy.

Rationale

One problem encountered when besieging a city far distant from Israel is the supply of food for the army. It is especially difficult to bring to the soldiers perishable foods, such as fruits. Without fruits the army will suffer from scurvy, a sickness resulting from vitamin C deficiency[20]. The simplest solution is to not destroy the fruit trees in the siege area, so that a plentiful supply of fresh fruit will be available. In addition, the fruit trees are sources of other nourishment needed by the besieging army, and they supply food without requiring attention by army personnel.

Furthermore, fruit may be of use as food for birds and animals, thereby maintaining the ecological balance. For example, birds control the insect population, which if not kept under control could spread disease. Thus, not cutting down the fruit trees may indirectly prevent the spread of disease in the area.

Law

Deut. 7 22   God will drive out the nations, occupying the territory promised to Israel, little by little. Otherwise the wild animals will increase in numbers.

Rationale

If the nations occupying the territory promised to Israel were destroyed within a short time, there would be much uninhabited land. Wild animals would then multiply to fill the void. In contrast, where civilized societies exist, wild animals are known to diminish in numbers.

There are two main reasons why large numbers of wild animals are not desirable. First, they can cause physical damage, and can kill people. Second, they can be a reservoir of disease microorganisms harmful to man. For example, animals are hosts to such illnesses as anthrax, rabies, psittacosis, brucellosis, leptospirosis, trichinosis, tularemia, and rickettsial diseases—all of which may be transmitted to man[21].

Law

Deut. 9 4–6   The enemy nations occupying the territory promised to Israel will be conquered by you, not because of your righteousness, but because of their wickedness; and because God wants to carry out His promise to your ancestors Abraham, Isaac, and Jacob.

RATIONALE

If the nation of Israel had been completely righteous, it would have been stronger than any other country for many reasons. The citizens would have been exceptionally healthy and tall, the army would have been organized according to the Biblical military regulations, and the people would have been educated and intelligent. In practice, however, not all the Biblical laws were properly observed, and therefore the nation of Israel, although strong, was not nearly as powerful as it could otherwise have been.

In contrast, the enemy nations were even worse off. There were numerous Biblical laws that were disregarded by these countries because of their wickedness. As a result, their citizens were not healthy, their armies were poorly organized, and their people were mainly illiterate.

Therefore, the military successes of the Israelites at the times of Moses, Joshua, and afterwards, were not because of the righteousness of the people, but because of the wickedness of the opposing nations.

Similarly at the present time, with the re-establishment of the State of Israel, the same thing can be said. It is not so much the righteousness of the Jewish nation that enabled the miraculous victories in 1948, 1956, and 1967, but the wickedness of the Arab nations. The typical Arab soldier, rather than being a fierce desert warrior, is an ignorant, listless, often disease-ridden peasant[22]. If, however, the Israeli citizens strictly observed the Biblical laws, then the Jewish nation would be even stronger, and the military miracles would be even more astounding.

Chapter Twenty-seven

ECONOMIC POLICIES

In this chapter are discussed those Biblical laws whose main purpose is to insure a sound economy for the country, and which are designed to eliminate poverty, prevent inflation, and encourage a high productivity for the nation. Included in economic regulations are laws concerned with land ownership, taxes, slavery, aiding one's fellow man, vow obligations, and agriculture.

Factors which are known to hurt the economy include: (A) failure of the society to provide job opportunities; (B) inability of certain individuals to contribute to the production processes; and (C) restrictions on individuals from participating in the productive processes, because of such factors as racial discrimination, or limitations imposed on women and the aged.[1]

The laws in the Pentateuch are aimed at eliminating just such things. Job opportunities are supplied by distributing the land equally among the people, thereby allowing anyone who so desires to work as a farmer. The existence of defective persons is eliminated by preventing disease, birth defects, accidents, and malnutrition. Finally, the Bible prohibits all types of discrimination, such as against aliens, widows, and the aged.

Observance of the Biblical regulations should lead to an extremely stable economy, where there would be no necessity for strikes and other types of public protests. The population would work efficiently and there would be close to 100 percent employment.

27.1 LAND OWNERSHIP

Laws

Num. 26 52–56	Apportion the land of Israel by lot to the twelve tribes (not including the tribe of Levi), and to their family subdivisions. The size of the property received shall depend on the number of individuals within each group.
Num. 18 20, 23; Deut. 18 1–2	The Levites and priests shall not be included in the apportionment of the land among the tribes.
Num. 35 1–8	The Israelites should give from their received land, according

to the size of their apportionment, 48 walled cities for the Levites. Each city shall have a surrounding field of 2,000 cubits, which begins 1,000 cubits from the city wall. The cities shall be for dwelling therein, and the surrounding fields for the cattle and other needs. Six of the cities shall be for refuge for manslayers.

Lev. 25 14–18, 23–34.
If you sell or purchase land do not wrong one another. You shall pay for the produce of the land according to the number of years of growing remaining until the next Jubilee year, when the land will return to its original owner. The sale of land is not a permanent sale, since the land belongs to God and you are just settlers on His property. If a poor person sells his land, then his nearest kinsman shall buy it back for him, or if the seller himself found sufficient funds he should buy back the land. The redemption price to be paid shall be the original purchase price minus the value for the years used. Otherwise the land shall remain with the purchaser until the Jubilee year.

A person who sells a dwelling house within a walled city may only redeem the house within one full year. Otherwise it remains permanently with the buyer. This law applies only to a walled city, and not to houses in cities without walls, nor to the walled cities of the Levites. Purchases from the Levite cities may be redeemed even after one year, and if not redeemed they return to the owner in the Jubilee year. No sales, however, may be made of the surrounding fields of the Levite cities, for these are a perpetual possession.

Num. 27 1–11; 36 1–13; Deut. 21 15–17
The following is the order of inheritance: sons; if there are no sons then the daughters inherit; next are brothers; then come the father's brothers; followed by the nearest relative.

When the sons inherit, the oldest son receives a double portion. This regulation cannot be modified by the father, even to the extent of giving the double portion to the oldest son of a different wife.

When the daughters inherit, they must marry men from within their own tribe, so that the property is not transferred to another tribe.

Deut. 25 5–10
If brothers dwell together and one of them dies without any child, then the live brother shall take the widow for a wife. The oldest son born from this union will bear the name of the dead brother, so the name will not be erased. If, however, the live brother does not want to take the widow for a wife, then she should go to the elders and state that her brother-in-

law refused to uphold the name of his brother. The elders shall speak to him, and if he still refuses then the widow should remove his shoe, spit in his face, and declare, "So shall be done to the man who does not build his brother's house." His name will then be called the house of him that had his shoe loosened.

Deut. 8 7–10; 11 10–12.

The land of Israel is a good land. It has streams, springs, and underground waters. It is a land of wheat, barley, vines, fig trees, pomegranates, olives, and honey. You shall not be wanting of anything in the land. Its stones are iron ore, and from its hills you may dig copper. You will eat, be satiated, and bless God for the good land. It is a land of hills and valleys. When rain comes you will have water to drink. God cares for the land all year long.

RATIONALE

The land regulations are designed to ensure an approximately equitable distribution of the land among the people. To achieve this aim, it is necessary not only initially to apportion the land among the inhabitants, but also to have regulations concerning its sale as well as concerning who is entitled to inherit. Without restrictions on sales and inheritance, it would not be long before the acreage of the nation would be under the control of a minority of the population.

An economic problem that arises in most countries of the world involves the inequitable distribution of the land. Often wealthy land owners are in possession of practically all the nation's acreage, while the majority of the people do not have any land of their own. As a consequence, the landless majority are dependent for work and housing on the wealthy minority. Even in countries where restrictions, such as high taxes, are placed on landholders, and as a result enormous estates are not that common, still much land speculation occurs, which has a negative influence on the national economy.

The Biblical laws are aimed at preventing the evils commonly associated with unequal distribution of the land. Each male over 20 years of age, of the original settlers in Israel, is to be given an equal share of the land. The only exception occurs with the Levites and priests, who are given cities in which to live, with a minimal amount of soil surrounding the city for agricultural purposes. However, the Levites and priests receive supplemental food, from taxes imposed on the other tribes (see Section 27.2).

Each family of the twelve tribes could use their acreage to supply more than enough food for their own needs. Housing, and even industry, could be built on their property. The need for renting is obviated in most cases, since everyone has their own land. If it happens that a family becomes poor to the extent that they cannot support themselves, then they could sell their land for a limited period, i.e., until the

Jubilee year, and thereby obtain enough funds. In general, ownership of land eliminates unemployment, since the landowner can always work productively in farming activities.

The Levites, who work not at farming but mainly at caring for the Temple area and the cities of refuge, only need property sufficient for housing, and some surrounding fields on the outskirts of the city for necessary agricultural pursuits. They receive 48 cities, i.e., four cities from each of the twelve tribes. Consequently the Levites are scattered throughout the nation, making it easier for the tithes to be distributed evenly among them without requiring excessively long transportation distances. It should be noted that the fields surrounding the Levite cities provide a cushion against air pollution.

Land speculation is eliminated by setting the price of purchased acreage at the value of the expected produce of the land until the next Jubilee year. When the Jubilee year comes, the land reverts to its original owner, thus giving the economy a fresh start. Although it is permissible to sell one's property, still it is not desirable. Therefore, the seller or his near relative is entitled at any time to redeem the property by payment according to the number of years remaining until the next Jubilee.

The above purchasing regulations apply to open fields. In cities surrounded by walls, land can be sold permanently, but only if it is not redeemed within the first year of the sale. These cities probably would be used mainly for housing and business. If, for example, the seller realizes that the sale was not to his benefit from a business viewpoint, he can redeem the land within one year. After the year is over, the sale is permanent. These laws do not apply to the cities of the Levites, since the Levites do not have additional estates outside the walled cities, and they need their property for housing. Therefore, the property of the Levites within a walled city has equivalent purchasing regulations to the property belonging to the other tribes. The fields surrounding the Levite cities cannot be sold at all since they are in a sense, property of the city governments, and are to be used for the benefit of all the inhabitants.

Other regulations, needed to maintain approximately equal estates among the population, involve the inheritance laws. The basic system is for the sons to inherit the property. The daughters, on the other hand, acquire land to live on by marrying men who have inherited estates. Since men can marry more than one wife, there would be few, if any, women without husbands; and therefore all the women would be cared for. The oldest son receives a double portion (i.e., twice the amount that each of the other sons receives) because his family will, on the average, eventually be the largest, since he will be first to marry and have children. In turn, his oldest son will be the first to marry, and may have sons before some of the father's brothers. Thus the eldest son's property will subsequently be divided into the most parts, and therefore he needs the largest estate. This explains why chronological age, rather than personal desires by the deceased father, determines who receives the double portion. Since the eldest boy receives the largest share, he is the one who undoubtedly is responsible for caring for his mother and sisters until they marry. It is of interest that first-born children tend to gain greater eminence in later life than their siblings, because of the differences in the interaction with the parents.[2] Perhaps, to encourage the oldest boy even more, he is given a double share.

If the father had no sons, but only daughters, then they inherit the property. However, they must marry within the tribe, for otherwise the property would be transferred to a different tribe, resulting in jurisdictional disputes. Similarly, if the father had no children, his nearest male relative inherits the estate, thereby keeping the land within the tribe, and allowing an orderly disposition of the estate.

Usually, if the deceased left no children, then the estate is inherited by his brother(s). However, an exception to this rule may occur when there is a widow. In such a case, the law requires the brother to marry the widow. The oldest son born from this union would be the one to inherit the estate. By this means a more equitable distribution of the land results. Furthermore, by marrying the woman, she would be provided support. Brothers are often alike in many respects, and the resulting marriage should be a happy one. Since men may have more than one wife, the brother can marry the widow even if he is already married. Note that this regulation applies only if the brothers dwell together, i.e., in the same tribal area. If, however, the brothers live far apart, as may easily happen with the Levites, or converts who have no inheritable land, then the requirement to marry the widow would not apply. It may similarly not apply if the brother is a permanent slave or has disappeared. Where the brothers do not dwell together, the widow is free to be married to whomever she wants.

Not necessarily will the brother want to marry the widow. He may not particularly desire the woman, or he may be more interested in his brother's inheritance which he would lose to a son who may be born from the widow. Therefore, the Bible exerts sociological pressure by the elders who speak to the brother and try to persuade him to marry the widow. If he still refuses, then the procedure is followed whereby he is shamed by having his shoe removed and by being spit upon in the face.

People should be aware, no matter what the piece of land they receive, that Israel is a good land. Observing the Biblical laws will result in good agricultural yields. Moreover, in certain cases rich mineral wealth of iron and copper lies buried in the ground. Be happy with the land because of the numerous benefits lying therein.

27.2 TAXES

The Pentateuch prescribes certain taxes to support the Levites, priests, and poor. The regulations concerning these taxes can be conveniently separated into two parts, namely tithes, and obligations to the priests.

27.2.1 Tithes

Laws

    Lev. 27 30, 32   One-tenth of the produce of the seed of the ground, the fruit of the tree, and the cattle and sheep is holy unto the Lord.

ECONOMIC POLICIES   629

Deut. 12 17–19; 14 22–27.	Each year you shall take one-tenth of your produce of the grain, wine, and oil, and eat from them only in the place selected by God. If it be too difficult to transport the food for a long distance, then you may exchange it for money, and use the money to purchase any type of food in the place selected by God. You and your children, slaves, and the Levites shall eat from the food and be happy. Do not forsake the Levites.
Num. 18 21, 24	Instead of an apportionment of land, the Levites receive from the one-tenth of the produce, in return for their work in the Temple area.
Lev. 27 31, 33	If a man redeems his agricultural tithe, he should add one-fifth of its value. A man shall not exchange one animal of the tithe for another, but if he does, then both animals become holy.
Deut. 14 28–29; 26 12–15	The tithe of the third year shall be given to the Levites, aliens, orphans, and widows, and shall be eaten within your settlements. Then you shall state that you have carried out the laws concerning the tithes, have not contacted the tithes with impure items, and shall ask God to bless the people and the land.
Num. 18 25–32	The Levites shall give one-tenth of the tithe as a gift for the priests. Afterwards, the Levites and their families may eat from the tithes wherever they may be.

RATIONALE

Usually the tithe laws are interpreted on the basis that there are two tithes each year, the first for the Levites, and the second to be eaten by the Israelites in Jerusalem or to be given to the poor. However, this distribution would result in the Levites getting too large a share. For example, if the average produce of each tribe were 100p per year (of which approximately 2p would be given to the priests) then the Levites would receive from the twelve tribes $12 \times 10p = 120p$ per year, of which 12p would be given by the Levites to the priests. The Israelites would end up each year with approximately 88 p (100p−10p−2p) and the Levites with 108p (120p−12p). Furthermore, additional portions would be given to the Levites every third year. Thus the Levites who hardly did any work on the soil, and are considered to be poor by the Bible, would receive about 25 percent more than the Israelites who worked industriously!

A more probable explanation, which would fit the Biblical wording more exactly, would involve only one tithe each year. From this tithe, the Israelites would take food for eating while in Jerusalem, mainly during the three pilgrimage festivals, and the remainder would go for the Levites. In the third year the Israelites would use their own food when eating in Jerusalem, and the tithe would be given to the Levites and the poor. This three-year cycle would be repeated a second time, followed by the Sabbatical year when no agricultural work was performed. From the calculation shown subsequently, it would result, assuming an average produce of 100p per tribe per year, that each Israelite tribe would end up with an average for a seven-year period of 78p, and the Levites with an average of 50.6p. Since the Levites could do supplementary work, besides work relative to the Temple, they could probably supply the additionally needed produce of 27.4p per year, thus resulting in a fairly equitable food distribution. It has here been assumed, for simplicity, that the number of Levites is approximately equal to the average of the number of persons for the other tribes.

Assume the situation where just enough produce is produced to feed the people for each seven-year period. The average tribe produces during non-Sabbatical years 100p of produce. Average annual produce set aside per tribe for the priests is approximately 2p. Average produce set aside for tithes per year per tribe is 10p. Assume each tribe on the average needs 78p of produce per year for eating. For two out of three years the tithe is used for food when staying in Jerusalem, and the remainder is given to the Levites. The third year the tithe is given for the Levites and the poor.

Each year there are about 20 days during which people stay in Jerusalem: one day for Passover sacrifice, seven days for Festival of Matzot, one day for Pentecost, seven days for Tabernacles, one day for Atzeret, and three days allowance for arriving one day in advance for each of the three pilgrimage festivals.

An average year has 365 days. Then 20/365 is approximately 0.055 of the year. During this time the people eat 0.055 of the total year's diet, or $0.055 \times 78p = 4.3p$. Since the total tithe is 10p this leaves 5.7p for the Levites per tribe per year. Since there are 12 tribes, the Levites receive $12 \times 5.7p = 68.4p$ per year during years when the tithe is used both for eating in Jerusalem and for the Levites. For the third year, the Levites receive $\frac{1}{2} \times 12 \times 10p = 60p$, based on the arbitrary assumption that half the tithe goes to the poor and the other half to the Levites. Over a six-year period the Levites receive $4 \times 68.4p = 273.6p$
$$2 \times 60p = 120.0p$$
$$\overline{393.6p}$$

of which one-tenth or 39.4p is given to the priests, leaving 354.2p. The average food available each year for seven years for the Levites is then $1/7 \times 354.2p = 50.6p$. The other tribes are each left with $100p - 2p - 5.7p = 92.3p$ for years when the Israelites eat the tithe in Jerusalem; and 88p for years when the tithe is given to the poor. The average for seven years is then $1/7 (4 \times 92.3p + 2 \times 88p) = 77.9 \approx 78p$. The shortage by the Levites of 27.4p per year (78p−50.6p) would be offset by the produce of the surrounding fields of the Levite cities.

Thus, in the case where there is just enough food for the population for a seven-year period, the Levites would receive a smaller but sufficient share. During years when there is an excess of food, part of which could be sold to neighboring countries, the Levites would receive a somewhat greater amount of food which would be more than enough for their needs.

For example, if the average produce were 125p per year per tribe (i.e., one and one-fourth times the needs of the entire population), then from similar considerations to those in the previous analysis, the typical tribe would end up with an annual average of 96.7p for a seven-year period, while the Levites would receive 69.9p. Similarly, if the average produce were 150p per year per tribe (i.e., one and one-half times the needs of the entire population), then the typical tribe would end up with an annual average of 115.6p per year per tribe, while the Levites would receive 89.2p.

Thus we see that the Bible provides a lesser amount of food for the Levites than for the other Israelites, although the amount received by the Levites should be sufficient for their needs.

It is noteworthy that the tithes are given from the grain, vegetables, fruits, wine, oil, and permissible animals. The resultant varied menu ensures a nutritionally balanced diet for the Levites, and prevents any deficiency diseases.

Part of the tithe was intended to be eaten by the Israelites in Jerusalem, so that there should be no food shortage when the entire population came to celebrate the three pilgrimage festivals. Every family would bring enough produce for its own needs, thereby preventing excessively high food prices. If, however, the distance to Jerusalem was so great for some families that it was impracticable to transport the required food, then it was permissible to exchange the tithe for money and to use the money to purchase food in Jerusalem. No penalty was incurred in such an exchange. Probably, such an exchange was limited to the approximate amount of food needed for the time of stay in Jerusalem. However, if it were desired to redeem the tithe, for other reasons, it was necessary to pay a one-fifth penalty. This penalty was to discourage, but not to prevent, such exchanges, and to impose a penalty in case cheating occurred. In the case of animals, it was not permissible to exchange one animal for another, otherwise people would tend to replace good animals with poorer quality ones. If one animal was replaced by another, then as a penalty they both become part of the tithe and cannot be redeemed.

The part of the tithe which would be in excess of the needs of the people for food in Jerusalem had to be given to the Levites. The portions received by the Levites did not have to be eaten in Jerusalem, since the food received was in place of an apportionment of land, and was equivalent to the produce grown by the Israelites on their estates.

The tithes of the third and sixth years are to be given to the aliens, orphans, widows, and Levites. The aliens, widows, and Levites do not have land of their own and therefore cannot raise produce. Widows, however, although they do not have land of their own, may be in charge of land inherited by their sons, but do not necessarily have the time and know-how to cultivate the soil. Similarly orphans probably have land, but may not have sufficient strength or capability to attend to farming requirements. It is therefore necessary to supplement the food for these classes of individuals. Naturally the food they receive does not have to be eaten in Jerusalem but can be eaten anywhere in the country.

After distributing the tithe of the third (and sixth) years it is necessary for the Israelites to make a statement that they have carried out the requirements for the tithes. It is particularly with the tithe of the third year that it is difficult to verify that the produce has been properly distributed. A person can always say, when confronted, that he gave the tithe to some unknown aliens, orphans, and widows. Therefore the Bible requires a statement that the tithe laws have been carried out. In contrast, a definite amount of produce is expected by the Levites from each Israelite family in the first and second years (and the fourth and fifth years), and cases where major cheating occurs can be detected fairly easily. Therefore, no statements are necessary, other than in the third (and sixth) year.

The Pentateuch imposes no restrictions on the purity of a person when eating from the tithes. An unclean as well as a clean person may partake of the food. However, the restriction is imposed that before the tithe is distributed it should not come in contact with a dead body or be placed in impure vessels (Deut. 26 14). These restrictions are to prevent the spread of disease upon distribution of the tithes.

It should be noted that the priests, even though originating from the tribe of Levi, are not included among the Levites in receiving the tithes. Instead, the priests receive special portions, as will be specified in Section 27.2.2. One of these special portions is the one-tenth of the tithe, given by the Levites to the Priests.

27.2.2 Priestly Portions

Not only the Levites but also the priests do not receive a land apportionment. Instead, both groups receive food from the Israelites. The portions given to the priests are varied, and are in addition to the tithes that the Levites give the priests, and which have been already mentioned in Section 27.2.1. These portions are given to the priests in payment for the services related to the Temple, and other tasks, which they perform (see Section 25.5.1).

LAWS

Ex. 22 28; 23 19; 34 26; Num. 18 12, 13; Deut. 18 4; 26 1-11.	The choicest first-fruits of the grain, wine, and oil, and the first ripe fruits of all that is produced by the soil, are to be brought to the sanctuary in a basket and given to the priest. The bringer should recite, "My father was a wandering Aramaean who went

ECONOMIC POLICIES 633

	down to Egypt...." Everyone in the priest's household who is clean may eat from the first fruits of the soil.
Deut. 18 4	The first fleeces of the shearing of your sheep shall be given to the priests.
Num. 15 17–21	The first of the dough (חלה) shall be given to the priests.
Ex. 13 2, 11–16; 22 28, 29; 34 19, 20; Lev. 27 26, 27; Num. 18 15–18; Deut. 15 19–22.	The male first-born of every animal belongs to the priest. No use is to be made by the Israelites of the first-born bull, sheep, or goat. In the case where the first-born animal is a bull, sheep, or goat, it is brought as a sacrifice when older than seven days, and its flesh is eaten by the priests in a clean place. However, if the animal has a blemish, then it is not brought as a sacrifice, and can be eaten in any location even by impure priests. The first-born of man or of an unclean animal is to be redeemed. Five shekels are paid to redeem a human or an unclean animal when above 30 days old; except that a sheep is given to redeem a donkey—otherwise the donkey is killed. The laws of the first-born are a remembrance of how God took the Israelites out from Egypt.
Lev. 10 12–15, 17; Num. 18 9–10. (Also see Lev. 2 3, 10; 6 9, 11; 7 9–10, for details of the meal-offering; Lev. 5 13; 6 19, 22 for details of the sin-offering; Lev. 7 6–7; 14 13 for details of the guilt-offering; and Ex. 29 28; Lev. 7 14, 31–34; Num. 6 20; Deut. 18 3, for details of the peace-offering.)	The parts of the meal-offering, sin-offering, and guilt-offering, which are not burned on the altar, are to be eaten by the priests (only males) near the altar, in the courtyard of the Sanctuary. The breast and right thigh of the peace-offering, as well as any accompanying cakes of fine flour, and the shoulder, the cheeks and the stomach, shall be eaten by the priests and their families, male or female, in any clean place.
Lev. 7 8	The skin of the burnt-offering belongs to the officiating priest.
Lev. 5 16; 22 14	A person who by mistake misused holy items, includ-

Num. 5 5–8	ing food, pays a one-fifth penalty in addition to the value of the item and gives it to the priest.
	A person who confesses that he stole from someone else should return to that person the principle plus a one-fifth penalty. If, however, the person against whom the trespass was committed had died and did not leave any heirs, then the principle and the one-fifth penalty are given to the priest.
Lev. 27 21; Num. 5 9, 10; 18 14, 19.	All holy gifts, and items made holy, belong to the priests. All contributions of holy gifts by the Israelites are for the priests and their sons and daughters.
Lev. 24 5–9	The twelve breads, put weekly on the table in the sanctuary, are to be eaten by the priests in a holy place.

RATIONALE

The portions provided for the priests obviously supplied sufficient food for their needs. One main item was the tithe from the Levites, which would be approximately one-half of one percent of the total produce of the country. Another important item was the first-fruits, and a third important item was the meat from the sacrificed animals. The amount of first-fruits to be given to the priests is not specified, and could be adjusted according to the needs of the priests. In general, the priests were supplied with a well balanced diet including fruit, vegetables, grains, bread, and meat. These foods were in payment for the services which the priests offered, and in compensation for the lack of inherited land for development. Furthermore, in addition to food, the priests were supplied with material for clothing, such as shearings from the sheep, and skins of sacrifices. Food and clothing were thus given to the priests, enabling them to function efficiently.

Of the food given to the priests, some items could be eaten only by the priests in the Temple area, and other items also by their dependents, such as by their slaves, sons, and daughters. Although the meat from many of the sacrifices, such as the sin-offering and guilt-offering, are only eaten by the priests in the Temple courtyard, still meat from the peace-offering and first-born permissible animals could be eaten in a clean place by all the members of the priests' families. Similarly, the received produce of the ground could be eaten by the families of the priests. Thus ample food supplies were designated, not only for the priests but also for the members of the household.

The priest who worked in the Temple received a greater supply of food than one who did not. This was to insure that a practicing priest would obtain sufficient food for his livelihood, as well as to guarantee that a non-practicing priest would have to work at some other beneficial task to supplement his income. The fact that little land was available to the priests and Levites guaranteed that if non-practicing they would work in a non-agricultural occupation, which would be beneficial to the society.

ECONOMIC POLICIES   635

Occasionally the priests received taxes which were neither food nor clothing. For example, they received payments from those who mistakenly misused holy items, and from those who wanted to atone for theft from persons who died without heirs. Furthermore, all types of holy gifts were given to the priests. In this way, the needs of the priests were well taken care of.

In general, the taxes to the Levites and priests are very beneficial to the economy. The taxes free the Levites and priests from agricultural pursuits, and allow them to maintain the Temple and religious rites, as well as to act as judges, officers, etc. needed for an efficient society (see also Section 25.5).

27.3 SLAVERY REGULATIONS

Two basic classes of slaves are specified in the Bible, namely a Hebrew slave and a heathen slave.

Laws

Ex. 21 2–6; The Hebrew male or female slave works for up to six
Lev. 25 39–43, 46; years, or until the Jubilee year if it occurs before six years
Deut. 15 12–18. of work are completed. The Hebrew slave is treated not as a slave, but as a hired servant or settler. He should not be worked rigorously. In the seventh year the Hebrew slave goes free, without any payment for freedom. If he was married before he became a slave, then his wife and children go free with him. If he was married after becoming a slave, his spouse and children remain with the master. When the Hebrew slave goes free, he should be furnished with possessions from the sheep, grain, and wine. If the slave states that he does not want to be free, but prefers to be a slave, then he should be brought to court, and a hole should be drilled with an awl through his ear unto the door or doorpost, and he shall be a slave until the next Jubilee year, when he returns to his inherited land.

Ex. 21 7–11 A special class of female Hebrew slave occurs when a man sells his daughter as a maidservant, to be married to the master or the master's son. In this case the maidservant does not go out after six years. If she was married to the master, and did not find favor in his eyes, then she should be redeemed, but not sold. If she was married to the master's son, then she should be treated as a regular daughter-in-law. If the master marries another wife, he should not detract from the level of food, clothing, and shelter supplied the maidservant. If

	the master does not marry her to himself or his son, and does not have her redeemed, then the maidservant goes free without any payment.
Ex. 22 2; Lev. 25 39.	An Israelite becomes a slave by being sold; either by his own accord because of poverty, or by court order because he has insufficient funds to pay for the crime of theft.
Lev. 25 47–55	If an Israelite be sold as a slave to a non-Israelite dwelling in the land of Israel, then it is the duty of the Israelite's relatives, especially his brother, uncle or cousin, to redeem him; or if the slave has sufficient funds then he should redeem himself. The price of redemption is the payment for the time remaining until he would automatically go free (e.g., after six years or in a Jubilee year, he would go free). The Israelite should not be worked rigorously as a slave to the non-Israelite.
Lev. 25 44–46	A heathen male or female slave may be purchased from the surrounding nations or from the non-Israelite settlers in Israel. These heathen slaves are a permanent possession and are an inheritance to your children. They may be worked with rigor.
Num. 31 18, 26–30; Deut. 20 11, 14	Heathen slaves may be obtained from the captives acquired upon conquest of nations distant from the land of Israel.
Ex. 21 20–21	If a heathen slave dies within a day of being punished by his master, then his master is subject to the death penalty. However, if the heathen slave survives for a day or two days, then no punishment of the master occurs since the slave is the property of the owner.
Ex. 21 26	If a master destroys the eye or tooth of his male or female slave, then the slave goes free in compensation for the damage.
Deut. 23 16–17	If a slave escapes to you for protection, do not return him to his master. Let him settle in a place suitable to him within your territory, and do not afflict the escaped slave.

RATIONALE

Although slavery is usually looked upon as a cruel practice, this is not the case in the Biblical form of slavery. A Hebrew slave, in practice, is a person who sells himself as a hired worker for at most six years. He is not to be worked with rigor, and must be treated properly. By selling himself as a slave, the person gains in several respects. He obtains a source of food, clothing and shelter for himself and his family. He learns how to perform certain tasks, thereby acquiring a new trade. Furthermore, he earns money which will be useful after his release.

When the Hebrew slave goes free, he is furnished with possessions such as sheep and grain, so that he can get started to earn a living on his own, and not end up dependent on charity. Probably the slave had sold his inheritable land previously because of poverty. With the money acquired from his work he may be able to redeem the land, especially because the price is now less since it is six years closer to the Jubilee year. If the slave was released in the Jubilee year, then he can immediately start anew, since his inheritable land returns to his possession at the same time.

A Hebrew slave who, because of his personality or other practical reasons, prefers to be a slave, is brought to court and has a hole drilled in his earlobe. It is necessary that the ear-drilling be agreed to by the court, for otherwise a master could make a temporary slave into a permanent one by simply drilling the ear against the slave's will. The pierced ear is a mark to designate a permanent slave, and can be accomplished with a minimum danger of infection and pain. In modern society, ear-piercing is often voluntarily done by women so they can wear earrings, thus showing the simplicity of the operation.

The special class of female Hebrew slave where the father sells his daughter, is really equivalent to the father obtaining payment for marrying his daughter to a particular person. If, however, after the sale, the master or his son does not marry the girl, or if she was married to the master but did not find favor in his eyes and was not allowed to be redeemed, then the girl goes free without any payment required. Thus, this class of female slave is nothing more than a modified form of marriage, where the wife has to work as hard as a maid-servant, and is legally protected from abuse.

An Israelite who sells himself to a non-Israelite brings about many problems with respect to observance of the Biblical laws. Therefore he should be redeemed as quickly as possible by his relatives. The responsibility falls on the relatives, since they are the ones who should have come to the support of the slave before he was in such a desperate condition that he had to sell himself into slavery. The same laws about going free, as well as not being worked to excess, apply to the Hebrew slave whether sold to an Israelite or non-Israelite.

In contrast to the laws regarding a Hebrew slave, a heathen slave can be worked hard and punished severely. He does not go free ordinarily, and is an inheritable possession. The laws regarding heathen slaves supply a source of cheap labor, solve the problem of what to do with war captives, and in the process raise the moral level of the slaves. Limitations exist, however, as to how severely the heathen slave can be punished. If any eye or tooth of the slave is destroyed, the slave automatically goes free. Furthermore, the slave cannot be punished so severely that he would die within the day, otherwise the owner is subject to death for murder (see Section 26.2.2.4).

One strong control of the treatment of slaves is that an escaped slave must be given refuge. Thus, if a slave, Hebrew or heathen, is treated poorly, he can escape, and thereby gain freedom. Hence a master would not want to treat his slaves too badly, for otherwise they would run away, and he would lose their manpower.

27.4 AIDING ONE'S FELLOW MAN

In numerous instances the occasion arises where assistance can be given to someone in need. A poor person may require a loan; an alien, orphan, or widow may need special help; a lost object may be found; or a person may encounter difficulty on the road. For all such occasions the Pentateuch prescribes definite procedures to be followed. Some underlying purposes for these regulations include compassion for one's fellow man and desire to maintain a high level of productivity for each individual. Many other benefits exist, which will be discussed in the ensuing sections.

27.4.1 Lending Laws

Laws

Ex. 22 24–26; Lev. 25 35–38; Deut. 23 20–21; 24 6, 10–13, 17.
If you lend money or any object to a fellow Israelite, do not take interest. If you take a garment from a poor man as a pledge for a loan, you must return it each day by sunset, because it may be the man's only garment for sleeping. He will bless you, and he otherwise might complain to God. If you take any item as a pledge, do not go into the house of the borrower to get it. Wait outside for the man to bring you the pledge. Do not take millstones or only the upper millstone for a pledge, because these are necessary tools for maintaining life. Do not take a widow's garment as a pledge. You may, however, take interest when lending to a foreigner.

Deut. 15 1–11
At the beginning* of every seventh year all debts of fellow Jews shall be remitted. You shall not require payment of debts, except from a foreigner. Do not refrain from lending a needy Israelite what he needs just because the year of remission of debts is nearing. As a result of observing these regulations, God will bless you, and there will hardly be any poor people in the land. The people of Israel will lend and rule over other nations, but will not need to borrow, and will not become subservient to other nations.

---

* Although the Biblical text states "at the end of seven years," the meaning is "at the end of the first moment of the seventh year, when according to the counting system seven years would have passed"; in other words "at the beginning of the seventh year." (See Sections 5.1.1 and 5.1.4.)

RATIONALE

The Biblical laws concerning lending money or objects to a poor person are intended to prevent the poor person from becoming poorer as a result of the loan. Thus, one should not lend at interest, because the borrower will have to pay back more than he borrowed, thereby often being in a worse financial condition. If an object is taken as a pledge to guarantee the return of the borrowed money, then the pledge must be returned when needed for practical necessities. A garment for sleeping must, for example, be returned every night so the borrower can function efficiently. A widow's garment should not be taken as a pledge because it might be her only spare garment. Furthermore, a work tool needed for a livelihood, such as a millstone, cannot be taken as a pledge, because otherwise the earning capacity of the borrower will be impaired, thereby making him even poorer.

Another factor of importance is the self-respect of the borrower. The lender must not enter the borrower's house to obtain a pledge, but must wait outside for the object to be brought to him. In this way the borrower maintains his self-respect and does not lose earning capacity because of a resultant poor mental attitude. In all these cases, not only does the borrower benefit in that he will probably be able to pay back the loan, but also the lender benefits because he gets his money back.

Despite all these laws, it may happen that a poor man will not be able to pay his debts. As a result, he might have to sell his inherited property or even himself as a slave. This would decrease the over-all productivity of the society. To prevent this, all debts of fellow Israelites are remitted at the beginning of the seventh year, to minimize the condition whereby the poor become poorer. People should not refrain from lending, however, even if the year of remission is near, and the loan will probably not be repaid; otherwise the purpose of the law to benefit the poor would be nullified.

By minimizing the number of poor people, the society is benefited. Goods can be purchased by the poor, thereby maintaining the productivity level of the nation and decreasing unemployment and underproduction. Moreover, poor people may out of necessity turn to crime, or may suffer from psychological illnesses. Eliminating poverty would prevent such pathetic situations.

There is another difficulty in lending on interest, even assuming that the poor person will be able to repay the loan plus interest. Interest results in the devaluation of the monetary unit. For example, if 100 shekels become 110 shekels after one year, then the value of the shekel will have decreased by ten percent. This will result in continuing inflation, which is the situation in practically every modern country of the world. A stable monetary unit having a definite purchasing power over long periods of time can only be maintained if the value of money is not decreased by taking interest.

Recently, in 1969-1970, consumer prices in the United States rose at an annual rate of 6 percent, the steepest rise in living costs in 20 years.[3] At the same time the going interest rates were the highest in many years. Beginning with 1971 interest rates were lowered somewhat, and the rise in living costs showed a corresponding slow-down to about 4 percent.[4] In effect, the United States performed a controlled experiment which showed that the rate of inflation increases with increasing allowable interest rates. Unfortunately, as a result of the experiment, unemployment doubled, business activity slowed, and the United States nearly underwent a major recession.

The laws of taking interest, and of releasing a borrower from debt in the seventh year, do not apply to a foreigner. Thus an Israelite can take interest from a foreigner, and vice versa. The reason for this exception can be explained by reciprocity; the foreigner will not lend to the Israelite without taking interest, therefore why should the Israelite lend to the foreigner without interest. Similar considerations apply to the fact that the laws on the year of remission do not apply to the foreigner. A more fundamental explanation of the exception is that the laws are made for the benefit of the society. Lending on interest to a foreigner allows a profit without affecting the buying power of the people within the nation of Israel, nor does the value of the monetary unit decrease since the interest arises from the productivity of the foreign country. Similarly, releasing the foreigner from his debt would only cause the Israelite lender to suffer, without a comparable enriching of the over-all national economy. Hence, the foreigner does not have his debt remitted.

As a result of observing these lending laws, a poor person does not become poorer upon borrowing, and often will be enabled to obtain a fresh start so he may gain financially. In this way, there will be few poor persons in the country, and the detriments that occur because of poverty are eliminated.

27.4.2 Aid for the Poor

There are two aspects to helping poor people. First, it is necessary not to take advantage of the unfortunate individual who because of his circumstances is easily oppressed. Second, methods have to be arranged whereby help is provided for the poor on a regular basis. The Biblical regulations consider both of these aspects.

Laws

Ex. **22** 20; **23** 9; Lev. **19** 33–34; Deut. **10** 19.	Do not wrong or oppress an alien in your country. Treat him as a native-born, love him as yourself. You know the feelings of an alien since you were aliens in Egypt.
Lev. **19** 13; Deut. **24** 14–15.	Do not oppress your neighbor. Do not oppress a poor hired worker, whether a citizen or an alien. Do not withhold the wages of a hired worker until the morning. Pay him on the same day, before the sun sets, because he is poor. Otherwise he may cry against you to God.
Ex. **22** 21–23.	Do not afflict the widow or orphan, because God will answer their cries.
Deut. **24** 17–18	Do not deprive aliens and orphans of justice. Remember you were slaves in Egypt.

Deut. 14 28–29; 26 12.	The tithe of the third year shall be given to the Levites, aliens, orphans, and widows, and shall be eaten within your settlements.
Lev. 19 9–10; 23 22; Deut. 24 19–22	When you reap the harvest do not reap the end of the field nor gather that which falls during preparing sheaves, nor gather forgotten sheaves. When beating the olive tree do not remove all the fruit. When gathering grapes do not glean the vineyard, nor gather left-over fallen grapes. Leave the remainders for the poor, widow, orphan and alien.
Ex. 23 11	In the Sabbatical year the poor may eat from the forsaken fields, vineyards, and olive trees.
Deut. 23 25, 26	When you enter another man's vineyard, you may eat as many grapes as you wish to satisfy your hunger, but you may not put any in your basket. When you enter another man's grain field you may pluck ears of grain by hand, but you shall not put a sickle to his standing grain.

RATIONALE

People who are most in need of assistance, and therefore the most subject to exploitation, are those without the means to earn a livelihood. For example, the alien does not have an estate of his own where he can raise agricultural produce. The widow also does not have her own land, and is dependent on the property that her sons inherit. She is in a particularly poor situation if she has no children. The orphan, too, is subject to exploitation since he may not be able to work the soil because of his young age. It is for these reasons that the alien, widow, and orphan need special consideration. In fact, in every society the widows and orphans are among those who have special problems of support.[5] In numerous cases, the guarantee of the rights of the alien, widow, and orphan will prevent poverty and suffering.

The alien is particularly vulnerable to prejudice, and may be discriminated against in employment and education. Love for the alien eliminates discontent by him, and indirectly may prevent criminal behavior, destructive tendencies, and riots, all of which are detriments to the society. For example, in the United States racism causes more fatalities, disabilities, and economic loss than any other single factor.[6]

The hired worker is another class of person easily oppressed. The day worker should be paid after each day's work, whether he is a citizen or an alien. Withholding the wages until the next morning might deprive him of the money he needs for necessities. Paying the hired worker on time may prevent crime, hunger, and extreme resentment.

Not only does the Bible have laws prohibiting discrimination against the poor, alien, widow, and orphan, but also has regulations designed to help them in times of need. Agricultural produce is supplied them in various ways. The tithe of the third and sixth years of a seven-year cycle are to be given to the Levites, aliens, orphans, and widows. As explained in Section 27.2.1, the amount of food for the aliens, orphans, and widows amounts to about one-twentieth of the nation's produce during those years. Moreover, each year the poor people are entitled to gather grain, fruit, and other produce purposely left over in the fields. The fact that the poor person works to collect the remnants allows him to obtain food without being obviously dependent on charity. If instead the leftover produce of the fields were collected and given to the poor, then he would be deprived of the opportunity to work for his food, and habits of laziness would be encouraged. It should be noted that undoubtedly not all the remnants in the fields will be collected. Whatever remains supplies food for beneficial animals, thereby maintaining the ecological balance; or decays and restores nutrients to the soil (see Section 27.6). Similarly, in the Sabbatical year the poor may eat from the produce that grows by itself in the untended fields. Thus we see that provisions are made to supply sources of food for the alien, widow and orphan annually, and to provide substantial supplements every third and sixth year.

One other valuable regulation is to be noted. Anyone entering someone else's field is entitled to take as much fruit as he can eat while in the field, or pluck with his hands, without tools, as much grain as possible. The amount of produce taken is negligible relative to the total amount of produce grown, but could be life-saving to a starving person, and would be of considerable benefit to one needing supplementary food. This law also has the additional facet that it prevents an owner from denying a worker in the fields food while working, thereby often enabling the worker to do a more industrious job.

Frequently emphasized in the Pentateuch is that the Israelite must show compassion for the poor because the Israelites were once slaves and aliens in Egypt, and therefore know at first hand how prejudice and oppression against the poor can lead to deterioration of the society.

27.4.3 Lost Objects

LAWS

Ex. 23 4; Deut. 22 1–3	If you come upon the straying ox or donkey of your enemy, return the lost animal to him. If you see the lost ox or sheep of your fellow countryman, do not ignore it, return it to him. If you do not know the owner of the lost object, then hold it in your possession until the owner claims the object. The law applies whether the object is a donkey or a garment or any other item.

RATIONALE

The return of lost objects is another way to help the economics of the society. The law requires the return of a lost item, even belonging to an enemy. The lost article should be taken to your house until the owner claims it, if you do not know who he is. In addition to the obvious benefits to the one who lost the object, there are the benefits gained by the friendship that may result. Many an enmity may turn into a friendship upon return of a lost item.

Moreover, if a lost article could be kept by the finder, this might lead to the purposeful taking of objects that are not really lost, and even to clear cut stealing. The thief could then claim that he found the object, and therefore need not return it. To prevent such occurrences, the Bible requires the return of lost items. (Also see Section 26.2.2.5 on Ex. 22 6–12.)

27.4.4 Emergency Aid

LAWS

Ex. 23 5; Deut. 22 4 — If you see the donkey of your enemy lying helpless under its load, then do not forsake your enemy. Help him to the extent that if you have to admit failure both of you will forsake the animal together. If you see the donkey or ox of your fellow countryman fallen on the road, help him to lift the animal up.

RATIONALE

Helping your friend or enemy, or their animals, is another way of helping the economy. Additional work is accomplished, and less wasted time occurs. An additional side product from this law, is the friendship and cooperation gained as a result. By helping an enemy's animal, a lasting friendship may be formed.

In modern times, the law would apply just as well to a stalled automobile. Assistance must be given to the driver of an automobile stuck on the road.

27.5 VOW OBLIGATIONS

The regulations involving vows do not obviously affect the economy. However, many aspects of the laws are concerned with factors relevant to the economy, and the topic is therefore treated as a subdivision of "economic policies."

LAWS

Deut. 23 22–24 — If you make a vow, do not put off its fulfillment, otherwise you will be guilty of sin. If you do not make a vow, you will not be guilty of sin. Mind what you say and do what you have promised.

Num. 30 2–17 — A man who makes a vow or swears to restrict himself should carry out his statement. A woman who makes a vow or imposes a restriction must also carry out her statements, except under the following special circumstances. When living in her father's house, her father can invalidate the vow or restriction on the day he hears it and the woman is excused.

If she marries, her husband can invalidate her vows or restrictions that she made either before being married or afterwards, but only on the day he hears the utterances. The vows or restrictions of a widow or divorcee have to be carried out. If a husband invalidates a vow or restriction more than one day after he hears it, then he bears the sin.

Lev. 27 1–29

If a man utters a vow according to the value of living persons, then the following valuations shall be used. Males from one month to 5 years—5 shekels; from 5 years to 20 years—20 shekels; from 20 years to 60 years—50 shekels; from 60 years and up—15 shekels. The corresponding valuations for females are 3 shekels; 10 shekels; 30 shekels; and 10 shekels. If the person who made the vow is too poor to give the prescribed valuation, then the priest should make a valuation according to the sum which the one who uttered the vow can afford.

If a vow be made of an animal suitable for a sacrifice, then the animal shall be holy and can not be exchanged. If the animal is exchanged for another, then both animals become holy. If the animal is unsuitable for a sacrifice, or if a house be sanctified, then the priest shall estimate the item's value. If the animal which is unsuitable for sacrifice or the house is redeemed by the donor, an additional fifth of the estimated value shall be added.

If an inherited field is sanctified, the value shall be estimated according to the seed required for sowing the field; land requiring a *homer* of barley seed is worth 50 shekels over a 50-year period. If the time remaining until the next Jubilee year is less than 50 years, then the price is calculated proportionately. If the one who made the field holy wants to redeem it, he shall pay the amount of the valuation increased by one-fifth. If the man who sanctified the field had previously sold it, and does not redeem it before the Jubilee year, then it will not be redeemable any longer. When the field goes out from the possession of the buyer in the Jubilee year, it goes to the priests as a permanent possession.

If someone sanctifies a field he purchased, then he pays according to the valuation by the priests based on the number of years until the Jubilee year; and in the Jubilee year the field reverts to the original seller.

All valuations shall be based on the sacred shekel which is worth 20 gerahs.

A first-born ox or sheep cannot be sanctified since it already belongs to God. A first-born unclean animal which was sanctified may be redeemed by paying one-fifth more than its valuation. If the animal is not redeemed it shall be sold at its estimated value. All objects, including slaves, animals, and fields, made *harem* to God by an individual cannot be sold or redeemed, and become most holy to God. All persons proclaimed by the community to be *harem* may not be redeemed, but must die.

RATIONALE

To have a properly functioning society, it is necessary that vows, or other types of oaths which people make, be carried out. Promises must be fulfilled, otherwise no one could trust his fellow man. However, circumstances may easily arise where the person, at the time he made the vow, was under stress, and therefore promised something unrealistic. This is particularly true of women, who because of their physical nature may be under tension at frequent intervals. For example, many women because of menstruation, pregnancy, nursing, or the menopause, experience varied emotional stresses. Furthermore, women are frequently dependent financially on their husbands or, if unmarried, on their fathers. Consequently, women may not be in a financial position, or may not have the freedom, to fulfill their vows.

To prevent the vows of women from becoming meaningless, the Bible has required that women just as well as men must fulfill their promises. However, in recognition of the nature of woman, permission is given to the father, if the girl lives in her parent's home, or to the husband, if the woman is married, to invalidate the vow on the day he hears of it. Naturally, if the vow is impractical it will be nullified by the man shortly after being told the details. Invalidation of a vow may be done only for a limited time, otherwise a woman could go to her father or husband to nullify her oath any time that the burden of the obligation became too great. As a result it would be impossible to rely on a woman's word.

The vows or self-imposed restrictions of a widow or divorcee must be carried out since she is not living with, and therefore not dependent on, a husband. However, if she remarries, then her new husband may invalidate the vow on the day he hears the details.

If a husband or father invalidates a vow not on the day he hears of it but at a later time, then the woman is absolved from guilt, and the man bears the sin.

When considering regulations involving vows, methods have to be prescribed for determining the values of living and inanimate items. Moreover, estimates have to be made on a reasonable basis, so that people who make vows do not become poor as a result. For example, if a vow be made to the Temple according to the value of living persons, then the amount of money to be given is as specified in the Pentateuch, rather than some much higher value based on the future earning power of the person. Values of living persons range from three shekels for a girl under five years old, to 50 shekels for a man between 20 and 60 years old. If the one who made the vow is too poor to afford even these modest valuations, then the priest estimates the person's worth according to his financial position.

When vows are made of animals suitable for sacrifices, the animals can be used for the Temple as they are, and therefore become holy and cannot be exchanged for money or other animals. If the animal is unsuitable for a sacrifice, or some other item such as a house is sanctified, then the priest estimates the object's value, and it is sold at the specified price. The proceeds from the sale are used for the necessities of the sanctuary. If the donor of the object decides to redeem it, he cannot buy it at the specified price but must pay an extra fifth of its valuation. This penalty is imposed so as to discourage people from giving to the sanctuary items, which they really want to retain, in order, for example, to receive an official estimate of the object's value.

A different problem arises if a person sanctifies his inherited field. Under ordinary circumstances the field may be given to the priests only temporarily, since it automatically reverts to its owner at the time of the Jubilee year. Furthermore, the priests estimate the value of the land not by the amount of produce, as is usually the case when a field is sold (Lev. 25 16), but by the amount of seed. This much lower valuation is to enable the owner easily to redeem his inherited portion. In fact, the owner has a right at any time to redeem the field, by paying a one-fifth penalty to the priests, even if the field had been sold by the priests to someone else. However, if at the time the owner sanctified his field for the sanctuary, the field was temporarily sold and not in his possession, and if the owner does not redeem the field from the priests before the next Jubilee year, then when the Jubilee year arrives the field goes directly from the temporary buyer to the priests as a permanent possession. In this manner, the ownership of a field may be permanently transferred to the priests.

On the other hand, a person who sanctifies a purchased field is required to pay immediately the valuation of the field to the priests. The field itself does not become transferred even temporarily to the priests, since at the time of the Jubilee year the field must revert to the original owner. In this case the valuation is based on the produce of the field rather than on the required seed.

A first-born animal of a permissible species cannot be sanctified since, as a first-born, its entire value is automatically destined for the sanctuary. However, a first-born of unclean animals (except for the donkey) may be sanctified, since only five shekels, its redemption price, would otherwise belong to the sanctuary (see Section 27.2.2). Once the unclean animal is dedicated, its actual value is estimated by the priest. It can then either be sold at that price, or redeemed by the donor for one-fifth more than the valuation.

A special class of vow called *harem* is also specified in the Bible. An object, or even a slave, animal, or field, made *harem* by an individual becomes most holy, and cannot be sold or redeemed. For example, a field made *harem* immediately becomes the permanent possession of the priests.

ECONOMIC POLICIES   647

If the community or leaders make a person *harem* then he must die and cannot be redeemed. Such a situation may occur for a murderer or the persons belonging to a nation whose people are required to be killed out (See, for example, Deut. 3 6; 7 2; 13 16; 20 17; Josh. 6 17; 8 26; 10 28; I Sam. 15 3).

Incidental to the laws about vows and oaths is the specification of the monetary value for certain items. For example, land requiring a *homer* of barley seed is worth 50 shekels over a 50-year period. Similarly, specific values are given for persons vowed to the sanctuary, depending on the age and sex of the person. Such valuation could not be stated in the Bible except if the value of the shekel did not change with time. This agrees with the assumption previously made that observance of the Biblical laws prevents inflation, and results in a stable monetary unit.

27.6 AGRICULTURAL ORDINANCES

A number of the regulations of the Pentateuch are designed to result in large agricultural yields. These regulations have among their main purposes the prevention of plant diseases, insect infestation, and nutrient deficiencies of the produce of the soil.

LAWS

Ex. 23 10–11; Lev. 25 1–12.	Six years you shall sow the land, prune the vineyards, and gather in the produce. In the seventh year the land shall rest and lie fallow. You shall not sow the field, nor prune the vineyard and olive grove. You shall not harvest the crop that grows by itself, nor gather in the grapes from the unpruned vines. However, what grows by itself may be used as food for you, your servants, your hired workers, the settlers who live with you, the nation's poor, your cattle, and the wild animals of the land. After seven cycles of seven years, i.e., after a total of 49 years, you shall proclaim on the tenth day of the seventh month, on the Day of Atonement, the start of the fiftieth or Jubilee year, by the blowing of a ram's horn. During the Jubilee year you shall not sow, nor reap that which grows by itself, nor gather in the fruit from the unpruned vines. However, you may eat from the field what grows by itself.
Lev. 25 20–22	If you ask what you are to eat during the seventh year, seeing that you will neither sow nor gather the harvest, the answer is that God will bless the produce of the sixth year so it will be sufficient for three years. In the eighth year you shall sow; but you shall eat from the old produce until the ninth year when the new crop will be gathered.
Lev. 19 9–10; 23 22;	When you reap the harvest do not reap the end of the field, nor gather that which falls during preparing sheaves, nor gather

Deut. 24 19–22.	forgotten sheaves. When beating the olive tree do not remove all the fruit. When gathering grapes do not glean the vineyard nor gather leftover fallen grapes. Leave the remainders for the poor, widow, orphan, and alien.
Lev. 19 19;	Do not sow your field with two kinds of seed.
Deut. 22 9.	Do not sow your vineyard with two kinds of seed, lest the seed and produce become unusable.
Lev. 19 23–25.	The fruit of a newly planted tree shall not be eaten for three years. In the fourth year its fruit shall be holy, for giving praise to the Lord. In the fifth year the fruit may be eaten to add to your fruit supply.
Deut. 22 10	Do not plow with an ox and a donkey together.
Deut. 25 4	Do not muzzle an ox while it is threshing the grain.
Lev. 19 19	Do not allow two different species of animal to mate together.
Deut. 22 6–7	When you come across a bird's nest, in a tree or on the ground, with fledglings or eggs in it and the mother bird on the nest, do not take the mother with the young. Send the mother bird away, and take only the young; then you will prosper and live long.

RATIONALE

The regulations concerning the Sabbatical and Jubilee years require that the land lie fallow and that the produce of the ground, vines, and trees not be gathered in. Letting the land lie fallow at the prescribed intervals replenishes the nutrients depleted from the soil, controls the population of insect pests, and eliminates plant diseases.

One major aspect of replenishment of the nutrients of the soil is the production of partially decayed material known as humus. As plants and animals die, and as leaves fall to the ground, their once living organic material decays by the action of bacteria and other microorganisms. As the decomposition proceeds, the chemical substances from which the living matter was originally composed are set free to replenish the soil. Moreover, humus increases the porosity of the ground, thereby allowing proper drainage, improved aeration, and better water retention.[7]

The Bible prescribes that during the Sabbatical and Jubilee years the produce which grows by itself not be harvested, so that humus production will occur. Similarly, during other years the Bible requires that some of the grain and fruit be left on the field to be collected by the poor, widow, orphan, and alien. Naturally, in many instances the remaining produce will not be collected, and will serve the secondary purpose of supplying organic matter for humus production.

It should be realized that a deficiency of any of the chemical elements necessary for plant growth may reduce the total growth of plants. In particular, deficiency diseases can be caused by lack of such elements as boron, calcium, copper, iron, magnesium, manganese, molybdenum, nitrogen, phosphorus, potassium, sulfur, and zinc.[8] The Pentateuch, in order to prevent such diseases in plants, and to ensure replenishment of the soil depleted by harvesting of crops year after year, prescribes the laws concerning the Sabbatical and Jubilee years.

Other even more important reasons for these regulations are to control insects and disease microorganisms. In years when no crops are grown, insects and disease microorganisms are deprived of most of their food supply, and are thereby greatly reduced in numbers, to the extent that they are not a problem to the crops for another six years. On the other hand, growing the same plant year after year tends to encourage insect pests[9] and disease microorganisms,[10] until the plant can no longer survive. It has, for example, been conjectured in the case of the aphid-borne virus, yellows disease of sugar beet, that the banning of seed production for one year can control the disease.[11]

The Biblical regulations require that the land of the entire country not be farmed during the same year. Thereby the insect pests and disease microorganisms throughout the nation are deprived of nourishment, preventing their spread from one area to another. If, instead, the Bible required only that each plot of land not be farmed once in seven years, irrespective of which plot in which year, then surviving insects and disease microorganisms could spread from a farmed to an unfarmed area during the following year, obviating much of the benefits.

The forty-ninth and fiftieth years are two consecutive years during which the land is not farmed. As a result the insect pests and disease microorganisms are reduced in numbers to an extremely low level. Moreover, depleted nutrients are replenished by natural processes to a greater extent than if the ground lay fallow for only one year. The fifty-year planting cycle helps guarantee that healthy, nutritious crops will be produced.

It should be realized that plant diseases not only harm the nation's crops but on occasion may also lead to sickness in man. Ergot, which is a fungus disease that infects cereals and other grasses, is a good example.[12] The ergot causes the seed kernels to be replaced by sclerotia, which contain alkaloids. When eaten, the infected grains have a powerful action on the nervous system and can produce gangrene or convulsions and, in severe cases, death.

At first, the Biblical promise that the agricultural produce of the sixth year will be so abundant that it will be sufficient for three years, seems difficult to explain. However, it should be recognized that with each year of farming the numbers of microorganisms in the soil increase, until they reach their maximum values in the sixth year. Now many of these organisms help replenish the nutrients in the soil. For example, certain bacteria which live in root nodules of leguminous plants, are known to convert the free nitrogen in the air into complex compounds useful for plant growth.[13] In the sixth year such nutrient replenishment would be at its maximum, thereby resulting in exceptionally large yields.

In the beginning of the Jubilee or fiftieth year, any estates that were sold are returned to their original owners (Lev. 25 28). The selection of the fiftieth year for the return of inherited estates is to simplify the procedure. Neither in the forty-ninth nor in the fiftieth years are crops grown on the soil. Thus, the return of the land is not complicated by disputes as to whom the crops of these years belong.

The prohibition against sowing with two kinds of seed, or in general the growing of hybrid plants, is to prevent the spread of insect pests and disease microorganisms. Hybrid plants are frequently developed in modern agriculture to produce greater yields and larger crops. However, these plants are usually subject to disease and insects, and lose their vitality after a few years. For example, the use of hybrid seed enabled the development of potatoes resistant to a particular nematode (microscopic worm). However, after a few years new types of nematodes developed which were capable of causing damage to the hitherto resistant potato plant.[14] Similarly, upon grafting one variety of potato upon another, the grafted plant contracted a disease called paracrinkle. The potatoes carried a virus which did no harm until grafting was attempted.[15] Moreover, many weeds harbor disease organisms and insects that attack desirable crop plants. Thus, the onion thrips often live in ragweed and mustards before attacking an onion crop.[16] Hence, the sowing of two plants together, or the development of hybrid plants, exposes one species to the insects and diseases carried by the other species, thereby frequently leading to spread of disease and insects.

Another problem with hybrid plants is the fact that they do not grow well on their own root systems. Such plants are propagated not by their seeds, but by means of grafting.[17] Thus, production of hybrid plants can result in nonproduction of satisfactory seeds for future use.

The reason why the fruit of a newly planted tree may not be eaten for the first three years is uncertain. It is known that a newly planted tree does not bear its first full fruit crop until three to twenty years after planting, depending on the type of tree.[18] Therefore the tree during its first three years may be considered as immature, possibly resulting in its fruit having unusual chemicals which are unwholesome for eating.

The prohibition against plowing with an ox and donkey together has sometimes been explained in terms of the difference in strength between the animals. The weaker animal would suffer pain when yoked with the stronger animal.[19] However, the questions then arise "Why only these two animals? Why only when plowing? Could not some arrangement be made so that the weaker animal would not be hurt?" Because of these difficulties it is obvious that the given explanation cannot be the correct one. A more probable reason is that during the plowing operation the fresh excrement from these two animals would be mixed together in the ground. This particular composite could be a fertile medium for growth of microorganisms detrimental to the soil and to plant life. Possibly a similar explanation can be given for the prohibition against muzzling an ox while threshing the grain. Some chemical may be produced by the ox, as a result of being muzzled, which would be excreted onto the grain making it more subject to disease microorganisms.

The prohibition against interbreeding two different species of animals can be explained in an analogous manner to the prohibition against sowing two different types of seeds together. First, an interbred animal may be able to harbor in its system microorganisms harmful to man, which may be transmitted either by insect vectors or directly through the air. Second, the offspring of the union is in all cases, with practically no exceptions, not capable of further procreating. Thus, there is inefficiency and waste in that the resultant animal is barren. Similar, better documented reasons, were presented previously for not growing hybrid plants.

The verse which forbids the taking of the mother bird with the young is the first record of a law for protection of birds.[20] If only the mother bird were taken and the young left, then either the eggs would not be hatched or the baby birds would die for lack of food. In contrast, if the mother bird is sent away, she can lay more eggs thereby increasing the bird population. In fact, there are many species of birds of which the mother bird will continue to lay eggs until a definite number has accumulated in the nest.[21] Thus, if the eggs or fledglings are removed, they are often quickly replaced with fresh eggs by the mother. It should be noted that it is particularly at the nest, when the birds are not flying, that they are most vulnerable.

Maintaining the bird population provides an indispensable check on the multiplication of insects, which would otherwise overrun and ruin the world.[22] Birds, because of their numbers and great mobility, concentrate quickly to control sudden outbreaks of insects. More than half the food consumed by the more than 1,400 species and subspecies of birds in North America consists of insects. As an example of the importance of birds, it has been recorded that an outbreak of crickets in 1848 in Salt Lake Valley, Utah, which threatened the crops, was eliminated by a sudden appearance of seagulls.[23]

Control of insects is important for many reasons. Insects are by far the most important agents of transmission of disease microorganisms. Few viruses could persist for long without insects.[24] They are involved in the transmission not only of plant sicknesses but also diseases of animals and mankind. Furthermore, insects destroy food while it is growing as well as in storage.[25]

Thus, the Biblical requirement to send away the mother bird is designed to protect the bird population, which in turn controls the insect population. If birds were not available to consume insects, then insects would flourish, destroy the food supply, and spread disease microorganisms throughout the world. Observance of the law to take only the young and not the mother bird, therefore results through a very indirect chain of events in allowing mankind to prosper and live long lives.

It is well known that weather, insects, and plant diseases are the three great natural hazards of crop production.[26] The Biblical laws are designed to provide protection against all three. Weather is controlled by bringing of sacrifices, which for example, maintain the needed rainfall (see Section 28.1). Insects are controlled by periodically letting the land lie fallow, and by maintaining the bird population. Plant diseases are eliminated by keeping insects under control, letting the land lie fallow, and not growing hybrid plants. Numerous other Biblical regulations, directly or indirectly, also control insects and prevent plant diseases. In these ways, the Bible assures a good agricultural yield, with a resultant stable economy.

In modern times, agricultural procedures are quite different from those prescribed by the Bible. Hybrid plants are developed to increase yields and to produce larger fruits and better quality grain. Replenishment of nutrients is accomplished by use of artificial fertilizers. Insects are kept under control by spraying large areas with insecticides. If certain insects acquire resistance to one insecticide, then another chemical is used. Plant diseases are somewhat more difficult to suppress. Numerous methods, such as rotation of crops, development of resistant hybrid varieties, and elimination of diseased plants, are often used.[27]

Nonetheless, there are many serious shortcomings to the above techniques. Continuous research has to be conducted to perfect new hybrid varieties, since the previously developed hybrid plants frequently lose their vitality after a few years, or succumb to insect pests and disease microorganisms. Overuse of fertilizers may lead to poor nutrient balance in the soil, and even to excesses of potentially harmful chemicals in the produce.[28] The chemicals in insecticides may injure plants,[29] kill off beneficial insects and animals,[30, 31, 32, 33] and cause poisoning to humans.[34, 35] Furthermore, plant disease arise every now and then which cannot be controlled by any of the known methods. Although modern agricultural practices have in general succeeded in achieving large yields and good quality foods, still the numerous harmful consequences which do occur indicate that the Biblical farming techniques will, when re-established, prove to be far superior.

Chapter Twenty-eight

RITUALISTIC PROCEDURES

Numerous laws and specifications are found in the Bible concerning such ritualistic procedures as the construction of the Temple, the sacrifices that are to be brought, festival requirements, and the design of the priestly garments. The reasons for many of the procedures and requirements are not easily discernible. All too often explanations have been suggested based on philosophical approaches, where the reasons are far from adequate. For example, the explanation is often given, based on the suggestion of Maimonides, that the purpose of the sacrifices was to wean the people away from idolatry. This explanation would imply that in modern times, where only in extremely rare situations in the world are sacrifices brought for purposes of idolatry, there is no longer a need for sacrifices. Such a conclusion is completely erroneous. There are very many practical reasons for the sacrifices and the other ritualistic procedures. An attempt is here made to provide numerous possible reasons for these laws. Naturally, as with many other explanations given concerning the rationale for the Biblical laws, only further research and greater scientific knowledge will prove or disprove these theories.

28.1 SACRIFICES

LAWS

The details of the sacrifices are quite involved. For simplicity, the different types of sacrifices have been arranged into tabular form. The basic types and their procedures are presented in Tables 28.1.1, 28.1.2, and 28.1.3. These basic types are the burnt-offering where the animal is burned completely, the peace-offering which is partly eaten by the bringer, the meal-offering which is usually composed of flour, and the sin- and guilt-offerings for expiation of transgressions. Suitable animals for sacrifices are cattle, sheep, and goats (Lev. 1 2; 22 19). Suitable birds are pigeons and turtle-doves (Lev. 1 14).

There are a number of other basic types of sacrifices which are listed in subsequent tables and have unique procedures. These are the installation-offering of the priests, purification-offering (involving two birds) for a leper or house, Passover offering, and the sin-offering on the tenth day of the seventh month brought by the high priest.

A second class of sacrifices are those brought at special times of the year, daily,

Table 28.1.1

Type	Suitable Animals	Part of Animal Sacrificed	Animal Preparation (and Other Requirements)
1. burnt-offering	bull, sheep, goat; male	entire animal except for the skin	skin the animal, cut it into pieces, wash inwards and legs with water
	turtledove, pigeon	entire animal except for the crop	partially separate by the wings
2. peace-offering	cattle, goat; male or female	fat on the inwards, kidneys and their fat, lobe above the liver	
	sheep; male or female	same as for cattle and goat, plus the fatty tail	
(a) thanksgiving-offering			the meat must be eaten on the day of the sacrifice, and not left until morning
(b) freewill-offering			the meat may be eaten on the day of sacrifice and the following day; any meat left to the third day must be burned, and not eaten lest the person be punished with excision

Basic Types of Burnt- and Peace-Offerings

Blood Sprinkling	Other Comments	References
around on the altar	skin of animal belongs to officiating priest	Lev. 1 1–13; 7 8; Deut. 12 27
drained onto side of altar	remove the crop with the feathers, kill by pinching head	Lev. 1 14–17
around on the altar	the meat of the animals is eaten by the bringer, except for the breast, which any priest may eat, and the right thigh which the officiating priest eats; the shoulder, the cheeks, and the stomach are given to the priests	Ex. 29 27–28; Lev. 3 1–5, 12–16; 7 28–36; Deut. 12 27; 18 3
around on the altar	as above	Lev. 3 6–11
	accompanying the thanksgiving-offering are unleavened cakes mixed with oil, unleavened wafers spread with oil, and leavened bread mixed with oil; one cake of each of the meal-offerings is eaten by the officiating priest, the rest is eaten by the bringer	Lev. 7 11–15; 22 29–30
		Lev. 7 16–18; 19 5–8

Table 28.1.2

Type of Sin	Person Sinning	Animal Sacrificed	Parts Sacrificed
Sin Offering			
1. inadvertant transgressing one of the negative commandments	high priest, bringing guilt on the people	young bull	the fat on the inwards, the 2 kidneys and their fat, and lobe above liver
	the entire Israelite community	young bull	same as above
	the ruler (of tribe. or of nation)	he-goat	same as above
	one of the leaders (מעם הארץ)	she-goat or female sheep	above plus fat tail from the sheep
2. not testifying; remaining impure; not carrying out an oath or vow	anyone	she-goat or female sheep	above plus fat tail from the sheep
	a poor person	2 turtledoves or 2 pigeons (1 as a sin-offering; 1 as a burnt-offering)	
	a very poor person	1/10 ephah of fine flour	handful of fine flour
3. inadvertent non-performance of a positive commandment	the Israelite community	young bull (as a burnt-offering), he-goat (as a sin-offering)	the fat on the inwards, the 2 kidneys and their fat, and the lobe above the liver
	anyone	she-goat of the 1st year	above plus fat tail from the sheep
Guilt Offering			
1. benefited from the holy objects, by mistake	anyone	ram (worth at least 2 shekels)	fat tail, fat on inwards, two kidneys and their fat, and lobe above the liver
2. transgressed one of negative commandments by mistake	anyone	ram (worth at least 2 shekels)	same as above
3. swore falsely about a deposit, pledge, robbery, oppressing neighbor, or a lost object	anyone	ram (worth at least 2 shekels)	same as above

Basic Types of Sin and Guilt Sacrifices

Comments	Blood Sprinkling	Other Retribution	Who Eats	References
skin, meat, head, legs, inwards, and dung burned outside camp	7 times, with finger, in front of veil of sanctuary; and on horns of altar of incense; all remaining blood poured at altar base		nothing eaten	Lev. 4 1–12; 6 23
same as above			nothing eaten	Lev. 4 13–21; 6 23
	with the finger on horns of altar; remaining blood poured at base of altar		officiating priest or other priests (male)	Lev. 4 22–26; 6 17–23
			officiating priest or other priests (male)	Lev. 4 27–35
	same as above	confess the sin	officiating priest or other priests (male)	Lev. 5 1–6
pinch off neck of sin-offering, do not separate; burnt-offering as usual	blood of sin-offering sprinkled on side of altar, remainder drained at altar base	confess the sin		Lev. 5 7–10
no oil or frankincense added		confess the sin	any priest eats remainder	Lev. 5 11–13; 7 10
burnt-offering, with meal and drink-offerings done as usual	with the finger on horns of altar; remaining blood is poured at base of the altar		officiating priest or other priests (male)	Num. 15 22–26
procedure does not apply to willful sinning	same as above		officiating priest or other priests (male)	Num. 15 27–31
	around on the altar	pay principle plus 1/5 penalty	officiating priest or other priest (male)	Lev. 5 14–16; 7 1–7
	around on the altar			Lev. 5 17–19; 7 1–7
	around on the altar	return object, plus 1/5 penalty, to owner		Lev. 5 20–26; 7 1–7

Table 28.1.3
Meal-Offerings

Type	Ingredients*	Amount Sacrificed	Who eats Remainder**	Other Comments	References
1. fine flour mixed with oil	fine flour, oil, frankincense, salted	handful	any priest		Lev. 2 1–3, 8–13; 7 10
2. baked in the oven	unleavened cakes of fine flour mixed with oil; or unleavened wafers spread with oil; salted	handful	officiating priest		Lev. 2 4, 8–13; 7 9
3. baked on a griddle	fine flour mixed with oil made into unleavened bread; salted	handful	officiating priest	break it into pieces, and pour oil on it	Lev. 2 5–6, 8–13; 7 9
4. of the stewing pan	fine flour with oil, salted	handful	officiating priest		Lev. 2 7–13; 7 9
5. of the first-fruits	grain dried in the ear by fire, groats of the fresh ear; oil, frankincense, salted	handful	any priest		Lev. 2 13–16; 7 10

* No meal-offering shall be made of anything that ferments, because no leaven or honey shall be burned as an offering.   Lev. 2 11

** A meal offering brought by a priest is completely burned, and not eaten.   Lev. 6 16

Saturday, and holidays. These sacrifices and their procedures are summarized in Table 28.1.4. Sacrifices brought under special circumstances are tabulated in Table 28.1.5. Typical special circumstances are purification after recovery from childbirth, leprosy, and oozing; purification of the Levites and priests; and sacrifice of first-born animals.

In general, Tables 28.1.1–28.1.5 are not complete descriptions of the sacrifices. The reader is referred to the original Biblical passages, as referenced in the Tables, for more detailed information. Particular points which have been omitted involve details on placing hands on the animals, and which parts of the animals are waved. In many cases, the rationale for numerous aspects of these sacrifices, other than procedural details, have been explained in previous chapters.

In addition to the descriptions of the sacrifices presented in Tables 28.1.1 to 28.1.5, there are many other relevant laws.

Ex. 20 21–22; 27 1–7; (Deut. 27 5–7)	The altar may be constructed from either earth or stones. If made of stones, the stones shall not be cut with an iron tool. The dimensions of the Tabernacle altar shall, however, be delimited by a copper-coated acaciawood framework.
Ex. 20 23	Do not go up steps to the altar, so that your private parts will not be uncovered.
Lev. 22 27	A newborn calf, sheep, or goat shall remain with its mother for seven days, and may be brought as a sacrifice when eight or more days old.
Lev. 17 1–9; Deut. 12 2–14, 26–27	Sacrifices may be brought only in the place selected by God for the Temple, not on every high place as done by the idol-worshipping nations. Anyone who brings a sacrifice other than near the Temple will be punished by excision.
Lev. 22 17–25; Deut. 15 21; 17 1	No serious blemish shall be found on an animal brought for a sacrifice, such as being blind, lame, mutilated, or having a running sore or skin disease. However, if the bull or sheep is overgrown or stunted it can be given for Temple purposes other than for sacrifices. Moreover, any animal having its testicles crushed, bruised, torn, or cut shall not be brought as a sacrifice, nor shall such an act be done to an animal in your land.
Ex. 23 18	The fat (*heleb*) of a festival offering shall not remain overnight until morning.
Lev. 2 13	Salt shall accompany all sacrifices.
Num. 10 10	On happy occasions, festivals, and the beginnings of the months, the priests sound the silver trumpets when bringing burnt-offerings and peace-offerings, so as to be a remembrance before God.

Table 28.1.4 Sacrifices at Set Times of the Year

Time of Year	Animals for Burnt-Offering (a)				Other Sacrifices	References
	Young Bulls	Rams	He-lambs of 1st Year	He-Goats for Sin Offering		
1. daily			2(b)			Num. 28 1-8
						Ex. 29 38-42
2. Saturday			2			Num. 28 9-10
3. New Moon	2	1	7	1		Num. 28 11-15
4. 14th of 1st month					Passover (c) offering	Num. 28 16
						Lev. 23 5
5. 15th through 21st of 1st month	2	1	7	1		Num. 28 17-25
6. Day of Omer (first sheaf)			1(d)			Lev. 23 9-14
7. Day of First-Fruits	2	1	7	1	first-fruit, (e) 2 he-lambs for a peace-offering	Num. 28 26-31
	1	2	7	1		Lev. 23 15-20

(a) Accompanying the burnt-offering, freewill-offering, and holiday sacrifices were meal-offerings and drink-offerings according to the following arangement:

Animal	Meal-Offering of Fine Flour Mixed with Oil	Oil Mixed with Meal-Offering	Wine for the Drink-Offering
he-lamb	1/10 ehpah	1/4 hin	1/4 hin

ram	2/10 ephah	1/3 hin
young bull	3/10 ephah	1/2 hin
(Num. 15 1–12; 28 1–29 39; Ex. 29 40–41)		

(b) The two he-lambs of the daily sacrifice were not brought at the same time of the day. One was brought in the morning, and one in the evening.

(c) The following are the requirements for the Passover sacrifice, which is a particular type of peace-offering brought by each family or group. It is brought on the fourteenth day of the first month, the spring month, and eaten at night time. Suitable animals are male sheep, goats, and possibly cattle. The blood of the animal should be smeared on the doorposts and lintels of the houses in Jerusalem where it is eaten. The animal should be roasted whole, without any broken bones. It should not be eaten with leavened bread, only with matzot and bitter herbs. None of the meat shall be left over until the next morning, and if left over the meat shall be burned. Only circumcised persons may eat the meat, not foreigners or aliens. If a person is impure and cannot bring the Passover sacrifice on the fourteenth of the first month, then he shall bring it on the fourteenth of the second month. A person who purposely does not bring the Passover sacrifice is punished with excision.
(Ex. 12 3–10, 21–27, 43 – 50; Num. 9 1–14; Deut. 16 1–7)

(d) The meal-offering for the he-lamb brought as a burnt-offering, on the day when the omer (first sheaf) was brought, was two-tenths of an ephah of fine flour, rather than the usual one-tenth as in all other cases. Nevertheless the accompanying drink-offering was one-fourth of a hin, as usual for a he-lamb.
(Lev. 23 12–14)

(e) On the Day of First-Fruits, two separate groups of sacrifices are brought. The first group (Lev. 23 15–20) is sacrificed at about the same time as the first-fruit offering. This offering consisted of two loaves of bread, each of two-tenths of an ephah of fine flour. With these are brought seven he-lambs, one young bull and two rams as a burnt-offering; one he-goat as a sin-offering; and two he-lambs as a peace-offering. The second group of sacrifices (Num. 28 26–31) were two young bulls, one ram, and seven he-lambs as a burnt-offering; and one he-goat for a sin-offering. Since the number of he-lambs and young bulls were not the same in the two burnt-offerings, it is obvious that two separate groups of sacrifices are meant.

Table 28.1.4 (continued)

Time of Year	Animals for Burnt-Offering (a)			He-Goats for Sin Offering	Other Sacrifices	References
	Young Bulls	Rams	He-lambs of 1st Year			
8. 1st of 7th month	1	1	7	1		Num. 29 1–6
9. 10th of 7th month	1	1	7	1	sin-offerings (f) of atonement	Num. 29 7–11
10. 7th Month						
15th day	13	2	14	1		Num. 29 12–16
16th day	12	2	14	1		Num. 29 17–19
17th day	11	2	14	1		Num. 29 20–22
18th day	10	2	14	1		Num. 29 23–25
19th day	9	2	14	1		Num. 29 26–28
20th day	8	2	14	1		Num. 29 29–31
21st day	7	2	14	1		Num. 29 32–34
22nd day	1	1	7	1		Num. 29 35–39
11. daily—incense was burned once in the morning and once in the evening on the altar for incense. Only incense was to be burned on this altar within the Temple.						Ex. 30 6–9

(f) On the tenth day of the seventh month the high priest performs an elaborate purification procedure, during which he wears garments made only from linen. He brings a young bull for a sin-offering and a ram for a burnt-offering. He also brings from the people two he-goats for a sin-offering and a ram for a burnt-offering. Then he selects by lot one of the he-goats for a sin-offering and the other one for sending away alive to the desert (Azazel). The high priest first slaughters the young bull for a sin-offering, places incense on burning coals inside the holy-of-holies, and using his finger, sprinkles blood from the young bull within the holy-of-holies upon the Ark cover, and seven times before the Ark cover. Then he slaughters the he-goat for a sin-offering, and sprinkles the blood as he did with the blood of the young bull. Similar sprinkling is done in the other room of the Temple, and on the horns of the altar for incense, for purposes of purification. Then the live he-goat, designated for Azazel, is sent to the desert. Finally, after a change to the high priestly clothing, the burnt-offerings of the rams are brought on the altar, as well as the fat of the sin-offerings. (Ex. 30 10; Lev. 16 1–34)

Table 28.1.5

Purpose of Sacrifice	Background Situation	Animals Sacrificed	Type of Sacrifice
sacrifice as a covenant with God		bulls	burnt-offerings peace-offerings
sanctification of the priests (sacrifices and procedures are repeated for 7 days)	purification procedure required of the priests before being able to bring sacrifices	young bull	sin-offering
		ram	burnt-offering
		second ram	installation-offering
sanctification of the priests	after 7 days of the previous procedure the priests began offering sacrifices on the 8th day	unleavened bread, unleavened-cakes mixed with oil, and unleavened wafers spread with oil.	installation meal-offering
		bull-calf	sin-offering of priest
		ram	burnt-offering of priest
		he-goat	sin-offering of the people

Sacrifices Brought under Special Circumstances

Procedural Details	Accompanying Items	Blood Sprinkling	Misc. Details	References
		half the blood was put in basins, and then thrown on the people; and half the blood was thrown on the altar		Ex. 24 4–8
the fats on inwards, on liver, and kidneys are burned on altar; the meat, skin, dung are burned outside the camp		blood placed, using finger, on horns of altar; remainder poured at base of altar	wash the priests; dress priests with priestly garments; anoint the high priest	Ex. 29 1–37 Lev. 8 1–36
cut into pieces, wash inwards and legs, burn entire animal on altar		throw blood around on altar		
the prescribed fats on tail, inwards, liver, and kidneys; and the right thigh; as well as one of each type of cake are burned; the breast is eaten by the priests; the meat is cooked and eaten with the cakes; anything remaining until the morning is burned	anointing oil, priestly garments basket to hold the unleavened items	blood placed on right earlobes, right thumbs and right big toes of the priests; remainder around on altar; blood from altar and anointing oil sprinkled upon priests and their clothes		
the prescribed fat, kidneys and liver were burned on the altar; the meat and skin were burned outside the camp		used finger to put blood on horns of the altar; remainder poured at base of altar	the bull-calf and ram were brought by the priests, while the he-goat, calf, lamb, bull, second ram and meal-offering were brought by the people	Lev. 9 1–24 Lev. 10 12–20
cut into pieces, washed inwards and legs, and burned entirely on the altar		thrown around on altar		
same procedure as for bull-calf; however the meat is eaten by priests				

Table 28.1.5 (continued)

Purpose of Sacrifice	Background Situation	Animals Sacrificed	Type of Sacrifice
		calf and lamb, both of first year meal-offering mixed with oil	burnt-offering of the people meal-offering
		bull and ram	peace-offering of the people
meal-offering on day of anointing of priest		1/10 ephah of fine flour	meal-offering baked on a griddle, entirely burned on altar
purification of woman after childbirth	(a) woman has waited 40 days after giving birth to a boy or 80 days after giving birth to a girl	lamb in its 1st year, and pigeon or turtledove	burnt-offering sin-offering
	(b) if woman is poor	2 turtledoves or 2 pigeons	1 for a burnt-offering and 1 for a sin-offering
purification of a recovered leper	(a) after recovery from one of the described forms of skin disease	2 birds (1 bird is not slaughtered)	
	(b) on the 7th day the recovered leper shaves the body's hair and washes his body and clothes; and on the 8th day brings the accompanying offerings	1 he-lamb, 1 ewe-lamb of 1st year 2nd he-lamb, 3/10 ephah of fine flour mixed with oil	guilt-offering sin-offering burnt-offering meal-offering

Procedural Details	Accompanying Items	Blood Sprinkling	Misc. Details	References
according to the usual procedure				
handful on the altar (in addition to the meal-offering accompanying the offering of the morning); remainder to be eaten.				
the prescribed fats, the tail, the fat on the inwards, the kidneys and liver, were burned on the altar; the breast and thigh to be eaten by the priests		thrown around on altar		Lev. 6 12–15
fine flour on a griddle, soaked with oil, in pieces; half in the morning, half in the evening				
				Lev. 12 1–7
				Lev. 12 8
the live bird, and cedarwood, scarlet and hyssop, are dipped into the diluted blood of the bird slaughtered over an earthen vessel containing fresh water	cedarwood, scarlet thread, hyssop, and an earthenware vessel	sprinkle the diluted blood 7 times on the recovered leper	the live bird is sent away	Lev. 14 1–7
first the guilt-offering is brought, accompanied by detailed sprinkling; then the sin-offering, then the burnt-offering and the meal-offering; the meal-offering is completely burned on the altar	1 "log" of oil	blood of guilt-offering put on tip of right ear, right thumb and right big toe of recovered leper; same done with the oil; also the		Lev. 14 8–20

Table 28.1.5 (continued)

Purpose of Sacrifice	Background Situation	Animals Sacrificed	Type of Sacrifice
	(c) the 8th day, if the recovered leper is poor	1 he-lamb 2 turtledoves or 2 pigeons	guilt-offering 1 as a sin-offering and 1 as a burnt-offering
		1/10 ephah of fine flour mixed with oil	meal-offering
purification of a house after visible growth of a microorganism has been eliminated	affected stones of the house were removed, and replaced by fresh stones, thus eliminating visible growth of microorganisms	2 birds (1 bird is not slaughtered)	
atonement for a man cured from oozing from his body	the cured person should count 7 clean days, wash his clothes and his body, and bring a sacrifice on the 8th day	2 turtledoves or 2 pigeons	1 for a sin-offering and 1 for a burnt-offering
atonement for a woman cured from unusual blood issue	she should count 7 days to become pure, and bring a sacrifice on the 8th day	2 turtledoves or 2 pigeons	1 for a sin-offering and 1 for a burnt-offering
atonement for having relations with a woman servant who should have been free	a man had sexual relations with a woman servant who should have been free, but was not; they are not killed for adultery, but he must bring a sacrifice	ram	guilt-offering
test of a woman suspected of unfaithfulness	a husband who suspects his wife of being unfaithful brings her to the priest and brings a sacrifice for her	1/10 ephah of barley meal	meal-offering of jealousy

Procedural Details	Accompanying Items	Blood Sprinkling	Misc. Details	References
as above	as above	oil is sprinkled 7 times in front of the Temple, and remaining oil is put on head of recovered leper as above		Lev. 14 21–32
the live bird, and cedarwood, scarlet, and hyssop, are dipped into the diluted blood of the bird slaughtered over an earthen vessel containing fresh water	cedarwood, scarlet thread, hyssop, and an earthenware vessel	sprinkle the diluted blood 7 times on the house	the live bird is sent away	Lev. 14 48–53
				Lev. 15 13–15
				Lev. 15 28–30
				Lev. 19 20–22
no oil or frankincense is is added to the meal-offering; a handful of the barley-meal is sacrificed	water in an earthen-ware vessel, and soil from the Temple area, to make bitter water for the woman to drink		dishevel the woman's hair, and make her swear	Num. 5 15–28

Table 28.1.5 (continued)

Purpose of Sacrifice	Background Situation	Animals Sacrificed	Type of Sacrifice
sacrifices of a Nazir (one who vows not to drink wine and other intoxicating beverages)	(a) if a Nazir becomes impure because of contact with a human corpse, then on the 7th day, when he becomes pure, he shall shave his head, and on the 8th day bring a sacrifice	2 turtledoves or 2 pigeons he-lamb of the 1st year	1 for a sin-offering and 1 for a burnt-offering guilt-offering
	(b) upon completion of the time vowed by the Nazir, prescribed sacrifices are brought; afterwards the former Nazir may drink wine	he-lamb of the 1st year; ewe-lamb of the 1st year; ram basket of unleavened cakes of fine flour mixed with oil, and unleavened wafers spread with oil	burnt-offering sin-offering peace-offering meal-offering (baked in the oven)
sacrifices brought by the leaders of the tribes to dedicate a new altar	the leaders of the tribes brought sacrifices upon completion of the altar	fine flour mixed with oil incense, 1 young bull; 1 ram; 1 he-lamb of the 1st year; he-goat 2 bulls, 5 rams 5 he-goats; 5 he-lambs of the 1st year	meal-offering burnt-offering sin-offering peace-offering

Procedural Details	Accompanying Items	Blood Sprinkling	Misc. Details	References
			the Nazir has to count his vowed time of abstinence again from the beginning	Num. 6 9–12
the hair of the Nazir is to be shaved off, and put on the fire under the peace-offering	meal-offerings and drink-offerings to accompany the burnt-offering and the peace-offering		the priest takes the cooked shoulder from the ram and one unleavened cake and one unleavened wafer, and puts them on the palms of the shaven Nazir; these parts are then waved and made holy, to be eaten by the priests	Num. 6 13–21
each tribal leader brought the identical sacrifices on successive days	1 silver dish weighing 130 shekels, and 1 silver basin weighing 70 shekels to hold the fine flour mixed with oil; 1 golden saucer weighing 10 shekels to hold the incense			Num. 7 10–88

Table 28.1.5 (continued)

Purpose of Sacrifice	Background Situation	Animals Sacrificed	Type of Sacrifice
purification of the Levites	the Levites were first purified by being sprinkled with cleansing water, shaving their body hair, and washing their clothes	young bull fine flour mixed with oil another young bull	burnt-offering meal-offering (accompanying the burnt-offering) sin-offering
sacrifice of first-born animal	the first-born male animals are holy	first-born male cattle, sheep, and goat	a type of peace-offering
preparation of purifying water from ashes of red cow	the purifying ash-water mixture is used to purify a person who became unclean by contact with a dead person	perfectly red cow (on which a yoke has not been placed)	

Procedural Details	Accompanying Items	Blood Sprinkling	Misc. Details	References
				Num. 8 5–12
the fats of the animals (*heleb*) are burned; the rest of the animal is eaten		throw their blood on the altar		Ex. 13 11–16 Num. 18 15–19 Deut. 15 19–23
burn the cow outside the camp, including the skin, meat, blood and dung; cedarwood, hyssop and scarlet are added to the burning cow; the ashes are set aside in a pure place; subsequently some of the ashes are added to water, and the mixture sprinkled using hyssop	cedarwood, hyssop, and scarlet thread	sprinkle with finger 7 times towards the Temple	the several officiating priests involved in the procedures, become impure and have to wash their clothes and bodies	Num. 19 1–22

Rationale

There are several primary and secondary reasons for the sacrifices. Primary reasons include weather control and purification from disease microorganisms. Secondary reasons include meat for the priests, psychological atonement for sin, and symbolisms for the festivals. It is probable that if the primary requirements for the sacrifices did not exist, then the secondary reasons would not have been sufficient cause to institute the elaborate sacrificial procedures. However, once the need existed for bringing sacrifices to control the weather and to eliminate certain types of disease microorganisms, then other benefits, which possibly could have been attained by other means, were also introduced. Thus, meat for the priests could have been given without having to burn parts of the animals on the altar; psychological atonement for sin could have been achieved by payment of a fine; and numerous other symbolisms for the festivals could have been devised. In the following paragraphs detailed explanations are presented to establish the proposed rationales.

The first reason for the sacrifices to be considered here, is control of the weather. The Bible promises that if the Biblical laws are observed then the rain will occur at appropriate times (Lev. 26 4; Deut. 11 14; 28 12). In the light of modern scientific advances in cloud seeding and other types of weather control, it is quite reasonable to assume that the vapors from the sacrifices help in the seeding of clouds.

Experiments to increase precipitation rely upon the hypothesis that natural precipitation is limited by a shortage of natural precipitation nuclei. In particular, silver iodide is the most common material tested. Silver iodide smokes, produced by burning a silver iodide-acetone solution, are often used to supply sublimation nuclei effective at temperatures colder than 23 F.[1] Although it has often been questioned whether the method of cloud-seeding has a significant effect on rainfall, recent data have established the efficacy of the technique. Based upon results of five years of testing, the National Science Foundation concluded that atmospheric seeding has been proved to increase the amount of rain, as well as to reduce the numbers of lightning strokes and hailstones in thunderstorms.[2]

It should here be pointed out that weather control is of extreme importance in ensuring an adequate agricultural yield; but neither too much nor too little rainfall is desirable for best results. An ample supply of water is necessary because it is needed for all the activities of plants. Thus, water is one of the raw materials used in photosynthesis, and constitutes from 10 to 98 percent by weight of plant cells.[3] On the other hand, wind-blown rain, flooding, lightning, and hail are among the elements of weather that may harm plants.[4]

Although silver iodide is the main seeding chemical presently used, the truth is that the attributes of a good seeding agent are not completely known. Besides silver iodide, such chemicals as vanillin, urea, and various steroids have been studied.[5] It has even been indicated that industrial air pollution may increase the frequency of rain.[6]

The weather in Israel, where there is much air moisture, but not that much rainfall, is particularly suited for artificial means of control.[7] It has been shown, for example, that spraying a silver iodide solution from an airplane into suitable clouds permits an increase of about 20 percent in the annual rainfall of Israel.[8] Furthermore, the weather in Israel has been shown to be predictable based on the extent of rain in October. Moderate rainfall in October is almost always followed by an exceptionally dry winter, while dry Octobers generally precede three month periods of above normal rainfall.[9]

The above data indicate that sacrifices may have a very significant effect on the weather in Israel. Sacrifices have to be burned only in Jerusalem, on a mountain, so that the emitted vapors will have maximum effect. Numerous natural body chemicals, such as steroids, may be vaporized in small amounts upon burning the animal parts. Around the month of October (specifically on the fifteenth to twenty-first days of the month of Tishri), a large number of burnt-offerings are brought during the Festival of Tabernacles. Very possibly these sacrifices are to suppress rainfall in October, so that three months of above normal rainfall will follow. In addition, burnt-offerings are brought daily throughout the year, with increased amounts on Saturdays and festivals, to maintain sufficient precipitation nuclei in the atmosphere. In the case of sin-offerings, guilt-offerings and peace-offerings, specific fatty parts of the animals, as well as the kidneys, are burned on the altar, perhaps because these parts supply a particularly high concentration of precipitation nuclei.

Since a scientific approach to weather control is just in its infancy, it is not as yet possible to explain the weather-control aspects of the sacrifices in great detail. Research on weather control, which is being conducted to an increasing extent throughout the world, should shed more light on the importance of sacrifices for the control of weather in Israel.

Sounding of the silver trumpets on special occasions may possibly also aid in controlling the weather. The resultant vibrations could disperse the vapors from the sacrifices, making the vapors more suitable for cloud-seeding. Alternatively, the sound waves from the silver trumpets could serve the useful purpose of keeping the insect population in the Temple area at a low level. It has for example been established that exposing adult Indian-meal moths and flour beetles to certain sound waves during the egg-laying period could reduce their reproduction by up to 75 percent.[10]

The second primary reason for the sacrifices is the purifying action obtained from such procedures as sprinkling and pouring of blood, sprinkling and rubbing with olive oil, burning of incense, and sprinkling of the ash-water mixture from the red cow.

The blood sprinkling and pouring procedures imply that the blood of different animals has antiseptic properties against specific disease microorganisms. Thus: (A) The installation-offering of the priests involved the placing of the blood of a ram on the right earlobes, thumbs and big toes of the priests, and the sprinkling of the blood upon the priests and their clothes. (B) The leper, after recovery from his skin disease, has the diluted blood of a bird sprinkled on him seven times; and then seven days later has the blood of a he-lamb, which was brought as a guilt-offering, placed on his right earlobe, thumb, and big toe. (C) The diluted blood of a bird is sprinkled seven times on a house after elimination of leprosy-type microorganisms. (D) The blood from burnt-offerings, peace-offerings, sin-offerings and guilt-offerings is sprinkled or poured around the altar. (E) Some of the blood of a sin-offering brought by the high priest or by the entire Israelite community is sprinkled on the veil of the sanctuary and on the horns of the incense-altar. Also, the blood of sin-offerings brought by the high priest on the Day of Atonement is sprinkled upon the Ark cover and elsewhere within the Temple. (F) The blood of the Passover sacrifice is smeared on the doorposts and lintels of the houses in Jerusalem where it is eaten.

The above listed blood-sprinkling rites may be interpreted in terms of antiseptic properties of the blood. It is, for example, used to purify the priests and recovered lepers from disease microorganisms. The placing of the blood on a few effective areas, such as the right earlobe, thumb, and big toe, is to distribute the blood but yet not to use excessive amounts. In the case of leprosy-type diseases, the blood of a bird is particularly effective in killing any residual disease microorganisms. The pouring of blood around the altar is to prevent the growth of pathogens near where the sacrifices are brought. Similarly, the sprinkling of blood on the Day of Atonement upon the Ark cover and elsewhere in the Temple is to kill any disease microorganisms that might perchance lodge in those areas. The blood of the Passover lamb, which is placed on the doorposts and lintels, is known to have prevented the spread of the pathogen responsible for the plague of the first-born (Ex. 12 13).

From a scientific viewpoint, blood when outside the body is not usually used for antiseptic purposes. However, the white blood cells are known to be devourers of many harmful microorganisms.[11] Moreover, the part of the blood called gamma globulin is known to contain antibodies, i.e., chemical substances which help fight disease.[12] Thus, there is some scientific evidence that blood may possess antiseptic properties, as is clearly indicated from the Bible.

The application of olive oil to the right earlobe, thumb and big toe, as well as to the head of the recovered leper indicates that the oil has antiseptic properties against the leprosy microorganism. In modern times, olive oil is often used for preservation of foods, such as in canning of sardines, to some extent substantiating its antiseptic properties.[13] The anointing oil, consisting of olive oil and spices (Ex. 30 22–25), which was used for anointing and installing the priests, also has antiseptic properties as is discussed in more detail in Section 28.3.

The incense, which was prepared according to a definite formulation (Ex. 30 34–38), also has antiseptic properties, as is strongly indicated from the Bible. Thus, on the Day of Atonement the high priest burned incense within the holy-of-holies so that he would not die (Lev. 16 13); and when at the time of Korah a plague was rapidly spreading throughout the population, it was stopped completely by using burning incense (Num. **17** 11-15). The burning of incense has also been interpreted as a procedure for counteracting disagreeable odors generated by the sacrifice of animals, and to exert a favorable psychological influence over the participants.[14] Another possible purpose for the incense is to repel insects from the Temple area.

The purifying action of the ash-water mixture prepared from the red cow has been elaborated on in Section 25.4.

It is also of interest to note that the bringing of burnt-offerings and peace-offerings stopped a plague at the time of King David (II Sam. **24** 21, 25), thus indicating that the burning of sacrifices, even without sprinkling of blood, has antiseptic properties.

In additon to the above-mentioned antiseptic purposes for the sacrifices, it was also necessary to take many precautions to prevent the sacrificial rites from becoming disease-spreading. Salt was added to all the sacrifices because of its preservative properties.[15] Meat from the sacrifices could not be left over until the next day, or in one instance until the third day, otherwise the chance of spoilage and harboring of insects would be great—especially if we realize that preservation by refrigeration is a relatively recent innovation. The thanksgiving-offering could be eaten only until the next morning because it was accompanied by unleavened cakes and leavened bread mixed with oil, which might hasten spoilage. The freewill-offering could be eaten until the third day since it was not accompanied with these other items (see Section 25.1.3). For similar reasons of possible spoilage, the animal fat (*heleb*) had to be burned on the holiday and not left until the following day. Moreover, no honey was to be burned on the altar, to prevent growth of disease microorganisms. Furthermore, with the exception of the thanksgiving-offering and the sacrifice on the Day of the First-Fruits, no leavened bread was to be burned on the altar, again to prevent growth of disease microorganisms.

Extra precautions had to be taken so that the priests were pure, and not potential disease carriers. They were not allowed to touch dead bodies, unless for a very close relative such as parent, child, brother, or unmarried sister (see Section 25.5.3). Sacred food could not be eaten unless the priest was pure, nor could he officiate unless pure (see Section 25.5.2). Similarly non-priests could not enter the Temple area unless pure (see Section 25.5.1).

The altar had to be made either from earth or stone—materials which could withstand the heat of the fire without damage, and which would not be potential sources of disease microorganisms. Stones cut with iron tools could not be used for the altar since, because of the hardness of stone, pieces of iron would become attached. Iron rusts quite easily, and may become a likely site for disease microorganisms; for example, the spread of tetanus bacillus is commonly associated with punctures by rusty nails.

Animals used for sacrifices have to be perfect, since any blemish on the animal may result from disease or a metabolic disturbance, or be a possible site for disease microorganisms. Not only lame and blind but also castrated animals could not be brought on the altar. Castrating of an animal was specifically prohibited since the animal may become diseased or more susceptible to disease as a result of the operation. Sacrificing such animals may spread illness, or produce unusual chemical products. On the other hand, an overgrown or stunted animal may be used for Temple purposes, other than for sacrifices, since its imperfection is caused by a hormone imbalance, and would therefore not spread disease.

If an animal is brought as a sacrifice other than at the Temple site, the detailed precautions prescribed by the Bible will in all probability not be followed, resulting in the spread of disease, and excision to the sacrificer.

Sacrificial animals are limited to cattle, sheep, and goats; and sacrificial birds to pigeons and turtledoves. Other animals or birds may not be as useful in cloud-seeding and weather control, and their blood may not have as suitable antiseptic properties. Also other animals may possibly spread disease microorganisms to the altar.

Only if the calf, sheep, or goat is eight days or older can it be sacrificed, for then the animal is sufficiently developed so that the body hormones are perfected, enabling the animal's blood to have the necessary antiseptic qualities. The young animal's rapid development is, however, contingent upon its being nursed by its mother, and therefore it must remain near her for the first seven days of its life.

A third, and fairly obvious reason for the sacrifices, was to supply food for the priests as well as for the Israelites. The priests ate the entire permissible parts of the animal from the sin-offerings, guilt-offerings, and installation-offerings. The peace-offerings were eaten mainly by the bringer, except for the breast and right thigh which were eaten by the priests, and the shoulder, cheeks, and stomach, which were given to the priests. Also, the meal-offerings, in general, were eaten by the priests, except for the handful that was burned on the altar. Only of burnt-offerings, and sacrifices brought by priests, was nothing eaten. Thus, for most of the different types of sacrifices, none of the edible parts were wasted. This served as partial payment for the priests for their time spent in officiating; as well as allowed peace-offerings to be eaten by the bringers to encourage this type of sacrifice. Sacrifices brought by priests were not eaten, to discourage corruption, whereby a priest would claim someone else's animal as his own so he could bring it as a sacrifice and eat therefrom.

In some cases, such as for the right thigh of the peace-offering, the sin-offerings, guilt-offerings and specific meal-offerings (baked in oven, baked on griddle, and of the stewing pan), the officiating priest had first priority in eating the food. In other cases, such as for the breast of the peace-offerings, and certain meal-offerings (fine flour mixed with oil, and meal-offerings without oil) any priest could eat therefrom. These rules encouraged priests to officiate but did not deprive other priests from obtaining food for eating.

It should be noted that the food supplied to the priests from the sacrifices included meat from cattle, sheep, and goats, as well as flour, bread, unleavened cakes of various types, olive oil, salt, and frankincense as a spice. These items provide most of the nutrients required by a person. With the supplementary foods received from the first-fruits and the tenth-of-the-tithes, a balanced diet was insured for the priests and their families.

A fourth reason for the sacrifices is psychological benefits. People who have sinned in error, that is people who do not desire to transgress but have done so unintentionally, would have guilty consciences for sins committed. By bringing sin-offerings or guilt-offerings, as the case may require, the guilt feelings are removed by a concrete act. Otherwise the feelings of guilt may possibly overwhelm a person to the point of making him sick (see Section 25.2). Similarly, if a person is happy, and wants to thank God for some benefit, he can bring a burnt-offering, thanksgiving-offering or a freewill-offering to express his appreciation in a concrete manner.

The requirement of bringing a sin- or guilt-offering will often cause a person to atone for his guilty act even in certain cases where the sacrifices are brought for purposeful sins. Thus, transgressions such as not testifying, remaining impure, not carrying out an oath, are purposeful sins requiring a sin-offering for atonement. Confession of the sin results in the benefit that the suppressed testimony is revealed, the person becomes purified, or the oath is fulfilled. Similarly, swearing falsely about deposits, pledges, or other objects requires the bringing of a guilt-offering for atonement. In addition, the contested object must be returned with a one-fifth penalty, thereby making restitution to the aggrieved party. Save for the above exceptions, sin- and guilt-offerings could only be brought for unintentional transgressions. Otherwise, many people would sin purposely, knowing that they could subsequently atone by bringing sacrifices.

It should be realized that bringing an animal as a sacrifice can be an expensive penalty for sinning. For a willful transgression, involving obvious harm to one's fellow man, such as swearing falsely about a deposit, pledge, or other object, it is desirable that the guilty person have to pay for a costly sacrifice. In other cases, such as not testifying, remaining impure, or not carrying out an oath, where the degree of guilt is not that obvious, it is more important that the suppressed information be revealed, the unclean person be purified, or the oath carried out, than the requirement of an expensive sacrifice. Therefore in these cases, if the person is poor, he can atone for his sin by bringing sacrifices of lesser value.

Since one of the reasons for the sacrifices is psychological benefits, it would be inappropriate that while the sacrifices are being brought the esteem of the priesthood be lowered. Therefore, the priest must not go up steps to the altar, for otherwise he may expose private parts of his body, leading to distraction, and even possibly to immoral acts. Furthermore, steps could lead to serious accidents. If a priest tripped while on the steps he could be seriously hurt, also resulting in distraction from the sacrifices being brought.

Table 28.2.1
Biblical Festivals

Biblical Name(s)	Occurrence Month	Day(s)	Days When Work is Prohibited	Manner of Observance	Historical Reason	References
Passover	1	14		Passover sacrifice, in evening, in the spring month, only for the circumcised, eaten in houses in Jerusalem	Exodus from Egypt	Ex. 12 3–10, 21–27, 43–49; 34 25; Lev. 23 5; Num. 9 1–5; 28 16; Deut. 16 1–2, 5–7
Passover (in the 2nd month)	2	14		Passover sacrifice for those who were impure or on a distant journey on the 14th day of the 1st month	Exodus from Egypt	Num. 9 6–14
Festival of Matzot (unleavened bread)	1	15 to 21	first and seventh; food preparation permitted	eat unleavened bread; do not eat leavened bread; otherwise excision; applies to alien also; observe the spring month; do not leave any leaven to be seen in your territory; all males go to Jerusalem	Exodus from Egypt; in spring	Ex. 12 15–20; 13 3–10; 23 15,17; 34 18,23; Lev. 23 6–8; Num. 28 17,25; Deut. 16 3, 4,8,16,17
Day of Waving the Omer	first Sunday after ini-			the sheaf of the 1st cuttings is brought to the priest in Jerusalem,		Lev. 23 9–14

Name	Month	Day	Sacred occasion	Ritual	Reason	References
(sheaf)		tial reaping of the harvest		and waved; a burnt-offering is then brought; do not eat from the fresh grain until after bringing the sacrifice		
Festival of Harvest; Festival of Weeks; Day of First-Fruits;		50th day after Day of Waving the Omer	day of the Festival	a meal-offering of the first-fruits of the wheat harvest, baked with leaven, is brought; be happy in Jerusalem; all males go to Jerusalem	remember you were slaves in Egypt	Ex. 23 16-17; 34 22,23; Lev. 23 15-21; Num. 28 26; Deut. 16 9-12, 16-17.
Day of Blowing the Shofar (ram's horn)	7	1	day of the festival	ram's horns are blown		Lev. 23 23-25; Num. 29 1
Day of Atonement	7	10	Day of Atonement; all work prohibited	afflict your souls, otherwise punishment of excision; day of atonement for all the people's sins; special sacrifices to purify Temple and altar		Lev. 16 29-34; 23 26-32; Num. 29 7
Festival of Ingathering; Festival of Tabernacles;	7	15 to 21	1st day	dwell in booths (*sukkot*); all males go to Jerusalem; on the first day take the fruit of hadar tree, palm branches, branches of thick trees, and willows of the brook; be happy for seven days	the Israelites dwelled in booths after Exodus from Egypt	Ex. 23 16-17; 34 22-23; Lev. 23 33-36, 39-43; Num. 29 12; Deut. 16 13-17.
Atzeret (closing day)	7	22	day of the festival			Lev. 23 36,39; Num. 29 35

A final reason for the sacrifices is their symbolic nature. The festival sacrifices (see Table 28.1.4) are brought to mark special holidays and occasions. For example, the omer offering marks the time when the year's grain produce can be eaten; and the New Moon sacrifices mark the beginning of the month. Because of the requirement of bringing sacrifices on set dates, care would be taken to develop a systematic calendar. Blowing of silver trumpets at the time when festival sacrifices are brought also marks the special nature of the holidays.

28.2 FESTIVALS

Explanations for the special features of each of the Biblical festivals are presented in the subsequent paragraphs. Rationales for the festival sacrifices are, however, not included since they have already been discussed in Section 28.1.

Laws

For simplicity, the festival regulations are summarized in Table 28.2.1. Included in the tabulation are the names, dates, manner of observance, and references for the holidays.

Rationale

The three main holidays, which all males are required to celebrate in Jerusalem, are the Festival of Matzot,* the Festival of Weeks** and the Festival of Tabernacles. These three holidays are dependent on events during the agricultural year, and are so arranged that they do not interfere with the country's agricultural produce. The Festival of Matzot occurs before the start of the grain harvest, the Festival of Weeks occurs after the wheat harvest, and the Festival of Tabernacles occurs after the fruit harvest. Thus the taking of extended holidays at these times of the year does not interfere with farming activities. It should furthermore be noted that these holidays occur in the warmer half of the year—not during the rainy season—so that travelling long distances to Jerusalem does not become a hardship.

In addition to resting once a week on Saturday (see Section 25.2), people need to take a vacation several times each year to provide renewed mental and physical vigor. The three pilgrimage festivals of Matzot, Weeks, and Tabernacles, are just the type of vacation needed. Each male brings gifts for the sanctuary (Deut. 16 16–17), and is commanded (especially for the Festivals of Weeks and Tabernacles when the harvestings are completed) to be happy in Jerusalem. The women, who may be indisposed, pregnant, nursing, or caring for young children, are not required to travel, but when able would naturally go along.

Food for the stay in Jerusalem is supplied from the tithe for four out of seven

---

* The Festival of Matzot is now commonly called Passover, but in actuality the term Passover, as used in the Pentateuch, refers to the Passover sacrifice brought the day before the Festival of Matzot.
** The Festival of Weeks is commonly called Pentecost.

years (Section 27.2.1) thereby ensuring a plentiful food supply for the pilgrims. Housing accomodations might involve setting up tents for the Festivals of Matzot and Weeks. Booths (*sukkot*) would however be used for the Festival of Tabernacles. To a great extent, the Pentateuch provides regulations to satisfy the food and housing needs of the multitude of pilgrims during these holiday periods.

A major problem could arise during the three pilgrim festivals, when the entire male population is located in Jerusalem. An enemy nation could select such a time for attacking and conquering the country. The Bible therefore states (Ex. 34 24) that the boundaries of Israel will be extended and no one will desire the land during these three pilgrimage festivals. As clarified in Section 26.3, the Israelites will, by observing the Biblical regulations, become militarily stronger than any other nation and will acquire natural defensible boundaries. Under such circumstances, it will be extremely difficult for an enemy nation to launch a surprise attack.

No work other than food preparation is allowed on the first and last days of the Festival of Matzot, and also on the first and last days of the Festival of Tabernacles if we include Atzeret. Moreover, no work is permitted on the one day of the Festival of Weeks. Now, as will be explained in a subsequent paragraph, the Festival of Weeks always follows a Saturday. Thus, we find for all the three pilgrimage festivals that a day of rest occurs upon arriving in Jerusalem for the holiday, and a day of rest occurs before leaving for home. Hence, the Bible provides rest days for the people so they will not become overexhausted from travelling. On the other hand, the one day festivals of Day of Blowing the Shofar and Day of Atonement only provide one day of rest since no travelling to and from Jerusalem is required.

In general, for all the festivals food preparation is allowed on the rest days. However, on the Day of Atonement, just as on Saturday, work involving food preparation is not permitted since it is a day of "affliction," with the implication that no food is to be eaten the entire day. It should be noted that food preparation had to be permitted for other festival rest days. Otherwise serious hardship could result in cases when the festival rest day preceded or followed the Sabbath. Many cooked foods would spoil when kept for more than one day, thereby detracting from enjoyment of the holidays.

Let us now explain the rationales for the particular features of the festivals, in the order presented in Table 28.2.1.

The Passover sacrifice, brought on the fourteenth of the first month was discussed to some extent in Section 28.1, and its details given in Table 28.1.4. The noteworthy feature of the sacrifice is that people who purposely do not bring it, either in the first or in the second month, are punished with excision. The implication is that some factor involved with the sacrifice prevents disease. The Bible particularly states that the placing of the blood of the Passover lamb on the doorposts and lintels, at the time of the Exodus from Egypt, prevented the spread of the pathogens responsible for the plague of the first-born (Ex. 12 13, 23). Moreover, the placing of the blood is a regulation to be observed for all generations (Ex. 12 24). Thus, some factor within the animal's blood prevents the spread of certain disease microorganisms, and thereby prevents premature death. Since the sacrifice can, if necessary, be brought in the second rather than the first month, it appears that the protection offered by the blood involves the individual within the house, and is not too dependent on the exact date during the spring month when the rite is performed. The protection would, however, not be achieved if the person is impure or is uncircumcised, for then the disease microorganisms might thrive on the person.

The Festival of Matzot has several unique requirements. These involve making sure that the holiday occurs in the early part of spring, that no leaven exists in the land, and that matzot and not leaven are eaten.

The requirement that the Festival of Matzot should occur in the spring, coupled with the correspondence of the holidays to the agricultural year, requires a solar calendar. However, the need for bringing sacrifices on the first day of the month, and the fact that the moon cycle is the basis of the length of the month, requires a lunar calendar. A suitable solution was obtained with the development of the Jewish lunisolar calendar. In this calendar, each month consists of 29 or 30 days, and each year consists of 12 months, except for leap years when a thirteenth month of 30 days is added. A regular lunar year contains 354 days, 11 short of the 365 days in a solar year. By having 7 leap years every 19 years, a complete lunisolar cycle is obtained (i.e., $7 \times 30 \approx 19 \times 11$). Because of the nature of the calendar there can be, during different years, a difference of as much as 29 days between the dates in the solar year that correspond to a fixed date in the lunisolar calendar. For example, the fourteenth of Nisan, when the Passover sacrifice is to be brought, can take place any day between March 26 and April 24. Similarly, for any fixed date in the solar calendar, the corresponding lunisolar dates can vary by up to 29 days during different years.

The requirement to eliminate all leaven from the land for seven days is designed to control, if not eradicate, the rat and mice population. Insects, other rodents, and disease microorganisms may possibly also be controlled by this means. At the beginning of spring, when food from the fields has been consumed during the winter, rats and mice are particularly susceptible to starvation by removal of the residual food supply. It is known, for example, that starving rats will devour each other, and thereby further their own destruction.[16] Rats and mice have a particularly strong liking for wet grain, and can often go without water for long periods as long as the food they eat contains a small amount of moisture.[17] The Biblical prohibition against having any leaven in the territory for seven days in the early spring thus deprives these rodents of their favorite foods, and leads to their starvation because other foods are not available.

In modern times, the rat population is controlled by elimination of garbage and extermination by poisoning.[18] Yet the complete elimination of the rat is not achieved because thorough removal of leaven for seven days in the early spring is not accomplished.

Mice, and especially rats, are very harmful creatures to man. Rats, for example, can carry as many as 35 different diseases. Their fleas spread bubonic plague which in the fourteenth century killed one out of every three persons in Europe. Rats also cause severe grain losses. In India they destroy about 25 percent of the crop in the field, and 25 percent of the grain in storage. Rats may be considered as the most injurious and universal pests of the human race.[19]

In addition to the regulation prohibiting leaven in the land, there is also the law prohibiting the eating of leavened grain. By this means, potentially harmful microorganisms within the person's digestive tract may possibly be deprived of essential nourishment, thereby preventing the occurrence of certain diseases. The prohibition against eating leaven for seven days has to be observed by the entire population at the same time, for otherwise disease microorganisms, even if eliminated from one person's system, may be later contracted from others.

The Day of Waving the Omer marks the beginning of harvesting the grain; an event which depends on the solar year. As explained previously, the corresponding dates in the lunisolar calendar, can differ during different years by as much as 29 days (or about four weeks). Thus it is impossible to specify an exact lunisolar date for the beginning of the grain harvest. In order to ensure that the Day of Waving the Omer is celebrated as soon as possible in the year, the Pentateuch prohibits the eating from the fresh grain until after bringing the sacrifice accompanying the waving ceremony.

The omer of grain is brought the day after Saturday, i.e., on the first Sunday following the beginning of harvesting. Fifty days later, also on a Sunday, occurs the Festival of Weeks, when the wheat harvest is essentially complete. The exact lunisolar date for the Festival of Weeks is not specified since it varies from year to year depending upon when the omer is brought.

The Day of Blowing the Shofar occurs on the first day of the seventh month. The reason for blowing the shofar on that day is not clear. Perhaps the emitted sound waves aid in weather control or in warding off insects, as previously suggested (Section 28.1) for the analogous case of blowing of the silver trumpets.

The Day of Atonement on the tenth of the seventh month involves self-affliction, such as fasting, in addition to the bringing by the high priest of special sacrifices to purify the Temple, the holy-of-holies, and the altar. The purification process, as explained in Section 28.1, probably involves the killing of microorganisms which may lodge in the Temple area during the year. In this manner, spread of disease is prevented.

Not eating for a full day on the Day of Atonement may be of benefit, not only in giving a rest to the digestive system, but also by ridding the digestive tract of particular pathogens. For example, there are numerous sicknesses, such as stomach viruses and ailments producing high fevers, where the individual often feels better and recovers more quickly by complete abstinence from food and drink. The Biblical requirement for the entire population to fast on the same day, may be to rid the population of certain disease microorganisms before they have a chance to produce any disease symptoms.

The Festival of Tabernacles is observed for seven days from the fifteenth to the twenty-first of the seventh month, followed by the one day holiday of Atzeret on the twenty-second of the seventh month. Atzeret, in certain respects, may be considered as the concluding day of the Festival of Tabernacles, although none of the features of the Festival of Tabernacles are to be observed.

The main features of the Festival of Tabernacles are the dwelling in booths (*sukkot*) and the celebrating with four specific plants. Booths are temporary structures which are covered not with a solid roof but with cut vegetation. These structures serve as housing for the multitude of pilgrims to Jerusalem, and have at this time of year the advantage over tents that they do not get as hot from the sun. The question, however, arises as to why it is not required to dwell in a booth on Atzeret.

The four specific plants to be taken by the people on the first day of the Festival of Tabernacles are the fruit of the hadar tree, palm branches, branches of thick trees, and willows of the brook. It is difficult to assign a beneficial purpose for this procedure. Perhaps the taking of these plants is purely symbolic, as a sign that all the year's agricultural produce has been harvested. Furthermore it may be a means by which the people can be happy on the holiday. Alternatively, the taking of these plants guarantees that care will be taken not to destroy the trees on which they grow, since the trees may possibly serve as food for some beneficial insects or microorganisms.

28.3 TEMPLE DESIGN AND COMPONENTS

The Tabernacle, the portable sanctuary in use for about 430 years, is described in detail in the Pentateuch. However, no dimensions and designs are given for the permanent Temple. The first actual plans for the Temple are presented in the Books of Kings and Chronicles, and were initially prepared by King David and transmitted in writing to his son Solomon (I Chr. **28** 11–19). A second Biblical set of plans for the Temple was revealed to the prophet Ezekiel (Ez. **40**–**43**), and represents the design to be used in construction of the Third Temple. No Biblical description of the Second Temple is given. Although the design of the Tabernacle is different in many respects from those for the First and Third Temples, still the basic features and principles are the same. For example, the dimensions of the Tabernacle are 30×10 square cubits, while the dimensions for the First and Third Temples are 60×20 square cubits (I Kings **6** 2; Ez. **41** 2, 4), i.e., the same ratios apply, although the dimensions of the Temple for the length and width are twice those for the Tabernacle. In general, the regulations concerning the Tabernacle are relevant to the design of the Temple, and therefore need to be studied in detail.

The historical periods in which these edifices were used are as follows: The Tabernacle was built in the desert (1473 B.C.E.) and continued in use until about the time of King David. The First Temple was built by his son, King Solomon

(995) and lasted until its destruction in 586. The Second Temple was built in 516 B.C.E. and was destroyed in 70 C.E. The Third Temple will be constructed in the near future.

LAWS

The main features of the Tabernacle and its accompanying vessels are summarized, for convenience, in Tables 28.3.1 and 28.3.2. Table 28.3.1 presents the dimensions and purposes for the structures and furniture, while Table 28.3.2 describes the smaller utensils and consumable items. In addition to the tabulated specifications, there is the regulation to fear the sanctuary (Lev. **19** 30; **26** 2); i.e., to show respect and observe the regulations concerning the Tabernacle.

RATIONALE

The Tabernacle, which was situated within the Tabernacle court, consisted of two rooms, namely the holy-of-holies and the holy place. The holy-of-holies is also called *devir* in I Kings **8** 6; II Chr. **5** 7; and the holy place is also called *heikhal* in I Kings **6** 5; II Chr. **4** 7, 8; Ez. **41** 4. In the holy-of-holies was placed the Ark containing the Tablets of the Covenant received by Moses from God. These tablets are a historical verification of the Divine origin of the Biblical laws, and are placed in the holy-of-holies for safeguarding. Nobody but the high priest may enter the room, and then only on special occasions such as the Day of Atonement.

In the second room of the Tabernacle, the holy place, were placed the lampstand for providing light at night, the table for holding showbread, and the altar for burning incense. As discussed in Section 28.1, the burning of the incense not only provided a pleasant fragrance but also had a purifying action, and probably prevented the growth of specific disease microorganisms and repelled insects. The showbread remained on the table for one week until eaten by the priests, and possibly allowed limited growth of beneficial microorganisms, such as molds, which helped to maintain freedom from disease in the sanctuary. Analogously, it is here suggested that the olive oil which was burned in the lampstand helped maintain a healthful atmosphere. It was necessary to have these three consumable items together in one room, i.e., the burning incense, the burning olive oil, and the showbread, to prevent the growth of disease-causing microorganisms.

On the other hand, an individual who for his own personal use prepares incense according to the proportions used in the sanctuary, is punished by excision. This prohibition implies that improper use of the incense can support the growth of disease microorganisms. For example, when King Uzziah transgressed by bringing incense for burning he was afflicted with leprosy (II Chr. **26** 16–21). Furthermore, the incense may possibly be a powerful drug, the fragrance of which can result in toxic effects when used improperly.

Similarly, the anointing oil, which was composed of olive oil and spices, was not allowed to be prepared for an individual's use, otherwise he would be subject to excision. Probably, when used under improper conditions, the anointing oil could

Table 28.3.1

Item	Purpose	Where Used	Dimensions (Cubits)		
			L	W	H
Ark	to house the tablets of the Covenant (עדת)	holy-of-holies	2.5	1.5	1.5
Ark cover (כפרת)	to cover the Ark	holy-of holies	2.5	1.5	
table	to hold the showbread	north side of the holy place	2	1	1.5
lampstand	to provide light	south side of the holy place			
incense-altar	for burning incense	in the holy place, in front of the veil (פרכת)	1	1	2
Tabernacle	to house the holy vessels	inside the Tabernacle court	30	10	10
holy-of-holies	room where the Ark stands	room in the Tabernacle	10	10	10
holy place	room where the table, lampstand, and incense-altar stand	room in the Tabernacle	20	10	10
altar	for burning sacrifices	in front of the door of the Tabernacle	5	5	3
Tabernacle court	to surround the Tabernacle and holy areas		100	50	5

Components of the Tabernacle

Construction Materials	Other Features	References
acaciawood overlaid with gold	2 poles of wood inserted into 4 gold rings on the sides; a band of gold all around	Ex. 25 10–16, 21; 26 33–34; 37 1–5; 40 3
pure gold	2 cherubim, with spreading wings, on the ends of the Ark cover	Ex. 25 17–22; 26 34; 37 6–9; Lev. 24 5–7
acaciawood overlaid with gold	a band of gold all around; a rim with a band all around; 2 poles of wood inserted into 4 gold rings on the sides	Ex. 25 23–30; 26 35; 37 10–16; 40 4, 22–23
pure gold	7 lamps for olive oil, to be lit each evening, and burn until the morning	Ex. 25 31–40; 26 35; 30 7–8; 37 17–24; 40 4, 24–25; Lev. 24 2–4; Num. 8 1–4
acaciawood overlaid with gold	a band of gold all around; 2 poles of wood inserted into 4 gold rings on the sides; horns are made on the altar	Ex. 30 1–10; 37 25–28; 40 5, 26–27
boards of acaciawood overlaid with gold; silver and copper sockets; multicolored linen curtains; goathair curtains; ram skins; porpoise skins; gold fasteners	the boards stand upright in the sockets; the structure was covered with curtains joined together with gold fasteners; skins of rams and porpoises were placed over the curtains	Ex. 26 1–37; 36 8–38. Ex. 26 33–34 Ex. 26 33, 35; 30 6
acaciawood overlaid with copper; stone or soil; copper	a copper grating reaching to half the altar's height; 2 poles of wood inserted into 4 copper rings; horns are made on the altar	Ex. 20 21–22; 27 1–8; 38 1–7; 40 6, 28–29; (Deut. 27 5–8)
acaciawood, linen curtains, copper sockets, silver hooks	the boards stand upright in the sockets; the curtains hang from silver hooks on the boards	Ex. 27 9–19; 38 9–20; 40 8,33

support the growth of pathogens. This is despite the fact that when properly used the anointing oil had antiseptic properties, as evidenced by its application to the Tabernacle and holy items, and its use for anointing the high priest.

The dimensions specified for the Ark, table, incense-altar, and altar (See Table 28.3.1) were undoubtedly for practical reasons. The Ark had to be large enough to house the Tablets of the Covenant. The table was a convenient height of 1.5 cubits (about 30 inches) and had sufficient area to allow the arrangement of two rows of six showbreads on its top. Similarly, the size of the incense-altar was suitable for the amount of incense burned. The altar for sacrifices was of much larger area than the incense-altar since large animals, and at times many animals simultaneously, had to be burned on its surface.

The altar upon which sacrifices were burned was situated in front of the Tabernacle in the open air. The vapors from the sacrifices could rise unimpeded to control the weather (as explained in Section 28.1). Moreover, this arrangement allowed the odors of burning animal flesh to be dissipated, thereby not becoming too unpleasant. Since the altar was in front of the Tabernacle, the fragrance from the burning incense masked any residual unpleasantness.

Great care had to be taken to prevent the growth of disease microorganisms near the altar. Purifying procedures, such as blood-pouring, had to be followed rigorously, and specific sacrificial routines, such as daily sacrifices, had to be conducted. Continuous fire on the altar had to be maintained so that the heat would kill any disease microorganisms which might otherwise grow on incompletely burned flesh.

The laver and its base were placed between the Tabernacle and the altar, so as to be conveniently located. The water within the laver was used for washing the hands and feet of the priests prior to their officiating either at the altar or at the Tabernacle. It is well known that washing can remove microorganisms, and thereby prevent the spread of disease. By such means, sickness was prevented, and the priests did not die as a result of serving in the Tabernacle area.

Specific tools and dishes were made to aid in such tasks as placing the showbread on the table, lighting the olive oil in the lampstand, and burning animals on the altar. The tools simplified the tasks and prevented accidents. In particular, without tools there would be a significant chance of the priests getting burns while officiating.

The design of the Tabernacle also took into consideration the aesthetics and durability of the structures. Reflective inert metals, namely gold, silver, and copper were used where appropriate. These metals do not corrode significantly, and therefore retain their high reflectivity and strength for extended periods. Similarly, acacia wood is a sturdy durable wood, and it was frequently overlaid with gold or copper for added protection and beauty. The curtains were made of white, blue, purple, and scarlet linen so as to have a colorful strong cloth. Additional protection for the Tabernacle curtains was obtained from the coverings of ram and porpoise skins. In general, the materials selected for use in the Tabernacle were ones that retained their aesthetic and structural properties for many centuries.

Table 28.3.2
Auxiliary Items for Use at the Tabernacle

Item	Purpose	Where Used	Constituents	References
showbread	memorial bread	placed every Sabbath on the table in 2 rows of 6 breads in the lampstand	2/10 ephah of fine flour for each of 12 breads; frankincense	Lev. 24 5–9
olive oil	fuel for the lamps in the lampstand		pure olive oil	Ex. 27 20–21; Lev. 24 1–4.
anointing oil*	for anointing the high priest, the Tabernacle, the Ark, the table, the lampstand, the altar of incense, the altar, and the laver	in Tabernacle area	500 shekels of myrrh, 250 of fragrant cinnamon, 250 of aromatic cane, 500 of cassia; one hin of olive oil	Ex. 29 7; 30 22–33; 37 29; 40 9–15
laver and base**	to hold water for the priests to wash their hands and feet	between the Tabernacle and the altar	copper	Ex. 30 17–21; 38 8; 40 7, 30–32
incense***	for burning	on incense-altar	fragrant spices: gum resin, aromatic shell, galbanum, and frankincense	Ex. 30 34–38; 37 29
tools for the table	to assist in placing the show bread	at the table	gold	Ex. 25 29
tools for the lampstand	to assist in burning the olive oil	at the lampstand	gold	Ex. 25 38–39
tools for the altar	to assist in burning sacrifices	at the altar	copper	Ex. 27 3

* An individual who prepares anointing oil as prescribed, or who uses it on an unqualified person shall be punished by excision (Ex. 30 32–33).
** The priests must wash their hands and feet before officiating, so they will not die (Ex. 30 19–21; 40 31–32).
*** An individual who prepares incense as prescribed, to smell thereof, shall be punished by excision (Ex. 30 37–38).

28.4 PRIESTLY GARMENTS

Laws

The priests are required to wear special garments when officiating. The ordinary priest wears only four articles of apparel, namely shorts, a tunic, a belt, and a hat. The high priest, in addition to the above items, also wears a robe, an ephod (a vest-like garment), a breastplate, and a gold plate on the forehead. Descriptions of the priestly clothes are summarized in Table 28.4.1.

Usually the Biblical terms "blue, purple, and scarlet" are interpreted as meaning *wool*-thread dyed these colors. However, if this explanation is accepted, it results in the high priest wearing two garments, the ephod and the breastplate, containing wool and linen threads. The Pentateuch expressly prohibits wearing a garment made of wool and linen (Lev. 19 19; Deut. 22 11). It seems quite astonishing that the high priest, who must maintain the utmost purity, would be made an exception to the rule and allowed to wear a combination of fibers that could lead to disease (see Section 25.4). As an alternate explanation, the terms "blue, purple, and scarlet" may be interpreted as meaning *linen*-thread dyed these colors. To some extent this is implied from the Biblical text where this succession of colors is followed by the word שש, meaning white linen. Further support for this interpretation is gained from Lev. 16 4, where the belt worn by the priests is called בד, i.e., linen (irrespective of color). From Ex. 39 29 we learn that the belt contained "blue, purple, and scarlet" in addition to white linen. Only if the terms "blue, purple, and scarlet" refer to linen dyed these colors, would the use of the word בד be justified (see Section 17.4.3).

The reason that the terms "blue, purple, and scarlet" have usually been interpreted as referring to wool thread may be the ease with which wool can be dyed. In contrast linen, because of the hardness and lack of penetrability of the fiber, has a very poor affinity for dye. Nevertheless, linen can be dyed on its surface quite satisfactorily.[20]

Rationale

Linen is the dominant fabric used in the priestly garments. This is because linen has a number of unique properties. First, it does not easily collect dirt and microorganisms on its surface, and therefore is especially hygienic and adaptable to sanitary use.[21] Second, linen is quite resistant to attack by bacteria and mildew.[22] Third, it does not build up static electrical charges, and as a result dust and smoke particles do not cling to the fabric.[23] All these properties are important for the clothes worn when bringing sacrifices. It is desirable that the clothes remain clean, do not absorb disease microorganisms, and do not retain the odor of the smoke from the burning sacrifices.

In contrast wool, which might be considered a likely alternative to linen, has

Table 28.4.1
Garments Worn by the Priests

Garment	Component Materials	Special Features	Order of Putting On*	References (in Exodus)
*High Priest***				
tunic	white linen		1	28 39; 39 27
avnet (belt)	white, blue, purple and scarlet linen		2	28 39; 39 29
robe	blue linen; blue, purple and scarlet linen for the pomegranates; gold bells	long sleeveless robe put on over the head, with alternating pomegranates and bells on the hem	3	28 31–35; 39 22–26
ephod (a vest-like garment)	white, blue, purple, and scarlet linen; gold; precious stones	2 precious stones, engraved with the names of the 12 tribes, were inclosed in settings of gold on the shoulder pieces	4	28 6–12, 25–28; 39 2–7; 18–21.
choshen (breastplate)	white, blue, purple and scarlet linen; gold; precious stones	12 different precious stones, in 4 rows of 3 stones, engraved with the names of the 12 tribes, were inclosed in settings of gold, and placed on the front of the breastplate	5	28 13–30; 39 8–21
mitznefet (hat)	white linen		6	28 39; 39 28
gold plate	gold; blue linen thread	the plate was engraved with the words "Holy to the Lord"; the plate was suspended from the *mitznefet* by blue thread, and rested on the forehead	7	28 36–38; 39 30–31

Table 28.4.1 (continued)

Garment	Component Materials	Special Features	Order of Putting On*	References (in Exodus)
Ordinary Priest:				
tunic	white linen		1	28 40, 39 27.
avnet (belt)	white, blue, purple and scarlet linen		2	28 40, 39 29.
hat (migbaat)	white linen		3	28 40, 39 28.
shorts	linen	the shorts extended from the loins to the thighs, and were also worn by the high priest	—	28 42, 39 28.

* Based on Ex. **29** 5–9; and Lev. **8** 7–9,13. Probably the linen shorts were put on before the other listed garments.
** On the Day of Atonement, the high priest initially wears the garments of the ordinary priest, except that he wears the turban-type hat (*mitzwefet*) (Lev. **16** 4).

many of the opposite properties. Viruses such as those causing polio or cowpox can live on wool for about three to five months.[24] Moreover, static can build up on wool to the discharge point. It has, in fact, been recommended that people who work in explosive atmospheres not wear wool.[25]

With respect to the latter point, it is known that fine dusts can often explode if ignited.[26] The dusts from incompletely burned ashes or from fine flour may, in unusual cases, be ignited by a spark from static on clothes. Use of linen, which does not build up large static charges, would prevent such occurrences.

Of interest, along these lines, is the case of the death of Uzzah, apparently from discharge of static electricity, when he touched the Ark to prevent it from falling (II Sam. **6** 7; I Chr. **13** 10). In that case, contrary to Biblical requirements, the Ark was being carried on a wagon, rather than by the Levites (see Num. **4** 4–6; **6** 9). The rubbing of the gold coating of the Ark against the material on which it stood during the transportation in the wagon, could have built up a lethal static-electricity charge.

Materials other than linen are found only in the clothing of the high priest. In particular, the other materials are gold threads, items of gold, and precious stones. Gold and precious stones are inert materials, and are unlikely to retain disease microorganisms. Moreover, these added items add greatly to the majesty of the high priest. The glitter from the gold, and the sparkle from the precious stones, coupled with the bright colors from the dyed linen garments, produce a remarkably aesthetic appearance.

The garments of the high priest also result in a melodious effect. When the high priest walks, the bells hanging from the hem of the robe, tinkle, thereby notifying others of his presence.

By these means the garments prescribed by the Bible make the high priest one of the most illustrious persons of the nation.

PART V

CONCLUDING REMARKS

On the previous pages we have shown in great detail that (A) the Biblical chronology is correct; (B) the individual books of the Bible are organized in a meaningful way; (C) the Biblical prophecies are actual revelations; and (D) great benefits to society arise from observing the laws in the Pentateuch. Thus we have established by four different approaches that the Bible is accurate, and its contents are true. An obvious conclusion from these analyses is that the Jewish religion, which is based on careful observance of the Biblical commandments, is the true religion.

At the present time, unfortunately, numerous Biblical laws are not being and cannot be observed, even by the most orthodox of Jews. Sacrifices cannot be offered, tithes are not to be separated, and purity requirements cannot be followed. These particular laws are examples of ones that should be reinstituted now that Israel is in control of the Temple Mount. Numerous other observances could also be initiated almost immediately if the appropriate religious climate existed.

One means for revitalizing the Jewish religion is to set up a Sanhedrin, or legislative body, for reinterpreting the Biblical laws. This group could eventually be substituted for the Knesset, or parliament of the State of Israel. Members of the Sanhedrin should be men of outstanding knowledge in Jewish and worldly subjects. On the average, they should be intellectually more capable than even the scholars who developed the Mishnah and Talmud. Decisions by the Sanhedrin would be binding on the Jewish people and the State of Israel.

It should be pointed out that in the analyses presented in this volume we have not always rigidly adhered to commonly accepted rabbinic interpretations. Otherwise it would have been impossible to develop many of the given explanations, and to solve numerous Biblical problems. For example, in the chronological section (Section 4.1) the length of rule of Joshua was calculated to be 52 years, rather than 28 years as usually is assumed. In Part II (Section 10.1), the authorship of Genesis was attributed to such key individuals as Adam, Noah, Abraham, Isaac, Jacob, Judah, and Joseph, rather than to Moses; although Moses may have been the final editor. In Part III (Section 21.2) the Messianic ruler of the Jewish nation was interpreted to be a person named David, and not necessarily a direct descendant of the famous King David. Finally, in the section dealing with the rationale for the

CONCLUDING REMARKS   697

Biblical laws (Section 27.2.1) it was concluded that only one tithe is to be taken each year from the agricultural produce, rather than two tithes as is the generally accepted explanation. These are examples of only a few of the numerous instances where straightforward interpretation of the Bible led to somewhat unexpected conclusions. The basic assumption has been that it is better to affirm the accuracy of the Bible, which is the source for the rabbinic interpretations—even if in the process some traditional explanations are disregarded—than rigidly to maintain the rabbinic explanations, and thereby undermine the faith in Biblical accuracy and the Jewish religion.

Let us examine the basis for the rabbinic interpretations. The first major work in the post-Biblical period, which records rabbinic decisions and conclusions, is known as the Mishnah. The Mishnah was completed circa 200 C.E., about 550 years after the time of Ezra and Nehemiah when the last books of the Bible were written. Traditional commentators such as Maimonides claim that the Mishnah carefully preserves ancient oral traditions going back to the time of Moses.[1] However, from a logical viewpoint one would consider it very unlikely that accurate knowledge and tradition could be transmitted orally for over 500 years from the time of completion of the Bible. Moreover, the Pentateuch was completed about 1434 B.C.E., over 1,600 years before the writing of the Mishnah. It would be even more remote that any traditional interpretations of the Bible from the time of Moses could have been preserved by word of mouth for so long a period.

Support for the absence of a detailed oral tradition is obtained from the chronological section (Section 6.1). There it is shown that the traditional duration of 420 years for the Second Temple is incorrect, and instead the Temple lasted 585 years. Associated with the chronological misconception are the placing by tradition of Daniel and Zerubbabel as contemporaries of Ezra and Nehemiah.[2] Such an historical error could only have arisen if in Talmudical times oral tradition from the time of Ezra and Nehemiah had been almost completely lost!

The problem then arises what is the basis for the development of the Mishnah. Examination of typical Mishnaic texts indicates that the Mishnah is a legal compilation, developed by brilliant scholars over many years, based on Biblical interpretation and prevailing practices. In addition, the level of scientific knowledge of that age, was applied to all types of practical situations that might arise. In general, the Mishnah attempts to specify and delimit what is and what is not permissible. The main traditions that may have existed and been incorporated into the Mishnah were based on prevailing practices that were handed down from generation to generation. Examples of such practices are the methods of slaughtering animals; how fringes are to be placed on garments; and how a booth for the Festival of Tabernacles should be built. On the other hand, theoretical interpretations of Biblical passages would undoubtedly have been lost over the hundreds of years elapsed.

Subsequent to the completion of the Mishnah, the Talmud (Babli and Yerushalmi) was developed to explain the Mishnah. Commentaries, such as those by Rashi, were later written to explain the Talmud, until finally, through a complicated series of developments, modern Jewish law was evolved. However, all these outgrowths have been mainly based on the Mishnah. In the legal development the Mishnaic and Talmudic conclusions have usually been accepted even if they somewhat contradicted the plain meaning of the Biblical laws. It is therefore quite possible that errors in Biblical interpretation, as incorporated in the Mishnah and Talmud could still prevail to the present time. As an example (see Section 27.2.1) the Bible nowhere mentions the giving of more than one tithe per year, yet the Mishnah and present-day teaching indicate that two tithes should be given, one for the Levites and one to be eaten in Jerusalem or given to the poor.

When a Sanhedrin, or authoritative legal body is convened, it will be necessary to make legal decisions not only based on Mishnaic, Talmudic, and later enactments, but also from a re-examination of the Biblical regulations in the light of modern knowledge. Great advances have been made in every field of learning, including Biblical interpretation, since the time of the Mishnah. There undoubtedly are many Jewish laws that need to be revised because of this advanced understanding. Moreover, it is of utmost importance that it be realized that the ultimate goal is the correct observance of every Biblical regulation. It is true that rabbinic interpretations have been made for the purpose of upholding, clarifying, and delimiting the Bible. However, many rabbinic conclusions have to be revised to agree more closely with the intent of the Pentateuch. The Bible (Deut. 17 8–11) gives authority to the judges and leaders of each generation to interpret the Biblical laws according to their understanding. It is therefore only reasonable, now that the Jewish state has been revived, that a complete re-examination of Jewish law be accomplished.

Nowadays, the laws derived from the Mishnah and Talmud are followed (as should be the case) even if the regulations clearly contradict Biblical statements. No modern rabbinic authority goes back to the Bible to decide a problem in a way contrary to prevailing interpretation. The farthest back anyone goes is to the Mishnah and Talmud. What is needed is a re-examination of the Biblical regulations, and the determination if the accepted interpretations properly express the intent of the Pentateuch. To a limited extent this was attempted in presenting Part IV concerning the rationale for the Biblical laws. However, since the stated conclusions are only one person's opinion, the presented interpretations can only be taken as a possible theoretical explanation. Instead, what is needed is for the entire Jewish legal development to be reviewed by a Sanhedrin, taking into consideration not only Talmudic law but also modern exegesis of the Bible. This does not mean that Talmudic explanations are to be discarded. In many cases no changes will be needed, and in other instances only slight modifications are warranted. Occasionally, however, major revisions will be necessary. Only by accomplishing such a task can we hope to observe properly all the Biblical regulations. Many of the Mishnaic and Talmudic interpretations which were warranted at the time they were made are no longer current and need revision. Nevertheless, until a Sanhedrin is convened, and until legal modifications are made, if any, Jewish law as now developed must be rigidly followed.

What is here being requested is that a Sanhedrin, or authoritative legal body, be convened, having members of greater knowledge and capability than the Mishnaic and Talmudic authorities. These modern scholars should use the Pentateuch as the main basis for their decisions. Under no circumstances is this suggestion meant to undermine rabbinic authority, but rather to strengthen it. By convening a Sanhedrin many antiquated interpretations of the Bible can be updated. In the process, the Biblical regulations will gain the support of the Jewish people, and will be observed. If this is not done, the modern generation will say that the Bible, as interpreted, does not recognize recent scientific advances. The older generation has to realize also that the Talmudic interpretations are not sacrosanct, and can be revised by a properly constituted legal body. Blindly following the usual Biblical interpretations could occasionally lead to non-beneficial results because of incorrect observance of the Bible, with consequent harm to the State of Israel.

ABBREVIATIONS

ANET	*Ancient Near Eastern Texts Relating to the Old Testament*
ARAB	*Ancient Records of Assyria and Babylonia*
ARE	*Ancient Records of Egypt*
CEN	*Chemical and Engineering News*
DOTT	*Documents from Old Testament Times*
EB	*Encyclopedia Britannica*, 1958 edition
EZI	*Encyclopedia of Zionism and Israel*
JE	*Jewish Encyclopedia*, Funk and Wagnalls Co., 1901–1907
JNES	*Journal of Near Eastern Studies*
TP	*Tiglath Pileser III* by Abraham S. Anspacher, 1912
WP	*Washington Post*

REFERENCES

INTRODUCTION

1. *EB*, Vol. 3, p. 508, under Bible.
2. *JE*, Vol. 3, p. 176, under Bible Exegesis.
3. For example, S.R. Driver, *Introduction to the Literature of the Old Testament*, 1897; published by Meridian Books, 1956.
4. *EB*, Vol. 2, pp. 232ff, under Archaeology.
5. Werner Keller, *The Bible as History*, William Morrow and Co., N.Y., 1957, Translated by W. Neil.
6. See e.g. M.L. Margolis and A. Marx, *A History of the Jewish People*, Jewish Pub. Soc., Phila., Pa., 1927, pp. 121, 201-2.
7. C. Darwin, *Origin of Species*, 1872; Mentor Books, 1958.
8. H.J. Sanders, "Chemistry and the Solid Earth", *CEN*, Oct. 2, 1967, p. 19A.
9. *EB*, Vol. 22, p. 468, under Trichinosis.

PART I
CHAPTER ONE

1. H.J. Sanders, "Chemistry and the Solid Earth", *CEN*, Oct. 2, 1967, p. 19A.
2. W.L. Stokes, *Essentials of Earth History*, 2nd ed., Prentice-Hall Inc., N.J., 1966, p. 146.
3. *ibid.* p. 15.
4. *EB*, Vol. 2, pp. 252, 255, 259C, under Archaeology.
5. A. Scheinfeld, *Your Heredity and Environment*, J.B. Lippincott Co., N.Y., 1965.
6. R.W. Prehoda, "Perennial Youth—A Forseeable Reality?", *Industrial Research*, Aug. 1966.
7. See e.g. *EB*, Vol. 2, p. 365, under Ark, where it is stated that before the rise of modern scientific views it was believed that there were fewer than 100 species of quadrupeds and fewer than 200 species of birds.
8. *EB*, Vol. 18, p. 951, under Rainbow.
9. *EB*, Vol. 18, p. 432, under Precipitation.
10. Paul A. Moody, *Genetics of Man*, W.W. Norton and Co., Inc., N.Y., 1967, p. 169.
11. Leonard Cottrell, *The Quest for Sumer*, G.P. Putnam's Sons, N.Y., 1965, p. 131.
12. George Roux, *Ancient Iraq*, World Pub. Co., Cleveland, 1964, p. 100.

13. *EB*, Vol. 10, p. 374, under Glacial Epoch.
14. Stokes, *op. cit.*, p. 33.
15. *ibid.*, p. 329.
16. Sanders, *op. cit.*, p. 35A.
17. "Microcontinents Sought", *Science News Letter*, Oct. 9, 1965, p. 229.
18. *Science News*, Feb. 28, 1970, p. 229.
19. Stokes, *op. cit.*, p. 154.
20. "Water Triggers Eruptions of Volcanoes", *WP*, Dec. 20, 1965, p. A3.
21. Roux, *op. cit.*, p. 139.
22. James G. Macqueen, *Babylon,* Robert Hale Ltd., London, 1964, pp. 155, 166.
23. D.W. Thomas, ed., *Archaeology and Old Testament Study*, Oxford Univ. Press, London, 1967, p. 44.
24. D. Diringer, *The Alphabet*, Philosophical Library, N.Y., 1948, p. 195.
25. *Panim el Panim*, No. 367, May 13, 1966, p.14.
26. *EB*, Vol. 13, pp. 701–2, under Language.
27. George B. O'Toole, *Case Against Evolution*, Macmillan Co., 1925.
28. R. Zdansky, "Mutations and Evolution", p. 631 in *Encyclopedia of X-rays and Gamma Rays*, G.L. Clark, ed., 1963.
29. Stokes, *op. cit.*, pp. 89–90.
30. O'Toole, *op. cit.*
31. *EB*, Vol. 21, p. 700, under Symbiosis.
32. R. Moore, *Man, Time, and Fossils*, A.A. Knopf, pub., 1953, pp. 317ff.
33. Sanders, *op. cit.*, pp. 28A, 29A.
34. B.F. Howell, Jr., *Introduction to Geophysics*, McGraw Hill Book Co., N.Y., 1959, p. 37ff.
35. M.J. Aitken, *Physics and Archaeology*, Interscience Pub., N.Y., 1961, p. 101.
36. Theodor H. Gaster, *Myth, Legend and Custom in the Old Testament*, Harper and Row, Pub., N.Y., 1969.
37. *ibid.*, pp. xxvi–xxxiii, 3–35.
38. *EB*, Vol. 7, p. 176, under Deluge.
39. See Gaster, *op. cit.*, pp. 82–128.
40. Ignatius Donnelly, *Atlantis: The Antediluvian World*, Revised ed., E. Sykes, ed., Gramercy Pub. Co., N.Y., 1949, p. 86.
41. D. Winton Thomas, ed., *DOTT*, Harper and Row Pub., N.Y., 1961, pp. 17–24.
42. Gaster, *op. cit.*, pp. 132–138.
43. Albert T. Clay, *The Origin of Biblical Traditions*, Yale Univ. Press, 1923, Chap. VI, p. 125.
44. Sidney Smith, *Early History of Assyria to 1000 BC*, 1928, pp. 17–18.
45. Giuseppe Ricciotti, *The History of Israel*, Vol. I, Bruce Pub. Co., Milwaukee, 1955, p. 159.
46. Samuel N. Kramer, *The Sumerians, Their History, Culture and Character*, Univ. of Chicago Press, 1963, p. 328.
47. E. Meyer, *Aegyptische Chronologie*, 1904.
48. J.H. Breasted, *History of Egypt*, 2nd ed., Charles Scribner's Sons, N.Y., 1909, p. 597.
49. Ira M. Price, O.R. Sellers, E.L. Carlson, *The Monuments and the Old Testament*, Judson Press, Philadelphia, Pa., 1958, p. 411.

50. Arnold J. Toynbee, *A Study of History*, Vol. X, Oxford Univ. Press, 1954, p. 182.
51. O. Neugebauer, "Origin of the Egyptian Calendar", *JNES*, Vol. 1, 1942, pp. 396–403.
52. J.H. Breasted, *ARE*, Vol. I, 1906, p. 28.
53. C. Leonard Wooley, *The Sumerians*, W.W. Norton and Co., N.Y., pp. 21–26.
54. Kramer, *op. cit.*, pp. 46–49.
55. Harrison Forman, *Changing China*, Crown Pub., N.Y., 1948, p. 12.
56. *EB*, Vol. 5, p. 519, under China, History.

Chapter Two

1. M. B. Rowton, "Date of Hammurabi", *JNES* **17**, 97 (1958).
2. E. Meyer, *Geschichte des Alterums*, 1901.
3. A. Poebel, "Assyrian King List from Khorsabad", *JNES* **1**, 247–306, 460–490 (1942); **2** 56–90 (1943).
4. Arnold J. Toynbee, *A Study of History*, Vol. X, Oxford Univ. Press, 1954, p. 169ff.
5. James B. Pritchard (ed.), *ANET*, third edition, Princeton Univ. Press, 1969, p. 564.
6. Rowton, *loc. cit.*
7. Poebel, *op. cit.* **1**, 247–306 (1942).
8. D.D. Luckenbill, *ARAB*, Vol. I, 1926, p. 88.
9. *ibid.*, Vol. II, p. 158.
10. *ibid.*, p. 152.
11. Leo L. Honor, *Sennacherib's Invasion of Palestine*, Columbia Univ. Press, 1926, p. 11.
12. *EB*, Vol. 11, p. 135, under Hammurabi.
13. *ibid.*
14. *ibid.*
15. Pritchard, *ANET*, Princeton, N.J., 1960, pp. 163ff.
16. W.W. Davies, *The Code of Hammurabi and Moses*, 1905.
17. G.R. Driver and J.C. Miles, *The Babylonian Laws*, Vol. II, 1955.
18. L.W. King, *History of Babylon*, Vol. II, 1915.
19. George Roux, *Ancient Iraq*, World Pub. Co., Cleveland, 1964, p. 172.
20. Giuseppe Ricciotti, *The History of Israel*, Vol. I, Bruce Pub. Co., Milwaukee, 1955, p. 3.
21. James G. Macqueen, *Babylon*, Robert Hale Ltd., London, 1964, pp. 49ff.
22. Ricciotti, *op. cit.*, Vol. I, pp. 121, 126, 128.
23. Pritchard, *ANET*, 1960, pp. 163ff.
24. Jack Finegan, *Light From the Ancient Past*, Princeton Univ. Press, 1959, p. 66.
25. George A. Barton, *Archaeology and the Bible*, 2nd ed., 1917, p. 332.
26. A. Leo Oppenheim, *Ancient Mesopotamia*, Univ. of Chicago Press, 1964, p. 157.
27. *New Scientist*, No. 310, Oct. 25, 1962, p. 188.
28. "Population—part 2", *CEN*, Oct. 14, 1968, p. 92.
29. *New Scientist*, No. 310, Oct. 25, 1962, p. 188.

Chapter Three

1. J.H. Breasted, *ARE*, Vol. I, 1906, p. 32.
2. F. Josephus, *Against Apion* I, 14–16.

3. J.H. Breasted, *A History of Egypt*, 2nd edition, 1909.
4. Breasted, *ARE*, 5 Volumes, 1906.
5. J. van Seters, *The Hyksos*, Yale Univ. Press, 1966, pp. 152–3.
6. W.C. Hayes, *The Scepter of Egypt*, Part II, Harvard Univ. Press, 1959, p. 42.
7. J.B. Pritchard, *ANET*, 1950, p. 253.
8. A.J. Toynbee, *A Study in History*, Vol. X, Oxford Univ. Press, London, 1954, p. 205.
9. G. Steindorff and K.C. Seele, *When Egypt Ruled the East*, Univ. of Chicago Press, 2nd ed., 1957, pp. 34–40.
10. Josephus, *op. cit.*, I, 14.
11. Hayes, *op. cit.*, p. 3.
12. S.W. Baron, *Social and Religious History of the Jews*, 2nd ed., Vol. I, Col. Univ. Press, N.Y., 1952, p. 37.
13. Breasted, *A History of Egypt*, pp. 211–229.
14. Josephus, *op. cit.*, I, 14–16.
15. Hayes, *op. cit.*, pp. 6–8.
16. G. Ricciotti, *History of Israel*, Vol. I, Bruce Pub. Co., Milwaukee, 1955, p. 149.
17. Breasted, *A History of Egypt*, p. 216.
18. Josephus, *op. cit.*, I, 14.
19. Pritchard, *ANET*, 1950, p. 231.
20. John M. Holt, *Patriarchs of Israel*, Vanderbilt Univ. Press. Nashville, 1964, p. 191.
21. Hayes, *op. cit.*, p. 9.
22. Steindorff and Seele, *op. cit.*, p. 91.
23. Hayes, *op. cit.*, p. 9.
24. Breasted, *A History of Egypt*, pp. 225–227.
25. *ibid.*, p. 252.
26. Steindorff and Seele, *op. cit.*, p. 34.
27. Hayes, *op. cit.*, p. 81.
28. Flinders Petrie, *History of Egypt*, Vol. II, 1917, p. 88.
29. Hayes, *op. cit.*, pp. 110–111.
30. *ibid.*, pp. 106–111.
31. Breasted, *ARE*, Vol. II, pp. 144–152.
32. Breasted, *A History of Egypt*, p. 283.
33. Breasted, *ARE*, Vol. II, p. 172.
34. Breasted, *A History of Egypt*, p. 320.
35. Breasted, *ARE*, Vol. II, p. 194.
36. *ibid.*, p. 172.
37. Breasted, *A History of Egypt*, p. 339.
38. Hayes, *op. cit.*, p. 140.
39. D. Winton Thomas (ed.), *Archaeology and Old Testament Study*, Oxford Univ. Press, London, 1967, pp. 4–5.
40. George A. Barton, *Achaeology and the Bible*, 2nd ed., 1917, pp. 345–348.
41. Thomas, *op. cit.*, pp. 6–7.
42. Barton, *op. cit.*, 7th edition, 1937.

43. I.M. Price, O.R. Sellers, E.L. Carlson, *The Monuments and the Old Testament*, Judson Press, Phila., 1958, pp. 210-211.
44. Holt, *op. cit.*, pp. 40ff.

CHAPTER FIVE

1. S.H. Taqizadeh, "Old Iranian Calendars Again", *Bulletin of Oriental and African Studies, 14*, 603(1952).
2. D. Winton Thomas, *DOTT*, Harper and Row Pubs., 1958, pp. 201-203.
3. T.H. Robinson, *A History of Israel*, Oxford, London, 1932(1957 edition), p. 455.
4. George Smith, *Assyrian Eponym Canon*, 1875, p. 2.
5. Thomas, *DOTT*, p. 80.
6. A. Akabya, סדרי זמנים לפי המסורת, 1943.
7. Abraham S. Anspacher, *Tiglath-Pileser III*, Columbia Univ. Press, 1912.
8. George Smith, *op. cit.*
9. Theodore Von Oppolzer, "Canon der Finsternisse" in *Denkschriften der Kaiserlichen, Akademie der Wissenschaften*, Vol. 52, 1887.
10. P. Van Der Meer, *Ancient Chronology of Western Asia and Egypt*, 1947, p. 14.
11. George Smith, *op. cit.*, p. 75.
12. Daniel D. Luckenbill, *ARAB*, Vol. I, 1926, p. 269.
13. A.T. Olmstead, *History of Assyria*, Charles Scribner's Sons, N.Y., 1923, p. 202.
14. Luckenbill, *ARAB*, Vol. II, p. 437.
15. *ibid.*, p. 2.
16. *ibid.*, p. 3.
17. Also see George Smith, *op. cit.*, p. 175, who argues that since Sargon commenced the fight against Samaria in his first year of reign, he continues to describe the events relative to the conquest of Samaria, even though the conquest occurred two years later.
18. Luckenbill, *ARAB*, Vol. II, pp. 142-3.
19. Olmstead, *op cit.*, p. 283.
20. Luckenbill, *ARAB*, Vol. II, p. 143.
21. *ibid.*, pp. 200-201.
22. Thomas, *DOTT*, p. 72.
23. W. Petrie, *History of Egypt*, Vol. III, 1905, p. 227ff.
24. J.H. Breasted, *A History of Egypt*, 2nd ed., 1909, p. 600.

CHAPTER SIX

1. *Seder Olam Zuta*, Chapters 7 and 9.
2. A. Akabya, סדרי זמנים לפי המסורת, 1943, pp. 197, 210.
3. *ibid.*, p. 196.
4. See e.g. A. Leo Oppenheim, *Ancient Mesopotamia*, Univ. of Chicago Press, 1964, p. 341.
5. Raymond P. Dougherty, *Nabonidus and Belshazzar*, Yale Univ. Press, New Haven, 1929, p. 7.
6. *EB*, Vol. 5, p. 655, under Chronology.
7. Dougherty, *loc. cit.*
8. D. Winton Thomas, *DOTT*, Harper and Row, Pubs., N.Y., 1958, p. 79.
9. *ibid.*, p. 80.

10. *ibid.*, p. 79.
11. *ibid.*, pp. 78, 79.
12. *ibid.*
13. James G. Macqueen, *Babylon*, Robert Hale Ltd., London, p. 145, 1964.
14. George A. Barton, *Archaeology and the Bible*, 2nd edition, 1917, p. 383.
15. Thomas, *DOTT*, p. 90.
16. H.W.F. Saggs, *The Greatness that was Babylon*, Hawthorn Books Inc., N.Y., 1962, p. 145.
17. H. Bengtson (ed.), *The Greeks and the Persians from the Sixth to the Fourth Centuries*, translated by J. Conway, Delacorte Press, N.Y., 1968, p. 8.
18. A.T. Olmstead, *History of the Persian Empire*, Univ. of Chicago Press, 1948, p. 109.
19. *ibid.*, p. 214.
20. I.M. Price, O.R. Sellers, E.L. Carlson, *The Monuments and the Old Testament*, Judson Press, Phila., 1958, p. 342.
21. Olmstead, *op. cit.*, p. 37.
22. Francis R.B. Godolphin (ed.), *The Greek Historians*, Vol. 2, Random House Pub., N.Y., 1942, pp. 633ff.
23. Jack Finegan, *The Archaeology of World Religions*, Princeton Univ. Press, N.J., 1952, p. 84.
24. Robert W. Rogers, *History of Ancient Persia*, Charles Scribner's Sons, N.Y., 1929, p. 103.
25. Percy Sykes, *History of Persia*, Vol. I, 3rd edition, Macmillan, London, 1930, p. 143.
26. *ibid.*
27. Olmstead, *op. cit.*, p. 108.
28. Rogers, *op. cit.*, p. 86.
29. Godolphin, *op. cit.*, pp. 626, 628.
30. *Cambridge Ancient History, Persian Empire*, Vol. 4, 1926, p. 663.
31. Rogers, *op. cit.*, p. 19.
32. Jack Finegan, *Light from the Ancient Past*, Princeton Univ. Press, 1959, p. 233.
33. G. Cornfeld (ed.), *Adam to Daniel*, Macmillan Co., N.Y., 1961, p. 502.
34. *EB*, Vol. 23, p. 986, under Zoroaster.
35. R.C. Zaehner, *Dawn and Twilight of Zoroastrianism*, G.P. Putnam's Sons, N.Y., 1961, p. 33.
36. *ibid.*
37. Rogers, *op. cit.*, p. 18.
38. William F. Albright, *From the Stone Age to Christianity*, 2nd ed., Doubleday, N.Y., 1957, pp. 359ff.
39. Also see George W. Carter, *Zoroastrianism and Judaism*, Gorham Press, Boston, 1918, p. 38.
40. Thomas, *DOTT*, pp. 260-265.
41. George Rawlinson, *Five Monarchies*, Vol. 4, 1867, p. 532.
42. George Rawlinson, *Ancient History*, 1900, p. 91.
43. Rawlinson, *Five Monarchies*, Vol. 4, 1867, p. 528.
44. Rawlinson, *Ancient History*, 1900, p. 91.
45. Olmstead, *op. cit.*, p. 376.

46. *Cambridge Ancient History, Assyrian Empire*, Vol. 3, 1929, p. 210.
47. Thomas, *DOTT*, pp. 260–265.
48. *ibid.*

CHAPTER SEVEN

1. JE, Vol. 10, 1907, p. 606, under Sabbatical Year and Jubilee.

PART II

CHAPTER TWELVE

1. D.W. Thomas, *DOTT*, Harper and Row Pubs., N.Y., 1958, p. 76.

PART III

1. Flavius Josephus, *Ant.* XI 8, par. 5.
2. Raphael Patai (ed.), *EZI*, Herzl Press and McGraw Hill, N.Y., 1971, p. 1043, under Six-Day War of 1967.

CHAPTER SIXTEEN

1. J.C. Stobart, *The Grandeur that was Rome*, 4th edition, revised by W.S. Maguinness and H.H. Scullard, F.A. Praeger, Pub., N.Y., 1961, p. 2.
2. F. Lee Benns, *Europe Since 1914*, 8th edition, Appleton-Century Crofts Inc., N.Y., 1954, pp. 133, 406.
3. George Rawlinson, *Religions of the Ancient World*, 1883, p. 55.
4. Collier's Encyclopedia, 1954 edition, Vol. 3, p. 525, under Boar.
5. Albert Carnoy, *Iranian Mythology*, 1917.
6. *EB*, Vol 6, p. 939, under Cyrus.
7. Herodotus, *The Histories*, translated by A. de Sélincourt, Penguin Books, 1954, p 66.
8. *JE*, Vol. IV, p. 403, under Cyrus.
9. *EB*, Vol. 21, p. 215, under Sphinx.
10. George Rawlinson, *Ancient History*, revised edition, 1900, p. 177.
11. J. Hirst, "Religious Symbolism of the Unicorn", *Archaeological Journal* 41, 233–4 (1884).
12. R. Ettinghausen, "The Unicorn", *Freer Gallery of Art, Occasional Papers*, Wash. D.C., Vol. 1, No. 3 (1950).
13. M.S. Dimand, *Handbook of Mohammaden Art*, 1947, p. 7.
14. *EB*, Vol. 22, p. 702, under Unicorn.
15. B. Wilson, "Rice of the Unicorn," *Cassels's Magazine* 33, 611 (1901).
16. *EB*, Vol. 2, pp. 856–7, under Babylonia and Assyria.
17. A. Nutting, *The Arabs*, Clarkson N. Potter, Inc., Pub., N.Y., 1964, p. 51.
18. See for example, M.L. Margolis and A. Marx, *History of the Jewish People*, Jewish Pub. Soc. of America, Phila., 1927, pp. 755, 756, 760.
19. Cyril Falls, *The Great War*, Capricorn Books, N.Y., 1959, p. 323.
20. Ettinghausen, *loc. cit.*
21. William Muir, *Life of Mohammad*, revised edition, 1912, pp. xciii, xciv.
22. *JE*, Vol. VIII, p. 645, under Mohammed.
23. *ibid.*

24. *ibid.*, p. 646.
25. Muir, *op. cit.*, p. lix.
26. *JE*, Vol. I, p. 597, under Angelology.
27. Muir, *op. cit.*, p. 473.
28. *EB*, Vol. 15, p. 646, under Mohammad.
29. J. Glubb, *Short History of the Arab Peoples*, Stein and Day, Pub., N.Y., 1969, p. 49.
30. William Loftus, *Chaldea and Susiana*, 1857, p. 320.
31. *EB*, Vol. 6, p. 939, under Cyrus.
32. See e.g., H.G. Wells, *Outline of History*, Garden City Pub. Co., N.Y., 1920, p. 270.
33. *EB*, Vol. 6, p. 940, under Cyrus.
34. *ibid.*
35. Wells, *op. cit.*, p. 323.
36. *ibid.*, p. 327.
37. *Botsford and Robinson's Hellenic History*, 5th edition, revised by D. Kagan, Macmillan Co., 1969, p. 318.
38. *ibid.*, p. 329.
39. *ibid.*, p. 327.
40. *ibid.*, p. 329.
41. *ibid.*, p. 330.
42. Wells, *op. cit.*, pp. 327-8.
43. Botsford and Robinson, *op. cit.*, pp. 342-3.
44. Wells, *op. cit.*, p. 333.
45. Botsford and Robinson, *op. cit.*, pp. 344-5.
46. Wells, *op. cit.*, map on p. 335.
47. Botsford and Robinson, *op. cit.*, p. 344.
48. Wells, *op. cit.*, p. 335.
49. Taylor, *History of Mohammedanism*, 1834, p. 75.
50. George Sale, *The Koran*, translated, F. Waine and Co., London, 5th edition, 1856, pp. 11ff.
51. Taylor, *op. cit.*, pp. 74-75.
52. *Encyclopedia of Islam*, 1934, Vol. IV, pp. 21-23.
53. Tor Andrae, *Mohammed, the Man and His Faith*, translated by T. Menzel, C. Scribner's Sons, N.Y., 1936, p. 150.
54. P.M. Sykes, *History of Persia*, 1921, p. 505.
55. *Encyclopedia of Islam*, 1934, Vol. II, p. 589, under Ka'ba.
56. William Muir, *Life of Mahomet*, Vol. II, 1858, p. 35.
57. Muir, *Life of Mohammad*, revised edition, 1912, pp. 27-31.
58. *ibid.*, p. 32.
59. *ibid.*, p. 403.
60. *ibid.*, pp. 358-9, 400.
61. *ibid.*, pp. 407-409.
62. Sale, *loc. cit.*
63. Muir, *op. cit*, revised ed., pp. 408-409.
64. *ibid.*, p. 412.
65. P.K. Hitti, *History of the Arabs*, 8th edition, Macmillan and Co., Ltd., London, 1963, p. 119.

66. Muir, *op. cit.*, revised ed., pp. ci, 469.
67. *ibid.*, p. ci.
68. *ibid.*, pp. 468ff.
69. Glubb, *op. cit.*, p. 30.
70. Sale, *op. cit.*, p. 83 of Introduction.
71. *ibid.*, pp. 4-5.
72. *JE*, Vol. VIII, p. 538, under Michael.
73. Muir, *op. cit.*, revised ed., p. 72.
74. Hitti, *op. cit.*, p. 100.
75. *EB*, Vol. 1, p. 567, under Alexander the Great.
76. Muir, *op. cit.*, revised edition, p. xxvi.
77. *ibid.*, pp. xlvii-xlviii.
78. *ibid.*, p. 518.
79. *ibid.*, p. 514.
80. *ibid.*, p. 55.
81. *ibid.*, pp. xiv, 72.
82. *ibid.*, pp. 480ff.
83. *JE*, Vol. VII, p. 150, under Jerusalem, Modern.
84. *EB*, Vol. 13, p. 7, under Jerusalem, History.
85. *ibid.*
86. *EB*, Vol. 12, p. 732, under Israel.
87. Patai, *EZI*, pp. 1192-1204, under War of Independence.
88. *Israel Digest*, American edition, Vol. X, No. 14, July 14, 1967, p. 4.
89. *Panim el Panim*, Nov. 24, 1967, p. 10.
90. *EB*, Vol. 13, p. 148A, under Jordan.
91. Patai, *EZI*, p. 1128, under Transjordan.
92. *ibid.*, p. 1129.
93. *ibid.*, pp. 80-81, under Armistice Agreements.
94. Patai, *EZI*, p. 1152, under United Nations and Palestine-Israel.
95. *Maariv*, August 9, 1970, p. 1.
96. Y. Gur, *Hebrew Dictionary* (in Hebrew), 2nd edition, Dvir Co., Ltd., Tel-Aviv, 1947, pp. 228, 537.
97. Patai, *EZI*, p. 1109, under Terrorist Organizations, Arab.
98. "Terror at the Olympics", *Newsweek*, September 18, 1972, p. 12.
99. *Maariv*, September 11, 1972, p. 3.
100. *EB*, Vol. 6, p. 940, under Cyrus.
101. *EB*, Vol. 7, p. 59, under Darius the Great.
102. *EB*, Vol. 17, pp. 555-6, under Persia.
103. Edwyn R. Bevan, e.g., frequently references passages from Chapter 11 in Daniel, in his book, *House of Seleucus*, Edward Arnold, London, 1902 (reprinted 1966 by Barnes and Noble, Inc., N.Y.).
104. Charles A. Robinson, *Ancient History from Prehistoric Times to the Death of Justinian*, Macmillan Co., N.Y., 1951, p. 183.
105. *ibid.*, p. 208.
106. J.B. Bury, *History of Greece*, 3rd edition, Macmillan and Co., Ltd., 1956, p. 268.
107. Herodotus, *The Histories*, Book VII, 22ff.

108. C.A. Robinson, *op. cit.*, p. 214.
109. Wells, *op. cit.*, pp. 333-336.
110. Rawlinson, *Ancient History*, p. 177.
111. *ibid.*
112. *ibid.*
113. *ibid.*
114. *ibid.*, pp. 178-179.
115. Bevan, *House of Seleucus*, Vol. I, p. 62.
116. Rappaport, *History of Egypt*, Vol. I, p. 30.
117. Rawlinson, *Ancient History*, pp. 180-183.
118. *ibid.*, p. 183.
119. *EB*, Vol. 12, p. 584, under Ipsus, Battle of.
120. M.L. Margolis and A. Marx, *History of the Jewish People*, Jewish Pub. Society, Phila., 1945, pp. 128-9.
121. Bevan, *House of Seleucus*, Vol. I, pp. 178-9.
122. *ibid.*, p. 179.
123. *ibid.*, pp. 180-183.
124. Rappaport, *op. cit.*, p. 154.
125. Bevan, *House of Seleucus*, Vol. I, p. 186.
126. Rappaport, *op. cit.*, p. 155.
127. Edwyn Bevan, *History of Egypt under the Ptolemaic Dynasty*, 1927, p. 204.
128. *Cambridge Ancient History*, Vol. 7, 1928, p. 723.
129. Bevan, *House of Seleucus*, Vol. I, pp. 313-314.
130. *ibid.*, pp. 315-317.
131. Pierre Jouguet, *Macedonian Imperialism and the Hellenization of the East*, 1926, p. 214.
132. *ibid.*
133. Bevan, *History of Egypt under Ptolemaic Dynasty*, pp. 227-8.
134. *ibid.*, p. 228.
135. Bevan, *House of Seleucus*, Vol. I, p. 319.
136. Bevan, *History of Egypt under Ptolemaic Dynasty*, p. 228.
137. *ibid.*, p. 256.
138. Margolis and Marx, *op. cit.*, p. 129.
139. Bevan, *House of Seleucus*, Vol. II, p. 32.
140. *ibid.*, pp. 36-37.
141. *EB*, Vol. 18, p. 733, under Ptolemies.
142. Jouguet, *op. cit.*, p. 250.
143. Flavius Josephus, *Antiquities of the Jews*, Book XII, Chapter IV.
144. *JE*, Vol. XII, pp. 167ff, under Tobiads.
145. Bevan, *House of Seleucus*, Vol. II, pp. 39-42.
146. *ibid.*, pp. 42-44. Also see, map in Vol. I, p. 74.
147. *ibid.*, p. 43.
148. *ibid.*, pp. 40-41.
149. *ibid.*, p. 44.
150. *ibid.*, pp. 45-46.
151. *ibid.*, pp. 46-47.
152. *ibid.*, pp. 57, 296.

153. *ibid.*, p. 134.
154. *ibid.*, pp. 90-91.
155. *ibid.*, p. 96.
156. *ibid.*, pp. 108-111.
157. *ibid.*, p. 114.
158. *ibid.*, pp. 119-120.
159. *ibid.*, pp. 111, 113.
160. *ibid.*, p. 125.
161. *ibid.*, p. 133.
162. *ibid.*, p. 120.
163. *ibid.*, p. 125.
164. *ibid.*
165. *ibid.*, pp. 125-126.
166. *ibid.*, p. 130.
167. Bevan, *History of Egypt under Ptolemaic Dynasty*, p. 282.
168. *Cambridge Ancient History*, Vol. 8, 1930, p. 498.
169. Bevan, *House of Seleucus*, Vol. II, p. 128.
170. *ibid.*, p. 133.
171. *ibid.*, p. 134.
172. *ibid.*, p. 135.
173. *ibid.*
174. *ibid.*
175. *ibid.*
176. *ibid.*
177. *ibid*, p. 136.
178. *ibid.*
179. *ibid.*
180. *ibid.*
181. *ibid.*, p. 137.
182. *ibid.*
183. Bevan, *History of Egypt under Ptolemaic Dynasty*, pp. 287-291.
184. Bevan, *House of Seleucus*, Vol. II, p. 141.
185. I Maccabees 1 20-24.
186. Bevan, *House of Seleucus*, Vol. II, pp. 142-144.
187. *ibid.*, pp. 144-145.
188. **II Maccabees 5 1, 11-16.**
189. I Maccabees 1 29-36.
190. I Maccabees 1 41-53.
191. I Maccabees 1 33.
192. I Maccabees 1 45-47.
193. Margolis and Marx, *op. cit.*, p. 137.
194. Bevan, *House of Seleucus*, Vol. II, p. 174.
195. I Maccabees 1 60-61; 2 46.
196. Bevan, *House of Seleucus*, Vol. II, pp. 174-175.
197. *ibid.*, p. 176.
198. I Maccabees 2 69; 9 3, 18.

199. Margolis and Marx, *op. cit.*, pp. 139-140.
200. I Maccabees 5; II Maccabees 12.
201. I Maccabees 6 18-31.
202. I Maccabees 7 5-11.
203. Margolis and Marx, *op. cit.*, pp. 138-139.
204. *ibid.*, pp. 149-150.
205. *ibid.*, p. 162.
206. Edward Fox, *William Hohenzollern and Company*, 1918, p. 85.
207. Baroness Von Larisch, *Behind the Scenes with the Kaiser*, Vol. I, 1922, p. 22.
208. Wells, *op. cit.*, p. 1008.
209. *EB*, Vol. 23, p. 623, under William II.
210. *ibid.*, pp. 623-624.
211. Fox, *op. cit.*, p. 236.
212. Von Larisch, *op. cit.*, p. 43.
213. *ibid.*, p. 106.
214. *ibid.*, p. 267.
215. *ibid.*, p. 328.
216. *Last of the War Lords*, G. Richards Ltd., London, 1918, p. 271.
217. Von Larisch, *op. cit.*, p. 356.
218. Virginia Cowles, *The Kaiser*, Harper and Row, Pub., N.Y., 1963, p. 194.
219. Von Larisch, *op. cit.*, Vol. II, 1922, pp. 225-226.
220. *Peace Handbooks*, Vol. VII, 41, London, 1920, p. 41.
221. *EB*, Vol. 11, p. 395, under Heligoland.
222. Rasmus Anderson, *Norse Mythology*, 1901, p. 296.
223. *EB*, Vol. 11, p. 395, under Heligoland.
224. *EB*, Vol. 11, p. 395, under Heligoland Bight.
225. *Peace Handbooks*, Vol. VII, 41, London, 1920, p. 30.
226. *EB*, Vol. 23, p. 752, under World War I.
227. Wells, *op. cit.*, pp. 1044-9.
228. *EB*, Vol. 21, p. 786, under Tanks.
229. *EB*, Vol. 1, pp. 469-470, under Air Warfare.
230. *EB*, Vol. 21, p. 492, under Submarine.
231. Wells, *op. cit.*, p. 1049.
232. *ibid.*, pp. 1048-1053.
233. Walter Langsam, *World Since 1914*, 1950, pp. 20-21.
234. Falls, *op. cit.*, Chapter III.
235. *EB*, Vol. 23, p. 765, under World War I.
236. *ibid.*, p. 757.
237. Thomas E. Lawrence, *Revolt in the Desert*, 1927.
238. *EB*, Vol. 23, p. 791C, under World War II.
239. Carlton Hayes, *Contemporary Europe Since 1870*, 1953, pp. 635-644.
240. *EB*, Vol. 23, pp. 791P-791S, under World War II.
241. George Mihan, *Looted Treasure*, 1944, pp. 9, 17.
242. James Lorimer, *Survival, the Salvage of Art in War*, 1950, pp. 262-265.
243. A. Blum and R. Tatlock, *Short History of Art*, 1926, pp. 5-13.

244. *EB*, Vol. 23, pp. 791B, 791P, 792C, under World War II; Vol. 14, p. 27, under Libya.
245. *EB*, Vol. 11, p. 598B, under Hitler, Adolf.
246. Jean Lugol, *Egypt and World War II*, 1945, p. 8.
247. Leon Poliakov, *Harvest of Hate*, 1954, pp. 110-114.
248. George F. Owen, *Archaeology and the Bible*, Fleming H. Revell Pub. Co., N.J., 1961, p. 166.
249. G.F. Rodwell, *Etna: History of the Mountain*, 1878, pp. 3, 7-9.
250. *EB*, Vol. 24, Plate 17, Map of Italy.
251. L. Shapiro, *They Left the Back Door Open*, 1944, p. 53.
252. *EB*, Vol. 23, p. 792D, under World War II.
253. *EB*, Vol. 23, pp. 792D-792E, under World War II.
254. Wells, *op. cit.*, Doubleday and Co., 1956 edition, Chapter 39.
255. Rufus Learsi, *Israel: A History of the Jewish People*, World Pub. Co., N.Y., 1949, Chapters 64-67.
256. Howard M. Sachar, *Course of Modern Jewish History*, Dell Pub. Co., N.Y., 1958, Chapter 17.
257. Learsi, *op. cit.*, p. 584.
258. *EB*, Vol. 8, p. 871, under Europe.
259. H.S. Hughes, *Contemporary Europe, A History*, 2nd edition, Prentice-Hall, N.J., 1966, pp. 22-24.
260. *Visitors Guide to the United Nations*, May 1954, p. 5.
261. For a picture of the Secretariat building, see e.g. Jacob A. Rubin, *Pictorial History of the United Nations*, Thomas Yoseloff, Pub., N.Y., 1962, p. 262.
262. A. Vandebosch and W.N. Hogan, *The United Nations; Background, Organization, Functions, Activities*, McGraw Hill Book Co., N.Y., 1952, p. 190.
263. For a picture of the Peace Palace, see e.g. Jacob A. Rubin, *op. cit.*, p. 184.
264. Vincent J. Esposito (editor), *Concise History of World War II*, F.A. Praeger, Pubs., N.Y., 1964, pp. 198-212.
265. Learsi, *op. cit.*, p. 648.
266. Patai, *EZI*, p. 1217, under White Paper of 1939.
267. *JE*, Vol. 10, p. 251, under Pseudo-Messiahs.
268. Patai, *EZI*, pp. 1143-1146, under United Nations and Palestine-Israel.
269. John W. Foster, *Arbitration and the Hague Court*, 1904, pp. 58-59.
270. Manley O. Hudson, *The World Court*, 1934, p. 2.
271. *Encyclopedia Americana*, 1965 edition, Vol. 13, p. 617, under Hague Court.
272. Cordell Hull, *The Memoirs of Cordell Hull*, Vol. II, Macmillan Co., N.Y., 1948, Chapter 116.
273. *ibid.*
274. *Encyclopedia Americana*, 1965 edition, Vol. 15, p. 231, under International Conferences.

Chapter Seventeen

1. See Section 18.4 where the basis for these dates is given.
2. R. Grossman, *Hebrew-English Dictionary*, Dvir Pub. Co., 1938.

3. Giuseppe Ricciotti, *The History of Israel,* Vol. I, Bruce Pub. Co., Milwaukee, 1955, p. 50.
4. "Water found in Jerusalem", *The Jewish Week,* Feb. 13, 1969, p. 3.
5. Raphael Patai (editor), *EZI,* Herzl Press and McGraw-Hill, N.Y., 1971, p. 1027, under Shekel.
6. J.H. Hertz (editor), *The Pentateuch and Haftorahs,* 1941, p. 80, comments on Gen. 23 7.

Chapter Eighteen

1. "Super Clean Nuclear Explosive", *WP,* May 12, 1968, p. A23.
2. "New Commercial Center for Bethlehem", *Israel Digest,* Vol. XI, No 17, Aug. 23, 1968, p. 2.
3. S. Grayzel, *History of the Jews,* Jewish Pub. Soc., Phila., 1947, p. 760.
4. "Petah Tikvah in the Plains of the Jordan", *Panim el Panim,* No. 497, Nov. 29, 1968, p. 9.
5. R. Patai (editor), *EZI,* p. 881, under Petah Tikva.
6. *ibid.,* p. 1221, under Wine Industry in Israel.
7. *EB,* Vol. 17, p. 142, under Palestine, Operations in.
8. Cyril Falls, *The Great War 1914–1918,* Capricorn Books, N.Y., 1959, p. 401.
9. Cyril Falls, *Armageddon: 1918,* J.B. Lippincott Co., Phila., 1964, pp. 141-2.
10. *ibid.,* p. 141.
11. Falls, *The Great War,* p. 405.
12. *EB,* Vol. 17, p. 140, under Palestine, Operations in.
13. Falls, *The Great War,* p. 324.
14. Rufus Learsi, *Israel: A History of the Jewish People,* World Pub. Co., N.Y., 1949, p. 578.

Chapter Nineteen

1. *EB,* Vol. 9, pp. 342–349, under Flag.
2. Claire Sterling, "Aswan Dam: Predictions Came True with a Vengeance", *WP,* Feb. 15, 1971, p. A18.
3. M.L. Margolis and A. Marx, *History of the Jewish People,* Jewish Pub. Soc., Phila., 1927, p. 679.
4. Raphael Patai, *EZI,* p. 444, under Hadera, and p. 1024, under Sharon.
5. *ibid.,* p. 881, under Petah Tikva.
6. Solomon Grayzel, *History of the Jews,* Jewish Pub. Soc., Phila., 1947, Chapter VII.

Chapter Twenty

1. Zev Vilnay, *The New Israel Atlas,* Israel Univ. Press, Jerusalem, 1968, p. 33.

Chapter Twenty-One

1. See e.g. J. D. Eisenstein, *Ozar Dinim u Minhagim,* 1917, (in Hebrew), under תחיית המתים, where it is stated that the Rambam asserts that there is no hint in the Bible about resurrection of the dead.
2. See also Joseph Albo, *Sefer Ha'ikkarim,* Book I, Chapter 23, who states that belief

in resurrection is not from the Bible, and is not a fundamental principle of Judaism, although the concept is well accepted.

Part IV

1. *JE*, Vol. IV, p. 181, under Commandments, the 613.

Chapter Twenty-Four

1. *EB*, Vol. 23, p. 115, under Veterinary Science.
2. *EB*, Vol. 7, p. 414, under Diptera.
3. "Egypt Hunts Drug to Halt Spread of Scourge of Nile", *WP*, March 20, 1969, p. E2.

Chapter Twenty-Five

1. Frederick Eberson, *Man Against Microbes*, 3rd edition, Ronald Press Co., N.Y., 1963, p. 388.
2. John D. Porterfield (ed.), *Community Health Its Needs and Resources*, Basic Books, Inc., N.Y. and London, 1966, p. 148.
3. Harold S. Diehl, *Healthful Living*, 7th edition, McGraw Hill Book Co., N.Y., 1964, p. 426.
4. C.E.A. Winslow, *Man and Epidemics*, Princeton Univ. Press, 1952, p. 141.
5. Eberson, *op. cit.*, p. 77.
6. Dr. T.R. Van Dellen, "Danger of Uncooked Pork", *WP*, June 4, 1969, p. B7.
7. Wilson G. Smillie, *Preventive Medicine and Public Health*, 2nd edition, Macmillan Co., N.Y., 1958, p. 141.
8. Winslow, *loc. cit.*
9. B. Silcock, "Indication of Tiny Disease Agent Challenges Concepts of Biology", *WP*, Jan. 26, 1967, p. A23.
10. *EB*, Vol. 22, p. 538, under Tularemia.
11. Eberson, *op. cit.*, p. 332.
12. Diehl, *op. cit.*, p. 433.
13. Porterfield, *loc. cit.*
14. K.M. Reese, "Don't Eat Huskies' Livers", *CEN*, May 3, 1971, p. 48.
15. Clara M. Taylor and O.F. Pye, *Foundations of Nutrition*, 6th edition, Macmillan Co., N.Y., 1966, p. 207.
16. Betty C. Hobbs, *Food Poisoning and Food Hygiene*, Edward Arnold and Co., London, 1953.
17. Dr. T.R. Van Dellen, "Shellfish Viruses", *WP*, Jan. 13, 1966.
18. Winslow, *op. cit.*, p. 137.
19. "Steamed Clams Cause Hepatitis", *WP*, April 1, 1967, p. B4.
20. "Warning Issued on Bay Food", *WP*, June 19, 1969, p. F1.
21. R.H. Clinton, "The Effect of Pollution", *Water and Wastes Engineering*, Oct. 1970, pp. 54–55.
22. "Oysters Don't Glow in Dark", *CEN*, July 19, 1971, p. 52.
23. "Most Tuna Safe to Eat", *WP*, Feb. 5, 1971, pA3.
24. "Ubiquitous Mercury", *Science News*, Nov. 7, 1970, p. 366.
25. "Fish Processors Scored", *WP*, May 22, 1971, p. A1.

26. "Woman on Fish Diet Suffered Mercury Damage to Brain", *WP*, May 21, 1971, p. A1.
27. Taylor and Pye, *loc. cit.*
28. "Scourge of Nile", *WP*, March 20, 1969, p. E2.
29. J. H. Hertz (editor), *Pentateuch and Haftorahs*, 1941, comments on Lev. 11 13–19.
30. Joel C. Welty, *The Life of Birds*, W.B. Saunders Co., Phila., 1962, p. 356.
31. Eberson, *op. cit.*, p. 264.
32. Diehl, *op. cit.*, p. 431.
33. C.H. Curran, *Insects in Your Life*, Sheridan House, N.Y., 1951, pp. 231ff.
34. *EB*, Vol. 8, p. 623, under Entomology.
35. Winslow, *op. cit.*, p. 167.
36. *EB*, Vol. 12, p. 418, under Insect Bites and Stings.
37. "Most Destructive Creature on Earth", *Reader's Digest*, Sept. 1967, p. 175.
38. "The Ubiquitous Mouse", *New Scientist*, No. 348, July 18, 1963, p. 127.
39. Dr. T.R. Van Dellen, "The Sick Mouse", *WP*, Oct. 25, 1965.
40. Kenneth Walker, *The Story of Blood*, Philosophical Library, N.Y., 1958, p. 191.
41. Eberson, *op. cit.*, p. 195.
42. "Report on Shechita", *Young Israel Viewpoint*, April 30, 1968, p. 8.
43. Mosheh Epstein, *Torah Verified by Science*, 1928, p. 37.
44. Lewis Herber, *Crises in our Cities*, Prentice Hall Inc., N.J., 1965, p. 130.
45. M. Frobisher, L. Sommermeyer, R. Fuerst, *Microbiology in Health and Disease*, 12th edition, W.B. Saunders Co., Phila., 1969, p. 407.
46. Diehl, *op. cit.*, pp. 143ff.
47. Hobbs, *op. cit.*, p. 33.
48. Winslow, *op. cit.*, p. 117.
49. V. Cohn, "Doctors Urge Watch on Effects of Drugs", *WP*, Oct, 23, 1970, p. A3.
50. Joshua Lederberg, "Must We Re-Educate Average Physicians", *WP*, March 29, 1969, p. A17.
51. *Science News*, July 11, 1970, p. 30.
52. M. Mintz, "Smokers' Life Cut, Data Find", *WP*, Sept. 12, 1967, p. A1.
53. Marvin A. Block, *Alcoholism, Its Facts and Phases*, John Day, Co., N.Y., 1965, pp. 21, 24, 35, 44, 55, 81, and 262.
54. Herbert A. Carroll, *Mental Hygiene, The Dynamics of Adjustment*, 4th edition, Prentice Hall Inc., N.J., 1964, p. 56.
55. *ibid.*, pp. 224–6.
56. Herber, *op. cit.*, p. 125.
57. *ibid.*, p. 140.
58. Carroll, *op. cit.*, p. 11.
59. "Racism Held Peril to Mental Health", *WP*, May 10, 1969, p. A3.
60. T.I. Rubin, "Psychiatrist's Notebook", *McCall's Magazine*, Nov. 1967, p. 16.
61. *ibid.*
62. T.I. Rubin, "Psychiatrist's Notebook", *McCall's Magazine*, August 1968, p. 20.
63. Walker, *op. cit.*, p. 202.
64. *EB*, Vol. 18, p. 667J, under Psychiatry.
65. W. Just, "Many Fear Cowardice, GI's Psychiatrist Says", *WP*, February 28, 1967, p. A1.

66. Carroll, *op. cit.*, p. 79.
67. Dr. T.R. Van Dellen, "Emotions and the Heart", *WP*, April 6, 1967.
68. *EB*, Vol. 18, p. 667, under Psychiatry.
69. Dr. T.H. Van Dellen, "Rest as a Remedy", *WP*, Dec. 26, 1966, p. B11.
70. J.D. Ratcliff, "Are You Getting Enough Sleep?", *Reader's Digest*, May 1967, p. 109.
71. M. Friedman and R. Rosenman, "Behavior: Missing Link in Coronary Mystery?", *Chemical Week*, Feb. 26, 1966, p. 86.
72. "Ambitious Found Prone to Heart Ills", *WP*, Nov. 25, 1968, p. A14.
73. *Panim el Panim*, No. 613, March 5, 1971, p. 9.
74. Carroll, *op. cit.*, pp. 31-35, 110-111.
75. "Exercise", *Consumer Reports*, March 1968, p. 41.
76. Herber, *op. cit.*, p. 42.
77. "Tokyo Curbs the Car, Beats the Smog", *WP*, Aug. 3, 1970, p. A1.
78. Herber, *op. cit.*, p. 16.
79. *ibid.*, p. 63.
80. S. Auerbach, "Reports Tie Air Pollution to Deaths, Asthma, Eczema", *WP*, Nov. 12, 1969, p. A3.
81. "Air Pollution Appears to Sicken Plants", *WP*, June 30, 1968, p. F6.
82. "The Pill and Blood Clotting", *Parade Magazine (of the WP)*, June 30, 1968, p. 10.
83. Porterfield, *op. cit.*, p. 47.
84. Frobisher, Sommermeyer, Fuerst, *op. cit.*, p. 437.
85. *EB*, Vol. 23, p. 43, under Venereal Diseases.
86. David Reuben, "Venereal Disease", *McCall's Magazine*, June 1971, p. 64.
87. "VD Menace Alarming", *Science News Letter*, Nov. 12, 1966, p. 402.
88. *Time Magazine*, Sept. 1, 1967, p. 32.
89. "Syphilis and Gonorrhea: The Differences", *WP*, Aug. 13, 1968, p. C1.
90. "As Standard of Living Rises, So Does Cancer Rate", *WP*, April 26, 1965, p. A19.
91. R.M. Deutsch, "Putting the Clues to Work", *Reader's Digest*, July 1965, p. 164.
92. "Cancer, Is Intercourse a Factor?", *Time Magazine*, Nov. 14, 1969, p. 77.
93. Zev Schostak, "Guide to the Jewish Family Laws", *Young Israel Viewpoint*, May 27, 1971, p. 13.
94. Amram Scheinfeld, *Your Heredity and Environment*, J.B. Lippincott Co., N.Y., 1965, p. 603.
95. *ibid.*, p. 36.
96. "Birth Defects Seen Tied to Mumps, Chicken Pox", *WP*, March 26, 1966, p. A3.
97. V. Apgar, "New Ways to Save Your Unborn Child", *Ladies Home Journal*, Aug. 1966, p. 46.
98. Dr. T.R. Van Dellen, "Smoking While Pregnant", *WP*, March 11, 1971, p. B10.
99. Scheinfeld, *loc. cit.*
100. *ibid.*
101. *ibid.*, p. 647.
102. "Study Notes Perils of Infants Born of Incest", *WP*, Sept. 28, 1965, p. A5.
103. Scheinfeld, *op. cit.*, p. 655.
104. *ibid.*, p. 36.
105. Dr. T.R. Van Dellen, "Misconceptions", *WP*, Jan. 16, 1965.
106. Dr. T.R. Van Dellen, "False Pregnancy", *WP*, March 14, 1968, p. F5.

107. C.J. Singer and E.A. Underwood, *Short History of Medicine*, 2nd edition, Oxford Univ. Press, N.Y., 1962, p. 360.
108. *EB*, Vol. 9, p. 264, under Fire.
109. Eberson, *op. cit.*, p. 195.
110. Diehl, *op. cit.*, pp. 357-8.
111. *EB*, Vol. 5, p. 721P, under Circumcision.
112. *ibid.*, p. 722.
113. *ibid.*, p. 721P.
114. *ibid.*, p. 722.
115. Diehl, *op. cit.*, pp. 357-8.
116. B. Spock, *Baby and Child Care*, Pocket Books, Inc., N.Y., 1957, p. 156.
117. "Four P.M. Found Best for Killing Pests", *WP*, Dec. 29, 1966, p. A7.
118. *EB*, Vol. 15, p. 252B, under Menstruation.
119. *EB*, Vol. 11, p. 36, under Gynaecology.
120. "Cancer, Is Intercourse a Factor?", *Time Magazine*, Nov. 14, 1969, p. 77.
121. S.G. Kohl, "The Expectant Mother", *Redbook Magazine*, Nov. 1967, p. 29.
122. Singer and Underwood, *loc. cit.*
123. W.W. Bauer and W.E. Schaller, *Your Health Today*, 2nd edition, Harper and Row, Pubs., 1965, p. 167.
124. *EB*, Vol. 13, p. 957, under Leprosy.
125. Wilson G. Smillie, *Preventive Medicine and Public Health*, 2nd edition, Macmillan Co., N.Y., 1958, pp. 273-274.
126. Hertz, *op. cit.*, pp. 460-465.
127. *EB*, Vol. 13, p. 957, under Leprosy.
128. Eberson, *op. cit.*, p. 212.
129. *ibid.*, p. 218.
130. *EB*, Vol. 13, p. 958, under Leprosy.
131. "Germ Warfare Lab Finds Beards Imperil Workers", *WP*, Aug. 22, 1967, p. C2.
132. Diehl, *op. cit.*, p. 325.
133. *ibid.*, p. 324.
134. *EB*, Vol. 18, p. 123, under Poison Ivy.
135. Edward D. Kilbourne and W.G. Smillie, *Human Ecology and Public Health*, Macmillan Co., 4th edition, 1969, p. 258.
136. "The Shocking Medical Menace that Few Escape", *Good Housekeeping*, Aug. 1966, p. 70.
137. *EB*, Vol. 16, p. 31, under Mutilations and Deformations.
138. Dr. T.R. Van Dellen, "Stigma of Tattoo", *WP*, May 31, 1967, p. D7.
139. Dr. T.R. Van Dellen, *WP*, Oct. 5, 1966.
140. Dr. T.R. Van Dellen, "Sycosis of the Skin", *WP*, May 14, 1971, p. B10.
141. Morris Fishbein (editor), *Illustrated Medical and Health Encyclopedia*, H.S. Stuttman Co., Pubs., N.Y., 1963, Vol. 7, p. 1665, under Rabies.
142. Bauer and Schaller, *op. cit.*, p. 433.
143. "Germ Warfare Lab Finds Beards Imperil Workers", *WP*, Aug. 22, 1967, p. C2.
144. Dr. Frank Falkner, "Getting Rid of Lice", *WP*, Dec. 23, 1969, p. B8.
145. "A Hundred Years of Hair", *WP*, May 21, 1971.
146. Bauer and Schaller, *op. cit.*, p. 460.

147. R.E. Rogers and E. Jacobs, "Report on Venereal Disease", *Redbook Magazine*, May 1970, p. 26.

CHAPTER TWENTY-SIX

1. John D. Porterfield, editor, *Community Health, Its Needs and Resources*, Basic Books Inc., N.Y. and London, 1966, p. 102.
2. *McCall's Magazine*, July 1966, p. 30.
3. Jim Mills, "Drugs, Drink and Driving, Deadly Mixture", *American Motorist*, Sept. 1967, p. 18.
4. Harry W. Hepner, *Psychology Applied to Life and Work*, Prentice-Hall Inc., N.J., 4th edition, 1966, p. 377.
5. Nicholas deB. Katzenbach (chairman), *Challenge of Crime in a Free Society*, U.S. Govt. Printing Office, Wash., D.C., 1967.
6. *ibid.*, pp. v–xi, 3–17, 31–35, 44–45, 55, 57, 69, 76, 88, 95–110, 118, 141, 146, 160–165, 279.
7. *ibid.*, pp. 10, 104.
8. *ibid.*, p. 95.
9. *ibid.*, p. 97.
10. *ibid.*, p. 141.
11. *ibid.*, pp. v–xi.
12. *ibid.*, p. 55.
13. E.H. Sutherland and D.R. Cressey, *Principles of Criminology*, 6th edition, J.P. Lippincott Co., N.Y., 1960, p. 171.
14. Katzenbach, *op. cit.*, p. 88.
15. Sutherland and Cressey, *op. cit.*, p. 203.
16. Andre Siegfried, *Routes of Contagion*, (translated from the French), Harcourt, Brace, and World Inc., N.Y., 1960, p. 29.
17. "Four P.M. Found Best for Killing Pests", *WP*, Dec. 29, 1966, p. A7.
18. "Risk of Typhoid in a Sanitary World", *New Scientist*, No. 332, March 28, 1963, p. 677.
19. Frederick Eberson, *Man Against Microbes*, 3rd edition, Ronald Press Co., N.Y., 1963, p. 195.
20. C.M. Taylor and O.F. Pye, *Foundations of Nutrition*, 6th edition, Macmillan Co., N.Y., 1966, p. 230.
21. Porterfield, *op. cit.*, p. 148.
22. William Tuohy, "Arab Officers Ill-Trained, Uninspiring", *WP*, Aug. 3, 1970, p. A14.

CHAPTER TWENTY-SEVEN

1. Burton A. Weisbrod, *The Economics of Poverty*, Prentice-Hall, Inc., N.J., 1965, p. 166.
2. "Achievement and Firstborns", *Science News*, Vol. 99, March 13, 1971, p. 182.
3. "Prices up 5.5% in 1970", *WP*, Jan. 30, 1971, p. A1.
4. "Cost Rise Slowed in April", *WP*, May 22, 1971, p. A1.
5. *EB*, Vol. 18, p. 383, under Poverty.
6. "Racism and Health are Linked", *WP*, April 24, 1968, p. A11.
7. G.M. Smith, E.M. Gilbert, et al, *Textbook of General Botany*, 5th edition, Macmillan Co., N.Y., 1953, p. 73.

8. J.E. McMurtrey, Jr., "Environmental Nonparasitic Injuries", in *Plant Diseases, 1953 Yearbook of Agriculture*, Wash. D.C., pp. 95–96.
9. Lester A. Swan, *Beneficial Insects*, Harper and Row Pub., N.Y., 1964, p. 346.
10. Clyde M. Christensen, *The Molds and Man*, Univ. of Minnesota Press, 3rd edition, 1965, p. 97.
11. "Sugar Beet Disease", *New Scientist*, No. 308, Oct. 11, 1962, p. 69.
12. Jessie I. Wood, "Three Billion Dollars a Year" in *Plant Diseases, 1953 Yearbook of Agriculture*, U.S. Dept. of Agriculture, Wash. D.C., p. 7.
13. Smith, Gilbert, et al, *op. cit.*, p. 328.
14. *Protecting Our Food; 1966 Yearbook of Agriculture*, U.S. Govt. Printing Office, Wash. D.C., p. 42.
15. Harold J. Simon, *Microbes and Men*, McGraw Hill Book Co., N.Y., 1963, p. 49.
16. C.G. McWhorter and J.T. Holstun, Jr., "Science Against Weeds", in *Protecting Our Food, 1966 Yearbook of Agriculture*, U.S. Govt. Printing Office, Wash. D.C., p. 75.
17. Smith, Gilbert, et al, *op. cit.*, p. 108.
18. *EB*, Vol. 9, p. 880, under Fruit Farming.
19. J.H. Hertz, editor, *Pentateuch and Haftorahs*, p. 844, comments on Deut. 22 10.
20. *EB*, Vol. 3, p. 636, under Birds, Protection of.
21. Joel C. Welty, *The Life of Birds*, W.B. Saunders Co., Phila., 1962, p. 138.
22. *EB*, Vol. 3, p. 626, under Birds.
23. Swan, *op. cit.*, pp. 103ff.
24. C.W. Bennet, "Viruses a Scourge of Mankind" in *Plant Diseases, 1953 Yearbook of Agriculture*, U.S. Dept. of Agriculture, Wash. D.C., p. 19.
25. C.H. Hoffmann and L.S. Henderson, "The Fight Against Insects" in *Protecting Our Food, 1966 Yearbook of Agriculture*, U.S. Govt. Printing Office, Wash. D.C., p. 27.
26. Wood, *op. cit.*, pp. 1ff.
27. P.R. Miller and H. McGrath, "Plant Diseases and Nematodes" in *Protecting Our Food Supply, 1966 Yearbook of Agriculture*, U.S. Govt. Printing Office, Wash. D.C., p. 45.
28. "Nitrates Found in Baby Foods", *WP*, March 17, 1968, p. C9.
29. McMurtrey, Jr., *op. cit.*, p. 95.
30. "First DDT, Now PCB", *Science News*, Vol. 98, Oct. 24, 1970, p. 332.
31. "Greatest Threat to Sea Life Called DDT", *WP*, April 30, 1970, p. A7.
32. "DDT, Weedkiller Escape Total Ban", *WP*, April 19, 1971, p. A22.
33. Hoffmann and Henderson, *loc. cit.*
34. *WP*, Aug. 22, 1970, p. A4.
35. V. Cohn, "Simple Chemicals May Harm Genes", *WP*, April 28, 1968, p. A1.

Chapter Twenty-Eight

1. *EB*, Vol. 18, p. 433, under Precipitation.
2. "Weather Seeding Declared Proven", *WP*, July 20, 1967, p. A9.
3. G.M. Smith, E.M. Gilbert, et al, *Textbook of General Botany*, 5th edition, Macmillan Co., N.Y., 1953, p. 205.
4. J.E. McMurtrey, Jr., "Environmental, Nonparasitic Injuries", in *Plant Diseases, 1953 Yearbook of Agriculture*, U.S. Dept. of Agriculture, Wash. D.C., p. 94.

5. "Weather Modification Bids for Research Money", *CEN*, Feb. 7, 1966, p. 43.
6. C.A. Gosline, L.I. Falk, E.N. Helmers, "Evaluation of Weather Effects", Section 5, in *Air Pollution Handbook*, Magill, Holden, and Ackley, editors, McGraw-Hill Book Co., 1956.
7. "Pouring Oil on Troubled Sands", *Reader's Digest*, Aug. 1966, pp. 171ff. (Condensed from the *Rotarian* by Ruth S. Knowles)
8. E.D. Bergmann, "Scientific Progress Has Overcome Frontiers and Arid Deserts", *Young Israel Viewpoint*, Vol. 7, No. 2, May 31, 1968, p. 8.
9. "Meteorology: Israel's New Prophet", *Time Magazine*, Dec. 16, 1966, p. 77.
10. C.H. Hoffmann and L.S. Henderson, "The Fight Against Insects", in *Protecting Our Food, 1966 Yearbook of Agriculture*, U.S. Govt. Printing Office, Wash. D.C., p. 31.
11. Justus J. Schifferes, *Healthier Living*, 3rd edition, J. Wiley, and Sons, N.Y., 1970, p. 139.
12. *EB*, Vol. 3, p. 749, under Blood Transfusion.
13. *EB*, Vol. 16, p. 775, under Olive Oil.
14. *EB*, Vol. 9, p. 915, under Fumigation.
15. *EB*, Vol. 19, p. 899, under Salt.
16. Dr. T.R. Van Dellen, "Rats", *WP*, May 22, 1970, p. D4.
17. W.W. Dykstra, "Damage by Rodents and Other Wildlife", in *Protecting Our Food, 1966 Yearbook of Agriculture*, U.S. Govt. Printing Office, Wash. D.C., p. 70.
18. "Rat Control Hinges on Technical Environmental Approaches", *CEN*, Aug. 28, 1967, p. 31.
19. "Most Destructive Creature on Earth", *Reader's Digest*, Sept. 1967, p. 175.
20. Isabel B. Wingate, *Textile Fabrics and Their Selection*, 6th edition, Prentice-Hall Inc., N.J., 1970, pp. 263, 270.
21. *ibid.*, p. 262.
22. *ibid.*, p. 263.
23. *ibid.*, p. 272.
24. *Today's Health*, May 1967, p. 10.
25. "Cotton Socks Safest", *CEN*, Sept. 4, 1967, p. 78.
26. *EB*, 1958 edition, Vol. 8, pp. 987ff, under Explosives.

Concluding Remarks

1. See Maimonides' introduction to the Mishnah.
2. *ibid.*

INDEX

Aaron, brother of Moses, 39, 41, 46, 51–54, 64, 66, 117, 130, 134, 139, 140, 142–145, 147, 148, 340
Abdi-hiba, 55, 56
Abdon, son of Hillel, 61, 168, 170–172, 307
Abdullah, Emir of Transjordan, 405, 449, 529
Abiathar, the priest, 179
Abigail, wife of David, 180
Abihu, son of Aaron, death of, 142–144, 148
Abijam, king of Judah, 74, 77, 78, 186, 189, 190, 334, 335, 350
Abimelech, son of Gideon, 60, 168, 171, 172
Abinadab, 182, 184
Abiram, rebellion by, 147, 148
Abner, 175
Abraham, 3, 19, 29, 34, 36, 39–42, 57, 117, 122, 123, 129, 131–135, 142, 153, 279, 344, 403, 487, 506, 514, 531
Absalom, son of David, 181, 182, 184, 230, 253, 257
Accident prevention, 597–599
Achaemenes, 100
Achan, 41
Achish, king of Gath, 180
Achor, valley of, 488, 515
Adad-narari III, king of Assyria, 91
Adam, 5, 6, 10, 17, 18, 22–24, 117, 122, 123, 129–132, 134, 135, 332, 340, 344, 385
Aden, 451, 523
Adoption, 37, 38
Adullam, cave of, 175, 179
Adultery, 482, 569–571
Agag, 101
Age for military service, 619
Age of people, 17
Age of world, xx, 3, 15, 16, 23

Agricultural ordinances, 549, 550, 647–652
Agur, son of Jakeh, 282, 299
Ahab, king of Israel, 74, 78, 88, 90, 186, 187, 189, 190
Ahasuerus, king of Persia, 67, 93, 99–103, 107, 118, 321, 322, 327, 328, 390
Ahaz, king of Judah, 76, 81, 83–85, 87, 89, 187, 194, 199, 210, 241, 243, 336, 342, 353
Ahaziah, king of Israel, 74, 186, 189, 190
Ahaziah, king of Judah, 72, 75, 78, 79, 82–84, 187, 189–191, 336, 351
Ahijah, the Shilonite, 122, 123, 185, 190, 335, 345, 350
Ahmose I, pharaoh who enslaved the Israelites, 48–50, 52, 56, 117
Ahmose, princess 48, 49, 53, 56
Ai, 55, 165
Alcoholic drinks, avoidance of, 561, 592, 594, 598
Alcoholism, 562, 563
Alexander Balas, king of Syria, 415
Alexander the Great, 102, 104, 108, 109, 115, 323, 356, 363, 367, 368, 372, 379–381, 386, 387, 413, 416, 417
Alexandria, 420, 427–429
Algeria, 451
Alien, 482, 563, 564, 581, 601, 629, 631, 632, 638, 640, 642, 648
Allenby, General Sir Edmund, 491
Alphabetical arrangement, 248, 253, 256, 309, 310
Alphabets, 13
Altar, 140, 154, 156, 159, 429, 450, 534, 679, 688–690; building of, 330, 465, 466, 654, 677; in Egypt, 499, 518, 532; as a memorial, 166; position of, 453; purification of, 467, 468, 477

Amalek, 137, 140, 147, 177, 179, 180, 618
Amarna age, 48, 49, 55-58
Amasis, pharaoh, 97
Amaziah, king of Judah, 75, 79, 80, 83, 187, 191, 336, 337, 342, 352
Amaziah, priest of Bethel, 245
Amenhotep I, 48, 49, 52, 56
Amenhotep II, 48, 55
Amenhotep III, 30, 48, 55, 56
Amenhotep IV (Ikhnaton), 30, 48, 55, 56
Amman, 522
Ammon, Ammonites, 158, 178, 184, 214, 231, 233, 249, 448, 498, 522, 528, 532
Ammon, Children of, 60, 182, 213, 249, 436, 437, 522, 523
Amnon, son of David, 182, 184
Amon, king of Judah, 76, 83, 188, 191, 338, 339, 342, 353
Amos, the prophet, 122, 240, 241; book of, 122, 124, 240, 242, 245, 246, 479, 487, 488
Amram, father of Moses, 39-41, 53, 56
Angel; of Arabia, see Gabriel; of Babylonia, 360, 409, 411, 413, 414, 443; Captain of the army of the Lord, 403; of copper, 453; dressed in linen, 325, 360, 407-413, 443-445; of England, 360, 443-445, 448; of Germany, 360, 443-445; of Greece, 360, 408, 413; of the Jews, see Michael; of Persia, 360, 408, 411, 413; of war, 166, 408
Angels, 102, 358, 360, 370, 372, 374, 375
Animal foods, 8, 550-556
Animals; creation of, 5; damages to or by, 612-614; diseases of, 552, 622; loss of species by, 11; for sacrifices, 646, 653-657, 659-674, 678; survival of Deluge by, 8, 10, 11; symbolism of, 325, 365-367, 372, 377, 378, 386, 498, 510, 516
Anointing oil, 676, 687, 690, 691
Anshan, 100, 368
Antediluvian leaders, 23-25
Antigonus, general of Alexander, 417
Antioch, 418, 419
Antiochus I, Soter, 415
Antiochus II, Theos, 415, 417, 419, 421
Antiochus III, the Great, 415, 419-425
Antiochus IV, Epiphanes, 415, 426-431
Antiochus V, Eupator 415
Antipater, 368, 416
Apadna, 438
Apophis, Hyksos ruler, 50

Apportionment of the land; see land distribution
Arab countries, 356, 365, 370, 371, 400, 401, 406, 448, 449, 451, 452, 477, 483, 512, 528, 530
Arabia, 195, 197, 364, 366, 372-375, 381, 437, 451
Arabian empire, 363, 367, 369, 371, 373, 375-377, 381, 387, 400, 448
Arad, king of, 147
Aram, 26, 79, 184, 193, 194, 196, 487
Aram-Naharaim, 254, 259
Aram-Zobah, 254, 259
Aramaic, 326, 331
Ararat, 17
Araunah, the Jebusite, 176
Arbela, battle of, 380
Ariaramnes, 100
Arioch, Nebuchadnezzar's captain, 361, 362
Ark, Noah's, 8
Ark of the Law, 62, 148, 151, 160, 163, 174, 178, 182, 184, 280, 341, 687-690, 695
Armistice agreement, with Israel, 405, 406, 449 500, 528, 529
Arrhidaeus, 368
Arsames, 100
Arses, king of Persia, 94
Art treasures, 437, 438
Artachshast, king of Persia, 100, 103
Artachshaste, king of Persia, 103-105
Artaxerxes I, 94, 102, 104, 108, 110
Artaxerxes II, 68, 94, 104, 105, 107-110, 118, 327-331
Artaxerxes III, 94
Asa, king of Judah 72-74, 77, 78, 186, 190, 332, 334, 335, 342, 350
Asahel, brother of Joab, 175
Asaph, musician, 123, 252, 256, 259, 260, 278-280, 343, 347
Ashdod, 194, 210, 491, 528
Asher; son of Jacob, 19; tribe of, 340
Ashkelon, 491, 528
Ashur, 132
Asia, 368, 416, 423, 451, 477, 530
Asia Minor, 360, 419, 421-424
Assar-uballit I, king of Assyria, 30, 32
Assurbanipal, king of Assyria, 89, 91
Assur-dan I, king of Assyria, 32, 33
Assur-dan III, king of Assyria, 91
Assur-nirari V, king of Assyria, 30, 33, 91, 247
Assyria, 26, 65, 85-87, 90-92, 193-199,

Assyria (continued)
  210, 249, 333, 367, 370, 475, 486, 492,
  498, 499, 502, 508, 518, 533, 534
Assyrian dates, 29-34, 86-92
Aswan Dam, 499
Athaliah, queen of Judah, 75, 79, 187, 190,
  336, 351
Athens, 426
Atomic bomb, 451
Atomic weapons, 484, 496, 530, 534
Austria, 437, 440, 441, 528
Austria-Hungary, 435, 448
Authorship of the Bible, 119ff
Avaris, 48, 50, 52
Avesta, 102
Azariah, companion of Daniel, 324
Azariah, king of Judah, 75, 79, 80, 81, 83,
  87, 88, 90, 187, 189, 191, 194, 199, 210,
  241, 243, 336, 337, 342, 352, 687
Azariah, son of Oded, 123, 350
Azariah, the priest, 123, 352

Baasa, king of Israel, 74, 77, 78, 186, 190
Babylon, Babylonia; 36, 38, 46, 85, 87, 91,
  93-98, 105, 107, 117, 118, 193-197,
  199, 210, 212-214, 229, 231, 233, 248,
  249, 300, 324, 325, 327, 329, 361-363,
  365-368, 370, 372, 373, 378, 380, 390,
  391, 407-414, 417, 419, 432, 444, 449,
  485, 486, 524; first dynasty, 27, 29, 57;
  formation of nation, 25-28; rivers of,
  255, 263, 281
Babylonian Chronicle, 82, 87, 96
Babylonian Exile, 69, 93, 105-108, 118,
  193-196, 199, 210, 281, 308, 323, 330,
  332, 333, 341, 386, 444, 519
Bactria, 99
Balaam, 122, 144, 147, 148, 158, 524
Balak, king of Moab, 524
Balconies, of the Temple, 458ff
Balfour Declaration, 491, 528
Baltic Sea, 436
Baruch, son of Neriah, 122, 123, 189, 191,
  213-215, 229-231, 345, 354, 355
Bashan, 487, 492, 503, 532; conquest of
  people of, 144
Bathsheba, wife of David, 174, 181, 182,
  184, 254, 342
Behistun inscription, 99-101
Belgium, 435-437, 441, 528

Belshazzar, king of Babylon, 94, 98, 99, 324-
  326, 366, 377, 389
Belteshazzar (Daniel), 407
Benefits for observance of Biblical laws, xxii, 535ff
Benjamin; son of Jacob, 19, 21, 42, 44, 136,
  230; tribe of, 44, 114, 171, 332, 341, 347,
  475, 483
Benjamin of Tudela, 377
Berenice, daughter of Ptolemy II, 418
Berossus list, 23, 24
Beth-Horon, 431
Bethlehem, 164, 485
Bible; accuracy of text, xx; authorship, xxi,
  119ff; correctness of, xx, 1; criticism, v, xix,
  xxi, 119, 323; organization, xxi, 119ff
Biblical laws, rationale for, vi, xx, xxii, 535ff
Bildad, the Shuhite, 123, 301, 302
Bilharziasis, 548
Birds; permissible, 550, 551, 554, 555, 557;
  protection of, 648, 651; for purification,
  587, 588; for sacrifices, 653; sent out after
  Deluge, 23; survival of Deluge, 8
Birth rate, 43
Black stone, in Ka'ba, 377, 381-383, 385,
  389, 446
Blasphemer, 142, 143
Blood avenger, 598, 599, 604
Blood; avoidance of, 556-558; covering of,
  557; issue of, 144; placing of, 683, 684;
  sprinkling of, 663-677
Boaz, husband of Ruth, 123, 306-308, 344
Bodily damages, 609-612
Booths (sukkot), 162, 681, 686, 697
Borrowing, 614
Boundaries; extending of, 607, 683; of Israel,
  36, 145, 365, 371, 412, 449, 474, 475,
  485, 496, 524, 529, 616
Bozrah, 504, 523, 524
Bribes, 601
Bronze age, 7
Bulgaria, 441, 451, 530
Burnaburias I, Kassite king, 30, 33
Burnt-offering, 154, 155, 159, 468, 470, 471,
  562, 583, 587, 588, 592, 633, 653-657,
  659, 660, 662, 664-673, 677-679
Busaire, 523

Cain, son of Adam, 6, 122, 130, 131, 134
Caleb, 59, 113, 166, 167, 170, 340, 392
Calendar; Arabian, 375; Babylonian, 68, 71;

Calendar (continued)
  Egyptian, 25, 47; Jewish, 101, 684, 685; lunar, 408, 684; Persian, 68, 101, 328, 329; solar, 20, 25, 47, 684; Zoroastrian, 68
Calf, golden, 139, 140, 143, 154, 402, 448
Cambyses I, 100
Cambyses II, king of Persia, 94, 99-101, 103, 105, 327, 328, 372, 415, 419
Canaan, son of Ham, 26
Canaan, land of; 38-40, 49, 52, 55, 56, 59, 117, 129, 133, 135, 137, 142, 146, 152, 165, 166, 278; entrance into, 46, 47, 117
Canaanites, conquest of, 144, 167, 617
Canada, 440
Cappadocia, 417, 426
Carchemish, battle of, 96
Carians, 378
Carmel, 503, 505
Cassander, empire of, 380, 387
Cease-fire, with Israel, 406, 450
Census, 43, 44, 144, 147-150, 175, 176, 181, 547, 548
Chaldeans, 241, 242, 248, 300, 326, 367, 390
Chambers, of the Temple, 454ff
Cherub, 409, 410, 460
Childbirth, 6, 144, 485, 501, 519, 568, 584, 666
China, 25-28, 451, 477, 489, 498, 530
Chronicles, book of, 71, 73, 82-84, 120, 123, 125, 126, 185, 189, 192, 240, 308, 331-355, 390
Chronicles of the Kings of Israel, 70, 71, 86, 185, 331-333
Chronicles of the Kings of Judah, 70, 185, 331-334, 336
Chronology; 1ff; of time of Abraham, 39ff; Biblical periods of, xxi, 1; of creation era, 16; of Israelites in Egypt, 46ff; of the Judges, 58ff, 168; of the kings, 65ff; of Second Temple, 93ff; summary of, 116-118
Churchill, prime minister of England, 447
Cigarette smoking, 561
Cilicia, 422
Circumcision, 36, 135, 165, 431, 472, 570, 581, 582, 680
Cities, walled, 627
Cleopatra, wife of Ptolemy V, 424, 426
Clitus, friend of Alexander, 416
Cloud seeding, 674, 675
Commandments; observance of, 540; six-hundred thirteen, 537; ten, 134, 137, 139, 141, 152, 448, 458, 539

Continents; formation of, 9, 10, 12, 22, 117; originally one, 9, 12
Contraception, 43, 568, 569
Converts to Judaism, 475, 510, 533, 581
Cooking-area, 465
Cooking-yards, 461, 462
Coracesium, 422, 423
Coregnancy, 72, 73, 77, 79-81
Courts (for judgment), 602
Courts of the Temple, 453ff
Craterus, 368, 416
Creation, Epic of, 22
Creation; six days of, 4, 5; of the world, 3, 4, 16, 116, 117, 130, 135
Crete, 498, 533
Crime control, 563, 597, 599-615
Cubit, 8, 453, 475
Curses, for non-observance of Bible, 536-537
Cush, 26, 132, 195, 249, 451, 498
Cushan-rishathaim, king of Aram, 60
Cutting of skin, 589, 590
Cyprus, 498, 533
Cyrus I, 100
Cyrus II, the Great, 93, 94, 99-101, 103, 105-107, 109, 114, 118, 193, 199, 231, 321, 324, 326-328, 330, 331, 341, 343, 356, 363, 366-368, 372, 378, 379, 386, 390, 407-409, 411, 415
Czechoslovakia, 437, 441, 451, 530

Damascus, 194-197, 213, 214, 249, 419, 490, 495, 528
Damesek-Eliezer, 38
Dan; son of Jacob, 19, 44; tribe of, 44, 171, 341
Daniel, 97, 98, 103, 105, 106, 123, 300, 323-325, 360-362, 365, 366, 371-374, 376-379, 384-386, 389-401, 407-415, 442, 443, 445, 697; book of, xxii, 123, 125, 323-326, 356-450, 477, 484
Darius I, 67, 94, 95, 98-100, 102-107, 109, 114, 118, 231, 240, 241, 249, 251, 321-324, 326-328, 331, 390, 391, 411, 413-415
Darius II, 94, 104, 107-109, 328
Darius III, 94, 95, 103, 104, 379, 380, 413
Darius, the Mede, 93, 98-100, 103, 107, 118, 328, 390, 414
Darius, the Persian, 103, 104, 107, 328
Dathan, rebellion by, 147, 148

David, king of Israel, 58, 61, 62, 71, 84, 113, 116, 117, 123, 172–177, 179–182, 184, 186, 190, 230, 252–263, 277–282, 304, 306–308, 311, 312, 334, 335, 340–343, 347, 392, 404, 472, 480, 485, 529, 686, 696

David, Messianic ruler, 197, 452, 453, 477, 485, 487, 489, 491, 493, 494, 497, 498, 502, 503, 509, 519, 529, 696

David, tower of, 304

Day of Atonement; see Festivals

Day of Blowing the Shofar; see Festivals

Day of the Lord, 357, 477, 479–483, 513, 529

Dead bodies, contact with; animal, 550–556, 558; human, 147, 552, 558, 561, 562, 579–581, 594–596, 605, 677

Dead Sea, 466, 467, 475, 478, 480, 483, 494, 523, 531

Dead Sea Scrolls, 126

Death punishment; 604–605, 608, 611, 636; by burning, 576, 595, 596; by stoning, 575, 596, 609

Deborah, judge, 59, 60, 122, 168, 171, 172

Debts, remission of, 638–640

Dedan, 26, 451, 523

Delian League, 416

Deluge, 8–13, 15–17, 20, 22, 23, 25, 27, 28, 66, 117, 131, 132, 135, 440

Demetrius I, Soter, 415

Denmark, 437, 441, 528

Desert of the Sea, 195

Detestable thing, 430

Deuteronomy; 122, 124, 129, 130, 150–152, 167, 168, 390, 396, 399, 482, 524, 525; early names for, 152–153, 156–164, 396

Devir, 687; see also holy-of-holies

Dietary restrictions, 5, 8, 144, 550–563

Dinah, daughter of Jacob, 19, 135, 136

Disease prevention, 549–596

Divorce, 569, 571, 577

Divorcees, 595, 645

Doorposts, 543, 544

Drugs, 561, 571, 598

Dry measure, 469, 607

Dumah, 195, 197

Eber, 18, 26, 57, 117, 132

Ecclesiastes, 123, 125, 311–321

Economic policies, 624–652

Eden, garden of, 5, 6, 22, 452, 507, 533

Edom, 131, 133, 198, 213, 214, 231, 233, 245, 249, 254, 255, 281, 311, 436, 437, 448, 452, 481, 482, 487, 498, 502, 504, 513, 522–525, 528, 531, 532

Educational practices, 543–545

Eglon, king of Moab, 60

Egypt; art of, 438; formation of, 25–26; modern, 364, 376, 405, 406, 437, 443–449, 451, 477, 481, 486, 492, 495, 496, 498, 499, 502, 508, 518, 528, 530–534, 616; return to, 546–548; river of, 36, 475; under the Pharaohs, 21, 25, 28, 39–44, 46–57, 92, 96, 97, 99–101, 117, 133–140, 147, 195, 198, 212–214, 229, 231, 233, 249, 369, 394, 397, 487; under the Ptolemies, 379, 417–422, 424, 426–430; under the Romans, 360

Egyptian dynasties; 47, 50, 137; eighteenth, 47ff

Ehud, son of Gera, 59, 60, 122, 168, 171, 172

Ekron, 491, 528

El Alamein, 437, 438, 443

Elah, king of Israel, 74, 186, 190

Elam, 26, 213, 229, 377, 498, 522, 524, 533

Elderly, respect for, 563, 565

Eleazer, son of Aaron, 41, 167

Elephantine papyrus, 104, 108

Eli, the priest, 61–63, 110, 168, 171–174, 177, 178, 182

Eliakim, son of Hilkiah, 197

Eliashib, high priest, 104, 108, 109, 330

Eliezer, son of Dodavahu, 123, 351

Elihu, 123, 300–303

Elijah (Eliyahu), the Tishbite, 122, 123, 186, 187, 189, 190, 351, 481, 529

Elijah (Eliyah), Messianic prophet, 251, 481, 495, 512, 529, 534

Eliphaz, the Temanite, 123, 301, 302

Elisha, the prophet, 122, 123, 187, 189, 190, 345, 351, 352

Elon, the Zebulunite, 61, 168, 170–172, 307

Emergency aid, 643

En-Gedi, 180

England; 435–438, 440, 443–448, 489–491, 498, 528; king of, 404

Enoch, son of Cain, 6

Enoch, son of Jared, 18, 24

Enosh, son of Seth, 18, 24

Entryways to Temple, 453ff

Ephesus, 423

Ephraim; son of Joseph, 42, 230, 521; tribe of,

Ephraim (continued)
   166, 168, 171, 340, 521; as representative of Israel, 197, 491, 521
Eponym lists, 86, 87, 90
Esarhaddon, king of Assyria, 33, 35, 87, 89, 91
Esau, 123, 131, 133-135, 340, 344, 483, 523
Esther; queen, 100-102, 321, 322; book of, 123, 125, 321, 322, 390
Esthonia, 441
Ethan, the Ezrahite, 123, 252, 261, 278
Ethiopia (also see Cush), 93, 197, 300, 301, 322, 437, 438, 449, 451, 477, 487, 489, 498, 528, 530, 532, 533
Eulaeus, regent for Ptolemy VI, 426, 427
Eulaeus River, 377, 378, 385
Eumenes, 417
Euphrates River, 36, 97, 281, 417, 475, 485, 486, 491, 496, 498, 502, 518, 531, 532, 616
Europe, 368, 416, 423, 441, 444, 449, 451, 477, 515, 528, 530
Eve, first woman, 5, 6, 10, 130
Evening-morning, 384, 388
Evil, concept of, 6
Evil-Merodach, king of Babylonia, 94, 97, 98, 107, 214, 215
Evolution, xx, 10, 13-16
Exodus; 39-41, 43, 44, 46, 47, 49-52, 54, 55, 59, 62, 64, 134, 137, 145, 146, 487, 524; date of, 3, 46, 52, 54, 68, 117; book of, 122, 124, 129, 136-142, 342, 390; early name for book of, 152-155, 163, 164
Ezekiel; the prophet, 84, 97, 122, 231, 233, 239, 240, 323, 453, 458, 460, 472, 497, 686; book of, 120, 122, 124, 231-239, 300, 390, 450-478, 493
Ezra, 69, 104, 107-109, 118, 123, 163, 164, 327, 330, 331, 333, 390, 697
Ezra-Nehemiah, book of, 104, 123, 125, 126, 326-332, 342, 343, 390

Family size, 43, 44
Fasting, 685
Fat (*heleb*); avoidance of, 556-558; for sacrifices, 659
Fear, 563, 565, 619, 620
Feisal, emir of Arabia, 437
Fence around roof, 597, 598
Festival sacrifices, 653, 659-663, 682
Festivals: 141, 472, 680-686; of Matzot, 68, 138, 327, 408, 630, 660, 661, 680, 682-684; Day of Waving the Omer, 660, 661, 680, 681, 685; of Weeks, 62, 408, 630, 661, 662, 681-683, 685; of Blowing the Shofar, 68, 408, 663, 681, 683, 685; Day of Atonement, 69, 239, 408, 409, 647, 662, 676, 681, 683, 685, 687; of Tabernacles, 68, 69, 155, 162, 327, 329, 408, 495, 532, 544, 545, 630, 663, 681-683, 686, 697; of Atzeret (Solemn Assembly), 329, 408, 630, 681, 683, 686
Finland, 441
Fire; damages by, 613; for purification, 580, 581, 690
First-born; 44, 45, 474, 627, 628, 633, 634, 645, 646, 654, 673; plague of, 54, 138, 139
First of dough, 474, 633
First of fleeces, 633
First-fruits, 474, 544, 545, 632, 634, 658, 660, 661, 679, 681
Fish; creation of, 5; non-permissible, 550, 551, 553, 554; survival of Deluge, 11
Food; permissible, 5, 8, 144, 550-563; spoiled, 558-561
Fossils, 10-12, 14, 15
France, 435-437, 440, 441, 483, 528
Freewill-offering, 558, 559, 654, 655, 660, 677, 679
Fringes, 145, 543, 544
Fruit trees, 622

Gabriel, angel of the Arabs, 325, 360, 375, 384-386, 388, 389, 400, 401, 403, 404
Gad, the prophet, 122, 123, 173-182, 334, 347, 348
Gad; son of Jacob, 19; tribe of, 86, 149, 166, 167, 340, 522
Gallipoli Campaign, 436
Gareb, hill of, 522
Gate of the Corner, 522
Gath, 179, 180, 254, 259
Gaza, 213, 421, 436, 480, 483, 491, 495, 498, 528, 532
Genealogies; 186; of Chronicles, 71, 81, 332, 333, 340, 341, 343-347; of high priests, 108, 145, 329, 330; of Moses and Aaron, 139
Generations; length of, 9, 41-43; number preceding the Deluge, 18, 23

INDEX 729

Genes, 10, 573
Genesis, 120, 122, 124, 129–136, 168, 342, 696; early name for, 152–154, 163, 164, 167
Gerar, 133
Germany, 433–441, 443–445, 448, 449, 528; East, 451, 530
Gershon, son of Levi, 39, 278, 340
Geshur, 182, 184
Gezer, 55, 56
Gezer Calendar, 70
Gibeah, city of, 171, 173
Gibeon, city of, 165, 175, 176, 181
Gideon, judge, 59, 60, 122, 168, 171, 172
Gilboa, 177
Gilead, 483, 487, 492, 532, 533
Gilgal, 166, 178
Gilgamesh, Epic of, 22
Goah, 522
God's names, 134, 142, 152, 153
Gog; 199, 450, 451, 477, 493, 503, 530; army of, 198, 406, 451, 452, 477, 479, 490, 495, 497, 500, 502–506, 508, 510, 511, 514, 517, 519, 520, 523, 526, 530, 531; war of, 243, 245, 362, 364, 365, 370, 371, 376, 406, 412, 449–452, 468, 475, 477, 479–496, 498–503, 506–508, 510, 512, 513, 516–520, 522, 524–526, 529–531, 533, 534
Goliath, 177, 179, 181, 306
Gomer, 26, 451
Goshen, 50
Governmental restrictions, 546–548
Great Assembly, 107, 110, 118
Greece, 26, 95, 104, 360, 365, 366, 368, 370, 372, 373, 377, 379, 380, 386, 387, 413–416, 432, 441, 449, 480, 491, 495, 517, 530, 531
Greek empire, 363, 367, 379, 380, 417
Greek history, 114
Guilt-offering, 465, 474, 562, 607, 633, 653, 656, 657, 666–668, 670, 678, 679

Habakkuk; the prophet, 123, 241, 242, 248; book of, 123, 125, 240, 242, 248, 479
Habiru, 55–57
Hachilah, 180
Hadadezer, king of Zobah, 281
Hadadrimmon, 493
Hadera, 515, 517, 528

Hadrach, 490, 491, 528
Hagar, wife of Abraham, 37, 135
Haggai; the prophet, 107, 118, 123, 240–242, 327, 390; book of, 123, 125, 240, 242, 249, 479
Hague, 442, 446, 447
Hair; cutting of, 473, 561–563, 589, 590, 592, 593; microorganisms in, 587, 593
Ham, son of Noah, 9, 18, 20, 21, 25, 26, 28, 132
Haman, 101, 107, 118, 321, 322
Hamath, 498, 533
Hammurabi; king of Babylonia, 29, 30, 34, 36, 38, 57, 117; Code of, 36–38
Hamon-Gog, valley of, 452, 531
Hananel, tower of, 522
Hanani, the prophet, 122, 123, 186, 190, 345, 350, 351
Hananiah, companion of Daniel, 324
Hananiah, false prophet, 67
Hannah, mother of Samuel, 174, 178
Haran, 38, 135
Harem, 474, 645–647
Harvest, failure of, 502, 503, 518
Hasmonaeans, 249, 431, 432, 444, 445
Hatnufer, mother of Senmut, 53, 56
Hatred, 563, 564
Hatshepsut, queen of Egypt, 48–50, 53, 54, 56
Hazor, 213, 214, 249
Health regulations, 549–596
Hebrew, original language, 6, 9, 13, 132
Hebron, 55, 62, 71, 72, 166, 175, 177, 180, 184
Hegira, 374
Heikhal, 458–462, 464, 465, 687, 689, 690
Hejaz, 405
Heleb; see fat
Helgoland, 434, 435
Heliodorus, 425, 426
Hellenism, 431
Hellespont, 421, 423
Heman, the Ezrahite, 123, 252, 261, 278
Herod, king of the Jews, 115
Herodotus, 99, 100
Herzl, Theodor, 515
Hess, Moses, 515
Hezekiah; king of Judah, 76, 81, 83, 84, 89–92, 113, 187, 189, 191, 194–196, 198, 199, 210, 241, 243, 249, 299, 333, 336, 337, 341, 342, 353, 392, 397, 399; men of, 123, 282, 299

Highways, from Israel, 498, 499, 505, 518, 533
Hinnom, valley of, 517
Hired worker, 640, 641
Hitler, 437
Holidays; see festivals
Holland, 433, 442
Holy covenant, 429, 430
Holy-of-holies, 144, 239, 458–460, 462, 465, 663, 687–689
Homs, 490, 528
Honey, 677
Horeb, 157
Horses, 11, 546–548; in Egypt, 51, 52, 54
Hosea; the prophet, 122, 240, 241, 489; book of, 122, 124, 240, 243, 244, 479, 488, 489
Hoshea, king of Israel, 73, 76, 81, 86, 88, 90, 187, 188, 191, 243
House of the Lord, 280, 479, 480, 484
Hozai, the prophet, 122, 123, 188, 191, 339, 345, 353
Huldah, the prophetess, 122, 123, 188, 189, 191, 345, 353, 354
Humus, 648
Hungary, 440, 441, 451, 528, 530
Hur, Israelite leader, 50, 123, 345
Hybrid animals, 651
Hybrid plants, 648, 650–652
Hyksos, 48–52, 56, 117
Hyrcania, 99, 101
Hyrcanus, John, high priest, 115
Hyrcanus, of family of Tobiads, 422, 426
Hystaspes, father of Darius I, 99–102, 106, 107, 118, 321, 328

Ibzan, of Bethlehem, 61, 168, 171, 172, 307
Ice age, 11, 12
Iddo, the seer, 122, 123, 185, 186, 190, 192, 333, 335, 343, 345, 350, 351
Idol worship; 448, 540–542, 605; by Abraham, 37, 38; of heavenly bodies, 381–383, 385; purification from, 67, 375, 446; by Solomon, 342; in Temple, 430
Imperfections of the world, 6
Impurity laws, 142, 144, 147, 551–553, 555, 559, 579, 580, 582–584, 587, 588; for priests, 474, 579, 591, 592, 594, 595
Incense, 461, 663, 664, 675–677, 687–689, 691
Incense altar, 458, 460, 461, 687–691

Independence; of Jewish nation, 407, 414, 432, 433, 444–446; War of, 405, 449, 507, 528
India, 93, 99, 322, 379
Indus, 417
Inflation, 639, 640, 647
Ingathering of the exiles, 199, 450, 452, 485, 490–492, 498, 501, 502, 505–507, 510, 512, 513, 517, 520, 521, 525, 527, 533, 534
Inheritance; of property, 145, 471, 472, 625, 627, 628; of physical traits, 6
Inherited defects, 571–574
Inner court, 453ff
Insecticides, 582, 652
Insects; control of, 648, 649, 651, 652, 675, 677, 685; as disease carriers, 555; not to be eaten, 550, 551, 555
Installation-offering, 468, 592, 653, 664, 675, 678
Interest, 638–640
Intermarriage, 572, 574
International Court of Justice, 442, 446, 447, 449
Intoxicating drinks, 473
Ionia, 378, 423
Ipsus, battle of, 417
Irad, son of Enoch, 6
Iran, 365, 449, 451, 477, 498, 530, 531, 533
Iraq, 364, 365, 376, 405, 449, 451, 486, 492, 495, 496, 498, 499, 502, 508, 518, 530, 531, 533, 534
Iron age, 7
Isaac, 19, 36–38, 42, 117, 122, 123, 129, 131–136, 142, 153, 344; birth of, 3, 40, 41
Isaiah; the prophet, 113, 122, 123, 187, 188, 191–195, 199, 210, 240, 337, 345, 352–354, 497, 505, 510, 513; book of, 121, 122, 124, 193–210, 215, 390, 497–518
Ish-bosheth, son of Saul, 63, 175–177
Ishmael, son of Abraham, 122, 123, 131, 133–135, 230, 340, 344, 385
Islam, 375, 377, 381–383
Island states, 424
Israel; kingdom of, 58, 70ff, 85, 86, 92, 118, 189, 193–196, 198, 240, 243, 245, 331; land of, 195, 198, 233, 372–376, 391, 394, 395, 402, 407, 448, 453, 476, 481, 488–491, 495, 515, 528, 531, 626; state of, 193, 323, 356, 357, 360, 364, 365, 370, 371, 376, 405–407, 412, 439, 444, 446, 448–452, 477, 479, 482, 483, 486, 487, 489, 491,

Israel (continued)
   492, 494, 498–500, 502–506, 508, 509, 513, 514, 516, 518, 519, 521–530, 532–534, 696, 699
Israelites, 40, 43, 46, 47, 50–52, 56, 57, 59, 117, 129, 137–140, 142, 145, 146, 148, 150, 151, 153, 165, 166, 171, 172, 278, 281, 371, 393, 394, 404, 432, 524, 525
Issachar; son of Jacob, 19; tribe of, 340
Issus, battle of, 379
Italy, 437–439, 441, 443, 449, 528

Jabal, son of Lamech, 6
Jabin, king of Canaan, 60
Jacob, 19, 21, 39–44, 46, 47, 49, 50, 117, 122, 123, 129, 131–136, 142, 153, 279, 340, 344–346, 383, 384, 403, 487, 505, 508, 514, 524, 525
Jaddua, high priest, 104, 108, 109
Jahaziel, son of Zechariah, 123, 351
Jair, the Gileadite, 60, 168, 171, 172
Japheth, son of Noah, 9, 18, 20, 21, 26, 28, 132
Jealousy, 564, 565, 576
Jebusites, 26, 167, 175, 176, 280, 403, 404, 491, 617
Jedidiah, 312
Jeduthun, chief musician, 123, 252, 258, 278
Jehoahaz, king of Israel, 75, 79, 187, 190, 397
Jehoahaz, king of Judah, 76, 81, 83, 188, 189, 191, 338, 354
Jehoash, king of Israel, 75, 79, 187, 190, 191
Jehoash, king of Judah, 75, 79, 83, 187, 190, 301, 336, 342, 351
Jehoiachin, king of Judah, 76, 81–84, 95, 96, 188, 191, 212, 214, 215, 232, 338, 354; exile of, 94, 98, 102, 107, 118, 184, 211, 239, 300
Jehoiada, the priest, 110, 301
Jehoiakim, king of Judah, 76, 81–83, 95–97, 188, 191, 211–213, 215, 229, 323, 324, 338, 339, 354, 361
Jehoram, king of Israel, 72, 74, 78, 187, 189, 190
Jehoram, king of Judah, 73, 74, 78, 79, 83, 187, 189, 190, 336, 342, 351
Jehoshaphat, king of Judah, 73, 74, 77, 78, 83, 186, 187, 189, 190, 334, 335, 342, 351; valley of, 480, 481, 496, 500, 530, 531
Jehozadak, high priest, 109, 332

Jehu, king of Israel, 75, 86, 88, 187, 189, 190
Jehu, son of Hanani, 122, 123, 186, 187, 190, 335, 351
Jephthah, the Gileadite, 61, 63, 122, 168, 171, 172
Jeremiah; the prophet, 85, 106, 122, 123, 189, 191, 210–215, 229–231, 240, 308–311, 345, 354, 390, 391, 393, 397–399, 407, 497, 523; book of, 122, 124, 188, 210–231, 300, 308, 309, 390, 391, 393, 394, 399, 519–524
Jericho, 55, 165, 166
Jeroboam I, king of Israel, 69, 71, 74, 77, 82, 154, 185, 186, 189, 190, 332, 333, 335
Jeroboam II, king of Israel, 73, 75, 79–81, 187, 191, 240, 241, 243, 245, 333
Jerusalem; 55, 56, 62, 67, 85, 91, 96, 97, 102–104, 106, 113, 158, 177, 182, 184, 194–199, 210–215, 231, 233, 239, 240, 247, 248, 279–281, 301, 304, 308, 311, 312, 322, 326, 327, 329, 330, 341, 373, 375, 390, 391, 393, 395, 396, 398, 399, 402–405, 409, 429, 430, 449, 454, 467, 475, 477, 480, 481, 483, 485, 488, 490, 491, 493–496, 498, 500–502, 504, 507, 508, 513, 514, 516, 521, 522, 528–533, 602, 629–632, 675, 680, 682, 683, 686, 698; daughters of, 305, 306
Jeshua, high priest, 109
Jesse, father of David, 497, 498, 529
Jethro, brother-in-law of Moses, 140
Jezreel, 177
Joab, general of David, 172, 254, 281
Job; righteous man, 123, 300–303; book of, 121, 123, 125, 300–303
Job opportunities, 624
Jochebed, mother of Moses, 41, 53, 56
Joel; the prophet, 122, 240–242; book of, 122, 124, 240, 242, 243, 479–481
Johanan, high priest, 104, 108, 109, 332
Joiada, high priest, 104, 108, 109
Joiakim, high priest, 109
Jonadab, son of Rechab, 213
Jonah; the prophet, 87, 122, 123, 187, 191, 240–242, 245, 247, 345, 352, 353; book of, 122, 124, 240, 242, 245, 247, 479
Jonathan, son of Saul, 63, 179, 180, 182
Jordan (country), 198, 364, 376, 405, 448, 449, 451, 452, 477, 481–483, 487, 492, 495, 496, 498, 499, 501, 502, 504, 505, 513, 522–525, 528–533

Jordan River, 150, 165, 166, 475, 478, 483, 523, 543
Joseph, son of Jacob, 19, 21, 40, 42, 46, 47, 49-51, 56, 57, 117, 122, 129-131, 133-137, 167, 230, 383, 384, 402, 448
Joseph, at time of Ptolemy V, 422
Josephus, the historian, 47, 50, 108, 114, 115, 323
Joshua, 42, 46, 47, 49, 55, 57-60, 64, 69, 112, 113, 117, 120, 122, 123, 129, 137, 138, 143, 144, 148-153, 164-168, 170, 278, 279, 344-346, 392, 402, 403, 448, 474, 524, 623, 696; book of, 56, 122, 124, 165-168, 170, 173, 342
Josiah, king of Judah, 67, 76, 81, 83, 85, 153, 163, 164, 188, 191, 210, 212, 230, 239, 241, 308, 338, 339, 353, 493
Jotham, king of Judah, 76, 80, 81, 83, 187, 191, 194, 199, 210, 241, 243, 333, 336, 337, 352
Jotham, son of Gideon, 122, 172
Jubal, son of Lamech, 6
Jubilee year, 69, 111-116, 141, 143, 472, 625, 627, 635, 637, 644, 646-649
Judah; son of Jacob, 19, 42, 122, 123, 129, 131, 133-136, 301, 340, 344; tribe of, 84, 114, 166, 170, 180, 332, 340, 341, 344, 475, 494
Judah; land of, 521; kingdom of, 58, 70ff, 85, 92, 118, 174, 175, 189, 193-199, 211, 214, 231, 233, 242, 243, 249, 311, 331-333, 340, 341, 350, 373, 393
Judah, the Hasmonaean, 431, 432
Judea (at time of Second Temple), 93, 95, 99, 102, 104, 107, 115, 118, 249
Judaea (conquered from Jordan), 452, 483, 485, 492, 493, 495, 496, 530, 531
Judges; 58ff, 116, 117, 171, 172, 307; book of, 56, 58, 120, 122, 124, 163, 168-173; appointment of, 140; power of, 168; regulations for, 600-603
Jupiter, 430

Ka'ba, 377, 381-384, 389, 446
Kalischer, Zevi Hirsch, 515
Kamose, pharaoh, 50, 52
Kassite dynasty, 30, 33, 34
Kedar, 195, 197, 213, 214, 249, 512
Keilah, 180
Kenite, 170

Keturah, wife of Abraham, 133
Khorsabad List, 30
Kidnapping, 605
Kidron; brook of, 522; valley of, 480
Kings; chronology of, 65-92, 116; book of, 70, 71, 73, 120, 122, 124, 126, 163, 184-192, 210, 230, 240, 308, 331-339, 341-343, 355, 390; regulations for, 174
Kings of Israel, 65, 70-81, 185-192
Kings of Judah, 65, 70-82, 185-192; ages of, 82-84
Kings of Judah and Israel, book of, 70, 71, 185, 331-333, 342
Kiriath-jearim, 174, 178
Kish, 11, 27
Kohath, son of Levi, 39-41, 278, 340
Koheleth, 311-313
Korah, 144, 147, 148, 278, 676; sons of, 41, 123, 252-256, 258, 259, 261, 278, 281
Koran, 375, 383, 387, 388
Koreish tribe, 382
Kuwait, 451

Laban, 133, 135
Labashi-Marduk, king of Babylonia, 94
Lachish, 55, 56
Lagash, 11
Lamech, son of Methuselah, 18, 24, 132, 135
Lamech, son of Methushael, 6
Lamentations, book of, 123, 125, 300, 308-311
Lampsacus, 423
Lampstand, 429, 458, 687-691
Lance, 484
Land; distribution, 166, 167, 450, 474-477, 533, 624-626; ownership, 471, 472, 624-628; purchase, 625; sanctification of, 644, 646; speculation, 627
Languages, confusion of, 9, 13, 22, 23, 117
Language families, 13
Laodice, wife of Antiochus II, 418
Larsa, 36; lists, 23-25
Lashes, 615
Latvia, 441
Laver, 690, 691
Lawrence, T.E., 437
Leader; regulations for, 468-472, 478, 534; respect for, 546, 548; selection of, 546, 547
League of Nations, 446
Leaven, 684

INDEX 733

Leavened bread, 559, 677, 680
Lebanon, 364, 376, 405, 406, 449, 451, 480, 492, 495, 499, 503, 505, 512, 530, 532, 533
Lemuel Melech, 282, 299
Lenaeus, regent for Ptolemy VI, 427
Lending laws, 638-640
Leonnatus, 368, 416
Leper, 144, 584-587, 590, 592, 666, 668, 676
Leprosy, 584, 585, 587, 590, 687; of garments, 585, 586; of stones, 587, 668
Levi; son of Jacob, 18, 19, 39-41, 46, 50, 117, 136, 137, 340; tribe of, 44, 278, 475
Levirate marriage, 625, 626, 628
Levites, 44, 148, 150, 151, 156, 158, 166, 332, 340, 343, 347-350, 353, 475, 477, 495, 517, 525, 533; age for serving, 592, 593; initiation of, 145, 147, 481, 482, 529, 672; land received, 624-627; portions for, 628-632, 698; requirements for, 472, 592-594; responsibilities of, 472, 590, 591, 627
Leviticus, 122, 124, 129, 142-144, 390, 524; early name for book, 152, 153, 155, 156, 162-164
Libya, 364, 376, 437, 438, 449, 451, 528
Life span of man, 5-7, 20, 41, 110, 516, 518, 534, 536
Liquid measure, 469, 607
Linen, 472, 473, 585, 586, 692-695
Lithuania, 440, 441
Locusts, 479, 480, 551, 555
Lost objects, 613, 614, 642, 643
Lot, nephew of Abraham, 36, 38, 122, 131, 132, 134
Lucius Scipio, 424
Lud, 517
Lunar years; see calendar
Luxemburg, 437, 528
Lycians, 378, 422
Lydia, 368, 378
Lysimachus, 380, 387

Maccabees, books of, 114, 115, 431
Macedon, 367, 368, 379, 386, 416
Machpelah, cave of, 39
Magnesia, battle of, 424, 425
Magog, 26, 450-452, 517
Malachi, the prophet, 123, 241, 242, 251; book of, 123, 125, 240, 242, 251, 390, 479, 481, 482

Manasseh, king of Judah, 76, 83, 85, 86, 89, 188, 191, 249, 336, 337, 342, 353
Manasseh; son of Jacob, 19, 230; tribe of, 86, 149, 166, 167, 340
Mandate, British, 404, 405, 407, 449
Manetho, historian, 47, 50
Manna, 84, 129, 137, 139
Manslayer, 598, 599, 625
Maon, wilderness of, 180
Marriage, limitations on, 575-577
Meal-offering, 465, 468, 474, 481, 587, 592, 633, 653, 658, 660, 664-673, 678
Meat; contaminated, 558, 559, 590, 677; and milk, 560
Mecca, 374, 382-385, 389
Medes, Media (also see Persia), 26, 100, 210, 214, 325, 367, 368, 378-380, 385, 390, 432
Medina, 367, 369, 374, 375, 382
Mediterranean Sea, 365, 366, 439, 475, 478, 480, 483, 486, 491, 494, 496, 499, 531, 616
Megiddo, valley of, 493
Mehujael, son of Irad, 6
Meleager, 368, 416
Memphis, 429
Menachem, king of Israel, 75, 80, 87, 88, 90, 187, 188, 191, 243
Menelaus, high priest, 430
Menstruation, 6, 494, 569-571, 582-584, 645
Mental health, 563-568
Mephibosheth, son of Jonathan, 182
Merari, son of Levi, 39, 278, 340
Merodach-baladan, king of Babylonia, 89
Meshech, 26, 450, 451, 517
Messiah, 279, 515; false, 445
Messianic Era, xxii, 126, 193-199, 231, 232, 242, 243, 245, 247-249, 251, 357, 432, 439, 450, 477, 479, 484-490, 495, 497, 499, 502, 505, 517, 519, 522-524, 527-534
Methusaleh, son of Enoch, 18, 20, 24, 130, 132
Methushael, father of Lamech, 6
Micah, idol of, 122, 171, 173
Micah; the prophet, 123, 241, 247, 485, 497; book of, 123, 124, 240, 247, 248, 479, 484-487
Micaiah, son of Imlah, the prophet, 122, 123, 187, 190, 351
Michael, angel of the Jews, 360, 372, 375, 408, 411, 413, 440

Midian, Midianites, 51, 52, 60, 144, 147, 148, 618
Midwives, 43, 44
Migdal-eder, 485, 533
Mikve Yisrael, agricultural school, 488, 515
Military needs, 563, 565, 597, 615–623
Mina, 383, 384
Miriam, sister of Moses, 39, 40, 46, 53, 144, 146, 147, 340
Mishael, companion of Daniel, 324
Mishnah, 696–699
Mizpah, 168, 431
Mizpeh, 179
Moab, Moabite, 158, 179, 184, 195, 197, 213, 214, 231, 233, 249, 306, 307, 436, 437, 448, 498, 501, 522, 525, 528, 532
Modin, 431
Mohammad, xxii, 323, 356, 357, 363, 367, 369, 374, 375, 377, 381–385, 387–389, 446
Monetary system, 469, 478, 534, 647
Mongolia, 451, 530
Monotheistic principles, 141, 539–542
Month; first, 68–70; length of Hebrew, 126
Mordechai, 99, 102, 103, 107, 123, 321, 322
Moriah, mountain of, 142
Morocco, 451
Moscow, 438
Moses, 39, 40, 43, 46, 52–54, 56, 58, 66, 69, 113, 117, 120, 122, 123, 129, 130, 134, 137–144, 146–153, 155–163, 165, 166, 211, 252, 255, 256, 261, 278, 340, 344–346, 395, 396, 402, 410, 482, 514, 525, 623, 696, 697; birth of, 46, 47, 51
Mount Ebal, 151, 165, 543, 544
Mount Etna, 439
Mount Everest, 8
Mount Gerizim, 151, 165
Mount Hor (in Jordan), 486
Mount Nebo, 151, 152
Mount Seir, 452
Mount Sinai (see Sinai)
Mourning; by Daniel, 408, 409; by priests, 595, 596; after War of Gog, 493, 496, 532
Murder, 598, 599, 602, 604, 605, 611
Musical instruments and accompaniment, 252, 257–263, 277
Mythology, 21–23

Naar, 59; age meant by, 230

Nabal, husband of Abigail, 180, 253, 259
Nabonidus, king of Babylon, 94, 98, 99
Nabopolasser, king of Babylon, 94, 105, 107, 241, 363, 370, 371
Nadab, son of Aaron, death of, 142–144, 148
Nadab, king of Israel, 72, 74, 186, 190
Nahor, father of Terah, 19
Nahum; the prophet, 123, 240–242; book of, 123, 125, 240, 242, 248, 479
Naomi, mother-in-law of Ruth, 306–308
Naphtali; son of Jacob, 19; tribe of, 340
Nathan, the prophet, 122, 123, 173–175, 177, 181, 185, 190, 254, 259, 312, 335, 345–350
Nations, formation of, 9, 25, 26, 117
Nazir, 561–563, 670
Nebuchadnezzar, king of Babylonia, 81, 94–98, 105, 107, 123, 210, 212, 213, 230, 231, 239, 324–326, 333, 360–363, 365–367, 371–373
Necho, pharaoh, 83, 213
Negeb, 483
Nehemiah; governor of Judea, 69, 104, 105, 107, 108, 118, 123, 164, 329–333, 341, 343, 347, 355, 697; book of, 328, 331, 342
Ner, 23
Neriah, father of Baruch and Seraiah, 214
Neriglissar, king of Babylonia, 94
Netherlands, 437, 528
New moon, 466, 471, 517, 532, 660, 661, 682
Nile River, 25, 51, 52, 56, 443, 449, 492, 499, 528, 531
Nimrod, 8, 26
Nineveh, 240–242, 245, 247, 248, 486
Nisan, first month, 17, 65–69, 96, 406
Noah, 8, 9, 16, 18, 20–22, 24, 27, 28, 66, 117, 122, 123, 129, 131, 132, 134, 135, 300, 344
No-amon, 240, 241
Nob, city of the priests, 179
No-man's-land, 405, 529
North, king of, 417ff
North Africa, 438, 443, 451, 477, 530
North Korea, 451, 530
North Sea, 434, 435
North Vietnam, 451, 530
Norway, 437, 528
Numbers, book of, 122, 124, 129, 144–150, 342, 390, 395, 524; early name for, 152, 153, 156, 163, 164, 395
Nutrient deficiencies, 571, 648, 649

Obadiah; the prophet, 122, 241, 242; book of, 122, 124, 240, 242, 245, 479, 482, 483, 523
Obed, son of Ruth, 306
Oded, the prophet, 123, 353
Olive oil, 675, 676, 687, 690, 691
Olives, Mount of, 480, 490, 493-495, 531
Oman; 451; Trucial, 451
Omar, 371, 372, 375, 376; Mosque of, 495
Omri, king of Israel, 74, 77, 186, 190
Onias I, high priest, 109
Organization of the Bible, 119ff
Ornan, threshing floor of, 480
Orphan, 482, 601, 629, 631, 632, 640-642, 648
Othniel, son of Kenaz, 55, 58-60, 117, 167, 168, 170-172, 340
Ottoman empire, 363, 364, 376, 448
Outer court, 453ff
Outermost wall, 453, 454
Overpopulation, 568

Palestine, 55, 97, 365, 373, 375, 376, 381, 404, 407, 417, 419-421, 426, 429, 436, 440, 444, 446, 448-491, 495, 515, 517, 527, 528
Panium, 421
Papyrus Sallier, 50
Parents; respect for, 608; crimes against, 608, 609
Parthia, 99, 101
Parysatis, queen-mother of Artaxerxes II, 105
Pashhur, son of Immer, 211, 219
Pashhur, son of Malchiah, 211, 219
Passover sacrifice, 67, 68, 146, 156, 159, 161, 165, 403, 468, 581, 582, 630, 653, 661, 662, 680, 682-684
Payments, as punishment, 605-615
Peace-offering, 468, 471, 558, 559, 562, 633, 653-655, 659, 661, 664-673, 677
Peace Palace, 447
Pekah, king of Israel, 76, 80, 81, 85, 87, 88, 187, 191, 194, 196, 243
Pekahiah, king of Israel, 75, 80, 187, 188, 191, 243
Peleg, son of Eber, 9, 10, 18, 26, 117
Pelusium, 427, 428
Pentateuch, 129, 134, 168, 467, 468, 519, 524-526, 529, 535ff, 697-699; early names of books of, 152-164

Perdiccas, 368, 416
Perez, son of Judah, 42, 130, 136
Pergamos, 426
Perjury, 603
Permanent Court of Arbitration, 446, 447, 449
Permanent Court of International Justice, 442, 446
Persia, Persian, 93-95, 98-103, 105, 107, 110, 126, 193, 195, 197, 199, 321, 325-329, 363, 365-373, 377-379, 386, 390, 391, 407, 408, 411-417, 419, 432, 449, 450
Petah Tikvah, 488, 495, 515, 517, 528
Pharaoh, 21, 47, 49, 51, 139; who enslaved the Israelites, 46, 117; of the Exodus, 46, 52, 117; at time of Joseph, 46, 47, 49, 117
Philip V, of Macedonia, 421, 423
Philistia, 195, 197, 213, 214, 231, 233, 249, 480
Philistines, 26, 60-63, 171, 172, 174-181, 184, 254, 259, 280, 281, 483, 487, 490, 491, 498, 532
Phoenicia, 422
Physical protection of the population, 579-623
Pilgrimage; Farewell, 375, 384; Greater, 383, 384; Lesser, 384
Plague, 552, 685
Plagues, 621; ten, 139
Plant diseases, 647-649, 651, 652
Pledge, 638, 639, 679
Plowshare, 484
Poisoning, from foods, 553, 554, 559-561, 652
Poland, 436, 437, 440, 441, 451, 528, 530
Pollution, air, 567, 627
Poor persons; aid for, 628, 638-642, 648; judgment of, 601
Popillius, ambassador of Rome, 429
Population in the desert; see census
Portugal, 441
Porus, ruler of India, 379
Priestly blessings, 591
Priestly garments, 464, 472, 592, 593, 692-695
Priestly portions, 145, 474, 521, 629, 632-635, 655, 656, 658, 659, 678, 679
Priestly statutes, 472, 590-596
Priests, 144, 148, 151, 156, 158, 166, 332, 464, 475, 477, 517; cities for, 533; high, 108-110, 143, 599, 693, 695; inauguration of, 142, 145, 467, 468, 481, 482, 495, 529, 592, 593, 664, 665; physical defects, 594, 596; requirements for officiating,

Priests (continued)
467, 592–594; responsibilities, 473, 478, 590, 591, 619, 620; special prohibitions, 534, 594–596, 677
Prison, 600, 606, 615
Property, public, 472
Prophecy, xxi, 356, 357
Prophets, false, 247, 494, 534, 541, 542
Prostitution, 569–571, 575, 577, 595, 596
Proverbs, book of, 123, 125, 281–300
Pruning-hooks, 484
Prussians, 434
Psalms, book of, 123, 125, 248, 252–281, 342, 390, 399
Pseudo-Smerdis, king of Persia, 94, 100, 101, 103, 105, 415
Psychological benefits of sacrifices, 469, 660, 679
Psychological measures, 563–568
Ptolemaic empire, 323, 356, 380, 381, 387, 413–415, 418, 429
Ptolemais, 420
Ptolemy I, Soter or Lagi, 47, 109, 110, 380, 387, 415, 417
Ptolemy II, Philadelphus, 415, 417, 418, 421
Ptolemy III, Euergetes I, 415, 418, 419
Ptolemy IV, Philopator, 415, 420, 421
Ptolemy V, Epiphanes, 415, 419, 421, 422, 424, 426
Ptolemy VI, Philometer, 415, 424, 426–428
Ptolemy VII, Euergetes II, 415, 428
Ptolemy, Greek historian, 93
Pul, country of, 517
Pul, king of Assyria, 86–88, 90, 91, 247, 340
Purification, 147, 674, 675, 696
Purim, 101, 107, 118, 322
Put, country of, 26, 451
Puzur-Assur III, king of Assyria, 30, 31, 33
Pyramids, 13

Rabbah, city of, 522, 523
Rabbah, land of, 255
Rabbinic restrictions, 537
Rabies, 552, 554, 556, 559, 590, 611
Rachel, 521
Radioactive dating, xx, 15, 16
Rainbow, 8, 9
Ramah, 521
Ramose, father of Senmut, 53, 56
Ramses II, 48, 57

Raphia, 420
Rats; control of, 684; impurity of, 551, 555, 556, 685
Rebekah, wife of Isaac, 38, 122, 131, 133–135
Rechabites, 211
Red cow, ashes of, 147, 494, 579, 580, 595, 672, 675, 677
Red Sea, 451, 475, 486, 491, 498, 524, 531, 616
Refuge cities, 145, 150, 166, 598, 599, 625
Rehoboam, king of Judah, 74, 77, 78, 82–84, 182, 184, 185, 190, 332–335, 341, 342, 350
Rephaim, valley of, 280
Resurrection, 439, 534
Reuben; son of Jacob, 19, 21, 340; tribe of, 86, 149, 166, 167, 340
Revenge, 563, 564
Reward and punishment; during lifetime, 535–537; after death, 102
Rezin, king of Aram, 85, 194, 196
Rhodians, 423
Rib-adda, ruler of Byblos, 55
Ritualistic procedures, 653–695
Rome, 360, 387, 424, 426, 428, 429, 432
Roosevelt, president of United States, 447
Rosh, 450, 451
Rothschild, Baron Edmond de, 488
Rumania, 436, 440, 441, 451, 530
Russia, 436, 438, 440, 441, 447, 451, 477, 489, 498, 528, 530
Ruth, 306–308; book of, 123, 125, 306–308, 342

Sabbath, 106, 147, 211, 261, 408, 409, 431, 466, 471, 510, 511, 517, 532, 566–568, 615, 660, 675, 682, 683
Sabbatical year, 111–116, 141, 143, 544, 545, 630, 638, 639, 641, 642, 647–649
Sabianism, 381–384
Sacrifices, 141, 159, 301–303, 401, 454, 464, 465, 467, 469, 534, 549, 651, 653–679, 690, 696; bringing of, 67, 142, 144, 384; meat of, to be eaten, 558, 559; reinstituting of, 450, 467, 468, 477, 480–482, 495, 529
SA-GAZ, 55
Salamis, battle of, 416
Salt, for sacrifices, 659, 677, 679
Samaria, 73, 77, 81, 89, 90, 92, 108, 194, 196, 240, 247, 422, 452, 483, 485, 520

Samson, son of Manoah, 61, 122, 168, 170–173
Samsu-iluna, ruler of Babylonia, 37, 38
Samuel; the prophet, 58, 61–64, 120, 122, 123, 168, 172–174, 177–180, 182, 211, 308, 335, 345–347, 404; book of, 120, 122, 124, 126, 173–184, 341–343, 355; length of rule, 62, 63, 117
San Francisco, 448
Sanballat, governor of Samaria, 108
Sanhedrin, 696, 698, 699
Sar, 23
Sarah, wife of Abraham, 36, 37, 135
Sargon II, king of Assyria, 89–92, 194
Satan, 102
Satrap, 100, 101, 379, 416
Saudi Arabia, 376, 451, 475, 498, 530, 532
Saul, king of Israel, 58, 61–63, 84, 117, 172–182, 253–255, 257, 259, 341–343, 347, 403, 404
Scopas, general of Ptolemy V, 419, 421
Secretariat building, 442
Sediment, from Deluge, 11
Seleucid empire, 323, 356, 380, 381, 387, 413–415, 418, 423, 424, 426, 427, 429, 430, 432
Seleucid era, 115
Seleucus I, Nicator, 380, 387, 415, 417
Seleucus II, Callinicus, 415, 419
Seleucus III, Soter, 415, 419
Seleucus IV, Philopator, 415, 425, 426
Semen, 144, 582, 583, 621
Senmen, 53, 54, 56, 117
Senmut, 53, 54, 56, 117
Sennacherib, king of Assyria, 33–35, 89–92, 113, 194, 198, 341, 397, 399
Septuagint, 20, 126, 127, 326
Seraiah, son of Neriah, 214
Serbia, 435, 436, 441, 528
Seth, son of Adam, 7, 17, 18, 24, 130, 131, 135, 525
Seti I, king of Egypt, 48
Sex prohibitions, 144, 568–578
Shallum, king of Israel, 75, 80, 187, 188, 191, 243
Shallum, son of Josiah, 211, 212 (also see Jehoahaz)
Shalmaneser I, 32–35
Shalmaneser II, 32
Shalmaneser III, 33, 86, 88, 90, 91
Shalmaneser IV, 33, 91
Shalmaneser V, 90–92

Shama, 477
Shamger, son of Anath, 60
Shamshi-Adad I, 30, 31, 33–35
Shamshi-Adad V, 91
Sharon, 56, 503, 505, 515, 528
Shatnez, 473, 586, 692
Sheba, 26, 300, 451, 512
Shebna, 197
Shechem, son of Hamor, city of, 135, 136
Shechem, city of, 168
Shekel, 469, 534
Shekel, half-, 149, 547, 548
Shem, son of Noah, 9, 18, 20, 21, 28, 117, 122, 123, 131, 132, 134, 135, 344
Shemaiah, the prophet, 122, 123, 186, 190, 192, 333, 335, 350
Shephela, 483
Sheshbazzar; see Zerubbabel
Sheshonk I (Shishak), king of Egypt, 78, 92
Shiloh, 166, 171, 172
Shinar, 498, 533
Showbread, 458, 687, 688, 690, 691
Shulamit, 304–306
Shuruppak, 11
Shushan, 101, 107, 118, 329, 377, 378, 438
Sicily, 439, 449, 528
Sidon, 420, 421, 480, 490, 495, 528
Sihon, king of the Amorites, 64
Silver iodide, 674, 675
Simeon; son of Jacob, 19, 21, 136, 340; tribe of, 170, 332, 340
Similarity of phrases (in books of Bible:) 120, 121; for Judges, 169–171, for Samuel, 182, 183; for Isaiah, 195, 200–209; for Jeremiah, 215–228, 309; for Ezekiel, 232–238; for Hosea, 243–245; for Amos, 245, 246; for Zechariah, 250, 251; for Psalms, 256, 264–277; for Proverbs, 282–299; for Lamentations, 308–310; for Ecclesiastes, 313–320
Simon, the Just, high priest, 108–110
Simon, of Hasmonaean dynasty, 407, 432
Sin-offering, 465, 467, 468, 470, 474, 562, 583, 587, 588, 592, 633, 653, 656, 657, 660, 662, 664–673, 678, 679
Sins, major, of Jewish people, 402
Sinai; desert of, 139, 140, 146; Mount, 134, 137, 141, 142, 145, 149, 448, 539; peninsula of, 475, 616
Sinew of the thigh vein, 559, 560
Singers' chambers, 454ff
Sin-muballit, father of Hammurabi, 38

Sisera, leader of Hazor, 170
Six-Day War, 356, 362, 405, 406, 412, 483–485, 495, 520, 530, 616
Six years, the, 362, 412; latter part of, 450, 484, 489, 495, 497, 520, 522, 524, 525, 530
Skills, origin of, 6
Skin disease, 552, 553, 584, 585, 587–589, 666–668, 687
Slaughtering of animals, 552, 553, 557, 558
Slavery, 605; regulations, 635–638
Slaves; becoming, 608, 618, 636; in Egypt, 39, 47, 51, 52, 54, 117, 137, 138; freeing of, 211, 213, 611; heathen, 635–637; Hebrew, 635–637; of priests, 593; treatment of, 610
Smoking, 561
Smyrna, 423
Sodom, 36, 132
Solomon, king of Israel, 58, 61, 64, 66, 77, 82, 84, 85, 92, 118, 120, 123, 174, 177, 182, 184, 185, 189, 190, 230, 252, 254, 255, 260, 263, 278–280, 282, 299, 300, 304–306, 312, 332, 334, 335, 341–343, 348, 392, 397–399, 404, 472, 686
Song of Songs, 123, 125, 304–306
Sothis, 25, 47
South, king of, 417ff
Spain, 441, 483
Species, 14
Speech, ability of, 6
Sphinx, 366, 368
Spies, 59, 144, 146, 147, 165–167, 402, 448
Stalin, premier of Russia, 447
Stalingrad, battle of, 438
Statira, wife of Artaxerxes II, 105
Stealing, 605–608, 613, 643
Stranger; see alien
Subjugation, periods of, 58, 59, 168, 171
Sudan, the, 364, 376, 451, 477, 530
Suez Canal, 436, 443, 475, 498, 502, 518, 616
Sumerian king list, 23–25, 27
Sumerian cities, 27
Susiana, 101, 321
Symbiotic relationships, 14
Synchronistic dating, 69, 70, 72, 189
Syria; ancient, 55, 97; under Seleucids, 418, 422, 425–432; under Romans, 360; modern, 364, 376, 405, 406, 449, 451, 477, 487, 492, 495, 498, 502, 530, 532, 533

Tabernacle; 137, 138, 140–142, 144, 163, 460, 465, 473, 690; cloud over, 148, 149; components of, 686–692; setting-up of, 139, 145, 146, 149, 403
Talmud, 326, 696–699
Tamar, daughter-in-law of Judah, 135, 136
Tamar, daughter of David, 182, 184
Tarshish, 26, 517; Traders with, 451
Tartan, general of Sargon, 194, 210
Tattoo, 589, 590
Taxes, 628–635
Teispes, king of Anshan, 100
Tel-el-Amarna letters, 30, 55
Teman, 300
Teman, in Edom, 523
Temple Mount, 247, 248, 398, 400, 453, 480, 483, 484, 496, 501, 502, 530, 532, 696
Temple, design of, 239, 453–467, 686–691
Temple, First; 67, 70, 111, 163, 173, 182, 184, 187, 280, 281, 398, 458, 459, 465, 480, 686; construction of, 3, 46, 61, 62, 64, 66, 72, 118; duration of, 82; destruction of, 3, 46, 85, 94, 95, 97, 106, 107, 109, 112, 113, 115, 210, 239, 240, 280, 308, 341, 393, 395, 409, 410, 432
Temple, Second; 1, 93, 107, 108, 111, 114, 116, 249, 390, 414, 429, 430, 432, 433; construction of, 103, 106, 107, 118, 242, 251, 327, 330, 389, 401, 687; duration of, xix, 93–95, 107, 697; destruction of, 115, 376, 535, 687
Temple, Third; 115, 239, 357, 402, 403, 449, 453–467, 477, 480, 510, 512, 527, 534, 686, 687
Tent-of-Meeting; see Tabernacle
Terah, father of Abraham, 19, 38, 117, 122, 131, 132, 134, 135
Terrorism, 406, 449
Terumot, 482, 529 (see also priestly portions)
Thanksgiving-offering, 558, 559, 654, 655, 677, 679
Thebes, 367, 368
Thrace, 421
Thutmose I, pharaoh, 48, 49, 52, 53, 56
Thutmose II, pharaoh, 48, 49, 53, 54
Thutmose III, pharaoh of the Exodus, 48–50, 53–57, 117
Thutmose IV, pharaoh, 48, 55, 56
Tiglath-Pileser I, king of Assyria, 32–35
Tiglath-Pileser II, king of Assyria, 86–91, 340, 370

Tigris River, 409, 443, 490, 524
Time spans; in Assyrian history, 35; in book of Daniel, 358, 359; of seventy years, 105, 106, 242, 391, 401, 402, 407, 409, 432
Tirzah, 77, 304
Tithes, 481, 482, 495, 529, 628-632, 634, 641, 679, 682, 696-698
Tobias, 422
Tobruk, 437
Togarmah, 26; house of, 451
Tola, son of Puah, 60, 168, 171, 172
Tower of Babel, 9, 13, 22, 23, 117, 131, 132
Tradition, oral, 697
Transjordan, 147, 405, 449, 529 (see also Jordan)
Tree of Knowledge, 5
Tree rings, for dating, 16
Tribes; Arab, 369, 374; Persian, 378; twelve, 475, 477, 478, 533
Trichinosis, xx, 552
Trumpets, silver, 145, 547, 548, 619, 659, 675, 682, 685
Tubal, 26, 450, 451, 517
Tubal-cain, son of Lamech, 6, 7
Tukulti-Ninurti I, king of Assyria, 32, 33, 35
Tularemia, 552, 556
Tunisia, 451
Turin Papyrus, 48
Turkey, 375, 436, 437, 441, 448, 451, 477, 490, 495, 528, 530
Turkish forces, 373, 376, 491
Twelve Prophets, book of, 122, 124, 126, 127, 240-251, 479-496
Tyre, 56, 57, 195, 197, 231, 233, 249, 278, 420, 480, 490, 495, 528

Unicorn, 366, 367, 369, 373
United Nations, 323, 357, 365, 404-406, 442, 446-449, 500, 528, 529
United States, 440, 447, 498
Ur of the Chaldees, 27, 29, 37, 40, 117, 135, 142
Uriah, husband of Bathsheba, 342
Uruk, 11
Utnapishtim, 22
Uz, land of, 300, 301
Uzzah, 695
Uzziah, king of Judah; see Azariah

Venereal disease, 473, 569-571, 574, 576, 580, 595, 596, 618

Vengeance, 526
Vineyards, 488, 495, 520, 528
Vow obligations, 141, 143, 145, 643-647; invalidation of, 643-645
Vulgate, 126

Washing; of body, 553, 556, 579, 582, 587, 592, 593, 621; of clothes, 551, 553, 579, 582, 586, 587, 592, 593
Water, from Jerusalem, 466, 467, 478, 481, 498
Wayward city, 541, 542
Weather control, 469, 651, 674, 675, 685
Wheat harvest, 62, 681, 682, 685
White Paper, 440, 444
Widows, 482, 574, 601, 628, 629, 631, 632, 638-642, 644, 648; as wives for priests, 473
Wilhelm II, leader of Germany, 433, 434, 448, 528
Witchcraft, 541, 542
Witnesses, laws concerning, 602-604
Wives; new, 620, 621; not many for ruler, 546, 547; of Solomon, 305, 306
Wool, 585, 586, 692, 695
Work, need to, 567
World War I, xxii, 323, 356, 357, 363, 364, 376, 433, 435, 436, 440-442, 448, 490, 495, 515, 528, 534
World War II, xxii, 322, 356, 357, 435, 437, 440, 441, 443, 444, 447, 449, 515, 517, 528
Writing, ability of, 6

Xerxes I, king of Persia, 94, 102, 105, 109, 415

Year; of accession, 72, 78, 93; agricultural, 65, 69, 70, 111, 112, 239; first day of, 17, 65-68, 111; first month of, 17, 65, 69, 96, 406; length of, 17, 20
Yemen, 451, 512
Yugoslavia, 441, 451, 530

Zadok, high priest, 468, 472
Zanzibar, 435
Zebulun; son of Jacob 19; tribe of, 170, 341
Zechariah, king of Israel, 75, 80, 187, 188, 191, 243

Zechariah; the prophet, 107, 118, 123, 240–242. 327, 492, 493; book of, 123, 125, 240, 242, 249–251, 390, 479, 490–495
Zechariah, the visionary, 123, 352
Zedekiah, king of Judah, 67, 76, 81–83, 95, 188, 189, 191, 211–215, 229, 239, 338, 342, 354, 398
Zelophehad, daughters of, 149
Zephaniah, son of Maaseiah, 211
Zephaniah; the prophet, 123, 241, 249; book of, 123, 125, 240, 248, 249, 479, 489, 490
Zerah, son of Judah, 41, 42, 136, 344
Zerubbabel, governor of Judea, 107, 118, 123, 249, 326, 327, 330, 331, 333, 343, 354, 355, 697
Zidon, 26, 55, 56, 197, 233, 249
Ziggurat, 13
Ziklag, 174, 180
Zimri, king of Israel, 74, 77, 186, 190
Zion, 247, 248, 253–255, 262, 278–280, 311, 481, 485, 491, 500, 503–505, 508, 511–515, 520, 532
Zionist movement, 515
Ziph, 180
Zobah, 184
Zophar, the Naamathite, 123, 301, 302
Zoroaster, advisor to Hystaspes, 102, 103, 107